SAINSBURY'S BOOK OF
FOOD

SAINSBURY'S BOOK OF
FOOD

FRANCES BISSELL

Photography by
CHRISTINE HANSCOMB

Published in the UK exclusively for
J Sainsbury plc, Stamford House,
by Webster's Wine Price Guide Ltd,
Axe and Bottle Court, 70 Newcomen Street, London SE1 1YT

First published 1989

ISBN 1 870604 03 2

Typeset by Black Bear Press,
Cambridge, England
Colour separations by Colourscan
Overseas Company, Singapore

Printed and bound in Italy by
Arnoldo Mondadori, Verona

Conceived, edited and designed by
Websters International Publishers

*Not all the foods featured in the book
are available from Sainsbury's*

CONTENTS

INTRODUCTION

If I had written this book when I first started to cook, it would have been much shorter with fewer and less interesting photographs. Twenty years ago I had never seen, let alone tasted, a persimmon. Fruit meant apples and pears in the autumn, oranges in the winter and strawberries in the summer. Lettuces were green then, and you ate them in summer for tea with cucumber, cress and tomato. Avocados were an expensive and rare treat. Fish was generally cod, haddock and plaice for every day, sole and turbot for special occasions, and salmon in the summer, mussels in the winter. Spaghetti bolognese was part of my repertoire of dishes, but not polenta, chick peas or chestnut flour. Nor did I think of making my own pasta in those days. Yogurt was just beginning to make its appearance in the shops. Apart from our own farmhouse cheeses, perhaps Brie, Roquefort and Parmesan were familiar, as were Gouda and Edam. Herbs and spices were few and far between, and fresh herbs were practically unobtainable outside the herb garden. Who would have imagined then that real vanilla pods, whole cardamoms, star anise, fresh lemon grass, fresh basil, coriander, dill, chervil and tarragon would be available, not just in specialist shops, but accessible to all who love good food?

That is what this book is about, the food that is more or less available to most of us, most of the time. It is not academic, but practical. If it is useful to know where an ingredient comes from, then I say so, otherwise I get on and describe how to choose, store and prepare it. The book is not encyclopedic either. The minute such a claim is made, someone somewhere is picking a luscious fruit from a tropical tree and deciding to export it for the first time. On the whole the book deals with familiar food, but there are some unfamiliar items that you may expect to see more of in the future. The chapters are organized alphabetically under each 'ingredient' heading. If you cannot find an item in the list, look it up in the index, where alternative names are given. Sometimes in an entry you will be referred to more information in another part of the book, either to another entry in the same chapter (in italics: 'See *Asparagus*', for example); or to another chapter (in capital letters: 'See FISH', for example) when you will find the same ingredient listed again.

Writing the book has given an extra focus to our family travels which in turn have provided me with much useful information. I really do love shopping. When we travel abroad we spend as much time in markets and supermarkets as others do in museums and art galleries. In California we saw at first hand how they use their huge variety of fish, herbs and vegetables in new and exciting ways. At the International Food Fair in Paris I was amazed at the range of preserved meats, hams, sausages and salami. In Alsace and Austria, and indeed, everywhere we have travelled over the last 18 months, we investigated cheeses. The markets in Ecuador and Colombia yielded riches, among other things, in the form of potatoes in many shapes, sizes and colours. We smelled our way round spice shops in Singapore and herb stalls in Bangkok. We visited the fish markets of Hong Kong and saw groupers and breams in literally every colour of the rainbow. The street markets of Shanghai and Guangzhou were heaped with vegetables of the kind you will see on page 23. In Taipei, the capital of Taiwan, a visit to the market stalls revealed rows upon rows of dried squid and cuttlefish. In Malaysia and Singapore we experienced the start of the durian season, and visited pineapple plantations in the Philippines.

Yet you do not have to travel far and wide for these ingredients. We are lucky to live in an age and a place which brings to our doorstep fresh produce of every kind, in rich profusion from every part of the world. True, this does take away the feeling of seasonality in our cooking which for some people is as important as cooking certain dishes for particular celebrations or cooking casseroles in winter and preparing salads in the summer. I quite often feel this way; the first produce of the season was always something to look forward to: Kentish strawberries in late June, mussels in September, asparagus in May, pheasants in October. But then, food has always been imported from abroad – Nell Gwynn was selling oranges 300 years ago. Perhaps we should just be thankful that we can pick and choose and enjoy a varied diet.

The key to eating well is not, as you might think, being able to cook like a television chef, but shopping carefully and creatively. By this I mean buying fresh, wholesome food in prime condition, and knowing how to store it, how to prepare it and how to cook it in the most appropriate way. Eating well does not mean eating expensively. A perfectly fresh piece of pearly white cod cooked with olive oil and garlic is easily the equal both nutritionally and gastronomically of a lobster thermidor, indeed some would say superior.

However much you might enjoy shopping, it can be time-consuming. But it is not necessary to shop every day since not all ingredients need be freshly bought. The heavier goods such as pasta, pulses, grains and flours can be bought in quantity

and variety and stored for some time in a dry cool store cupboard or larder; and they only need replacing when you run out. One is usually more limited by lack of space than the shelf life of these products. Salt and sugar also keep well, as do most vinegars and oils. Thus with careful planning, this sort of large scale food shopping need only be done infrequently, leaving precious time for those things which really are best freshly bought, such as most of the fruits and vegetables, fish and meat.

Our diets have changed. Meat and two veg are no longer what we want to eat every day or, indeed, have the time to prepare. We have been influenced by the food we eat on holiday and we want to eat the same things at home: fish dishes like the ones we eat in the Mediterranean, marvellous bean and pasta dishes from Italy, paella like those in Spain, the deep-fried squid that we enjoy in Portugal and succulent grilled skewers of lamb that we eat in Greece and Turkey. Now we are able to recreate these dishes at home. We may not have the sun, the local wine and the live bouzouki music, but at least we have the produce with which to make a creditable hummus and taramasalata to go with the lamb kebabs.

With this huge array of produce at our disposal we can also look afresh at our own traditional recipes and dishes. With the roast pork why not try Chinese-style stir-fried vegetables? Or with the roast beef consider roasting some yam or colocassi. Try plantain chips instead of potato chips. Use fragrant Oriental herbs and spices such as lemon grass and galangal when you poach or steam a piece of cod – the combination is exquisite.

There are purists who believe it is quite wrong to cross culinary boundaries in this way. Yet while I respect this view, I cannot agree with it. I feel that all this wonderful food is there to be tasted and cooked and enjoyed however you want to use it.

Finally, I should mention that we have described in the text and photographed some items that have been part of our traditional diet but are now either subject to some uncertainty (for example, certain unpasteurized soft cheeses) or actually banned in Britain (as in the case of calves' brains and sweetbreads). The reader needs to be aware that risks do arise from time to time in food production and should take authoritative and up-to-date advice issued by government departments and other responsible authorities. However, the fact that a given food may be considered a problem in one country does not necessarily mean that it is not safely available in others where different circumstances may apply.

During the course of writing this book, I have used many sources from the great Roman gourmet Apicius to the works of my food-writing colleagues and contemporaries. Of particular help when I have consulted them have been Catherine Brown, Antonio Carluccio, Alan Davidson, Anna del Conte, Peter Graham, Jane Grigson, Robin Howe, Elizabeth Lambert Ortiz, Daphne MacCarthy, Sri Owen, Roger Phillips, Patrick Rance, Claudia Roden, Ann Rosenzweig, Yan Kit So, Tom Stobart and Alice Waters. I am grateful to them all. My parents taught me how to shop for food and how to enjoy it. My part in this book is dedicated to them with love and gratitude.

Frances Bissell

VEGETABLES

There is nothing in the food world quite as varied as vegetables. They come in a huge array of colours, shapes, sizes and from a vast range of habitats. Nowadays, more than ever before, we seem to be introduced to a new vegetable almost every week, and old familiar faces appear in new guises. Tiny yellow pear-shaped tomatoes are seen alongside cherry tomatoes and beef tomatoes. Red and green peppers, once rare and exotic themselves, are joined by yellow, orange, black, white and purple peppers. The size of our vegetables is also changing. Prizes may be given for the fattest leek and the largest cauliflower, but in culinary terms 'small is beautiful'. Tiny carrots, pencil-slim leeks, miniature corn cobs and egg-sized cauliflowers have become fashionable. They taste good too and are tender.

The edible part of the plant may be the root, as with parsnips and carrots, or the seed and pod, such as peas and beans, or the leaf, as it is with spinach, cabbage and lettuce, the stem, as with celery and chard, the shoot, as with asparagus, or even the flower, which is the case with broccoli and cauliflower. Tomatoes, marrows, aubergines and peppers are really fruits, but we treat them as vegetables.

NUTRITION

Vegetables are very important to a balanced diet. They provide plenty of bulk or fibre which satisfies and also helps the digestion of other foods. Some, such as potatoes and parsnips, provide carbohydrates, in the complex form of starch, which is much slower in digestion and absorption and is thus more satisfying over a longer period. Some vegetables, such as pulses, provide protein, but on the whole, vegetables are low in protein, as they are also in fat.

The main nutritional value of vegetables is in their mineral and vitamin content. To a greater or lesser degree they contain calcium, iron and phosphorus. Vitamin A is present in green vegetables and in yellow or orange vegetables, particularly carrots. Vitamin E is present in moderate amounts in leafy vegetables. The water-soluble vitamin C is present in many types of vegetables, roots, leaves and 'fruit vegetables' such as peppers and tomatoes. Some of the B complex of vitamins is present, particularly in green leafy vegetables and potatoes.

COOKING VEGETABLES

If you cook vegetables in water, the water-soluble vitamins are, as you would expect, gradually leached out into the water. Save this for other purposes such as soup, but in any case, for preference, use as little water as possible. Many vegetables can be eaten raw, but they can also be cooked by almost every method: steaming, poaching, boiling, stewing, frying, baking, braising, even grilling and barbecuing are all suitable methods for appropriate vegetables. Above all, do not overcook them.

All vegetables should be thoroughly washed and scrubbed before use to get rid of any dirt. Organic vegetables are grown without artificial chemical aids and some claim that they taste better. They do not usually look quite as pristine as the conventionally grown product because they can be more susceptible to slug, insect and disease damage.

BUYING AND STORING

Whatever you choose should look appetizing and good enough to eat with minimum preparation. Leafy vegetables should look green not yellowing. Leaves should be sound, not slimy, holey, browning, or wilted. Root vegetables should be firm, not limp, with no damp or shiny patches, spade marks or other surface damage. Tomatoes and peppers should have taut, shiny skins and should be firm and unbruised.

Harder vegetables keep much better than soft or leafy vegetables. Certain cabbages and cauliflowers can be stored for up to a week in the salad drawer of the refrigerator, but all vegetables are best, as far as flavour and nutrition are concerned, the fresher you eat them. Most salad vegetables – including fennel, chicory, celery and asparagus – will keep for several days in the refrigerator, at the bottom, but will gradually begin to wilt or go limp and lose their appeal. Carrots, parsnips and potatoes will keep for a week or two in a cold dark place in a wire basket, without much sign of deterioration provided they are undamaged to start with.

Strong-smelling vegetables such as leeks should be kept away from other food, and should not be refrigerated, unless wrapped. If buying ready-packaged vegetables remove them from any close-fitting wrapping, since the change of temperature to a domestic setting may cause them to sweat and ultimately start to rot with the accumulation of moisture.

The page numbers in brackets at the end of an entry refer to the relevant photograph.

ACORN SQUASH *des moines squash, tabee queen*

This winter squash is shaped like an acorn but rather larger, up to 8in (20cm) long and 4–5in (10–12cm) thick, and can weigh up to 2lb (1kg). It has a smooth, hard rind which is widely ribbed and changes from dark green to orange during storage. The pale orange flesh is quite firm in texture, slightly sweetish and there is a large seed cavity. Bake it whole, stuffed with a spiced minced meat and rice mixture; or peel it, cut it in chunks and boil or steam until soft, then mash with plenty of black pepper and butter.

Choose specimens that are heavy for their size and free from blemishes. Like all winter squashes, acorn squash has good keeping properties. A whole undamaged specimen will keep for weeks, if not months, in a cool airy place, such as a dry cellar or garage. Check them out occasionally. See also *Squash*.

AKEE *ackee*

Akee is a Caribbean fruit eaten as a vegetable, best known for its role in the classic West Indian dish akee and saltfish. It is the shiny, red, pear-shaped fruit of an evergreen tree which, when ripe, splits to reveal three black seeds encased in three segments of creamy-yellow soft flesh – the only part that is edible, and then only when just ripe. When unripe or overripe it is poisonous. Outside the Caribbean it is usually only available canned in brine. Before cooking, soak it for an hour to remove some of the saltiness, rinse and drain well, then remove the pink membrane before cooking and discard the water in which it is boiled. When cooked the flesh looks rather like scrambled eggs and has a lemony flavour. Akee is also used with okra, breadfruit and other vegetables and seafood.

ASPARAGUS

Asparagus comes in different sizes, from the thinnest spoke – known as sprue – to the fattest jumbo. The buds should be tight, the spears a good even colour with a firm, unwrinkled appearance; long, pale, woody stems will mean a great deal of waste. In Britain and America we seem to prefer the thin green variety while on the Continent the pale, fat, blanched stalks with yellow or purple buds are very popular.

Ideally, cook asparagus with its feet in water and its head in steam. There are special tall narrow asparagus pans which enable you to cook them upright tied in bundles. However, you can cook the spears flat in a frying pan. Whichever method you use, wash the asparagus thoroughly beforehand and cook in boiling salted water for about 10 minutes, depending on the size, until tender (test by piercing the lower part of the stem with a sharp knife). Use the tough stalks in a soup. Cook and eat asparagus as soon as possible after buying it.

Asparagus is so delicious that it deserves its own special place in a meal rather than being treated simply as an accompaniment to fish or meat, or as a garnish. On a French menu, the word *argenteuil* means that asparagus plays an important part in the dish (the town of Argenteuil supplied grand Parisian kitchens with asparagus in the last century). In Germany the *Spargelfest* (asparagus feast) is a feature in many restaurants during May and June.

Asparagus is best served neither hot nor cold, but just tepid and dressed with vinaigrette, hollandaise sauce or mayonnaise. One of my favourite ways of serving and eating it, as a simple supper dish, is with boiled or steamed new potatoes and a fried, poached or boiled egg. (27)

AUBERGINE *brinjal, eggplant*

Long popular in Mediterranean countries and southern Asia, aubergines have come into our kitchens relatively recently, although they were originally introduced into Britain at the end of the sixteenth century. White aubergines may account for the alternative name of eggplant. I have also found tiny viridian green aubergines from Mauritius that look like underripe tomatoes. It is usually a shiny deep purple, roundish or cylindrical with a rounded base and sometimes quite large, over 1lb (500g) in weight. A smaller, thinner, paler purple variety streaked with green or cream is also fairly common, and even smaller purple and yellow varieties are becoming available.

Aubergines can be found most of the year. Look for a firm, bright, shiny skin without wrinkles or brown patches. The stalk end should still be green and fresh-looking. Store them in the salad drawer of your refrigerator.

For most recipes aubergines do not require peeling – unless you prefer them that way – and I have never found them bitter enough to need salting and draining. However, some people do: slice or cube them, salt the cut surfaces and leave to drain for 30 minutes to an hour, then rinse and dry them thoroughly. Salting does seem to make them absorb less of the oil in which they are cooked. Oil, particularly extra virgin olive oil, is best for cooking them in. They have such an affinity with other Mediterranean flavours that it seems quite wrong to cook them in butter.

Aubergines feature heavily in Greek and Turkish cooking – moussaka *must* include aubergines and the lovely Turkish dish, *imam bayildi* – stuffed aubergines – could not exist without them. Use them also in highly flavoured stews such as ratatouille, or on their own simply sliced and fried or grilled over charcoal. Sliced aubergines make delicious fritters, which in Japan form part of the famous *tempura*, a collection of shellfish and vegetables dipped in batter and deep-fried. Aubergine has a particular affinity with acid foods such as tomatoes. Stuff it, bake it and serve it with a tomato and cheese sauce. Or dice it small and cook with sausagemeat and tomatoes for a tasty pasta sauce. (11)

AVOCADO

This pear-shaped fruit has buttery-yellow flesh rich in oils (and calories), and a large inedible single stone. It is a large-scale commercial crop in Israel, California, Florida, the West Indies and throughout the southern hemisphere.

There are many varieties of avocado, some small, brown and knobbly-skinned (Hass), some smooth green and truly pear-shaped (Fuerte), others about the size and shape of an ostrich egg or, at the other end of the scale, there are tiny sausage-shaped avocados with only a slim central quill rather than a large stone. The same test for ripeness applies to all: they should yield to gentle pressure at the stalk end, but should not be squashy, nor should the inedible skin be broken, bruised or blackened. To halve an avocado cut through to the stone around the fruit lengthways using a stainless steel knife, then twist the two halves against each other to separate them. Brush the exposed surface with lemon, lime or other acid such as vinegar to prevent discoloration. Ripe avocados will keep for no more than a few days. To ripen unripe ones at home, keep at room temperature.

Although people keep inventing recipes for cooked avocado, I prefer it simply dressed with olive oil, lemon juice, salt and pepper, and spooned out of the shell. Occasionally I stuff chicken breasts with slices of avocado and Mozzarella cheese before baking them. A classic speciality of Mexican cooking is *guacamole* – a thick sauce or dip of avocado mashed with lime juice, chilli and herbs. (*11*)

BAMBOO SHOOT

I never appreciated how much work goes into preparing fresh bamboo shoots until I saw women labouring over them in the markets in

Fruit Vegetables

1 PLANTAIN (UNRIPE)	10 AVOCADO (POLLOCK)
2 AVOCADO (ISRAELI)	11 AUBERGINE (SMALL
3 AUBERGINE (PURPLE)	PURPLE)
4 AUBERGINES	12 AUBERGINES
(GHANAIAN)	(AFRICAN
5 AVOCADO (FUERTE)	EGGPLANT)
6 AVOCADO (HASS)	13 AVOCADO (KENYAN)
7 AUBERGINES	14 AVOCADO (RYAN)
(CHINESE)	15 GREEN BANANAS
8 AUBERGINES	16 BREADFRUIT
(YELLOW)	17 AUBERGINES
9 PLANTAINS (RIPE)	(STRIPED)

Shanghai. The central shoot of the bamboo plant is brown and shaped like a slightly narrow rugby ball. Fibrous and with overlapping, closely wrapped young leaves, it is shaved with a knife as if one is sharpening a pencil. Then the white central core is par-boiled to destroy the hydrocyanic acid (a bitter poison) it contains. Finally, it is sliced, then cooked again for just five minutes in fresh water. We rarely see the fresh article in the West, but there is a tolerable canned version. It bulks out dishes and adds little flavour, but an agreeable crunchy texture which is so important in Oriental cooking.

BANANA LEAF AND FLOWER

The leaf of the banana plant is dark green and glossy. It can be huge, up to 10ft (3 metres) long and 2ft (60cm) wide but it can, of course, be cut into much smaller pieces. After being slightly warmed to increase its suppleness it makes a wonderfully exotic wrapping for the type of food that lends itself to being cooked *en papillote* (in a parcel) – chicken, fish, even fruit – and gives the food a delicate flavour all its own – more than can be said for foil or greaseproof paper. But do not eat the leaves, even when 'cooked' in this manner.

The flower of the banana plant is edible. Peel off the outer petals to reach the tender heart. Slice it thinly in salads or add to a mixed stir-fried vegetable dish. See also *Green Banana*. (*23, 43*)

BEAN SPROUT

These are the highly nutritious sprouts of mung beans. They can be steamed, used in stir-frys, or added in small quantities to mixed salads. Keep them in the refrigerator and use within a day of purchase. See also SPROUTING BEANS, PEAS AND SEEDS, page 99.

BEETROOT *beet*

This ruby-red root vegetable, which is available all year round, is not one of my favourites. It is at its best in those fine soups – particularly borsch in all its variations – so beloved by Russian and Scandinavian cooks. I dislike pickled beetroot in salads, but raw beetroot, peeled, grated and

mixed with a mustardy mayonnaise or olive oil and lemon juice, or tossed with lamb's lettuce and walnuts, does make a refreshing winter salad. Beetroot are often bought ready-boiled, but you can also buy them raw and cook them yourself.

To ensure even cooking, pick vegetables of roughly the same size; make sure that the roots are not damaged and that the skin is intact. Cut off the leaves about 2in (5cm) above the root. All this preparation, which also applies when steaming or baking them, will help to prevent the beetroot from 'bleeding' and losing colour. Boil them in very lightly salted water for 30–40 minutes, until tender, then allow them to cool slightly and rub off the skins. Cooked beetroot should be eaten within two to three days and stored meanwhile in the refrigerator. Uncooked beetroot will keep quite well in a cool, dark, airy place.

Apart from the lovely rich colour it gives to soups, beetroot juice can be used to colour homemade pasta. Young beetroot tops can be cooked and eaten as a green leaf vegetable. There are also golden yellow and white types, and a reddish variety with white rings which can be prepared in much the same way as the red variety. (*18, 43*)

BREADFRUIT

As its name suggests, breadfruit is an important staple food crop. It originated in South-East Asia and the South Pacific islands, where it grows in profusion, and was introduced to the West Indies in the 1790s by Captain Bligh.

Eaten as a vegetable, the fruit looks something like a round or oval melon with a thick, rough, yellowish green rind which ripens to brown. Inside the flesh is creamy and starchy. It is usually peeled, and the seeds discarded, before being baked or boiled, or sliced and deep-fried like chips. When roasted, the flavour lies between bread and potatoes with a slight sweetness and dense texture. It can be served as a substitute for potatoes, and is an excellent vehicle for rich spicy stews and sauces.

Breadfruit is high in carbohydrate and a good source of all vitamins other than vitamin A. It does not keep well and should be cooked as soon as possible; it is never eaten raw. (*11*)

BROAD BEAN *fava bean*

The time to enjoy homegrown broad beans is from the end of May to early July. Earlier in the spring they are imported from Spain, Egypt and Cyprus. The pods should be pale green with a satiny bloom, and feel soft and tender. The beans inside should be small and not fully mature. Quickly boil or steam them in their pods and eat whole. In Italy young broad beans are shelled and eaten raw with Pecorino cheese, though this can be dangerous, because certain types of broad bean contain toxic substances which are only neutralized in cooking.

As the season progresses the pods become thicker, longer and coarser, and the beans themselves develop quite a tough, fairly indigestible outer skin. It is a good idea to cook them lightly, then rub off the skin before completing the cooking. Whatever the age of the beans, cook them immediately after they are shelled. After buying they will keep a day or so in the vegetable drawer of the refrigerator.

The classic herb to serve with beans is summer savory. Indeed, the two are often grown together since the herb helps to keep blackfly away from the young beans. (*13*)

BROCCOLI *calabrese, sprouting broccoli*

There are two types of broccoli: calabrese which has large densely packed, blue-green heads and few outer leaves, and sprouting broccoli which is leafier with smaller, looser purple or white heads. Both are often sold simply as 'broccoli'. Cape broccoli is not broccoli at all, but a type of

Beans, Peas and Pods

1 BROAD BEANS	9 SWEETCORN
2 BROAD BEANS	10 SOYA BEANS
(MANGETOUT)	11 GUNGA PEAS
3 YARD-LONG BEANS	12 OKRA
4 BABY SWEETCORN	13 MANGETOUT PEAS
5 RUNNER BEANS	(GUATEMALAN)
6 RUNNER BEANS	14 MANGETOUT PEAS
(CANADIAN	(ENGLISH)
WONDER)	15 MANGETOUT PEAS
7 FRENCH BEANS	(SUGARSNAP)
8 FRENCH BEANS	16 PEAS
(DWARF)	

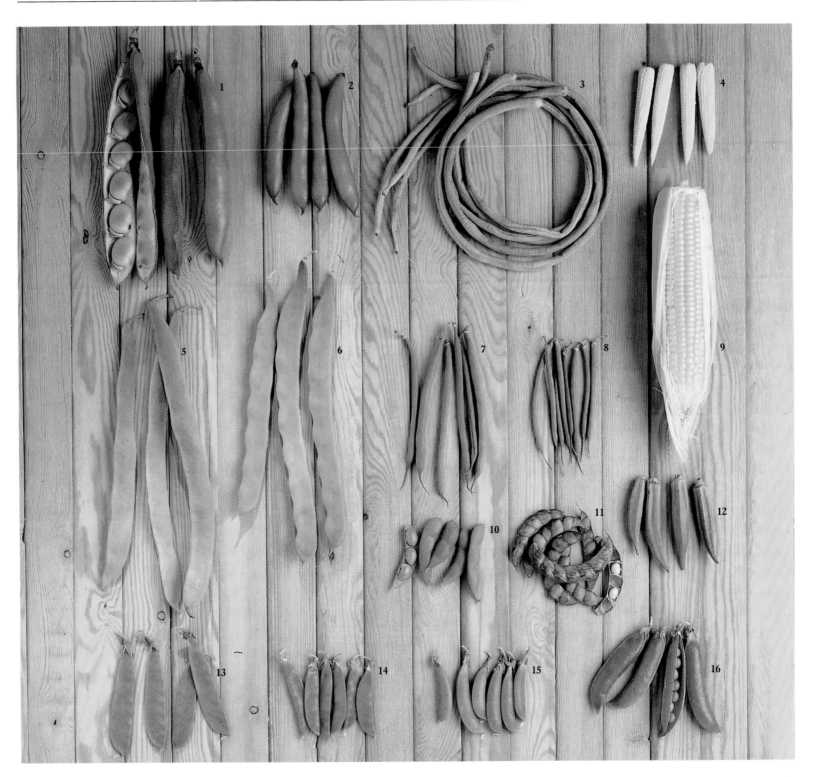

cauliflower with a purple head. Broccoli is available for most of the year. The home-grown season for sprouting broccoli is February to May, and for calabrese from June to November.

Broccoli's richly vivid colour and agreeable crispness make it a marvellous accompaniment to both meat and fish dishes. It is also an excellent source of vitamin C – more so even than oranges – and is also rich in vitamins A and B. However, it must be properly cooked to retain these properties. Steaming for just a few minutes over boiling salted water is best. Consider serving broccoli as a salad vegetable. The florets can be eaten raw or lightly blanched, with a vinaigrette or mayonnaise. I have made soup with broccoli, tarragon and pears – which is an intriguing combination.

When choosing broccoli make sure it looks firm and healthy, with stalks that are neither unduly woody nor dry and wrinkled. The flower heads should be tightly packed, with no sign of yellowing. If you keep it longer than a couple of days, even in cool dark conditions, it will begin to turn yellow and will not be worth cooking. To prepare it for cooking, peel the stalk only if it is thick and tough; a vegetable peeler pares off the thinnest layer. (*15*)

BRUSSELS SPROUT

These little cabbages are not my favourite vegetable, but I seem to be alone in this prejudice since they feature on the grandest tables at Christmas and Thanksgiving. As their

Brassicas

1 SPRING GREENS
2 BRUSSELS SPROUT TOPS
3 CAULIFLOWER
4 KOHL RABI (PURPLE)
5 CABBAGE (DUTCH WHITE)
6 BROCCOLI (CALABRESE)
7 CAULIFLOWERS (DWARF)
8 CABBAGE (SAVOY)
9 CABBAGE (RED DRUMHEAD)
10 CAULIFLOWER (ROMANESCO)
11 CABBAGE (RED)
12 KALE
13 KOHL RABI (GREEN)
14 CABBAGE (MINI-SAVOY)
15 BRUSSELS SPROUTS
16 CABBAGE (CELTIC)
17 CABBAGE (HISPI)
18 CAULIFLOWER (CAPE BROCCOLI)
19 KOHL RABI
20 BRUSSELS SPROUTS

name indicates, they probably originated in Belgium, where they were sold in the markets of Brussels as early as the thirteenth century.

They have a sweetish nutty flavour and, indeed, are often served with chestnuts at Christmas. I've also tasted them shredded finely and stir-fried Oriental style in a wok with ginger and garlic. Shredded sprouts cooked this way, and mixed with mashed potato make a rather superior bubble and squeak. For those who grow their own, sprout tops can be cooked like spring greens.

For even cooking choose ones that are as near as possible all the same size, and look for clean, tight firm buds, with no sign of yellowing or slime. Trim the outer leaves and base of the stalk if necessary (cutting a cross in the stem is a waste of time), wash them well and cook them for about 10 minutes in a covered pan containing just enough lightly salted, boiling water to cover them. This will best conserve the nutrients they contain. Eat them as soon as possible after buying. (*14–15*)

BUTTERNUT SQUASH

A winter squash, this one looks like a large, smooth, cylindrical peanut with a slightly bulbous base, and grows up to 1ft (30cm) long. Peel off the hard, pale butterscotch-brown skin before cooking. See also *Squash*. (*44*)

CABBAGE

Cabbage belongs to the brassica family which also includes cauliflower, broccoli, kohl rabi, brussels sprouts, spring greens, Chinese leaf and many Oriental greens. One of the oldest known vegetables, it was being eaten by the Chinese several thousand years ago.

There are many varieties, with different cropping times, so they are available most of the year. Look for firm fresh leaves without slime or insect damage. Winter cabbages such as the red, white and Savoy should be solid and firm in the centre. Stalks of all cabbages should be clean and unbruised. Although you will probably discard the outer leaves, it is better to buy cabbage with some still attached as they protect the centre of the cabbage and help keep it moist.

Raw cabbage is a good source of vitamin C and some vitamin A, and is low in calories. In winter, when lettuces might not be so readily available, firm red and white cabbages make good substitutes in salad. Slice them thinly or grate the heart and dress it liberally with good oil and wine vinegar or lemon juice.

Cabbage can be cooked in different ways. The one way *not* to cook it is to boil it long and hard in lots of salt water; the nutrients leach out and the smell of sulphur pervades the kitchen. To prepare hearted cabbage for cooking remove the outer leaves and cut the cabbage into quarters,

then slice into thin shreds, put into a colander and rinse thoroughly. To prepare leafier spring cabbage simply separate the leaves, pile them together and shred. Rinse thoroughly.

After washing there will be enough water clinging to the cabbage to allow it to cook slowly in its own juices in a covered pan with some added butter, olive oil, goose fat or whatever appeals. Herbs and spices go in at this stage too. Alternatively, stir-fry the cabbage and serve it while still a little crisp. It can become a surprisingly sophisticated vegetable. Stir-frying or braising with a few lavender buds, a sprinkling of brown sugar, a dot of butter and a hint of lemon juice turns it into a very special dish. It also goes well with aniseed flavours such as tarragon, fennel, aniseed itself, and Chinese five-spice powder.

Preserved cabbage is a feature of many cuisines. In the markets of Hong Kong and China there are pickle shops selling bunches of pickled cabbage. In Korea *kimchee*, pickled cabbage, is served at all times of the day. Alsace and Germany vie with each other to claim the best sauerkraut – salted and fermented white cabbage.

Cabbage is still an important part of the East European diet and is essential for such hearty, delicious dishes as *golubtsi* – rolled cabbage leaves stuffed with pork. Cabbage, particularly the white winter cabbage, and pork is a good combination. This applies whether the cabbage is pickled or fresh, and the pork fresh or cured as in ham, bacon or sausages.

Red cabbage is a classic accompaniment to game dishes and to roast pork. The best way to cook it is to shred it finely and braise it very slowly (for three or four hours) with some thinly sliced onion and the same quantity of apple, a little stock, brown sugar, red wine and wine vinegar. In the best version I have ever tasted, a friend replaced the red wine with port, and kept adding it to the pot until almost a whole bottle was used — extremely extravagant but wonderful.

Leafy spring cabbages should be bought for immediate consumption and certainly not kept for more than a couple of days. Firm cabbages will keep in a cool place for up to a week, but there will be some moisture loss in the outer leaves. (*14–15*)

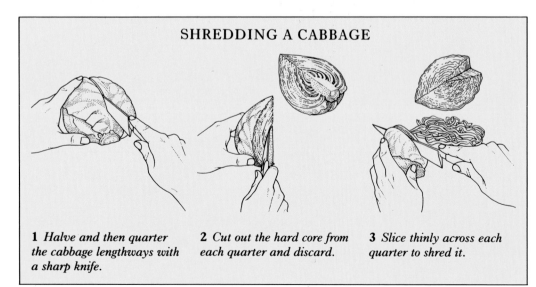

SHREDDING A CABBAGE

1 *Halve and then quarter the cabbage lengthways with a sharp knife.*

2 *Cut out the hard core from each quarter and discard.*

3 *Slice thinly across each quarter to shred it.*

CALLALOO *calalou, callalo, callilu*

Callaloo is a generic name given to the large, green leafy tops of the taro and malanga families of edible tubers which include the dasheen, eddo, and tannia or coco yam among others. 'Cook it just like spinach,' I was advised when I first came across it, but then I was told how callaloo is turned into a soup of the same name, made with milk, okra, salt pork, spices and coconut milk. No spinach is ever that good! But in fact spinach can be used in recipes calling for callaloo, as can chard. Buy for consumption on the same day; wash it quickly, chop coarsely and do not overcook. (*43*)

CAPER

These are the flower buds of the white-flowering, low-growing caper bush native to the Mediterranean region. The buds are picked when full, but still firm and unopened, and preserved in vinegar and salt, or salt alone. The mother of a Sicilian friend preserves them in olive oil – most delicious – with the bonus of an unusually flavoured oil to use in salads. The flavour develops only after they have been pickled. They are imported in jars, mainly from Spain and Italy and should always be kept submerged in the pickling liquid after opening.

Capers are used as an adjunct to sauces and other dishes, such as the traditional English leg of mutton with caper sauce. They are also important in *pasta con le sarde*, the Sicilian pasta with sardines, and in black butter sauce for skate or calf's brain. Try them also with veal, chicken and salmon dishes. They are much used as a flavouring in the cooking of Provence where the best ones, known as *non pareilles*, come from. *Tapenade* – capers, olives and anchovies pounded to a paste with olive oil – is named from the Provençal word for capers, *tapéno*.

CARDOON

This is a favourite white vegetable in southern Europe, but little known in Britain. A member of the thistle family, like the globe artichoke – whose flavour is somewhat similar – the cardoon resembles a large head of celery with long, white fleshy ribs and silvery green leaves.

Only the inner stalks, ribs and tender heart are eaten. Remove the tough outer stalks and any that are wilted or stringy. Strip the leaves from the remaining stems. Cut the stems into 3in (7cm) pieces and drop them into water to which you have added a little vinegar to prevent them darkening. Drain and rinse well before cooking in boiling stock or water for about 30 minutes or until tender. Serve with a tomato, butter or cheese sauce, as you wish. Small pieces can be cooked, then dipped in batter and deep-fried to form part of an Italian *fritto misto* (mixed vegetables deep-fried in batter). The tenderest parts can also be eaten raw.

This is such a rare and unusual vegetable that you are likely to want to cook it as soon as you get it home and not even think about storing it, but it will keep for a week or so in a cool place.

CARROT

'Eat up your carrots, they'll make you see in the dark.' As a child that piece of logic was quite lost on me, but I now know that carrots *are* one of the best possible sources of vitamin A, which is essential for the ability to see in dim light. They also contain vitamin C, dietary fibre, mineral salts and trace elements.

Recently it has become possible to buy carrots by the bunch again with their attractive leafy tops, and also small carrots harvested when young and full of flavour. It is sometimes possible to buy named varieties of carrot, which enables you to choose different ones for different purposes. Parisienne is a short, round stumpy carrot with a lovely sweet flavour. It can be cooked whole. Supreme Chantenay is more conical in shape, smooth-skinned and deep orange in colour; it has a very concentrated flavour. Mokum is a hybrid variety, slender, medium-sized, very crisp and juicy. Zino is a large, sweet, exceptionally juicy carrot which, because of its size, is ideal for making juice. Nantes is an early cropping carrot, slender with a narrow core, and with a slightly coarse texture.

Carrots are available most of the year, both homegrown and imported. New carrots need only vigorous scrubbing or a light scraping. Main-crop carrots will probably need peeling, as thinly as possible. When choosing either variety, look for well-shaped, smooth-skinned spe-cimens. They can be stored in a cool, dark, dry, airy place for up to a week.

Both new and main-crop carrots are delicious raw, the latter being particularly sweet. Cooking times will depend on the type of carrot, the recipe and personal preference. They can be boiled, steamed or braised in a little stock or butter to serve separately. They are also an important ingredient in vegetable stews such as Irish stew, boiled beef and carrots, and vegetable soups. I have a recipe for carrot and peach soup that I often serve, garnished with rosemary or thyme flowers for summer dinner parties. Carrot soups can also be flavoured with orange or mint. Carrots go very well with a number of herbs; cold in a salad they get a fillip from fresh mint and chives, parsley, coriander or basil. Grated raw carrot dressed with an oil and lemon vinaigrette is delicious.

Sweet main-crop carrots make a lovely moist cake, can be used in pies with lots of spices – rather like a pumpkin – can be grated into fruit cakes and puddings, and used in jam and in other delicious desserts such as carrot halva from India. (*18*)

CASSAVA *manioc, yuca*

A tropical plant cultivated for its starchy roots, cassava looks somewhat similar to the yam, with a tough brown, often waxed skin and creamy white or yellow hard flesh. There are two varieties, bitter and sweet. Bitter cassava is poisonous until cooked.

Cassava may be cooked and eaten as a potato substitute (peel it very well), but it is also often processed into cassava flour – *farina* – for making bread, cakes and dumplings, or, best of all, cassava wafers. Other by-products are tapioca, *cassareep* (a syrup used in Caribbean cookery) and *gari* (cassava meal, also important in the Caribbean) and Brazilian arrowroot – an edible thickening agent. (*18*)

CAULIFLOWER

Cauliflower seems to me little more than an uppity cabbage, but it is widely available, even during winter when more exotic and interesting vegetables are in short supply. When buying, look for a firm, compact head with white or

creamy white curd (flowers), a firm stalk and fresh-looking, bright green leaves. Any with speckling or brown patches on the curd, and those with slimy or bruised stalks, may have begun to rot. Yellowing leaves are a sign of age.

Several green-flowered varieties are available, notably Romanesco and Alverde, as well as dwarf white ones. A purple-headed variety is known, confusingly, as Cape Broccoli. As well as being a suitable vegetable accompaniment to meat dishes, cauliflower can be served as a starter or separate course, in a soup or a soufflé, in the famous cauliflower cheese or in fritters. I quite like it *à la grecque*, lightly cooked and dressed while still warm with olive oil, wine vinegar and seasonings.

It keeps its shape and retains its flavour better if steamed rather than boiled. When stir-frying, break off the florets, and thinly slice the stalk before cooking the two together. The green-flowered varieties are more delicate than standard cauliflower, and cook more quickly. (*15*)

CELERIAC *celery knob, celery root*

It is surprising that such a delicious vegetable is not more popular. True, it has an unprepossessing appearance, rather like that of a rough turnip, but it tastes like a particularly sweet and

Roots and Tubers

1 BEETROOT (GOLDEN BEET)	17 TARO
2 BEETROOT	18 EAST INDIAN ARROWROOT
3 BEETROOT (BABY)	19 TURNIPS (SNOWBALL)
4 RADISHES (RED GLOBE)	20 TURNIPS
5 HAMBURG PARSLEY	21 NAVETS
6 RADISHES (FRENCH BREAKFAST)	22 CARROTS
7 CASSAVA	23 CARROTS (FINGER)
8 SWEDE	24 CARROTS (PARISIENNE)
9 YAM (WHITE)	25 PARSNIPS
10 SWEET POTATOES	26 SALSIFY
11 RADISH (BLACK)	27 EDDOES
12 YAM (CUSH-CUSH)	28 TANNIA
13 YAM (YELLOW)	29 LOTUS ROOT
14 TURNIP	30 HORSERADISH
15 CELERIAC	31 COLOCASSI
16 WATER CHESTNUTS	32 DASHEEN

nutty celery. Only the celeriac root is eaten. In fact, it is rarely sold with the top, which looks like an underdeveloped head of celery (though celery and celeriac are not parts of the same plant). Like many root vegetables it is available mainly in the winter. Avoid very large specimens, which may be woody, or hollow and woolly. It is a fairly tough beast, with a stringy, hard, knobbly skin that needs careful peeling with a sharp knife.

Celeriac can be boiled in water or stock, and steamed or fried after par-boiling. To serve as a salad, blanch it briefly in boiling acidulated water, then shred it or slice it into strips, or cube it, and dress it with a sharp mustardy vinaigrette. It is particularly delicious when combined with shellfish in mayonnaise flavoured with orange or mustard. Celeriac can be added to soups or casseroles and substituted for celery in many dishes. It is an excellent accompaniment to game, particularly when cooked and mashed with potatoes and plenty of garlic. (*18*)

CELERY

Now that celery is available all year it has become an important ingredient for spring soups, salads and stir-frys, as well as being an excellent winter vegetable.

There is 'white' celery which has white or greenish-white stalks and greenish-yellow leaves, and there is 'green' celery which really *is* green. Whatever the variety, the stalks should feel as if they would snap easily. If flexible and rubbery they are stale. Look for firm straight stalks which are not bruised.

Most celery is now sold washed, trimmed and 'sleeved' in polythene. It keeps best in its sleeve in the refrigerator. Just occasionally, in the winter months, a gardening friend gives me some homegrown earthed celery, raised in traditional trenches. The wonderful flavour and crispness repays the effort required to wash away the dirt. Celery is delicious raw, on its own or with cheese, traditionally Stilton.

Sometimes celery is sold trimmed right down to the centre as celery hearts. These are marvellous cooked slowly in the oven in a little stock and served with a meat dish – though you can prepare full-size celery the same way. The flavour of celery is a perfect complement to roast beef or ham.

Do not discard the leaves, particularly in winter when fresh herbs are scarce. Chop them up and stir into soups and casseroles. In Italy celery is used mainly as a herb, the flavour being vital to *ragù* sauces, such as that for spaghetti bolognese.

Chinese celery, which is more like the original wild celery, is thinner and has a more delicate flavour than European celery, but can be used in the same way for flavouring and is even better than European celery in Chinese dishes. The Chinese name is *heung kun*. (*27*)

CHARD *leaf beet, leaf chard, swiss chard*

This member of the beet family is grown for its stem, a broad, creamy white rib, ending in somewhat coarse green leaves. There is also a crimson-stemmed variety – rhubarb chard. The leaves are cooked separately, perhaps in a soup or a flan, or as a substitute in spinach recipes – although chard is more robust. Chard stems have a delicate, distinctive flavour and can be served on their own, like asparagus, with an appropriate sauce. To retain all the flavour, steam them lightly until just tender.

Look for tender ribs and leaves which indicate youth and freshness. Older specimens will be stringy and not nearly as good, nor as rich a source of vitamins and minerals. It is used in Italian and French recipes, particularly the latter which combine it with pork, in terrines, pâtés and sausages. (*43*)

CHICORY *radicchio (red leaf), witloof (white leaf)*

There is understandable confusion over chicory and endive, which belong to the same family.

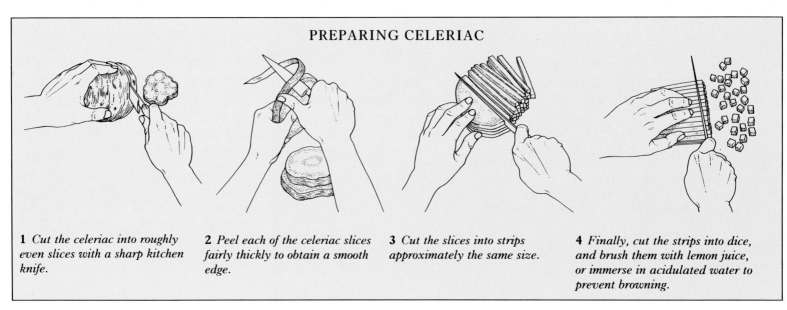

PREPARING CELERIAC

1 *Cut the celeriac into roughly even slices with a sharp kitchen knife.*

2 *Peel each of the celeriac slices fairly thickly to obtain a smooth edge.*

3 *Cut the slices into strips approximately the same size.*

4 *Finally, cut the strips into dice, and brush them with lemon juice, or immerse in acidulated water to prevent browning.*

The first is *Cichorium intybus*, the second *Cichorium endivia*. What we call chicory is the pale, compact, spear-shaped plant that the French call *endive*. What we call endive or frisée – the large, loose-headed, sometimes frizzy, lettuce-like plant – the French call *chicorée* or sometimes *chicorée frisée*.

Chicory is grown on a small scale in Britain but is mostly imported from Belgium and Holland. One of the prettiest sights in a French market in winter is the wooden boxes of chicory. The neat, pale shapes look so clean and crisp and appetizing against the soft, dark blue tissue paper which protects them from the light. They are mostly used in salads, so look for crisp, white, firm specimens, in tightly packed cones with yellow leaf tips. Avoid any that are beginning to curl and open out, that have damaged leaves, or leaf tips that are turning green. To prepare for salads, break off the leaves carefully and rinse them.

Because of its slight bitterness chicory is also a good vegetable to serve with a rich meat dish, braised in the oven. Alternatively, serve it on its own with a cheese sauce, quickly browned under the grill.

To prepare it for cooking, trim off the base. Very large or fat chicory can be sliced down the middle; otherwise cook it whole. Wash it thoroughly, blanch for three or four minutes, then drain and cook according to your recipe.

Dried chicory root is still used as a coffee substitute or as an addition to coffee.

Radicchio is the Italian name for red chicory, several varieties of which are now quite widely available. Another type of red chicory also reaches us from Holland, from early spring to mid-May. Unlike most radicchio this is exactly the same shape and size as the conical, white chicory variety known as witloof, and has a delicious nutty flavour.

Chicory should be kept for not more than a few days in the salad drawer of the refrigerator. See also *Radicchio*. (*30*)

CHILLI *chile, chili*

Chillies are small, hot members of the capsicum family. Originating in Mexico, they were quickly introduced into the rest of the tropics by the great fifteenth-century explorers, bringing colour, heat and spice to the bland preparations of cassava, yam, corn and rice which are still the main staples of these areas. Chillies are a feature of the cooking of Mexico, Central and South America, North and West Africa, India, Thailand, South-East Asia and parts of China, not to mention California, Texas and Louisiana. To the unwary, they can bring tears and blisters.

There are hundreds of varieties, over 150 in Mexico alone, although relatively few find their way into the shops. If you come across a chilli you have never seen before, it is safest to assume that it is hot until it proves otherwise. Appearance is some guide. Dark green chillies tend to be hotter than pale green ones, and hotter than red, because on ripening to red they sweeten – although 'sweet' is a relative term. Also sharply pointed thin chillies tend to be hotter than short blunt ones. But there are exceptions in all categories and it is even possible to get mild and hot chillies from the same plant. Proceed with caution, and take note that some parts of the pod are hotter than others; the tip is milder than the seeds and membranes. Discard both the latter if you are chopping chillies. Wear thin rubber gloves and prepare them under water. Afterwards, wash your hands, knives and chopping board very thoroughly and, whatever you do, take particular care not to let any part of the chilli go near your eyes.

Having said all that, chillies are great fun to use! Here are some that you might come across:

Anaheim About 4in (10cm) long, and thin with a blunt end. They may be red or green and can be quite mild.

Ancho The dried red version of the poblano chilli; fairly mild.

Cayenne Longish, thin and red, these are often called finger peppers.

Cherry Round red or green chillies which are usually sweet but can sometimes be hot.

Chili negro About 5–7in (12–18cm) long, these have wrinkled black skins and a distinctive earthy flavour.

Chipotle Smoked *jalapeño* peppers which give a distinctive extra flavour to the dish. They lose none of their hotness in the smoking process.

Jalapeño Red or green, quite short and blunt. Probably the best-known hot type in Mexican and Tex-Mex cooking.

Poblano These resemble darker, more mis-shapen green peppers or capsicums and are much used in Mexican dishes; they are hot.

Rocotillo or **West Indian** These are also called bonnet peppers and do resemble squashed yellow, green or red bonnets; very hot.

Serrano Small, thin, red or green Spanish chilli; hot or mild.

Thai The tiniest peppers, about ½in (1cm) long and sharply pointed; very pretty in green, white, orange and red; extremely hot. These are also called bird peppers, apparently because they are much liked by mynah birds!

Yellow wax Pale, waxy yellow. Some – Hungarian wax peppers – are hot; the mild ones are called banana peppers.

When following authentic national recipes that call for chilli, do not assume that you have the same tolerance for chilli as the writer of the recipe. Use only a fraction of the recommended amount to begin with, then gradually add more according to your taste. In that way you will be able to enjoy exotic and wonderful dishes without risking teary, blistering misery. Enjoy couscous from North Africa with a pungent *harissa* – an intensely flavoured red sauce – made from chilli and other spices. Make up your own version of *chilli con carne* – beef with chilli and red beans. Experiment with fragrant, heady dishes from Thailand and Indonesia, or the easy and delicious Sichuan vegetable recipes from China, such as stir-fried green beans with garlic and chilli.

A chilli also makes a decoration far superior to tomato rosettes. Take a long thin chilli (or two or three if you can get different colours) and with a sharp knife make a cut about ½in (1cm) from the stalk end to the point, four or five times, until the 'petals' curve back towards the stalk. (*37*)

CHINESE CHIVES *flowering chives, garlic chives, gau choy fa, kuchai*

This is the flowering stem of a member of the onion family, sometimes used with the flowers and sometimes without. When cooked it has a wonderful garlic and onion flavour. Although it is often cut up and stir-fried it is delicious served whole as a side dish to accompany noodle soup. The hollow angular stems are up to 15in (38cm) long and the white flower buds about ¼–½in (5mm–1cm) long.

Their flavour and shape make them an excellent substitute for chives in Western cooking, with potatoes, omelettes, risottos, scrambled eggs, fish dishes and poultry. I have used them to make a very pungent savoury green sauce mixed with pine nuts, Parmesan cheese and olive oil, like *pesto*, which is marvellous with fish and pasta. But do try them on their own, also. They will keep well enough for two or three days in the salad drawer of the refrigerator. (*23*)

Chinese Flat Cabbage *tsai goo choi*

This looks like a stunted, flattened *pak choi*. It has the same ivory stems and soft, dark green leaves but grows close to the ground, only a few inches high. In flavour and texture it is a little coarser than *pak choi* but can be cooked in the same way. See also *Pak Choi*.

Chinese Flowering Cabbage *choy sum*

This yellow-flowering member of the cabbage family is not as sturdy looking as Chinese kale, but it is perhaps the most common vegetable in Chinese restaurants. When steamed it is crisp and tender and has a most delicious, delicate flavour.

Choose flowering stems with bright smooth leaves and firm juicy-looking stalks. (*23*)

Chinese Kale *Chinese broccoli, gaai laan*

The white flowers distinguish this green vegetable from *choy sum*, or Chinese flowering cabbage. Choose specimens with flowers in bud rather than fully open, and soft green leaves with a fine greyish-white bloom to them. The firm stem is tender, delicate and full of flavour, like broccoli. Generally speaking the same cooking methods apply for all the Chinese brassicas: plenty of heat for a short time. (*23*)

Chinese Keys

Despite its name this strange-looking root, like a small vegetable octopus, is not generally used in Chinese cookery. It is a member of the ginger family and has an aromatic scent and distinctive sweet flavour that are used to good effect in Thai and Indonesian curries and pickles. (*23*)

Chinese Leaf *peking cabbage, po tsai*

We see two types of this delicious crunchy vegetable: the one longer and more pointed, the other shorter with a barrel-shaped head. Both have long, pale, tightly wrapped, crinkly serrated leaves with crisp, white, broad-based stems. Imports from Israel, Spain and Holland, and homegrown supplies, mean that it is available all year and it is particularly welcome in succulent winter salads when there are fewer varieties of lettuce about.

Chinese leaf is also good cooked in stews and stir-frys. It has a mild, delicate, slightly cabbage-like flavour but not the smell while cooking. It keeps well for a week or so in the salad drawer of the refrigerator. (*23*)

Chinese Mustard Cabbage *gai choy, swatow mustard*

This is a strong, mustardy flavoured cabbage used by Cantonese cooks as a soup ingredient, after blanching it or turning it into preserved cabbage like sauerkraut. It is a pale green stalky cabbage which resembles an escarole in leaf shape. Because the heads are mainly stalk they are heavy for their size. (*23*)

Chinese Spinach *amaranth, een choy*

This is one of the many leafy greens given the name callaloo in Caribbean cooking. Several varieties are sold here in bunches, with roots, some with green leaves, some with maroon-centred purple leaves. As its name suggests it can be cooked and served like spinach, or as a soup or vegetable dish, but its flavour is only vaguely reminiscent of its namesake, and indeed it is not a related vegetable. Choose fresh-looking, leafy plants. Brief cooking is all that is needed, whether it be boiled, steamed or fried. It is not a salad vegetable.

Chinese Water Spinach *ung choy*

This vegetable does indeed resemble spinach. It has soft green arrowhead leaves and a firm, crunchy, hollow stem. When cooked, this distinctive texture is maintained, which makes it an unusual and agreeable vegetable dish. Because of its high moisture content, particularly in the stalks, water spinach should be used soon after purchase, certainly within two or three days. Avoid any with blemished or slimy stems. Before cooking cut off the tougher bottom portion of the stem. (*23*)

Christophine *chayote, cho-cho, chow-chow, vegetable pear*

A pale green, ridged, pear-shaped vegetable, the christophine is a native of Central America and the Caribbean now grown as a commercial crop in California and becoming more widely available in Britain. It is also grown in North Africa.

Like many other members of the gourd family, christophine is rather bland; to say it is delicate is doing it a kindness. Its main virtue is that the firm, white flesh provides plenty of bulk but is low in starch. It combines well with other vegetables in spicy, peppery dishes such as couscous. Like marrow, it can be boiled, baked, fried, stuffed, and served with a cream or a tomato sauce. I have sliced and quickly fried young specimens in butter, then baked them in a quiche flavoured with mature cheese and a generous amount of sage.

Choose them as small as possible, firm and unblemished and of similar size. Store in the vegetable drawer of the refrigerator. It is not necessary to peel them if they are being baked, stuffed or fried, but do peel them thinly if they are to take on the flavour of whatever they are cooked with. The single central seed is edible. Caribbean and South American Creole recipes are the best source of inspiration. Otherwise cook it as you would courgettes or other small squash. (*45*)

Colocassi

This is a member of the same species of tubers which includes dasheen, eddo and taro and is a valuable source of carbohydrate. They can be cooked and served in many of the same ways as potatoes: roasted, fried, baked or boiled.

Colocassi looks rather like a large, brown, rough-skinned carrot with a prominent pale stalk. It is characteristic of Greek Cypriot cooking, where it is often teamed with pork or chicken. (*19*)

COURGETTE

Courgettes are baby marrows. Homegrown courgettes are available from mid-June until October, with imports from Spain, France, Italy, Israel and Egypt available through the rest of the year. They are small, cylindrical vegetables, and are found in a range of sizes, up to 8in (20cm) long and 1–2in (2·5–5cm) thick. The colours range from tender pale green to deep, rich green and there are also yellow varieties.

My favourite courgettes are the tiny, finger-sized ones; they are exquisite thinly sliced – in rounds or lengthways – and dressed with oil, a little sea salt and a sprinkling of lemon juice. At this size they need no cooking. Slightly larger ones are good, again thinly sliced and quickly fried in a fruity olive oil. They are also delicious dipped in batter and deep-fried as in an Italian *fritto misto* (mixed vegetables fried in batter). The larger they get the less flavour they have and so need more attention: cook them perhaps with a cheese sauce or with other vegetables in a traditional ratatouille. The larger sizes can be hollowed out, stuffed and baked.

Whichever size you choose, look for firm, smooth, shiny specimens. To prepare them for cooking simply slice off both ends. Do not peel them, as this would lose some of the vitamins, and the niacin content. Buy courgettes in small quantities, keep in a cool larder or the vegetable drawer of the refrigerator, and eat them within three or four days.

Courgette flowers are a treat but, unless you grow the plant, a rare one. Italian markets in June have them in profusion, piles of golden trumpets delicately heaped on stalls. If you do have the opportunity of cooking them, stuff them with a rice and herb mixture, gently folding over the petals to seal them, and place

Oriental Vegetables

1 MOOLI
2 CHINESE CHIVES
3 CHINESE WATER SPINACH
4 CHINESE FLOWERING CABBAGE
5 PAK CHOI (SHANGHAI)
6 CHINESE KEYS
7 PAK CHOI
8 CHINESE LEAF
9 CHINESE MUSTARD CABBAGE
10 CHINESE KALE
11 BANANA FLOWER

them in an oiled dish with a little more olive oil dribbled over, cover with foil and bake. Or you can stuff them with Ricotta cheese and deep-fry; or bake them with a tomato sauce. Occasionally, in elegant restaurants, you will see a dish consisting of a small, fanned out, sliced courgette with the stuffed flower still attached, sitting in a pool of delicately coloured sauce. See also *Marrow*. (*25*)

CRESS

It was a source of wonder to me as a child to see tiny plants growing from seeds I had scattered on a damp piece of flannel. This is still as good a way as any of having a constant supply of a fresh salad ingredient, but you can also buy cress growing in small trays or boxes and simply cut off what you require.

Cress is either sold with rape or as a mixture with rape and mustard. Mustard and cress are sometimes sold together, but since it germinates faster than cress, mustard is usually sold on its own. Cress is the more feathery and delicate sprout, mustard a darker green with two small heart-shaped leaves.

Cress makes a good salad ingredient and a pretty garnish, but its crisp freshness is perhaps most appreciated in sandwiches. (*30*)

CUCUMBER

Native to southern Asia, cucumbers almost certainly first came to Britain with the Romans, who carefully tended them in their villa gardens. Cucumbers were not reintroduced on a large scale until the sixteenth century when, as now, they were used raw in salads, pickled or cooked.

The most common variety is a long, slim, straight vegetable with a smooth, dark green, slightly glossy skin, but there are also ridged and even 'warty' ones. Some are more yellow or white than green. Cucumbers are homegrown, mainly under glass, from February to November, and imported from the Netherlands, Spain and the Canary Islands. Small quantities of short, stubby cucumbers for making pickles or gherkins are also imported from Cyprus and the Middle East.

Choose firm, stiff cucumbers; any that wobble when you pick them up and lightly shake

them are old and will be bitter and rubbery. A good cucumber will be moist, juicy and crisp inside, with a good proportion of flesh to seed. Only peel it if it is essential to the recipe, because the skin aids digestion and you will lose a good portion of the dietary fibre, vitamin C and mineral salts. It will keep in the vegetable drawer of the refrigerator for up to six or seven days, but it is so much better when fresh and crisp.

Cucumbers have always been credited with being cool and refreshing, which is not surprising since they are 96 per cent water. Once seen as an essential part of the 'English' salad, the cucumber is now often used as a vegetable in its own right. Delicious salads of cucumber, yogurt and garlic, such as *cacik* from Turkey and *raita* from India, are borrowed from Oriental cooking. Diced and cooked in butter, it also makes a good companion to chicken.

To draw out some of the water content of cucumber, cut it in half, scoop out the seeds, slice paper-thin and sprinkle with sea salt. Rinse after an hour and squeeze dry in a clean tea towel. It can then be served as a salad with an appropriate dressing, but it is also a revelation fried quickly in butter and served with fish. Another way of preparing it is to peel it, then shave off long strips with a sharp swivel peeler and salt them. (*25*)

CUSTARD MARROW *custard squash, cymling, patty pan, scallop*

One of the most attractive of the squashes, the custard marrow is a disc-shaped summer squash with a scalloped edge. Pale green when young, it turns white as it matures, although there are also brilliant yellow varieties which really do resemble fluted custard pies. When young they have a lovely flavour reminiscent of courgettes, and they are at their best eaten when about 4in (10cm) in diameter rather than allowed to mature. Rather, halve them horizontally and stuff them. See also *Squash*. (*45*)

DANDELION

Dandelion has diuretic properties which give it, in France, the name *pissenlit*. The English name comes from *dent de lion*, or 'lion's tooth' which aptly describes the jagged leaves. Dandelion

grows wild all over Europe, America and Asia and is an excellent 'free food'. It is rich in vitamin A, iron and calcium and is one of the most nutritious of all green plants. Dandelions are also cultivated in northern Europe, particularly France and Belgium, and these are paler through blanching, more tender and less bitter than the wild variety.

Dandelions make a delicious addition to winter and early spring salads; indeed our ancestors used to serve them as a spring tonic to purify the system after a diet of heavy winter food.

They can also be cooked and served with a little grated cheese and fried onion and garlic. Perhaps the nicest way is half cooked, half raw, that is in a wilted salad with hot bacon fat and slivers of bacon mixed in.

If you pick your own leaves, do so in the spring before the flower forms, when the leaves will still be tender. Do not pick them from the roadside, as they will have absorbed petrol fumes. (*30*)

DASHEEN

This large, round root vegetable, similar in shape to swede, and the same species as taro, is much used throughout the tropics as a starchy equivalent of potatoes. Peel off the coarse bark-like skin and boil or bake until tender. The leaves are often sold as callaloo. (*19*)

DRUMSTICK

Drumsticks look like long ridged beans but are in fact the unripe seed pods of a small tree, native to north-west India. The inside has the same sort of

Cucumbers and Marrows

1 COURGETTES (YELLOW)	7 GHERKIN (RIDGED)
2 CUCUMBER (LONG)	8 MARROW (STRIPED)
3 COURGETTES (WHITE)	9 GHERKIN
4 CUCUMBERS (MINI)	10 COURGETTES (BABY)
5 MARROW (GREEN BUSH)	11 GHERKIN (SMOOTH)
6 COURGETTE FLOWERS	12 COURGETTES (ROUND)
	13 COURGETTES
	14 CUCUMBER (RIDGED)

mucilaginous quality as okra when cooked and a pleasant asparagus flavour. They are best treated like asparagus, boiled and then sucked and scraped with the teeth.

Look for specimens roughly the same size, scrub and then string them. Large versions will need 25 minutes' cooking as they can be up to ½in (1cm) thick and 20in (50cm) long. They can be cut up before or after cooking.

DUDI *bottle gourd, calabash, doodhi, lokhi, woo lo gwa*

These gourds come in a variety of shapes – not always resembling a bottle. All have pale green hard skins, smooth to the touch, sometimes faintly ridged. The flavour is mild and slightly cucumbery. Cook them as you would summer squashes; they can also be stuffed and baked. See also *Squash*.

EAST INDIAN ARROWROOT

This is a large starchy root — a member of the *Tacca* family. It is occasionally used in Chinese and South-East Asian cooking peeled, diced and stir-fried with other vegetables and pork. (*19*)

EDDO

The eddo is a small round potato-like tuber – a variety of taro. It is used a great deal in the Caribbean and in West African cooking. It has a pastier consistency than potatoes and a sweeter, nuttier flavour but is used in similar ways. Peel (use gloves because the peel contains a skin irritant) and bake or boil it, or parboil and add to spicy stews or vegetable curries. (*19*)

ESCAROLE *broad-leafed endive*

This salad green is the least bitter member of the chicory family and grows in a loose-leaved head rather like a lettuce. The broad-edged and fluted leaves are bright green on the outside – in some varieties tinged with red – and a pale yellow in the centre.

Look for firm white central ribs and crisp fresh leaves. Avoid limp, discoloured specimens. Like all salad greens escarole should be used soon after purchase, but can be stored in

the salad drawer of the refrigerator. If, despite your best efforts, it loses some of its crispness, refresh it by sitting it in a large bowl of iced water for an hour or so. Soaking salads is not a process I like to recommend as it leaches out vitamins and minerals, but, if it has become limp, it has probably lost much of those anyway. See also *Chicory, Frisée.* (*30*)

FENNEL *fennel bulb, Florence fennel*

The sweet aniseed flavour of fennel is like no other vegetable I know. As its name suggests Florence or Florentine fennel came to Britain from Italy, probably in the seventeenth century, although it had been enjoyed long before that by the ancient Egyptians, Greeks and Romans. It is available throughout the year.

Fennel resembles a squat celery stalk; most of the feathery fronds are cut off by the time they reach us. In the market in Palermo they sell fennel that still has its yard-long stalks and fronds and these are also used in various dishes. The bulb is white with overlapping ridged leaves. Look for ones that are well rounded. Flat-bellied ones are immature. Specimens should not show any bruising or broken leaves and they should look dry, but not, of course, dried out.

Although a rather expensive vegetable, it is worth buying from time to time to serve on its own as a separate vegetable course, Italian style, perhaps with cheese sauce using one of the lovely Italian cheeses such as Fontina or Caciotta. I make a little fennel go a long way by dicing it small and cooking it with chopped shallot or onion in a creamy risotto.

Fennel gives a special crispness and flavour to salads and the trimmings can be chopped up and used in soups, or cooked with fish or chicken.

Eat fennel as fresh as possible, although it will keep in the salad drawer of the refrigerator for a few days. Cut surfaces will brown when exposed to the air, so if you slice it drop the pieces into acidulated water immediately. See also HERBS, page 100, and SPICES, page 110. (*27*)

FRENCH BEAN *green bean, haricot vert*

We are all familiar with the small, thin green beans which are available all the year round.

They became quite a cliché in cooking in the late 1970s to mid-1980s when the vogue for miniature vegetables was at its height. They are extremely tasty when fresh, but it is sad that we seem to see little of the wide variety of beans that is available in other countries. In France and Italy you find small, round, waxy yellow pods, broad, flat yellow pods, violet and deep purple bean pods which turn green on cooking and green beans streaked with purple. (But you can buy seed and grow your own.)

The French beans we are most familiar with are occasionally homegrown but frequently imported from Kenya, Cyprus, Spain and Egypt. When they are sold loose check for freshness by snapping one: it should snap easily and be fresh and juicy. The pod will be a clear, rich green with a slight bloom to the skin. The smallest scarcely need topping and tailing. Larger specimens can be cooked whole or broken into even lengths. Boiling, steaming and stir-frying are all good cooking methods. They can be served as an accompaniment to meat and fish dishes. Try them as a salad or starter dressed when warm with oil, vinegar and garlic. Summer savory and basil go particularly well with French beans. (*13*)

FRISÉE *curly endive*

This member of the chicory family looks like a large, loose-headed, open lettuce with thin, crinkly, branching leaves ranging from a good bright green on the outside to a pale greenish yellow at the heart.

It has the characteristic bitterness of its cousins, chicory, escarole and dandelion, and is an excellent salad green, on its own or mixed with other leaves. Look for crisp, fresh-looking

Stalks and Shoots

1 CELERY
2 GLOBE ARTICHOKE (ENGLISH)
3 GLOBE ARTICHOKE (FRENCH)
4 GLOBE ARTICHOKE (ENGLISH)
5 GLOBE ARTICHOKE (ENGLISH)
6 GLOBE ARTICHOKE (AMERICAN)
7 ASPARAGUS
8 ASPARAGUS (SPRUE)
9 FENNEL ROOT
10 FENNEL BULB (FEMALE)
11 FENNEL BULB (MALE)

specimens and avoid any with wilted, slimy or discoloured leaves. They are best bought for immediate use but will keep, wrapped, in the salad drawer of the refrigerator for two or three days. See also *Chicory*. (31)

FUZZY MELON *hairy cucumber, tseet gwa*

This looks something like a rather large courgette. It is dark green with a mass of tiny hairs on the surface. Inside, the flesh resembles that of cucumber but is not as moist. Fuzzy melon is a type of winter melon used a great deal in Cantonese cooking, but also in India, Japan and South-East Asia. Because it is fairly bland it soaks up other flavours and is generally cooked in homespun dishes with, for example, pork and mushrooms, either braised or stir-fried. It is most important to get rid of the hairy skin first as this would otherwise act as an irritant. Vigorous scrubbing or the swivel potato peeler will do the trick. See also *Squash*. (45)

GARLIC

This is a member of the large allium family to which chives, onions, shallots and leeks also belong. Although some is grown in Britain, mainly in the Isle of Wight, it is most often imported from France, Spain, China and Italy. There are white-skinned, pink-skinned and purple-skinned varieties – the purple-skinned is generally considered to be superior. Garlic is available all year round since, like onions, it can be dried and stored. However, fresh new season's garlic is a wonderful treat to look forward to, sometimes as early as the end of April when the first Italian bulbs reach us. Then it can be cooked as a vegetable. One head or bulb of garlic will contain eight to ten plump cloves. The skin is so tender and moist that only the very outer layer need be removed. Casserole the cloves with chicken and squeeze the soft cooked garlic on to the chicken before you eat it. A classic French recipe calls for 40 cloves of garlic to be cooked with the chicken – if the cloves are cooked the smell will scarcely be noticeable on the breath.

Garlic can also be used more traditionally, and in smaller quantities, to season salads, pasta sauces, soups and casseroles. If you are frying garlic to flavour a casserole do not let it burn or

even get brown as this renders it inedibly bitter. Use it in pâtés and terrines and to flavour butter. Any such dishes have a fairly short shelf life in the refrigerator as the garlic tends to turn them rancid after a while. When using old garlic you will probably notice that it is beginning to shoot, that is, a green tip is showing through at the pointed end. The garlic can still be used but cut the clove in half and completely remove the small green shoot, which is strong and bitter.

For crushing garlic I advise against using a garlic press. The acid in the garlic can react with the metal to produce a sharp flavour. In addition the press is very difficult to clean so you risk getting bits of garlic dried in the holes which will produce off-flavours. Instead peel and roughly chop the garlic on a chopping board, sprinkle with a tiny bit of salt and crush with the point of a knife held flat. Alternatively, crush it in a pestle and mortar. If you use these implements for other things wash them well after use as the smell of garlic is very tenacious.

Raw garlic is claimed to have valuable medicinal properties, antibiotic and antiseptic as well as anticoagulant. In the past it was also used to ward off evil spirits and was thought to be an excellent safeguard against vampires.

Garlic is widely used to most delicious effect in Mediterranean cooking. Think of the rich garlicky flavoured sauces of Greece and Provence: *skordalia, rouille* and *aïoli*. Think of those wonderful garlic soups of Spain, Italy and Malta, which are little more than bowls of hot broth, or even water, with some torn up bread and plenty of olive oil and garlic, sometimes a whole egg, or sometimes a little ham. A neatly plaited bunch of garlic will keep well through the autumn and winter in a dry airy place. (35)

GHERKIN

A member of the same family as cucumber and courgette, this looks like a small, squat, somewhat rougher cucumber. Some varieties are warty-skinned, others ridged. Usually pickled, it is traditionally eaten with salt beef. (25)

GLOBE ARTICHOKE

The globe artichoke is a member of the thistle family. At its best it should look fresh and the

head, made up of tightly overlapping club-shaped leaves, should be firm. Some varieties, particularly those from Brittany, have an almost round, pale green head; others, from Cyprus and Egypt, are more elongated and range through green and purple (green varieties are less bitter than purple). Miniature artichokes – about 2in (5cm) long – from California and France are delicious eaten whole. In the south of France they eat them raw dipped into a piquant dressing such as an anchovy vinaigrette. Of course, if you grow artichokes, you can pick them at a tender age rather than waiting for them to become fully grown – when some weigh close to 1lb (500g).

Artichokes are rich in iron, mineral salts and vitamins, and low in calories. There is, however, very little that is edible on the artichoke and you may wonder whether it is worth all the fuss and bother of preparing it. Indeed it is. It has a unique flavour, which somehow 'sweetens' everything you taste with it or immediately after, which incidentally applies to wine too. Do not serve wine with artichokes. It is a wonderful vegetable to serve boiled as a first course. Dip each leaf into a mayonnaise or vinaigrette and scrape off the soft fleshy base with your teeth. When you get to the centre pull out the inedible hairy or spiky choke a tuft at a time or slice it off with a sharp-edged spoon or knife. Cut up and eat the base or *fond* with the remaining sauce. Part of the stalk too is sometimes tender enough to eat.

Eat artichokes as fresh as possible, ideally the day you buy them. If you keep them longer treat them as flowers: cut off a little of the stalk and stand them in water for an hour or so to refresh them. To prepare, wash them thoroughly, remove any discoloured leaves and boil in salted water or steam until tender – usually at least 30 minutes – when an outside leaf will come away easily if gently pulled. Drain them well. Serve hot or cold on a plate with a small pool of sauce or dressing.

Restaurants often serve artichokes with the leaf tips cut off so that the top is flat, but it is not necessary to do this unless you are preparing the spiky variety.

Artichokes can be hollowed out and stuffed, and the trimmed bases make exotic receptacles for salad ingredients or poached eggs. The very small varieties make good centrepieces for salads, and you can eat them choke and all. I once had thinly sliced artichoke bases cooked in a risotto – they were delicious. The Roman way is to flatten young artichokes, dip them in batter and deep-fry them. They are available most of the year, but homegrown ones are at their best in July and August. *(27)*

GOLDEN NUGGET SQUASH

This is a well-flavoured squash, found in the autumn. It grows to about 1lb (500g), is spherical and slightly fluted. Its lovely bright orange skin makes it perfect as a miniature jack-o'-lantern, and its sweet, pale orange flesh can be used to make a spicy pie or soup, or it can be baked with a rich cheese sauce. See also *Squash*. *(44)*

GREEN BANANA

These are the unripe version of the sweet yellow bananas we eat for dessert. As bananas ripen from green to yellow to brown-patched yellow, the starch converts to sugar and they become a sweet fruit. While still green they have a slightly nutty flavour and can be used as a starchy vegetable in place of plantains or, indeed, potatoes or any other staple. They are usually boiled until soft, whole and unpeeled, then peeled and mashed. A cheese sauce is one of the ways of dressing up this rather bland vegetable. I would be inclined to add it to hot spicy stews.

Most bananas come to us from the West Indies, and occasionally from the Canary Islands. *(11)*

GREEN ORIENTAL RADISH

The first time I ever came across this pale green root, in my sister-in-law's kitchen in Hong Kong, I thought it was a type of turnip. It does taste a little like one. But no, it is a cultivated radish, growing up to 8in (20cm) long and 3in (7cm) in diameter. Both skin and flesh are green. Choose it as you would any root vegetable, looking for firm unblemished specimens. Reject any with worm holes. It is a very good soup ingredient and can also be peeled, sliced and cooked as you would cook kohl rabi.

GUNGA PEA *cajan pea, pigeon pea, red gram*

These are dark brownish-red peas which come from small, twisted, slightly hairy pods. They are an important food in the tropics, particularly Africa, India and the West Indies. Although usually sold dried fresh ones are sometimes available. When fresh, the peas are green, four or five to a pod. They are more like mature beans than peas, and have a nutty flavour and mealy texture. They can be added to vegetable soups and are also good in chicken soup and casseroles. See also DRIED PULSES, page 94. *(13)*

HAMBURG PARSLEY *parsley root*

This is a delicately flavoured root vegetable which looks rather like an underdeveloped parsnip, and is used particularly in Germany in soups and stews. You can also cook it like carrots: remove the leaves, scrub it, slice it unpeeled and boil in salted water until tender. Use the leaves instead of parsley. *(18)*

HORSERADISH

One of the toughest beasts in the vegetable garden, this is well-nigh impossible to pull up, so deep and entrenched is the knobbly, irregular root. It is also one of the more difficult raw ingredients to handle. When you peel it, as you must, and grate it, the vapours irritate and make your eyes water.

Horseradish is used as a condiment particularly with roast beef and other robust meat dishes. See also SPICES, page 110. *(19)*

JERUSALEM ARTICHOKE

The jerusalem artichoke and the globe artichoke are not even remotely related. Once upon a time someone decided that the two vegetables had a similar flavour and christened this tuber 'artichoke' too. 'Jerusalem' is probably a corruption of *girasole* (the Italian for sunflower), to which family the jerusalem artichoke belongs.

The tubers grow underground to an average weight of about 3oz (75g). They are rather knobbly and irregular in shape with light beigy-brown or purply-red skins. If buying them loose choose unbruised ones and, for easy preparation,

those of the most regular shape and size. To prepare scrub them, boil or steam until tender and *then* peel. If, for a particular recipe, you have to peel them first, drop them into water to which you have added a little lemon juice or vinegar to stop them browning.

Cook in gratins, soups or purées, or roast with a joint of meat as you would cook potatoes. Prime specimens can be scrubbed, thinly sliced (unpeeled) and eaten raw, dressed in a salad. The crisp, sweet flesh is rich in carbohydrate, minerals and vitamin C. *(29)*

JICAMA *yam bean*

This root vegetable is a native of Central America, although it is also used a good deal in Oriental cooking. It has a crisp, juicy texture and slightly sweet, fruity flavour. It is eaten raw, peeled and sliced in salads, cooked like potatoes, or stir-fried. In Mexico raw slivers are served as an appetizer, first dipped in lime juice and dusted with salt and powdered chilli. *(29)*

KALE *borecole*

Kale is a useful winter standby, being one of the hardiest of the cabbage family and able to withstand frost. It is a sprouting plant, rather

Roots

1 JICAMA
2 JERUSALEM ARTICHOKE (PURPLE)
3 JERUSALEM ARTICHOKE

like broccoli or spring greens, without a heart. The curly leaf kale is the most widely available. Cook it as you would cabbage, in just a little salted water, and not too long as the leaves are relatively tender. It has a very pronounced flavour and is best cooked with other strong flavours such as bacon, garlic and cheese. (*15*)

KANTOLA

This bitter gourd is widely used in Chinese, Indian, Sri Lankan and South-East Asian cooking. Bright spring-green in colour, kantolas are about 2in (5cm) long and 1¼in (3cm) thick. The flesh sweetens on ripening and the seeds, which are edible when young, harden. Because of their knobbly skin kantolas need plenty of scrubbing under cold running water to get rid of any dirt lodged in the grooves, but go gently so as not to break the skin. Soak in salt or blanch to get rid of the greater part of their bitterness then cook them like courgettes or use in stir-frys or vegetable curries. (*45*)

KARELA *bitter gourd, bitter melon*

Prepare and cook this in the same way as kantola. It differs in size from kantolas, being about 7in (18cm) long and 3in (7cm) thick. Karelas come with slightly different characteristics. The Indian karela is thin, darker, bitter and more pointed than the Chinese one. The Thai karela is white when immature. (*45*)

Salad Leaves

1 LETTUCE (QUATTRO STAGIONI)
2 PURSLANE
3 CHICORY (WITLOOF)
4 RADICCHIO
5 LAMB'S LETTUCE
6 CRESS
7 SALAD BURNET
8 LETTUCE (LITTLE GEM)
9 DANDELION
10 ESCAROLE
11 WATERCRESS
12 LAND CRESS
13 ROCKET
14 NASTURTIUM LEAVES
15 ESCAROLE (RED)
16 LETTUCE (BUTTERHEAD)
17 LETTUCE (CRISP LETTUCE)
18 LETTUCE (COS)
19 LETTUCE (FEUILLE DE CHÊNE)
20 LETTUCE (LOLLO ROSSO)
21 LETTUCE (LOLLO BIONDO)
22 FRISÉE

KOHL RABI *turnip-cabbage*

This member of the cabbage family is quite popular in Europe and Eastern Europe but less so in Britain and America. When young and still relatively small, no bigger than a small apple, it has a nutty, crisp sweetness, reminiscent of turnip and cabbage (hence its alternative name) but rather nicer than either.

It is a root vegetable, usually sold with the broken stems jutting out from the top of the root, but sometimes with the leaves intact; these can be steamed or boiled like turnip or beet greens. It is smooth, round and pale green in colour, or sometimes purple. Fresh ones will still have a slightly youthful bloom about them. Choose the smallest you can find. Steam or boil them whole for about 15–20 minutes depending on the size, then peel them just before serving with sauce or melted butter. Slice and stir-fry very small ones or serve them raw in salads.

Most recipes for turnip will also adapt very well to kohl rabi. (*15*)

KUDZU

This starchy root is used in South-East Asian cookery. It is irregular in shape, rather like a yam, although the skin is less bark-like. The flesh is white and sweet like a beet and when boiled the cooking liquor will take on this sweetness. The root itself stays fairly tough unless you have a very young specimen and cut it up small.

LAMB'S LETTUCE *corn salad, mâche*

This delicate green leaf is becoming increasingly available as a salad green. It is not a true lettuce but originally a weed native to most of Europe. It has been cultivated largely in France and Italy as a winter salad vegetable, although it is now available all year round. It is rather expensive, but it is light in weight so a little goes a long way.

Lamb's lettuce is sometimes sold loose in whole plants with a little of the root system still attached, but usually the leaves are separated and packed. It is preferable to buy it whole since it is a fragile plant which bruises easily.

If you buy it whole sit it in a bowl of iced water for an hour or so. That will not only freshen it up but will help draw out the sand in which the plant grows which gets lodged in the base of the stem. There is no merit in cooking this sweet little leaf. Enjoy it as it is, as part of a salad. Or use it as a garnish for cold dishes. (*30*)

LAND CRESS *American cress*

Similar to watercress in flavour, this is a useful winter salad leaf. Simply wash it and discard the coarser stems. (*30*)

LEEK

Leeks, which first appear in the autumn and early winter, are one of my favourite vegetables. Tender baby leeks quickly steamed or boiled, then dressed with a vinaigrette and eaten when tepid, are one of the best salads imaginable. Or you can cut them into short lengths and add to light summer vegetable soups; or stir-fry them whole with young beans, peas, baby corn cobs and carrots. When buying older leeks make sure that they have not developed a woody core. Use mainly the white part; the green tops can be used in soups.

Unlike commercially grown leeks, which are planted differently, homegrown ones can be difficult to clean properly as soil gets lodged between the leaves. If the recipe calls for sliced leeks, simply rinse the slices thoroughly under a running tap, or stand them for 15–20 minutes in a bowl of water. If you need whole leeks, make slits in them at intervals and cover with water to soak out the soil.

Their delicate yet distinctive, mildly oniony flavour makes them a perfect accompaniment to all meat dishes, particularly poultry and fish. They will take cream, cheese or butter sauces, and can be turned into delicious soups such as cock-a-leekie, Welsh *caul*, Flemish leek soup and *vichyssoise*, the cold creamy leek and potato soup. Quiches, pies and omelettes, indeed many kinds of egg dishes are perfect vehicles for leeks. (*35*)

LETTUCE

Lettuces now come in a whole range of colours from the palest green Iceberg to the rich russet brown of Feuille de Chêne, also known as Oak Leaf. Whatever type you buy the same signs of freshness and quality apply: the leaves should be firm and crisp, with no sign of browning at the edges and no sign of slime or insect damage. When preparing them discard any wilted outer leaves, carefully wash the leaves you are using and dry them thoroughly by draining them on a clean tea towel or in a salad spinner or shaker. Use most lettuces within a couple of days, although Iceberg and Little Gem can be kept for five to seven days in the salad drawer of the refrigerator.

There are basically three types: round hearted lettuces also known as cabbage lettuces (which can be butterheads, with soft fleshy leaves, or crispheads, with crisp juicy leaves); the long lettuces known as Cos and the cutting lettuces where you simply pull off the leaves that you require from the growing plant.

Round Lettuce

Batavia A large crisphead type lettuce with pale green or red-tinged leaves.
Buttercrunch A superbly crisp and delicious lettuce, dense-hearted and sturdy.
Butterhead Crisp and most popular of all.
Continuity A well-flavoured lettuce with red-tinged leaves.
Crisp lettuce A delicious, hardy lettuce, large with a good firm crisp heart.
Four Seasons, Quattro Stagioni A red-leaved lettuce with fine, neat, curled leaves. It has a loose heart and good flavour, and keeps well.
Iceberg Large and pale, somewhat resembling a winter cabbage with its crisp, densely packed leaves. It has very little flavour, although it does have an agreeable crunchy texture and generally keeps well.

Long Lettuce

Cos, Romaine A tall lettuce with thick, firm leaves with a stout central rib.
Little Gem, Sucrine A small, Cos-type lettuce with sweet, crisp, compact hearts. It has a better shelf life than most lettuces.
Winter Density Another small Cos-type lettuce with crisp dark green heart.

Cutting or Loose-Leaved Lettuce

Feuille de Chêne (also called **Oak Leaf** or **Red Salad Bowl**) A delicately flavoured salad which is good mixed with other leaves. It comes in both green and red varieties.
Green Lollo, Lollo Biondo A lettuce with very frilly green leaves streaking down to pale green in the centre; sometimes develops a heart.
Green Salad Bowl A useful cut-and-come-again lettuce, with frilled leaves and no heart.
Red Lollo, Lollo Rosso A red, equally decorative version of Green Lollo.

If you grow lettuces you may well have a glut at the end of summer, which is an excuse for making lettuce soups and dishes of braised lettuce, but most of us will be content to eat them in cooling and refreshing salads. (*30*)

LOOFAH *Chinese okra, silk melon*

The angled loofah is an edible gourd used in Chinese, Indian and South-East Asian cooking. It resembles a boomerang-shaped cucumber with ridges but, confusingly, can also be straight. Inside it has spongy, creamy white flesh with slippery seeds. To prepare, peel off the ridges with a potato peeler or remove the skin altogether if tough. Cook in the same way as fuzzy melon. See also *Squash*. (*45*)

LOTUS ROOT

The underwater rhizome of the lotus flower, this looks like a string of fat sausages. Its sweet, crunchy texture and lacy appearance when sliced make it a very agreeable addition to a plate of mixed stir-fried or steamed vegetables or braised pork in Chinese cookery. At Chinese New Year slices of the root are candied and served as sweetmeats. Whole lotus roots take about two hours to cook. Canned lotus roots are not as crisp or fresh tasting but the pretty, lacy effect is still there and less time is needed for cooking. (*19*)

MANGETOUT PEA *snow pea, sugar pea, sugar-snap pea*

Mangetout are now available most of the year. There are two types: flat-podded and round-podded. The latter are usually called sugar-snap peas, the former mangetout. Preparation and cooking methods are the same, although sugar-snap do keep a little better than mangetout after picking and they taste a little sweeter. Asparagus peas are similar to sugar-snap and mangetout peas in that they are cooked and eaten whole, although strictly speaking they are not a pea at all, but a member of the vetch family.

Look for small crisp bright green specimens with fresh-looking stalks. Mangetout pods should be flat with only a hint of a row of gentle swellings where the embryo peas lie. Sugar-snap peas have small, well-rounded pods. Do not store them for more than a day or two, well wrapped in polythene in the refrigerator.

To prepare them for cooking simply top and tail them, removing as much string as you can from the edges. Cook them in as little water as possible or steam or stir-fry them.

They are delicious eaten on their own but make a pretty decoration for light meat, poultry and fish dishes. Chervil, basil, mint and parsley go well with mangetout. For a more unusual dish, combine them with shellfish or mushrooms in a light salad starter. One summer dish I particularly like is a soup made of older, larger, coarser Moroccan mangetout cooked and sieved, in which some of the new season's English crop, no more than an inch or two long, are served whole in the soup. (*13*)

MARROW *table marrow*

The sad thing about this intrinsically rather delicate and attractive summer squash is that it was so often allowed to grow to monstrous proportions, which made it entirely devoid of flavour or texture, so that it became little more than a large container of water.

If you can find small marrows, no more than a foot long, which are firm and unblemished, their sweet freshness will be enhanced by cooking them sliced, in butter or olive oil and herbs, or by stuffing them with a mixture of cooked rice, chopped lamb and mint, for example, and baking them. Marrows can also be turned into chutney or jam.

There is also something called marrow rum, a large marrow is filled with sugar, after a slice has been cut off the top and part of the inside hollowed out. It is then suspended in a pillow-case from a ceiling hook and after suitable fermentation time a hole is poked in the bottom of the marrow and the 'rum' drips through. See also *Courgette*. (*25*)

MOOLI *daikon, rettiche, white radish, winter radish*

Despite looking like a large smooth, clean, white elongated parsnip, mooli is a variety of the same species as radish. It contains twice as much vitamin C as red radishes but less iron and calcium. It has an agreeable fresh, slightly bitter, peppery taste which makes it very appetizing in a salad, peeled and sliced or grated.

Unlike other radishes, mooli is also good cooked but because of its high water content it is a good idea to salt it after peeling and cutting up. Let it stand for 30 minutes or so, then rinse well and steam or boil it until tender.

Those familiar with fine Japanese and Chinese cooking will know that the mooli is an excellent vegetable for carving – into flowers, dragons and phoenix. (*23*)

NASTURTIUM

If you grow nasturtiums the leaves can be an unusual addition to the salad bowl. The round leaves are slightly fleshy with an agreeable peppery flavour, not unlike watercress. But watch out for blackfly lurking underneath. You can also shred them and add to scrambled eggs or omelettes. The flowers are edible too, and the green seed pods can be pickled and used like capers. (*30*)

NAVET *french turnip*

These small, flattish, tender turnips are available in the spring and summer. Their flavour is much more delicate than that of the winter turnip, tasting something like a young kohl rabi, and they are good served plainly cooked with some of the richer meats such as lamb, pork and duckling.

Really fresh unblemished specimens do not need peeling, so the lovely pale purple and white colours of the skin will be preserved in the finished dish. I like to enhance the slight sweetness of the turnip by slicing it thinly, par-cooking it in a little water, then adding orange juice and butter and letting it caramelize. This is delicious served with grilled meats.

Young turnip tops also make excellent spring greens which require little cooking and are rich in vitamins. See also *Turnip*. (*18*)

NETTLE

This hedgerow plant was a welcome addition to our ancestors' kitchens after a long hard winter when few greens were to be had. Like dandelions, nettles had the reputation of being a good spring tonic. Recipes for nettles are essentially rustic as they are not commercial plants.

When you pick them, wear gloves and gather well away from the roadside as anything growing there will have absorbed petrol fumes and much else from passing traffic. Take only the young tips of the nettles. The coarse lower leaves and stalks are not edible. Wash the nettles and cook them, tightly covered, in the water that clings to them. Once cooked the sting has gone and they can be used in all manner of dishes.

An intriguing Welsh recipe I came across calls for a lovely mixture of whatever you can find to make a purée of garden greens: bolting lettuce, dandelions, turnip tops, nettles, anything fresh and green. In Burgundy one of the famous chefs makes a stunning dish of snails in a nettle purée – real hedgerow food that. The best nettle dish I have ever encountered was in the tiny village of Triora perched up in the forest behind the Ligurian riviera. There, nettles were combined with spices and Ricotta cheese as a stuffing for ravioli. (*43*)

OKRA *bamia, bhindi, gumbo, ladies' fingers*

Okra is the American name for this edible seed pod belonging to the hibiscus and mallow family. The small, tapering, five-sided pods are about 3–4in (7–10cm) in length. Choose firm, small, bright green ones that still have a fresh-looking bloom, and that snap cleanly and do not bend. Avoid any that are browning at the edges and tip.

To prepare for cooking, wash and dry them, and carefully pare off the stalk without breaking the seed pod. Inside are tiny edible seeds and a sticky juice. When cooked, the okra gives a rich silky finish to stews and soups. It is the main component of the gumbos (stews of meat or seafood and vegetables) of Louisiana and the southern United States and is also found in Indian and Caribbean cookery. It is delicious stewed with onions, aubergines, tomatoes and garlic; serve it hot or cold. (*13*)

OLIVE

Olives are among the world's oldest fruits and have been cultivated in the Mediterranean region since about 3000BC. They are hard-stoned fruit used for seasoning and as appetizers. You very rarely see fresh olives for sale. They are very bitter and must be treated to remove the bitterness and pickled before they are edible. There are basically three kinds: green, violet and black. Green olives are picked and processed when they are unripe. They are often pickled with herbs and spices and sometimes stuffed with slivers of red pepper or almond. Violet-coloured olives are not quite fully ripe, while the black shiny olives are picked fully ripe when they are brownish pink, then fermented and oxidized to achieve the jet black finish.

Olives are sometimes sold loose from a marinade of oil flavoured with garlic, herbs and lemon peel. These are delicious on their own and can be added to casseroles. Olive flesh can be chopped finely and used as a spread as in the Provençal *tapenade*. Whole black olives can be baked into bread, as in Turkey. Loose olives should be used up within two or three days. Olives packed in brine will keep, unopened, for a year or so. See also OILS, page 121. (*34*)

Olives

ONION

This is the vegetable that cooks never allow themselves to run out of. And it was probably ever thus, as onions have played a major part in the mythology, medicine and cuisine of all the world's major civilizations.

With the exception of spring onions, most of the onions on sale have been allowed to dry out slighty, hence their crisp, papery skin. Choose firm dry specimens with thin light skins, which may or may not be peeling off. Avoid any that are obviously damaged, are soft or show signs of dampness, and any that are beginning to sprout green shoots.

If you have plenty of storage space then a bunch or two of firm sweet onions hung up in a dry airy place is a good idea. Otherwise, since they are used so frequently, it is best to buy them on a regular basis.

Even the ordinary brown onion can vary enormously in skin colour from pale straw colour to dark brown. The flesh varies from greenish-white to creamy yellow. Bulb onions come to Britain from many countries including Spain, Hungary, Chile, Italy, Australia and the Netherlands, and we grow about as much as we import. Spanish onions, which are much milder, have the largest bulbs. When they are finished, in about May or June, the same type of onions are imported from the southern hemisphere.

Beautiful onions with white papery skins are sometimes available. They are mild and sweet, as are the rich dark purple-red onions which are delicious raw and can also be cooked. However they do keep some of their purple colour so you need to think about the appearance of the finished dish.

The tree onion or Egyptian onion is the sort of plant you might grow rather than buy. It is a curious object with small bulbs instead of flowers and larger bulbs underground. It has something of the taste of garlic about it.

The Welsh onion, and its close relation the Japanese bunching onion, known as *chang fa* in Chinese, grows in clusters of approximately six stalks, resembling both chives and leeks. Both leaves and stems are delicious.

For pickling use any small bulb onions, but the brown-skinned, white-fleshed varieties are the most popular for this. Pickling onions are perfect for adding whole to stews, casseroles and such classic dishes as *boeuf à la bourguignonne*. They are sometimes called pearl onions or button onions.

Peeling onions under water is said to prevent tears. Another remedy is to leave the root end on right until the last stroke of the knife; and some people recommend chewing a piece of bread as you peel. Onions can be coarsely grated as well as chopped and sliced. Onion juice can be extracted – rather wastefully it must be said – by squeezing a half onion on a lemon squeezer. If you want to fry onions do not chop them in a food processor. Too much liquid is released and the onions will steam rather than fry.

When adding onion to the stock pot, include a piece of the inner brown skin as this adds a good golden colour, but do not overdo it or a bitter flavour may develop. You can also add colour by frying a thick slice of onion until quite browned on each side and then adding it to the stock. Onions brown readily because they contain sugar which begins to caramelize once it reaches a certain heat.

As well as adding essential flavouring to most savoury dishes, onions are marvellous vegetables in their own right: traditional French onion soup, Alsace onion tart, German *Zwiebelkuchen* (onion tart), onion and potato soup, onion and bread sauce, stuffed onions, baked onions, fried onion rings. I love to cook them slowly with red wine, raisins and herbs such as thyme or marjoram, and serve them with an equally slow-cooking pot roast. See also *Shallot, Spring Onion*. (*35*)

PAK CHOI *bok choi, spoon cabbage*

Originally from China, this member of the cabbage family is now also cultivated in Holland. It is identifiable by its long, white, slightly ribbed leaf stalks which – like celery – are bunched together from a central root. The oval leaves are quite thick and fleshy, mid green on the upper surface and paler underneath.

Occasionally baby *pak choi* can be found and that is a great delicacy, cooked whole. Shanghai *pak choi* is a smaller plant with the same overall shape and pale green, lightly ribbed stems. All have an excellent mild, very uncabbage-like flavour when cooked. They lend themselves best to stir-frying or steaming, but can be boiled. Whichever method is used cook the leaves and stems quickly to retain flavour and texture.

Pak choi fits naturally into the context of a Chinese meal but use it also as a substitute for cabbage or cauliflower in Western meals. (*23*)

PARSNIP

You will look through dozens of French recipe books before you find a recipe for parsnips, and in Italy parsnips are fed to those pigs destined to become San Daniele and Parma ham; but in Britain we still like it as a winter vegetable. The Americans cook it in the same fashion, as a rich sweet glazed vegetable for the festive table at Christmas. Look for regularly shaped roots with unblemished skins and no rusty patches. They will keep in a cool airy place for several days.

Some very tiny specimens sold as baby parsnips, are beginning to be available. These can be be scrubbed and cooked whole. Peel the older ones thinly and cut into slices, strips and chunks. Roast them with a joint of beef, or add to soups and soufflés. Best of all I like them cooked and mashed with potatoes, garlic and butter or olive oil and spiked up with cardamom and black pepper. (*18*)

The Onion Family

1	FRENCH RED ONIONS	9	CHINESE RED ONIONS
2	ITALIAN RED SALAD ONIONS	10	WHITE GARLIC
3	SPANISH ONION	11	PURPLE GARLIC
4	WHITE ONION	12	LEEKS
5	ENGLISH BROWN ONIONS	13	LEEKS (BABY)
6	PEARL OR BUTTON ONIONS	14	SPRING ONIONS (LARGE)
7	SHALLOTS	15	SPRING ONIONS (SMALL)
8	PICKLING ONIONS	16	WELSH ONIONS

PEA

This is the British summer vegetable *par excellence*. The pod should be bright green, with a fresh satiny look to it, and round and full, but not hard as this indicates a rather mature pea. By the time the pod has lost its bright green colour the pea will be starchy and lacking in sweetness.

Cook such peas slowly and make them into a soup or purée with chunks of ham and with plenty of flavouring to liven them up.

Fresh green peas are a traditional accompaniment to duckling in both Britain and France. In France they are cooked with a little bacon, spring onions and shredded lettuce. One of my favourite Indian dishes is *muttar paneer*, a curry

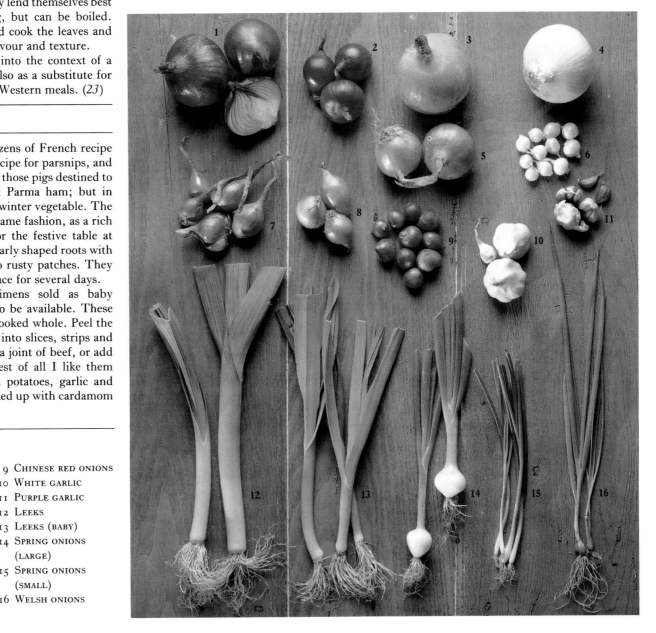

of fresh peas and soft white homemade cheese.

Petits pois are mainly peas picked when very young. The pods are small and sweet, and the young peas inside are very sweet and tender. See also *Mangetout Pea*, and DRIED PULSES, page 94. (*13*)

PEA SHOOT *dao minu, pea tendril*

If you are in Hong Kong during January and February you will come across these tender delicacies. They are nothing more than the growing tip of ordinary pea plants. At the beginning of the season they are enormously expensive and are always treated as a rarity. I love their soft, tender green leaves and their delicious pea flavour. They are usually served with other rare ingredients, *con poy* (dried scallops) or crab roe, for example.

PEPPER *bell pepper, capsicum, sweet pepper*

The pepper family includes not only the large, sweet, mild peppers now so familiar, but literally hundreds of varieties of hot chilli peppers.

Sweet peppers are somewhat squarish, hollow pods, with a pointed or blunt concave end. About ½ inch (1cm) of stalk is usually left on. Originally we could get only green and then red peppers, which are a riper version of the green ones; but new strains with vivid and surprising colours have been developed – yellow, orange, white, even black; and in Holland I have seen beautiful elongated lilac ones. Look for shiny, plump unwrinkled specimens and avoid any which have soft spots. Placed in a plastic bag, they will keep well in the refrigerator. Before cooking them remove the seeds, the white membrane and stalk.

Peppers have many culinary uses, apart from brightening up salads with their thinly sliced rings. Italian pepper salads are delicious: peel the vegetables by grilling the skins until charred, or hold them over a gas flame and then rub off the skin. Then slice the peppers into long broad strips and marinate in plenty of olive oil with additional seasoning for a few hours before serving. Cooked and sieved, they also make colourful sauces. Serve yellow, green and red pepper sauces with steamed or poached fish for a very modern and light dish.

Peppers are also used in ratatouille and added to chicken and pork casseroles. Stuffed peppers are found in Middle Eastern, Mexican, European and Chinese cooking. See also *Chilli*, and SPICES, page 110. (*37*)

PLANTAIN *kayla*

The plantain belongs to the same family as the banana we eat as a fruit. It looks similar but is much larger, starchier and blander. It changes colour from green to yellow to black, becoming sweeter as it ripens, and can be eaten at any of these stages although it must be cooked first to make it palatable. It is best fried in butter when the skin is almost black and the flesh very soft. Depending on the recipe plantains can be cooked in their skins or peeled first. Or you can slit them and insert butter under the skin, then wrap them in foil and bake. Use them also in savoury or sweet dishes, or to replace potatoes as a starchy accompaniment. Plantains combine well with other ingredients, are good with spicy sauces and can be added to stews and casseroles of meat, fish or poultry. Plantain chips or crisps, prepared in the same way as potato crisps, make a crunchy snack.

Plantains are sold unripe (green), half-ripe (yellow) or ripe (black). Green plantains will ripen if kept in a light airy place such as on a window sill. Like bananas they should not be refrigerated. It is better to buy them unripe and ripen them off at home.

Plantain is a good source of carbohydrates, dietary fibre, potassium, carotene and vitamin C. The best recipes come from the Caribbean, Central and South America and Asia. In Guatemala, for example, plantains are peeled, cooked, mashed and mixed with flour and seasoning to form a dough which is rolled into circles, filled with cheese and deep-fried. (*11*)

POTATO

Like the tomato and the pepper, which belong to the same botanical family, the potato was one of the edible treasures introduced to Europe from South America by the Spanish invaders. But it took 200 years for it to be really accepted. Gradually potatoes became an important food source throughout Europe. In Ireland, in the

nineteenth century, it became almost the only food available and when harvests failed people starved or emigrated in thousands.

In France the eighteenth century military pharmacist Parmentier is credited with having popularized the potato. Thus whenever you come across a dish described on a French menu with the word *Parmentier,* expect to find potatoes in it.

The potato can be grown at a higher altitude and in colder climates than any other food crop except barley, and is said to produce more food per acre than any other northern food crop. It came originally from the Andes, where the Incas were familiar with it 2000 years ago. Today it is still an important crop in Peru, Ecuador and Colombia. The main market in Bogotá, Colombia, has a whole section devoted to potatoes; countless varieties, in different shapes, sizes and colours, each appropriate to a particular dish.

The potato is a starchy tuber which grows, several to a single plant, underground. They are sold, whole, in their skins, sometimes loose, sometimes packaged, sometimes washed, sometimes not. In shape and size they vary enormously. Large Desirée can weigh 1lb (500g); new season's new potatoes can weigh less than ½oz (15g). The colour of the skin ranges from an almost parchment-like cream through yellow, brown, pink, red, purple and even to black. The skin's texture can be smooth or netted. There may be 'eyes' (from which the new shoots would have appeared) surrounded by different colours.

The flesh of the potato varies from milky white to cream, pale yellow, deep yellow, or

Peppers and Chillies

1 YELLOW PEPPER	10 CHILLIES (KENYAN)
2 ORANGE PEPPER	11 CHILLIES (BONNET
3 RED PEPPERS	PEPPERS)
4 PURPLE OR 'BLACK'	12 RED PEPPER
PEPPER	13 RED WESTLANDS
5 WHITE PEPPER	PEPPER
6 GREEN PEPPER	14 GREEN WESTLANDS
7 HUNGARIAN WAX	PEPPER
PEPPERS	15 GREEN CHILLIES
8 SMALL BLACK	16 RED CHILLIES
PEPPERS	17 ORANGE CHILLIES
9 SMALL GREEN	(THAI)
PEPPERS	18 INDIAN CHILLIES

SELECTED POTATO VARIETIES

The following varieties are illustrated in the photograph opposite.

Alcmaria (1) First early. All-rounder with good flavour. Best in salads; boil or steam.

Arran Pilot (2) White-fleshed, white-skinned first early. Firm flesh; good in salads; also suitable for chips and baking.

Asperge (3) Second early, also known as *la ratte* and *cornichon*. Yellow skin and waxy, creamy flesh. Excellent in salads or steamed and served hot.

Ausonia (4) Second early of Dutch origin. Waxy texture; boil or steam.

Belle de Fontenay (14) Pale yellow skin with very yellow flesh. Fine-grained flesh keeps its flavour when cooked. Steam or boil; serve hot or cold. Use in stews. Good in salads.

Cara (5) Large round main-crop with creamy flesh. Good all-rounder; best baked or boiled.

Carlingford (6) White-skinned, firm white flesh. Best hot or cold in salads. Tends to flouriness on the outside and hardness in the centre.

Catriona (7) Yellow-skinned second early. Cream-coloured, well-flavoured flesh with floury texture. Bake, roast or steam.

Civa (8) First early of Dutch origin. Waxy flesh; boil or steam.

Cleopatra (9) First early of Dutch origin. Suitable for either boiling or steaming.

Diana (10) Red-skinned, waxy, early main-crop variety. Boil or steam.

Duke of York (11) Yellow-skinned with pale yellow flesh.

Dunbar Standard (12) White-skinned, cream flesh.

Estima (13) Second early. Pale yellow skin and flesh. Ideal for baking; also suitable for boiling.

Golden Wonder (15) Dark brown russetted skin and pale yellow flesh. Best for baking; also suitable for salads and mashing.

Jersey New, Royal Kidney, International Kidney (16) Second early with creamy-yellow skin and flesh. Boil or steam; serve hot or cold. Flesh is tender rather than firm; best served whole.

Kennebec (17) White-skinned, creamy-fleshed main-crop. Good all-rounder.

King Edward (18) Large main-crop; pale skin with pink flashes. Cream-coloured, floury-textured flesh. Excellent all-rounder; less good in salads. Good for roasting.

Marfona (19) Second early. Best for baking; can also be boiled. Unsuitable for roasting.

Maris Peer (20) Second early with white flesh and skin. Very good flavour. Best boiled or steamed; excellent for salads.

Maris Piper (21) Popular main-crop. Thin white skin and cream-coloured flesh. Good flavour. Excellent for boiling, mashing and baking; also suitable for chipping and roasting. Not good for salads.

Morag (22) Main-crop, with pale skin and white, waxy flesh. Boil, bake or steam.

Nadine (23) Second early Scottish variety. Boil or steam.

Pentland Dell (24) Popular main-crop, long oval with white skin and creamy white flesh. Suitable for chips, mashing, roasting and baking. Little flavour; close, firm texture.

Pentland Javelin (25) First early. Very white, smooth-skinned, milky white-fleshed first early. Boil or steam; suitable for salads.

Pentland Squire (26) Main-crop. White-skinned, occasionally russetted, white-fleshed. Floury texture and good cooking qualities; perfect for baking; also boil or mash. Not recommended for salads.

Red Pontiac (27) American variety with dry floury texture, suitable for boiling.

Romano (28) Popular main-crop with red skin and cream flesh. Fairly good all-rounder, not exciting, but suitable for all cooking methods.

Roseval (29) French favourite, main-crop with red skin, yellow flesh and excellent flavour. Fine, firm-fleshed with excellent cooking qualities; steam, boil, fry or use in salads.

Shetland (30) Second early Scottish variety. Flesh and skin darken as it matures. Boil or steam.

Spunta (31) Second early with white skin and pale lemony flesh, firm, waxy yet moist. Suitable for chips and shallow frying; best boiled or parboiled and then finished off by frying.

Vanessa (32) Versatile first early, with very attractive pink skin and pale yellow flesh. Very good flavour. Boil, steam or bake.

Wilja (33) Second early with fair flavour; good all-rounder. Holds its shape when cooked and particularly suitable for boiling or steaming. Use in salads or casseroles; also mash, bake or roast. Yellow, netted skin and pale yellow flesh.

OTHER VARIETIES

Bintje Whitish-yellow skin, with yellow flesh. Suitable for all cooking methods; excellent for chips and in salads.

Charlotte Pale yellow skin and yellow flesh. Firm, waxy texture and good flavour. Excellent in salads, hot or cold.

Desirée Very popular red-skinned main-crop. Pale yellow flesh. Excellent all-rounder, particularly good for mashing and roasting and firm enough for salads.

Edzell Blue White flesh and blue skin; steam or boil. Serve in its skin to enjoy its unusual appearance.

Elvira Italian early; cream skin and flesh. Best in salads. Steam or boil; serve in its skin.

Epicure First early, white, pink-tinged skin, white creamy flesh. Round potato with very good flavour. Best for salads, boiling or mashing.

Home Guard First early. White skin and white flesh, short oval potato. Slightly more floury than most new potatoes; boil or fry.

Kerr's Pink Very good main-crop potato suitable for most types of cooking, considerably less so for salads.

Kingston Main-crop. Good for boiling. Pale yellow skin and cream flesh.

Maris Bard First early. White skin, firm waxy white flesh. For boiling, chipping and salads.

Pentland Hawk Main-crop suitable for most cooking methods, but particularly good for mashing and baking. Good keeping qualities.

Pentland Ivory Main-crop with very white skin and flesh. Mash or bake.

Pink Fir Apple One of the best flavours; main-crop with many characteristics of new potatoes. It has a very elongated tuber, slightly knobbly with one blunt end and the other more pointed. Pinkish-yellow flesh; nutty, earthy taste; firm, waxy texture; flesh still translucent when cooked. Good keeping properties. Excellent in salads; also boil and use in stews.

Shelagh Main-crop Scottish variety with cream flesh and particoloured skin with a tinge of pink in the eyes. Waxy. Boil or steam.

Sirtema Oval first early; yellow skin, pale yellow, firm flesh and good cooking qualities; good in salads and casseroles. Boil or steam; or parboil then shallow fry.

Ulster Sceptre First early, elongated oval potato with white skin and flesh; good firm potato that cooks well by most methods; best for boiling, steaming or in salads.

Charlotte, Desirée, Elvira, Shelagh and Pink Fir Apple are illustrated on page 40.

pinkish yellow. The texture, when cooked, can be floury, watery, mealy, creamy or waxy, in various degrees. Different potatoes are generally suited to specific cooking methods, although a number of varieties can be considered good all-rounders.

There are three main types of potato crop: first earlies, second earlies and main-crop. As their name suggests, the earlies are available first, from late May, and are usually referred to as 'new' potatoes. Main-crop potatoes are available from September until the following June. It is probably impossible to calculate how many varieties of potatoes there are worldwide but it will number in the thousands. How sad then, that just five varieties account for almost three-quarters of the main-crop potatoes which are planted commercially in Britain. Fortunately, as interest in potatoes grows, more varieties are finding their way into our shops.

There can be few more versatile vegetables than the potato. It can be cooked almost any way you can think of. Its own flavour and texture is restrained and this makes it a perfect vehicle for other foods, flavours and textures. The very highest realms of gastronomy welcome the potato, where it is combined in exquisite fashion with *foie gras*, with oysters, or with caviar. Cheese and butter or herbs and olive oil make a potato baked in its jacket an inexpensive yet highly appetizing dish. The potato is nutritious, being an important source of vitamin C, complex carbohydrate, dietary fibre, some protein and essential minerals. Plain boiled, steamed and baked potatoes are, contrary to common belief, low in calories.

Buying potatoes Look for the freshest samples. If you can find newly dug potatoes, they are wonderful. If they are 'new' potatoes the skin should rub away easily and is probably already flaking off. The skin will look tight, as if the potatoes are bursting with freshness. Main-crop potatoes should be free of damage, of both mechanical and insect variety, and clean, with smooth tight skins. Do not buy if the skins feel dry and wrinkle when you touch them. Do not buy any that are beginning to sprout or turning green. This means they have been exposed to the light and toxins are being formed under the skin.

New potatoes are best used soon after buying. If you have to store them for a few days, put them in a cool, dark, airy place. Main-crop potatoes are often sold in polythene bags. Transfer them to a large, stout brown paper bag and keep it folded over. Except for the very oldest, thick-skinned, scabby specimens you can scrub potatoes and cook them in their skins before peeling them. The skins of new potatoes can be eaten along with the flesh, and the crisp skin on a potato baked in its jacket is delicious. Potatoes for chips are customarily peeled first. (*38, 40*)

Potatoes

1 PINK FIR APPLE	4 DESIRÉE
2 SHELAGH	5 CHARLOTTE
3 ELVIRA	

PUMPKIN

This is perhaps the best known of all the winter squashes. Pumpkins are native to America but have been known in Britain since the sixteenth century.

These hard-skinned, brilliant orange vegetables can grow to an enormous size; one specimen weighed in at 400lb (125kg). Usually they are more manageable: 'pie pumpkins' can be found at around 6lb (3kg) and the variety Jack-Be-Little is tiny, up to 2lb (1kg) in weight. Even so, many pumpkins are larger than the average household might want unless a pumpkin lantern is required and so it is often sold by the piece. If buying it this way check that the orange flesh is firm, not fibrous. As well as the traditional pumpkin pie, filled with spices and brown sugar, pumpkin makes a delicious soup, particularly when cooked in the shell, and is also extremely good peeled, chopped into chunks and cooked in rich meat stews in the South American fashion.

Pumpkin contains a great deal of water and cooks down to about half its bulk. (*45*)

PURSLANE

This is a small plant with stiff, reddish stems and crisp, succulent, smooth, fleshy rounded leaves. Its mild flavour and unusual texture make it an excellent addition to the salad bowl, but it is also very good as a cooked vegetable. Its scarcity makes it unlikely to be used very often as a vegetable, however, which is a pity as it was a favourite summer dish of our ancestors. Occasionally, it can still be found during the summer months. Buy it for immediate use while it is still crisp and fresh.

It is a good source of iron but also, like sorrel, has a high oxalic acid content and should not be eaten in large quantities. Oxalic acid inhibits the absorption of calcium and magnesium. (*30*)

RADICCHIO *red chicory*

Not to be confused with red-leaved lettuces, radicchio is the Italian name for chicory in general, although in Britain it is applied to the red, round-headed, compact types. There are several varieties: Treviso has long pointed leaves, red at the edges with a broad white rib. Castelfranco is a very decorative variety with green leaves streaked with red, and an inner head of red and white.

All the red chicories are excellent in salads as they add an agreeable bitterness and firm texture. In Italy, however, particularly around Trieste, Treviso and Venice, where it is a local winter crop, it is not unusual to come across it in a wide variety of cooked dishes. It makes a marvellous stuffing for ravioli when chopped and wilted in a little olive oil and mixed with Ricotta and Parmesan cheese. I like it shredded and stirred into a dish of steaming hot spaghetti, with oil and garlic, and have used it in delicious risottos. Charcoal-grilled, it is fabulous. Sadly, the rich colour is lost in cooking; the pretty red leaves fade to a rather dull autumnal brown, but the flavour remains.

Look for bright, firm, crisp, unblemished leaves and clean stalks. Keep it no longer than you would lettuce, well wrapped and in the salad drawer of the refrigerator. (*30*)

RADISH

I do not think there is a cookery writer who has lived in France for any length of time who does not have an unfading memory of a plate of crisp red and white radishes, with their tufts of tender green leaves left on, eaten with crusty bread, salt and pale, creamy, unsalted butter. The radishes in question are the small, slender, elongated French breakfast variety, which seem to have a nutty sweetness that the round radishes lack. They are eaten as a simple starter in the summer, for this is when radishes are at their best. Look for small, firm, bright specimens and avoid any that are limp or damaged in any way. If you can, buy them in bunches with the leaves still attached as these are obviously a good guide to freshness. The larger radishes may be over-mature and rather tasteless. Red, red and white, and white radishes are available. They are eaten raw in salads. I would not recommend cooking radishes. See also *Mooli*. (*18*)

ROCKET *arugula, roquette, rucola*

This is an old-fashioned salad herb that is now enjoying a great revival in Britain and America. Judging from the abundance of rocket in Italian and French markets it has never gone out of fashion there.

It is a small plant with irregular, slightly fiddle-shaped leaves which resemble radish or young turnip tops. They have a distinctive peppery taste which makes them an excellent addition to salads although they can also be cooked, quickly in olive oil, and stirred into a bowl of pasta. Rocket is often to be found as a component of *salades composées* in French and English restaurants. In Italy it is often served with *carpaccio*, the thin slices of raw beef served with shavings of pungent Parmesan cheese and a dribble of olive oil. (*30*)

RUNNER BEAN

When they were first introduced to Britain from South America in the early 1600s runner beans were grown as ornamental climbing plants and the bright red flowers were used in bouquets and posies. It was only in the last century that they were grown as a vegetable.

Homegrown runner beans are available from July until about October. When choosing them, look for fresh, firm, bright green specimens. They should not be giant-sized, should snap easily and not be very stringy. If you can find very small, young runner beans, these are good raw in salads. Otherwise they need cooking to soften the fibre and make them palatable. Before cooking, top and tail them and remove the long, fibrous strings. As new stringless varieties become available this may not be necessary. Do *not* slice or worse shred, the beans before cooking. If you do, much of the goodness will be leached out of them. Cook them whole and then cut up if necessary.

The very large stick-like beans have little to recommend them, being rather bland and lacking in character, not to mention stringy. Herbs and spices will be needed to cheer them up, or a good salad dressing. (*13*)

SALAD BURNET

Another rare salad herb which you are more likely to find on the Continent than in Britain unless you grow it yourself. I have seen boxes of it on sale in the wholesale market in Amsterdam, where it was labelled *pimpernel*, and destined for the city's grandest restaurants. The tiny toothed leaves, rather like strawberry leaves, have a sharp, nutty, cucumber flavour, useful in salads but also in sauces and soups. Butters and cream cheeses can be flavoured with salad burnet, and it can also be infused in vinegar. (*30*)

SALSIFY *oyster plant, vegetable oyster*

Like its close cousin scorzonera, salsify is little appreciated in Britain and America. In Europe it is widely available in markets, food shops and restaurants when it is in season from autumn to late spring. It somewhat resembles a very long, thin, tapering carrot and is sold in bundles often without the leaf tops. The skin is earthy, brownish and rough, the flesh creamy white.

One of its names, the vegetable oyster, is thought to stem from a similarity in flavour, although I do not detect this. It is, nevertheless, an extremely good winter vegetable, especially with pork, chicken and game.

The tender white flesh discolours when exposed to air, so it is best to scrape each root and drop it into a little vinegar and water. Parboil, drain, cut to the desired length and then finish cooking it until tender. Alternatively, scrub the roots well, cook them in their skins and then peel them. Serve *au naturel* or with a rich creamy or lemony sauce; dress in a vinaigrette and serve cold as a salad; or combine with prawns, scallops or even oysters.

SCORZONERA *black salsify*

This is, like salsify, a member of the daisy family and is cultivated for its roots. Scorzonera is bigger than salsify and the skin is much darker, but should be cooked and prepared in the same way. Its flavour and texture is perhaps a little more intense, but otherwise there is very little difference. Do not be put off by the bundle of dirty-looking roots. The effort preparing them is more than repaid by the discovery of a winter vegetable far superior to most. (*18*)

SEA KALE *silver kale*

This plant is native to most coastal areas of Britain and Western Europe and is not widely available commercially. It is cultivated for its thick celery-like stalks and also the broad leaves, similar to rhubarb but paler. If you do cook the leafy tops, do so separately as they take far less time to cook than the stalks. They are also eaten raw in salads like young spinach.

It is preferable to steam rather than boil the stalks, to best appreciate their delicate flavour, and serve them as you would asparagus with any of the appropriate sauces.

If you are lucky enough to find sea kale in the shops (which should not be confused with sea kale chard) make sure that the stalks are firm and ivory white with no damage or discolouration. Keep it for a couple of days at most in a cold, dark, airy place.

SEA KALE CHARD *sea kale beet*

Sea kale chard is one of the beet varieties, like swiss chard, which are cultivated for their chards or mid ribs rather than their roots. Steam them until tender, then cut up and serve with melted butter or a butter or oil-based sauce.

SHALLOT

The true French shallot resembles a bulb of garlic more than a small onion. It has a papery russet skin, is somewhat conical in shape and is often made up of two or more 'cloves'. Shallots are quite indispensable to authentic classic French sauces and other dishes. I love their mild yet concentrated flavour and occasionally flavour a bottle of wine vinegar by steeping a shallot in it. See also *Onion*. (*35*)

SORREL *French sorrel*

This soft leafy green herb is so sour that it may be used to curdle milk and make junkets. A frothy sorrel soup, a creamy sorrel omelette, a rich yet sharp sorrel sauce to go with salmon are all classic French dishes. Fortunately it is slowly becoming more available here. If you do see it, look for the freshest, firmest leaves possible and do not keep for more than two or three days, well wrapped in polythene, in the salad drawer of the refrigerator. Because of its high oxalic acid content, which inhibits absorption of magnesium and calcium, sorrel should not be eaten in large quantities, not that you are likely to get the chance. Use its fresh astringent flavour to good effect in salads, potato dishes and egg dishes.

There is another plant sometimes called sorrel, and also known as roselle. It is a type of hibiscus and its pink flowerheads are used in the West Indies both as a vegetable and as a herb to flavour a traditional Christmas drink. It has a sweet-sour flavour. (*43*)

SOYA BEAN *soja, soybean, soy pea*

Fresh soya beans are usually only available commercially in the areas in which they are grown: China, South-East Asia and parts of the United States in the late summer, with very little in Britain. There are something like a thousand varieties cultivated in South-East Asia, in several sizes and colours: yellow, green, brown and black.

Cook it as you would cook other beans, bearing in mind that it has a very delicate bland taste. See also DRIED PULSES, page 94. (*13*)

SPINACH

Most of our spinach is homegrown and, with some imports from Europe, available all year round. It has been grown in Britain as a salad green and a vegetable for at least 400 years, and is believed to have originated in Asia.

Spinach is an excellent source of vitamins A and C. However, it also contains oxalic acid and one should not eat it in the quantities prescribed by Popeye's creators in the 1930s! To me it has always seemed something of a luxury, special-occasion vegetable. It is prepared in large quantities since it cooks down to a shadow of its original bulk, and it goes well with lots of butter, cream and exotic spices.

Young tender spinach leaves are excellent raw in salads. When choosing, look for firm, fresh, crisp deep green leaves without blemishes, insect damage or slime. Always use spinach within a day or so of buying it, and until you do so, store it in a cool place. To prepare wash it well in several changes of water to remove any grit and soil and shake it dry. Remove any central ribs if these are tough. Cook it briefly until just soft in the water that clings to its leaves; do not add any. Drain it well, and press out excess liquid in a sieve. To use as a cooked vegetable, buy 8–10oz (250–300g) per person. About half that amount of young spinach is enough to serve raw in a salad.

Spinach is found in the traditional recipes of many countries: in Middle Eastern pastries, in delicious vegetable curries from India, in sweet French tarts, in Spanish omelettes and in any dish described as Florentine. It goes beautifully with eggs, particularly in a simple dish of poached eggs on a bed of cooked spinach. The flavour of ham is an excellent foil for it and it can be used in numerous fish and shellfish recipes. It is not always obvious what vegetable to serve as an accompaniment to a fish dish. Spinach never fails to please. It is well worth all the washing and rinsing it needs before cooking. (*43*)

SPINACH BEET *beetgreen, spinach green*

Although it slightly resembles a coarser version of spinach, this vegetable is actually a form of beetroot that is grown solely for its leaves.

Look for fresh leaves and clean, milky white stalks. Remove the stalks when washing it. The leaves, when blanched, can also be used for wrapping things, rather as you might use vine leaves. It can be shredded and added to thick vegetable soups for extra winter vitamins, or substitute it in recipes for chard. (*43*)

SPRING GREENS

Despite their name, spring greens are now available year-round, although they tend to be more popular in the winter, perhaps because they go well with the more wintry casseroles. They are non-hearting cabbages with all the nutritional qualities of the cabbage, and a particularly good flavour. They should be bought for eating within a couple of days. I like spring greens with braised beef or pork, but also braised with chunks of smoked bacon and slivers of sun-dried tomatoes. See also *Cabbage*. (*14*)

SPRING ONION *salad onion, scallion*

These are available all year round and are useful in winter salads when there are few other greens about. They are sold in bunches or pre-packed. Look for clean specimens with firm white bases and undamaged green tops. Any sliminess indicates that they are less than fresh. The thinner the spring onion, the milder it will be. To prepare it for salads chop off the roots and remove the topmost part of the green, then use whole or sliced. Spring onions can also be cooked in stir-fried dishes and in omelettes. Young spring onion tops are an excellent substitute for chives. (*35*)

Leaf Vegetables

1 BANANA LEAF	7 NETTLES
2 SORREL	8 BEETROOT TOPS
3 SPINACH BEET	(GOLDEN BEET)
4 CALLALOO	9 TURNIP TOPS
5 SPINACH	10 BEETROOT TOPS
6 VINE LEAVES	11 CHARD

SQUASH

Cucumbers, melons, marrows, courgettes, pumpkins, gourds and squashes all belong to the same family of vegetables. Some are used for decoration only, but most members of this family are edible.

The two main types are summer squash and winter squash. With year-round availability these terms are no longer very helpful but it is useful to know that summer squashes are, in general, small, quick-growing, with thin skins, soft seeds and pale flesh. Courgettes are characteristic of this type, as the pumpkin is the perfect example of the winter squash with its tough, much darker rind and flesh and hard seeds.

Summer squashes, when young and tender, require no peeling and quick cooking. Cook them as you would courgettes and match them with other sunny summery flavours such as tomatoes, basil and garlic.

Winter squashes are usually peeled before being cut up in chunks and cooked, at their best baked but they can also be added to stews and soups. In Britain squashes are something of a neglected vegetable which is a pity when you consider that they are almost as good a source of vitamin A as carrots, and are often just as sweet and firm. Yet they are far more versatile too, particularly the larger ones that can serve as a cooking container as well as a basis for an exciting dish. Think about a squash soup, spiced up with lots of good flavours from herbs and nutmeg, enriched with a little meat and served in the hollowed out rind. American cookery books are far more adventurous. I came across a delicious recipe for a baked squash pie in which mashed winter squash is flavoured with ginger, lemon juice, and crushed aniseed.

Among the Oriental gourds there are mild and bitter varieties; loofah, dudi, fuzzy melon and tindoori are mild, kantola and karela are on the bitter side. These squashes are described under their separate headings. (45)

Squashes, Pumpkins and Gourds

1 SQUASH (ONION)
2 WINTER MELON
3 PUMPKIN (TABLE KING)
4 PUMPKIN (JAMAICAN)
5 PUMPKIN (WEST INDIAN)
6 PUMPKIN (LONG-NECKED)
7 BUTTERNUT SQUASH
8 TURBAN SQUASH
9 SQUASH (YELLOW BIRD)
10 PUMPKIN (GELE REUZIN)
11 SQUASH (CROWN PRINCE)
12 SQUASH (PONCA)
13 SQUASH (RED KURI)
14 VEGETABLE SPAGHETTI
15 MOSCHATA SQUASH
16 WINTER SQUASH
17 GOLDEN NUGGET
18 SQUASH (HONEY DELIGHT)
19 PUMPKIN (NEW ZEALAND)
20 PUMPKIN (HOIKOIDO)
21 CUSTARD MARROW
22 MARROW (LITTLE GEM)
23 CHRISTOPHINE
24 SQUASH (GEM)
25 CUSTARD MARROW
26 SNAKE GOURD
27 LOOFAH
28 KANTOLA
29 PUMPKIN (JACK-BE-LITTLE)
30 FUZZY MELON
31 PATTY PAN (YELLOW CUSTARD MARROW)
32 KARELA
33 CHINESE BITTER MELON
34 SQUASH (HERCULES WAR CLUB GOURD)

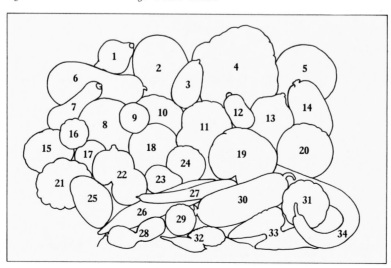

SWEDE *rutabaga*

This is a large winter vegetable of the cabbage family, grown for its roots and its leaves. It is very similar to turnip in flavour and texture, and can be used interchangeably in recipes (in northern parts of Britain it is called turnip). But the swede's flesh is pale orange, that of the turnip creamy white.

When buying swede look for smaller rather than larger specimens, which are likely to be coarse and woody inside. Avoid any that are damaged or broken or show signs of worm damage.

It can be peeled and roasted with a joint of meat, cooked in soups, added to casseroles or turned into a rather more elegant version of mashed swede with plenty of cream or butter, nutmeg and a little ginger to give it the class it generally lacks. In Scotland mashed swede and turnip – 'bashed neeps' – is the traditional accompaniment to haggis. (*19*)

SWEETCORN *corn-on-the-cob, maize*

Sweetcorn comes from maize, the tall grass thought to have originated in Mexico. This is a delicious vegetable when it is really fresh. It has a sweet juiciness unlike anything else. Sweetcorn is quite high in carbohydrate, and contains protein, dietary fibre, mineral salts, vitamins A and C (and some of the B group).

When buying sweetcorn look for creamy, tightly packed, juicy kernels on a plump well-rounded cob. If buying it still in the husk make sure that this is soft and tender, pale green with a bloom on it, and that the corn silk (the tassel at the end) is brown, fine and silky.

Corn is best simply boiled by dropping it into boiling water for five to eight minutes – having first stripped it of its husk and silk – then served with melted butter. Do not add salt to the water as this may toughen the kernels. A pinch of sugar can be added if you doubt the sweetness of the corn. It can also be very successfully barbecued. For dishes such as corn fritters or crab and sweetcorn soup I would use frozen corn.

Baby sweetcorn, harvested when immature and eaten whole or sliced lengthways, is often included in Thai and other Oriental recipes. It can be almost white, or yellow. Particularly

delicious simply stir-fried with other vegetables, it should never be overcooked or it will become tough and lose its sweetness. Use it also in salads, boiling it first for about three minutes and combining it with the dressing while still warm. Look for fresh, plump specimens; avoid any that look wrinkled and dried out. (*13*)

SWEET POTATO

Native to tropical America, sweet potatoes have now become an important food crop in South-East Asia, China and Japan and are a staple in the southern United States. Indeed there it is referred to simply as potato and the white potato is called the Irish potato.

The skin of this elongated tuber may be pinkish or yellowish in colour and is delicate. There are several types of sweet potato. The flesh can range from mealy to moist, and from almost white to deep yellow in colour. It is best, if possible, to boil or bake sweet potatoes in their skins and then peel them, as some of the varieties can take on an unappealing greyish tone if cooked peeled. Choose smooth plump potatoes with unwrinkled skins. They will keep well for up to a month in a cool dry airy place.

You can cook them as you would potatoes but their delicious sweetness makes them wonderfully versatile, not only in soups and casseroles, but in sweet dishes, pies, breads and in puddings. I was first introduced to sweet potatoes when I sat down to my first American Christmas dinner. With the turkey, cranberry sauce and cream gravy was served a dish of candied sweet potatoes – translucent, golden brown chunks of rich sticky sweetness to be eaten in small helpings They can also be mashed with lots of butter and black pepper. (*19*)

TANNIA *coco yam*

One of the starchy tubers that is an important food source in the tropics, tannia can grow up to 10lb (5kg) in weight but is usually smaller – 2–3lb (1–1·4kg). It has a rough hairy brown skin, with a bulbous end and a tapered end. Peel and cut it up before boiling. Like most of these tubers, it is often made into a bland purée which serves as an excellent foil for all kinds of spicy meat or fish dishes. (*19*)

TARO

This is a rough brown-skinned tuber similar in appearance to yam. It is essentially the same as an eddo but larger and originated in South-East Asia and India. It is peeled, sliced and boiled like potatoes. In a cool dry place it will keep for three or four months. See also *Eddo*. (*19*)

TINDOORI

These small mild gourds are members of the cucumber family and indeed resemble gherkins in appearance and cucumber in flavour. The largest ones are no more than 3in (7cm) in length and 1½in (3·5cm) in diameter. They have green skins, either pale, or dark with paler stripes, and moist crisp pale green flesh with many seeds. Eat them in salads, but be careful, some varieties are slightly bitter and it is not possible to tell which are which from their appearance. They are most often used in Indian cookery as pickles, side dishes or in vegetable curries. See also *Squash*.

TOMATO

It seems that at long last, growers are beginning to hear our plea for tomatoes that taste like tomatoes. For many years that seemed to be the least important attribute. People wanted tomatoes to look good, which meant they had to be large, with a bright regular surface, had to be disease-resistant, had to ripen at the same time

Tomatoes

1 GREEN STUFFING TOMATOES (UNRIPE)	10 ORANGE TOMATOES (GOLDEN BOY)
2 LARGE PINK TOMATO	11 SMALL RED TOMATOES
3 PINK TOMATOES	12 CHERRY TOMATOES
4 GREEN (UNRIPE) TOMATOES	13 SMALL CHERRY TOMATOES
5 BEEFSTEAK TOMATO	14 YELLOW TOMATOES
6 PLUM TOMATOES	15 YELLOW CHERRY TOMATOES
7 RED TOMATOES (GARDENER'S DELIGHT)	16 YELLOW PEAR TOMATOES
8 TIGERELLA TOMATOES	17 YELLOW CURRANT TOMATOES
9 LARGE ORANGE TOMATO	

as their neighbours. Fortunately, things are changing.

Now you can find the sweet little cherry red or yellow tomatoes which still have a hint of that glorious tomato fragrance that you get when you brush past a plant in the greenhouse.

Beef tomatoes – extra-large varieties – are usually imported from Holland. They are sometimes more irregular in shape and are used in salads for their firm texture – sadly however, they can lack flavour. Marmande-type tomatoes from Provence, France and Morocco do sometimes reach our shelves and these are a rare treat to be snapped up, as are the plum tomatoes which are occasionally available at the end of the summer. These have the best flavour for sauces and soups, and have a denser, less watery flesh than the round varieties. Yellow tomatoes can sometimes be found and these are delicious. Even rarer are the tiny cherry and pear-shaped yellow tomatoes which are a boon to those who like miniature vegetables for garnishes.

Tomatoes ripen off very quickly. If you put one ripe tomato in a bowl of green tomatoes it will ripen them. But unripe green tomatoes can make a spicy chutney.

It is possible to buy tomatoes all year round, but the bulk of the homegrown crop comes on to the market in the late summer. That is the time for experimenting. Try making tomato ices, tomato and fruit soups, herb and tomato sauces

for pasta, tomatoes with exotic stuffings, tomato juice for breakfast and tomato jam. Best of all slice them, sprinkle with sea salt and a little olive oil and cover with shredded basil for one of the most perfect summer dishes ever. When a recipe calls for the addition of lemon juice I have occasionally used the juice which runs from tomatoes, not the pulp from around the seeds. It has a very agreeable acidity – more neutral than that of lemon and lime – which makes it particularly useful for marinating raw fish. Tomatoes feature largely in Italian and Spanish cooking, are essential in many Provençal dishes including ratatouille and add a hint of the warm South in winter casseroles.

I could not live without canned tomatoes which I use for soups, sauces and casseroles. Sun-dried tomatoes are another useful form of preserved tomato. They have a dense texture and highly concentrated flavour which is marvellous when added to slow-cooking casseroles. A very simple pasta sauce can be made by cutting sun-dried tomatoes into thin strips and stirring them with olive oil and crushed garlic into a bowl of freshly cooked pasta. (*47*)

TURBAN SQUASH *buttercup squash*

This unusual vegetable, a winter squash with a turban-like formation at the flower end, is one of the most delicious of the squash family. It

has firm, dry, sweet, deep orange flesh which makes lovely soups and will provide an excellent filling for a sweet pie, pumpkin fashion. See also *Squash*. (*44*)

TURNIP

This is another member of the cabbage family grown mainly for its root in Britain. The tops, when young and tender, have a delicious peppery taste and are much loved in Europe and the southern United States where they are sold as turnip greens and cooked like other greens.

Turnips have a nutty delicate sweetness when young. Once allowed to grow much bigger than a tennis ball they lose some of their sweetness and take on a much coarser texture and taste. I once had thinly sliced raw turnip as part of the *mezze* – mixed hors d'oeuvres – in a Cypriot restaurant and was surprised to find it as good as apple; cool, crunchy and delicious.

Emphasize their sweetness by cooking them in thin slices with a little fruit juice and butter. They become lightly caramelized and make a good accompaniment to winter dishes. Or serve them raw, sliced or grated in a vinaigrette.

Young turnips are sometimes sold in bunches in the spring and summer. Good specimens will have smooth undamaged skins of pale purple or white shading into green. They will not need peeling. Main-crop turnips will be larger and

SKINNING TOMATOES

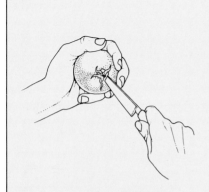 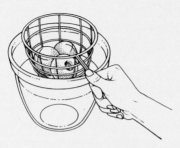 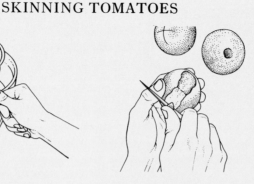 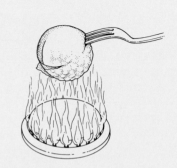

1 *Remove the green calyx and a small piece of the tougher core. Cut a cross in the other end of each tomato.*

2 *Lower the tomatoes into a basin of water which has just been boiled, and leave them there for about 30 seconds.*

3 *Drain the tomatoes and peel back the skin. It should come away very easily.*

4 *Alternatively, skin tomatoes by holding them over an open flame for 15 seconds or so.*

need peeling. Again look for undamaged specimens and avoid any that are spongy or have worm holes. See also *Navet*. (*18, 43*)

VEGETABLE SPAGHETTI *spaghetti squash*

This makes an excellent one-pot supper dish for two! It resembles a honeydew melon, ovoid, with a thin hard rind, pale creamy-white or bright yellow. Inside are flat seeds which are usually young enough to be edible and, its most distinctive feature, a mass of tangled, spaghetti-like threads. To cook it pierce a hole in one end with a skewer to stop it exploding and boil or bake it for about 40 minutes. Check for tenderness by piercing it again with a skewer. Cut it in half horizontally and pour on a meat or tomato sauce. Eat it just as you would a bowl of spaghetti. See also *Squash*. (*45*)

VINE LEAF

Fresh vine leaves are rarely sold commercially, but if there is a vine growing nearby, a few leaves removed in the early summer will not hurt the plant and they are a pleasure to cook with.

Choose soft green leaves that are not in any way beginning to coarsen in texture or darken in colour. The leaves will be smooth on top and a little frizzy underneath. If you want to stuff them choose ones with as little indentation as possible, remove the stalk and blanch them in boiling water for three minutes.

The use of vine leaves in cooking probably goes back as far as the cultivation of vines, and is a particular feature of Greek and Middle Eastern dishes. They will impart some of their tart grapy flavour to whatever is cooked with them, so wrap them around quails, sardines, red mullet, chicken breasts and other small pieces of meat or fish before baking; or set a joint of meat on top of a bed of vine leaves for roasting. Try cooking vegetable casseroles in a pan lined with vine leaves. When they are stuffed, as in the Middle East, with spiced rice and meat mixtures, the vine leaves are eaten along with the stuffing.

Fresh vine leaves will keep well for a few days in the salad drawer of the refrigerator. If you buy packets of brined vine leaves soak them in hot water for 20–30 minutes, rinse well and dry on kitchen paper before use. (*43*)

WATER CHESTNUT *ma taai*

These are small corms up to 2in (5cm) across with dark brown skin and triangular leaf scales. Mainly used in Chinese cooking, they have a crunchy, moist texture and a sweet, slightly earthy, nutty flavour. They can be eaten raw or cooked and are often to be found in sweet dishes or minced with meat to provide texture for the fillings in *dim sum*, those exquisite little morsels which are steamed or fried and served for lunch in Cantonese restaurants. Western cooks have adopted water chestnuts, wrapped in bacon and grilled, as an interesting hors d'oeuvre.

Chinese water chestnuts must be carefully peeled before use and only those with crisp white flesh should be used. (*19*)

WATERCRESS

Almost all our watercress is homegrown, most of it in Hampshire and Dorset. It is the most widely used of all the cresses, which are, as you would imagine from their tart peppery flavour, members of the mustard family. It is rich in iron, calcium and vitamins A and C, although one would need to eat it in large quantities to absorb one's daily iron ration.

Watercress does not keep well and is best eaten within 24 hours of purchase. Avoid wilting or yellowing cress which indicates that it is no longer fresh. Pick watercress in the wild only from free-flowing streams, and only if you are sure the stream cannot have been polluted by sheep droppings – when there is a danger of liver fluke; wash it thoroughly.

As well as being a traditional salad ingredient and sandwich filling watercress combines well with eggs, in omelettes, quiches or even a simple dish of scrambled eggs. Use it finely chopped to mix with butter and serve it with grilled fish or meat. Even better, make it into a purée and serve it as a sauce. Watercress can be used to make delicious soups, hot or cold. (*30*)

WINTER MELON *Chinese bitter melon*

Winter melon is another of those wonderful container vegetables like pumpkins and vegetable spaghetti. Although it can be cooked, Western-style, as you would other summer squashes (after peeling, of course) or stir-fried in Chinese dishes, it is at its majestic best as the centrepiece of a Cantonese banquet as Winter Melon Pond. This is a soup slowly braised in the partially hollowed-out melon – good stock containing pork, goose, Yunnan ham, crabmeat and all manner of other delights. The skin is intricately carved with dragons, phoenixes or Chinese characters wishing the guests a long life and other auspicious greetings. (*45*)

YAM

Living in Nigeria for a year I became very familiar with yams. Too familiar. *Fufu* (a kind of thick yam porridge) was not an exciting dish. For some reason, although it bears a passing resemblance to mashed potatoes, it is not something I could eat every day, unlike mashed potatoes. And although it acts as an excellent foil to hot peppery stews as its soft blandness soothes in a most effective fashion, the yam is not a particularly good staple, being largely starch with little in the way of vitamins and minerals.

Yams come in all sizes and shapes, some irregular, some cylindrical and weighing anything up to 12lb (5·5kg). They are sold whole or in pieces. The skin is usually brown and bark-like, rough and sometimes slightly hairy. The flesh can vary: white, yellow, even purple, the white being the finest. They can be peeled, boiled and mashed with butter and seasonings, or wrapped in foil, unskinned, and baked, when they are absolutely delicious. (*19*)

YARD-LONG BEAN *asparagus bean*

These resemble French beans and can be prepared and cooked the same way. The striking difference between them and their more familiar cousins is that they do indeed grow up to a yard long. In flavour they are more like runner beans than French beans.

They are sold in bundles. Look for springy, firm, bright green specimens with the smallest possible swellings. This means that the beans inside the pod are still young and tender. The whole bean is eaten, pod and all, although in northern China the plants are allowed to grow to maturity for the beans inside and not the pod. The beans are then dried. (*13*)

SEA VEGETABLES

When steaming a whole fish I often lay it on top of a bundle of seaweed – of the coarse dark bladder-filled variety – in the bottom of the fish kettle where it permeates the steam with a wonderfully fragrant, healthful, minerally scent which combines perfectly with the flavours of the fish. But seaweed can be eaten, too. It is a major feature of Japanese cooking: the essential ingredient (with or without bonito fish flakes) in *dashi*, the stock which is the basis of much Japanese food, from the soup served at breakfast, lunch and dinner to sauces and numerous other dishes. In Wales one of the traditional dishes is laverbread, not a bread at all but a mass of washed and cooked seaweed. Seaweed is also used in Chinese cooking, and is beginning to be adapted to the Western table, particularly in fish dishes where it contributes visual appeal as well as a new flavour and texture.

The Japanese consider seaweed to be an important element in their diet and indeed it.is crammed full of many of the vitamins we find in vegetables (abundant vitamins of the B complex, C, E and K varieties) as well as being rich in minerals such as calcium, iodine, iron, magnesium, potassium, sodium, copper and zinc. High-quality protein is found in seaweed, and some of it is a useful gelling agent.

Most seaweed is sold dried, and in this form it keeps indefinitely. Reconstitute it by soaking in water and boiling it until soft.

AGAR-AGAR *kanten*

Indirectly an ingredient in the famous Chinese bird's nest soup, agar-agar is obtained from various types of seaweed, including *Gelidium japonicum*, found in the Far East. There it is used as a foodstuff, sold after processing into thin, transparent white sheets, strips and sticks from which it is made into soups and jellies, both sweet and savoury. It is used in *yokan*, a Chinese sweet made with bean jam. (Chinese swallows also use the seaweed to build their nests.) It is a useful vegetarian alternative to gelatine.

ARAME *sea oak*

Dark greenish-brown seaweed rich in calcium and with a delicate mild flavour. It is sold dried and shredded and can be an ingredient in traditional Japanese *miso* soup (made from fermented soybean paste and water). Soak for five minutes, then simmer for about 30 minutes.

CARRAGHEEN *Irish moss*

This is a reddish-purple seaweed, and should be bought sun-bleached out to a yellowy pink. It grows in fan-like branches and fronds around Atlantic coastlines in America and Europe and in its natural state is tough and almost translucent. It is still widely used for its gelling properties in Ireland where, for example, it is cooked in milk, which is then strained to make a set blancmange mould. It can also be used as a thickener in soups and stews.

DULSE *dillisk*

A reddish-brown seaweed found all around the Atlantic coastline, it is still used in Ireland and parts of Scotland. Street vendors in Edinburgh 100 years ago used to sell 'dulse and tangle', dulse mixed with another seaweed, kelp, and sweetened. The great chef Soyer used it in St Patrick's soup and thus introduced it to classical cooking. Because of its salty, tangy flavour, it needs a bland foil and is therefore excellent with potatoes, as in the Irish dish 'dulse champ', a mixture of mashed potatoes, dulse cooked until soft, and plenty of butter. It can also be eaten raw in salads, especially with a vinaigrette dressing, and makes a spectacular garnish.

HIJIKI *hiziki*

One of the most agreeable of Japanese seaweeds, with a tasty sweetish flavour, this is usually only available dried. It looks like a mass of fine, curly brown shreds and needs no soaking and very little cooking as it is bought pre-cooked. In Japan it is either simmered with vegetables, or fried and then simmered. Add it to any mixed vegetable stew.

KELP *kombu, konbu, laminaria*

Although this is the generic name for most of the brown seaweeds, kelp has many picturesque names in Britain such as sugarware, fingerware and grockle, but it is also found all over the world, East as well as West, and in the southern hemisphere. Cooked or raw, kelp has an excellent flavour and it has the valuable property of helping to soften other foods. It is worth buying some to cook with dried pulses.

One large-leaved, succulent, brownish-green type of kelp, *kombu*, is best known as an ingredient in Japanese cooking, where it is very widely used for poaching and stewing. Japanese *kombu* is usually dried or pickled or shaved thin in dry sheets for wrapping *sushi*.

LAVER *nori*

Perhaps the best known of the edible seaweeds in Britain, laver is a strong survivor of traditional regional cooking. It is widely used in Wales; in Scotland and Ireland (sloke) and Cornwall (black butter). After the lengthy process of washing, soaking and long cooking, a dense, dark purée called laverbread is produced. In Wales it is rolled in oatmeal and fried in round flat cakes to be served for breakfast with bacon. It is delicious! A little mixed with stock and the juice of a Seville orange makes traditional laver sauce for Welsh lamb or mutton.

A tiny amount spread on small triangles of hot toast makes an exquisite hors d'oeuvre, especially if topped with an oyster, shrimp or freshly steamed mussels. I also use it to enrich shellfish sauces, and indeed any fish dishes. It makes an unusual ingredient in a fish stuffing, or a mousseline.

Laver is used a great deal in Japanese cooking in the form of *nori*, which is delicious and fairly sweet. The seaweed is processed by being chopped, flattened and dried on frames like paper. There are many varieties. It can be black, purple, dark green or dark red, and in various thicknesses. It is used to wrap the delicate small parcels of vinegared rice and fish that are eaten as *sushi*, and it is served at breakfast time to wrap one's rice. You can make the sheets more pliable by laying them between layers of damp kitchen paper. I wrap small fish fillets in *nori* before steaming them. Held over a flame, or put under the grill very briefly, the sheets of *nori* will crisp and can then be crumbled over seafood or other salads. Or cut them into shreds to decorate and flavour soups or salads.

SAMPHIRE *glasswort, marsh samphire, sea asparagus*

Not strictly speaking a seaweed, samphire grows in marshy shallows, salty mudflats and along the shoreline in bright green fleshy tufts about 10in (25cm) high. It can be eaten as a vegetable with fish, or it makes a delicious start to a fishy meal, boiled until tender, then dipped in melted butter and eaten with the fingers. Don't add salt to the cooking water, as it is already salty enough.

SEA LETTUCE *lettuce laver, sea laver*

In spite of its alternative names, this is not from the same family as laver. It is bright green in colour and does, indeed, have the appearance of lettuce leaves. The fleshy parts can be cooked by washing it thoroughly and wilting it in butter. Take care not to collect stringy green sea lettuce plants as these are not suitable for eating.

WAKAME

Dark green mild flavoured and softer textured than many seaweeds, *wakame* is more akin to a conventional green vegetable. It is sold dried or pickled and can be cooked and eaten finely chopped in salads or soups, or simmered with other vegetables. It is traditionally shredded and added to Japanese *miso* soup. *Mekabu* is the basal sprout of *wakame*. Strong-flavoured and creamy, it is used to make a 'tea', or deep-fried.

Sea Vegetables

1 DULSE
2 KELP (*KOMBU*)
3 WAKAME (*MEKABU*)
4 ARAME
5 HIJIKI
6 KELP (*LAMINARIA*)
7 CARRAGHEEN
8 SAMPHIRE
9 WAKAME
10 LAVERBREAD
11 NORI
12 KELP (*KOMBU*, SHAVED FOR WRAPPING *SUSHI*)
13 AGAR-AGAR

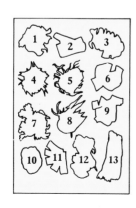

FRUIT

No food satisfies all the senses in quite the same way as fruit does. The sight of a well-displayed stall of fruit in a Mediterranean street market is enough to stop you in your tracks. The feel of the smooth bloomy skin of a fresh peach, the smell of an absolutely ripe pineapple, the sound of a crunchy apple when you bite into it; fruit provides feasts for all of the senses, not just our tastebuds.

Fruit provides a ready source of energy because it is rich in sugar (fruit sugar or fructose), and minerals and vitamins are present in most fruits. Fruit is also a good source of dietary fibre, both in the edible skin and in the water-soluble fibre called pectin found in certain fruits such as apples and quinces. Almost all fruit is low in calories.

BUYING AND STORING FRUIT
Above all fruit should look fresh and appetizing. If it is plump, firm, heavy for its size and unwrinkled, these are signs of freshness and good moisture or juice content. Soft fruit such as berries should look dry and full; avoid those with signs of mould or wetness, including any leakage in the packaging. Whether the fruit skins are edible or inedible make sure that they are not bruised, split or broken or with signs of insect damage.

Many fruits will ripen successfully at home which is useful since most of us do not have the opportunity to shop every day. Bananas, for example, are often sold immaculately pale yellow, tinged with green. These need to be ripened to a warm yellow marked with brown and will do so if kept in the fruit bowl.

Citrus fruit keeps well, for a couple of weeks if necessary, but the skins will begin to toughen and wrinkle and you will lose some of the essential oils. So if you want the fruit for the zest, use it within a few days.

Pineapples and melons are best eaten just chilled but this is something of a problem. Their scent is so penetrating that they must be well-wrapped, or they pass on their flavours to other refrigerated foods.

Smell is a good indication of ripeness, which is fortunate because some fruit does need to be bought and eaten when ripe. Melons should smell melony and fragrant. Although they will keep quite well for a week

or so, they will not ripen if bought underripe. Hard fruit such as apples and pears, as long as they are bought unblemished, will keep for a few weeks in the refrigerator.

Any fruit stored at room temperature will ripen and deteriorate quicker than if stored in a cool place, because the water content gradually evaporates and with it the sweet juiciness which makes the fruit so delicious. Some fruits are best bought for immediate consumption. All the soft berry fruits fall into this category. All fruit should be carefully washed before eating and cooking.

FRUIT IN THE KITCHEN
Perfectly ripe fresh fruit in season needs no cooking or other adornment. Most fruit can be eaten raw (sloes and rowanberries are two of the exceptions), but it is an exciting ingredient to experiment with in the kitchen.

Fruit can have a place in any part of the meal. Fruit cocktail or a half grapefruit may be served as an appetizer or perhaps figs or melon with Parma ham. Try mango slices with smoked fish and pink grapefruit with

Apples

1 RED DELICIOUS (AMERICAN)	20 FIESTA
2 TYDEMAN'S LATE ORANGE	21 LORD LAMBOURNE
	22 INGRID MARIE
3 RED DELICIOUS (ENGLISH)	23 KIDD'S ORANGE RED
	24 ORLEANS REINETTE
4 JUPITER	25 LORD DERBY
5 STARKING	26 WINSTON
6 JONAGOLD	27 GALA
7 EGREMONT RUSSET	28 ST EDMUND'S PIPPIN
8 MCINTOSH	29 BRAEBURN
9 CRISPIN	30 IDARED
10 NORTHERN SPY	31 STURMER PIPPIN
11 JAMES GRIEVE	32 EMPIRE
12 ROYAL GALA	33 BRAMLEY'S SEEDLING
13 SUNSET	34 KATY
14 DISCOVERY	35 ASHMEAD'S KERNEL
15 COX'S ORANGE PIPPIN	36 LAXTON'S FORTUNE
	37 FUJI
16 LAXTON'S SUPERB	38 GOLDEN DELICIOUS
17 HOWGATE WONDER	39 SPARTAN
18 SPLENDOUR	40 BLENHEIM ORANGE
19 GRANNY SMITH	

smoked salmon. Refreshing fruit or fruit and vegetable soups are an excellent beginning to a summer dinner party. Fruit can accompany many meat dishes. Fruit with fish is less usual. Mackerel with gooseberries is familiar, but also try rhubarb or cranberries.

Fruit and cheese is a classic combination. Try Wensleydale with apple pie, Roquefort or Parmesan with a juicy pear. There is almost no end to the wonderful sweet dishes that can be made with fruits, either singly or in combination, from the simplest compote or fruit salad, to airy confections using spun sugar and crisp pastry to set off berry fruit, through the fools, trifles, ice-creams, sorbets, soufflés, mousses, pies, cakes and pastries.

Our eating of fruit used to be governed by the seasons: gooseberries in May, cherries in June, soft berry fruits in July and August, September for the tree fruits and blackberries, a late harvest of raspberries in October, and then nothing new throughout the winter and spring except stored apples and pears. As transport methods have improved, more fruit has become available, not just tropical fruit but familiar fruit in the opposite season: strawberries and peaches from the southern hemisphere in the midwinter, for example. We are very lucky now to have a fruit harvest from all over the world at our disposal.

The page numbers in brackets at the end of an entry refer to the relevant photograph.

STONING FRUITS

To remove the stone from fruits such as apricots and peaches, cut around the centre of the fruit through the crease with a sharp knife. Twist the halves against each other and lever out the stone.

APPLE

There are few taste sensations quite as thrilling as biting into the first homegrown apple of the season. True, it brings with it thoughts of autumn rather earlier than one might wish, but what a wonderful, invigorating crunch and sweet, subtle fragrance after the soft summer berries, rich apricots and mellow peaches.

As well as being excellent dessert fruit, apples are used in cooking in many countries. Our own roast pork with apple sauce and apple charlotte pudding are also well-known examples. In Normandy, France, apples are a major feature of cooking, usually combined with cream, butter and Calvados. Cooked apples are a traditional accompaniment to grilled black and white pudding served during Christmas and New Year in France, and in Germany and Scandinavia they are served with roast goose.

Apples are a good source of vitamin C and, in the form of pectin, of water-soluble dietary fibre. Because of their high pectin content, apples can be used in jelly- and jam-making and, in this respect, can be usefully combined with other fruit low in pectin.

Some apples are well suited to the British climate and there are something like 600 homegrown varieties, although most of these are little known. However, about 50 varieties of apple are available and these, together with apples imported from all over the world, ensure that we have year-round supplies.

If you are buying apples for consumption within a week, look for those with unbruised and unbroken flesh and with no sign of insect damage. No special storage is needed; the fruit bowl is an adequate place, unless the room is hot and dry when the apples will begin to lose some of their crispness. Apples can also be stored in a polythene bag in the refrigerator if you like to eat your apples chilled.

If you pick your own apples and need to store them for longer periods, treat them very carefully. The apples should be perfect and free of blemishes; handle them as little as possible in picking and packing. Place them in trays, not touching, or in baskets, or indeed in polythene bags with a couple of ventilation holes. Store in a cool, dry place. See also DRIED FRUIT, page 82. (*52*)

APRICOT

This small blushing fruit has given its name to one of the sunniest, most delicate colours of the spectrum: not pink, not yellow, not orange, but a mix of all three. The skin is soft and tender with a matt bloom. The flesh is juicy, slightly firmer than a peach, and usually the same colour as the skin. The large, brown, inedible stone can be removed and cracked to obtain the kernel; when sweet, this can add an agreeable almond flavour to the cooked fruit.

To be enjoyed at their best apricots should be picked from the tree at the perfect point of ripeness and eaten fresh while still warm from the sun that ripened them. That is rarely possible in Britain! We have to make do with what we are sent from France, Spain, Greece, Italy and Turkey. Because the apricot is a delicate fruit when ripe, it is usually picked and transported underripe, pale and rather firm, reaching us in June, and on sale for most of the summer.

Choose apricots with the warmest colour, a slight blush and pink or orange hues – these are the ripe fruit (if they are very pale or tinged with green they will be underripe). Do not store them for more than a few days. They will soften and wrinkle very quickly in the fruit bowl, particularly with other ripe fruit close by. If you do need to keep them for a few days store them in a polythene bag in the salad drawer of the refrigerator.

Ripe apricots are delicious eaten raw and in fruit salads. They do not need peeling. Poach slightly underripe apricots in syrup, sweet wine or a mixture of honey and lime juice to bring out their flavour, and serve them hot or cold, with or without cream or yogurt. Best of all bake apricots in a tart with a light glaze on top.

Apricots are versatile. Do not restrict their use to desserts and puddings. Having reached Europe from their native home in China, they passed through many cultures and many usages. Middle-Eastern cooking includes apricots in meat dishes, particularly lamb, the tartness of the fruit offsetting the rich meat perfectly.

Fresh and dried apricots are a good source of dietary fibre and are rich in potassium. Fresh apricots have a high vitamin A content. See also DRIED FRUIT, page 82. (*73*)

APPLE VARIETIES

Ashmead's Kernel Hard, dry aromatic, richly-flavoured, sweet white flesh and skin that is russetted on greenish yellow, with some brownish-red flushing or stripes.

Blenheim Orange Crisp, dry, aromatic yellow fleshed apple, with a sweet, slightly tart flavour. Although a dessert apple, it cooks well.

Braeburn Attractive red dessert apple from New Zealand.

Bramley's Seedling Best-known cooking apple, but I do not find it the best, as it disintegrates quickly in cooking. However, many people particularly like the thick mushy purée it produces. I use it for apple sauce, but not for pies or baked apples. A large, often irregular-shaped apple, with a deep green skin, sometimes flushed with reddish brown. Creamy yellow, acid flesh.

Cox's Orange Pippin Dull-flavoured if picked too early; but otherwise richly aromatic, with lovely russetted skin and crisp, juicy, creamy yellow flesh when ripe. A wonderful dessert apple, also excellent for cooking.

Crispin Large apple with greenish-golden skin, sometimes flushed with orange. Crisp, firm, white flesh, agreeably tart.

Discovery Refreshing flavour and crisp white flesh, with green skin flushed with rosy pink, and occasionally some russetting. Best kept refrigerated and eaten slightly chilled (but *not* icy cold) to bring out its flavour.

Egremont Russet Golden russetted skin, wonderfully scented, nutty, white flesh and a fine, hard texture. One of the best eating apples; also excellent in pies and tarts.

Empire Light-textured and juicy American red dessert apple. Crisp, green-coloured flesh.

Fiesta Bred from Cox's, to which it is similar in flavour. It has a golden-yellow skin almost covered with light red stripes and flushes. Crisp, juicy flesh.

Fuji New Zealand apple similar to Cox's, with crisp, juicy, aromatic white flesh and a hint of acidity.

Gala Tough yellow skin, slightly russetted sometimes and flushed with a light, bright red or orange; crisp, sweet juicy flesh.

George Cave Sweet aromatic dessert apple with white, crisp flesh and green skin, flushed with rosy crimson.

Golden Delicious Can be an excellent all-round apple when ripe; use for cooking, making sorbets, ice-creams and sauces, and as a dessert apple. Large and well-shaped, its skin is pale green to yellow gold,

often flushed with pale orange when ripe; juicy, sweet, crisp flesh.

Granny Smith A versatile apple that keeps well. Usually a dessert apple, but particularly suitable for cooking, being tart and refreshing and only moderately sweet. Its hard, crisp, greenish-white juicy flesh retains its shape when cooked. The skin is tough and a bright, deep green.

Howgate Wonder Large, relatively sweet cooking apple with a creamy white, firm, aromatic flesh.

Idared White-fleshed but without much interest to the texture; as good for cooking as for eating. Indifferent flavour.

Ingrid Marie Greenish-white flesh tinged with yellow, firm, crisp and juicy.

James Grieve Pale yellow dessert apple, flushed and striped with red, with tender crumbly, creamy flesh, delicious to eat raw or cooked.

Jonagold Large yellow dessert apple, with hints of green and bright red. Crisp, juicy, well-flavoured white flesh. Also good cooker.

Jonathan Good all-round apple. Bright red skin streaked with orange; creamy white flesh, sometimes tinged with red. Juicy, slightly tart, suitable for pies and eating raw.

Jupiter Juicy apple with a flavour similar to the Cox; greenish-yellow skin that is flushed and striped with reddish-orange.

Katy Very attractive crisp apple, with good flavour, pale green, ripening to yellow, flushed with bright scarlet and flecked with deeper red.

Kidd's Orange Red Most attractive apple, quite small with a yellow skin heavily flushed with crimson and scarlet stripes, and cream, finely-textured crisp flesh full of sweet, aromatic, even flowery flavour. Perfect for toffee apples.

Lady Williams Crisp, sweet dessert apple. Fragrant with a pale green, yellow and red skin, flushed, striped and streaked in any combination.

Laxton's Fortune Deliciously sweet and aromatic apple with crisp, creamy white flesh, and pale green skin flushed and striped with red.

Laxton's Superb Medium-large apple with a yellowy-green skin, flushed with crimson. White, crisp flesh and sweet aromatic flavour make this an excellent eating apple.

Lord Derby Large green cooking apple with taut, creamy-white flesh.

Lord Lambourne Large greenish-yellow dessert apple flushed with red, with firm, crisp flesh and a slightly sweet, aromatic flavour.

McIntosh First developed in Canada, a good apple for making apple sauce, for baking and for pies. With its white, juicy, crisp, aromatic flesh, slightly tart flavour ripening to a mild sweetness, it is also an excellent eating apple. Bright deep red, with some green russetting.

Northern Spy Marvellously versatile, juicy, yellow-fleshed apple. Use for pies, apple sauce and baked apples. Also very good eating.

Orleans Reinette Large, magnificent fruit, with golden russetted skin lightly flushed with red. Sweet, aromatic, yellow flesh.

Red Delicious A bright red apple, sometimes in solid colouring, sometimes striped. Good eater, with juicy, somewhat crumbly, yellowish-white flesh and a slight refreshing tartness. Fairly tough skin. The homegrown variety is sweeter than its American counterpart and not as red.

Royal Gala Crisp, sweet, red-striped apple.

St Edmund's Pippin Delicious garden variety with unfortunately short shelf life, therefore not available commercially.

Spartan Striking-looking apple, of medium size, pale yellow with a dull purple-red flush that ripens to a brighter maroon. Very white, fine, crisp and well-flavoured flesh.

Splendour Yellowish-white flesh which is firm and sweet, slightly acid and a little rich.

Starking Firm, sweet, yellow flesh; yellow skin, liberally flushed and striped with deep red.

Sturmer Pippin Very good cooking apple with thin, firm, tart flesh and rich aroma; also excellent dessert apple. Smooth, shiny green skin, sometimes flushed with a dull, reddish brown.

Sunset Attractive golden skin with an orange-red flush. Crisp, firm yellow flesh with a mild aromatic flavour.

Tydeman's Late Orange Golden yellow with a reddish-orange flush. Aromatic, sweet flesh.

Winesap Excellent all-round apple. Sweet, juicy and slightly tart, it makes a good dessert apple but is also excellent in pies. It has a deep, clean red flesh, tinged with yellow, and some russetting around the stalk.

Winston Greenish-yellow apple, with some russetting and light red flushes. Firm, crisp, very white flesh, with a pleasing tartness underlying the mild, sweet flavour.

Worcester Pearmain Pale yellow-green apple that is flushed with scarlet and russetted. Its crisp, sweet, white flesh is intensely perfumed, with hints of strawberries.

ARBUTUS *tree strawberry*

The coat of arms of the city of Madrid depicts a brown bear picking fruit from a small tree. The tree is the arbutus and the fruits are small, scarlet, granular berries, not unlike strawberries at a fleeting glance. You are unlikely to come across them in shops, although the tree can be grown in sheltered parts of Britain. It is native to

Soft Fruit

1 BLACKCURRANTS
2 TAYBERRIES
3 GOOSEBERRIES (LEVELLER)
4 GOOSEBERRIES (COOKING)
5 RED RASPBERRIES
6 REDCURRANTS
7 YELLOW RASPBERRIES
8 STRAWBERRIES (CALIFORNIAN)
9 WHITE CURRANTS
10 LOGANBERRIES
11 BLUEBERRIES
12 STRAWBERRIES (ENGLISH)
13 YELLOW *FRAISES DES BOIS*
14 BLACKBERRIES
15 *FRAISES DES BOIS*
16 SMALL ENGLISH STRAWBERRIES

the United States, southern Europe, and also to Killarney, where it grows 'by the waters of Leane', according to the old Irish folk song. Their sweet soft flesh is mild with a hint of vanilla and no acid to speak of. They are much used in liqueur- and sweet-making.

ASIAN PEAR *nashi*

A superb eating fruit with a crisp, grainy texture like a pear and wonderfully juicy, appley flavour, Asian pears look like rather large yellow-skinned apples. They are best eaten slightly chilled, and make a marvellous addition to fruit salads. (*59, 60*)

BABACO

A very recent arrival on our shelves, the babaco originated in the Andean belt of South America, then began to be cultivated in New Zealand and, more recently still, in Guernsey. It is a large fruit, some 10in (25cm) long, pointed at one end and blunt at the other, with five slightly concave sides. When unripe the skin, which is edible, is pale green, ripening to a rich yellow all over. The flesh is a very pale orange-pink, moist and juicy. I find it rather bland, though it can be refreshing on a hot day, like a melon. There is a slight scent of strawberries and pineapple to the fruit when cut but none of the flavour. The babaco is related to pawpaw, and similarly contains valuable enzymes which aid digestion, as well as a good supply of vitamin C.

Babaco has good keeping qualities which make it a good standby for a fresh fruit dessert. However, it requires a good deal of livening up with sugar, citrus juice or spices. (*59, 60*)

BANANA

This rather homely fruit has never enjoyed a high regard in classic cooking, but its sweet nutritious flesh encased in its hygienically sealed skin make it one of the best convenience foods ever. Apart from the familiar dessert banana you can sometimes find apple bananas, a dwarf variety with a faintly appley flavour.

Considering the banana's exotic provenance – the Canary Islands, the Windward Islands and even further afield – it is strange that it should be suited to very traditional domestic dishes such as trifle, tea breads and, perhaps best and simplest of all, the bananas on toast of childhood teas, or sliced over breakfast cereal.

American cookery occasionally combines bananas with meat or other savoury dishes, such as the fritters served with chicken Maryland. A breakfast of grilled bacon, waffles and pancakes and fried bananas can make a rather good start to the day. For an easy pudding fry bananas in butter, sprinkle with sugar, flame with rum and serve with cream.

Bananas are rich in carbohydrate, some iron, and all the vitamins except vitamin D. When unripe the skin is pale yellow with a greenish hue, and the fruit is starchy and bland; when it ripens to a rich yellow mottled with brown it becomes deliciously sweet. Overripe bananas (when black and squashy) are *not* good to eat.

Do not keep bananas in the refrigerator. They go quite black, and their smell pervades everything. See also DRIED FRUIT, page 82. (*59*)

BILBERRY *blaeberry, whinberry, whortleberry*

Late summer is the time to go picking bilberries on the moors in Yorkshire, Devon, Scotland and Wales, and in the North-East. It was a favourite childhood excursion for me, as these small smooth purple berries seemed so much more exotic than the ubiquitous blackberry.

What wonderful tarts and pies they made, eked out with apple if they were scarce, or just packed with bilberries if there was a good picking. The flavour is at once sharp and sweet and fragrant. They also make excellent jam and jelly, particularly when mixed with a fruit richer in pectin. Muffins, scones, pancakes and fritters are all good uses for this lovely, short-season wild fruit. A few bilberries, lightly crushed and stirred into thick yogurt, make a wonderfully easy pudding. And bilberry ice-cream is richly flavoured and a stunning colour. They do not keep well so eat them soon after picking or buying. See also *Blueberry*.

BLACKBERRY *bramble*

A sweet, black, juicy fruit made up of tiny drupelets, the blackberry is a native of Britain, Europe and other temperate zones. It grows wild in woodlands and hedgerows from late July to the first frosts, although people used to be warned not to eat blackberries after the end of September because then, according to legend, 'the devil is in them'. Wild blackberries have a delicious sweet yet tart flavour, are small and firm and have rather a lot of seed to flesh. Cultivated blackberries taste almost as good and are rather more fleshy and juicy.

When buying them look for firm fruit that is glossy black all over with no green and red patches and with no sign of mould. Do not keep blackberries more than a day or so and hull them (pull out any remaining stalk or calyx and the pithy hull will come away with it) before using them. They are very good in jams and jellies, pies, tarts and crumbles, mixed with apple or not. Blackberries make excellent sorbets and ice-creams. Crushed in vodka they make a delicious liqueur, a spoonful of which turns a glass of dry sparkling white wine into a rather fine cocktail. Or steep crushed blackberries in a pint of wine vinegar, for a fruity addition to a salad dressing. Firm but ripe blackberries make a rather pleasant addition to an autumn salad. (*56*)

BLUEBERRY

Blueberries belong to the same family as bilberries and are similarly small, round and dark bluey black with smooth bloomy skins. They can be used in the same recipes, although they are slightly blander and benefit from a squeeze of lemon or lime juice.

In the United States, where they grow wild, blueberry cheesecake, blueberry bread, blueberry muffins, blueberry pancakes, blueberry shortcake are all traditional recipes using this luscious fruit. I like to make blueberry jam in the autumn and pot it in small jars to give as Christmas presents. I have also used them with other soft fruits in an excellent variation on summer pudding. Blueberries are fairly robust and stand up well to many different treatments; try crumbles with an almond topping, pies and tarts flavoured with a sprig of mint, or steamed sponge puddings.

They keep rather better than the other soft fruits and undamaged specimens will last for a few days in the refrigerator. (*56*)

CAPE GOOSEBERRY *Chinese lantern, physalis*

These small golden berries enveloped in a thin, papery husk used to be a winter treat from warmer climates. Now we get them from several countries at different times of the year. They seem to be a permanent feature of the *petit four* plate in grand restaurants, where they are served as sweetmeats, prepared by folding back the husk (which is not eaten) and dipping the fruit in fondant icing. They are quite delicious like this. For a simpler after-dinner treat serve them raw – still in their husks – and let your guests peel back the papery covering and dip them in a little sugar, if liked, before eating them. The flavour is similar to that of a soft ripe gooseberry, tart and mildly scented. They also make an excellent – if expensive – jam, or a purée to flavour creams and cakes.

Cape gooseberries will keep for a few days in a cool place or the refrigerator. (*58*)

CHERIMOYA *chirimoya, custard apple, soursop*

There are several varieties of this large family of fruit: the cherimoya or chirimoya, the anon, annona or custard apple, and the soursop or guanabana.

The cherimoya has a green smooth skin marked with what looks like indented fingerprints. The somewhat grainy flesh is creamy and sweet, with a slight orange flavour. It has a number of shiny, black, inedible seeds.

The custard apple is shaped like a rounded pine cone with soft, scale-like protruberances. The skin is green, darkening to patchy brown as it ripens. The pale custardy flesh has a deep mellow flavour.

The soursop is the largest of the three. It is pear-shaped, very dark green and covered in short fleshy ridges or spines. The pulp is juicy and richly flavoured, with more natural acidity than the other two fruits, hence its name. In South America it is grown on a commercial scale to produce pulp for wonderfully refreshing drinks and ice-creams.

Most imports of cherimoya and custard apple reach us from Brazil and Spain. Despite their robust appearance they are very fragile and should be handled carefully if the fruit is not to break open. If not fully ripe when you buy them (that is, if they do not yield to slight pressure) put them in a brown paper bag in the kitchen. Do not keep them long once ripe, no more than three or four days in the refrigerator.

The best way to eat this fruit is in its most natural state. Cut in half down the length of the fruit and eat the creamy white flesh with a spoon, discarding the shiny black seeds. The flavour is complex: creamy, custardy, vanilla, but for all that, not at all bland, and with a slight hint of acidity. I do not see the point of adding it to milk-based desserts as one is occasionally advised to do, but it makes a delicious sorbet. (*59, 60, 77*)

CHERRY

The old road from Freiburg in southern Germany to Basel in northern Switzerland is called the Baseler Landstrasse. For much of its length it is lined with cherry trees to supply the local distilled cherry spirit (Kirschwasser) industry. It also supplied us hungry students when we travelled its length by motor scooter. Sharp, sweet, fleshy fruit with juice that stains the lips, the fingers and everything they come in contact with, cherries are a summertime treat worth waiting for. There are two main types: sweets and sours. The first are eaten raw or cooked, the second are usually cooked, in desserts or to accompany savoury dishes.

There are said to be over 300 varieties of sweet cherries and 600 varieties of sour cherries, but it

Tropical Fruit

1	GUAVAS	16	CHERIMOYA
2	CAPE GOOSEBERRIES		(CUSTARD APPLE)
3	BABACO	17	KUMQUATS
4	PAWPAWS	18	MANGOES
5	DURIAN	19	RAMBUTANS
6	JACKFRUIT	20	TAMARILLOS
7	SAPODILLAS	21	PEPINO
8	LOQUATS	22	BANANAS
9	MANGOSTEENS	23	PITAHAYAS
10	STAR FRUIT	24	PASSION FRUIT
11	APPLE BANANAS	25	KIWI
12	PINEAPPLES	26	LONGANS
13	GRANADILLAS	27	GINUPS
14	ASIAN PEARS	28	KIWANOS
15	LYCHEES		

is rare to find more than two or three types for sale at a given time.

Sweet cherries The group known as Guignes, or Geans, have soft, tender, juicy flesh and include Waterloo, Elton, Eagle, Early Purple and Black Tartarian. The Hearts or Bigarreaus have firm, sweet flesh and include the Windsor, Schmidt and Mezel varieties as well as the White Heart cherries, of which the best known is the pale Napoleon.

Sour cherries These are the Morellos and Amarelles such as Montmorency, early Richmond and King Amarelles. Both Morellos and Amarelles have soft flesh and juice of varying acidity, from the almost sweet Montmorency to the bitter Kentish cherry.

When shopping for cherries examine the stems, if present, as these are good indicators of freshness. They should be green and flexible. Dry, brown, brittle stems tell you that the cherries were picked some time ago. This is not surprising perhaps; they are imported from all over the world: Turkey, Greece, the United States and the southern hemisphere in winter, as well as from France and Italy. Red varieties are ripe when they are deep red; white and yellow varieties when they are flushed with pink. Avoid fruit that is too soft, or bruised or split. Do not keep cherries for more than two or three days, or up to six days in the refrigerator.

It is hard to better cherries eaten raw. However, they do find their way into a great variety of cooked dishes from all over the world. In classic recipes cherries are often served with duckling and other poultry such as quail. Any dish described on a menu as 'Montmorency' will

Tropical Fruit Slices

1	PASSION FRUIT	13	STAR FRUIT
2	LONGAN	14	PITAHAYA
3	LYCHEE	15	BABACO
4	SAPODILLA	16	CHERIMOYA
5	LOQUAT		(CUSTARD APPLE)
6	KIWI	17	MANGO
7	MANGOSTEEN	18	KIWANO
8	TAMARILLO	19	GRANADILLA
9	KUMQUAT	20	PEPINO
10	GUAVA	21	PAWPAW
11	ASIAN PEAR	22	DURIAN
12	RAMBUTAN	23	JACKFRUIT

be accompanied by cherries, originally of the Montmorency variety, which came from a small town of the same name just outside Paris that used to supply the Paris market at Les Halles with cherries.

In Scandinavian and Eastern European cooking cherries are made into soups, both hot and cold. They are also used to fill the dumplings sometimes served with these soups as in the Russian *vareniki*. One of my favourite puddings, *kissel*, also comes from Russia, a clear dark fruit extract thickened with potato flour which sets to a soft delicate jelly when chilled. Other soft fruit can be substituted for the cherries. *Clafoutis* is a harvest dish from the Limousin and Auvergne in France, a batter pudding filled with sweet black cherries and baked in the oven – a substantial ending to a meal after a hard day in the fields. (*73*)

CITRON

This is a large, lemon-shaped fruit of the citrus family, up to 8in (20cm) in length. The peel – rough-textured and greenish to golden yellow – and the pith are the important elements as it is a fruit used solely for candying, crystallizing or otherwise preserving. The pulp is very sour. (*67*)

CLEMENTINE

A cross between the tangerine and the bitter orange, this popular 'easy-peeling' citrus fruit is not quite as sweet as the tangerine, and is almost seedless. It makes a marvellous addition to a fruit salad and, because of its thin loose skin and lack of pips, is very economical. The juice of a clementine is fragrant and sweet but with a distinct hint of acidity, which makes it a welcome addition to the breakfast table. That

same acidity makes clementines suitable for adding to mixed citrus fruit marmalades. Sorbets and ice-creams made from clementines will have a good depth of flavour. Their only drawback is that they are so small you need to squeeze a great many to get even a pint of juice.

Look for deep orange, shiny-skinned, plump fruit, and avoid any that look dry or slightly shrivelled. If using them for marmalade thoroughly scrub and dry the skins to remove any preservatives. (*67*)

CRAB APPLE

The small sharp fruits of the wild apple tree, which looks so delicate in the spring with its pink and white fragrant blossom, crab apples can be yellow, red or greenish red depending on the type of tree. Because they are so attractive when in blossom, in leaf and in fruit, crab apple trees are often to be found in gardens and orchards.

The fruit is usually no more than 1in (2·5cm) in diameter, with a large proportion of core to flesh. It is not worth eating raw, and most crab apples are mouth-puckeringly tart. They make brilliant, clear, jewel-like jellies, to be eaten with hot toast or scones. But if you add herbs to the syrup as it cooks you will have delicious and unusual jellies to serve with meat such as roast pork or pheasant. (*61*)

CRANBERRY

The largest producers of these tart, rich ruby-red berries are in the United States, in New England especially, but also in Wisconsin, the Canadian border area and the West Coast states of Washington and Oregon. A smaller version of the better-known American cranberry also grows in boggy parts of Scotland and the north of England. The Scandinavian lingonberry is of the same family and can be used instead of

Autumn Fruit

1 HAWS
2 DOG-ROSE HIPS
3 ROSEHIPS (ROSA RUGOSA)
4 SLOES
5 CRANBERRIES
6 QUINCES
7 CRAB APPLES (GOLDEN HORNET)
8 CRAB APPLES (TORINGO)
9 MEDLARS
10 JAPONICA QUINCES

cranberries in any of a multitude of recipes – they are rarely eaten raw.

North American Indians used cranberries to make pemmican, a mixture of meat and fruit which was dried to provide a useful winter food. It was they who introduced the fruit to settlers from the Old World who quickly adopted it, together with the wild turkey. Even today in the United States celebration meals such as Thanksgiving and Christmas would not be complete without roast turkey and cranberry sauce.

Cranberries are hardy and, because they store so well, have a long season from autumn to Christmas and beyond. They are normally in the shops from early November. Look for shiny full berries and avoid packs that contain squashed or wizened ones.

Cranberries are more sour and bitter than any other fruit, but their high pectin content makes them an admirable candidate for the preserving pan. I like to combine them with sweeter fruits and one year made a very successful cranberry and persimmon jam which turned out a rich garnet colour. Use them with sliced pears in a pudding or a pie, or instead of raisins in tea breads and scones. They also make delicious ice-creams and even better sorbets and water-ices. When making sweet dishes cook cranberries until they pop before you add the sugar, otherwise the skins will remain tough.

Their distinctive tart flavour makes cranberries equally suitable for savoury dishes. A few lightly cooked berries can be added to a rich meaty gravy for roast duck, game dishes, lamb or chicken. Make a cranberry sauce to accompany a fish that needs a little livening up – a rainbow trout, for example.

Fresh cranberries will keep well-covered, in the refrigerator for up to ten days if you first remove damaged fruit. *(61)*

CURRANT

These delicious soft berry fruits, available in July and August, are almost entirely home-grown. Blackcurrants and redcurrants are the most widely available. The rarer, less acid, and very beautiful white currants are an albino strain of the red variety. When you can get white currants, poach them very gently in a light syrup, perhaps flavoured with a liqueur, and

serve them with ice-cream and almond biscuits. They also look very pretty frosted or glazed and used to decorate cakes and fruit salads.

Redcurrants and blackcurrants are marvellous for jams and jellies because they have good setting qualities and do not need long cooking, which helps to retain their fresh flavour. Redcurrant jelly is an essential ingredient of Cumberland sauce, the traditional accompaniment to certain lamb and game dishes. Another good jelly to accompany meat and game dishes is made with blackcurrants and fresh mint leaves. Blackcurrant syrups and cordials are a popular winter remedy against colds and coughs, and no wonder, because they are rich in vitamin C.

Fruit soups and desserts all benefit from the addition of these fresh, tart, fragrantly herby fruits, and redcurrants combine particularly well with sliced peaches and nectarines, both to look at and to eat. To detach the berries from the stems ready for use simply run a fork down the length of the stem held over a bowl. *(56)*

CURUBA *banana passion fruit*

A type of passion fruit popular in Colombia and occasionally available, it is rather elongated in shape with a soft yellowy-green skin and orangy pulp. Slightly tart, but with a rich, powerful and delicious flavour like that of the more familiar passion fruit, it definitely needs a little sugar; good in sorbets. See also *Passion Fruit*. *(77)*

DAMSON

This small plum-like fruit with its deep blue-purple skin and delicate bloom can be picked from the hedgerows, but is also available commercially from August to October.

Because of its relatively large stone it is not a particularly suitable fruit for eating raw, although it has a very good flavour. Use it to make delicious damson jams, pies, tarts, fools, ice-creams and sorbets. Damson cheese, which is like a very solid jam that you cut with a knife or spoon, is a marvellous traditional sweetmeat.

If I were lucky enough to have a damson tree I would try some more exotic uses. Damsons could take the place of prunes in the Touraine dish of pork fillets with prunes cooked in one of the soft white wines of the Loire. A Moroccan

lamb *tagine*, or stew, with stoned damsons and almonds would be heavenly; and a spicy damson chutney would go well with grilled, roast or curried chicken. See also *Plum*. *(79)*

DATE

How I love the dates we are now lucky enough to find on sale during the winter months! I don't mean the small sticky dried ones packed in long wooden 'lace'-lined boxes that are a traditional Christmas treat, nor the smooth-skinned fresh dates from Israel. No, the ones I really like are the medjool dates from Egypt and California. They are large, up to 2in (5cm) long and at least 1in (2·5cm) in diameter. The dark golden-brown skin is slightly wrinkled and encases a rich sweet, dense flesh. They are expensive, but one or two instead of a pudding or *petits fours* at the end of a meal will not break the bank. They are also delicious served with cheese, either a soft fresh cheese or something like a tasty farmhouse Lancashire. It is also possible to buy semi-dried dates on the stem, from Tunisia and Morocco. These are almost as good, but not quite as richly fleshily opulent, and not quite as large.

Fresh Israeli dates straight from the palm are sometimes available. Green and smooth when unripe, they gradually ripen through a pale to a deeper yellow then to a rich golden brown. When pale yellow they are still somewhat underripe and have a bitter tannin in their skins. The flesh, however, is pale, sweet and crisp; eating it is almost like munching raw sweetcorn. If you keep them for a few days they will begin to soften, darken and become more translucent. This is when they start to develop that familiar honey smell and flavour.

At about 70 per cent, the carbohydrate content of dates is higher than in any other fruit. The date stone is inedible. To remove it, split open the date lengthwise and ease it out with the point of a knife. This leaves a useful cavity to hold stuffing, such as cream cheese, date purée, or a mixture of chopped nuts, grated cheese, what you will. Dates are very good combined with walnuts or pecans in tarts, and in the traditional date and walnut loaf. In California I came across one of the most unusual ways of using dates with savoury dishes. A young chef in San Francisco served duck breast on a purée of dates, then topped and glazed it with a hollandaise sauce. He may have been influenced by the Roman gourmet Apicius, as dates with meat were a strong feature of Roman cooking. See also DRIED FRUIT, page 82. (*63*)

Dᴜʀɪᴀɴ

A huge fruit, weighing up to 10lb (4·5kg), with a greenish-brown skin which is a mass of short sharp spikes. Inside the thick woody rind are up to five segments of pale yellow, creamy flesh which is rich and custardy. It is eaten raw. The large brown seeds are roasted or boiled.

When buying a durian steer clear of split fruit for two good reasons: it indicates that the fruit is overripe, and the smell is overpowering and offputting unless you are accustomed to it. Never store the fruit with other foods.

To prepare the fruit for eating use a large sharp knife to quarter it, then scoop out the flesh and seeds with a spoon. Beware of the juice getting on to your clothing – it leaves an indelible stain. It is traditionally used in jams and cakes; in Indonesia the unripe fruit is cooked as a vegetable. Here, however, it is never likely to be more than a rare late-spring to midsummer treat, so enjoy the unadulterated flavour by eating it raw. The creamy soft flesh is delicious – rich with an unusual aftertaste which some people describe as gamy, some as cheesy. It is most appreciated by those whose diet is rich in hot chillies and spices to which it acts as a foil. (*59, 60*)

Eʟᴅᴇʀʙᴇʀʀʏ

Near my home there is a small clump of elder bushes, intertwined with brambles, and they provide a rich source of flavours for my kitchen. In the autumn I pick a panful of blackberries and clusters of elderberries, cook them with a little sugar and sieve them to make a thick sauce for fools, cream desserts, yogurts and ice-creams. The same sauce, kept slightly tart, is good with

Mediterranean Fruit

1 Dᴀᴛᴇs (Hᴀʟʟᴀᴡɪ)	5 Pʀɪᴄᴋʟʏ ᴘᴇᴀʀs
2 Dᴀᴛᴇs (Iʀᴀǫɪ)	6 Pᴏᴍᴇɢʀᴀɴᴀᴛᴇs
3 Dᴀᴛᴇs	7 Fɪɢs
4 Dᴀᴛᴇs (Sɪᴀʀ)	8 Fɪɢs (Kᴀᴅᴏᴛᴀ)

game. Elderberries alone combine very well with pork. I also flavour vinegar with elderberries for use in autumn salads, which are especially good when a few walnuts are added. They are not, to my knowledge, available commercially, but they grow everywhere. Pick your own but not from bushes close to traffic-congested highways. Strip the berries off the stalks with a fork.

FEIJOA *pineapple guava*

Originally from Brazil and central South America, the feijoa is now also cultivated in New Zealand and in the south of France. It is 2–3in (5–7cm) long and oval in shape. When unripe the skin is a brightish green, not unlike an avocado; when ripe it becomes a duller greenish red. Its alternative name is pineapple guava but, except for its guava-like texture, it bears little relation to either of them. When green it has a flavour somewhat reminiscent of banana, when ripe that of a strawberry. The best way to eat it is to enjoy its novelty: cut it in half, scoop the flesh and seeds out and lightly season with lime juice. It is usually available around Christmastime.

If you ever come across it in great abundance, then use it in jellies, preserves, purées, fools, pancake fillings and tarts. (*77*)

FIG

Figs epitomize the Mediterranean, its climate, its food, its way of life. It is not particularly refreshing, nor does it have a very strong flavour, but it is a fruit to be eaten slowly and savoured, from the luscious mouthfuls of soft pink flesh to the tiniest edible seeds. Some people peel figs, or discard the skin, but it is perfectly edible. If the skin is so bruised and damaged that you want to remove it, then the fruit inside is probably quite spoiled too. Look for firm unblemished fruit which just yields when you hold it in your hand without pressing it. It can be a number of colours from pale green and golden yellow to deep purple.

Figs, especially Kadota, the most important Italian variety, can be served with Parma ham, a good combination. If there is a glut and you can buy them at a much lower price than usual, make fig jam; or gently poach them in wine or syrup. See also DRIED FRUIT, page 82. (*63*)

GINUP *mamoncillo, Spanish lime*

This round, green, tropical fruit, about 1½in (3cm) across, grows in bunches like grapes. It has the vivid green dimpled skin of a tiny lime but despite its alternative name, by which it is known in Florida, it is not a lime. The structure and texture of the whole is very like a lychee, and the flavour is not dissimilar, although they do not belong to the same family. Peel off the hard leathery skin to reveal the jelly-like pink flesh which you simply chew off the central seed. It is sweet with a slight tang. Don't get the juice on your clothes as the stain is irremovable. (*59*)

GOLDEN APPLE

This is something of a misnomer, because this is not an apple, but a golden plum-shaped fruit which grows several to a branch. It is small, about 1½in (3·5cm) long and 1in (2·5cm) in diameter, with a delicate skin. It has a distinctive flavour, sweet yet slightly acid, and a wonderful fragrance. A tropical fruit, it is popular in the West Indies, Central and South America, the southern United States, as well as India, South-East Asia and the Pacific. The skin and pulp are eaten and the large single stone discarded. It is used to make jams, jellies and syrups, and is also added to curries and chutneys. (*77*)

GOOSEBERRY

The first green gooseberries are available from late May onwards and they last through until August. They are rarely eaten raw. Sweet yellow-green Levellers come on to the market in July and occasionally the large yellow or red dessert gooseberries are available. Gooseberries are a good source of dietary fibre and rich in pectin, which makes them an ideal fruit for jams, chutneys and jellies. They are comparatively inexpensive and when there is a glut I make them into jelly; not as economical as jam but I love its pale pinky-gold colour. At the beginning of the season I flavour a few jars with elderflowers. Later I make a darker, fragrant jelly by stewing and infusing lavender heads with the fruit.

An agreeably tart gooseberry sauce is traditionally served with mackerel, and rather less traditionally with deep-fried Camembert wedges. Try the sauce with other fish dishes and rich meat dishes such as roast pork. Gooseberry pies and tarts are also delicious.

When cooking the fruit for jelly-making there is no need to top and tail, but for any dish that contains the whole berry use a sharp knife or scissors to trim them.

The gooseberry juice which drips through the jelly bag has a tartness which makes it an interesting substitute for lemon or lime juices. I use it in salad dressings, marinades and fish sauces. (*56*)

GRANADILLA *grenadilla*

This is a member of the passion fruit family, but is larger and rounder with a smooth, brittle orange skin and greyish pulp and seeds – the edible part. It is used in the same way as passion fruit but the flavour is somewhat blander. See also *Passion Fruit*. (*58, 60*)

GRAPE

With very few exceptions grapes grown expressly for wine-making do not appear on the table, and vice versa. Wine grapes are smaller, sharper tasting and have tough skins. Some varieties, however – the Chasselas and the Muscat come to mind – are cultivated both for the table and for wine-making. Among the varieties you may come across are Flame Seedless, Alphonse Lavalleé, Belgian Royal, Thompson Seedless, Muscat, Italia (black and white) and America. Many are rather dull, though the exceptions are remarkable.

There is at least one truly delicious grape widely available today and that is the Muscat. A perfect ripe Muscat grape is the very essence of the fruit. It is large and pale green, shading almost to a golden yellow. When fully ripe it may have a golden-bronze tinge and then it will taste like nectar, the flavour perfectly captured in the natural sweet Muscat wines of Provence, from Frontignan and Beaumes-de-Venise, and in the Muscat wine from the Greek island of Samos. Black and red Muscat grapes are also available occasionally.

Grapes can be bought all year round, but they are little used in cooking. In classic French cooking, *sole Véronique* is garnished with grapes. Peeled, halved and de-pipped, Muscat grapes also make a good accompaniment to the more delicate game birds, such as partridge and quail, and to poultry.

The larger grapes are very good in open tarts made with sweet shortcrust pastry. Peel them first, either by scalding them very briefly, or with a small sharp knife if the skins are loose. Squeeze the pips out or, if firmly lodged, halve the grape and scoop them out with a spoon.

Red or white grapes can be matched with a similar wine to make delicious grape jellies. I would not waste a fine wine on this, but a Moscatel de Valencia or Moscato d'Asti would be perfect. If using a dry red wine some extra sugar may be needed.

On the whole I would just as soon eat grapes as they are, lightly chilled, with wet walnuts and English farmhouse cheese, a lovely autumn treat. See also DRIED FRUIT, page 82. (65)

GRAPEFRUIT

A large, yellow-skinned, tart-flavoured member of the citrus family, grapefruit is now available all the year round, from Cyprus, Florida, California, Israel, and from the southern hemisphere. White- (pale yellow) and pink-fleshed varieties, such as Ruby Red, are available. There is also a special green-skin variety called Sweetie which is less tart. Choose fruit that is heavy for its size – a sign of juiciness – with plump skin and a good, grapefruity smell.

Chilled fresh grapefruit or freshly squeezed grapefruit juice is an excellent thirst-quencher or appetite whetter at any time of the day, not just breakfast time. The sharp refreshing flavour is so good that it is a great pity to mask it with sugar, sherry, glacé cherries or syrup.

Grapefruit does not improve with cooking. However, it has a place in salads served as a first

Grapes

1 FLAME SEEDLESS
2 ALPHONSE LAVALLÉE
3 COLMAR
4 BELGIAN ROYAL
5 THOMPSON
  SEEDLESS (GREEK)
6 ITALIA (BLACK)
7 THOMPSON
  SEEDLESS (ISRAELI)
8 ITALIA (WHITE)

course. The sharp, but not sour flavour marries well with fish, shellfish, cooked offal such as sweetbreads or chicken livers, indeed, anything with a pronounced flavour and rich texture. Pink-fleshed grapefruit with smoked salmon is a most perfect combination. A platter of different smoked fish sliced and arranged with segments of pink and white grapefruit or Sweetie makes a sumptuous first course for a dinner party. The citrus note in the grapefruit is not as sharp as that of the lemon or lime and does less damage to the accompanying wine.

A little grapefruit juice can also be used for marinating fish before cooking it – not one of the delicate, expensive fish but one which needs some pepping up, such as mackerel. Marinate in four to five tablespoons of juice for no more than 20–30 minutes or the acid will 'cook' the fish.

Grapefruit marmalade is one of the best versions of this breakfast-time favourite, and the crystallized peel makes an elegant sweetmeat to serve with after-dinner coffee. (*67*)

GREENGAGE

The greengage is a small green plum named after Sir William Gage who brought them back from France in the eighteenth century, and is my favourite member of the plum family, with the exception, perhaps, of the golden Mirabelle.

Fully ripe (when a golden tinge shows through the skin) they are delicious eaten raw as a dessert fruit. Poach them in syrup for something a little richer. Greengages can also be made into a purée or mixed with cream or custard to make ice-cream and greengage jam is one of the very best. See also *Plum*. (*73*)

GUAVA

From the magical garden where I spent a couple of years as a child I remember guavas being small, soft-skinned, fragrant, pale yellow, pear-shaped fruit. Once cut open the fruit was even more fragrant and the flesh pink, softly grainy, with flat crunchy seeds. The smaller and pinker they were, the more flavour they had. Those were the true 'wild' guavas. Guavas today seem to be bigger, greener – that is, less ripe – and less scented. More often than not the flesh is a pale creamy white, and moist but not what I would

call juicy. Fully ripe guavas have yellow skin and a warm fragrance.

Guavas, available from about November to April, come from Central and Southern America, the Caribbean and Thailand. They are fragile, so handle them with care and use soon after buying. The simplest way to eat them is to cut them in half, sprinkle with a little lime or lemon juice and eat the flesh and seeds with a spoon, discarding the skin – though some people do eat this too. Ice-creams, sorbets, jams and jellies can all be made with guavas alone, or combined with other fruits. It has something of the scent of a quince and it goes similarly well in apple dishes such as pies and sauces for meat, game and poultry. (*58, 60*)

HAW

This is a small dark red berry, the fruit of the hawthorn or May tree. Haws are rather tart in flavour, but can be made into a jelly with crab apples, or a sauce for mutton and lamb. (*61*)

HIP *rosehip*

This is the bright orange-red seedpod of the rose picked in the autumn. Hips used to be an important source of vitamin C for country people, being 20 times richer in this respect than oranges. They are not eaten raw but the whole fruit can be made into a syrup, sweetened with honey, or a tart, bittersweet jelly to serve with roast duck or turkey. (*61*)

JACKFRUIT

Originally a native of southern Asia the jackfruit is a variety of breadfruit now grown in most parts of the tropics. It can grow very large, to a weight of well over 20lb (9kg), but smaller ones are marketed. It is irregularly shaped but roughly oval, and the densely spiny skin ripens from green to brown. The rather musty sweet aroma intensifies as the fruit ripens.

The rather bland pulp has more of the characteristics of a staple carbohydrate than a dessert fruit. It can be eaten raw when ripe and sweet, but is more usually cooked and served with curries and other meat dishes. The numerous edible white seeds can be dried and ground

to provide a type of flour or roasted and eaten like chestnuts, in which case they should first be boiled and the water thrown away. (*59, 60*)

JUJUBE *Chinese date*

This yellowish-green, olive-shaped fruit comes mainly from Thailand and is available most of the year. Rich in vitamin C, the fruit can be eaten raw or dried when it tastes like a date. (*77*)

KIWANO *horned cucumber, horned melon, jelly melon*

One of the most striking of the newer fruits, the kiwano originates from Africa but is being developed commercially largely in New Zealand. It is roughly ovoid in shape and covered in irregular sharp spikes protruding from the skin or rind, which is a bright yellowy orange and very tough. Cut into it with a sharp

Citrus Fruit

1 CITRON	10 CLEMENTINES
2 UGLI FRUIT	(SPANISH)
3 POMELO	11 CLEMENTINE
4 RUBY GRAPEFRUIT	12 LEMON (SPANISH)
5 PINK GRAPEFRUIT	13 LEMON (CYPRUS)
6 WHITE GRAPEFRUIT	14 NAVEL ORANGE
7 SWEETIE	15 BLOOD ORANGE
GRAPEFRUIT	16 SATSUMA
8 NAVELINA ORANGE	17 LIMES
9 VALENCIA ORANGE	

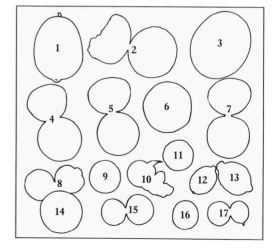

knife and you will find a mass of bright green jelly, encasing edible seeds, which you eat with a spoon. It is like eating the seedy core of a cucumber and the flavour is similar. (*59, 60*)

KIWI *Chinese gooseberry, kiwi fruit*

The kiwi used to be considered rare and exotic, appearing in exquisite dishes cooked by the world's best chefs. Then the less gifted took it over and began to use it in inappropriate ways and it fell out of favour for a while. However, it is delicious eaten raw. Even the skin is edible – just. But I usually cut it in half, or cut the top off like a boiled egg, and use a teaspoon to scoop out the rich bright green flesh with its central rosette of tiny black edible seeds. One fruit has more than the adult's daily requirement of vitamin C. The flavour is sweet, but with a surprising amount of acidity backing it up. It is so acid, in fact, that it dissolves aspic and gelatine, so do not use it in recipes including these ingredients.

Kiwis are particularly welcome in the winter when summer fruits are over. Because they are so hardy, they have a long season, being kept in cold storage for months on end. Supplies come from New Zealand, but also from Brazil, Italy, France and the Channel Islands.

The promoters of kiwi fruit would have us believe that it is perfect with everything: better with Parma ham than figs or melon, the ideal accompaniment to chicken dishes, the only garnish for a salmon, sliced with the thin rings overlapping in the manner of scales. But its acidity clashes with and even alters some flavours and textures (such as wine and cream), and it should not be used indiscriminately. (*59, 60*)

KUMQUAT

Peach blossom and kumquats are auspicious symbols for the Chinese lunar New Year when beautiful little kumquat trees with glossy green leaves are sold in street markets in Hong Kong. Kumquats symbolize gold and good fortune.

They are small fruits, no bigger than a large olive, and somewhat similar in shape. The skin looks very much like that of an orange (although it is not, technically, a member of the citrus family), but it is thinner, and edible. You pop the whole fruit into your mouth and eat skin and pulp, discarding the seeds as neatly as possible. It makes a refreshing mouthful after a rich meal, being both astringent and sweet. It has an intense, deep fragrance as you bite into the flesh and release the essential oils. There are hints of orange, orange blossom, bergamot and lime.

Whole kumquats cooked with poultry or fish enhance the finished dish because the flavour comes from the scented oils in the skin.

They can also be preserved. Wash, scrub and dry them, prick all over and pack into a preserving jar. Half-fill with sugar syrup and top up with vodka. After two or three months you will have delicious fruit to add to fruit salads, and a wonderful liqueur. (*59, 60*)

LEMON

The market in Palermo, Sicily, on New Year's Eve is a wonderful sight – stalls piled high with nothing but lemons in all shapes and sizes, some with green patches, some with leaves and twigs still attached. And the scent stops you at three paces, sharply fragrant, fruity and soft. That is what lemons *should* smell like. Lemons of the same intensity grow on Gozo, an island near Malta, where my parents live. They make them into that quintessentially English delicacy, lemon curd, and give it to friends on the island, who welcome this culinary curiosity into their Mediterranean repertoire. These lemons also make exquisite marmalade and candied peel and can be preserved in salt and oil to add an authentic flavour to North African and Middle Eastern dishes.

Fresh lemons flavour lemon meringue pies, ice-cream, lemonade, water-ice and sorbet, hot and cold soufflés, sponges, tarts and one of my favourite recent discoveries, Shaker lemon pie. This old recipe from Ohio uses sliced lemons, macerated overnight in plenty of sugar, then mixed with egg yolk and baked in a pie. It is wonderfully, mouth-puckeringly lemony.

Lemons are indispensable culinary aids. A few drops of juice make all the difference to mayonnaise and oil-based salad dressings, to smoked salmon, to stewed and raw fruit dishes, to various sauces and gravies, and to fish and poultry dishes. Lemon juice also prevents discoloration when applied to the cut surface of fruits such as bananas and pears.

The fruit we buy in the shops keeps quite well because it has been treated to preserve it from rot and the other evils that attack fresh fruit – scrub them well if you intend to use the skin. It is not necessary to keep them in the refrigerator and, in any case, a bowl of lemons brightens up the kitchen no end.

Choose fruits that feel heavy for their size. Small thin-skinned ones will be juicier, larger knobbly ones will have more peel and pith in proportion to flesh, but these are perfect for candying and preserving as, in this case, it is the essential oils in the skin you want to preserve, not the juice. A delicious method of extracting the flavour is to peel a lemon with a good skin very thinly, taking off only the zest. Put this into a half bottle of gin, vodka or any white fruit spirit, stopper it and leave it for a month. You will then have a fragrant pale yellow spirit which is excellent for cooking fish or poultry.

Luckily, lemons are available all year round, from Italy, Spain, Cyprus and 'Mediterranean' parts of the southern hemisphere. (*67, 72*)

LIME

The main supplies of this small green citrus fruit come from Brazil, Florida and the Caribbean. Unlike its cousin the lemon, it grows in tropical and sub-tropical climates, and is associated with many dishes of, for example, India and South-East Asia. Sharp lime pickle is delicious eaten in tiny bites with tandoori chicken, and Thai papaya salad is enlivened with hints of lime and chilli. Key lime pie from Florida is made similarly to a lemon meringue pie.

It can be used as a substitute for lemon in most dishes, but has an even more piercingly sour flavour, so use less of it.

When choosing limes look for the same qualities as in lemons – heavy for their size with plump, unblemished skin. (*67*)

LIMEQUAT

This is a cross between a kumquat and a lime. It is a small bright green fruit with thin edible skin and sharp fragrant flavour. Use as kumquats in cooking. However, beware. They are extremely sour and I find them quite inedible raw, unlike kumquats. (*77*)

LOGANBERRY

The loganberry is one of many hybrids derived from the wild blackberry or, in the United States, dewberry, and the domestic red raspberry. There are some slight differences in the fruit but selection and preparation are the same for all of them.

Boysenberries were developed from the strawberry, raspberry, dewberry and loganberry, and most closely resemble large plump blackberries, with similar glossy drupelets.

Loganberries are larger, softer and darker red than raspberries and with a hint more acidity. They are named after Judge Logan in whose Californian garden the first plant was discovered 100 years ago.

Youngberries are hybrids of the dewberry and loganberry and are not yet widely cultivated.

When choosing any of these berries look for sound, firm, dry, fully ripe specimens. Do not keep them longer than 24 hours as their fragrance and flavour soon disappear.

The fruit grows high off the ground so they should not be dirty, and do not require washing, which really does drain them of flavour. Remove squashed or mouldy fruit you find, along with any stalks or leaves.

Use the fruit in a variety of ways: fresh with a little sugar and cream, in jams, jellies, pies, sorbets, soufflés and ice-creams. Slightly over-ripe fruit can be crushed and steeped in wine vinegar to make an excellent fruit vinegar for cooking. Like blackberries they go well with some game dishes – particularly wild duck. (*56*)

LONGAN

Not unlike the lychee to which it is distantly related, the longan grows in clusters on branches and is a small fruit with a fairly smooth pale brown skin which encloses a sweet juicy translucent flesh. It grows in South-East Asia and other tropical parts including China, where it is particularly popular – the name means dragon's eye. I have eaten it in a delicious fruit soup when the liquid was a syrup made with jasmine flowers. If you are ever lucky enough to get them they will be expensive. Eat them as they are, peeling away the brittle shell, and discarding the stone. (*59, 60*)

LOQUAT *Japanese medlar*

These small Mediterranean fruits are quite fragile and their pale orange skin often looks spotted with brown bruises. They come from a beautiful dark green-leafed tree and are only 1½in (3cm) long, with waxy-looking skin, soft apricot-coloured flesh and a large inedible stone. They make one of the most subtle and delicious ice-creams I have ever tasted. Their flavour is slightly astringent, with a resinous hint, not unlike a mango. (*58, 60*)

LYCHEE *litchi*

A dish of lychees shared between friends is a very agreeable way to end a meal. The brittle, rough, pinkish shell cracks easily when pressed between thumb and finger, and can be peeled off cleanly to reveal the pearly white fruit inside. The sweet flesh has a slight grape-like texture but is a little more chewy and delicately scented. Deep within the flesh is a long, shiny, oval, brown, inedible seed. Alternatively, shell and stone a large quantity and serve them chilled swimming in a light syrup.

Look for fruit with as much pink or red on the skin as possible; they will be sweet and ripe. If the shell is pale beige or has a greenish hue the fruit is likely to be underripe. If it shows signs of turning brown, it is overripe, or has been stored for too long. (*59, 60*)

MAMEY

A spherical fruit, some 6–8in (15–20cm) in diameter, the mamey is a native of the American tropics. It has a rough, almost cork-like skin, earthy brown in colour, which is removed before eating, and best peeled back in segments. The flesh inside is scented, rich and sweet, and a bright deep yellow with hints of pink and orange, and contains several large inedible pits covered in bitter rough brown skin. It is best eaten raw, with a squeeze of lime and lemon but it also makes a particularly good jam.

MANGO

The mango is native to the Far East, the Indian sub-continent and South-East Asia. The Portuguese took it to Brazil centuries ago and from there it spread throughout South and Central America, the Caribbean and Florida. It also grows in East and West Africa.

But Thailand is the place for mangoes of every shape, size and colour, from small heart-shaped yellow ones, no bigger than a baby's fist, to pale, lemony-green ones shaped like an elongated 'S' which you peel and eat like a banana. There is a huge variety of mangoes – some 2500 types in all. Alfonso, Amélie, Bombay, Haydon, Julie, Kent, Langra, Manilla, Petacon, Romain and Zéphirine are the varieties most often seen.

They vary considerably: some mangoes are

PREPARING A MANGO

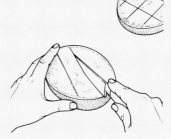

1 *Cut through the mango lengthways ½in (1cm) from each side of the centre to free the stone.*

2 *Cut the flesh from around the stone. Then make evenly spaced criss-cross cuts through each side section.*

3 *Take each side section in both hands and bend it back to separate the cut cubes. Remove these with a spoon.*

ripe when the skin is still green or green flushed with red; others when they become red-gold or pale yellow. Ripe mangoes give gently when you squeeze them lightly in the palm of your hand. The skin – which is inedible – should not be wrinkled or spotted with black.

The flesh of a ripe mango is a rich golden yellow, and oozing juice. Good mangoes are not too fibrous. I love the slightly resinous flavour that edges its luscious sweetness into a taste that is unique. A mango doesn't taste a 'little bit like a peach with a hint of pineapple', it tastes majestically of itself!

Mango is delicious eaten as it is, or it can be turned into the most glorious mousses, purées, ice-creams, sorbets and salads. Slightly underripe mango works well in a *salade composée* – a mixed salad served as a first or main course – combined with smoked meats or fish, or with shellfish. Ripe and underripe mangoes also make excellent chutney and pickles – a fruity mango chutney being particularly good with a mellow farmhouse cheese and crusty bread. See also DRIED FRUIT, page 82. (*58, 60*)

MANGOSTEEN

The mangosteen is not related to the mango. But you realize that as soon as you look at it. It is hard to believe that this unprepossessing little fruit is one of the most delicious of tropical fruits. It is the size of a small apple with a leathery, purplish-brown, inedible skin. Four small, hard, curved leaves with a central stalk make up the calyx. The skin and pith is thick for the size of the fruit, and a deep, bright, staining pink. This encloses the fruit itself – five pearly white, translucent segments in the centre of which are two inedible stones. The flavour is exquisitely sweet and fragrant with a lively touch of acidity.

It is too rare and delicate a fruit to mask its beauty with cream or syrup. Eat it as it is: cut round the top third, lift it off and scoop out the flesh with a small spoon. (*59, 60*)

MEDLAR

The small, brown fruit of this deciduous tree native to temperate Europe is most likely to be encountered in an old-fashioned garden, or growing wild. It is shaped like a large, flattened rosehip with an open end, and is about the size of a crab apple. The skin is rough and russetted.

It is eaten raw when it is overripe, not to say rotten – a state which is known as bletted – when the hard flesh softens and sweetens to a brownish purée which still has an edge of tannic astringency. When less ripe they can be made into ice-creams or jellies. One year I made some delicious medlar jelly with a bag of windfalls from a friend's garden. Some were soft and ripe, some still hard. This seemed to be a good combination. (*61*)

MELON

There are many varieties of melon available at different times of year, and they vary enormously in size, shape and colour of both skin and flesh:

Cantaloupe has an irregular sectional green skin and a pale green or orange flesh.
Charentais is my favourite. It is a type of cantaloupe with a roughish, pale green skin, a fragrant peachy-orange flesh when ripe, and is round rather than ovoid. It makes a wonderful sorbet.
Galia is spherical with a netted skin, which turns from green to brownish when ripe, and darkish green flesh.
Honeydew melons have smooth white or bright yellow ridged skins and pale greenish-yellow flesh, and are refreshing if a little tasteless.
Khoob melons from Iran are similar to pineapple melons, but usually larger.
Ogen is a round, sectional melon with green skin and flesh. Raw Ogen melon blended with cooked courgettes, herbs, cream and stock makes an unusual and delicious summer soup.
Piel de Sapo is a type of honeydew melon; its name means 'toad's skin'.
Pineapple melon has an orange netted skin and a luscious orange flesh with a distinctly pineapply scent.

When ripe all melon varieties should yield to slight pressure at the stalk end, and some have an unmistakable melony scent.

Chilled melon is good for breakfast or as a starter, but I like it best to end a meal. Combine it with other summer fruits, such as redcurrants, raspberries or wild strawberries, or perhaps a mixture of all three in a melon shell splashed with a little strawberry liqueur. Or scoop balls out of three different-coloured melons and put them in a honey syrup in a glass bowl. Melons combine well with fresh mint. I once made a powerfully refreshing melon and mint sorbet.

Take care that melons are well covered if stored in the refrigerator, otherwise they impregnate everything around them with their heady scent. See also *Watermelon*. (*71*)

MULBERRY

These luscious purple-black berries are twice as good and twice as big as blackberries. But they are fragile, ripening and dropping from the tree before there is time to pick them. If you are lucky enough to obtain some eat them as they are with a little cream. Mulberry-flavoured vinegars and vodkas are particularly good.

NECTARINE

This smooth-skinned peach is perhaps the most delicious of all stone fruit. The flesh is very juicy with a pronounced peachy, almondy flavour and

Melons

1–4	WATERMELONS	11	OGEN (ENGLISH)
5	HONEYDEW	12	PIEL DE SAPO
6	PINEAPPLE MELON	13	GALIA (UNRIPE)
7	KHOOB	14	GOLDEN
8	GALIA (RIPE)		WATERMELON (CUT)
9	GOLDEN	15	CHARENTAIS (CUT)
	WATERMELON	16	CHARENTAIS
10	OGEN (DUTCH)	17	OGEN (ENGLISH)

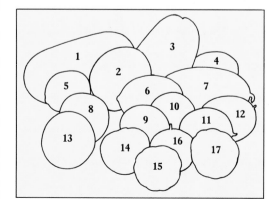

a good balance of sweetness and acidity. The skin ranges from white to yellowy orange to pinkish red. The white-fleshed varieties are particularly fine.

When ripe, nectarines are best eaten raw and unpeeled as an inexpensive dessert fruit. In cooking, the delicate flavour and firm texture are lost. Slightly underripe nectarines can be gently poached in syrup for a short time and then chilled. A bowl of sliced nectarines in fresh orange juice, white or red wine or Champagne is

Citrus Fruit

1 VARIEGATED LEMON
2 SWEET LEMON (CUT)
3 SWEET LEMON
4 SEVILLE ORANGE
5 TANGERINE (MINEOLA)
6 SHAMOUTI ORANGE

a splendid way to end a summer dinner.

The most efficient way of peeling the fruit, if you need to, is to pour boiling water over it and leave immersed for 30–40 seconds, then remove the fruit and peel the skin away effortlessly. However, this does tend to cook the outer layer, so I prefer to peel nectarines with a knife. See also *Peach*, and DRIED FRUIT, page 82. (*73*)

ORANGE

Spain, springtime and oranges remain inextricably linked in the mind. The first whiff of orange blossom in southern Spain in early spring is truly memorable.

The oranges I like best are the ones that come early in the year from the Mediterranean, from Spain, Morocco and Cyprus. Of course, they also come from Florida, Israel and the southern hemisphere. But summer oranges do little for me. I'm content to wait until the dark winter months, for the large, sweet, almost seedless Navel and Navelina oranges and the smaller blood oranges with red-flushed skins and deep ruby-coloured juice. These last make brilliant sorbets and *granitas*, and are essential to *sauce maltaise*, a mayonnaise flavoured and coloured with blood oranges – delicious with cold fish or shellfish, poultry and vegetables. Valencia is the world's most important variety, and is good for both eating and juicing. Shamouti is a Mediterranean variety available in the winter.

Peeled and thinly sliced orange rings, bathing in a little of their own juice, make a simple and economical dessert. A sprinkling of orange flower water lifts it into another class altogether. Oranges can also be successfully combined with savoury ingredients – thin onion rings, olives, cucumber slices, Mozzarella cheese and smoked fish – to make unusual salads.

Bitter Seville oranges are best for making marmalade. They have a short season in January and should be bought up when you can find them. Seville orange is the correct ingredient for duckling with orange sauce. The bitter acidity of the fruit is a marvellous foil for the rich succulent meat. Fresh orange juice can also be used as a marinade – for white fish or salmon, for example – but do not overdo it as the acid will 'cook' the fish.

The best of the orange flavour comes not from

the juice but the essential oils contained in the thin outer layer of skin, the zest. Before using it, scrub, wash and dry it. Extract the zest by grating the skin over a plate or, if using a sweet recipe, rub a cube of sugar hard over the skin until it is impregnated. Orange zest can be cut up and ground with sugar to make a delicious orange sugar for use in sponge cakes and custards. A thin strip of zest added to a casserole or fish soup will impart a wonderfully warm flavour. And if you are squeezing oranges for their juice, save some of the skins for candying or crystallizing.

Fresh-tasting homemade orange jelly with a few peeled fruit segments suspended in it makes another inexpensive dessert. Orange tarts and ice-creams are also good; and a few slices of orange add colour to fruit salad.

To make neat peeled orange slices, slice the oranges on to a plate to catch the juice, and then snip round with a pair of sharp kitchen scissors to remove the peel, pith and membrane.

Ortaniques are a cross between the orange and tangerine, and are unique to Jamaica. They are sweet and very juicy, thin-skinned 'easy-peelers' and can be used in the same way as oranges. (*67, 72*)

PASSION FRUIT *maracuya*

The true passion fruit (*Passiflora edulis*) in its natural fresh ripe state is a smooth ovoid about 3in (7cm) long with either a reddish-purple leathery skin or a pale yellow skin. The fruit is green when unripe. Originally from Brazil, the passion fruit is now widely cultivated in Kenya and in South America, notably Colombia where it is known as maracuya. By the time it reaches us it is often somewhat shrivelled in appearance. It is not true that the wrinklier they are the better; they are just older. The leathery skin encloses a thin reddish pith surrounding a white membranous lining which encloses small edible crunchy seeds, each one set in a fragrant, intensely flavoured, sweet-sour and translucent pulp, dark greenish orange in colour.

To get to the sweet pulp cut the top off the fruit like an egg, and spoon out the interior. Both pulp and seeds are edible. If you just want the pulp, rub through a fine sieve with a tablespoon of boiling water which will help to remove the pulp from the seeds. Add the pulp to fruit salad.

The juice can be used for marinating. I find it particularly successful with game such as venison and pheasant, and I add the marinade to the sauce or gravy at the end.

Passion fruit curd, ice-cream and sorbet are perhaps the most effective ways of using this delicious fruit. See also *Curuba* and *Granadilla*. (59, 60, 77)

Stone Fruit

1 CHERRIES (NAP)
2 CHERRIES (MORELLO)
3 NECTARINES (SILVER GEM)
4 CHERRIES (RAINIER)
5 APRICOTS
6 NECTARINES (ITALIAN)
7 CHERRIES (BING)
8 PEACHES (ITALIAN)
9 NECTARINES (FANTASIA)
10 CHERRIES (BRADBOURNE)
11 GREENGAGES
12 NECTARINES (RED DIAMOND)
13 PEACHES (RED TOP)
14 PEACHES (ELEGANT LADY)

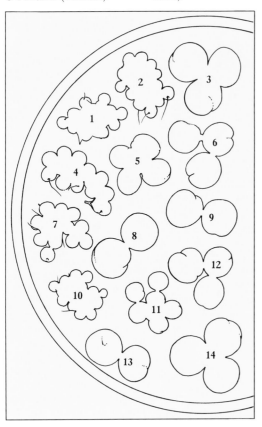

PAWPAW *papaya*

Where I lived in Nigeria we had a pawpaw tree growing outside the kitchen door. Lime trees were also abundant around the compound. Instant breakfast! I am ashamed to say that after a while I became bored with the morning ritual, reaching up with a pole to hook down a ripe fruit, cutting it in half, scooping out the small black seeds and cutting up a lime to squeeze over it. The fruit was always meltingly ripe, fragrant, deep peachy orange and sweet enough to need no other accompaniment – the perfect pawpaw. The seeds at the centre of the fruit, though edible, are very peppery.

Although some varieties grow to an enormous size, up to 20lb (10kg), the ones we find most often weigh about 12–16oz (375–500g), and are an elongated pear shape, sometimes slightly angular. The inedible skin turns from green to yellow as it ripens. A traditional test of quality is to look at the stalk end of a green pawpaw; if it has a ring of yellow round it will ripen. If not, you will always have an unripe fruit.

Pawpaw, as well as containing vitamin A, is a rich source of the powerful enzyme papain which breaks down protein, so pawpaw juice acts as a meat tenderizer when added to marinades. In Nigeria we used to wrap tough beef in the pawpaw skins discarded from breakfast. By extension, pawpaw sorbet or half a pawpaw at the end of a meat-rich meal is an excellent digestive.

Pawpaw combines well with other tropical fruits. For special meals around Christmastime I make a fruit salad with pawpaw, mango, kiwi fruit, passion fruit, a few Muscat grapes and anything else that looks and smells good. In Thailand, where they are plentiful, unripe pawpaws are shredded to make a refreshing pale green salad mixed with lime juice, chillies and other ingredients. They can also be pickled or preserved, and when unripe can be stuffed and baked as a savoury dish. *(59, 60)*

PEACH

This sweet juicy fruit, which originated in China, needs plenty of sun to ripen it fully, and most of our supplies come from Spain, Italy, France and the United States. Several varieties can be obtained: yellow-fleshed, pink-fleshed and perhaps sweetest of all, the small white-fleshed peaches. Some are cling peaches – which means that the flesh tends to cling to the stone – and some are of the freestone variety.

When choosing peaches look for undamaged and unbruised specimens. The slightest bruise or even firm fingermark will cause the fruit to deteriorate rapidly. The soft yellow, velvety skin, flushed with red, should not be wrinkled or dry and the fruit should be firm but not hard. They keep reasonably well in a fruit bowl for two or three days, but it's best to use them quickly as their fresh flavour soon dissipates. They can be eaten raw or cooked.

To skin peaches, many cooks advise you to immerse them in boiling water for about 30 seconds, after which the skins should come off easily. This is effective but it does slightly cook the fruit, which is not important if they are to be cooked anyway, but if eating them raw peel them with a very sharp knife to retain maximum flavour. To remove the stone, slice them in half around the stone through the groove, and twist the two halves against each other (see page 54). One half will come clean away. Lever the stone out of the other half with a knife.

A peach sliced into a wine glass topped up with Champagne is a delightful classic dessert. More simply, steep peeled sliced peaches in fresh orange juice or a little apple juice. Use the small white-fleshed peaches whole.

American cookery books are full of peach recipes – pies, puddings, cobblers, ices, fluffs, compotes, preserves, jams and jellies in abundance. Spiced peaches make a good accompaniment to cold smoked meats. Slightly underripe peaches can be made into excellent chutneys and combine well with oranges to make a richly flavoured marmalade. Fresh peaches, raspberries and vanilla ice-cream combine to make the classic dish *pêche melba*, created by the chef Escoffier in honour of the Australian opera singer, Dame Nelly Melba. See also DRIED FRUIT, page 82. *(73)*

PEAR

Although there are said to be over 5000 named varieties of European pear and 1000 American ones, almost all descended from the common pear, there are very few varieties on sale at any one time. Pears which crop well, pack well and eat well are what we are offered. Fortunately, some of these are extremely good:

Anjou is a large chunky fruit with a greenish skin that turns yellow as the pear ripens. It is often russetted. The flesh is juicy and sweet. Use for dessert and culinary purposes.

Beurré d'Amantis, Beurré Hardy and **Beurré Bosc** are medium-sized fruit. Golden russet skin and juicy, slightly acidic flesh that is creamy white with a pink or yellow tinge. (Beurré means 'buttered'.)

Beurré Dumont A large, heavy, russetted, slow-ripening pear with firm grainy flesh. A good cooking pear.

Beurré Superfin Large, long, hard, green pears when underripe and lightly russetted all over, this is a very superior variety. When ripe it still has a tough skin, golden green in colour, but also firm yet sweet, very juicy flesh with a nice hint of acidity. The graininess so common in many pears is scarcely perceptible. It's much too good for cooking. Serve it on its own or with a fine piece of cheese.

Black Worcester A dark, knobbly, forbidding-looking cooking pear. Heavily russetted all over but you can just detect a shadow of its deep purple skin underneath. It has firm grainy flesh.

Bristol Cross A delicately shaped pear, half russetted, green turning to yellow when ripe. The flesh is juicy and sweet and slightly grainy in texture.

Comice or **Doyenne du Comice** is large and roundish; the skin is yellow with a greenish tinge, speckled and russetted, sometimes with a red blush. The flesh is soft, creamy white, very juicy, fragrant and full-flavoured. It is best eaten raw as a dessert pear.

Pears

1 BEURRÉ BOSC	9 FORELLE
2 RED BARTLETT	10 NAPOLEON
3 WILLIAMS BON CHRÉTIEN	11 ZÉPHERINE GRÉGOIRE
4 RED WILLIAMS	12 WINTER NELIS
5 BRISTOL CROSS	13 PACKHAM'S TRIUMPH
6 BLACK WORCESTER	14 COMICE
7 CONFERENCE	15 LAXTON'S FOREMOST
8 BEURRÉ DUMONT	16 BEURRÉ SUPERFIN

Conference is long and tapering, the skin green with brown russetting, and the flesh very juicy and sweet with a firm, sometimes grainy texture. It is an excellent all-purpose pear and as a bonus, it keeps very well.

Forelle Green with a dark red flush on one side. It has a grainy flesh and a distinctive fresh flavour even after long storage. Recommended for cooking, or with cheese if a crisp pear is liked.

Laxton's Foremost One of the largest pears, green and lightly russetted, it ripens to a deep all-over yellow. The flesh is juicy with a nice sharpness underlying the sweetness. The texture is characteristically grainy and a pale cream with a touch of pinkish yellow. It quickly becomes overripe and this is not always apparent from the outside because it becomes soft and brown from the inside out, with no evident blemishes on the outer surface.

Napoleon Small, squat and regular in shape, this has a bright clear green skin with no russetting at all. It ripens slowly to a yellowish green. A dessert pear rather than a cooking pear, with soft, sweet, juicy flesh.

Packham's Triumph A slow-ripening pear, green, firm and lightly russetted, ripening to a clear yellow over a period of weeks. Very soft succulent flesh. Smooth and sweet with the acidity of pear drops. A fine dessert pear.

Red Bartlett has a shiny skin, speckled rather than russetted, turning from green with a red flush to yellow with an extensive red flush. When ripe the texture is soft and buttery. The flavour is good and it is a very juicy pear.

Red Williams Almost identical in characteristics to the Red Bartlett.

Williams Bon Chrétien (Bartlett) is medium-sized with yellow speckled skin flushed with pink. Use for culinary or dessert purposes.

Winter Nelis A small, round, russetted pear which remains quite green. It has a sweet grainy flesh which holds its shape reasonably well when cooked. I use it underripe in game casseroles.

Zépherine Grégoire A beautiful name for a rather small, plain pear. It is squat and dumpy with no distinctive marking but it does have a good flavour and juicy flesh.

Pears of one sort or another are always available, although I particularly like to use them in the autumn with other seasonal ingredients such as nuts. Walnut or almond and pear tarts are delicious. Pear sorbet with a hint of distilled pear spirit is a good way to finish a substantial autumn or winter dinner.

Use pears in cakes, tarts and puddings, to grate into tea breads and for making ice-cream. Pears are good in winter salads, adding a rich but unaggressive fruitiness. For this reason, too, I love to cook pears with game. A few quarters pot-roasted with a partridge and then rubbed through a sieve to make the sauce provides an amusing dinner for two on the 'first day of Christmas'. Pears, with a little pear spirit, are also excellent with venison. Homemade pear-flavoured vinegars and vodkas can be made in the autumn to give as Christmas gifts.

Perfectly ripe, sweet, juicy pears make one of the finest desserts served, as they are in Italy, with good cheese. Gorgonzola is traditional but try also a not-too-mature Parmesan or a farmhouse Lancashire. See also DRIED FRUIT, page 82. (75)

PEPINO

Creamy yellow and streaked with purple, an elongated oval with a smooth, taut shiny skin, you might at first sight mistake this for an aubergine. In fact, the pepino, like the aubergine, potato and tomato belongs to the large *Solanaceae* family. The flavour of the fruit is sweet and slightly acid and it is probably best eaten cooked. It should be peeled first, whether eating it raw or cooking it, because the skin is somewhat bitter. Cooked with a little sugar or honey, the pulp is delicious with ice-cream or as a filling for a cake. (59, 60)

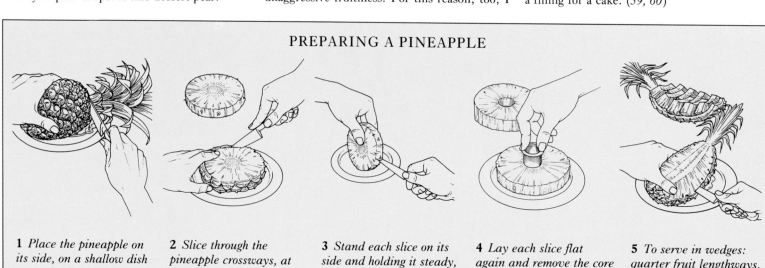

PREPARING A PINEAPPLE

1 *Place the pineapple on its side, on a shallow dish to catch all the juices, and holding the fruit steady, cut off the leafy crown.*

2 *Slice through the pineapple crossways, at intervals of about ½in (1cm). Then cut away all of the tough 'rind'.*

3 *Stand each slice on its side and holding it steady, carefully flick out the small, woody eyes with the tip of the knife.*

4 *Lay each slice flat again and remove the core with a small pastry cutter, apple corer or a small, sharp kitchen knife.*

5 *To serve in wedges: quarter fruit lengthways. Remove core. Separate fruit from rind and cut into wedges as shown.*

PERSIMMON *kaki, Sharon fruit*

This can be one of the trickiest fruits to buy. Confusingly, there are two varieties which at a certain stage of their development look identical – rather like large, squarish, deep orange tomatoes. The true persimmon is mouth-puckeringly bitter and sour when firm, and full of tannin. As it ripens it becomes soft, translucent and 'swollen' looking. In other fruit it would be considered overripe, but this is the time to buy and eat persimmon. Sadly, we rarely see them in this state of splendour since they spoil very quickly and many people are reluctant to buy them because they look so overripe.

But it is a magnificent fruit, available in late October to December. Buy it, chill it, slice off the top and scoop out the sweet fruit pulp – almost a jelly – with a teaspoon. It needs no other embellishment. The pulp does, however, mix well with cream to make fools, mousses and iced soufflés.

Sharon fruit is a variety specially bred to be palatable in a conventional state of ripeness. It is sweet but perhaps not quite so luscious as the persimmon and can be used in salads, fruit and savoury. When kept for several days it softens and can be eaten like a persimmon. (77)

PINEAPPLE

I have a perfect pineapple in front of me. It comes from Ghana, but it might have come from the Ivory Coast, Central America, Hawaii or any number of tropical countries. The rough skin 'carved' into neat lozenges is a warm orange gold. The plume is a firm, fleshy grey-green, with a soft bloom to the leaves. One pulled gently from the centre comes away easily. This, and the distinctive smell of pineapple, show that it is ripe. It weighs about 2lb (1kg), which is medium size. Recently, tiny 'individual-portion' pineapples have become available. These are just as sweet and fragrant, and make delicious desserts, hollowed out and filled with a mixture of pineapple flesh and a creamy custard, or syrup and other tropical fruits.

Kirsch and other spirits or liqueurs are often sprinkled on pineapple when it is served in wedges or slices and this certainly helps if the fruit is lacking in flavour but, in truth, a perfectly ripe pineapple needs nothing else.

Pineapple is occasionally cooked with meat dishes, notably pork, both in European, American, particularly Hawaiian, and Chinese cooking. A small amount in a rich spicy fish or chicken curry would not be inappropriate either. Ices, custards and mousses all benefit from its powerful flavour and delicate colour, but do not use pineapple with gelatine or it will never set. Vanilla, ginger, coconut, butter, rum and black pepper are all flavourings that combine well with pineapple – not all at the same time, of course.

This lovely fruit is a good source of vitamin C, dietary fibre and one of the pepsin enzymes which breaks down protein (that's why the gelatine doesn't set). It is therefore good to serve after a meat-rich meal as an aid to digestion. Fine steaks can be marinated in pineapple juice to tenderize them. Surprisingly, little of the flavour remains with the meat. (59)

PITAHAYA

The fruit of a Central and South American cactus, this looks like a rubbery crimson grenade. It is quite heavy for its size and the skin bears leaf scars or slight scales. Inside the densely packed soft flesh is a truly startling fluorescent pink with a mass of tiny edible black seeds. There is no doubt that spoonfuls of flesh added to other fruits in a compote or fruit salad will provide brilliant colour contrast but on the other hand, shocking pink is not a particularly appetizing colour for food. It does not have a distinctive flavour – quite mild, quite sweet, quite pleasant – and is improved by a sprinkling of lime juice, sugar and even a touch of ginger.

It also comes in a yellow version, equally bright, rather more like a cactus and rubbery looking. Although of no great gastronomic appeal it is rich in fibre and vitamin C. Cut in half lengthways and eat the flesh with a spoon. (58, 60)

PLUM

This is a late summer stone fruit, much of it homegrown, though the season is extended with imports from France, Italy, Spain and the United States. The plum is something of a workhorse in the kitchen. It never seems quite to

Tropical Fruit

1	JUJUBES	7	YELLOW PASSION FRUIT
2	LIMEQUATS	8	TIENTSIN PEAR
3	FEIJOAS	9	CHERIMOYA
4	CURUBAS	10	CHERIMOYA (SOURSOP)
5	PERSIMMONS		
6	GOLDEN APPLES		

have reached the heights of peaches and apricots but a good ripe dessert plum is a luscious delight. I soon come to regret the spaces in my store cupboard in winter if I do not make at least a few jars of plum jam: green from the green plums such as the gages, Early Laxtons, Pershore Yellow Eggs and Warwickshire Drooper, red from Opal, Cherry Plum and some of the less ripe Victorias; and a rich dark red to purple jam from the River's Czar, Early Prolific, Pershore, Monarch and Marjorie's Seedling.

Plums vary in size from not much more than 1in (2·5cm) long to a good 3–4in (7–10cm). Whatever their shape, colour or size, look for firm, plump, unwrinkled specimens, which still have a bloom to them if possible. They will keep well for up to a week at room temperature if bought while firm, but will continue to ripen. Buy ripe plums for immediate consumption. Plums are eaten raw or cooked, and unpeeled.

Plums make wonderful pies and tarts, and preserved in wine or cider vinegar they are delicious with cold ham and turkey. Cook them into a thick sweet-sour sauce to serve with pork or to use in Oriental dishes. Add them North African style to meat casseroles where the combination of meat, fruit and nuts is rich, fragrant and delicious. Dried as prunes, they are even more versatile. See also *Damson* and *Greengage*, and DRIED FRUIT, page 82. (79)

POMEGRANATE

Although the pomegranate has been of great symbolic significance in many cultures and religions over thousands of years it has not enjoyed much of a culinary reputation, although some of the uses to which it is put today clearly come from its original home, the Middle East and Central Asia. Now it is cultivated in South America, the Canary Islands, California, the Middle East and the Mediterranean and supplies reach Britain from August to December. It is the first 'exotic' fruit I tasted as a child. The individual seeds had to be removed with a pin.

It is a fine fruit to look at, with its tough, leather-like, burnished, glowing skin, ranging from a warm brownish-yellow to a deep true crimson. It feels good to hold, solid, heavy, slightly angular and looks distinctive with its crown-shaped calyx. The fruit can be cut in half to reveal a yellow suede-like pith and translucent fleshy cells of juicy red enclosing white seeds. Clusters of cells are separated by a thin yellow membrane, which like the pith and to a lesser degree the seeds, is exceedingly bitter, being full of tannin.

The red fruit can be used to decorate and flavour ice-creams, mousses and fruit salads. Extract the juice by gently but firmly pressing each half over a lemon squeezer. It is not a good idea to use an electric or even mechanical means of extracting the juice as this breaks down the seeds and membrane and makes the juice taste too bitter.

With the juice you can make grenadine, a lovely pomegranate syrup traditional in France and Italy for flavouring long drinks and ices. Use the juice on its own to make a marvellous water ice or a dessert jelly.

Pomegranate juice is one of the best marinades I know. It has a real depth of distinctive flavour and gives colour to the final sauce as might a light red wine. Best of all it has just the right balance of acidity which, for me, is preferable to that of lemon or lime. I use it to marinate game, poultry and lamb. At Christmas I like to prepare non-traditional recipes using traditional ingredients. One year it was pheasant breasts marinated in pomegranate juice and walnut oil, finished off on a charcoal grill. Another year it was sliced pan-fried turkey breasts, marinated in pomegranate juice, and served with a delicate sauce decorated with pomegranate seeds. (63)

POMELO

This is a type of citrus fruit, larger than a grapefruit, pear-shaped and with a much thicker, greeny-yellow skin and membrane. Both should be removed before serving the fruit

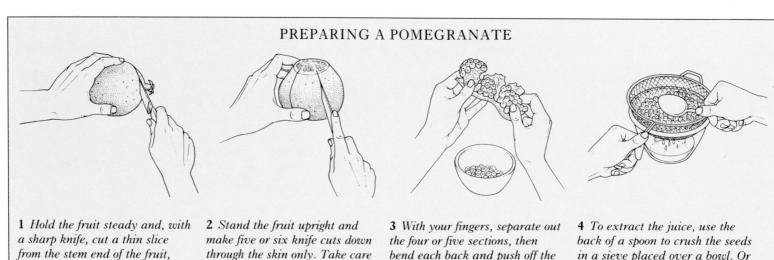

PREPARING A POMEGRANATE

1 *Hold the fruit steady and, with a sharp knife, cut a thin slice from the stem end of the fruit, revealing the juicy scarlet seeds close-packed inside.*

2 *Stand the fruit upright and make five or six knife cuts down through the skin only. Take care not to puncture the seeds as you do this.*

3 *With your fingers, separate out the four or five sections, then bend each back and push off the seeds. Remove the bitter pith and membranes and discard.*

4 *To extract the juice, use the back of a spoon to crush the seeds in a sieve placed over a bowl. Or halve the fruit and use a lemon squeezer.*

raw or using in a made-up dish. Its flesh is refreshingly sharp and sweet, and not quite as juicy as that of the grapefruit. The skin can be candied or added to citrus marmalade. (67)

PRICKLY PEAR *barbary fig, Indian fig*

Prickly pears are the fruit of a type of cactus. They ripen from green to yellow to a deep rosy-apricot colour, and are about 3in (7cm) long and ovoid in shape. Minute hairs protrude from the skin like small sharp needles which can become embedded in your hands.

Wear rubber gloves to handle them. Drop the fruit into a bucket of water, then remove by spearing with a fork or sharp knife. With another sharp knife cut off a thin slice at the top and bottom and slit the skin lengthways without piercing the flesh too far. Peel back the skin, remove the fruit and place it in a bowl. The yellow or pinkish flesh contains edible, crunchy, but quite hard seeds. The fruit has a sweet, mellow, warm flavour that marries well with other fruit in compotes and fruit salads, or it can be eaten with a squeeze of lemon or lime. The fruit can also be cooked and sieved and the purée used for sauces, ices, jams, cake fillings or moulded jellies. (63)

QUINCE

Sometimes in late autumn you can buy these large golden-yellow fruits, intensely fragrant and with a light fuzzy-grey down on their skins. They belong to the same family as the apple and the pear (*Rosaceae*) and in shape can resemble either one. The hard, dry flesh of the quince is a creamy yellow; the seeds and core are very large and coarse.

Plums

1 STANLEY
2 MARJORIE SEEDLING
3 SULTAN
4 ENGLISH RED
5 PRESIDENT
6 CASSELMAN
7 VICTORIA
8 MONARCH
9 FRIAR
10 PERSHORE YELLOW EGG
11 SANTA ROSA
12 POND'S SEEDLING
13 BURBANK
14 RIVER'S EARLY PROLIFIC
15 DAMSONS

The quince is not for eating raw. Its greatest property apart from fragrance and flavour is the amount of pectin contained in the seeds, so it makes the most marvellous jams, jellies and marmalades. Indeed, the word marmalade comes from *marmelo*, the Portuguese word for quince. Quince can also be added to fruit less rich in pectin to help give a good set. A few slices added to an apple or pear tart will give an extra depth of flavour. Quinces in a bowl give a whole house a wonderfully rich autumnal smell. You can use the small, golden, apple-shaped fruit of the ornamental japonica quince in the same way.

Add the fruit to meat casseroles, or make a sauce for roast pork along the lines of apple sauce. A few pieces put inside a chicken before you pot-roast it with a little cider gives an exquisite and unusual flavour.

Quince is perhaps best known for the fruity paste made from the pulp cooked long and slowly with sugar. It's called *cotignac* or *pâte de coing* in France, and *membrillo* in Spain. The latter is often served with soft cheeses or fresh goat's cheese – an excellent combination.

Preserve some of the flavour of quinces by extracting it into a spirit. Cut them into chunks or use small ones whole (wash and wipe them thoroughly to get rid of the down before chopping them). Pack them into a wide-necked decanter or a preserving jar. Cover the fruit with gin, or even better *grappa* (a marc or grape brandy made in Italy); stopper and keep for at least a couple of months to make a good digestive as well as flavouring for fish, chicken and sweet dishes. (*61*)

RAMBUTAN

A distant cousin of the lychee, the rambutan originated in Malaysia but is now cultivated in the United States and parts of South-East Asia. It is about 2in (5cm) in diameter, with a dark red-brown skin covered in soft hairy spines. The brittle skin can be broken open with a knife or the fingers and then peeled away to expose the pearly-white, sweet, translucent flesh. In taste and texture it resembles the lychee and, like it, contains an inedible brown stone.

It is a fruit best eaten raw but it can also be served in a light syrup on its own or with other fruit. (*59, 60*)

RASPBERRY

This family of soft fruit includes the wineberry with its small, bright orange-red berries and the salmonberry which is an American wild raspberry. Black raspberries are sometimes found, also known as the blackcap, but the true raspberry is usually a soft, warm crimson red, with velvety drupelets. The yellow or white raspberry is now rarely available commercially, but well worth looking out for as it has a fine, delicate flavour.

Homegrown raspberries come on to the market in June and July, followed by another crop as late as October.

If you are lucky enough to have lots of raspberries make them into delicious jams and jellies, but otherwise it is a pity to cook this exquisite summer fruit. Serve raspberries with cream, on their own or sprinkled with claret or port and a little sugar. Combine them with strawberries and blueberries in a bowl and serve with *sabayon*, a foamy sauce. Serve a mixture of raspberries and melon chunks in a hollowed-out melon shell. Make a pastry containing ground almonds or hazelnuts and bake a sweet pastry shell to hold a mound of raspberries and cream. Serve them with homemade meringues. Crush and sieve ripe raspberries to make a sauce to serve with ice-cream or to make an ice-cream or sorbet. Fill a sponge cake with raspberries and cream. Lastly, they are an important ingredient in the traditional English summer pudding – a mixture of red soft fruits, lightly cooked then chilled inside a bread casing which takes on the brilliant colour of the juice – utterly delicious!

What about raspberries in savoury dishes? Raspberries have a degree of acidity that makes them an appropriate partner for some meat dishes, particularly lamb and duck, either whole or crushed and used in the sauce or marinade. Contrary to popular belief fruit vinegars are not a recent invention; raspberry vinegar has been around for a very long time. It makes a refreshing drink, diluted with cold sparkling water, as well as being a delicious addition to a vinaigrette.

As with all soft berry fruits, do not buy more than you need for immediate use (although they do freeze well) and avoid buying packs with damaged or overripe fruit. (*56*)

RHUBARB

At a certain point in the year, in the late winter and very early spring, this is the only fresh homegrown fruit available (although strictly speaking it is not a fruit but the sweet stalk of the rhubarb plant). Early rhubarb is forced into growth and has long, thin, red and pink stems with pale yellow, sickly-looking leaves. It's not very exciting to look at, but make the most of its fresh spring-like flavour and turn it into a glorious pie or tart. Serve with a vanilla or ginger cream, both perfect flavours to complement rhubarb. Rhubarb sorbet or ice-cream made from the pink forced rhubarb is delicate and refreshing.

One of the best ways of using rhubarb I ever came across was as a chilled fruit soup, clear, pink, and with a marvellously clean refreshing taste. It was served instead of a sorbet between the fish and meat courses.

Main-crop rhubarb is much coarser than early rhubarb, with deep red skin, and a good if tart flavour. It is a useful filler for family puddings, pies and crumbles. Use this clean tartness to advantage in combinations with rich meats – a rhubarb sauce for pork, a few batons of poached or fried rhubarb with sliced duck breast.

Rhubarb is also good in jams and jellies, although only main-crop rhubarb has enough pectin to set on its own.

Rhubarb is hardly ever eaten raw. Never eat rhubarb leaves as they are poisonous. (*81*)

ROSE APPLE

A pretty tropical curiosity, this strikingly beautiful, waxy, pink fruit does indeed have the colour and fragrance of the rose. Its shape is that of a somewhat top-heavy apple and it has the same crispness of flesh. Use it for decoration as it does not have a great deal of flavour.

ROWANBERRY

Rowanberries are a brilliant scarlet, growing in clusters on the rowan or mountain ash tree. They are not sold commercially but you might find a tree in your street or neighbourhood. Use the fruit for making a wonderful jewel-like jelly to serve with meat, poultry and game.

SAPODILLA

A small oval fruit with rough, brown, inedible skin, the sapodilla should not be eaten until it is really soft and ripe, when the white flesh darkens to creamy yellow and becomes very delicious with a custardy vanilla flavour. When unripe the flesh is bitter with tannin, and grainy like an unripe pear. *(58, 60)*

SATSUMA

A type of orange of Japanese origin, the satsuma belongs to the same group of 'easy-peelers' as the clementine. Pale orange and the shape of a slightly flattened sphere, it is juicy, slightly tart and almost seedless. Peel and eat it raw, or use it in fruit salads, jams and marmalades. *(67)*

SLOE

The sloe is the fruit of the native blackthorn bush, a member of the plum family. The fruit is small, blue-black with a slight bloom to it and a bitter-almond, plummy flavour. It is not usually picked until November or after the first frost, which slightly cracks the skin. Then it is suitable for packing into jars and covering with gin. By Christmas you will have sloe gin. You can pick the fruit earlier but then you will have to do the work of the frost and prick the skin all over yourself with a fork.

Sloes can also be made into jams and jellies and combined with other fruit for the same purposes. They are much too sour to eat raw. *(61)*

STAR FRUIT *carambola*

This pretty, waxy, pale yellowy-green fruit – about 3–5in (7–12cm) long – is a teaser which promises much and yields little. Sliced horizontally, unpeeled, but with the central seeds removed, the elegant five-pointed 'stars' can be used to decorative effect in fruit salads. They are supposed to have a refreshing sweet-sour flavour. To me they taste like vaguely citrusy peapods and have the same sort of texture. Some trees bear sweeter fruits, others more acid ones, and there's no way to tell which you are buying. *(59, 60)*

STRAWBERRY

The large, bright red fruit we know today has developed over the centuries from the tiny wild fragrant fruit that grows all over Europe and other temperate areas. Of course, the wild or alpine strawberry, *fraise des bois*, is still to be found, growing on wooded banks and enjoyed for its warm musky flavour. Sweet, white vanilla-flavoured strawberries are also occasionally available.

Cultivated strawberries come in many different varieties: small, large, globular, conical, some with a neck, some with a concave top, some with more hairs and seeds than others, some hollow, some dense, and with varying degrees of colour. Look for fruit that is bright, firm and unblemished with a fresh green calyx; eat it on the same day.

If you have to wash the fruit do so very quickly, and before you remove the calyx, otherwise water will get into the fruit and destroy the delicate flavour. This is best enjoyed uncooked, with or without cream and sugar, or yogurt, syrup or wine. Eat strawberries as they come, or piled in a pre-baked pie shell or on a sponge base. *Fraises des bois* are served in France with *crème fraîche*, or drowned in red Bordeaux wine.

Also use strawberries for delicious ice-creams and sorbets, and to make jam. Remember, however, that they are very low in pectin, and it will not set unless you add lemon juice or some other acidic fruit. I once combined them with the left-over extract of a batch of gooseberries I'd cooked for jelly and this was a particularly good combination.

American cookery books give recipes for strawberry shortcake and strawberry cobbler, but also combine it with avocado in savoury starters.

Strawberry-flavoured vinegars and liqueurs can be made by infusing your chosen liquid with plenty of strawberries and keeping it in a dark place for several weeks. *(56)*

TAMARILLO *tree tomato*

Originally from South America, this fruit is now grown in a number of tropical and sub-tropical countries. The best version of tamarillos I have ever eaten was cooked for me by a New Zealand chef. The fruit had been peeled, sweetened and baked and was served with a fine, warm *sabayon* sauce. Eaten raw the fruit is very acidic, even when ripe.

The fruit is smooth, egg-shaped and 2–3in (5–7cm) long with a tough but thin orange-red skin which should be peeled off. It contains more vitamin C than the average orange.

Tamarillo purée can be sweetened and made into a wonderful ice-cream, or salt and spice it to serve with fish or poultry as a sauce. It can also be made into jams and pickles. *(59, 60)*

TANGERINE

This is the generic name for a number of small citrus varieties with fragrant, loose, orange skin, otherwise known as mandarin oranges.

This is the fruit of childhood Christmases,

Rhubarb

1 FORCED RHUBARB   2 MAIN-CROP RHUBARB

DRIED FRUIT

when it was wrapped in silver paper and put in the bottom of the pillowcase or stocking hung up at the end of the bed. Not long ago I was bought some tangerines from Uruguay in the middle of summer, and smelling them with my eyes closed I was immediately transported to sharp frosty December days when we eat tangerines with nuts and figs.

Mineolas can be used in exactly the same way as oranges. Hybrids of the grapefruit and tangerine, they resemble the orange in size and colour, though they have a distinctive bulge at the stalk end, and no seeds. They are 'easy-peelers' like tangerines, and have a good extra touch of acidity. (72)

TAYBERRY

Large, rich, bright purple berries with a long conical shape, these are hybrids of blackberries and raspberries, and were developed in Scotland. In scent and flavour they are like ripe blackberries. (56)

TIENTSIN PEAR

This is a most handsome fruit with its long elegantly curving stalk and rounded pear shape. It is largish, weighing 6–8oz (175–250g) with a pale yellow, slightly rough skin. It is delicately russetted. The flesh is firm, sweet, crisp and juicy with a grainy texture, best eaten raw, slightly chilled at the end of a spicy meal. (77)

UGLI FRUIT

A hybrid of the grapefruit, the orange and the tangerine, this 'sad sack'-shaped, greeny-yellow-skinned fruit most resembles the grapefruit but the skin is loose and it is sweeter. It is also juicy and delicious. Use it like grapefruit. (67)

WATERMELON *tiger melon*

Watermelons are truly spectacular in appearance with their glossy dark green or striped skin and brilliant pink flesh dotted with tiny black seeds. They have a refreshing sweet flavour, but are more water than substance; capitalize on this by chilling and serving them in ice-cold wedges on a hot day. See also *Melon*. (71)

Many types of fruit are available dried. Whereas fruit in its natural state is bursting with fresh, sweet juices, dried it changes character completely. It becomes dense, concentrated in flavour and often not particularly attractive to look at, being wrinkled and leathery.

Dried fruit is sometimes treated with sulphur dioxide to help preserve it further. Fruit that has been so treated will be identifiable from the label. In a cool, dry, well-ventilated place, dried fruit will keep for 18 months.

Dried fruit is an excellent source of dietary fibre, and although much of the moisture has been removed, most of the nutrients found in the fresh fruit are retained (apart from vitamin C). A handful of plump raisins makes a very satisfying, healthy snack, and a ready source of energy, the reason being that dried fruit is crammed full of concentrated fruit sugar.

Dried fruit is higher in calories, volume for volume, than fresh fruit. When rehydrated, or soaked in water, the nutritional value of dried fruit approximates that of the fresh fruit. Some fruits absorb a good deal of water, some less so: tree fruits such as apples and pears increase by between three and five times their volume after soaking, vine fruits such as currants and raisins by about twice their volume.

USING DRIED FRUIT

Not all dried fruit is soaked before use. Dates are delicious as they are, just eaten out of the box or packet, or better still from the palm twig on which they are sometimes sold. They can also be made into sweetmeats by removing the stone and stuffing them with almond paste. Figs, too, often with a light honey glaze, are sold as dessert fruit, as are raisins.

Vine fruits Raisins, currants and sultanas are all dried grapes. Currants are dried black grapes (originally from the province of Corinth in Greece, hence the name); sultanas are dried green, usually seedless grapes; raisins come in various shapes and sizes, depending on the original grape type. While they can be soaked and cooked, vine fruits are most often used in their dried, concentrated form. In Britain they have an important place in the store cupboard as an essential ingredient for rich fruit cakes and puddings, the spectacular Christmas pudding and the more homely 'spotted dick'. They are

used in tea breads, biscuits, Eccles cakes and currant buns, and traditional mincemeat cannot be made without them. A few sultanas or raisins plumped out in a little rum make a plain vanilla ice-cream into a special occasion dish. Try them, too, to give a subtle sweet note to savoury dishes; in stuffings and sauces.

Tree fruits Reconstituted, such fruit can be used as you would the fresh fruit – in apricot jam, prune tart, fried apple rings to go with pork or sausages, peach ice-cream, nectarine sorbet. They all make marvellous purées and sauces, fools and mousses once soaked and cooked. You can soak them in hot tea, red or white wine, cider, all of which change the flavour of the finished dish. Soak the fruit for an hour or two by pouring boiling liquid over them, then simmer until just tender. The soaking liquid can be reduced to make a syrupy sauce or used as part of the liquid in the recipe you are using for the dried fruit.

Dried fruits are often sold in mixed packs and these make very good winter fruit salads or compotes for breakfast. When soaked and cooked you can use them in a delicious fibre-rich pudding using wholemeal bread to line a pudding basin, then filling it with the mixed fruit as if making a summer pudding. I serve this as an alternative to traditional Christmas pudding.

Prunes, apricots and pears go particularly well with meat dishes. I cook venison with dried pears and a splash of *eau de vie de poire* goes in at the end of the cooking. Apricots go marvellously with pork and lamb dishes – I stuff a loin of pork with apricots, walnuts and rice, and cook lamb stews in the North African style, adding apricots and almonds. From Elvas in Portugal and Agen in France we get some of the very best prunes. In the Loire Valley pork is cooked with the local fruity white wine and prunes to make a succulent rich dish. Prunes make delicious sweetmeats too. Soak and cook them, remove the stones and fill them with almond paste wrapped around a piece of walnut or even better fill them with dense, sweet purée of prunes.

Hunza apricots are a very special dried fruit and look nothing like the familiar, squashed, translucent orange apricots. These are small, beige, nut-like fruits which come from wild apricot trees in the valleys of Afghanistan and Kashmir. They have an intensely sweet, toffee-like flavour when eaten as they are, and their stone is much easier to crack open than that of domestic apricots, which makes them doubly valuable. When you have soaked and poached them, extract the kernel from the stone and use this too in the finished dish. You can use Hunza apricots in all manner of dishes, but I like them stewed with a separate bowl of thick strained yogurt. Tart cherries are dried in the United States where they are a popular addition to cakes and muffins.

Other dried fruit Although dates and figs are often eaten as they are, they also have an important place in the kitchen. Both are excellent chopped up, mixed with nuts and spices and added to a tea bread mixture. In fact, one of the useful standbys in my kitchen is a glass jar of my own dried fruit and nut mixture. I vary it from time to time but usually have figs, apricots, Muscatel raisins, almonds, walnuts. Sometimes I add peaches and prunes or dates. This makes an instant mincemeat, it makes fast fillings when mixed with cream and butter, or exotic ice puddings when stirred into vanilla ice-cream; it flavours soufflés and sweet omelettes, stuffs apples and pears before they are baked, and can be mixed with melted chocolate, rolled into balls and served as *petits fours*.

Dried mangoes, pawpaw and bananas can be added to this mixture too, or used on their own as you might use apricots or figs. Bananas are very good in tea breads and soufflés. Dried mangoes make a marvellous addition to chutneys and curries, but are even better chopped up with other fruit in a traditional English fruit cake.

Dried Fruit

1 Unsulphured whole apricots	12 Mango pieces
2 Apricots	13 Bananas
3 Hunza apricots	14 Dried figs
4 Nectarines	15 Moist boxed dried figs
5 Pears	16 Greek currants
6 Stoned dates	17 Malaga Muscatel raisins
7 Whole dates	18 Australian raisins
8 Peaches	19 Californian raisins
9 Apple segments	20 Australian sultanas
10 Apple rings	
11 Large californian prunes	

*F*UNGI

Fungi are among the most curious, interesting, useful and delicious foods; mushrooms are fungi. Through the ages they have been the object of worship and of myth, and have enjoyed an important place in many cuisines, literatures and pharmacopoeia.

Fungi belong to a particular class of plant life that feeds off living, dead or decaying organic matter. The part of most edible fungi that we see above the ground is actually the fruiting body of the plant. Beneath the surface is a far-reaching network of thread-like filaments – the mycelium – through which the fungus draws its nutrients. There are many thousands of different types of fungus. Only a few are edible, some are actually poisonous and many are simply not worth bothering with. Very few of the edible types are cultivated – indeed, many are very difficult to cultivate – and many of the most delicious kinds can only be gathered from the wild, from heaths and paths, fields and woodland, even city parks and suburban lawns.

In general fungi of all types favour dark, damp habitats, such as forest floors rich in leaf litter, though each type has its favourite 'host' plant or environment. Chanterelles and ceps are said to favour beech woods, field mushrooms grow best in meadows where cows or horses have been grazed. Some fungi, such as morels, can be gathered in spring, but most emerge in the misty months of early autumn, before the frosts set in. They should always be picked in the very early morning, before flies and other predators – and other pickers – have had a chance to get to them.

In Europe, Scandinavia and Russia mushroom hunting is a major pastime, and people are expert at identifying them. In Britain, except among the Italian, Czech and Polish communities, there seems to be little interest in picking them, although ceps, chanterelles and morels are found in many parts of the country. Where I live in North London, a group of us found 17 edible varieties including ceps, puffballs, blewitts, oyster mushrooms and beefsteak fungus in our local parkland one morning. However, we were with experts, who were able to identify everything. *On no account should you pick and eat any fungus from the wild unless you can positively identify it. Take an expert with you, or a reliable and detailed guidebook. There are some fungi which are deadly poisonous, and others which make you ill, and some of the edible varieties are easily confused with inedible ones.* Cooking them does not destroy the toxins. My advice has to be, if in doubt *do not* pick them.

Fortunately there is an ever-increasing range of cultivated fungi available, and some of the better wild varieties are gathered by experts to be sold commercially (unfortunately, because of the difficulties of obtaining them, these are always expensive). It is possible to extend your culinary range even further by using dried mushrooms. Ceps, morels and chanterelles can be bought in dried form and added to sauces, soups, stuffings, omelettes, in fact, to most of the dishes in which one would use fresh mushrooms. Reconstitute them first by soaking them for about 30 minutes in a bowl of warm water.

Mushrooms deserve a prominent place in our diet. They have low salt, no cholesterol, no carbohydrates and no fat, but contain vegetable protein, and valuable vitamins such as B1, B2 and niacin and minerals such as potassium. They lose some of their vitamins in the cooking medium, so it's worth saving it to use in a sauce or stock.

Mushrooms, when mature, have an intensely savoury and concentrated flavour which comes from glutamic acid, the naturally occurring flavouring agent which is related to monosodium glutamate. The flavour is most intense in wild mushrooms, but also in the cultivated shiitake. It is not lost in preservation, and indeed becomes more concentrated in dried mushrooms. Although the best, such as ceps, are expensive, just one or two pieces of dried cep added to the somewhat bland cultivated mushrooms in a casserole or a mushroom soup or sauce will make an enormous difference to the flavour.

As fungi in general contain a good deal of water, much bulk is lost in cooking and you will need a larger quantity per person than you might think.

There are certain properties common to all mushrooms and they need similar treatment when it comes to preparation and storage.

Cultivated mushrooms need no washing and there is no waste on them. Simply wipe them with kitchen paper before using them. Prepare wild mushrooms by cutting off the gritty base of the stem if necessary – you can do this in the field as you gather them – then brush them with a soft brush to remove any grit or sand, rinse quickly under cold running water and pat dry.

Mushrooms do not keep well: certainly no longer than three days in the refrigerator. Wild fungi will not last even this long; eat them the same day if possible. If you have kept them too long and they look damp, you can rescue them by spreading them out on kitchen paper in a warm place and allowing

Fungi and Mushrooms

1 BLEWITT	12 GREY CHANTERELLE
2 SHIITAKE	(GIROLLE)
3 CHANTERELLE	13 CULTIVATED CUP
4 HONEY FUNGUS	MUSHROOM
5 AMETHYST DECEIVER	14 CULTIVATED
6 CHAMPIGNON DE	BUTTON MUSHROOM
PARIS (PINK)	15 BAY BOLETUS
7 FLAT MUSHROOM	16 JEW'S EAR
8 YELLOW OYSTER	17 OYSTER MUSHROOM
MUSHROOM	18 CEP
(PLEUROTTE)	19 BEEFSTEAK FUNGUS
9 JAPANESE OYSTER	20 HORN OF PLENTY
MUSHROOM	21 MOREL
(HIRATAKE)	22 PHOLIOTTE
10 SHAGGY PARASOL	23 BLACK TRUFFLE
11 CHAMPIGNON DE	24 WHITE TRUFFLE
PARIS (WHITE)	25 PIED DE MOUTON

them to dry out completely. Reconstitute them when you are ready to use them by pouring boiling water over them.

If you manage to acquire a large quantity of mushrooms which you can't use up immediately you can dry them, marinate them or pickle them for future use; or you can freeze them.

AMETHYST DECEIVER (*Laccaria amethystea*)

A very common, small, delicate woodland mushroom, found from late summer to early winter. The stem and cap are a lilac colour as you would expect from the name. It can be cooked with other mushrooms in a mixed mushroom stew or served as a garnish to other dishes.

BEEFSTEAK FUNGUS (*Fistulina hepatica*)
ox-tongue fungus

You need to look high up for this one as it grows on trees – very often chestnut or oak. A close examination explains its name. It does indeed resemble a piece of meat: steak, tongue or liver. It has a good flavour and texture. I cook it like liver, slicing it into fingers, tossing them in seasoned flour, then frying in olive oil or butter.

BLEWITT (*Lepista nuda*) *wood blewitt*

This is one of the few wild fungi that has traditionally been gathered in Britain, although it is a tradition that has largely petered out nowadays. The stem, cap and gills are an unmistakable bright lilac blue. They have a fresh clean flavour that combines excellently with potatoes. Blewitts are related to the Japanese *matsutake* mushroom and can be substituted in any recipe requiring it.

CEP (*Boletus edulis*)

This is the penny bun, or in Italian, little pigs (*porcini*) and in French, *cèpe*. It has a round brown cap and thick white stem widening at the base. It is one of the best of all mushrooms, with a deep rich flavour and soft yet resistant texture when properly cooked. I first came across it when staying with a friend in the Languedoc many years ago. We went out into the woods and

brought back enough to cook for a filling for the most wonderful omelette.

Because ceps taste so good it is a mistake to swamp them in garlic and wine; just a little butter and finely chopped parsley is all they need, with the merest hint of garlic. As a sauce for tagliatelle or other pasta, as a filling for ravioli or as the flavouring for a risotto, ceps are a major feature of Italian cooking during the autumn and winter months. Some people remove the spongy gills before cooking, but this is not essential. Ceps lend themselves to pickling, marinating and drying.

Bay boletus (*Boletus badius*), found in conifer woods, is a somewhat inferior variety, but still good. Several other members of the boletus family are also edible.

CHANTERELLE (*Cantharellus cibarius*) *girolle, pfefferlinge*

This is one of the most attractive of all fungi. Found in woodland areas, particularly of beech and oak, the chanterelle is a deep yellow, sometimes with an apricot tinge, sometimes the pure yellow of egg yolk. It has a concave cap and fluted edge which tapers into the stem. I have never been able to detect the 'apricot' smell ascribed to them; to me they smell clean and earthy. They need gentle cooking to avoid toughening and are best sliced after thorough rinsing and brushing. Because they are expensive, they are perhaps best used as an adjunct to a main dish. I have had them with lamb fillets, with chicken breasts and in many similar dishes. The way I like to cook them is slowly, in the oven, or in a deep frying pan, layered with thinly sliced potatoes, salt, a little pepper, some parsley and butter. The flavour is absorbed into the potatoes in a most delicate way. Of all herbs tarragon is the one that most complements the flavour of chanterelles, but use only a tiny amount.

Grey chanterelle or *girolle* (*Cantharellus cinereus*) can be cooked in the same way. Dried chanterelles are excellent for adding to sauces and casseroles.

Chanterelles are very similar in colour to the false chanterelle (*Hygrophoropsis*) though the latter is distinguishable by its well-formed gills. False chanterelles are very inferior in quality and may cause indigestion.

CHESTNUT MUSHROOM (*Agaricus bisporus*)
champignon marron, champignon de Paris, Paris brown, Paris pink, Paris white

This is a variety of the common cultivated mushroom similar in shape to the cup mushroom, with a slightly thicker stem and perhaps a more spherical cap. The stem is pale and the cap a soft even brown, or creamy white. It needs no peeling, merely wiping, before preparing it. Use it in Oriental dishes, with veal or chicken, in sauces and soups, in fact, you can regard it as an all-purpose mushroom.

CULTIVATED MUSHROOM (*Agaricus bisporus*)

There are several varieties of cultivated mushroom and they are sold at different stages of maturity.

Button This is the immature stage when the mushroom has just popped its round white head through the growing medium. There is almost no stem, and the cap is velvety and white. At this stage the mushrooms are good eaten raw, whole or sliced, in salads, or dressed in olive oil and vinegar. They can be used to make soups and sauces, or added to omelettes, risottos or soufflés. It has to be said that they have only a very mild flavour, some would say bland, and respond well to other flavours, such as garlic, herbs, spices, wine vinegar, olive oil or soy sauce, which they absorb readily.

Closed cup At a further stage in its development the mushroom's membrane breaks as it grows in size but the pale pinky fawn gills are not yet visible. The cap is still milky white. It can be kept pale by adding a touch of acidity to whatever it is being cooked in – white wine, wine vinegar or lemon juice. Like the button mushroom the closed cup remains pale when cooked. It can be anything up to 2½in (6cm) in diameter. At this size closed cup mushrooms can be used in the same way as button mushrooms. The closed cup is the most suitable stage at which to use the cultivated mushroom in Chinese cooking. It is excellent in stir-frys.

Open cup At this stage the mushroom is quite mature, with brownish pink gills and a darkening speckled cap and is very good for stuffing and baking. Some people like to peel it and remove the stem, but if you do this, be sure to

use the debris in stock as it has an excellent flavour. Open cup mushrooms are generally sliced before cooking.
Flat By this stage the cap has opened out completely and is often quite flat. These mushrooms have the most pronounced flavour but because the gills are now brownish black, the skins perhaps a little frayed and the stalks quite dark, they are often held to be inferior to their paler relatives. The contrary is true. They have a superb flavour. These are the ones I use to make mushroom soup. They are marvellous for breakfast just grilled with a little bacon, or with a poached egg served on top. If they are large and not too flat they can be stuffed with breadcrumb and herb mixtures. Some people peel off the skins of flat mushrooms, but unless they are very ragged or bruised, this is not at all necessary.

ENOKITAKE (*Flammulina velutipes*) *enoki*

Originally only found in Japan, these tiny pale mushrooms, which resemble clusters of bean sprouts, are being cultivated in Europe and the United States. They have little flavour but look good in Oriental soups and stir-fried dishes and can be added to salads. They need no more than a minute's cooking.

FAIRY RING MUSHROOM (*Marasimus oreades*) *mousseron*

This grows in rings on lawns and other areas of short cropped grass. The mushrooms are small, ½–2in (1–5cm) across the cap, and have slender stems. They can, however, be very easily confused with a poisonous mushroom of similar appearance so I would not pick them myself, but you can sometimes buy them. It is a tasty little mushroom to add to various dishes including egg dishes or mixed mushrooms. You can also buy them dried.

FIELD MUSHROOM (*Agaricus campestris*)

This is the mushroom which is to be found in open grassy areas, even lawns and parks, during the summer and autumn. It belongs to the same family as the cultivated mushroom and can be used as an all-purpose mushroom in the same way. Use as soon as possible after picking.

HONEY FUNGUS (*Armillaria mellea*)

Very common, this is a long-stemmed, yellow-capped wild mushroom that grows in large clusters on tree trunks and stumps. It has an astringent taste when fresh and must *always* be cooked.

HORN OF PLENTY (*Craterellus cornucopioides*) *trompette*

Not a common mushroom, this is funnel-shaped with a fluted edge and deep gills. Dark brown to black in colour, it has a good rich flavour to add to soups and stews, and to provide contrast to pale, creamy dishes. The horn of plenty is often available dried and can be used as fresh after reconstituting in water.

HORSE MUSHROOM (*Agaricus arvensis*)

A large white mushroom which grows in open fields in the autumn, this resembles the field mushroom and the cultivated mushroom in appearance, but has a more concentrated flavour with a slight hint of aniseed. It can be used in the same way as the cultivated mushroom.

JEW'S EAR (*Auricularia auricula-judae*)

A type of fungus which grows on tree stumps. It looks like a series of very shallow oval cups – in fact, like ears! It can be used instead of its Chinese cousin, wood-ear or cloud-ear mushroom (*Auricularia polytricha*), in stir-fried dishes and soups. Wood-ears are generally only available dried and need soaking for about 30 minutes in warm water before use. They have a crunchy, yet gelatinous texture.

MATSUTAKE (*Tricholoma matsutake*) *pine mushroom*

Highly prized and extremely expensive, this Japanese mushroom grows wild among pine trees on mountain slopes, but has also been cultivated in Japan since as long ago as AD199. They are large – up to 10in (25cm) across – and reddish-brown with succulent meaty flesh. If they are available at all in the West they will be dried, canned or pickled. Fresh matsutake

would be simply grilled – perhaps with a few pine needles – and served with a sweet or piquant sauce, such as soy or *mirin*, a sweet thin liquid made from rice and alcohol.

MOREL (*Morchella esculenta, Morchella vulgaris*) *morille*

This, with the cep and the chanterelle, is for me right at the top of the class of mushrooms. It is a spring mushroom and is to be found in many parts of the British Isles. In appearance it is unusual, with a conical cap covered in irregular indentations giving it a spongy or honeycomb appearance. The stem is a ridged creamy white, the cap, cream to buff. I have seen wonderful large morels, almost hand-sized, in a restaurant in Amsterdam. The chef was about to stuff them with a creamy chicken mousseline before cooking them. Morels are indeed excellent in chicken and veal dishes. They are always cooked and never eaten raw.

ORANGE PEEL FUNGUS (*Aleuria aurantia*)

I have a soft spot for this one as it is among those I found on a mushroom hunt in rough heath in a local suburban park. It grows on bare soil at roadsides and looks for all the world as if a passing motorist tossed a handful of orange peel out of the window. You would need a lot to make a dish, and it is thus perhaps best used as a garnish. It really is quite striking. It is in season in early autumn to early winter.

OYSTER MUSHROOM (*Pleurotus ostreatus*) *hiratake, pleurotte*

Found in the wild growing on dead logs and tree stumps, the oyster mushroom is now being cultivated and so is becoming more widely available. The colour of the fan-shaped cap gives the mushroom its name. Some might feel that it has a slippery oystery texture when cooked. It is a pale fawnish grey, though there is also a peacock-blue-capped variety. *Pleurotus cornucopiae* is a closely related mushroom occurring on elms, which also has a yellow-capped variety. A version of oyster mushroom is widely cultivated in Japan where it is called *hiratake* or, commercially, *shimeji*. It is grown in a special way to produce long stems and small caps. It is cooked with rice or floated in clear soups.

The oyster mushroom is best used in dishes with other ingredients because it would be rather expensive to serve it as an individual vegetable. Tear the cap into long triangular pieces following the lines of the gills, or use the very small ones whole. I like to fry them quickly in a little olive oil and serve them still hot on a plate of salad leaves. They go very well with eggs and are particularly good with shellfish. Use them also in Oriental cooking.

I find there is very little difference in taste between the wild and the cultivated varieties. It is superb in both cases, quite pronounced and savoury despite the mushroom's delicate appearance. But it cooks down to a mere shadow of its former self as it is full of moisture. Oyster mushrooms are also sold dried and need minimal soaking in hot water to reconstitute them.

PARASOL MUSHROOM (*Lepiota procera*)

Some parasols grow to a size of 10in (25cm) in diameter and are one of the largest of the wild mushrooms. Found in summer and autumn, it is a delicious mushroom and one that dries very well for use in the winter months. I like to bake it in the oven, layered with potatoes and other mushrooms, or as part of a mushroom lasagne. It is closely related to the much more common shaggy parasol in which the scales on the cap are much more pronounced. However, unless you are sure which is which, or have bought the parasol mushroom from a reliable source, it may best be avoided since the shaggy parasol (*Lepiota rhacodes*) can cause gastric upsets.

PHOLIOTTE (*Agrocybe aegerita*)

This sweet-smelling mild-flavoured fungus has long slender stems, and smooth, round, yellow caps. It used to be cultivated by the Greeks and Romans on poplar wood and is now cultivated in a semi-artificial way in Southern Europe.

PIED DE MOUTON (*Hydnum repandum*)
hedgehog fungus, wood hedgehog

A lovely creamy-yellow fleshy fungus, this grows in the wild but is sometimes gathered commercially. The flesh is firm, succulent and tangy and can be sliced or diced, fried in butter and stirred into omelettes or scrambled egg or risotto. It remains pale in colour, and retains much of its bulk when cooked.

PUFFBALL (*Langermannia gigantea*) giant puffball

From golf ball to football size, these soft spherical fungi are found in woodlands and fields in late summer and autumn. When mature they change from creamy white to a chocolate brown, and eventually explode and send all their spores, like fine dust, shooting into the air. They are not edible at this stage. The smaller puffballs are the most appealing. Once they get much bigger than a cricket ball, although still white, firm and with an appetizing smell, I find them rather woolly inside. The small ones are excellent sliced, dipped in egg and breadcrumbs and fried. They taste delicate, sweet and, well, mushroomy. They can also be diced and simmered in stock and wine with the addition of chives and tarragon.

SHIITAKE (*Lentinula edodes*) black forest mushroom, flower mushroom, winter mushroom

Another Oriental mushroom, this is now cultivated in Britain, Holland and the United States and can be bought fresh or dried. It has a pronounced meaty mushroomy scent and flavour. The cap has a velvety texture and a tan colour, sometimes faintly veined or spotted with pale cream scales. The gills are white, the stem quite tough. Its powerful flavour makes it admirably suited to strong meat dishes, pork or beef casseroles for example, as well, of course, as all Oriental dishes requiring mushrooms. Do not wash or peel them, simply wipe the caps and stalks before cooking.

Although shiitake can be eaten raw, cooking brings out their unique flavour and texture. They should be cooked gently and for not too long, as they may begin to toughen. These mushrooms are excellent when cooked with ordinary cultivated ones, their flavour permeating the blander mushrooms. Cooked with butter, garlic and parsley and piled on hot toast, they make one of the best instant meals I know.

STRAW MUSHROOM (*Volvariella esculenta*)
paddy-straw mushroom

In Chinese their name means double mushroom and that is exactly what they look like, two mushrooms end to end. They are small and greyish-brown with a pale stem. When cooked they are slippery and delicious and an essential ingredient in many Chinese dishes. They adapt very well to Western cooking, and can be used in the same way as cultivated mushrooms.

TRUFFLE (*Tuber aestivum, Tuber magnatum, Tuber melanosporum*)

Depending on the quality of the annual harvest the price of truffles can be anything up to £600 a pound. At this level, my interest in them becomes somewhat academic.

There are three types: the Perigord truffle, *Tuber melanosporum*, the white truffle, *Tuber magnatum* and the summer truffle, *Tuber aestivum*. Only the last grows in Britain; it is quite rare and usually found under beech trees in chalky soil in late summer and autumn. It is good to eat, and can be used in the same way as the more superior truffles.

The black truffle from Perigord is the one that most of us only ever come across as a minuscule nugget in a slice of *pâté de foie gras*. But it has a natural affinity with eggs, particularly omelettes and scrambled eggs. It also goes with other delicate dishes such as fish and chicken. In its natural state it is knobbly, black as a lump of coal, and earthy. Like the other truffles it grows underground and must be dug up once you know where to dig. Dogs and pigs can be trained to hunt them by smell. Truffle flies hover over buried truffles and are a good indicator of the whereabouts of this precious fungus.

The white truffle grows in northern Italy, and when it is in season, from late autumn, it is found in many marvellous dishes. Unlike the black truffle, it should not be cooked, simply cleaned by brushing it hard. Mostly it is grated – at vast expense – over fresh pasta or risotto or, traditionally, in the Piedmontese speciality *fonduta*, a fondue made with white wine and Fontina cheese. White truffles have a pungent smell and flavour, unlike anything else, and once experienced never forgotten.

NUTS

Nuts are the fruits of various types of trees. Although many different kinds are now available all year round there are seasonal variations. Some nuts are available fresh – referred to as 'green' – but most are dried to enable them to store well, and this is how they are usually sold.

Nuts are a very good source of energy, being high in protein, carbohydrate and fat, and thus extremely high in calories. Although they are delicious to eat as a snack, and a healthy natural food, it is all too easy to pile on the calories quite without thinking.

Despite their tough appearance, nuts do deteriorate and should not be kept for months on end. Buy them in relatively small quantities, store them in an airtight container in a cool place, and use them up within a few weeks. Avoid any with damp, mouldy looking shells – these can be dangerous as they are a possible source of toxins. In general, choose nuts that feel heavy for their size. Light nuts may indicate that the kernel has lost moisture and begun to wither. Most nuts can be bought either in the shell or shelled, and some are further processed by blanching, flaking or grinding. Some nuts, such as chestnuts, are cultivated for flour. If using nuts in recipes it is preferable to buy them in the shell and prepare them yourself. Time-consuming perhaps, but you are likely to get a fresher end product. Good nuts taste sweet, have a crisp texture and a plump appearance. Stale nuts will taste rancid and unpleasant and look shrivelled.

Many types of nut are cultivated as much for their oil as the nut meat. These include walnuts, hazelnuts, peanuts and almonds. See also OILS, page 121.

ALMOND

The almond belongs to the same family of trees as the plum, the peach and the apricot. According to some, it originated in the Middle East, to others in China or Japan, but it is now cultivated commercially in many parts of the world including Spain, Italy, Portugal, North Africa, California and Australia. It is one of the earliest-flowering trees and is to be found all over southern Europe in spring dusting the landscape with a fine powdering of snowy white blossom. The nut, as it matures, is enclosed in a pale jade-green velvety case, which falls away when the fruit (the nut) is ripe in its tough, fibrous shell, the colour of ginger biscuits. The shell is a narrow oval shape, with one pointed end and one rounded, and is sometimes difficult to crack.

The kernel is clothed in a tight-fitting, brown skin which is easily removed by a process known as 'blanching': pour boiling water over the kernels, leave them for a few minutes then drain them and rub off the skins. You can then split the kernel lengthways. They are delicious eaten raw or cooked, the elegant, tapered Jordan almonds having the most delicate flavour.

Depending on the recipe, almonds can be used whole, split, flaked, chopped or ground, with their skin still on or blanched. Whole or split blanched almonds are served with any dish described as *amandine*, such as trout. They are also one of the classic ingredients of the fragrant Moroccan *tagine*, or stew. Indeed, almonds are widely used in Arab cooking and in all those regions, such as Spain, Sicily, Portugal and Malta, which at one time came under Arab influence. They are also important ingredients in several classic pastries and sweetmeats – nougat, praline, Spanish *turrón* and Italian *panforte*. Ground almonds can be used in place of flour to make moist cakes – such as Derbyshire Bakewell puddings – and crisp light biscuits as well as macaroons. They are, of course, the main ingredient of almond paste, or marzipan. Almonds were widely used in medieval cooking during Lent when meat was forbidden. They were made into 'white' dishes, of which the nursery pudding blancmange is a survivor.

There are two types of almonds, sweet and bitter. The latter are poisonous and should not be eaten raw. They are also extremely bitter and tongue-numbing. It is impossible to tell from looking at the tree which will be sweet and which bitter; those with almond trees on their land hope that fortune has smiled upon them and given them sweet almonds. Bitter almonds are very good in baking, however. The volatile toxins are destroyed by heat and bitter almonds somehow help to concentrate the flavour of sweet almonds which are combined with them. See also OILS, page 121.

BRAZIL NUT

The brazil nut we know with its tough brown three-sided shell looks quite different growing on its tree in the tropics. The nut did indeed originate in Brazil and it still comes mainly from the dense tropical rain forests of Brazil and the Amazonian regions of neighbouring countries. Some two dozen such nuts are tightly packed into a large, hard brown casing, which splits open when ripe and scatters the nuts. Brazils are used mainly as dessert nuts, but also in confectionery. They contain a large quantity of oil so they go rancid very quickly. Because of their size, they are quite easy to grate and can be added to good effect to cakes and biscuits.

Closely related and similar in appearance to the Brazil nut is the Paradise or Sapucaya nut which is also native to South America. It is slightly sweeter in flavour and has a shell that usefully can be cracked by hand.

CANDLE NUT

Part of their Latin name, *moluccana*, gives a strong hint of their origins, the Spice Islands, which are now part of Indonesia. Round, creamy, oily nuts, they have a texture and flavour similar to that of macadamias, which can be substituted for candle nuts in Malaysian and Indonesian recipes. They are roasted and crushed, then mixed with other ingredients to give texture and richness to soups and curries.

Mildly toxic when raw, candle nuts should always be cooked.

CASHEW NUT

We never see cashews in their undried state in Britain and almost certainly would not recognize them if we did. Originating in South America, the cashew tree is now widely grown throughout the tropics. The fruit – the cashew 'apple' – has large shiny smooth lobes, rosy-pink, red or yellow in colour, whose flesh can be eaten raw or made into jam or a refreshing drink. At the apex of the fruit is a small kidney-shaped, hard brown shell which encloses the cashew nut.

The nut is eaten as a snack, but it also has a place in Chinese cooking, for example in the well-known chicken and cashew nuts dish.

CRACKING A COCONUT

1 *Hold the coconut in one hand or steady it on a firm surface. Pierce two eyes with a skewer.*

2 *Pour off the milk into a small bowl and store in the refrigerator.*

3 *Using a strong hammer, hit the coconut all round its centre. Lever open the halves.*

4 *Break up the halves. Lever the flesh from the shells with a knife. Peel using a swivel peeler.*

CHESTNUT *sweet chestnut*

This large, leafy, attractive tree grows in most temperate climates, as does the horse chestnut tree with which it is often confused, and whose fruits are inedible though not poisonous. The trees are distinguishable by their very different leaf shapes and also by the green casings which hold the shiny brown nuts. The sweet chestnut casing is covered in fine prickly spines; the horse chestnut casing in fewer very sharp spikes.

One of the most familiar street smells in winter is of chestnuts roasting over a brazier, and to me it immediately brings back childhood memories of roasting chestnuts on a shovel set over a coal fire on Sunday afternoons. Chestnuts are an important food; they provide starch, and can be ground into a flour for use in baking and cooking. They are also used in the making of a luxury item, *marrons glacés* – chestnuts soaked in a concentrated sugar syrup until they become translucent.

Chestnuts are rarely eaten raw, but they can be steamed or boiled, and made into a purée to serve with game, or chopped to make a stuffing for turkey. Sweetened chestnut purée – which is usually available in cans – combines marvellously with chocolate to make rich puddings.

Unlike most nuts, chestnuts bought in their shells are always recently picked and in their fresh, undried state. Consequently they have a short shelf life and should be eaten within a week or so of purchase.

Before cooking, chestnuts must be peeled and skinned. It's almost impossible to do this successfully when they are completely raw, so first par-cook them by roasting them in the oven for five minutes or so (nick the shells with a sharp knife, or they will explode), or by bringing them to the boil in a pan of water. Remove the shells and the inner pale brown skin – which you can rub off with a tea towel – while they are still hot.

Alternatively, by-pass the entire process and buy dried, skinned chestnuts and soak them overnight before cooking. See also GRAINS, CEREALS AND FLOURS, page 128.

COCONUT

My first meeting with a fresh coconut is a taste memory I treasure. A hot tropical night in Singapore found us at the hawkers' stands where delicious food is prepared and served to eat immediately: Chinese soups, Malay kebabs, Singaporean noodles, all the dishes of that wonderfully mixed cuisine. And to drink with it? Large, fresh green coconuts were shaved down to a manageable size with a machete, a slice taken off the bottom to allow it to stand flat and a lid taken off the top, for you to drink the clear sweet refreshing juice through a straw, and then scrape out the thin layer of jelly-like, immature flesh with a long-handled spoon.

Nuts

1 CASHEWS, SHELLED
2 PISTACHIOS, SHELLED
3 PINE NUTS
4 CANDLE NUTS
5 HALF GREEN COCONUT
6 TIGER NUTS, DRIED
7 PISTACHIOS IN SHELLS
8 WATER CHESTNUTS
9 PEANUTS, SHELLED
10 PEANUTS IN SHELLS
11 LOTUS NUTS, WHOLE
12 MACADAMIAS, SHELLED
13 ALMONDS, SHELLED
14 CHESTNUTS PEELED
15 WHOLE GREEN COCONUT
16 LOTUS NUTS, PIECES
17 MACADAMIAS IN SHELLS
18 ALMONDS, BLANCHED
19 ALMONDS IN SHELLS
20 CHESTNUTS, UNPEELED
21 CHESTNUTS IN SHELLS
22 HAZELNUTS, SHELLED
23 PECANS, SHELLED
24 JORDAN ALMONDS, SHELLED
25 ALMONDS IN GREEN OUTER CASING
26 CHESTNUT IN CASING
27 HALF MATURE COCONUT
28 HAZELNUTS
29 PECANS IN DYED SHELLS
30 BRAZIL NUTS, SHELLED
31 FRENCH 'WET' WALNUTS
32 WALNUTS, KILN-DRIED
33 KENTISH COBNUTS
34 PECANS, UNDYED
35 BRAZIL NUTS IN SHELLS
36 WET WALNUT IN CASING
37 ENGLISH DOUBLE 'WET' WALNUTS
38 WHOLE MATURE COCONUT

These young coconuts bear little resemblance to the coconut we know best in Britain, which is the mature fruit with a hard shell covered with tough brown fibres. Inside the nut is lined with a thick layer of dense, white flesh, and contains maybe a small cupful of thin sweetish liquid. Occasionally you can find green coconuts, or more often turning brown, which are at the stage between the very immature ones, and fully mature nuts. These young coconuts have more substantial flesh which has not yet hardened. It makes the most wonderful ice-cream: scoop or cut it away from the shell and blend it with cream and sugar syrup to taste before freezing it. Cubes of it are also very good in tropical fruit salad. I like to shred long curls from it over salads of all kinds, particularly shellfish. Coconuts are rich in vitamins, proteins and natural oils. However, unlike many plant oils coconut oil is a saturated fat and high in cholesterol.

The coconut grows all over the tropics and it is widely used in the cooking of these regions. On the Caribbean coast of Colombia it is cooked with coconut milk and rice to make a rich-tasting, savoury accompaniment to shellfish, and also made into a succulent and sweet pie. In India, Sri Lanka and most of South-East Asia the juice and flesh are used in stews, soups and curries. Coconut has long been a feature of cake- and confectionery-making in Britain and the United States, where it is used more often in its desiccated or dried state.

It is very easy to use a 'fresh' coconut and well worth it. Choose one which is heavy for its size, with plenty of juice in it when you shake it close to your ear. An empty coconut is probably one that has been around for a long time and it will almost certainly be rancid inside. Make sure there is no sign of mould around the three 'eyes' in one end of the nut. Carefully pierce two of the eyes. Drain the clear liquid into a jug for future use (try it in exotic tropical cocktails).

There are several ways to crack the nut. Putting it in a plastic bag and banging it on a stone step or concrete floor is a rough and ready method that works perfectly well. You can hold it horizontally in both hands and crack it down hard on one of its three barely visible ridges. This will split it. Or hold it with the other, pointed end on a hard surface and bang it round the circumference with a hammer. The brown

skin on the flesh should also be peeled off. The nut can then be grated or chopped, by hand or in a food processor. You can keep it fresh by putting it in a container, covering the pieces with water or the juice from the nut, covering tightly and refrigerating. Grated fresh coconut can be used in biscuits, cakes and pastries. It is especially delicious very thinly sliced and combined with shellfish salads.

To make coconut milk – not the same as the juice inside the nut – grate a coconut and cover it with boiling water. Allow to cool then squeeze through fine muslin to obtain as much milky liquid as possible. A further, weaker extract can be made by repeating the process.

You can also buy blocks of compressed creamed coconut which can be reconstituted to make coconut milk for use in curries and other dishes. Simply cut off a slice and put it in a jug with boiling water. Make it as strong or weak as you like. See also COOKING FATS, page 238.

GINGKO NUT

In appearance this is a small, shiny, pale nut, somewhat like a fat, smooth, foreshortened almond. It has a hard shell which houses a delicious nut. It is used in Chinese and Japanese cooking, in both sweet and savoury dishes and is often to be found in celebratory food for the important Chinese festivals.

HAZELNUT *Barcelona nut, cobnut, filbert, Kentish cobnut*

The feast day of St Philibert, 22 August, is the day on which the cobnuts or filberts in the hedgerows are said to be ready for picking. Turkey is the largest producer of hazelnuts in the world, although supplies also reach Britain from the United States, Italy and Spain, particularly the variety known as the Barcelona nut which is larger than the others, and rounded at one end with a blunt point at the other.

The Kentish cobnut is a type of hazelnut which is sold in its freshly picked state, with a pale green, slightly brown shell, and still in its green husk. The kernels are sweet and juicy and are best eaten raw dipped in a little salt.

More usually hazelnuts are sold dried, when their shells are very hard and brittle. Inside, the

roundish sweet nut is encased in a thin brown edible skin. They can be enjoyed raw, just cracked and eaten with cheese, but they also have a place in the kitchen. Grind them coarsely for use in and on cakes and in crumble toppings for sweet and savoury dishes. Grind them finely and mix with flour to make cakes, biscuits or meringues. More unusually, sauces can be thickened with finely ground hazelnuts. One of the best uses I have come across was devised by a clever young Italian chef who pounds them with garlic and oil as a sauce for pasta.

Where a recipe calls for skinned hazelnuts, roast them lightly in the oven for ten minutes and rub off the skins with your fingers, or with a clean tea towel. See also OILS, page 121.

LOTUS NUT *lotus seed, med bua*

These are the seeds of the lotus, an Asian plant closely related to the water lily. A feature of Thai cooking, they have a slightly almondy flavour and are generally cooked to a purée and added to soups, desserts and puddings. In Chinese cooking, they are often served whole in a sweet clear soup at the end of a meal as a dessert.

MACADAMIA *Queensland nut*

Native to the woodlands of Australia, macadamia trees were introduced to California and Hawaii in the middle of this century and subsequently to Latin America.

In its natural state the macadamia is covered with a green coating, easily removable. The shell which houses the nut is extremely hard to crack, but when done it reveals a small, round, crisp nut, almost white and buttery. It is sold both in its raw state and roasted in oil, usually coconut oil. It can be grated or sliced and used in cakes, tarts or confectionery, but it is expensive, and I for one prefer to eat it as it is.

PEANUT *groundnut, monkey nut*

Although it is not, strictly speaking, a nut but a member of the pea and bean family which grows underground, the peanut's culinary position lies closer to that of the nut than the bean. On the other hand, when I lived in Nigeria where it grows in great quantity, it was a cheap staple and we would often, at the end of the month when funds were low, eat a stew of fresh peanuts and chillies with rice. This may explain why I would be quite happy never to see a peanut again.

It is, nevertheless, a highly nutritious natural product from which a high quality cooking oil, groundnut or arachide oil, is derived. Peanut butter is made from ground peanuts, with or without salt. Indonesian and other South-East Asian cooking makes use of peanuts in flavoursome stews and sauces – notably for *satay*, small pieces of meat or chicken, marinated, skewered and grilled. In the West it is mostly eaten roasted and salted as a snack. See also OILS, page 121.

PECAN NUT

Becoming more generally available, the pecan is a native of the United States and belongs to the hickory family. The nut is enclosed in a smooth brittle shell – sometimes dyed pinkish-brown – and is similar in shape to a large olive. The nutmeat inside is in two halves, each one of which is lobed, rather like a walnut, but more tightly packed. When fresh it is sweet and richly flavoured, much used in sugary pie fillings – especially the celebrated pecan pie from the American South – and in cakes and confectionery, but is equally good raw.

PINE NUT *pine kernel, pine seed*

These small creamy coloured nuts are the fruits of the stone pine which grows in sandy areas around the Mediterranean basin but particularly in Spain. The nut is found in the base of the scales which form the pine cone. Harvesting is difficult and the pines are not extensively grown which makes the nuts a luxury item in the kitchen. It is well worth investing in them occasionally, particularly if you are also able to lay your hands on a good supply of fresh basil and garlic. Then you can make *pesto*, that rich, pungent sauce from Liguria in Italy, which is so good with pasta. Pine nuts are also mixed with other ingredients such as spinach and Ricotta cheese to make a filling for ravioli. In Catalonia they are used in turkey stuffing. Cakes and biscuits in Sicily and Malta use pine nuts. Buy them in small quantities and use quickly because their high oil content makes them turn rancid rapidly.

PISTACHIO

These lovely pale-green-fleshed nuts with purply skins, which originated in the Middle East, have given their name to a green food colouring, but it's far better to enjoy the flavour of the real thing. In classic French cooking they are used in terrines. Italian mortadella sausage contains pistachios, which give it an attractive appearance when sliced. Pistachios are also used in ice-creams, desserts and confectionery, especially in nougat and Turkish delight and the Greek sweetmeat known as *halva*.

TIGER NUT *chufa, earth almond*

Not really a nut, but this small wrinkled tuber, grown underground, derives one of its names from the fact that it has sweet crisp nutty white flesh somewhat reminiscent of almonds. It seems to me, but probably isn't so, that the entire world consumption of *chufas* takes place in and around the city of Valencia in Spain. There cafés, or *horchaterías*, sell a refreshing, sweet, milky drink called *horchata de chufa*, made from ground *chufas* and water.

WALNUT

Perhaps one of the most versatile of all nuts, the walnut deserves a place in every kitchen. Not only do walnuts make excellent cakes and biscuits, but when finely ground and mixed with eggs, butter and sugar they produce exquisitely rich pie fillings. Fine ice-creams, confectionery, toffee, chocolates – the list of sweet things that are enhanced by walnuts is endless. But they are also good in savoury dishes – whole in salads, ground to make sauces, combined with chicken in Chinese dishes, and in one unusual dish from Shanghai where a walnut brittle is flavoured with freshly ground black pepper.

In France, especially in the south-west where there are plenty of walnut trees, walnut oil is produced, expensive but worth it because of the superb flavour it adds to salad dressings and other sweet and savoury preparations.

In Alsace in October, just after the start of the grape harvest, small cafés or *Weinstube* offer fresh or 'wet' walnuts and new wine, the cloudy just-fermented grape juice. Wet walnuts do not keep and should be eaten soon after buying. In England especially, wet walnuts are sometimes salted and pickled. They become very soft and black with a sharp, salty flavour, and are usually served with cold meats, or with cheese.

In the United States there are several types of walnuts: the large pale-shelled one we know, which is there called the English or California walnut; the black walnut which has a very dark brown shell with pronounced ridges and a very oily strongly flavoured nut, and the butternut, or white walnut. North American Indians used butternut oil in their cooking, as well as the nut meat. See also OILS, page 121.

WATER CHESTNUT *ling gok*

Often confused with the tuberous vegetable of the same name, authentic Chinese water chestnuts are unmistakable, at least in appearance. The creamy white nuts are generally sold encased in their black horned shells that are extremely difficult to crack. They are rather sweet and starchy and must be cooked before eating, either boiled like a vegetable, or braised in soups and stews. Use shelled nuts within a day or two as they quickly become rancid.

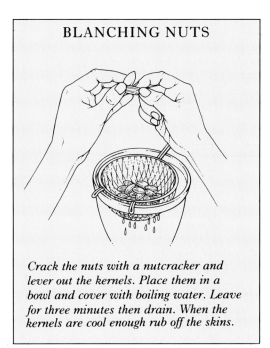

BLANCHING NUTS

Crack the nuts with a nutcracker and lever out the kernels. Place them in a bowl and cover with boiling water. Leave for three minutes then drain. When the kernels are cool enough rub off the skins.

DRIED PULSES

Do not be put off buying dried peas and beans by all the mystique attached to them. To soak or not to soak? And for how long? Do you really need to cook them for hours and hours? Can you use the pressure cooker? Once these questions have been dealt with, the whole world of pulse cookery opens up. And it *is* a whole world. From Boston, the original home of the baked bean, to Mexico and its re-fried beans, from the *dhal* (lentil) curries of Madras to the bean cakes of Nigeria, there is not a continent, scarcely a country, which does not have its traditional recipes using this marvellous food. Inexpensive, nutritious, versatile, these are all important properties of the huge range of pulses now available. You can recreate traditional English pease pudding, northern European split pea and ham soups and, my own favourites, the richly flavoured slow-cooked stews – *cozidas* of Portugal, the *ollas* and *fabadas* of Spain, the cassoulets of South-West France, and the *pasta e fagioli* of Italy.

Although often served alone, pulses combine well with other ingredients and flavourings. Because they are without a strong taste of their own, they are well matched with powerful or rich flavours, whether they be tomatoes, garlic, olive oil and herbs of southern Europe, the *garam masala*, and curry spices of the Indian subcontinent, the chillies and coriander of Mexico, Brazil, the south-western part of the United States and the Caribbean, or the smoked hams and sausages of northern Europe.

Pulses are rich in protein but they do not constitute a complete protein in themselves. When combined with grain, however, they do form a first-class protein which makes them eminently suitable for vegetarian cookery. This combination of pulse and grain protein is found in the Caribbean dish, 'rice and peas', the 'red beans and rice' of New Orleans, the *pasta e fagioli* of Italy and, indeed, in any good homemade bean soup served with a thick slice of wholemeal bread. Apart from protein, pulses contain carbohydrates, not to mention vitamins (particularly B) and minerals (notably iron).

Once cooked they keep well in a covered container in the refrigerator, and reheat well.

They are a good standby for adding to soup made, for example, from a chicken carcase and a few vegetables. They will fill out a casserole very nicely, or will make an extra salad ingredient. Many pulses can also be sprouted to produce highly nutritious vegetables to add to stir-fried dishes and to mixed salads (see page 99).

PREPARATION

Soaking Although for a very long time recipe instructions have told us to soak dried beans overnight, I am not convinced that this is any longer necessary. The purpose of soaking is, of course, to put back into the beans the moisture which was deliberately removed in order to preserve and package them. The older the beans (they will continue to dry out during storage), the more soaking they will need. It makes sense therefore to buy your pulses from a source which has a rapid turnover. Sometimes, particularly in France, it is possible in the late autumn to buy dried beans such as flageolets that are labelled 'new season'. These need only a short soaking time before cooking.

Lentils, because of their small size and flat shape, do not need soaking. Chick peas and soya beans, however, are particularly dense and these, I find, do require longer soaking. It will do no harm to soak them overnight, whereas some of the other beans would fall apart in cooking if they were soaked as long.

It is always a good idea to put the beans or peas in a sieve and rinse and shake them under cold running water before soaking them, although these days you should not need to sort through for hidden pieces of stone or grit.

There are three main methods of soaking. One is to cover the beans with plenty of cold water and soak them for up to eight hours depending on the bean variety. The second is to cover them with plenty of boiling water and soak for about two to three hours. The third is to bring a pan of beans in water to the boil very slowly, hold it there for two minutes, then turn off the heat and cover for an hour or so.

Initial boiling *This is important: dried kidney beans (both red and black) contain toxins on the outer skin when raw. After soaking they must be put into a saucepan, covered with plenty of cold water, brought to the boil and boiled vigorously for 15 minutes. Drain, rinse and continue the preparation. The toxins contained in the beans are rendered harmless by boiling. Soya beans should also be pre-boiled vigorously for one hour, as they contain a substance that prevents the body absorbing protein.*

Cooking Even soaked pulses need cooking thoroughly if they are not to be tough and tasteless, not to mention indigestible.

There are those who believe that a pressure cooker is the answer, because this cooks the beans thoroughly in a short time to retain the maximum amount of nutrients. Others believe beans need to be cooked slowly and gently until tender, absorbing the flavours and aromas of the other ingredients cooked with them. On the whole I favour this latter method. The kind of dishes I make with beans are those warming soups and casseroles for autumn and winter days which do need slow cooking. On the other hand, cannellini beans for a refreshing bean and tuna fish salad could certainly be cooked quickly in a pressure cooker, or at a brisk rate in a saucepan of boiling water.

Season with salt only at the end of cooking as salt has a hardening effect, but do leave enough time, say 10 to 15 minutes, for the salt to be absorbed and meld with the flavour of the beans. Contrary to some commonly held opinions, sodium bicarbonate is not required in the cooking of pulses and if used it destroys some of the vitamin content.

Pulses

1 BORLOTTI BEANS	14 BLACK KIDNEY BEANS
2 BROWN LENTILS	15 NAVY BEANS
3 YELLOW SPLIT PEAS	16 CANNELLINI BEANS
4 PINTO BEANS	17 GREEN LENTILS
5 FLAGEOLETS	18 BROAD BEANS
6 MUNG BEANS	19 SPLIT RED LENTILS
7 ADUKI BEANS	20 BROWN BEANS
8 HARICOT BEANS	21 CHICK PEAS
9 RED KIDNEY BEANS	22 SOYA BEANS
10 BLACK-EYED BEANS	23 GUNGA PEAS
11 FUL MEDAMES	24 BUTTER BEANS
12 BLACK SOYA BEANS	25 PUY LENTILS
13 GREEN SPLIT PEAS	

ADUKI BEAN *feijoa bean*

Widely grown in China and Japan, the aduki bean is also available here. Small, red and shiny, it is delicious in salads, mixed with other vegetables, and also, because of its size, makes a good stuffing. However, because of its unique and rather sweet flavour, it is commonly used as an ingredient in sweet dishes. Ground to a flour it is used in cakes, bread and pastry. The aduki bean is also the basis of the red bean paste used to fill Cantonese *dim sum* and to make a sweet dessert soup. It may also be very successfully sprouted.

BLACK BEAN *black kidney bean*

These shiny, black, kidney-shaped beans with a slightly sweet flavour are the essential ingredient of the majestic Brazilian *feijoada*, a rich stew which also contains dried beef, smoked pork, tongue and pigs' ears and trotters, flavoured with chillies and garlic. Use them also in black bean soup with plenty of ground cumin and coriander.

BLACK-EYED BEAN *black-eyed pea, cowpea*

Small, cream-coloured and creamy flavoured, roundish beans, with a black 'scar' where they were joined to the pod, giving them an attractive appearance. I first came across them in Indian cooking, made into a deliciously fragrant and spicy curry. In the southern United States they are eaten mixed with rice. In Nigeria they are cooked, drained and ground to make *accra*, or bean cakes, a dish which is also found in the Caribbean.

BORLOTTI BEAN

These are my favourite beans, to look at, to cook and to eat. They are oval in shape and quite plump, with a thin, pinkish, pale brown skin, deep maroon streaks and a bitter-sweet flavour. As their name suggests, they are an Italian variety of the common bean (*Phaseolus vulgaris*). I use them in all Italian recipes which call for beans: pasta and bean soup (*pasta e fagioli*) and minestrone soup. They also look good in mixed bean salads.

BROAD BEAN *fava bean*

Flat and, as their name suggests, broad, these beans when dried can be up to 1in (2·5cm) long. They are rather floury in texture and, to me, are but a pale shadow of their fresh selves. Together with butter beans, they are my least favourite dried bean. However, they share the nutritional qualities of the rest of the pulses and do well in richly flavoured meat stews of lamb or beef rather than paler meats. See also VEGETABLES, page 9.

BROWN BEAN *Dutch brown bean*

These are a very tasty variety of the common bean, a plump warm brown, and are found in many Scandinavian and northern European recipes, particularly those using ham or bacon in bean soups and stews.

BUTTER BEAN

Large, cream-coloured, sweetish-flavoured beans with a soft floury texture when cooked, these are very good added to mixed bean salads and to rich meaty stews. They are particularly high in potassium.

CANNELLINI BEAN *Italian haricot bean, white kidney bean*

Creamy-white, fairly slender and elongated kidney-shaped versions of the common bean, slightly larger than the haricot or navy bean, these are also related to the larger French Soissons and, like them, have a fluffy texture when cooked.

I find them very good all-purpose beans; in soups, salads and even in a cassoulet. It is the bean to use for *tonno e fagioli* (Italian tuna fish and bean salad), and *fagioli all' uccelletto*, where the beans are stewed with sage and tomatoes, and in an even simpler dish with olive oil, onion rings, garlic and parsley.

CHICK PEA *chana, garbanzo*

These are pale golden hard peas, knobbly rather like hazelnuts. When cooked they have a wonderfully rich nutty flavour and are to be found in tasty rustic casseroles in North Africa (couscous), Spain (*caldo gallego*), India (*kabli chana*) and many other parts of the world. In the Middle East they are part of the staple diet and are often made into a flour. Chick peas are an essential ingredient of *hummus bi tahini*, a lightly seasoned Greek dip of cooked ground chick peas, *tahini* (a paste made of toasted ground sesame seeds), oil, garlic and coriander. In Egypt they are made into a snack which is cooked and sold by street vendors.

I like to use them in casseroles of tripe and pigs' trotters or mixed meat stews in the Spanish style which include greens such as spinach and spicy sausages. They go very well with lamb. Chick peas probably do need more soaking and cooking than any of the other pulses, with the exception of soya beans. They can also be sprouted.

FLAGEOLET *green haricot bean*

When properly prepared, these small pale green, sometimes white, kidney-shaped beans – which are young haricot beans removed from the pod before they are ripe – are the most delicate and fresh tasting of all the pulses. They should not be overwhelmed with herbs, spices or chillies. To taste them at their very best, soak and cook them gently until just tender, toss in butter or olive oil, and serve as the main vegetable to accompany a nice garlicky roast leg of lamb or roast veal.

Flageolets are also the perfect ingredient in a mixed bean salad consisting also of fresh green beans, red kidney beans and perhaps some haricot beans.

FUL MEDAMES *field bean, foul, ful*

The Egyptian word for bean is *ful*, from the Latin *phaseolus* – which is also the derivation of *flageolet* (French), *fagioli* (Italian) and *fassoulia* (Greek). They are a small, plump, light brown broad bean with a full, nutty flavour, which needs long, slow cooking after soaking. *Ful medames* is often described as the national dish of Egypt and is cooked and served in many ways, most usually flavoured with plenty of cumin, olive oil, raw onion and served with hard-boiled egg; but also in other savoury dishes.

PREPARING PULSES

Type of pulse	Soaking time in hours	Pre-boiling in minutes	Simmering time in hours	Cooking time in pressure cooker in minutes	Most classic and traditional uses
ADUKI BEAN	3–4	15	1–1½	10	casseroles and soups, but also sweet cakes, bread, Chinese 'red bean paste', sprouts
BLACK BEAN	3–4	15	1½–2	10	Brazilian *feijoada* stew amd soups
BLACK-EYED BEAN	3–4	15	1–1½	10	curries and other strongly flavoured dishes
BORLOTTI BEAN	3–4	15	1–1½	10	Italian dishes, tuna & bean salad, *pasta e fagioli* (pasta and bean soup)
BROAD BEAN	3–4		1½–2	10	vegetable soup, purées
BROWN BEAN	3–4		1½–2	10	cooked with bacon or ham in casseroles
BUTTER BEAN	3–4		1–1½	10	rich meat stews
CANNELLINI BEAN	3–4		2	10	soups, salads, casseroles
CHICK PEA	5–8		2½–4	25	*hummus, couscous,* soups, stews, especially tripe dishes
FLAGEOLETS	3–4		1–1½	10	as a vegetable, often served with lamb
FUL MEDAMES	5–8		2½–4	20	Egyptian dishes, bean salad
GUNGA PEA	3–4		¾–1	10	Caribbean rice and peas
HARICOT BEAN	3–4		1–1½	10	cassoulet, *cocido*
LENTILS—BROWN,			½–¾	10	in soups, salads and as a vegetable
GREEN, PUY,			½–¾	10	in soups, salads and as a vegetable
YELLOW					
RED			½	6	in soups, salads and as a vegetable
LIMA BEAN	3–4		1–1½	10	*succotash,* in soups, salads and as a vegetable
MUNG BEAN	3–4		1	10	sprouts
NAVY BEAN	3–4		1–1½	10	Boston baked beans
PINTO BEAN	3–4		1–1½	10	Mexican re-fried beans, Asturian bean stew
PEAS: GREEN SPLIT	1–2		¾	10	pease pudding
YELLOW SPLIT	1–2		¾	10	split pea and bacon soup
WHOLE GREEN	1–2		¾	10	mushy peas
RED KIDNEY BEAN	3–4	15	1½–2	10	*chilli con carne*
SOYA BEAN	5–8	60	3½–4	25–30	sprouts, as a vegetable, in soups and salads, to make bean curd and fermented black bean

Even these simplest of 'rules' cannot be adhered to slavishly. Much depends on the length of time beans have been stored. The figures given here are simply 'averages'. You might come across a very fresh batch of brown beans which cook in scarcely an hour, or discover a jar of cannellini beans that you've had in your store cupboard for a year or two (though you really should not keep them that long). They may need closer to three hours gentle simmering.

97

GUNGA PEA *Congo pea, Jamaica pea, pigeon pea*

Said to come originally from Africa, this may be borne out by their other name, Congo peas, or that may simply be a corruption of gunga peas. They are small, round, slightly flattened peas, beige in colour, flecked with brown. They are the essential ingredient in 'rice and peas', one of the staple dishes of the Caribbean, the cooking of which can vary from island to island. See also VEGETABLES, page 9.

HARICOT BEAN *white bean*

Small, white, plump roundish beans which cook to a melting tenderness yet still retain their shape, these are the beans to use in slow cooking dishes such as cassoulets, and the casserole dishes of South America, Spain and Portugal. Haricot beans can also be used in bean salads and vegetable soups. They are suitable for purées. With little flavour of their own they absorb other aromas and flavours readily. Cannellini, flageolets and navy beans are all types of haricot.

LENTIL *dhal*

These come in different sizes and colours: red, yellow, green and brown. The tiny grey-green lentils from Puy in France are the most superior. They are not easy to find but worth hunting out as they have a very distinctive flavour, keep their shape and colour when cooked and are an excellent autumn or winter vegetable. I prepare them as a salad or as a vegetable either flavoured with ham or bacon or moistened with olive oil, and serve with a game stew or – a more unusual combination – with smoked fish.

The larger, flat brown or green lentils are not quite so fine, but they also keep their shape well and can be used in the same way. They are especially good in lentil and bacon soups, as indeed are the yellow and red lentils. These last two cook down to a smooth purée and are used a great deal in Indian cooking to make rich, mildly spiced dishes to go with meat and vegetable curries. These are often called *dhal*, which is also the general Hindi term for split lentils, peas and other pulses (when whole they are called *gram*). In Germany lentils are used in excellent winter soups with sausages.

LIMA BEAN *Madagascar butter bean*

There are two varieties, small creamy white kidney-shaped beans (also known as Madagascar butter beans) and the pale green limas which are an essential ingredient in *succotash*, the native American mixed vegetable dish in which the other main ingredient is corn. The two are combined after cooking with butter, seasoning and sometimes cream. Lima beans are suitable for soups, casseroles and salads.

MUNG BEAN *green gram, moong*

These are to be found whole or split and are one of the smallest of the beans. They are olive green and chunky looking with a fresh flavour and creamy texture. The whole beans are excellent for sprouting – these are the familiar 'bean sprouts' – but also cook well in soups and casseroles and are suitable for making into purées. Mung beans are widely used in Oriental and Indian cooking where they are also ground to provide an excellent flour.

NAVY BEAN *Yankee bean*

These were the original baked beans, a product which probably developed from the deliciously rich and mellow stew of Boston baked beans. There are those who consider that that dish in turn came from the French cassoulet, rather than a native American dish, and certainly it has much in common with it – a slow-cooked stew of haricot beans, pork and preserved goose. Use navy beans as all-purpose beans.

PEA *blue pea, marrowfat pea, split pea*

Split peas cook quite quickly and need little soaking if any. Both yellow and green varieties make excellent soups, particularly those flavoured with a knuckle of bacon or a ham-bone that are typical of Scandinavia and northern Europe. Green split peas are the main, almost the only ingredient of that very old dish from the north of England, pease pudding, a very dense purée of cooked dried peas, seasoned then steamed and served with roasts, particularly pork or baked ham. Green peas are also available dried whole, and these peas are essential for

another classic English dish, pea purée or mushy peas. See also VEGETABLES, page 9.

PINTO BEAN

A rich orange-pink bean with rust-coloured flecks, this is aptly called the painted (*pinto*) bean. It was the original ingredient of the Mexican refried beans, *frijoles refritos*, but is now used for many recipes, and other beans are sometimes substituted in the Mexican dish.

RED KIDNEY BEAN

These are a dark red-brown kidney shape which keep their shape and colour when cooked. In fact, if you are cooking a mixture of beans that includes red kidney beans, you should cook these separately as they have a tendency to colour other foods cooked with them. They are excellent in mixed bean salads and stews, including *chilli con carne*, the spicy hot stew from the south-western part of the United States whose main ingredients are beef (or venison), cubed rather than minced, and chillies as hot as you can stand.

SOYA BEAN

A power house of nutrition, soya beans are crammed full of protein, fat, vitamins and minerals. Unlike other beans, they have little starch. They are very dense and take a long time to cook, but once cooked are very digestible. They are, not to put too fine a point on it, bland, and need plenty of distinctive flavours cooking alongside them: tomatoes, garlic, thyme, or flavoursome curry spices. Even then they are not my favourite bean. They can be made into a purée, added to soups and casseroles, or ground fine and used to give texture to loaves, or raw and sprouted.

Soya beans are also used to produce many other foodstuffs: flour, 'milk', 'textured vegetable protein', which is used as a meat substitute, bean curd (*tofu*), oil, soya sauce and *miso*, that fermented soya bean paste so essential to Japanese cooking. The small black soya beans are also fermented to make the salty black beans of Chinese cooking. See also VEGETABLES, page 9, and OILS, page 121.

SPROUTING BEANS, PEAS AND SEEDS

These are easy to prepare at home and make a welcome addition to salads and stir-fried dishes with their crisp texture and deliciously nutty but refreshing flavour. They are also highly nutritious being exceptionally rich in most of the elements necessary to a healthy diet – protein, fibre, vitamins, minerals and starch.

A large jam jar, a piece of muslin and an elastic band is all you need, though it's worth buying a special 'sprouter' if you do this a lot. Use beans, peas or seeds intended for sprouting or eating, and not those for planting as they may have been specially treated with preservatives. Only the whole 'seed' will sprout so split peas and other split pulses, such as lentils or mung, cannot be used.

The following are suitable for sprouting: aduki beans, chick peas, lentils, linseed, mung beans, soya beans and snow beans (which need pre-soaking for a few hours), as well as seeds such as alfalfa, poppy, sesame, fenugreek, sunflower, pumpkin, and even some cereal grains, especially wheat which sprouts very easily.

Fresh sprouts will keep in the bottom of the refrigerator for up to a week in a covered container.

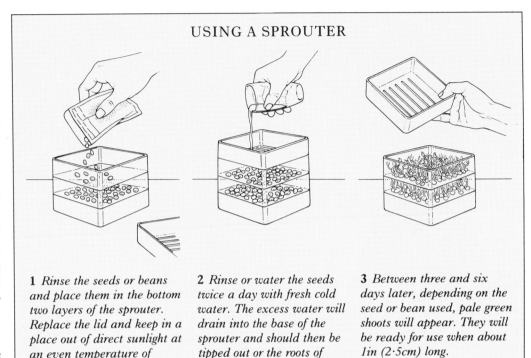

USING A SPROUTER

1 *Rinse the seeds or beans and place them in the bottom two layers of the sprouter. Replace the lid and keep in a place out of direct sunlight at an even temperature of 50–70°F (13–21°C).*

2 *Rinse or water the seeds twice a day with fresh cold water. The excess water will drain into the base of the sprouter and should then be tipped out or the roots of sprouts will rot.*

3 *Between three and six days later, depending on the seed or bean used, pale green shoots will appear. They will be ready for use when about 1in (2·5cm) long.*

Seeds and Sprouts

1 SOYA BEAN SPROUTS
2 FENUGREEK SPROUTS
3 LINSEED
4 MUNG BEAN SPROUTS
5 ADUKI BEAN SPROUTS
6 PUMPKIN SEEDS
7 ALFALFA SEEDS
8 SNOW BEAN SPROUTS
9 BLACK POPPY SEEDS
10 WHITE SESAME SEEDS
11 WHEAT SPROUTS
12 LENTIL SPROUTS
13 ALFALFA SPROUTS
14 SNOW BEANS
15 WHITE POPPY SEEDS
16 BLACK SESAME SEEDS
17 CHICK PEA SPROUTS
18 SUNFLOWER SEEDS

Herbs

Despite their lack of importance as a source of nutrition, herbs contribute hugely to our enjoyment of food. They add scent, flavour and colour to such a degree that it is hard to imagine certain dishes without their traditional herbs. Tomato salad without basil would be unthinkable. *Gravad lax* would not be *gravad lax* without dill. And without chives a potato salad is a poor dish indeed.

The flavour of the herb comes from the essential oils stored in the leaves, stem and flowers, which are released through heat or when the 'seal' is broken as the leaf is crushed. Try it with a leaf of basil, sage or tarragon. Carefully pick and smell the leaf, then crush it between your fingers and notice how much more powerful is the smell.

FRESH AND DRIED HERBS
Herbs can be bought fresh, and the freshest of all is a herb that you pluck from the growing plant, so, if possible, grow these small, inexpensive treasures on a sunny window-sill or balcony. You do not need lots of space or an elaborate herb garden.

The next best thing is to buy fresh herbs and use them immediately. Sometimes only the leaves are used: basil for salad, tarragon or parsley for a sauce, but add the stalks to soups, or use them to enhance the flavour of a stock. It is an easy matter to fish them out at the end of cooking time.

Keep herbs fresh for a few days by wrapping them in a little damp kitchen paper and putting them in a polythene bag in the salad drawer of the refrigerator. Put large bunches of herbs, such as parsley or coriander, in a jug of water and keep out of direct sunlight.

Herbs

1	ANGELICA	11	BASIL
2	DILL	12	FENNEL
3	COMFREY	13	FENUGREEK LEAVES
4	CORIANDER	14	BALM
5	CHERVIL	15	LEMON GERANIUM
6	CURRY LEAVES	16	SCENTED GERANIUM
7	OPAL BASIL	17	CHIVES
8	LOVAGE	18	ROSE GERANIUM
9	HYSSOP	19	BORAGE
10	ROCK HYSSOP	20	BAY

You can buy dried herbs or dry your own. From experience I find that the ones which dry best are the rather tough ones, which when fresh are pungent and oily: sage, bay, lavender, rosemary, marjoram and thyme fall into this category. The more delicate herbs such as chervil, basil and tarragon do not dry so successfully – though they can be frozen. Or rather, they can be dried perfectly well, but little of the characteristic scent and flavour remains.

To pick herbs for drying, choose a hot sunny day before the herbs have flowered, when they will be at their peak. Wait until the sun has dried the dew but has not been up so long that the plants are beginning to wilt. Cut the plant with part of the stem and take care not to bruise the leaves as the essential oils will escape. Blanch the herbs briefly, tie in small bunches and dry in an airy cupboard. Most modern kitchens are too full of humidity for this method to work well there, however pretty it may look. The bedroom is probably as good a place as any. (See also page 106.) Alternatively, spread the herbs on trays, turning them occasionally, until they are completely dry. They can also be dried in a very low oven, but only dry them, do not allow them to heat. Once dry, pack the herbs into glass containers which can be closed to give an airtight seal. Best of all is to use tinted glass since the herbs should be stored away from light and heat. Six to nine months is the maximum keeping time.

HERBAL INFUSIONS
Apart from flavouring food, herbs are also used to make very pleasant tisanes or herbal infusions that are said to have many therapeutic qualities, depending on the herb used. An infusion of mint aids digestion; camomile tea will help you to sleep; an infusion of basil holds travel sickness at bay; and combinations of herbs are used to make reviving morning teas and soothing evening teas.

ANGELICA

Many of us only know angelica as the small sweet crystallized or candied strips of green packed into clear plastic boxes for use as a decoration for cakes and trifles. It is a tall, leggy biennial plant with a sturdy stem and slightly shiny bright green leaves with the shape of celery leaves and greenish-yellow flowers in its second summer. As well as candying the tender sweet-tasting stems, you can cook them in pies with tart fruit such as rhubarb or apple to reduce the acidity, and the leaves are attractive in salads or finely chopped and mixed with mayonnaise or cream cheese for dips or spreads.

ANISE *sweet cumin*

It is the seed of this annual leafy plant, native to the Eastern Mediterranean, that is most familiar to us, but the leaves can also be used in salads, to flavour cooked vegetables such as carrots, fish soups and pickled vegetables. See also SPICES, page 110.

BALM *lemon balm*

This small bushy perennial herb with slightly hairy serrated leaves is valuable for its pronounced lemon flavour and fragrance. It has a natural affinity with fish, poultry, veal, vegetables, indeed with anything that you might want to match to a lemon flavour. Its leaves can be used whole in salads, chopped into stuffings, in marinades and to scent the steam in which you might cook a fish or chicken. As a herbal infusion or tea, lemon balm is soothing, refreshing and delicious. Creams, syrups and custards can be infused with its lemony flavour in a most agreeable way. It loses its flavour almost entirely when dried.

BASIL *genoa basil, sweet basil*

This semi-hardy annual has long been one of the cornerstones of Mediterranean cookery. There is nothing like it for bringing the scent and flavour of the warm south to a northern kitchen. It was one of the ingredients I used to look forward to most when it arrived in our shops in late May or early June, all the way from Italy. Now it is imported from warmer countries most of the year round, and we have our own homegrown supplies in high summer.

Basil has a warm spicy smell and flavour that does wonders for a tomato salad and many other dishes, particularly summer vegetables and salads. The soft, shiny green leaves are the main ingredient of *pesto*, the thick paste made by pounding basil with Parmesan and Pecorino cheeses, pine nuts and olive oil. This is widely used in Italy in Ligurian and Genoese dishes, such as *trenette al pesto* – a simple and exquisite preparation of thin flat noodles served very hot with the fragrant sauce stirred in. A similar sauce, called *pistou*, is popular further to the west in France, around Nice.

Basil leaves give a wonderful flavour to a tossed green salad. It is better to shred them by hand rather than chop them as this helps to retain more flavour. In hot dishes add basil leaves at the last minute (prolonged cooking reduces their potency). Put basil in omelettes and other egg dishes, mix it with garlic and olive oil and stir it into hot pasta, or use it in sauces for fish, veal and chicken. It is always worth experimenting with basil. I have cooked noisettes of lamb with a white wine sauce flavoured with basil that suited the meat to perfection.

Apart from the sweet basil there is a beautiful deep purple, well-flavoured variety called opal basil, a tiny-leaved, low-growing bush variety, and Neapolitana, which has very large crinkled leaves and a powerful flavour that is particularly well suited to *pesto*. Very decorative, and delicious, ruffled basils are also to be found, both purple and green; and some with different aromas overlaying the characteristic basil scent – lemon basil, anise basil, cinnamon basil and spice basil.

BAY

This attractive ornamental evergreen tree is a member of the laurel family. Its leaves are an indispensable ingredient of the *bouquet garni*, the small bundle of herbs which also includes thyme and parsley, tied together with string or in a knot of muslin, and used to flavour soups and casseroles. These *bouquets* can be bought ready made, but many people like to make up their own, adding other herbs if appropriate to a particular dish. For example, a sprig of dill might be added to a *bouquet* used to flavour a fish dish.

Fresh bay leaves will be quite firm and shiny, with a dull surface underneath and a distinct fragrance. They can be used in marinades, to flavour meat or game terrines and pâtés, or soups and stocks. Bay leaves are particularly good as a flavouring for many carbohydrate dishes – potato soup, bean stews and risottos. But do not think of them only as a flavouring for savoury dishes. A bay leaf buried in a jar of sugar, or tucked under the pastry lid of an apple pie, or cooked with a rice pudding gives a wonderful fragrance to the finished dish.

BERGAMOT

Bergamot belongs to the same family as mint. It has few culinary uses, but the lemon-scented leaves can be added to salads and fruit cups, and the pink, white or purple flowers can be crystallized. Bergamot tea is a soothing, soporific bedtime drink.

BORAGE

Very much a summer treat, borage flowers are first and foremost a visual delight – brilliant blue or lilac and star-shaped with tiny black stamens. They look beautiful scattered over a salad or floating in a crystal bowl of chilled punch, or they can be frozen in ice-cubes for winter drinks. The rest of this annual plant is fairly coarse looking and extremely hairy. A faint but palatable cucumber flavour is present in the flowers and the leaves. Capture some of this by finely chopping the tenderest leaves into cream cheese, mayonnaise or egg salad. But be warned: if you use anything except the tiniest leaves and fail to chop exceedingly fine, the hairs will irritate your mouth and throat. Coarser leaves and stems can be used when making a vegetable stock.

CHERVIL

This small annual herb makes a wonderful addition to the cook's repertoire. I love to use it in delicate fish dishes. The leaves are soft-textured, lacy and rather fan-like, similar to but more fragile than flat-leaved parsley. But, once picked, chervil wilts and yellows very quickly and so should be used as soon as possible. The flavour resembles that of parsley with a hint of aniseed, and is particularly good in all egg and cream dishes, with fish, shellfish, poultry and vegetables.

Unlike many herbs, chervil does not dry well, and loses its flavour rapidly, so if you're using the leaves in cooking, add them near the end. It does freeze well, however, either in chopped leaf form or pounded into a herb butter.

Chopped up with parsley, tarragon and chives, fresh chervil is one of the classic *fines herbes* – a herb mixture much used in French cooking, being added to salads, omelettes and butter sauces and sprinkled on soups.

CHIVES

This is one of the four *fines herbes* of classic French cooking. Who could imagine potato salad without chives snipped into it to give a delicate, mild oniony flavour? The slender green spikes of the chive plant can also be used to impart their flavour to butters, cheeses, creams and sauces, in which chopped onions would be too strong, and in all egg dishes. It does not tolerate heat well, so is always added at the end of cooking. Lengths of chive make very attractive decorations, for example, on a fish fillet in a sauce. Long chives are sometimes tied round bundles of cooked beans or baby vegetables for added decorative effect. The pretty lilac-pink pompom flowers are edible and look good in salads, while the petals can be scattered on smooth vegetable soups.

STORING HERBS

Wrap fresh herbs in damp kitchen paper and place in the refrigerator. They will keep well for a few days.

COMFREY

This is a member of the borage family and, like that plant, has a coarse stem and leaves. The bell-shaped white, yellow or pinkish-purple flowers can be used in salads for decoration. The large young leaves can be dipped in a light batter and fried, or cooked like spinach, but it's only worth doing if you have lots of them.

CORIANDER *Chinese parsley, cilantro, Greek parsley*

Every part – seeds, leaf, stem and root – of this intensely aromatic and exotic herb, can be used in cooking. If I had a ready supply of them I would also use the pretty lacy flower heads in dark green leafy salads for flavour and contrast. The fresh seeds are delicious in fish or vegetable dishes and the roots can be mixed with other root vegetables in stews, casseroles and curries.

Coriander is an essential ingredient in many Indian, Chinese, Portuguese, Greek, Turkish and North African dishes such as curries, *hummus* and couscous. Its intensely aromatic spicy flavour marries well with meat dishes including chillies. It has also found a niche in the modern kitchen both as a garnish instead of parsley, and as a flavouring in fish dishes and root vegetable casseroles, for example, and with poultry. It is also much used in the 'new' American cooking, where it is more often referred to as *cilantro* (its Spanish name) which indicates a borrowing from Mexican cooking, where the herb is predominant. Both the feathery upper leaves and the broader lower leaves are used, and usually added towards the end of cooking. It freezes well. See also SPICES, page 110.

COSTMARY *alecost*

Its strong camphor, minty scent and flavour make this a herb more suitable for pot-pourris and scenting linen than using in the kitchen where it would overpower most dishes. However, it does have digestive qualities and it can be interesting to experiment with minute quantities in place of mint, using the youngest, tenderest leaves. It has long been used in home-brewing to clear and preserve ale.

CURRY LEAF

A bright, shiny green leaf, this resembles the bay leaf and should not be confused with the silvery-grey-leaved curry plant which, though it does have a distinctive 'curry' scent, is usually grown only for ornamental purposes. Curry leaves are used in many Indian and South-East Asian dishes to which they impart a pronounced spicy curry flavour. The chopped leaves are fried in oil until crisp, then the other ingredients are added.

DILL *dill weed*

Both the seeds and feathery leaves of this hardy annual are used. It has a strong distinctive flavour with slight aniseed overtones, and is most commonly used with fish dishes such as the traditional Scandinavian *gravad lax* and the more modern derivative marinated fish dishes. I find it also goes very well with chicken, in cream sauces, in egg dishes and with fish soups, potato and other root vegetable soups. It is best added towards the end of cooking to obtain maximum flavour. It is delicious with raw cucumber or blended with cream and cottage cheese. Fronds and the seeds can be steeped to make a well-flavoured vinegar to use in salad dressings and mayonnaise. See also SPICES, page 110.

FENNEL

This belongs to the same family as dill and has similar feathery leaves, flower heads and seeds, but an even more pronounced aniseed flavour. In Mediterranean cooking, particularly the fish soups of Marseille, fennel is often used in conjunction with a splash of *pastis*, the milky aniseed-flavoured spirit. The tall, sturdy plant grows wild all over the Mediterranean. One of the best uses to which it can be put in the kitchen or, better still, barbecue, is to grill fish or meat on top of the upper stems and leaves so that some of their fragrance is absorbed as the fish cooks.

CHOPPING HERBS – FOUR METHODS

1 Use sharp kitchen scissors to snip up the leaves over a board or plate.

2 Use a mezzaluna – a special curved, double-handled blade – and rock it from side to side over the leaves.

3 Use a sharp kitchen knife to chop coarsely. Bunch leaves up against blade and chop with knife against your fingers.

4 To chop finely, place leaves in a heap. Use knife point as a pivot while chopping backwards and forwards across the pile.

Fennel is particularly useful in counteracting the oiliness of some fish, such as sardines and mackerel.

I like to cook whole heads of yellow flowering fennel with a boned pork joint, covering it with milk and cooking it slowly in the oven, Italian style. It is delicious.

Use fennel leaves or seeds to flavour vinegars and oils, but it's best of all fresh, chopped into green salads, used with fish, eggs, poultry, pork and veal, or to flavour creams and butters for sauces.

Fennel is usually a bright green plant, but there is also a handsome, bronze version which can be used in the same way. See also VEGE-TABLES, page 9, and SPICES, page 110.

FENUGREEK LEAF *methi*

The soft green clover-like leaves of the fenugreek plant are used both as a herb and a vegetable in Indian cooking where the rather bitter flavour combines well with other spices. The taste of the leaves is something like eating a very lightly curried walnut. It is a valuable herb, being even richer in iron than watercress. At the two-leaved sprout stage it can be used very successfully in salads. See also SPROUTING BEANS, PEAS AND SEEDS page 99.

GERANIUM LEAF *pelargonium, rose geranium, scented geranium*

These cheerful summer flowers which brighten up our balconies and window boxes come in a huge range of varieties. Some have surprisingly small, quite inconspicuous simple flowers, unlike their larger, opulent red and pink cousins. But they do have a range of wonderful scents. One with oak-like leaves has the spicy smell of incense, while a very delicate spiky leaf has a rose-lemon scent. Others smell of apple, orange, pine, peppermint and rose. These make wonderful and unusual additions to many dishes.

I use the 'sweeter' scents to flavour creams, custards, sugars, jellies, sorbets and jams, by infusing the leaves in syrup or liquid. When baking pies, sponge or fruit cakes, a few leaves laid underneath the pastry or cake batter impart a subtle scent and flavour. Use orange- or lemon-flavoured leaves under rich fruit cakes.

Some of the spicier leaves are excellent in fish soups or casseroles, in game pâtés or with rabbit or chicken – used in much the same way as a bay leaf. See also EDIBLE FLOWERS, page 108.

HYSSOP *rock hyssop*

One of the less common herbs, hyssop is similar, in certain respects, to rosemary and lavender. It is strongly flavoured and aromatic, with slight hints of liquorice and anise. To me its appeal lies in the way it perfectly counteracts rich meat dishes, particularly offal such as kidneys and liver (it is excellent for adding to pâtés). It is also delicious with lamb and rabbit, when simply cooked in the Mediterranean style. In very small quantities it works well in robust fish dishes such as stews and in soups heavy with garlic and tomatoes.

KAFFIR LIME *makrut*

These aromatic leaves from a type of lime tree add one of the most distinctive flavours to Thai and Indonesian cooking. They are equally distinctive in appearance, like a figure of eight with two leaves joined together base to tip. The leaves and rind of the fruit are used in Thai cooking, but only the leaves in Indonesian cooking.

LAVENDER

The scent of lavender comes not only from the flowers but is contained in the stalks and leaves. It is not a plant which springs to mind immediately as a culinary ingredient, but I have used it often in my recipes and find it excellent. Use it sparingly as you would rosemary. It has the same intensity of fragrance in its essential oils. A sprig of leaves can be used to scent the steam in which you are cooking chicken or rabbit. A few sprigs tucked around a joint of lamb before it is roasted will give it an exquisite flavour without overpowering the meat itself. See also EDIBLE FLOWERS, page 108.

LOVAGE *sea parsley*

This hardy perennial, old-fashioned pot herb deserves to be given a much more prominent place in cooking. I love its shiny glossy foliage,

toothed and lobed like celery leaves, and its intensely savoury celery flavour. Stem, leaf and seeds can all be used – in soups, stocks, sauces and salads. It is also an excellent marinade ingredient, particularly for the lighter meats such as veal, pork and chicken, and it livens up root vegetables – potatoes best of all. Add the chopped leaves to a potato soup or potato omelette, or stir into a potato salad. The seeds can be used in the same way, and are especially good with mashed potatoes.

MARJORAM *oregano*

Marjoram and oregano belong to the same family and have similar properties and culinary uses. (Oregano is also known as wild marjoram.) The most common varieties of marjoram are the savoury pot or French marjoram and sweet marjoram, which really does have a sweeter flavour. With a concentration of essential oils, marjoram and oregano add a powerful flavour to whatever you cook with them. I like to have a bunch in the kitchen just to smell.

One of the nicest presents I have ever been given was a bunch of *rigani* from Greece, where friends had been out to gather this wild marjoram on the hillside. I used it in fish dishes, homemade tomato sauces and omelettes, to flavour oils and vinegars and generally to make my kitchen smell like a Greek taverna for a few weeks. Quite wonderful.

Marjoram (or oregano) is traditionally used to flavour the tomato pulp which is spread on pizza dough. It makes a good addition to a marinade

Herbs

1	PURPLE SAGE	13	GINGER MINT
2	SWEET CICELY	14	APPLE MINT
3	MELILOT	15	TARRAGON
4	ROSEMARY	16	WINTER SAVORY
5	SPEARMINT	17	OREGANO
6	TANSY	18	PEPPERMINT
7	BOWLES MINT	19	BLACK PEPPERMINT
8	PINEAPPLE SAGE	20	CURLY PARSLEY
9	MYRTLE	21	SILVER POSY THYME
10	SAGE	22	THYME
11	FLAT-LEAVED PARSLEY	23	LEMON THYME
12	PINEAPPLE MINT	24	MARJORAM

for lamb and furred game, and a sprig of it adds a pleasant fragrance to a roast. It is also good with vegetables, especially marrow and potato.

MELILOT *sweet clover*

This prettily named plant, derived from *meli* the Greek word for honey, is a member of the clove family. It is more often used as a medicinal or cosmetic herb, and smells fresh and sweet. Use a little in stuffings, pâtés and sausages.

MINT

I have to declare a strong prejudice against the traditional uses of mint in English cooking, particularly with roast lamb or new potatoes or peas. On the other hand, cooking fish with mint is a revelation. Try steaming a skate wing over a fresh mint infusion, and serving it in a warm salad dressed with walnut oil, wine vinegar and chopped mint leaves. I love mint tea, real fresh mint ice-cream, chopped mint in a stuffing for vegetables or vine leaves, crystallized or frosted mint leaves added to summer drinks and fruit salads, a few leaves added to the fruit when making blackcurrant jelly, or tucked into a bilberry pie. For these dishes there is a large

variety of mint: spearmint, pineapple mint, apple mint, Bowles mint, lemon mint, peppermint, ginger mint, some with overlaying flavours, some with variegated leaves. Pennyroyal is a type of mint with a strong peppermint flavour and scent.

MYRTLE

This spicy sweet herb with incredibly fragrant white flowers and leaves is one of those hot-weather plants like rosemary and lavender in which the essential oils are very concentrated. Myrtle is not much used in cooking, which I think is a pity. Twigs of myrtle are marvellous used as aromatic fuel for a barbecue of lamb, pork or spicy sausages; or tuck a few sprigs around a joint of lamb when roasting it. A few leaves and the black berries can be added to marinades and stuffing. The sturdy fragrant leaves retain their flavour when dried.

PARSLEY

Two kinds of parsley are now widely available: curled parsley and flat-leaved parsley, both a vivid green. The latter has a more pronounced flavour but they can be used interchangeably in

almost any savoury dish, making it the most widely used herb. It is also a rich source of carotene, vitamin C, iron and mineral salts.

Use parsley in large quantities to make delicious soups and sauces where it is the main ingredient rather than playing a merely decorative role. Finely chop it with garlic and mix with butter not only to stuff into snail shells, but to flavour grills and to mix with vegetables. Add it to a *bouquet garni* to flavour soups and casseroles. Use it in marinades and stocks and do not forget that there is much concentrated flavour in the stalks, which should not be wasted – they are ideal for use in a *bouquet garni*. If you have plenty of parsley, fry it until crisp to make a marvellous accompaniment to fish. It can be dipped in batter first but this is not necessary. Fried parsley is also traditionally served with Wiener Schnitzel. An alternative way of preparing parsley is to cook it in a small amount of stock, make a purée of it and whisk in a little butter to make a delicious vegetable to serve with chicken or veal. Also use flat-leaved parsley in salads.

ROSEMARY

I once had leg of veal cooked with rosemary over an open fire in an old restaurant in the hills above Trieste. It was one of the most perfect marriages of flavours I have ever come across, the aromatic oils of this evergreen shrubby herb complementing the rich yet delicate flavours and texture of the meat. More traditionally, rosemary flavours roast lamb, but try it too with sausages, pork or rabbit. Use a little finely chopped in bread dough, risottos, stuffings, or potato salads.

This is a very powerful, intensely aromatic herb and should be used in moderation. It is best to remove the dark green spiky leaves before serving the dish. If you do use it chopped up it should be *very* finely chopped.

Rosemary can also be used in sweet dishes. Tuck a sprig of rosemary in a jar of sugar; or grind rosemary flowers with sugar. Infuse it in creams, custards and syrups or use it as a flavouring for delicate water ice. One of my favourite ways of poaching pears is to peel them, then add a little honey to the liquid in the saucepan and a sprig of rosemary. Once cooled, decorate the pears with rosemary flowers.

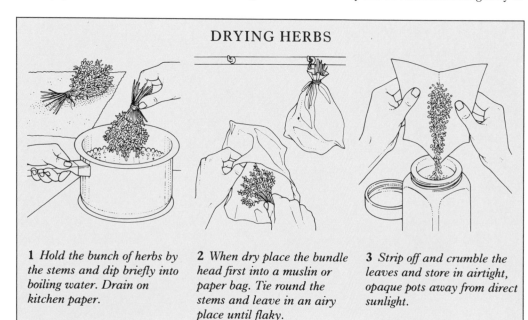

DRYING HERBS

1 *Hold the bunch of herbs by the stems and dip briefly into boiling water. Drain on kitchen paper.*

2 *When dry place the bundle head first into a muslin or paper bag. Tie round the stems and leave in an airy place until flaky.*

3 *Strip off and crumble the leaves and store in airtight, opaque pots away from direct sunlight.*

USING HERBS

Angelica Young stems used for their sweetening qualities; also candied, to decorate cakes and trifles. Add chopped leaves to salads.

Balm Add the chopped leaves to salads, desserts and fruit cups; use in stuffings for poultry and game; good with fish, veal, vegetables.

Basil Add at the last minute. Use in tomato dishes, in salads, with soft cheeses, *pesto* sauce, pasta, vegetable soups, asparagus or broccoli, egg dishes and with lamb.

Bay Long cooking best releases the strong, distinctive flavour. Part of the classic *bouquet garni*. Use in *court bouillons*, stocks, casseroles and pot roasts, fish and vegetable dishes. Also in desserts.

Bergamot Add the chopped leaves to salads. Crystallize the flowers and use as cake decorations.

Borage Add the young leaves and flowers to salads and drinks. The flowers can also be crystallized as cake decoration.

Bouquet garni This is a bundle of herbs – classically comprising thyme, parsley and bay, though it can vary. Use to flavour soups and casseroles, and remove after cooking.

Chervil Use in salads, *fines herbes*, soups, stews, meat sauces, with vegetables, and in egg, chicken or cheese dishes. Excellent in herb butter with grilled fish. Prolonged cooking destroys the flavour.

Chives Mildest of the onion family. A garnish for salads, soups and vegetable dishes; add to egg, cheese, poultry and fish dishes.

Comfrey Use flowers in salads and as decorations.

Coriander Add chopped fresh leaves to spiced dishes such as curries – towards end of cooking. Goes well with roast pork. Use also in Middle Eastern dishes, and casseroles, chutneys and apple pie.

Costmary Use instead of mint, and in brewing.

Curry leaf Fresh curry leaves are used in curries, the ground dried leaves added to curry powder mixes.

Dill Do not subject its mild caraway flavour to prolonged heat. Use in fish marinades, in salads, sauces and soups. Good with potatoes, chicken, egg dishes.

Fennel Good with oily fish and fatty meats such as pork, or in sauces and apple dishes. Use chopped fresh leaves in salads.

Fenugreek leaf Use in curries.

Fines herbes A classic mixture of herbs used in French cooking – usually parsley, chervil, tarragon and chives. Use in omelettes, sauces and salads.

Geranium Use the scented leaves to flavour sorbets. Crystallize the flowers for decoration.

Hyssop Use in rich meat dishes, especially offal, pâtés, rabbit, lamb.

Lavender Use flowers and stalks in moderation with rabbit, fish and lamb.

Lovage The chopped leaves combine with other strongly flavoured herbs in soups, stews and stuffing; use alone in tomato sauce for pasta. Good with root vegetables, especially potatoes.

Marjoram and **oregano** Fresh, dried or ground leaves keep their flavour well, even when subjected to heat. Use in sauces to accompany pasta, in stuffings for vegetables. Good with pork, poultry, game and fish, also tomatoes.

Melilot Use in moderation in stews or in a marinade for rabbit, or in stuffings and pâtés.

Mint Best with vegetables, in mint tea and mint ice-cream. Also good with fish.

Myrtle Good with roast lamb, pork, sausages, and in marinades and stuffings.

Oregano See Marjoram.

Parsley Principal ingredient of *fines herbes* and *bouquet garni*. Good with vegetables and fish dishes, or in stocks and sauces. Use fried as a vegetable and fresh in salads.

Rosemary Very strongly flavoured; use sparingly, finely chopped, in stuffings for meat and game. Insert sprigs into roast mutton, lamb, pork or game; remove them after cooking. Also in sweet dishes: creams, custards, poached pears.

Sage Use fresh or dried. Very powerful flavour even after long cooking, so use sparingly. Excellent combined with tomatoes, garlic, olive oil. Best with fatty meats such as pork or duck, and with offal such as kidneys and liver.

Sassafras Louisiana cuisine, gumbos.

Savory Bean and pasta soups and stews, meat casseroles.

Smallage Substitute for celery in soups and stews.

Sweet cicely Leaves used in fruit puddings containing tart fruits such as gooseberries, rhubarb or plums will reduce the amount of sugar necessary. Use sparingly in salads.

Tansy Once used in cakes and custards.

Tarragon Ingredient of classic *bouquet garni* mixture, and *sauce béarnaise*. Use fresh chopped leaves in salads.

Thyme Used in *bouquet garni*, in stuffings, meat casseroles, marinades, and to flavour pasta sauces. Good with fish, chicken and game.

Woodruff Add to fruit and wine cups.

SAGE

Although not a subtle herb, sage deserves a better fate than in the often dry-as-dust sage and onion stuffing. It is really a hot climate shrub by nature, particularly a Mediterranean one, the sun concentrating its aromatic oils. It pairs very successfully with other Mediterranean flavours, such as garlic, tomatoes and olive oil.

A little sage shredded into vegetable soups and beef or pork casseroles is excellent. Some of the best stuffed pasta dishes of the Emilia-Romagna around Modena and Mantova are served with melted butter in which a few fresh sage leaves have been heated. In fact, it is to be found most often in Italian cooking, with quickly fried calves' liver, with veal and with kidneys. Closer to home, it is traditionally used to flavour and colour cheeses, such as Derby and Lancashire, and with roast pork and duck. Once, at a reception, I took something from a plate without really looking, and ate it: a revelation – sage leaves which had been dipped in a light batter and deep-fried.

This soft, slightly furry, silvery green leaf comes in many varieties. I particularly like the golden sage, a variegated leaf.

SASSAFRAS

The sassafras tree belongs, like the bay, to the laurel family, and its leaves are used in the cooking of Louisiana, where dried and powdered sassafras leaf is the main ingredient in *filé* powder, a flavouring and thickening agent essential in the making of those wonderful Creole stews called gumbos.

SAVORY

The German word for savory, *Bohnenkraut*, means 'bean herb', and this gives a clue to how it is most often used – with beans of every variety: typically fresh green beans, dried haricot and flageolet beans. With a flavour slightly reminiscent of thyme and rosemary, that is, aromatic and pungent, savory should be used with a light hand if it is not to overpower whatever is cooked with it. There are summer and winter savories, both with similar flavours. It is one of the few herbs whose flavour, when dried, is retained or

EDIBLE FLOWERS

even improved, because it loses some of its biting pungency. I like it in rich bean and pasta soups and meat casseroles.

SMALLAGE *herb celery, sedano*

A little-known herb today, smallage is wild celery, from which was bred the more familiar vegetable. The flavour is similar to but more bitter and pungent than that of celery. It is a useful herb for flavouring soups and stews in the absence of celery, but not to eat raw in a green salad, for example; it is too strong for that.

SWEET CICELY

This is a tall, many-stemmed perennial plant with soft, toothed, lacy leaves and tiny white flowers clustered on a broad umbrella-shaped flower head. The leaves are aromatic and have a delicate flavour akin to anise and liquorice. The leaves are attractive enough to add to a salad plate, but sweet rather than savoury and so perhaps more suited to cooking with fruit: apple pies, dried fruit compotes and gooseberry fools, for example.

TANSY

An extremely bitter herb, with a rather dank musty smell, tansy was widely, and to my mind inexplicably, used in earlier times. There are recipes for its use in cakes and custards. It was perhaps something that was felt to be good for you, for there are numerous medicinal uses for it recorded in herbals. The cakes and custards were no doubt an earlier version of the 'spoonful of sugar to make the medicine go down'.

TARRAGON

A constituent of the classic *fines herbes*, tarragon is one of the most important herbs in the kitchen. Be sure that you use the true French and not Russian tarragon, which has a coarse, rank flavour. French tarragon has slender green leaves and the authentic flavour is difficult to describe – aromatic, intensely so when crushed, with a slight hint of aniseed, and strangely 'cooling'. If you bite into it, the tongue tingles a little and feels almost as if it has been ever so slightly anaesthetized for a second or two.

Like basil, tarragon has many uses. It is an essential ingredient in a number of classic French sauces, particularly *sauce béarnaise*. A few sprigs put in when you pot-roast a chicken makes all the difference. It is excellent in sauces for fish and vegetables and can be infused in vinegar for a vinaigrette. For a truly magnificent salad, chop and crush a few leaves with a little salt and add them to a bowl of green salad leaves dressed with walnut oil and lemon juice. Above all other herbs tarragon is the one that adds a touch of class to a dish. But use fresh tarragon if you possibly can. Dried tarragon loses so much of the character of the fresh herb that it is scarcely worth shelf space.

THYME

The very tiny, greyish-green leaves of this low-growing, shrubby herb are full of an intensely aromatic essential oil which gives a deep, rich flavour to slow-cooked dishes such as *daubes* and casseroles. Thyme is one of the ingredients of a *bouquet garni* together with parsley and bay and is, without doubt, one of the most important kitchen herbs. Beef, pork and lamb casseroles would simply not taste the same without it. Thyme is cooked with them, and also used in their marinades, as it is with furred and feathered game.

There are many varieties of thyme, both wild and cultivated, the 'common' thyme as well as flavoured thymes, with overtones of lemon, orange and even caraway. Lemon thyme is a particular favourite of mine which I think goes perfectly with fish, especially those types that need a little help in the way of flavouring such as farmed salmon and rainbow trout. Its lemony, spicy flavour also goes marvellously with some of the richer fish – a sprig tucked inside a sardine before it is grilled does wonders.

WOODRUFF *sweet woodruff*

This is not so much a culinary herb as an addition to wine cups, particularly in Germany where it is added to young Rhine wine and served as *Maibowle* on 1 May. It is a sweet fragrant herb, with flowers and leaves reminiscent of freshly cut hay.

The use of flowers in cooking is a centuries-old tradition in Britain and elsewhere, one that lingers on and deserves to be revived. Flowers add much pleasure to food; they are delightful to look at and, in many cases, to eat.

However, some words of warning first. Even if you know a flower to be edible, such as a rose, do not use it for culinary purposes if you think it may have been sprayed with harmful substances. Secondly, do not eat anything that you cannot identify just because it smells as if it would taste good. Finally, many of the flowers traditionally used in cooking, such as violets, primroses, mallow and cowslips, are wild flowers. The countryside is no longer carpeted with wild flower meadows. Those that remain are part of our dwindling natural heritage and must be preserved at all costs. Do not even pick wild flowers, let alone uproot them. It may be illegal to do so. It is certainly antisocial. Fortunately, specialist seed merchants can supply wild flower seeds, so there is no reason why you should not grow your own if you want to make violet syrup or cowslip wine.

Many of our garden flowers, also, can be used in the kitchen in different ways. From a herb garden can be picked the flowers of rosemary, thyme, borage, marjoram, lovage, fennel, coriander, bergamot and many others. These add colour and delicate flavours to salads. They make some of the most attractive decorations too. One of my summertime favourites is chilled peach and carrot soup with rosemary flowers scattered on the surface. Nasturtium, marigold, pansy and chicory flowers can also be used in salads, as can rose petals, geranium petals, violas and even the petals of the day lily and hollyhock.

I have to admit that I am much more interested in actually cooking with flowers, extracting their essence, as it were, and in some cases their colour. Without going to the lengths of distillation and decoction, it is possible to borrow at least one technique from the perfumer's art, that of *enfleurage*, and simplify it to produce flavoured butters. All you do is wrap a piece of fresh, unsalted butter in muslin, bury it in a bowl of flower petals, cover and leave it in a cool place for about 12 hours. Then unwrap the butter, which is delicious on toast or teatime scones. Other teatime delicacies are flower jams or jellies made by adding washed flower petals, shredded if you like, to the liquid and sugar. Apples and rosehips, for example, make the perfect base for rose jelly. Elderflowers combine deliciously with gooseberries in fools and jams. They can also be fried in batter, and, of course, make an excellent 'Champagne'.

Flavoured sugars for ice-creams, sorbets, custards and junkets can be made by grinding one part clean, dry petals to two to four times their volume of sugar. The proportion depends on the strength of the flower's scent. Lavender will take plenty of sugar, violets and mimosa will take less.

Fresh flower petals can be infused in a heavy sugar syrup to make a wonderful flavouring for cakes, sorbets and soft drinks, among other things. The very best flowers to use are the intensely fragrant ones: lavender, old-fashioned scented roses, clove carnations or pinks, scented white jasmine (the kind used to make jasmine tea) and violets. Primroses, elderflowers and mimosa will also flavour but to a lesser extent. I talk about flavour, but what happens is that the butter or ice-cream or junket somehow tastes exactly as the flower smells.

I use flowers mostly in sweets and puddings, but there are two I use frequently in savoury dishes: pot marigolds and nasturtiums. They are particularly good finely chopped, with one or two of their leaves, and added to cream cheese, omelettes, soufflés or vegetable terrines. Shredded into a risotto or a hot dish of pasta and olive oil they make a delicious, unusual and eye-catching dish.

Some of the most fragrant flowers, such as rose and lavender, can be used to flavour white wine vinegars.

Edible Flowers

1 HOLLYHOCK
2 ROSE
3 ROSE
4 BERGAMOT
5 CHINA ROSES
6 PANSIES
7 CLARY SAGE
8 LAVENDER
9 HOLLYHOCK
10 VIOLAS
11 MARIGOLDS
12 WILD MALLOW
13 MARJORAM
14 HEARTSEASE
15 MINT
16 BORAGE
17 OREGANO
18 TANSY
19 MALLOW
20 FENNEL
21 MEADOWSWEET
22 NASTURTIUMS

SPICES

Spices are the dried, intensely aromatic parts of certain plants – usually the seeds, pods, berries, roots, stems, buds, bark or even sap. Their insignificant size and appearance belie the importance of spices throughout the ages. Originating often in faraway places, they have been the subject of dangerous voyages of exploration, long-drawn-out wars and centuries of empire-building. Considering how difficult they were to obtain it is hardly surprising that they were very precious, and locked away in my lady's closet until relatively recent times when the coming of the steam ship meant that import costs went down. Even today saffron is very, very expensive because its production is small, labour-intensive and dependent to a large degree on climate and season. Fortunately other spices are readily available and inexpensive enough for us to experiment with their warm fragrant scents and flavours in our cooking.

They are sold whole or ground, in small or large quantities. How you buy them will depend on how much you use them in your cooking. With black pepper, for example, which I like to grind myself, I buy the largest pack I can afford. I use a lot of pepper and although, as with all spices, the volatile essential oils fade, those in peppercorns do seem to retain a good deal of their pungency.

Buy those that are used less frequently in small quantities and whole if possible, to be ground when required. Use a pestle and mortar or even a small electric coffee grinder kept only for grinding spices. Ground spices may be a quick labour-saving alternative, but some may quickly lose their flavour, scent and colour so it is preferable not to keep them for more than six months. Keep all spices, whole or ground, in airtight glass jars, preferably with tinted glass, or in clear jars in a closed cupboard, away from heat and light.

AJOWAN *ajwain, bishop's weed, omum*

Used mainly in Indian cooking, greenish-brown ajowan seeds are a little larger than celery seeds, and have a strong aroma of a rather coarse thyme. If a recipe calls for ajowan, you could certainly substitute thyme leaves, pounded with the rest of the ingredients, for a similar effect.

ALLSPICE *Jamaica pepper*

Not to be confused with 'mixed spice', allspice is a member of the 'pimento' or pepper family. It is a berry about the size of a small pea, round, with a rough brown coat. Its name very probably comes from the fact that when it is ground it tastes like a mixture of clove, cinnamon, nutmeg and, perhaps, ginger and pepper. It is one of the most pleasing and versatile additions to any spice rack. I use a few berries in my pepper grinder, along with black peppercorns.

Allspice goes with sweet or savoury ingredients. It adds a warm subtle spiciness to cakes, biscuits and pies. Grind it coarsely and use in a winy garlicky marinade for game, pork or beef; or add it to a casserole. A delicately spiced vinegar can be prepared with a few allspice berries and it is one of the usual components in pickling spices used for vegetables, such as onions and cabbage, and for fish and meats – herring and spiced beef, for example.

Whole Spices

1 CASSIA BARK	22 BLACK MUSTARD SEED
2 DILL SEED	
3 MUSTARD SEED	23 ANISEED
4 FENNEL SEED	24 LIQUORICE STICKS
5 CORIANDER SEED	25 SAFFRON
6 GALANGAL ROOT	26 CLOVES
7 CUMIN SEED	27 NIGELLA SEED
8 GREEN CARDAMOM PODS	28 FENUGREEK SEED
	29 NUTMEG AND NUTMEG WITH MACE 'CAGE' OR ARIL
9 HORSERADISH FLAKES	
10 AJOWAN SEED	30 STAR ANISE
11 TURMERIC ROOT	31 LEMON GRASS (DRIED)
12 GRATED HORSERADISH	32 LEMON GRASS (FRESH)
13 ANNATTO SEED	33 CINNAMON STICKS
14 CARAWAY SEED	34 VANILLA PODS
15 FENNEL POLLEN	35 GINGER ROOT (FRESH)
16 BLACK CARDAMOM PODS	36 GINGER ROOT (DRIED)
17 SLICED LIQUORICE ROOT	37 PRESSED TAMARIND
18 CELERY SEED	38 TAMARIND SEEDS
19 ALLSPICE BERRIES	39 TAMARIND PODS
20 JUNIPER BERRIES	
21 MACE BLADES	

3

4

5

6

8

9

10

11

16

12

13

14

15

19

20

21

22

23

26

27

28

29

30

31

32

36

37

38

39

ANISE *aniseed*

I remember aniseed balls from my childhood – marble-sized, round, hard sweets which changed colour as you sucked them and which contained a real aniseed when you got through to the centre. As I sipped my *pastis* on a café terrace in Paris years later, the two taste sensations locked together. It is a flavour I love, but must take care not to overdo; not everyone is as fond of it as I am.

A Mediterranean plant, it is much used in the cooking of the region (as well as in its drinking, in *pastis*, *ouzo* and *anisette*). It turns up in sweet and savoury dishes alike, in pastries and breads, with fish and with meat. Occasionally I use anise in place of fennel seeds, when making breads and pastries for example, or for adding to a fish dish. If you don't have any anise, but happen to have some *pastis*, a splash of that will do the trick. See also HERBS, page 100.

ANISE PEPPER *farchiew, Sichuan pepper*

Very hot and peppery, but in spite of the name this is not actually a pepper, but the dried red berries and husks of a type of ash tree. It is an ingredient of Chinese five-spice powder and is particularly associated with the fiery cuisines of the Sichuan and Hunan provinces of China, and is often sold as Sichuan pepper. It is very pungent in aroma with some of the numbing effect of cloves rather than the hotness of black pepper. It should be roasted and ground before use. *Sansho* is a Japanese spice powder produced from the dried leaves of the same plant, used as a seasoning for cooked food.

ANNATTO *achiote*

This small reddish-brown seed is the fruit of a tropical South American tree, contained in a prickly seed pod, something like a large beech nut. It is widely used in South American cooking and can be bought in powdered or in seed form and is used for colouring and to a lesser degree for flavour. The seed can be gently heated in oil or, more usually, lard which takes on a rich orange colour. This is then cooled and stored and used for cooking. Although edible, it has little flavour, and its culinary value is limited to its colouring properties. A commercially produced 'natural' colouring called 'annatto' is used to tint, among other things, cheese such as Leicester and Cheshire, and fish such as smoked mackerel fillets and kippers. The seed is widely used in South American cooking.

ASAFOETIDA *giant fennel, heeng, hing, stinking gum*

Once you smell this devil's dung, as it is known colloquially, you are unlikely to forget it. But if you like Indian or Middle Eastern food you will need to come to terms with its odour, which disappears in the cooking process. Native to Iran and Afghanistan, asafoetida comes from a 10ft (3m) high plant – a type of fennel – the milky sap of which solidifies into this pale rust-brown resin which darkens with age. This is the spice that, despite its fearful stink, in minute quantities does a great deal for exotic vegetable, fish and meat stews, but can also be used in more homely dishes such as mashed potato.

Departing from my usual advice on spices, buy this one in its powdered form rather than in solid chunks, which you will have to chip with a hammer before you can even grind it down. Spare yourself the experience of preparing it and keep it in an airtight tin.

CARAWAY SEED

A member of the extensive umbellifer family, there are hints of anise, fennel and chervil in the flavour of this small oval greenish-brown seed. It is widely used in German and Austrian cooking, both in sweet and savoury dishes: cakes, biscuits, goulashes, soups, fresh cabbage and sauerkraut, pork and sausages; and even to flavour cheeses and liqueurs. I have to say it is my least favourite spice and one I can detect immediately, however light the hand that introduced it into the dish.

In British cookery it is used most often in rather plain worthy seed cakes.

CARDAMOM *elaichi, ilaaichee, lachee*

Apart from its traditional place in Indian, Arab and North African cookery, where it is used to delicious effect in curries and Moroccan stews, cardamom is also used in northern Europe, especially in Scandinavia and Germany, where it is an occasional ingredient in cakes and pastries as well as in pickling brines. It adds fragrant spicy undertones to all these dishes.

It is essential to buy cardamom whole, still in its pod, which is about ¼in (5mm) long, sometimes rounded but sometimes slightly faceted, blunt at one end, pointed at the other. The pod will be pale green, creamy beige or dark brown and hairy. The first two have the most flavour, the dark brown pods are rather larger and coarser. The slightly sticky seeds inside are massed together in small brown chunks. If you rub them between your fingers they will separate. You can use them like that, or grind them to a fine powder, as and when you need it; once ground it quickly loses its flavour.

Although one of the most expensive spices, cardamom amply repays experimenting with in your cooking. Try it instead of vanilla as a flavouring for ice-cream. Make a cardamom-flavoured custard to serve with fruit poached in wine. Grind it into Christmas cakes and puddings. Use it in custard tarts in place of nutmeg. Try it in pumpkin pie. Use it in slow-cooking meat stews or sprinkle on lamb just before grilling or frying it. Use it in pâtés or terrines. Cook it with some of the duller vegetables; you will not believe how it can improve, say, a purée of carrot and turnip, or a dish of cabbage. I would be quite happy, too, to replace caraway in seed cakes with cardamom seeds.

Cardamom is also used in the Middle East to flavour tiny cups of strong dark coffee, and in India to flavour strong, sweet, milky tea. This is a deliciously refreshing drink to make at home, using loose Ceylon tea (not bags) and adding a good pinch of cardamom seeds to the pot. Try them, too, in mulled wine or spiced ale.

CASSIA

This is not unlike cinnamon. In fact, it is often called Chinese cinnamon, being one of the ingredients of Chinese five-spice powder. However it has a slightly less fine and less aromatic flavour than cinnamon and is best kept for savoury dishes. Like cinnamon it is the dried bark of an evergreen tree. It is sold in powdered form or in pieces.

CELERY SEED

The tiny dried seed heads from the celery plant are a useful way of adding the flavour of celery to soups, sauces and vegetable dishes, if you do not have fresh celery available. If you like celery salt you can make your own by grinding salt and celery seed in the proportions you prefer. It is an intensely savoury spice, and needs to be used carefully if the dish is not to be overpowered.

CHINESE FIVE-SPICE POWDER

This compound of anise pepper, cassia, fennel seed, star anise and cloves, all ground to a fine powder, has a powerful anise aroma and flavour, bordering on liquorice. It is an essential ingredient in much Oriental cooking – especially in any dish using pork or chicken, and in stir-frys. Used in small quantity it is almost indefinable, but you miss it if it's not present.

CINNAMON *daal cheenee, taj bhooko*

The dried rolled bark of a tropical evergreen tree native to Sri Lanka, southern India and the West Indies, cinnamon is sold either in small pale brown 'sticks', or in powdered form. In Singapore I bought it once in its more natural state. In one of the tiny spice shops along Beach Road they were selling it in 2ft (60cm) lengths. The stick form is what you need for spicy meat or vegetable casseroles, but the sticks are quite difficult to grind, so the powdered form (buy in small quantities as it can lose its flavour) is useful for cakes, pies and puddings.

Apart from using it to give a lovely flavour to cakes and buns, infuse it in a syrup for poaching fruit, or add it to a cinnamon custard, or better still cinnamon ice-cream. It is particularly good with apples and with chocolate. I like to add it to a chocolate cake mixture. It is also often used in special coffees, such as the *café brûlot* of New Orleans, a spiced black coffee flamed with Curaçao and Cognac.

CLOVE *lawaang, long*

Native to the islands of South-East Asia, and one of the most familiar of all spices, cloves are used in many cuisines, in both sweet and savoury dishes. We are perhaps most familiar with seeing these dried flower buds of the evergreen clove tree spiked into apples, or marching all over an impressive-looking ham. The French use cloves to flavour *blanquette de veau*, the classic creamy veal stew, by sticking cloves into an onion cooked with the meat. This method can be used to flavour other types of stews and casseroles, and even bread sauce, provided you do not overdo it. Try adding a single clove to a *bouquet garni*. It marries wonderfully well with apples – apple sauce and apple pie – and is also used with cinnamon in hot spiced wines and punches.

Cloves contain a very powerful and aromatic essential oil (eugenol). Oil of cloves is used in dental preparations and as an analgesic against toothache, so it's not the sort of flavour one wants to be too aware of.

Ground cloves are probably more useful than whole for baking, but it is still preferable, if possible, to grind them yourself – the easiest part to grind is the central bud if it hasn't fallen out of the clove. Cloves are a common ingredient of pickling solutions, and are also found in sweet and sour cucumbers or plums.

CORIANDER *dhania*

The small, round, ridged brown seed of the coriander plant is sold whole or powdered. It has a warm, savoury flavour which I find indispensable when making spicy meat or vegetable stews in the Moroccan style. Coriander is also an important ingredient in Indian and South-East Asian cooking, and in those spicy dishes in the classic French repertoire labelled *à la grecque* – cooked with selected herbs and spices, and served very cold. It is not an overwhelming spice and deserves to be much more widely used. For instance, you can flavour a *court bouillon* with it when cooking fish, or grind a little into a butter sauce to serve with grilled or poached fish. It is a fine pickling spice, too, imparting a very good flavour to homemade pickled and spiced fruits. See also HERBS, page 100.

CUMIN *jeera, zeera*

This is the small, ridged, parchment-coloured seed of a small annual herb, and has a distinctive, mildly hot, sweetish flavour and aroma. I once published a recipe for black bean soup and a reader enquired if I really meant to put in a tablespoon of ground cumin rather than a pinch. He had enjoyed black bean soup whenever he'd had it in the United States, but had never been able to reproduce the rich spicy flavour. Cumin is the answer. I use the seed in vegetable stews, couscous and other North African dishes. But it is excellent, too, in ground form. Use just a pinch with grilled duck breasts, for example, or to flavour a mayonnaise to serve with shellfish. It is an exciting, versatile spice and one I wouldn't be without.

DILL SEED

Dried dill seeds taste similar to caraway seeds, but milder; they keep their flavour very well and are excellent to use in fish dishes during the winter when fresh dill is unavailable. These small, oval, pale brown seeds with a ridged surface can be used just as successfully in the delicious *gravad lax*, the Scandinavian cured salmon dish. Try preparing other fish such as herring and mackerel in the same way. Dill seed is also very good with potato dishes, hot and cold, and root vegetables, and is the traditional flavour for pickled cucumbers. Try scattering a tablespoon of dill seed on to a coleslaw salad – delicious. See also HERBS, page 100.

FENNEL SEED

These come from both kinds of fennel: the feathery annual herb, sweet fennel, and the bulbous and perennial Florence fennel, eaten as a vegetable. The former is the one to grow yourself. Just before you harvest fresh fennel seeds ready for the winter, the flower heads are covered with a mass of yellow pollen. In Tuscany fennel pollen is avidly collected from the wild to sprinkle on grilled and roast meats or to impart a subtle flavour to soups and stews.

Fennel seeds are very sweet and anise-liquorice flavoured. In a number of Mediterranean countries the seeds are sprinkled on top of bread dough before cooking and this makes delicious breakfast rolls. The seeds can also be used instead of anise seeds, for example, in the richly flavoured Mediterranean fish soups and stews such as *bourride* and *bouillabaisse*. In

113

Florence, from where we get the bulbous vegetable, fennel seeds are used in one of the salamis called *finocchiona* in much the same way that black peppercorns are used in others. Use them to flavour oily grilled fish, such as sardines, or pork. See also VEGETABLES, page 9, and HERBS, page 100.

FENUGREEK SEED *methi*

After an unfortunate experiment in my kitchen many years ago when I overdid the fenugreek, I am now more inclined to use these small, tan-coloured, pebbly, rather pungent seeds to sprout and eat in salads instead of in cooking. They can also be used in pickles and chutneys. Native to India and south-eastern Europe (the name means 'Greek hay'), it is an especially important ingredient in Indian and Sri Lankan cooking, both on its own and, more often, as part of a compound of spices which make up curry powder and give it its characteristic smell. The seeds must be lightly roasted before grinding. See also SPROUTING BEANS, PEAS AND SEEDS, page 99, and HERBS, page 100.

GALANGAL

This rhizome of the same family as ginger, which looks rather like the horny foot of some large and exotic bird, does have a mildly peppery ginger flavour. There are two varieties, greater (*laos*) and lesser (*kenchur*), the lesser galangal having the more intensely spicy flavour. It is one of the most important ingredients in the curries of South-East Asia, particularly Indonesia, Malaysia and Singapore. It can be found as a fresh root, a dried root or ground. Prepare the fresh root as you would ginger: peel it thinly, slice or chop it finely. Use it up within a week.

GARAM MASALA *gorum moshla*

Like Chinese five-spice powder, *garam masala* is not a spice but an intensely aromatic mixture of ground spices used in the making of some Indian dishes (the name means 'hot spice mixture'). It is available commercially, ready mixed but it is, of course, possible to grind and mix your own *garam masala*, indeed several of them: one for poultry, one for fish, one for

vegetables, changing the proportion of spices to suit the type of dish. As a basic guide, a typical all-purpose *garam masala* will probably contain cumin, coriander, cardamom and black pepper. For fish dishes you might try a mixture of ginger, turmeric, cardamom, cumin and coriander. This would also go extremely well with vegetables and white meat dishes. Chilli, black pepper, cloves, cardamom, cumin and nigella seeds would be a suitable mixture for red meats. To prepare a *garam masala*, dry-roast the whole spices over a low heat in a heavy pan, cool them and grind to a powder. Store it in an airtight container and use up within a month or so. Unlike curry powder, *garam masala* is always added towards the end of the cooking time, and can be sprinkled on to the finished dish as a seasoning.

GINGER *adar, adrak*

Ginger was known to Western cooks earlier than almost any other spice. It was especially popular in medieval times as an ingredient of ginger-bread – then an exotic treat, and has been used in British cooking for hundreds of years, a tradition that has survived in cakes and biscuits such as parkin and ginger snaps. Fortunately root ginger is now widely available, and even for baking you can grate the fresh root and use it instead of ground ginger. It is an essential ingredient in all manner of Chinese dishes (especially stir-frys), and in Indian and Arab dishes.

Its flavour is hot and spicy but at the same time sharp and refreshing. I use it in rabbit or chicken casseroles, with shellfish dishes, with cooked cabbage dishes, and in plum or green-gage crumble. When buying a fresh root look for the smoothest and plumpest. Pare off the skin very thinly with a potato peeler and chop or grate finely. The unpeeled root will keep for up to six weeks tightly covered with foodwrap in the refrigerator. Ginger is available as a sweetmeat, preserved in syrup or candied.

HORSERADISH

Dried horseradish root is a good substitute for the fresh article. It is used to flavour sauces for such things as roast beef, smoked fish, chicken and eggs. See also VEGETABLES, page 9.

JUNIPER

As well as being the main flavouring for gin, these small purply-black berries – the fruit of a European evergreen bush – are very useful in marinades and casseroles. I tend to use them more in savoury dishes than sweet, but see no reason why their spicy, pine-scented resiny aroma and flavour should not enhance some of the rich mixtures used for fruit cakes and Christmas puddings, especially if you then sprinkled on a few spoonfuls of gin before wrapping up the cake for storage. Juniper has a particular affinity with coarse game pâtés. Much used in German and northern European cooking, juniper is excellent with rich, robust dishes, anything with cured pork or sausages, or hams, or furred game such as venison and wild boar. It is a flavouring of which I am very fond, particularly in winter dishes. Crush the berries with the back of a spoon, or with a pestle and mortar, before using.

LEMON GRASS *takrai*

A most distinctive ingredient in many dishes of South-East Asia, particularly Thailand and Vietnam, fresh, dried and powdered lemon grass is increasingly available in the West. The bulbous base and first 4–5in (10–12cm) of the stem of this lemon-scented broad-leaved grass is the part used in the kitchen. The root can be crushed or sliced; the stems are used whole and removed before serving. Dried lemon grass should be soaked for a couple of hours before use. Its main flavouring constituent is the same

Ground Spices

1 CUMIN	12 POWDERED MUSTARD
2 YELLOW MUSTARD	13 FENNEL
3 CHINESE FIVE-SPICE POWDER	14 MACE
	15 MIXED SPICE
4 TURMERIC	16 CLOVES
5 SAFFRON	17 HORSERADISH
6 CINNAMON	18 SUMAC
7 NUTMEG	19 CORIANDER
8 BLACK MUSTARD	20 ANNATTO
9 STAR ANISE	21 ALLSPICE
10 FENUGREEK	22 LEMON GRASS
11 GINGER	23 GARAM MASALA

as that found in lemon zest, so it is possible to substitute lemon for lemon grass. As you would expect it is excellent with fish and light meat dishes, and also in sweet dishes. I infuse it in the milk for custards and milk puddings and also use it to flavour a delicious sweet soufflé.

LIQUORICE

Liquorice is a native shrub of temperate and Mediterranean regions. Its strong aniseed flavour – extracted from the roots – has long been used in the making of sweets and drinks, but it has few other notable culinary uses. It is available as a dried root or powder or as sticks of concentrated black extract.

MACE *tavitri*

Mace is actually part of the nutmeg plant. It is the reddish-orange 'aril' covering the ripe seed – the nutmeg – and not surprisingly it has a similar, though more delicate, flavour. It is usually sold separately in fragments or 'blades', or ground into a powder, but one year an enterprising herbalist had the brilliant idea of packaging individual nutmegs still surrounded by their brittle lacy covering of mace. It made a perfect small Christmas present. I am still using up those I was given.

Mace is particularly useful for flavouring pale and delicate dishes such as clear soups or sauces, also jellies, from which it can then be removed whereas a sanding of the darker coloured nutmeg might spoil the appearance of a dish. It is traditional in British potted meats and fish, as well as in milk puddings, in French *boudins blancs* (white sausages) and in Italian cheese sauces.

MUSTARD SEED

This comes from one of three plants, black mustard, brown mustard or white mustard, the first two having more flavour than the last. Apart from being the main ingredient of mustard, mustard seed is also used as a pickling spice and an ingredient in some Indian dishes, and the seed can be sprouted and used at the two-leaf stage as one half of mustard-and-cress. See also MUSTARD, page 119.

NIGELLA *kalonji*

This tiny black seed comes from the flower of which the familiar 'love-in-the-mist' is one variety. It is a rather mild-flavoured spice, slightly peppery, slightly 'spicy' in a vague sort of way. It is used in Indian and Middle Eastern cooking. Both the Indian name, *kalonji* and the German name *Schwarzkümmel* mean black cumin, but nigella is not the same thing as black cumin, nor is it the same as onion seed which it closely resembles.

NUTMEG *jaiphal*

This is the ripe brown seed of the nutmeg plant, a large evergreen tree native to the tropics, especially Indonesia and the Philippines. It has a warm, sweet, nutty flavour. One of the most delicious uses of nutmeg I have ever come across is in some of the exquisite stuffed pastas of northern Italy. Sometimes it is mixed with the filling, sometimes it is sprinkled on the pasta after it has been tossed in melted butter. It is a perfect match, particularly for those stuffed with pumpkin or spinach.

Nutmeg is also an important ingredient in *béchamel* or cream sauces and in pumpkin pie fillings and indeed in many cakes, pies and puddings. Curd cheese tarts and rice pudding positively demand it. Try it in savoury dishes, too, with meat, poultry and vegetables. It is also the perfect partner for cooked cheese dishes, from fondue to Welsh rarebit. Grate it at the last minute because the essential oils are volatile in the extreme, and the flavour is quickly lost.

PEPPER

Two quite distinct spices come under this heading: cayenne, paprika and chilli powder (or chilli pepper) made from the red peppers of the *Capsicum* family, and peppercorns of various colours which are the fruit of the vine pepper (*Piper nigrum*).

Cayenne This comes from a hot red chilli pepper, and is probably named after the part of tropical South America where it originated. It is very finely ground from the fruit of one of the most pungent varieties of chilli, *Capsicum frutescens*. Not only has the dried flesh been

ground but also the seeds, which are the hottest part of the plant. It should be used sparingly – in traditional British cooking a sprinkling of cayenne added a certain piquancy to dishes such as kedgeree and devilled kidneys.

Chilli powder (*choora mirch, goora lanka*) Some maintain chilli powder is simply dried hot chillies ground to a powder, used for instance in *chilli con carne*, the spicy hot meat dish, originally from Mexico but now part of the common culinary repertoire. Others say it is a compound spice mixture, containing chilli as one of its constituents but also herbs and spices such as oregano and cumin, and even cocoa powder. A similar compound is used for Mexican dishes such as *mole poblano* (turkey with a spicy chocolate sauce). To flavour meat, poultry, egg and fish dishes you can make your own compound or grind your own chilli powder. Wear rubber gloves when doing this, and take care not to touch your eyes or mouth – some chilli peppers can be very hot. If buying chilli powder, read the label carefully to see exactly what it contains, and whether it is hot or mild.

Paprika This is the ground red powder of the dried ripe *Capsicum annuum*. Mild and hot peppers are used and you need to check the label carefully to see what it is you are buying, but it is always much milder than cayenne or chilli powder. Paprika is important in Hungarian and Austrian cookery where it is used in *goulash* and other meat stews. It is also widely used in Spanish cooking, in sauces, in sausages and in fish dishes. Because of its mild flavour and striking appearance, it is often used as a garnish on pale creamy dishes like egg mayonnaise.

Peppercorns Green peppercorns are the unripe fruit of *Piper nigrum* and have a milder flavour than black or white peppercorns. They are preserved in several ways, either by freeze-drying or dehydrating or potting in brine or vinegar. The latter is not much use, the harsh vinegar blotting out the subtle pepper flavour. Green peppercorns make a good sauce for rich meat dishes, particularly duck and pork, and are excellent pounded and mixed with butter to flavour grilled steaks or lamb.

White peppercorns have been allowed to ripen, then the skin and outer flesh are removed. They are hot but less fragrant than black pepper.

Black peppercorns are green peppercorns

picked undersize and then allowed to dry whole. They are relatively mild and intensely aromatic.

Pepper is one of the most important spices, and is fundamental to most of the world's finest cuisines, including those of the West where it has been well-known and highly treasured since ancient times. It adds a flavour of its own, but more importantly it brings out the flavour of other ingredients in a most striking way. This is perfectly demonstrated by slicing fresh strawberries and grating black pepper over them.

Use black and white peppercorns freshly ground in a peppermill as they quickly lose their aroma. See also *Anise pepper*, and VEGE-TABLES, page 9, (*Chilli* and *Pepper*).

PINK PEPPERCORN

Something of a controversy has surrounded this spice. In France, the United States and Britain it became *the* fashionable ingredient, until it was suddenly rumoured to be dangerous to eat – in large quantities it is mildly toxic. In fact, it is not a pepper but the processed berry of a South American relative of the extremely nasty poison ivy. It seems to have crept back into favour. I like its slightly resinous flavour and use it with fish, poultry, game and pâtés.

RAS EL HANOUT

This is a Moroccan spice mixture used in meat and game dishes as well as with rice and couscous. The spices can be combined according to personal taste and availability. The most refined Moroccan mixture might have as many as a hundred ingredients in it, including those thought to have aphrodisiac qualities. A home-made mixture might include allspice aniseed, cardamom, cayenne, cloves, cumin, galangal, gingers, mace, nutmeg, orris root and peppers and even some dried flowers such as rosebuds.

SAFFRON *kesar, zafraan*

This is the costliest spice in the world. The dark orange and red stigmas of a purple-flowering crocus are used and, to yield 1lb (500g) of saffron, up to a quarter of a million flowers are harvested by hand. The best saffron comes from La Mancha in Spain where the producers have

Pepper

1 CHILLI POWDER
2 PAPRIKA
3 CRUSHED PINK PEPPERCORNS
4 WHITE PEPPERCORNS
5 BLACK PEPPERCORNS
6 CAYENNE
7 PICKLED GREEN PEPPERCORNS
8 GREEN PEPPERCORNS
9 PINK PEPPERCORNS
10 WHOLE RED CHILLIES
11 CRUSHED CHILLIES
12 ANISE PEPPER
13 GROUND WHITE PEPPERCORNS
14 GROUND BLACK PEPPERCORNS

banded together to maintain quality control, in effect to establish a system of controlled appellation, La Mancha Selecta. Saffron also comes from Egypt, Iran, Kashmir, Morocco and India. One of the most wonderful presents I have ever been given was a large packet of saffron filaments carefully chosen for me in the spice market in Marrakesh by an expert. You can also buy it in powdered form.

Saffron's happiest marriage is with rice – in Spanish paellas, Italian risottos, northern Indian pilaus and Iranian rice dishes. It is also used in Mediterranean seafood dishes, notably *bouillabaisse*, the fish stew from Marseille.

Saffron used to grow in England, around Saffron Walden, which gave rise to some traditional English uses, such as saffron buns. I like to experiment with it as I love its strong slightly bitter flavour and pungent sweet scent; but it can be overpowering if you are not used to it. The best way to extract the flavour and brilliant yellow colour is to infuse it in a little boiling water or stock then stir it into the dish.

SEVEN-SPICE PEPPER *shichimi togarashi*

This is a Japanese ground mixture of seven flavourings. Anise pepper, sesame seeds, flax seeds, rape seeds, poppy seeds, dried tangerine or orange peel and ground *nori* seaweed are the most usual ingredients, but they can vary. There should be two hot spices and five aromatic ones. It is used to season cooked food, especially grilled meats and fish, and noodles.

STAR ANISE

An important ingredient in Chinese cooking, this contains the same essential oil as anise but looks quite different. Consisting of the fruits and seed pod of an evergreen tree, it is often used whole so that the pretty star-shaped pod adds a decorative effect to the finished dish. Star anise is used in classic Chinese dishes, such as red-roasted duck and pork, and in its dried form it is an ingredient of Chinese five-spice powder, the other four being cassia, cloves, fennel seed and anise pepper. The overall flavour is almost overwhelmingly anise liquoricy, but with deeper spicy undertones. Because of its glamorous appearance, star anise is finding its way into modern English and American cooking, not to mention the cooking of those French chefs who have worked for a time in the Far East.

SUMAC

This attractive plant is grown in North America and other temperate regions, but it is the dried seeds of the Mediterranean species that are used as a spice and play an important role in Lebanese and Turkish cooking. In Arabic recipes sumac is preferred to lemon.

The distinctive taste is both astringent and fruity – like a mild fruit vinegar – and, indeed, the juice extracted from the seeds is used as a dressing for salads, and as a marinade. In red powder form it can be used to season grilled meats and spicy fish dishes or stews.

TAMARIND *imlee, Indian date, taytool*

This is the pulp that fills the pod and surrounds the seeds of the tropical tamarind tree. It is dark brown and slightly sticky with an acidic taste that is very refreshing. Usually it is sold in a compacted or dried form from which pieces are cut or broken off as required, being soaked in hot water and pressed through a sieve to produce a sour liquid to add to curries and other Indian dishes. Other acids such as vinegar and lemon juice do not make effective substitutes because the tamarind has a very distinctive flavour. It is also an ingredient of chutneys, jams and jellies.

TURMERIC *haldee, haldi*

Fresh turmeric root looks very like ginger, being a smaller rhizome of the same family. Cut it in half and you will see the brilliant orange flesh, which dries to a dull yellow and is ground to produce the familiar yellow powder much used in Indian cooking, and misused in the inexpensive curry powders. Occasionally it is used in place of saffron to obtain a lovely golden yellow. This is a great mistake for it has nothing like the same flavour as saffron, but rather a warm spicy taste and aroma. Imagine that in a paella! But it is, of course, perfectly appropriate in a pilau.

Turmeric is also used commercially in pickles and relishes and, indeed, is an essential ingredient for many homemade pickles, such as pickled cucumbers and piccalilli. I have also used the grated fresh root with fish and in pale dishes that benefit from its bright colouring and very lightly spicy flavour.

VANILLA

Vanilla pods are the dried, cured seed cases of an orchid plant, and usually sold whole – singly or in pairs – in long glass containers like test-tubes. Once you have used real vanilla pods you will find it hard to go back to using a flavoured essence out of a bottle.

There are many ways to extract the flavour from the pod, depending on how you want to use it. The simplest is to keep two or three pods in a large jar of sugar. These will give a distinct vanilla flavour to the sugar and will last for up to a year if you keep the jar topped up. For a more pronounced vanilla effect infuse a pod in scalded milk or cream for a vanilla sauce or custard or for rice or other milk puddings – it is wonderful in tapioca pudding. The pod can then be removed, washed and dried, and used again. The most extravagant method, and you really have to do this to make good vanilla ice-cream (it should be said, there is no better), is first to infuse the pod in the custard, then remove it, split it down its length and, with a knife point, carefully scrape out the sticky black seed mass and put it back into the custard. The seeds will separate and the ice-cream will have the characteristic tiny black specks of real vanilla ice-cream. The pod will still contain enough essence to flavour sugar.

Although it is almost always associated with sweet dishes vanilla is not in itself sweet. I have used it to flavour sauces and stock for shellfish, notably scallops. It does not meet with universal approval; the scent of vanilla is so associated in our taste memory with sweetness that it can come as a shock to some to find it in a savoury dish. I shall persevere.

WASABI

A Japanese condiment, this is the ground root of a type of horseradish, usually only available in powdered form in the West. It is very sharp and fragrant. The powder is mixed to a paste with water, and served with *sashimi*, paper-thin slices of raw fish and shellfish.

MUSTARD

Mustard spice is generally ground then, with other ingredients, mixed into a paste (mustard) and used either in cooking or as an accompaniment – especially to meat.

Black mustard seed – the hottest and most pungent – was for centuries the traditional mustard-making seed. It has now largely been replaced by the shorter, brown mustard seed – a shade lighter in colour and slightly less pungent. White mustard seed is creamy-yellow and has a much cooler, milder flavour. Most condiment mustards are based on brown or white seeds or a blend of both.

There are many excellent varieties of mustard available. Apart from coarse-grained types, the trend towards new mustards includes all kinds of flavoured ones featuring ingredients as varied as horseradish, honey, chilli and Champagne.

The uses of mustard are so numerous and various that it is worth keeping several jars in the store cupboard (but not too long as it begins to darken and dry out after a few months, even in a cool airy place).

Purists say that vinaigrette should contain nothing but oil, vinegar, salt and pepper, but most of the mustard used in our house goes into vinaigrettes. I like to use a little Dijon mustard for this. Mustard also brings out other flavours. Try a minute quantity in a spice cake, gingerbread or chocolate cake.

In Italy sweet mustard syrups are used to preserve fruits – *mostarda di Cremona* has large pieces of mixed crystallized fruit suspended in a rich sweet glaze. This is traditionally served with plain boiled meats.

But try it in other ways. Spread a thin layer of Dijon or tarragon mustard over a rack of lamb and then press in some breadcrumbs before roasting it. Mustard is also an essential ingredient of the French dish *lapin à la moutarde* (rabbit casserole where the rabbit is coated in mustard before cooking). Try preparing chicken in the same way.

ENGLISH MUSTARD

Traditional English mustard comes in powder as well as 'made-up' form. It is based on brown (dehusked) and white seeds blended with wheat-flour and a little turmeric for colour. Smooth, pungent and very hot indeed, it is the classic relish for roast beef and ham and also goes well with other meats and mature hard cheese. To mix the powder into a paste, add cold water and let it stand for 15 minutes so that flavour and heat develop fully; for a milder version, use milk instead of water. Mustard made up from powder becomes stale after about four hours.

FRENCH MUSTARD

France is famous for its Dijon, Meaux and Bordeaux mustards. Dijon, possibly the mustard capital of the world, produces the staple 'cooking' mustard for dressings and sauces and ideal partner for all meats. Dijon mustard is made from black (or brown) seeds, blended with salt, spices and white wine or verjuice (from unripe grapes). It has a clean, sharp, medium-hot taste and, because the seeds are dehusked, an unexpectedly pale colour: creamy yellow-grey.

Bordeaux – popularly known as 'French mustard' and dark-brown in colour – is also made from black and brown seeds mixed with sugar, vinegar and herbs, especially tarragon. Its mild, aromatic flavour goes well with poultry and cold meats. Meaux mustard is prepared from mixed mustard seeds. It has a grainy texture and a medium-hot fruity spicy taste that suits pork pies, bacon and sausages.

GERMAN AND AMERICAN MUSTARDS

German mustard – complementing frankfurters and all the other sausages – is typically dark with a sweet-sour pungency and medium heat, although hotter strengths are produced. Regional variations include a pale, mild sweetish mustard in Bavaria – indispensable with Munich's white sausage, *Weisswurst*. American mustard – based on white seeds with sugar, vinegar and turmeric – is yellow, mild and sweet and has a soft, almost liquid consistency.

Mustards

1 MEAUX MUSTARD
2 BLACK MUSTARD
3 RED WINE MUSTARD
4 DIJON MUSTARD
5 AMERICAN MUSTARD
6 GERMAN MUSTARD
7 EXTRA-STRONG GERMAN MUSTARD
8 MILD BAVARIAN MUSTARD
9 FRENCH MUSTARD
10 HERBED DIJON MUSTARD
11 CHILLI MUSTARD
12 ENGLISH MUSTARD

Salt

Salt is an essential ingredient in the kitchen. Indeed it is vital to life as it maintains the body's fluid balance and the activity of muscles and nerves. In cooking, only you know how much salt is appropriate for you, since some of us like salt more than others. That is why recipes say 'season to taste'. Taste and adjust the seasoning in the last few minutes of cooking. If you add salt too liberally in the early stages, it is usually impossible to rectify your mistake.

Salt is used in processing foods as varied in taste as meat products, some canned fish and vegetables, butters, cheeses and breads, many of which do not as end products taste salty. In this way our bodies and our palates become accustomed to taking in and tasting more salt than we may realize. To counterbalance this I use far less salt in my cooking than I used to. It is surprising how quickly one begins to appreciate the true taste of ingredients.

Apart from its use in cooking as a flavour enhancer, salt is one of the most important agents for preserving food. Food that is preserved in salt, whether ham, bacon, or fish, undergoes chemical changes which cure the flesh, usually by drawing out the moisture content. Sometimes the preparation involves dry salting, sometimes brining in which a solution of salt and water is used. Salt cod, smoked salmon and Parma ham are examples of salt-cured foods.

The pickling process, whether on a commercial scale or in the domestic kitchen, relies heavily on salt. Most foods which are pickled have a certain moisture content. This must be reduced otherwise the vinegar becomes diluted and will not preserve the food. It is therefore salted before the vinegar is added.

ROCK SALT

In prehistoric times there were huge saline underground lakes which eventually dried out leaving great seams of impacted salt – rock salt. This is boiled down and crystallized to varying degrees of fineness.

Crystal rock salt can be used both in cooking and on the table. Crush the crystals in a salt mill.

Kitchen salt or **cooking salt** is refined rock salt and is suitable for all culinary purposes.

Low sodium salt For those who are on a low-sodium regime, a salt which has a lower level of sodium chloride (sometimes with potassium to replace it) is available. It looks like table salt and can be used in the same way.

Table salt is finely ground and refined rock salt with the addition of the chemical magnesium carbonate to make it free running. Without this salt becomes damp and compacted.

SEA SALT

There are some ancient salt pans on many Mediterranean islands where you can gather large sparkling white crystals of pure sea salt. And, if you stand there long enough, you can watch it being made by nature. As the waves wash over the rocks and recede, some water is left behind in the pools. The sun evaporates the liquid, and the salt emerges as crystals.

Sea salt is much more widely available than it used to be, and good sea salt – such as that from Maldon in Essex – is well worth the extra expense. It has a real 'salty' taste which means you use less of it. When buying sea salt you have a choice of whole crystals or fine or coarsely ground crystals. Maldon salt tends to be in small flakes, which I like to sprinkle directly on to food, particularly in salads where I enjoy its crunch. Or it can be ground in a special grinder. Sea salt can be used in cooking and in preserving or kept for table use only. Coarse sea salt sprinkled on bread rolls before baking them gives an agreeable crunchy texture to the crust.

SPICED AND HERBED SALTS

These are compounds of salt and other flavourings. Some contain celery seeds, some garlic. Others containing a mixture of spices are intended for use when cooking meat or fish. I make seasoning salts at home, blending herbs and spices with the salt in a pestle and mortar.

Salt

1 KITCHEN SALT	5 SEA SALT
2 CELERY SALT	6 MALDON SALT
3 LOW SODIUM SALT	7 TABLE SALT
4 ROCK SALT	

OILS

In culinary terms oils are edible fatty substances in liquid form derived from a number of plant sources: from seeds such as pumpkin, cottonseed, rapeseed, safflower and sunflower; from cereals such as corn; from fruit such as the olive; and from nuts such as walnut, hazelnut, almond and coconut. All oils are an extremely concentrated form of energy. One tablespoon (15ml) contains 125 kilocalories. Important fatty acids are also present. Fatty acids can be one of three kinds: saturated, mono-unsaturated and poly-unsaturated. Certain oils – safflower, sunflower, corn, grapeseed and soya – are low in saturated fats and high in polyunsaturates and are therefore healthier. Some – palm oil and coconut oil – are very high in saturated fats (see COOKING FATS, page 238, for these oils), and should not be used in high quantities. Oils are also slow to digest and, when combined with other foods, delay their digestion too.

Oils can be extracted either by simple mechanical means (crushing or pressing) or by further processing, usually the application of heat.

Virgin oils are those obtained from a cold pressing, usually the first pressing. These oils are sold unrefined, have the most characteristic flavour and are the most expensive. After the first pressing more oil is released by the application of heat, up to a third and fourth pressing in the case of olive oil. These subsequent pressings extract substances that impart a harsh flavour to the oil, and refining is necessary to deodorize, clean and filter them. These will then be sold as 'pure' or 'refined' oils. Such oils are suitable for general cooking purposes but add no distinctive or characteristic flavour to the dish.

For flavour use extra virgin olive oil, cold-pressed sesame oil, and cold-pressed nut oils. Or use the essential oils of citrus fruit, such as lemons, oranges and grapefruits.

Although certain oils are suitable for certain uses, it is also a matter of taste. I find olive oil too strong for mayonnaise, but others would use nothing else. I like pumpkin seed oil in a salad dressing but some might find it too thick, dark and strong. With certain delicate and expensive oils, such as the nut oils, it

makes no sense to subject them to the kind of heat used in frying as it will destroy their flavour and scent. Far better to use a blander oil such as groundnut or sunflower.

When storing oils do not keep them much beyond the sell-by date. They will gradually lose their flavour and become rancid. Protect them from the harmful effects of heat and light by storing them in a cool dark place. From this it follows that oil keeps best in a can. But do not keep in the refrigerator – some oils, such as olive and walnut, solidify if they get too cold.

Although oils for cooking are stable at high temperatures, not enough is known about the chemical reactions which take place when oil is re-used and thus subject to repeated heating and cooking. For this reason I do not recommend that you use oil more than two or three times. Nor should it be re-used for cooking different types of food. For example, keep the same oil for re-using with fish, but do not use it for meat or vegetables as it may very well transfer off-flavours.

As well as the natural oils, it is also possible to buy flavoured oils. But it is also very easy to make these oils yourself by infusing herbs or spices in a jar of a good-quality neutral oil such as sunflower or groundnut, or a more fully flavoured oil such as olive. Keep for a few weeks to let the flavour develop.

ALMOND OIL

This is a pale clean oil with a fairly neutral flavour and, it has to be said, not much taste of almonds. It is mainly used in baking and confectionery. I find it useful for oiling baking tins or soufflé dishes when making very delicately flavoured sponges or soufflés, or for oiling a marble slab on the rare occasions when I make sweets. Used alone it is not enough to give an almond flavour to cakes and biscuits. For that you need to use almond essence, or, of course, almonds themselves. See also NUTS, page 89.

AVOCADO OIL

Extracted from the inedible stone of the avocado, this is a very neutral oil. It is almost colourless and aromaless. It has no flavour of the

rich buttery avocado, although it does feel and taste like a very oily oil. To my taste it has a chemical flavour. Although it is used for culinary and cosmetic purposes, I find little to recommend it. See also VEGETABLES, page 9.

CORN OIL *maize oil*

This is one of the most economical and widely used of all edible oils. It is a deepish, golden-yellow, with quite a strong flavour. It is technically suitable for all culinary uses including baking, but is not pleasant in salad dressings and mayonnaise, and for frying I prefer one that is lighter in texture, such as groundnut oil or sunflower oil.

COTTONSEED OIL

Mostly used in cotton-growing areas as it is a by-product of this process, cottonseed oil is also used as a packing oil in commercial food production. It is said to impart a characteristic flavour to Egyptian dishes. Cottonseed oil is sometimes an ingredient in those highly refined oils labelled 'cooking oil' or 'vegetable oil'.

FRUIT OIL

These are rather different from the rest of the oils in this section in that they are used for flavouring and not for emulsifying (as in mayonnaise), lubricating (as in salad dressings) or cooking (as in deep-frying). They are the essential oils stored in the skin of citrus fruits. Grapefruit, lemon and sweet orange oil are quite remarkable for their aroma and concentration. Just a drop is needed to permeate a dish with the scent and flavour of the fruit. I sometimes use them with a dash of spirit such as gin or vodka to flavour a sauce for fish or chicken. They are delicious stirred into custards or creams for cake filling. They are less successful when cooked, in cake batters, for example, because they are so volatile they simply disappear.

GRAPESEED OIL *grape-pip oil*

A pale, delicate, quite neutral but pleasant tasting oil, extracted from grape pips, is quite widely available. It is excellent for frying and for general culinary use, and is the oil I normally use for making mayonnaise. If you want to use some of the more unusual and intensely flavoured oils such as hazelnut or sesame but find them too strong, then grapeseed oil is excellent for diluting them; mix the two until you have the combination you want.

GROUNDNUT OIL *arachide oil, arachis oil, peanut oil*

When I tasted this oil for the first time, when I lived in Nigeria, I was surprised and delighted to discover that it tastes nothing like peanut butter. Rather it is a very fine oil for all culinary uses: frying, baking, salad dressings and mayonnaise. It is used a great deal in French and Chinese kitchens, which is certainly a reliable indication of its quality.

HAZELNUT OIL

An expensive but delicious oil, this is one of the many nut oils which are now becoming available outside their area of production. It is too expensive to use on anything but the finest salads, with very little well-aged wine vinegar or lemon juice added, and maybe a few crushed hazelnuts. It is a richly flavoured, nutty brown oil which marries beautifully with fish in, for example, a marinade for a raw fish salad that is then served with the marinade. I have also, extravagantly, used it as the shortening when baking with ground hazelnuts. It works very well, but I have the impression that some of the flavour is lost when the oil is heated. However, it has such a powerful flavour to begin with that there is always more than enough deal left. See also NUTS, page 89.

OLIVE OIL

Whole books have been devoted to the subject of olive oil. Many myths are attached to it and many claims are made for its health-giving properties. It is also important nutritionally, as it contains a high proportion of mono-unsaturated fats and vitamin A. And we should not forget, too, that to savour a fine fruity olive oil is one of the great gastronomic experiences.

First, let's look at the labelling of olive oil:

'pure olive oil', 'virgin olive oil' and even 'extra virgin olive oil'. How confusing! It's even more confusing to realize that different olive-oil-producing countries have their own system of grading and labelling rather like wine. There is a move to standardize the labelling so that we have simply 'virgin olive oil' and 'pure olive oil'. In the EEC, however, virgin olive oil is divided into several categories dependent on the level of acidity in the oil, that with the lowest acidity being the most highly prized and the most expensive. 'Extra virgin' olive oil – the top category – has a maximum acidity of 1 per cent, followed by 'virgin' olive oil with a maximum of 2 per cent.

Anything labelled simply 'pure' will undoubtedly be refined olive oil. This is not as nice as it sounds. It will have been cleaned, filtered, deodorized, in other words stripped of its character from a third or fourth pressing using heat as well as mechanical means to extract the oil. This is then flavoured with a percentage of virgin olive oil. 'Light' olive oil is that produced by the last pressing, and has the nutritional qualities of pure olive oil, but with a very mild flavour.

The colour of olive oil varies from the paler yellow of these 'refined' oils to the deep golden oils of Spain and the limpid greens of Tuscany. If possible choose extra virgin olive oil, but be prepared to pay a higher price for it. As with most things you get what you pay for.

Olive oils from single olive groves, produced and bottled on the estate, are as highly prized as fine clarets. Like wine, olive oil varies from year to year; it is dependent on the climate, the soil and the type of olive and it varies from country to country. Spain is the largest producer, followed by Italy, Greece, Tunisia, Turkey, Portugal, Morocco and France. There is much discussion about where the best olive oil comes from. There are those who maintain that there is no finer oil than that produced in the small family-run properties around Lucca in Tuscany. On the other hand the Tuscan olive groves were decimated by frost a few years ago, and considering that olive trees need at least a decade before they are producing well, one does begin to wonder where the olives for much of the current Tuscan olive oil are actually grown. Some say that the oil produced from the olives around Nyons in

Provence is the finest. I like olive oil which comes from Lérida near Barcelona for general purposes, that from Portugal for salad dressings and that from Liguria for fish dishes. Olive oil is far from being a standardized product and that in itself perhaps accounts for much of its reputation. Discovering a 'new' olive oil is still a matter of great excitement for me.

I use a great deal of olive oil, and would be lost without it in my kitchen. I use it for frying food, as a marinade, in salad dressings and even in baking. It can make marvellous shortbread, for example. Except for the really delicately flavoured ones, such as the light Ligurian oil, I find it just too rich and overpowering when combined with the egg yolk in mayonnaise. On the other hand it is delicious as a sauce on its own, stirred into pasta with a little chopped garlic and some black pepper, floated on top of a thick vegetable soup or mixed with hot vegetables instead of melted butter. Use virgin olive oil to replace butter when mashing potatoes and you will realize how indispensable it is. See also VEGETABLES, page 9.

PINESEED OIL *pine nut oil*

Produced in France, this is a light brown oil, with a distinct flavour of pine nuts and excellent flavour. It makes a marvellous oil for dressing salads, dipping artichoke leaves or tossing vegetables in. Above all, it tastes expensive, and it is, which makes it difficult to recommend rather

Oils

1 SAFFLOWER OIL	14 CORN OIL
2 SOYA OIL	15 ALMOND OIL
3 OLIVE OIL WITH BASIL	16 GRAPESEED OIL
4 VEGETABLE OIL	17 EXTRA VIRGIN OLIVE OIL
5 HAZELNUT OIL	18 GRAPESEED OIL WITH HERBS
6 SUNFLOWER OIL	
7 PINESEED OIL	19 PUMPKIN SEED OIL
8 RAPESEED OIL	20 ORANGE OIL
9 LIGHT OLIVE OIL	21 SESAME SEED OIL
10 OLIVE OIL	22 GROUNDNUT OIL
11 VIRGIN WALNUT OIL	23 WALNUT OIL
12 OLIVE OIL WITH HERBS	24 TOASTED SESAME OIL
	25 LEMON OIL
13 AVOCADO OIL	26 GRAPEFRUIT OIL

than, for example, walnut oil or hazelnut oil. It costs about four times as much as hazelnut oil. See also NUTS, page 89.

PUMPKIN SEED OIL

This is a thick dark brown oil, with the same colour as soy sauce or balsamic vinegar. It has a slightly toasted flavour with a distinct hint of pumpkin seed. It has something of the character of a good sesame seed oil but with an altogether different flavour. Steiermark in Austria is a major source of pumpkin seed oil and it is very popular in that country. It makes a good powerful salad dressing if mixed with other robust flavours, is delicious sprinkled on hot vegetables and also on fish.

RAPESEED OIL *colza oil*

Bright yellow fields of rape produce Britain's only homegrown source of edible oil. It was introduced as a crop by the Romans to provide oil since olives would not grow in Britain.

It is a bland, neutrally flavoured oil, suitable for frying, baking and other uses. It is lower in saturated fats than most other commonly used fats. It is sometimes inaccurately called mustard oil because the rape plant, like mustard, is a member of the brassica family and confusingly has very similar yellow flowers.

SAFFLOWER OIL

This bright rich yellow, rather thick oil comes from the seeds of the safflower (also called false saffron). It is of great nutritional value, being higher in polyunsaturated fats (75 per cent) than any other oil, low in saturated fats, and an excellent source of vitamin E. It is best used for cooking with other strongly flavoured ingredients. I find it too strong to use in mayonnaise or salad dressings.

SESAME SEED OIL

Cold-pressed unblended sesame oil is a rich, light brown colour with a distinctive smell and strong nutty flavour. Indeed many people find it too strong and so a teaspoon mixed with a couple of tablespoons of grapeseed oil is sufficient.

Sesame oil keeps extremely well since it contains a substance which prevents it going rancid.

Toasted sesame oil, which has a deep golden colour, is an important ingredient in Japanese and Chinese cooking. It is used more as a seasoning, flavouring or marinating ingredient than as a cooking medium, as it burns at a relatively low temperature.

SOYA OIL

The invaluable soya bean produces a cooking oil that is inexpensive and of high quality, although not exciting. It has little flavour, but its very neutrality makes it a useful all-purpose oil.

SUNFLOWER OIL

High in polyunsaturates and with 33 per cent mono-unsaturates (the neutral fatty acids), sunflower oil is perhaps the best all-purpose oil. It is tasteless and pale yellow, also light in texture, which makes it excellent for frying, as an ingredient in salad dressings and as the oil for mayonnaise, mixed with other more highly flavoured oils if liked.

VEGETABLE OIL

Unfortunately the constituents of vegetable oil are not necessarily listed on the label and manufacturers can make up their own combination of oils. It may contain corn oil, safflower oil, rapeseed oil, cottonseed oil, or soya oil in any proportions. It may also contain coconut oil or refined palm oil, both of which are very high in saturated fats. It is usually very economical, and has very little flavour and aroma, which makes it popular as an all-purpose cooking oil.

WALNUT OIL

This deliciously nutty oil is made in France – in the Dordogne, Périgord and the Loire – and also in Italy. Production is small, and it is therefore an expensive oil. It does not keep too well and, once opened, it should be stored in a cool place to prevent it from turning rancid, but not in the refrigerator as this can cause it to solidify and change colour, though the labels will sometimes tell you otherwise.

High in polyunsaturates and rich in iodine, it is wonderful on salads and should be mixed with only a hint of good vinegar or lemon juice and a few crushed walnuts. In South-West France they use cider vinegar in walnut oil vinaigrettes. I have also used walnut oil in baking to add an extra depth of flavour. It is particularly good, for example, in a walnut and coffee cake, but use it also in breakfast breads with a chopped walnut and raisin mixture, in pastry for a walnut tart, or to make crisp walnut biscuits. Walnut oil mixed with lime juice and onions also makes a marvellous marinade for raw fish. It flavours sauces and marinades for chicken and is delicious over hot vegetables. See also NUTS, page 89.

OILS AND THEIR USES

	Frying	Salads	Baking	Grilling	Flavouring
ALMOND			•		
CORN	•			•	
COTTONSEED					•
FRUIT			•		•
GRAPESEED	•	•	•	•	
GROUNDNUT	•	•		•	
HAZELNUT		•	•	•	•
OLIVE	•	•		•	•
PINESEED		•	•		•
PUMPKIN SEED		•		•	•
RAPESEED	•	•	•	•	
SAFFLOWER	•	•		•	
SESAME		•		•	•
SOYA	⊖		•	•	
SUNFLOWER	•	•	•	•	
VEGETABLE	•				
WALNUT		•	•	•	•

Vinegars

The word vinegar comes from the French *vin aigre*, 'sour wine'. Wine turns to vinegar when it is exposed to the air and the alcohol in the wine reacts with a bacteria to produce acetic acid. The wine no longer has a 'winy' flavour and aroma, but a sharp and agreeable 'vinegary' flavour. The bacteria grow on the surface of the vinegar creating a thick skin, known as the vinegar 'mother', which is sometimes used as 'starter' for a new batch. Vinegar is produced not only from wine but also from other types of alcohol: beer and cider are the most common.

There are those who maintain that you should not let vinegars cross culinary boundaries, that wine vinegar alone should be used in French, Italian and Spanish cooking, rice vinegar in Oriental cooking, cider vinegar in traditional American cooking. While I agree that fish and chips need malt vinegar and *sushi* needs rice vinegar, there is room for flexibility. I am sure wine vinegar would be more appropriate to Californian cooking than cider vinegar.

Vinegar is indispensable in the kitchen. Its original use centuries ago was for preserving vegetables and fruits through the winter months and it is still one of the main preserving agents in pickles and chutneys. It is also valuable as a flavouring in its own right. Good, well-flavoured vinegars are essential in salad dressings and mayonnaise – better for this purpose than lemon juice which can cause stomach upsets. They are also added to some sauces, such as *hollandaise*, *sauce diable*, and Chinese sweet-and-sour sauces. Vinegar is often used in marinades for meats and fish. Some vinegars, notably cider vinegar, are said to have remarkable medicinal properties, and some are used in drinks.

Balsamic Vinegar *aceto balsamico*

Wonderfully dark and mellow, with a sweet-sour flavour, balsamic vinegar is made only in and around Modena in northern Italy ('balsam' simply means 'balm' and refers to the smooth, soothing character of the vinegar). There are two kinds: *industriale* – the commercial version – and *naturale*, which is still made by traditional methods, in small quantities and aged for at least 15–20 years in wooden casks. There are reputed to be some exquisite vinegars of well over a hundred years old still in the possession of the families who originally produced them.

The vinegar is made from grape juice concentrated over a low flame and fermented slowly in a series of wooden barrels, beginning with large chestnut or oak barrels and moving each year into progressively smaller barrels in a variety of different woods.

Balsamic vinegar is expensive but a little goes a long way. Just a drop or two with some extra virgin olive oil makes a fine salad dressing. Do not mask the flavour with garlic and herbs and other flavours. Good mellow vinegars such as these can be surprisingly useful as a condiment to add to rich meaty soups or casseroles. Again, only a drop or two is needed. A classic dish from Modena is sliced strawberries simply sprinkled with a little balsamic vinegar and left to macerate for half an hour or so before serving.

Cider Vinegar

To make cider vinegar, pure apple juice is fermented into cider which is exposed to the air so that it sours and is thereby converted to acetic acid – in other words vinegar. It is a clear pale brown vinegar, although unpasteurized versions can be cloudy, and the apple taste is quite strong. It is suitable for salad dressings if you like the flavour, but I find it best of all for pickling fruits – pears and plums spiced with cloves and cinnamon sticks, and the cider vinegar sweetened with one of the dark sugars.

Fruit Vinegar

Raspberry vinegar, pear vinegar, blackcurrant vinegar, strawberry vinegar: the list of exotic new vinegars which have appeared in the last few years seems endless. They are, of course, not new. Look through any Victorian or even much earlier cookery book and you will find a recipe for raspberry vinegar. Then it was used, more often than not, as the basis for a refreshing drink. Now it is used in salad dressings and particularly in sauces made from pan juices, for example, when you are frying calves' liver or duck breasts. It tastes very good, too, used as part of a basting mixture when roasting ham, duck or other fatty or rich meats.

Make fruit vinegar by steeping fresh fruit in wine vinegar and then straining it. For a more concentrated flavour repeat this process with a second batch of fresh fruit in the same vinegar.

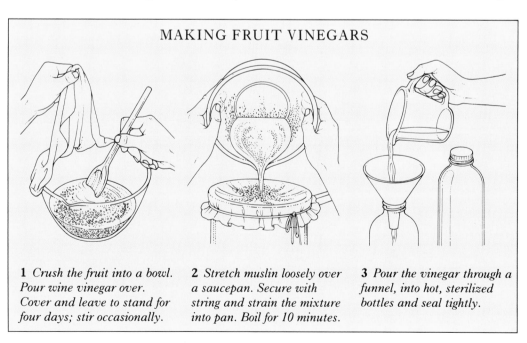

MAKING FRUIT VINEGARS

1 *Crush the fruit into a bowl. Pour wine vinegar over. Cover and leave to stand for four days; stir occasionally.*

2 *Stretch muslin loosely over a saucepan. Secure with string and strain the mixture into pan. Boil for 10 minutes.*

3 *Pour the vinegar through a funnel, into hot, sterilized bottles and seal tightly.*

HERB VINEGAR

Subtle yet distinctive flavours can be added to salad dressings by using red or white wine vinegar in which herbs have been steeped. Tarragon vinegar is perhaps the most popular, but there is no limit to the herb-flavoured vinegars you can make. Basil vinegar, thyme vinegar, rosemary vinegar and lavender vinegar are ones I have used and enjoyed in salad dressings and in mayonnaise. Tarragon vinegar is particularly good in sauces based on eggs or butter, and is, indeed, an essential ingredient of *sauce béarnaise*. It is important to use healthy, unblemished herbs, bought or picked at their peak of freshness. To make herb vinegars, simply steep a bunch of fresh herbs in wine vinegar in the bottle.

MALT VINEGAR

Just as wine vinegar is the everyday vinegar of wine-producing areas, and rice vinegar the everyday vinegar in those areas which produce rice wine, malt vinegar is commonly used in

Vinegars

1	SEAWEED VINEGAR	17	MALT VINEGAR
2	ROSEMARY VINEGAR	18	LIGHT MALT VINEGAR
3	RASPBERRY VINEGAR	19	WHITE WINE VINEGAR
4	BALSAMIC VINEGAR	20	ROSE PETAL VINEGAR
5	THYME VINEGAR	21	BRANDY VINEGAR
6	TARRAGON AND RED WINE VINEGAR	22	JAPANESE RICE VINEGAR (MITSUKAN)
7	PICKLING VINEGAR	23	BLACKCURRANT RED WINE VINEGAR
8	WILD BRAMBLE VINEGAR	24	SPICED MALT VINEGAR
9	HONEY AND CAPER VINEGAR	25	RIOJA VINEGAR
10	LEMON VINEGAR	26	CIDER VINEGAR
11	STRAWBERRY RED WINE VINEGAR	27	SHERRY VINEGAR
12	BOUQUET GARNI VINEGAR	28	BROWN RICE VINEGAR
13	PEAR VINEGAR	29	CHAMPAGNE VINEGAR
14	GARLIC RED WINE VINEGAR	30	JAPANESE RICE VINEGAR (TOGAZU)
15	DISTILLED MALT VINEGAR	31	TARRAGON VINEGAR
16	RED WINE VINEGAR	32	GREEN PEPPERCORN VINEGAR

Britain and northern Europe, the 'beer belt'. It is made from soured, unhopped beer. In its natural form the vinegar is pale and usually sold as light malt vinegar. It may be coloured brown by the addition of caramel and will sometimes be called brown malt vinegar.

In the same way that wine vinegars can be flavoured, so too can malt vinegar. It is most usual to find it flavoured with spices such as black and white peppercorns, allspice, cloves and tiny hot chillies. Often this is sold as pickling vinegar, since in Britain it is malt vinegar that is usually used in the preparation of pickled onions, pickled walnuts and mixed vegetable pickles such as piccalilli.

Use distilled malt vinegar to pickle particularly watery vegetables which are likely to dilute the vinegar. The vinegar is concentrated by distillation so that it has a higher proportion of acetic acid than the usual four to six per cent. Distilled or white vinegar can also be made from other grains and is mostly used for pickling, though in Scotland it is used in the same way as ordinary malt vinegar.

On the whole the malt vinegars are best restricted to pickling and making preserved or bottled sauces such as tomato chutney. The malt flavour is too strong as a seasoning or for salad dressings. On the other hand who could think of sprinkling wine vinegar on fish and chips? It has to be malt vinegar for that.

RICE VINEGAR

Rice vinegar is made from soured and fermented rice wine. There are rice vinegars from China which are sharp and sour, and rice vinegars from Japan which are quite different: soft, mellow, rounded, almost sweet. Indeed, if you are planning to substitute a Western vinegar (cider vinegar is the best alternative) for Japanese rice vinegar in a Japanese dish, you will need to sweeten it a little. For a really authentic flavour in Oriental cooking, when making seasoned rice for *sushi* for example, rice vinegar is essential. Always use Japanese rice vinegars with Japanese dishes, and Chinese rice vinegars with Chinese dishes. Fortunately it is also delicious in Western dishes, and makes a perfect vinaigrette with, for example, one of the fine nut oils.

Like other vinegars, rice vinegars are some-times made into flavoured vinegars: with soy sauce, *dashi* (Japanese soup-stock), or *mirin* (a sweet rice wine for cooking) as the base, and then additions of grated ginger for *shogazu* vinegar, bonito flakes for *togazu* vinegar, toasted sesame seeds for *gomazu* vinegar and chillies and onions for *nanbanzu*. Horseradish, mustard, citron and white radish, or daikon, are also used as flavourings for rice vinegar.

Most rice vinegar is a clear straw colour. Brown rice vinegar is made from wholegrain rice and is a clear deep dark brown with a wonderful mellow flavour.

WINE VINEGAR

Orléans in the Loire valley in France is the home of the wine vinegar industry, where the traditional lengthy fermentation processes are still followed. Any vinegar made by the Orléans process, wherever it comes from, will be expensive but of superior quality.

Wine vinegar – which is the strongest natural vinegar with an acidity of about 6·5 per cent – is made from any wine untreated with preservatives. Not surprisingly regions that are noted for a particular wine type also produce related vinegars. Among the more readily available wine vinegars are Champagne vinegar which is pale, light and delicate; Rioja vinegar, usually a red vinegar, which is rich, mellow and very full-bodied; and sherry vinegar, a nutty brown vinegar matured in wooden barrels by methods similar to those used for sherry itself, and particularly full and rounded. All these vinegars, of course, are especially suited to their local dishes, but are also excellent in all manner of salads. In other wine-making regions, interesting new wine vinegars are being made. In California, for example, they are making a Zinfandel vinegar from the local grape variety. Brandy vinegar is also available.

The more expensive wine vinegars, such as Orléans vinegar and sherry vinegar, are best used alone, but the more widely available red and white wine vinegars are the ones to use for experimenting with additional flavours.

Wine vinegars can be flavoured with fruit or herbs and also with honey, garlic, shallots, chillies, peppercorns, cloves, cinnamon, flower petals, and even seaweed.

GRAINS, CEREALS AND FLOURS

Named after Ceres, the Roman goddess of grain, cereals are the world's single most important foodstuff. These edible seeds or grains grow in many varieties throughout all climatic zones, from the hardy barley of Northern Europe, and the wheat of temperate regions to the maize and rice of sub-tropical and tropical areas. The most common cereals are barley, corn, oats, rice, rye and wheat. Others, such as buckwheat and millet, are not true cereals but are used in the same ways.

NUTRITION

Cereals are our most important source of carbohydrate, but also contain some proteins, fats and vitamins. Three important elements make up the grains – the outer husk or bran, the endosperm which is the starch-bearing and largest part of the grain, and the germ which contains the new growth and is the grain's source of protein. Whole-grain products are exactly what they say: they contain all parts of the grain, and are therefore richer in

fibre and protein than the refined products. Fibre is tough and indigestible, and should not be given in large quantities to infants. For the rest of us, fibre is an essential part of our daily diet. Generally in the Western world we eat too many processed foods. Eating plenty of unrefined cereal products helps to achieve a more balanced diet.

COOKING WITH CEREALS

It is not difficult to eat cereals and their products. Think of all the good things which come from our bakeries: breads, cakes, croissants, Danish pastries, muffins, teacakes, biscuits, pies – all these have a cereal base, usually of wheat flour. Imagine an Oriental diet without rice, an Italian one without pasta and polenta, a Scottish one without haggis, porridge and oatcakes – impossible!

I love to experiment with different flours when I'm baking; mixing refined and wholemeal; or adding oatflakes to white flour. Try using rye and barley flours in your bread dough with a good proportion of wheat flour to add the gluten which is necessary for an elastic smooth dough. Sometimes I add soaked whole grains of wheat to the dough for a lovely nutty texture.

Cooked rice dishes such as risotto are very familiar, but try making similar dishes with barley and wheat. These grains are also excellent added to thicken vegetable soups, almost making them into a meal.

As well as providing the whole grains and flours cereals are sometimes processed to give grits, groats or flakes. These cook quickly and are useful in milk puddings and breakfast cereals. You can make your own very good and inexpensive breakfast cereal of the muesli type by mixing rolled cereal flakes, plain or toasted, with nuts and dried fruit.

Cereal Products and Flours

1 WHEAT FLAKES	22 RYE FLAKES
2 PEARL BARLEY	23 MALTED BROWN
3 ARROWROOT	FLOUR
4 RICE BRAN	24 CHESTNUT FLOUR
5 SEMOLINA	25 BROWN RICE FLOUR
(WHOLEWHEAT)	26 BARLEY FLOUR
6 OATMEAL (MEDIUM)	27 CORNMEAL
7 WHEATGERM	28 BROWN RICE FLAKES
(NATURAL)	29 SOYA BEAN FLAKES
8 MILLET FLAKES	30 POTATO FLOUR
9 WHITE HOMINY	31 PORRIDGE OATS
10 BLUE CORNMEAL	32 KUDZU STARCH
11 SEMOLINA	33 WHOLEWHEAT FLOUR
12 PLAIN WHITE FLOUR	34 HOMINY GRITS
(UNBLEACHED)	(FINE)
13 RYE FLOUR	35 SOYA FLOUR
14 SAGO	36 ROASTED
15 WHEAT BRAN	BUCKWHEAT
16 CORNFLOUR	37 BESAN FLOUR
17 SOYA BRAN	38 POLENTA
18 COUSCOUS	39 YAM FLOUR
19 SWEET POTATO	40 BUCKWHEAT FLOUR
FLOUR	41 GROUND RICE
20 BULGAR	42 TAPIOCA
21 BARLEY FLAKES	

ARROWROOT

A fine white powder that is over 80 per cent starch, obtained from processing the maranta root, arrowroot is used chiefly as a thickening agent for sauces. When it is mixed with cold water or other liquid and then added to the sauce and heated, the starch granules swell to a jelly, a property which makes arrowroot particularly suitable for thickening clear meat or fruit sauces. Arrowroot can also be mixed with cake flour or used on its own in the making of cakes and biscuits. Because the powdered grains are very fine, arrowroot is easy to digest, and so has always been used in dishes for delicate or convalescent appetites.

BARLEY

One of the most ancient of cultivated cereals, barley is grown over a wide area and used in many cultures and cuisines. It is malted for use in brewing and distilling. It is also subjected to several processes to produce flakes, a wholemeal flour and, perhaps best known in the British kitchen, pearl barley.

Whole grain barley with only the outer husk removed is used, for example, in Scots barley broth where it is cooked with mutton and vegetables. In fact, lamb is often combined with barley – as are mushrooms. The whole grains, when cooked, have a delicious nutty and slightly chewy character. Sometimes I make a version of risotto with barley grains, combining them with a homemade stock, dried mushrooms and herbs. The grains need longer cooking than rice, up to two to three hours, and will never become soft.

Pearl barley is a more polished, refined form of the grain, with more of the husk removed, and this does cook more quickly. It is an excellent addition to winter vegetable soups (requiring about 1½ to 2 hours' cooking time) and thickening, flavouring and adding an interesting texture.

Barley flour makes tasty teatime breads and scone-like mixtures. It is also used as a thickening for soups and sauces made with milk, and has a low gluten content.

BESAN FLOUR

This fine, pale yellow flour, used in Indian cookery, is made by grinding *chana dhal* – which looks like small yellow split peas. In fact, if you cannot find either the ready-ground, slightly sweet flour or split dried *chana dhal*, you can substitute yellow split peas and grind them yourself. Crush them before putting them in the grinder to avoid damaging the blades. Finally sieve out the husks.

Use besan as a thickener for soups and curries, or simply add water to make a batter to coat foods, especially fish, for frying.

BRAN

This is the outer layer of any cereal. Wheat bran is the most common, but rice bran, oat bran and soya bran can be found. It is usually separated out from the grain during the milling of flour, and may be fine or coarse. It also varies in colour, from pale to dark brown. As a valued source of fibre it is used to enrich breads and crisp breads, or toasted and marketed as a cereal.

BUCKWHEAT *beechwheat, saracen corn, sarrazin*

This small triangular 'grain' is actually the seed of a plant related to rhubarb, and is milled into flour and groats of varying degrees of fineness. It is rich in vitamins A and B, calcium and carbohydrates. Fertile soil is not required for this hardy plant, which probably originated in Siberia and Mongolia. Buckwheat, as *kasha* – in which the roasted grain is prepared similarly to cooked rice – is something of a staple in Russia and Poland, where it is used in meatless dishes.

Buckwheat flour is grey coloured with darker speckles and has a rather strong flavour. It is used to make dumplings, accompanied by a vegetable sauce or served with meat stews, or it is served sweetened as a breakfast cereal with milk. It is also an essential ingredient for *blinis*, the light, yeast-risen pancakes that are the traditional Russian accompaniment to caviar.

In France buckwheat is known as *sarrazin* and cultivated in Brittany. There the flour is used to make the delicious *galettes* (flat bread or cake baked on a griddle) and *crêpes* with savoury fillings. The *crêpes* with sweet fillings are made from *froment* or wheat flour.

In the United States buckwheat flour is used for delicious breakfast 'bakes' such as pancakes, muffins and crumpets, which are served hot with plenty of butter and maple syrup.

BULGAR WHEAT *bulgur, burghul, cracked wheat, pourgouri,*

This is one of my favourite cereals. I began to use it when we lived in a part of London with a large Greek-Cypriot community and used to enjoy this light, moist, yet fluffy, nutty-tasting cracked wheat as an accompaniment to grilled lamb kebabs.

Because the wheat grain has been partially processed, that is, cracked by boiling, it absorbs moisture readily and therefore cooks relatively quickly.

Bulgar wheat is excellent served in place of rice or potatoes with grills, roasts and casseroles. Use it also as an unusual base ingredient for a chicken or turkey stuffing, spiced with chopped nuts, apricots, garlic and coriander. A lovely summer salad dish can be made by cooking and cooling the wheat, then mixing it with olive oil, onions, herbs and other good things.

Dried bulgar wheat, finely ground and sieved, is the main ingredient (with raw lamb) in the Lebanese national dishes *kibbeh* (a smooth minced meat paste with finely chopped onions and seasoning) and *tabbouleh* (a salad of bulgar, onion, tomatoes, herbs, lemon and olive oil).

CHESTNUT FLOUR

Chestnuts and the chestnut flour ground from them used to be staples in Corsica, and the poorer parts of France and Italy, when the countryside was rich in sweet chestnut trees. With urbanization, pollution and blight, it is now rare to come across dishes made with chestnut flour.

However, if you are lucky enough to find it, chestnut flour makes marvellous cakes, bread and biscuits, sweet and savoury soufflés. It can also be mixed with chocolate for delicious puddings. I even use it in pasta dough when making lasagne layered with a game sauce. See also NUTS, page 89.

CORN *maize*

Corn used to be the generic name for all grains, but now is synonymous only with maize. There are many varieties, soft, hard, and different colours.

Cornmeal is widely used as a staple in corn-growing parts of the world, both as human feed and animal feed. Indeed it is one of the largest crops in the United States. The southern states make most use of this lovely golden meal in the kitchen in the form of cornbread, spoonbread, corn cakes, corn sticks and battercakes.

Cornflour or **cornstarch** is the finely powdered white starch extracted from maize kernels. It is so fine that it is generally used as an excellent thickening agent, particularly in sweet or savoury sauces. Some cakes and biscuits are also made with cornflour.

Polenta is the name given to the same fine golden cornmeal in Italy, where it is made into a soft, savoury, porridgy mass (also called *polenta*) which is served with fish, game and meat dishes. Alternatively it is allowed to cool, then sliced and grilled or baked. A similar dish, called *mamaliga*, is made in Romania.

Hominy When the golden hull has been removed from corn and the remaining kernel dries, it becomes hominy. The whole kernel is then softened by cooking it in water or milk, after which it can be fried, baked, served with a sauce, or added to a casserole. It should be cooked overnight, then added to boiling, lightly salted water and simmered very gently until tender, which can take up to five hours. This is an excellent grain to add to a slow-cooking pork casserole, the kind that stews away in the oven overnight.

Grits are ground hominy, a relatively fine, whitish, gritty cereal which is made into breakfast dishes, or accompanies meat dishes. Grits are cooked in water to a mushy consistency and typically served with bacon and eggs. Whole grain grits have less of the husk removed and thus retain slightly more fibre, flavour and texture.

Blue cornmeal While most maize (corn) kernels are yellow, one variety has a stunning blue-black colour. When ground, this becomes blue cornmeal. Originally it was a staple used only by the North American Indians. Now it is available commercially in the United States, where it has become a very popular, not to say fashionable food on the east and west coasts, and in the south-west. It is used mainly in making tortillas and small pancakes.

Popcorn is a small variety of hard yet edible corn with cobs about 6in (15cm) long. When dry heat is applied to corn in a covered but not hermetically sealed pan, the moisture and air inside the kernel expands, forms steam and explodes to turn the kernel literally inside out, so that the starchy white part is outermost. It is eaten as a snack, salted, or sweetened or rolled in butter or syrup.

KUDZU STARCH

Very similar in texture to cornflour, which is an excellent substitute, kudzu starch is processed from the root of the kudzu vine. An important ingredient in Japan where the kudzu plant grows wild, it is used to thicken soups and stews and give them a glossy finish. It can also be used to coat food before deep-frying, which gives a lighter result than batter.

MILLET

Millet has been cultivated across Asia, North Africa and Southern Europe for thousands of years, but it is little used in the British kitchen. This is a pity. It can be cooked, as it is in parts of Russia and Central Europe, with milk, water or stock, and served as an accompaniment to rich spicy casseroles, or as a soothing and nourishing breakfast dish. Consider using a handful of the small, round, golden grains in vegetable soups to thicken them and provide extra food value. (Millet grains swell considerably, so beware of using too many.) Millet flakes are also available, and these cook more quickly than whole grains.

OATS

This cereal grass flourishes in damp, cold, northerly climates and has been an important staple in Scottish, Irish and Northern European diets for centuries. Highly nutritious, it contains not only carbohydrates, protein and fat, but is a good source of iron, potassium and vitamin B. When cooked it has a characteristic jelly-like consistency, as water-soluble fibre, gums and pectins are released during cooking.

Oatmeal, which is the cut groat or kernel, is available in various grades, distinguished by size and texture. The largest and coarsest is pinhead, then rough, medium, fine and superfine. The most usually available grades are pinhead, medium and fine.

Fine oatmeal, almost like a flour, makes excellent biscuits, such as oatcakes, and can be used to thicken soups and sauces. But in order to use it in bread-making (for example, to make lightly risen bread) it needs to be mixed with wheat flour as the gluten content is not high.

It was after a visit to Scotland that I came to appreciate the qualities of the different types of oatmeal, and indeed porridge itself. I had always thought this a rather sticky, dull dish until I began to make it with oatmeal rather than oatflakes. The meal has a texture and flavour that is lacking in the flakes because they have been steamed and rolled. Brose, a traditional Scottish dish like porridge, is a mixture of oatmeal, hot water, milk or other liquid and a little butter to enrich it. Bannocks – Scottish griddle cakes – are also made with oatmeal. One of the most unusual oatmeal dishes I have come across is skirlie, which is oatmeal fried with onion in fat or oil. Sometimes served as an accompaniment to a meat dish (I first had it with a haunch of venison), it also makes an excellent stuffing.

Oatflakes or **rolled oats** as they are also known, and even the larger jumbo oatflakes, being processed, do cook more quickly than all except the finest oatmeals – about four minutes instead of up to 30 minutes for pinhead or medium oatmeal porridge.

Oat flakes or oatmeal are also used in other breakfast dishes such as the Swiss muesli. The oats can be lightly toasted first.

Experiment with the various types of oatmeal or flakes in bread- and cake-making to achieve different textures, and in crumble toppings for sweet and savoury dishes. Oatmeal is essential for making parkin, that rich sticky gingerbread from Yorkshire, flapjacks and, of course, oatcakes. Dip fish or meat in oatmeal instead of breadcrumbs before frying. It is most traditionally used in this way to coat filleted herrings.

Oat bran is the outer casing of the seed and fruit of the oat kernel, and can be mixed with oatmeal or rolled oats in porridge, or used as a breakfast cereal, added to other flours in baking.

POTATO FLOUR *farina, fecula, potato starch*

An ultra-fine, soft, white powder, potato flour is the pure starch obtained from soaking pulped or grated potatoes in water. The liquid is eventually strained off, leaving the cellulose behind and this is discarded. The starch suspended in the liquid sinks to the bottom and is collected and dried. It can be used alone or mixed with ordinary wheat flour in baking bread or potato scones, and the same mixture gives a dry light texture to cakes.

Potato flour is particularly useful as a thickening agent in sauces as it needs gentle cooking and for a much shorter time than wheat flour; also, it has no flavour. This is a great advantage when thickening sauces made from fruits or vegetables when long cooking of the starch would reduce the fresh flavours of the primary ingredient. Potato flour should be gently simmered, not boiled, after adding it to a sauce, and even then only for a couple of minutes, otherwise it will thin out again. As a thickener potato flour can be substituted for cornflour in the same quantities, and one-and-a-half times the quantity of wheat flour. In fruit puddings, such as the Russian *kissel*, potato flour gives a clean, smooth, transparent appearance. Potato flour is also useful to those on a gluten-free diet.

RICE PRODUCTS

Ground rice is creamy-white and grainy, similar to semolina, but paler. It is used mainly in sweet dishes such as milk puddings, and in cake- and biscuit-making – where it adds an agreeable sandy texture to such recipes as shortbread.

Rice bran is the outer husk of the rice grain. It should be used in the same way as wheat bran.

Rice flour is very finely ground and pulverized rice, available either white or brown. Because it is one of the softest powders produced the white flour is also used in the cosmetic industry as a base for face powders and eyeshadows.

Rice flour can be used as a thickening agent and as an ingredient in cakes and puddings. In Oriental cooking, it is used to make a dough from which noodles are cut, both narrow and broad. Rice flour rolls, stuffed with prawns or pork, are a feature of the Cantonese snacks *dim sum* and resemble Italian cannelloni. See also RICE, page 134, and NOODLES AND DUMPLINGS, page 144.

RYE

A cereal grass similar to wheat, rye will flourish in harsher conditions and has long been a staple grain in Northern Europe, Scandinavia, Eastern Europe and Russia. As well as being milled to make flour and other products such as rye flakes and rye bran, rye is also used in the United States to make rye whiskey, in the Netherlands to make Holland gin and in Russia to make *kvass*, a slightly alcoholic, sour-sweet beverage.

Rye produces a darker flour than wheat but is in no way inferior nutritionally. Although it can be used alone to make bread, rye flour has a low gluten content and therefore makes a slightly less elastic dough than wheat flour, and for this reason the two are often combined.

I love the rich flavour of rye bread, sometimes called black bread, and find it the perfect accompaniment to the raw, salted, cured or marinated fish dishes of Scandinavia.

There is also a white rye flour, but as most of the bran has been removed, it lacks that distinctive strong rye taste.

SAGO *pearl sago*

This is the starch extracted from the pith of the sago palm and various other tropical palms. It is a staple food in many of the Pacific islands. In Europe and America it is generally used in milk puddings and to thicken sauces. As a flavourless, easily digestible starch, sago is an ideal food for invalids and convalescents. The appearance of the small, pearly white granules gives the product its more usual name of pearl sago.

Whole Grains

1 WHEAT BERRIES
2 BUCKWHEAT
3 CORN
4 BARLEY
5 MILLET
6 RYE
7 OAT GROATS
8 MALT BARLEY

SEMOLINA

This grainy, pale creamy yellow flour ground from durum or hard wheat has a higher protein and gluten content than flour produced from soft wheat and is the main ingredient of dried Italian pasta. Because it is a hard flour to work by hand or in domestic machinery, it is almost impossible to make pasta at home using only semolina. I combine it with strong flour, using just under one part semolina to two parts strong flour. (See also PASTA, page 137.)

Semolina is also used to make *gnocchi* – small dumplings – and milk puddings, and in biscuits. **Couscous** is semolina grains that have been rolled, dampened and coated with finer wheat flour. This enlarges the individual grains and keeps them separate in cooking. The couscous that is available commercially has already undergone this process mechanically and simply needs moistening (which allows the grains to swell and soften), then steaming.

Couscous is the staple of the North African diet and has given its name to a wonderful dish composed not only of the soft, tender mound of yellow grains, but the fragrant vegetable stew which accompanies it, also meats which can be a combination of grilled spicy sausages, lamb, meatballs, kidney, chicken, or, more simply, lamb stewed with the vegetables. There is a special pot called a *couscoussière* which allows the vegetables to be cooked in the pot, on the stove, and the grains to be steamed above them.

The cereal can also be used in a salad, moistened, then mixed with herbs, onions, chopped tomato and olive oil.

SORGHUM

A large number of sorghum species are grown worldwide. Some are suitable only as animal feed and some, such as sweet sorghum, for the extraction of syrup, widely used in the United States for cooking purposes. In India white-grained sorghum is used to make a flat unleavened bread with a faintly nutty taste.

Sometimes species of this cereal grass are described as millet, but millet and sorghum do not belong to the same family. The grain sorghums are mainly used on a commercial scale for the extraction of their oil and starch.

SOYA FLOUR *soybean flour*

One of many products derived from the soya bean, this flour is higher in protein than any other type of flour, or indeed many other food stuffs, and so is very nutritious. It is available in full-fat, medium-fat and low-fat forms. The first two should be refrigerated or stored in a cold dark place to prevent them turning rancid, and used up within six months.

Soya flour does not contain gluten, so it can be used by those on a gluten-free diet. It can also be combined with wheat flour in bread- and cake-making for a more nutritious end product. It gives a creamy texture to soups and sauces.

TAPIOCA

This is a starchy product of the tropical root cassava, or manioc. It is carefully prepared from the dried root, because some fresh roots contain hydrocyanic acid. The manufacture of tapioca involves heating and drying, so losing the toxicity. It is available in flake form, granulated (ground flakes), and as pearl tapioca.

Tapioca pudding is probably the best-known, if not always best-loved, manifestation of this pale, rather bland cereal. It has been known as 'frogs' spawn' to countless consumers of school dinners. In fact, a well-made, creamy rich tapioca pudding has much to commend it. I have experimented with a lighter version by thinning down a vanilla tapioca pudding with rich milk or cream, chilling it and then stirring in a few summer berries or slices of tropical fruit. Cooking the tapioca with coconut milk rather than with a vanilla pod is also a pleasant variation.

Tapioca gives body to soups and stews and is sometimes used to fill out meat loaves.

WHEAT

Wheatgerm, wheat bran, wheat flakes, flour, wholewheat or wholemeal flour, plain flour (all-purpose flour), strong flour and self-raising flour are just some of the derivatives of wheat – one of the most important food crops in the world. Bread, pasta, pastry, pies, cakes, buns, biscuits, breakfast cereals – none of these would be possible without wheat.

There are hard and soft wheats, each produc-

ing different kinds of flour. The type of flour is also affected by the processes it undergoes and it is important to choose the right one for the purpose in hand.

White flour is not usually labelled as such, but rather as plain flour; this contains about 75 per cent of the wheat grain, sometimes less. Because most of the bran and wheatgerm has been lost during the milling process, the flour is not as nutritious as wholewheat flour. White flour can be 'plain' or 'all-purpose', which is suitable for sauces, as a thickening agent and for pastry; it can also be 'self-raising' which, by the addition of leavening or raising agents, is suitable for light, airy-textured cakes and puddings.

White flour milled from soft wheat is suitable for biscuits and cakes because of its low protein and delicate texture when cooked, and it will sometimes be labelled 'cake' or 'sponge' flour. 'Strong white flour' has been milled from hard or durum wheat which has a higher protein content, and more gluten which gives an elastic dough. This makes it the most suitable flour for yeast cookery, particularly breads, also some pastry and pancake batter; in fact, anything that is required to rise and increase in volume.

Wholewheat or **wholemeal flour** is any 100 per cent flour, milled from the whole grain, with nothing added or removed, so all the nutrients of the grain are intact. It can be used for making breads, cakes and pastries.

Stoneground flour is simply flour that has been ground between two stones in the old-fashioned way rather than milled in a steel roller mill. This gives the flour a better flavour, but it does not last as well, so buy it in small quantities unless you use it regularly.

Malted wheat flour is a brown flour with a distinctive sweet nutty flavour and texture obtained by adding malted wheat grains. It may also contain crushed rye grains.

Wheatgerm is the heart of the grain. It can be bought in its natural state or toasted. Add it to mixed breakfast cereals. It is highly nutritious.

Sprouted wheat is a fairly recent development. The whole wheat grain is germinated to boost the protein and vitamin content and the starch is converted into natural sugar. The sprouted wheat is then mixed with other ingredients such as chopped fruit, nuts, seeds or grains and baked into a dense, moist loaf. See also *Semolina*.

133

RICE

An annual cereal grass, rice is the staple food of about half the world's population. It grows on marshy flooded land where wheat and other cereals will not grow, particularly in the Indian subcontinent, China, Japan, South-East Asia and the south-eastern part of the United States. It also grows in the wide, fertile Po valley in Piedmont in north-west Italy and in the low-lying area around Valencia along the Spanish Mediterranean coast. Small amounts are grown in the Camargue, the wild marshy region in southern Provence in France.

In certain very poor parts of the world rice is the sole source of food for many people, in others it ekes out small quantities of meat or other proteins. One way and another, more rice is eaten overall than any other single food. Where the economy flourishes, rice is turned into fine dishes, mixed with costly spices and other flavourings. Consider the *pullao* of the Moghul court in India, cooked by artists who had learnt their skills from the Persians; it survives today in much of the northern Indian cooking to be found in India itself and in other countries. Italian risotto with shaved white truffles and Spanish paella with fine rare saffron are two further examples of how a simple staple can be transformed into some of the world's finest dishes.

There is no doubt that rice does have extraordinary qualities. It soothes and nourishes, as in the traditional British rice pudding and that favourite Chinese breakfast dish *congee*, or rice gruel. It absorbs other flavours and enhances them as in some Persian and Arab dishes where meat, fruit and rice are cooked together with herbs and spices. Eaten with hot spicy Indian curries or piquant Thai dishes, it cools and refreshes. It provides a bland base against which to set all the exotic textures of a Chinese banquet – the crunchy, the shiny, the gelatinous, the velvety, the crisp, the soft, all of which are experienced at their best when taken with a morsel of rice.

Rice has given its name to the *rijstaffel* or 'rice table'. A popular dish or meal in Holland much influenced by Indonesian cooking, it is a large platter of spiced rice which is accompanied by small dishes of hot spicy curries, relishes and chutneys. Any dish described as *alla milanese* in an Italian restaurant will probably have rice as an accompaniment – Milan is at the heart of the rice-growing region. Fortunately so many varieties of rice are now available that we can recreate some of these culinary experiences at home.

As well as its many traditional uses, rice has an important role in the modern kitchen. It cooks relatively quickly with little or no special preparation in advance and thus makes an excellent staple to serve occasionally with meat or fish instead of potatoes. Because of its absorbent qualities it goes particularly well with casseroles which have plenty of sauce. Indeed the rice and sauce together is so good, that I would often prefer to have just that, without the meat. I love it with chicken casseroles cooked with a creamy, lemony sauce with mushrooms in it. A couple of spoonfuls of rice added to a pan of soup will thicken it most agreeably. Clear chicken soup or tomato soup with rice are delicious.

Often, cold left-over rice is used in salads. These can be very tasty. Even better though is to make up the salad while the rice is still warm; in this way it absorbs some of the flavours from the dressing. Experiment with cooked rice in savoury stuffings in place of breadcrumbs. It is particularly good as a stuffing for vegetables such as peppers and aubergines when mixed with herbs, onions and perhaps a little meat. I use rice also to stuff squid which I then bake in olive oil and white wine.

PREPARING RICE

Rice is relatively inexpensive, easy to cook and, contrary to popular belief, is not fattening. It also supplies many important nutrients, especially B vitamins and minerals such as potassium and phosphorus.

There are many kinds of rice. Some are distinguished by the size of the grain: long, medium or short. Some are described by their origins, such as Patna rice and Java rice. Different types of rice are cooked in different ways and have different powers of absorption. For example, a medium- or long-grain rice will absorb three times its weight in water; a short-grain rice is far more absorbent: 1oz (25g) of rice will take almost 1 pint (600ml) of milk. So certain rices are more suited than others to particular dishes.

Rice used to be sold loose from hessian sacks, and recipes always told you to wash it until the water ran clear to remove any fine grit or stones and the coating of talc it had often been given. Packaged rice is, of course, perfectly clean. A preliminary rinsing will get rid of any powdered starch which clings to the outside of the grains, but even this is not absolutely necessary.

Before looking at some of the types of rice available, a word about cooking. In fact a few words. Although rice *is* easy to cook, there are perhaps as many methods of doing it as there are cooks. Methods also vary with the dish. Dishes like risotto and paella require constant attention and stirring in order to blend all the flavours and produce a particular consistency. A *pullao* requires the rice to be left undisturbed to give it a fluffy, separate grain. There are cooks who believe that you should cook rice rather like pasta in a large quantity of lightly salted boiling water. When the rice is just done it is drained and spread out on a clean cloth to dry and separate.

My preferred method is to cook rice by absorption. I use Patna or Basmati – about 2oz (50g) per person. Sometimes I turn the rice in a little oil or butter in the saucepan first and then pour on two parts water to one part rice, add a little salt, bring it to the boil, cover with a tight-fitting lid and turn down the heat as low as possible. About 18–20 minutes later you have perfectly cooked rice. Brown rice will take 40–45 minutes. It can be cooked on top of the stove or in a moderately low oven. I find this method gives perfect results every time.

Rice

1 GLUTINOUS RICE (WHITE)	6 ARBORIO RICE
2 GLUTINOUS RICE (BLACK)	7 CARNAROLI RICE
3 WHITE LONG-GRAIN RICE	8 BASMATI RICE (WHITE)
4 BROWN LONG-GRAIN RICE	9 BASMATI RICE (BROWN)
5 FLAKED RICE	10 WHITE SHORT-GRAIN RICE
	11 WILD RICE

ARBORIO RICE

The classic risotto rice from Piedmont in northern Italy, this is one of the best types of all (it is graded *superfino*), because it can absorb a great deal of the cooking liquid without becoming too soft. Although classed as long grain in Italian terms it is actually of medium to long grain, a little shorter than Basmati rice. The grain is slightly plump and irregular, translucent at the edges with a white hard core which is what produces the distinctive risotto texture: creamy but with a slight bite. It is one of the most expensive rices but well worth hunting out.

Other Italian risotto rices are Carnaroli, Roma and Baldo. All are classed *superfino*. There are three other grades of Italian rice. *Fino* is a long-grain rice also used for risotto; *semifino* a medium-length round-grain rice used for hors d'oeuvres and boiled as a side dish (Vialone, Nano and Padano are well-known varieties); and *ordinario*, small round grains suitable for soups and puddings (varieties are Originario and Balilla).

BASMATI RICE

A slender long-grain brown or white rice, this is grown in the foothills of the Himalayas; its name means 'fragrant'. Of all the rices I use, it is the one which for me has the most distinctive aroma and flavour – healthy, appetizing and with a real hint of 'fragrance'. This is the rice to use for savoury dishes, such as *biriani* or rice salads, when you want very light, fluffy separate grains, and for when you want to use rice simply as an accompaniment.

BROWN RICE

This is the whole rice with only the outer tough husk removed. The layers of bran are retained, keeping the rice brown, and giving a characteristic nutty flavour and chewy texture. It is available in long, medium and short grain. Because it is less refined it needs more cooking than white rice, up to 45 minutes, though this can be reduced by pre-soaking. It is richer in minerals and vitamins than white rice and is a source of the B vitamins thiamine, riboflavin and niacin, as well as calcium and iron. It also contains more protein. Brown rice can be substituted for white rice. Increase the cooking time and allow for the fact that brown rice absorbs about four times its volume in liquid.

CAROLINA RICE

A long-grain rice variety originally cultivated in the state of Carolina in the United States, this swells a good deal during cooking. Like all long-grain rices it cooks dry and fluffy, but it is also good in sweet milk puddings and in stuffings for vegetables like peppers and vine leaves. It is more usually known as American long-grain rice.

CONVERTED RICE *par-boiled rice*

This is a long-grain white rice partially steam-cooked before milling which has the effect of forcing nutrients from the bran to the inner part of the rice grain so that they are retained in the milling process. This is good, tasty rice which cooks to fluffy, dry separated grains.

FLAKED RICE

Processed white or brown rice is put through rollers to produce these lightweight flakes of rice. It is mainly used in making puddings, its main virtue being that it cooks quickly, but it can also be added to a muesli mixture.

GLUTINOUS RICE *sticky rice, sweet rice*

This is a short- to medium-grain rice with a high starch content much used in Chinese and Japanese cooking. Black (unpolished) and white varieties are available. Its name is entirely descriptive of its texture. Rather than the grains being fluffy and separate, they stick together slightly, making it easier to eat with chopsticks. It is used for both sweet and savoury dishes.

JAVA RICE

One of the shorter of the long-grain rices and similar to Carolina rice, this is an all-purpose rice, but being so absorbent it is particularly good in puddings and baked rice dishes.

PATNA RICE

This is an excellent rice to cook as an accompaniment to Indian food. It cooks to fluffy, dry, separate, milky-white grains which also makes it a very good all-purpose rice for salads, stuffings and dry rice dishes. It is a smooth long-grain rice that retains just a hint of firmness in the centre when cooked and takes flavourings very well: spices, saffron, butter, flaked almonds, herbs.

PUDDING RICE

A short-grain rice sold specifically for milk puddings and rice desserts. The grains swell and absorb a great deal of liquid and cling together in a creamy, rich consistency.

THAI FRAGRANT RICE

These young, tender rice grains are favoured by the Thais and Vietnamese; the rice does indeed have a particularly special fragrance. It is usually served on feast days.

VALENCIA RICE

This is the paella rice *par excellence*, but is not widely available outside the region. It is a short- to medium-grain rice with good qualities of absorption. It does not become creamy when cooked, but it produces a very tender melting swollen grain.

WHITE RICE

This is the general name for polished, or pearled, rice. This is rice that has been milled to remove the husk and the bran. It can be bought as short, medium or long grain as well as in more specific varieties such as Basmati, Arborio and so on. In general, short-grain varieties are best for sweet puddings, medium-grain varieties are best for savoury risottos that require a creamy texture, and long-grain is best where dry separate grains are needed. 'Enriched' rice is simply white rice with some of the nutrients, notably iron and the B vitamins, put back after the polishing process.

WILD RICE

These long, slender, black grains are not, in fact, a rice at all. Wild rice is an aquatic grass which grows along lakesides and rivers in Canada, northern California and the northern part of the United States.

At one time it was harvested by many Indian tribes – the Algonquin, the Chippewa, the Fox, the Sioux and the Winnebago – who fought for control of the best wild rice lakes and rivers. Because of the difficulty of reaching it – by small, two-man canoes – it was a precious crop. Although traditional production methods are still used in certain areas, it is now being cultivated on a commercial scale, and mechanically harvested, with the result that it is becoming increasingly available.

It is a delicious food and although still rather expensive a little wild rice goes a long way. You can feed up to six people with about 4oz (125g) of wild rice, as it absorbs four times its volume of liquid. Serve it in the same ways as as you would rice. It is particularly good as an accompaniment to game and poultry and makes a marvellous stuffing when combined with a few nuts, herbs and other ingredients.

Wild rice will take anything from 35–60 minutes to cook (as you do rice) depending on whether you like it chewy or tender. You can also soak it in water overnight to reduce the cooking time and also increase its volume when cooked.

Compared with rice and wheat, wild rice is extremely nutritious. Its protein, approximately 14 per cent of the whole, contains all nine essential amino acids and is particularly rich in one of them, lysine. It is a good source of fibre, low in calories and gluten free.

PASTA

The mixing of flour and water to form a paste which is then kneaded and cut into lengths or shapes is one of man's earliest culinary inventions, and one common to a number of races. The Etruscans, the ancient Greeks and the Shang dynasty in China some 3500 years ago, all left records in the form of paintings or manuscripts which show that pasta was a staple food in their diet. A visit to the Museo Storico degli Spaghetti, a museum devoted entirely to pasta in Pontedassio in the northern Italian region of Liguria, should be enough to convince anyone that Marco Polo did not bring the art of pasta-making back with him from China as is commonly thought. He was already familiar with it and recognized the 'good lagana' or lasagne he encountered on his travels there. A long history of pasta-making also exists in Spain, Israel and in Arab countries, as well as in Russia and Mongolia. It is a perfect simple recipe which cannot be improved upon and which today is very like the pasta made hundred of years ago.

ITALIAN PASTA

The word *pasta* means paste or dough and Italian (or Italian-type, since good pasta is also made outside Italy) pasta is made from semolina from durum or hard wheat mixed with water. The dough is then kneaded and rolled out into flat sheets before being shaped and cut in various ways depending on whether the pasta is being made commercially or at home. Semolina is a hard flour to work by hand and so homemade pasta is better made with a mixture of flours.

Pasta secca Factory-made or dried (*secco*) pasta is first pressed through a die or *trafila* into many shapes and sizes. The pasta is then dried and sold in packages. Look for the words 'durum wheat' or *pasta di semola di grano duro* on the label. Pasta made from soft wheat is soggy when cooked. The pasta will be clear yellow in colour and sometimes it will have a few tiny dark flecks in it. This is an indication that the wheatgerm has not been removed but ground up in the flour, which adds to the already relatively high protein content. However a large amount of flecks may mean that it contains a good deal of bran which makes the pasta rough and harsh.

Pasta all' uovo All fresh pasta made at home is made with eggs which are needed to bind together the flour and water. Emilia-Romagna in northern Italy has long been famous for its homemade pasta and it was traditionally made daily in each home. It is now easy to buy fresh egg pasta which has been made commercially. While much dried pasta is simply made from durum wheat flour and water, some also has the addition of egg. When sold in Italy it must have five eggs per kilo (about 2lb) of flour. Dried *pasta all'uovo* can be used in the same way as its plainer cousin.

Fresh versus dried pasta In recent years 'fresh' pasta has become very popular. It is wrong to assume, however, that because it is 'fresh' it is better than dried pasta. If fresh pasta is made entirely from durum wheat then it is as good, nutritionally speaking, as dried pasta. However, durum wheat flour is hard to handle, particularly on a domestic scale, and it is often mixed with soft wheat flour to make it easier to work. This reduces the protein content and the absorbent qualities and increases the starchiness of the finished product. For the short shapes or the long flat or round pastas to serve with sauces, I do not think you can beat dried pasta made from 100 per cent durum wheat. If I could only take one type of pasta with me on a desert island, it would be a spaghetti made from durum wheat flour with the wheatgerm left in it.

Wholewheat pasta With the growing interest in health foods, it seemed an obvious step to produce a healthier pasta, using the whole wheat grain, which would provide more protein, more nutrients and more fibre. Wholewheat pasta has always been made in the Veneto in north-eastern Italy, where it is known as *bigoli*, and in appearance it resembles a large-gauge spaghetti. Wholewheat pasta, in particular spaghetti, lasagne and other shapes, is now made on a commercial scale by some of Italy's larger pasta manufacturers, mainly for the export market. It is also made in Britain and elsewhere. Wholewheat pasta has a rich brown colour and because it contains so much more fibre than the more refined product, it takes longer to cook.

Coloured pasta Green sheets of lasagne and green tagliatelle have been familiar for a long time. The pasta is coloured with either spinach juice or powder. Other vegetable colouring, usually tomato purée, is used to produce orange pasta; red or pink pasta is coloured with beetroot juice and yellow pasta with saffron or turmeric. All flavourings are natural ones. Apart from the green and orange pastas, most other coloured pastas are likely to be found only as homemade pastas, or as fresh pasta from specialist sources.

In Venice black pasta is a famous dish and is produced by colouring the pasta dough with the ink from squid or octopus. It is traditionally served with a sauce made from the squid. Chocolate pasta went through a fashionable period not too long ago, not as a sweet, but as a savoury dish. I must admit to a fondness for it, and have often made it to accompany the darker game dishes such as pigeon, hare and wild duck. Purists tend to dismiss these variations, believing that the original, simple product cannot be improved upon. They may well have a point.

PASTA AND NUTRITION

Contrary to common belief, pasta itself is not a 'fattening' food and it is considered to be nutritious and healthy. The average portion in Italy is reckoned at 100g (3½oz) dry weight of pasta containing 350 kilocalories but remember that in Italy pasta is eaten as a first course before the main course. The same amount of cooked pasta contains about 115 kilocalories. It can contain about 14 per cent protein depending on the type of wheat flour used and on whether the wheatgerm is removed or left in. About 70 to 80 per cent is carbohydrate, and pasta contains virtually no fat (less than 1 per cent). The B vitamins, and minerals potassium and iron are also present. Pasta made from durum wheat will absorb as much as three times its weight in water, unlike that made from soft wheat flour which will absorb about twice its weight in water.

Pasta is a satisfying food, both in the immediate eating and in its digestion. The carbohydrates it contains are complex ones which take time to digest and which are satisfying over a much longer period than the simple carbohydrates to be found in much over-refined food.

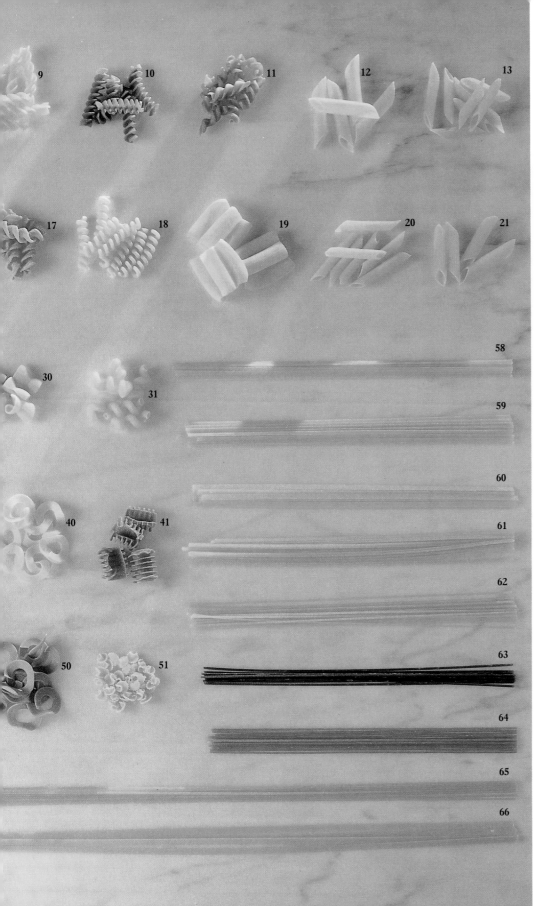

Pastas for Boiling

1 FUSILLI
2 ZITI COL BUCO
3 MACCHERONI
4 MACCHERONCELLI
5 MAFALDINI
6 TRIPOLINI
7 FARFALLE
8 NASTRINI
9 FUSILLI
10 SPINACH FUSILLI
11 WHOLEWHEAT FUSILLI
12 PENNONI
13 PENNE RIGATE
14 ASSORTED 'SAFARI' PASTA
15 MEDIUM-SIZED FARFALLE
16 ELICHE
17 TOMATO FUSILLI
18 FUSILLI BUCATI
19 'DESIGNER' PASTA
20 MEDIUM-SIZED PENNE
21 MEDIUM-SIZED PENNE RIGATE
22 TAGLIOLINI FINI A NIDO
23 ZITI
24 TUBETTI LUNGHI
25 CORNETTI
26 WHOLEWHEAT TUBETTI LUNGHI
27 ORECCHIETTE
28 SPINACH FARFALLE
29 CASARECCIE
30 PLAIN, TOMATO AND SPINACH FIOCHETTI
31 CAVATAPPI
32 SPINACH TAGLIATELLE
33 RIGATONI
34 DITALINI RIGATI

35 TUBETTI
36 DITALONI RIGATE
37 CONCHIGLIE RIGATE
38 CONCHIGLIETTE RIGATE
39 ROTELLE
40 CIRCULAR NOODLES
41 WHOLEWHEAT RADIATORI
42 PAPPARDELLE
43 ELICOIDALI RIGATE
44 PLAIN, TOMATO AND SPINACH GNOCCHETTI DI ZITA
45 CHIFFERI PICCOLI RIGATI
46 PIPE RIGATE
47 LUMACHE RIGATE GRANDE
48 GNOCCHI PICCOLI
49 CRESTE MEZZANE
50 CIRCULAR SPINACH NOODLES
51 FUNGHINI
52 TAGLIATELLE
53 FRESH FETTUCCINE
54 FRESH SPINACH TAGLIARINI
55 FRESH TOMATO TAGLIOLINI FINI
56 CONCHIGLIE RIGATE
57 SPINACH CONCHIGLIE RIGATE
58 BAVETTINI
59 LINGUE DI PASSERI
60 TAGLIARINI
61 TRIFOGLI
62 VERMICELLI
63 SPINACH SPAGHETTI
64 WHOLEWHEAT SPAGHETTI
65 SPAGHETTI
66 TAGLIATELLE

PASTA IN THE ITALIAN KITCHEN

Each part of Italy has its own specialities, and each season brings different sauces. In the north where much game is hunted in the autumn *pappardelle alla lepre* (broad flat noodles with hare sauce) is a special treat to look forward to in one of Milan's many small restaurants. *Pasta con le sarde* is a great speciality of Palermo in Sicily where pasta is served with sardines, wild fennel, raisins and pine nuts. Genoa's speciality is *trenette al pesto*, thin flat ribbons of pasta served with a rich green sauce of basil, olive oil, pine nuts, garlic, Parmesan and Pecorino. Then there are the delicious baked pastas such as *lasagne al forno*, which is sheets of pasta layered with meat sauce and béchamel and then baked to a golden brown, and cannelloni pasta tubes filled with spinach and ricotta cheese and baked with a cheese or tomato sauce.

All pasta, whether dried or fresh, can be divided into two main groups – pasta for soups (*pasta in brodo*) and pasta served with a sauce (*pasta asciutta*).

Pasta for soups The type of soup will determine the size of the pasta. A clear, mild soup or *brodo* (broth) will take tiny pasta shapes which are often labelled *pasta in brodo* or *pastina*. The range is enormous and many shapes have fanciful names. There are alphabets, numerals, melon seeds (*seme di melone*), small shells (*conchigliette piccole*), small rings (*anellini*), and small stars (*stellette*), to name a few. More hearty soups such as minestrone or *pasta e fagioli* (pasta and bean soup) will take thicker shapes or broken-up lengths of spaghetti. The pieces of pasta

Pastas for Stuffing and Baking

1	TORTELLINI	9	AGNOLOTTI
2	RAVIOLI	10	CANNELLONI
3	SPINACH TORTELLONI	11	WHOLEWHEAT RAVIOLI
4	TOMATO TORTELLINI	12	SPINACH RAVIOLI
5	SPINACH TORTELLINI	13	DRIED SPINACH LASAGNE
6	CAPPELLETTI	14	DRIED LASAGNE
7	UNFILLED CAPPELLETTI	15	FRESH SPINACH LASAGNE
8	TORTELLONI		

should not be much bigger than the other soup ingredients such as chopped vegetables.

Pasta for boiling This is the largest pasta group and the range is enormous. Most of these shapes are sold as dried pasta. There are flat noodles such as tagliatelle, long, thin pastas such as spaghetti, hollow tubes such as *maccheroni* and the smaller, pretty shapes such as bows (*farfalle*) and shells (*conchiglie*). Some pastas are smooth and others ridged. These pastas can be served plain, with a small amount of olive oil put into the warmed dish before adding the cooked pasta or with a large knob of butter put on top of the pasta to melt slowly. Or there are many sauces designed for serving with these pastas, either stirred in or served separately.

Pasta for stuffing Fresh pasta, whether homemade or commercial, comes into its own as stuffed pasta or *pasta ripieni*. In Emilia-Romagna, a rich farming region, each town has its own speciality and purists still make it fresh each day and roll it out by hand. Although I love the *tortellini* of Bologna, my favourite are the *tortellini di zucca* of Mantova – small, plump pasta pillows filled with a mixture of pumpkin, nutmeg, cheese, almonds and fruit. They are served as a savoury but their sweet spiciness comes down in a direct line from the princely kitchens of the Middle Ages. Ravioli, *agnolotti*, *tortelloni*, *tortellini* and *cappelletti* are just some of the types of stuffed pasta you will come across.

The fillings vary from region to region and from one season to the next. One of the best and most common fillings for stuffed pastas is spinach or chard, finely chopped and mixed with Ricotta and Parmesan or Pecorino, some garlic and often a hint of nutmeg. In Bologna a rich meaty filling is made from mortadella sausage, pork or veal, or both, and chicken or turkey meat. In Trieste and the Veneto where radicchio grows, it is used as a filling for ravioli, mixed with cheese. Such rich pastas are served with a very simple sauce, or usually just olive oil or melted butter, in which a few sage leaves have been infused.

Pasta for baking There are several excellent pasta dishes made by baking alternate layers of pasta and sauce in the oven or *al forno*. *Lasagne al forno* is the most famous example.

The sheets of lasagne usually have to be precooked briefly in boiling water before being assembled with usually a meat sauce and béchamel. Try lasagne layered with fish, shellfish or vegetables in an appropriate sauce. It is now possible to buy lasagne which is ready to use without precooking.

COOKING PASTA AT HOME

Pasta is a marvellous base on which to build delicious sauces, limited only by your imagination, or by the contents of your store cupboard. A couple of garlic cloves, a can of anchovies, some extra virgin olive oil and a little fresh parsley is all you need to turn a packet of pasta into a fine tasty dish. Herbs and canned tomatoes will also make a quick simple sauce. An egg and a couple of rashers of bacon will produce that classic Roman dish, *spaghetti alla carbonara* (charcoal burners' spaghetti). However, pasta is most emphatically not a vehicle for using up a collection of soggy leftovers that you cannot think what to do with. That is not to say that a careful look through your refrigerator might not produce the makings of an excellent sauce. Whenever I cook hare or rabbit I always make sure that there will be enough meat left over to shred and heat up in extra gravy to stir into some freshly cooked pasta. The remains of a ham on the bone which has reached the 'too-difficult-to-carve' stage can be picked off and heated up with cream and *petits pois* to make a quick, easy and very good sauce for tagliatelle.

Storing pasta Dried Italian durum wheat pasta will keep for up to two years without losing its flavour although it is unlikely that anyone would want to keep a food item that long. It does indicate, however, what a useful

Pastas for Soup

1	STELLETTE	8	SEME DI MELONE
2	SEME DI PEPERONE	9	RISI
3	EXTRA SMALL STELLETTE	10	ALPHABET AND NUMERALS
4	PEPE BUCATO	11	EXTRA SMALL CORALLINI
5	SPINACH OCCHI DI PERNICE	12	CONCHIGLIETTE PICCOLE
6	FEDELINI TAGLIATI		
7	ANELLINI		

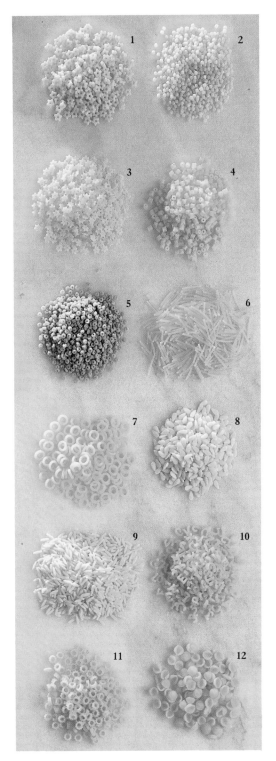

standby it is. Pasta must be stored in a dry, dark place and thus is best kept in its original package or in a tin, not in a decorative glass jar displayed on the kitchen shelves. Dried pasta made with eggs does not keep as well. Fresh pasta can be frozen successfully.

HOW TO COOK DRIED PASTA

There is the classic method of cooking dried pasta, and a newer method evolved by the president of one of Italy's largest pasta manufacturers which is the one I now always use because it is economical and produces good results.

The classic method This requires about 10 pints (6 litres) of boiling, salted water for each 1lb (500g) spaghetti. The pasta is folded and twisted into the fully boiling water. As it softens on contact with the water it bends and you can 'fold' it into the pan without having to break it. Never break the longer pieces of pasta. When the pasta is completely submerged and the water at a full rolling boil, stir the pasta from time to time with a long fork to make sure it is not sticking to the pan, and boil it for the time stated on the packet. The length of time will depend on how thick the pasta is, how dry it is and, therefore, to some extent, on the humidity or otherwise of the storage conditions. It can take up to 15 or 20 minutes to cook. (There are also some quick-cook dried pastas which do not take as long.)

Although it is sometimes recommended that you add oil to the cooking water to stop the pasta sticking together, I do not advise this as it also stops the sauce clinging to the pasta. It is far better to use plenty of water and to stir the pasta while it boils.

After about three-quarters of the cooking time has elapsed, test the pasta to see whether it is done by fishing a piece out of the water and biting into it. It should feel a little elastic and slightly firm to the bite, or *al dente*. Remember that different shapes take different times to cook. As soon as it is done to your liking, add a cup of cold water to the pan to halt the cooking process. Drain the pasta in a large colander and return it to the warm pan. When draining pasta it is important not to drain it so thoroughly that it dries out and sticks together. A little water should still cling

to it which will then mix with the sauce. Never rinse pasta.

Stir in the sauce or seasoning and carefully pour it into a heated serving dish. Serve immediately on heated plates or in shallow soup-plates with sloping sides.

The newer method This also requires a large saucepan full of boiling, salted water but once the pasta has been folded into the water and the water brought back to the boil, it is boiled for two minutes only. Then switch off the heat and cover with a very tight-fitting lid. You can also place a tea towel between the pan and the lid to ensure a good fit. Leave to stand for the full cooking time stated on the packet. The pasta is then drained and served in the usual way. Using this method means the pasta will be perfectly cooked and not in the least bit soggy. Because it has not been subjected to the same agitation as in the classic method fewer of the nutrients and less of the starch have leached out into the water. This means that more goodness has been retained and the outside of the pasta is not too sticky when drained. It is also a method which economizes on fuel since the cooking time is so much less than for the classic method.

Cooking fresh pasta Freshly made pasta is still full of moisture and requires far less cooking time to soften it. Sometimes it needs only a minute or so and sometimes up to five, depending on the type.

CHOOSING A SAUCE

Different pasta shapes determine the method of cooking and the type of sauce served with it. Smooth, slender spaghetti will not hold a thick, chunky sauce very well but is best suited to a light, simple dressing of olive oil or a fresh tomato sauce. Thick sauces need the kind of pasta that will trap it in its folds, curls and hollows. For these sauces choose *penne rigate* (ridged quills) or *rigatoni* (thick, hollow, ridged tubes) or the snail- and shell-shaped pastas. Spiral pasta shapes such as *fusilli, eliche, tortiglioni, spirale, cavatappi* and *riccini* are also excellent for serving with substantial sauces. Pastas with fluted, wavy edges like the *cresti di gallo* (cock's comb), *festonati* (festoons) and *lasagne festonate* (festooned lasagne) also hold a sauce well.

However, there is really no hard and fast rule and you can eat any shape with any sauce.

Some well-known sauces Here is a list of the most common sauces for pasta.

al pesto A speciality of Genoa, this strong sauce uses basil, olive oil, pine nuts, garlic, Parmesan and pecorino cheese. Often served with *trenette*.

all' arrabiata A sauce of tomatoes, bacon and red hot peppers.

all' aglio e olio With chopped garlic and olive oil.

all' amatriciana A bacon, tomato, olive oil and onion sauce originating from Amatrice in Abruzzo.

alla carbonara A dish from Rome with ham, eggs, black pepper and sometimes cream.

alla marinara A fresh tomato and basil sauce, often served with *fettuccine*.

alla napoletana A sauce from fresh tomatoes, garlic, onion and olive oil.

con ragù A meat sauce from Bologna (hence Bolognese sauce in English) served with tagliatelle. *Spaghetti alla bolognese* is not an Italian combination.

PASTA NAMES

The question of names for pasta can be a minefield for the unwary who try to claim a definitive and accurate list of pasta names and translations. *There is no such thing.*

What I know as *fusilli*, another may recognize as *tortiglioni*, and yet another as *eliche*. And are they 'spirals', 'screws' or 'spindles'? Some Italian pasta guides label *vermicelli* or 'little worms' as the long pasta which is one grade thicker than spaghetti. Others maintain that *vermicelli* is thinner than *spaghettini* (itself thinner than spaghetti), while yet others claim that this thin pasta should be called 'angel's hair' (*capelli d'angelo*) rather than little worms. Show a pasta shape to five Italians and I am convinced you will be given five different names. Confusing it may be, but the naming of pasta is highly descriptive and amusing. Little ears (*orecchiette*), little boots (*stivaletti*), elderflowers (*fiori di sambuco*), twins (*gemelli*), little celery stalks (*sedanini*), flying saucers (*dischi volante*), priests' hats (*cappelletti di preti*) are some of my favourite names, and the list is literally endless.

A SELECTION OF PASTA SHAPES

Here is a list of some readily available pastas, some rarer ones and some with amazing names. It is *not* an exhaustive, exclusive or encyclopedic list. Estimates suggest that there are over 200 shapes with perhaps 600 or more names. But new shapes are being added all the time because in the large pasta factories, it is the privilege of the pasta maker to introduce a new shape and to give it a name. This is the age of designer pasta! Remember too that names for pasta shapes can vary from one region of Italy to another and between manufacturers. Some hints are given by the various suffixes which denote the size of the pasta. *Etti* or *ette* means small as in *orecchiette*, *spaghetti* and *farfallette* (little ears, little strings and little butterflies); *ini* or *ine* means very small as in *lumachine* and *sedanini* (tiny snails and tiny celery); and *oni* or *one* means large as in *lumacone* and *farfalloni* (large snails and large butterflies).

Agnolotti Small, round pasta shapes with a meat stuffing.
Anelli, -etti, -ini 'Rings'. Smaller ones are popular in soups.
Bavette, -ini Thin, oval spaghetti.
Bigoli Wholewheat spaghetti from the Veneto in north-eastern Italy.
Bozzoli 'Cocoon-like' small shapes.
Brichetti 'Small bricks'.
Bucatini Long hollow pasta, thicker than spaghetti.
Cannelloni Large, short tubes for stuffing and then baking. Probably originating in Piedmont, cannelloni are made from egg pasta.
Capelli 'Hair'. Fine, long spaghetti. Capelli d'Angelo is the finest version; sold in small nest-like bunches it is added to soup.
Cappelletti 'Little peaked hats'. Made from egg pasta, these stuffed shapes are similar to tortellini.
Cappelletti di preti 'Little priests' hats', similar to tortellini except the pasta is cut into squares before stuffing and shaping.
Casareccie Small, twisted pasta from Sicily.
Cavatappi Ridged pasta in twists.
Chifferi, -ini, -otti Small, curved pasta tubes.
Conchiglie, -ette 'Shells' in various sizes. Can be smooth or ridged.
Corallini 'Small rings'.
Cornetti Small tube pasta.
Cravatte, -ine 'Bows' in various sizes.
Cresti di gallo, cresti mezzane Shapes resembling a cock's comb. Various sizes.
Dente d'elefante 'Elephant's tooth'.
Dischi volante 'Flying saucers'.

Ditali, -ini 'Little thimbles'.
Eliche Twists or spirals.
Elicoidale Similar twists or spirals.
Farfalle, -ette, -ini, -oni 'Bows' or 'butterflies' in various sizes.
Fedelini Similar to vermicelli.
Festonati 'Festoons'.
Fettuccine Long narrow ribbon noodles made from egg pasta. A speciality of Rome and often confused with tagliatelle which are slightly wider.
Fiochetti 'Little bows'.
Fiori di sambuco 'Elderflowers'. Small shapes used in soups.
Funghini Small pasta shapes with wavy edges.
Fusilli 'Corkscrews' or spiral-shaped pasta.
Gemelli 'Twins'. Two short pieces of spaghetti twisted together.
Gnocchi, -etti Small, slightly curved pasta tubes but, confusingly, gnocchi are also dumplings, usually made from potato, spinach or semolina.
Gramigna Small, ridged tubes of pasta slightly curved. From Emilia-Romagna.
Lasagne, -ette Broad sheets of pasta, about 2in (5cm wide), for baking. The green version is very popular. Can be bought pre-cooked and sometimes has wavy edges. Usually made with egg pasta.
Lingue di passeri 'Sparrows' tongues'. Long, narrow pasta.
Linguine 'Small tongues'. Similar to spaghetti but slightly fatter. Often accompanies seafood.
Lumache, -celli, -ine, -oni 'Snails' in different sizes.

Maccheroni, -celli, -cini Slightly curved tube pasta of varying lengths. Often baked in pies. In English often called macaroni.
Maccheroni alla chitarra Not macaroni but flat ribbon pasta made with a special utensil resembling a musical instrument. A speciality of the Abruzzo region.
Maltagliati 'Badly cut'. Small, irregular shapes added to thick soups.
Maniche Short tube pasta.
Nastrini 'Small bows'.
Nidi Nests of pasta.
Occhi di lupo 'Wolf's eye'.
Occhi di pernice 'Partridge's eye'.
Orecchiette 'Tiny ears'.
Paglia e fieno 'Straw and hay'. Long, thin noodles of green and yellow pasta.
Pappardelle Broad egg noodles from egg pasta, sometimes with wavy edges. Often served with game sauce.
Pastina Small pasta shapes for broth soups.
Penne, -ini, -oni 'Quills'. Tubular macaroni of various sizes. Can be cut diagonally at both ends. Both smooth and ridged varieties.
Pipe Curved tubular pasta.
Radiatori Thick, ridged pasta like radiators.
Ravioli Stuffed pasta squares with serrated edges. Traditionally filled with spinach and Ricotta but often nowadays a meat filling is used. Made with egg pasta.
Riccini 'Wavy' or 'curly' pasta.
Rigatoni Fat, tubular pasta, mostly ridged. Often used for baking.
Risi Small, rice-shaped grains. Used in soups.

Rotelle 'Wheels'.
Ruote, -ini 'Wheels'.
Sedanini 'Little celery stalks'.
Seme di melone 'Melon seeds'. Used in soups.
Seme de peperone 'Pepper seeds'. Used in soups.
Spaghetti, -ini, -oni Long, thin, string-like pasta.
Spirale Spiral-shaped pasta.
Stelle, -ette, -ini 'Stars' in various sizes, used in soups.
Stivaletti 'Little boots'.
Tagliarini Flat, thin, ribbon-like pasta.
Tagliatelle Flat, ribbon noodles made from egg pasta. There is also a green version. A speciality of Bologna and often confused with fettuccine.
Tagliolini Thinner version of linguine. Often used in soups.
Timballo Pasta with sauce and cheese baked as a pie.
Tortellini, -oni Tiny, stuffed shapes made from circles of pasta and folded to resemble small ears. A speciality of Bologna. Larger ones are confusingly called tortelloni.
Tortelloni Small squares of stuffed pasta. Also large tortellini.
Tortiglioni Spiral-shaped pasta.
Trenette Flat, thinner version of linguine. Often used with seafood and with pesto sauce.
Trifogli Long, flat, ridged pasta.
Tubetti Often called elbow macaroni. Short, slightly bent tubes.
Vermicelli 'Little worms'. Thinner than spaghetti.
Ziti, -oni Wide, tube pasta. Can be smooth or ridged.

NOODLES AND DUMPLINGS

Noodles are a type of pasta made from flour, eggs and water, or just flour and water, and cut into flat strips of varying shapes and sizes. They are very popular in the Far East, in particular China, where there are literally hundreds to choose from, and in central Europe (the word 'noodle' derives from the German word *Nudel*).

ORIENTAL NOODLES

In China, Korea, Japan and Vietnam noodles and sheets of pasta dough are made from the staple grain of the area, thus rice noodles, wheat noodles and dumpling wrappers, buckwheat noodles and noodles made from mung bean starch are found in the region. Chinese noodles have since been introduced to Hong Kong, Taiwan, Thailand, Indonesia and Singapore and from there to the rest of the world wherever Chinese cooks have gone in any number. Japanese and Korean noodles are less well-travelled but are becoming more available in the West. Japanese and Korean noodle dishes are often served cold.

Oriental noodle dishes can be used in a number of ways: as the basis of hot, steaming soups; served with sauces and other ingredients, stir-fried and garnished with shredded meats, seafoods and vegetables, and tossed. Noodles are often eaten at every meal, not just dinner. One of the finest breakfasts I have ever eaten was a bowl of *yifu* noodles, some pickles, *po lih* tea and a glass of soya milk, sitting at a picture window 30 floors up overlooking the city of Shanghai.

BUYING AND COOKING NOODLES

Oriental noodles are sold dried, fresh and precooked and come in an enormous range of shapes and sizes, often tied in long bundles or coiled into square packages. Allow 3–4oz (75–125g) of noodles or one compressed square or round per person. Apart from egg noodles, they are mostly available in the West only in dried form but always buy fresh ones if you can find them. Fresh and precooked noodles will keep for up to three days in a refrigerator, well covered in foodwrap. They can also be frozen and defrost quickly when dropped into boiling water. Dried noodles keep well, like pasta, for up to a year in a cool, dark place such as a larder or cupboard.

Some noodles need soaking in water to soften them before cooking, which is usually divided into two stages. They are parboiled or steamed first and then rinsed quickly in cold water. Their final cooking may be stir-frying, further simmering or steaming, or adding to soup dishes. Cooking times vary depending on the type of noodle. Oriental wheat noodles require less cooking than Italian ones because they are made from soft wheat rather than durum wheat. Noodles made from rice flour and bean flour are also quick to cook.

ARROWROOT VERMICELLI

These are thin, white, brittle Oriental noodles which are usually sold in bundles. Traditionally they are used as soup noodles.

CELLOPHANE NOODLES *bean thread noodles, harusame, pea starch noodles, transparent noodles*

Ground mung bean flour is the usual staple used to make these wiry, hard, translucent noodles, common to most Oriental cooking. A Japanese version, *harusame*, is made from rice or potato flour. In their dried form they look like shredded cellophane and before cooking should be soaked in water for about 15 minutes. They will finally absorb about four times their weight in liquid and so are ideal for sauced noodle dishes. Cellophane noodles are usually cooked as part of a savoury dish to be served with rice. They can also be tied together and deep-fried.

DUMPLINGS

There are several ways of using a flour-and-water dough other than making noodles and Italian-style pasta. In German-speaking countries and other parts of central Europe, small flour-and-water dumplings are a popular addition to soups and stews, as indeed they are in certain British stews such as Lancashire hot-pot and Irish stew.

Knödeln are small dumplings found in Alsace, Austria and Germany. They are served hot with cream or melted butter as a separate course, like pasta in Italy, or made in small sizes and cooked in clear soup. *Nockerln* are similar but they are served in soups and stews, and sometimes replace potatoes. Generally such dumplings are something you make at home, and are not available ready-made like pasta and noodles.

EGG NOODLES

Made with wheat flour and egg, these are perhaps the most commonly used of all Oriental noodles, whether in soups, with sauces or stir-fried. They can vary in size and shape from thin and round to broad and flat. Dried egg noodles are often sold in compressed rounds or squares ('parcels'). Allow one per person.

GNOCCHI

These small Italian dumplings are often confused with the dried pasta shapes resembling small elongated dumplings which are also called *gnocchi* or *gnocchetti*. *Gnocchi* can be made from mashed potatoes, potato flour or polenta as well as from wheat flour. There are many regional variations, including the well-known Roman speciality *gnocchi alla romana* made with semolina. *Gnocchi* are usually poached in boiling water and then baked briefly in the oven and served with a cheese, meat or tomato sauce.

MAULTASCHEN

Looking exactly like a large square ravioli, *Maultaschen* are a speciality of Swabia in southern Germany. Filled with a light meat and parsley mixture they are often served in broth. The name means 'slap in the face' which is exactly what you are likely to get unless you cut it up before putting it to your lips.

NOUILLES

These are the French version of Italian egg noodles. Made as thin, flat strips they are sold dry or fresh, and usually accompany meat, poultry and game dishes.

RICE NOODLES *rice vermicelli*

Rice noodles are more common than wheat noodles in southern China and in Cantonese restaurants, since this is the rice-growing area of the country. They are used as soup noodles and also in sauced dishes with meat and vegetables. Thin, white, and slithery if fresh, rice noodles are sometimes available fresh in the West (use within a day of purchase) but they are mostly sold dried in bundles. Dried rice noodles should be soaked for about two hours until they are soft before parboiling quickly.

RICE PAPERS *spring roll wrappers*

These are thin, dry, brittle almost translucent circles made from rice flour and water which are used in Vietnamese and Thai cooking to make spring rolls. The wrappers are softened by dipping in or brushing with water, and then filled with, for example, pork, shrimp, water chestnuts or bean sprouts, before being rolled up and steamed or deep-fried.

RICE STICKS

These are broader, ribbon-like noodles, made by mixing ground rice and water. The dough is rolled and steamed into thin sheets before being loosely folded and cut. Fresh rice sticks should be used within a couple of days but dried ones will keep for several months if kept in an airtight container. Rice sticks make one of my favourite dishes, 'Singapore fried rice sticks' or *kway teow*. It is a tasty mixture of prawns, shredded roast pork, peppers and seasoning.

SOBA

Thin, flat, greyish-brown Japanese noodles, these are made from mainly buckwheat and varying amounts of wheat flour. They are very popular in Japan where they are a principal fast food, used in hot broth soup with vegetables in winter and eaten cold with a simple dipping sauce in summer. Simple to use and nourishing, they are available fresh, dried or precooked.

SOMEN

These are very fine, glossy, white Japanese noodles made from wheat flour which cook very quickly, in only two to three minutes. They are sold dried and are usually served chilled in summer with a dipping sauce.

SPÄTZEL *Spaetsel, Spätzle*

These soft irregular-shaped noodles from Alsace, Austria and southern Germany are made by mixing flour, water and sometimes egg and rubbing it through a special sieve into boiling water. *Spätzel* are usually made at home.

UDON *udong*

These are long, narrow, ribbon-like Japanese noodles made from wheat flour. They can be bought dried, fresh or precooked and are sold in bundles. They vary in thickness and may be square, round or flat. Do not need pre-soak.

WHEAT NOODLES

Wheat is the primary grain in northern China and wheat noodles made without egg are sold in bundles or compressed into square packages.

WONTON WRAPPERS

The Chinese version of Italian ravioli is *wonton*, a small dumpling made from wheat flour paste rolled out wafer-thin and stuffed with finely minced savoury fillings. The wrappings, about 3in (7cm) square, are sold fresh or frozen. *Wonton* can be boiled and served in soup, steamed as a snack, or stir-fried in hot oil.

YIFU NOODLES *efu noodles, yi noodles*

These are round yellow egg noodles woven into a round cake and are sold precooked. They are used for soup noodles and stir-fried dishes.

Oriental Noodles

1 FRESH EGG NOODLES
2 DRIED EGG NOODLES
3 CELLOPHANE
   NOODLES
4 PARCEL-SHAPED
   SPINACH NOODLES
5 PARCEL-SHAPED EGG
   NOODLES
6 PARCEL-SHAPED
   WHEAT NOODLES
7 RICE STICKS
8 FLAT RIBBON RICE
   STICKS
9 WHOLEWHEAT
   NOODLES
10 WONTON WRAPPERS
11 FRESH RICE STICKS
12 EGG NOODLES
13 UDON
14 SOMEN
15 SOBA

FISH

Fish comes from all over the world, in all shapes, sizes and colours: from the lazy flat fish such as skate, which feed on the bottom far out in the ocean, to the small silver herring which roam in vast shoals around our shores; from the vivid coral trout to the bright blue parrot fish of the Seychelles. We also get river and lake fish, fresh and dried fish, salted and smoked fish. Shellfish, smoked fish and salted fish are dealt with separately (see page 169, page 177 and page 181) but these are the main categories of fresh fish:

Round sea fish This is a large group which includes such familiar fish as cod, haddock, whiting, herring and mackerel and more exotic creatures such as John Dory and red mullet from the Mediterranean and parrot fish from tropical waters. They can be tiny like whitebait or huge like sharks. Their distinguishing features are their rounded body shape with eyes at each side of the head and the fact that they swim dorsal fin uppermost.

Such fish are usually sold whole, in fillets or in cutlets (steaks).

Freshwater Fish

I BREAM (FRESHWATER)	7 TROUT (BROWN)
	8 SALMON TROUT
2 PERCH	9 CATFISH
3 ST PETER'S FISH	(FRESHWATER)
4 SALMON (WILD)	10 PIKE
5 TROUT (RAINBOW)	11 CARP
6 SALMON (FARMED)	12 EEL

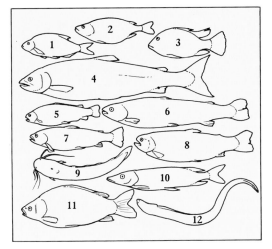

Flat sea fish Sole, halibut, turbot, plaice and dabs are among this group. They swim on their sides, have both eyes on top of their head and usually have one white side, the blind side, and a darker upper surface coloured to camouflage them within their habitat. Except for very large fish, such as turbot and halibut which can be cut into steaks, and skate which is sold in pieces (wings), flat fish are usually sold whole or filleted.

Freshwater fish Some of these fish, such as the pike, live out their entire life cycle in the lakes and rivers in which they were hatched. Others, such as the salmon, live as adults in the sea and then return to the river of their birth to spawn. Freshwater fish is not available in the shops in such variety but those lucky enough to know an angler may occasionally be offered some.

CHOOSING FISH

Many fishmongers will bone or fillet your fish for you. Fish is best bought absolutely fresh, and you can recognize this first by its appearance. A fresh fish will still have its natural colouring. If it was full of brilliant blues and greens, you should still see them. Colours fade as the fish looses its freshness. Steely mackerel begins to look dull. Salmon loses its silvery sheen. Rainbow trout starts to lose its moist coating. In a fresh fish the eye will look full and bright. White, sunken or dry eyes are signs that the fish is no longer fresh. The gills should be red. Also, a fresh fish is stiff and firm with its scales tightly fitting. When it is no longer fresh it becomes limp and its scales begin to flake off. The smell is also important. Fresh fish has a most agreeable smell: a breath of ozone, iodine and sea air. Any hint of an unpleasant smell should warn you off.

It is as important to select the right size and cut for fish as it is for meat. This will to some extent be governed by the recipe you are using, the method of cooking, and the fish itself. Large fish can be poached whole but should be cut into steaks for grilling, whereas small fish can be grilled whole.

Whether you leave the head on or have it removed is a matter of personal taste. Do make sure you take the head and bones home with you, however, as well as any other bones

the fishmonger can spare. These will make excellent stock, either for a sauce to serve with the fish or a fish soup the next day.

COOKING METHODS

Cooking fish is not difficult at all. In many ways, it is much easier to cook than meat and it cooks much more quickly, making it an excellent food if you are in a hurry. Whereas meat is cooked to tenderize it, fish is already tender. All you need to do is to cook it sufficiently to make it palatable, by which I mean just to the point of 'setting' the proteins in the fish, almost as you do when cooking an egg. Overcooking spoils fish, making it tough, dry and unpleasant. If a fish flakes off the bone very easily, it is almost overcooked. It should have lost its pearly translucence but still be moist and juicy.

In certain countries raw fish is popular. *Sashimi* and *sushi*, two of the best-known Japanese dishes, involve raw fish; *gravad lax* from Scandinavia, *ceviche* from South America and 'maatjes herrings' from the Netherlands are all fish that have undergone no cooking whatsoever. The first time I tasted raw fish in a Japanese restaurant I was amazed at how truly delicious it was: a firm yet melting texture, cool, fresh and full of flavour, it converted me completely and I now serve raw fish at home.

Fish that you serve raw must be absolutely fresh. Most people are unlikely to be able to obtain fish within a few hours of being caught. It could well be up to two days old, but if it has been carefully handled it should be quite safe. Buy it for using the same day and do not store it. This applies whether the fish is to be eaten raw or cooked. At a pinch you can keep it, well-wrapped, towards the top of the refrigerator for 24 hours but I would not recommend this as a regular practice. Wrap it in a clean, damp tea towel and then in foil. Before cooking the fish, rinse it carefully and dry it again.

Frying and deep frying This is suitable for small whole fish such as sprats, whitebait and dabs, and for fillets and cutlets such as salmon, cod and haddock. They can be breaded, or battered or rolled in flour first or not as you wish.

Grilling Small whole fish are suitable, also mackerel, herring, red mullet, Dover sole, and fillets and cutlets of larger fish such as salmon, turbot and halibut.

Baking, or cooking in foil, paper or roasting bag (*en papillote*) These are appropriate methods for stuffed whole fish: salmon, grey mullet, shad, and for rolled fillets of plaice, sole, lemon sole; also for monkfish tail and thick cutlets of salmon, conger eel or turbot.

Braising in a sealed pan is suitable for halibut cutlets, small monkfish tails, thick salmon cutlets, red mullet, in fact, anything that needs a moist cooking medium without too much liquid.

Poaching Medium to large whole fish, can all be poached: salmon, salmon trout, trout, sea bass, grouper and snapper.

Steaming is suitable for small to medium fish such as trout and sea bass, and for medium to thick cutlets of salmon and conger eel.

Casseroling Use rich meaty fish (in pieces), such as monkfish and conger eel.

PREPARATION

All fish should be gutted and cleaned before cooking. Some fish need to be scaled first.

REMOVING FINS AND SCALES

Cut off the fins with strong scissors. Hold the fish by its tail, preferably over newspaper or the kitchen sink, and scrape away the scales – working towards the head. Then rinse thoroughly.

The scaly fish include herring, salmon, salmon trout, sea bass, grey mullet, red mullet, snapper and carp. Some fish are completely smooth, such as mackerel, tuna and monkfish. They can be skinned or not, as you wish. Keeping the skin on during grilling helps keep the fish moist. Other fish have tough skins but the scales are not loose; turbot, sole and halibut come into this category. Again, you can skin them or not as you wish.

When the fish has been cleaned and gutted make sure that all the blood and any dark skin has been removed from the stomach cavity round the backbone. Rubbing it with a little salt will remove any traces. If left it will give a slight bitterness to the cooked fish. For the same reason the gills are usually removed before cooking.

NUTRITION

Fish is an excellent source of easily digestible protein, so much so that it was often recommended as suitable food for invalids and convalescents. It is a delicious food to include in your diet at least two or three times a week. B vitamins, iron, calcium, fluorine and, in sea fish, iodine are present in varying degrees, depending on the type of fish. The fat content in fish is of the unsaturated type. White fish is very low in fat and even oily fish such as trout has less than meat or poultry.

The page numbers in brackets at the end of an entry refer to the relevant photograph.

ANCHOVY

Fresh anchovies are rarely found outside Mediterranean fishing ports because they are small delicate fish, easily spoiled, and need to be eaten or processed soon after catching. They are oily fish, related to the herring family, silvery, slim, rounded, and up to 6in (15cm) long.

Fresh anchovies are easy to clean and prepare. Bend and snap the backbone behind the head and as you pull the head away, most of the innards come too. Use a knife, or even a thumbnail, to split and fillet the fish. The strong unusual flavour is best enhanced by simple cooking – baking, grilling or frying in shallow or deep oil – or marinating and eating raw. Lemon,

garlic, olive oil and other Mediterranean flavours are best. You can also cure anchovies at home. After filleting them, pack in layers of salt and keep them covered in the refrigerator. See also DRIED AND SALTED FISH, page 181. (*150*)

ANGEL FISH *fiddlefish, shark-ray*

The angel fish is a member of the shark family. It has wide pectoral fins which when spread out resemble wings – of an angel no doubt. It grows up to 20lb (9kg) in weight and is usually sold in the markets skinned and without the head.

For those who do not like fish because of the bones this is the fish to serve. The backbone is a set of cartilaginous knobs with no other small sharp bones. It is cut into steaks which can be grilled, baked, casseroled, or dipped in batter and fried. The wings are thicker than skate wings but just as sweet and appetizing. Poach them gently, then fry them and serve with a brown butter sauce. Or serve as a salad, just warm, dressed in olive oil and sherry vinegar with salad leaves.

BARRACUDA *becune, sea pike*

It is hard to believe that this fierce fish belongs to the same family as the meek-looking grey mullet. Small versions grow to about 12in (30cm), but some are 4–5ft (120–150cm) long. It has large jaws, strong sharp teeth and a slender streamlined body with small scales. The back is dark in colour, some brown, some greenish, some bluey grey, depending on the species, with a pale underbelly.

The barracuda has firm white and well-flavoured flesh. Steaks can be grilled, fried or barbecued and then marinated Portuguese-style, or eaten hot or cold. Whole fish can be poached or baked. (*166*)

BASS *sea bass, sea perch*

A large round fish which grows up to 40in (100cm) long and can weigh up to 20lb (9kg), sea bass belongs to a large family of fish common to most of the world's fishing grounds. It is a handsome fish, not unlike a salmon in appearance, but a darker, steely rather than silvery grey, with a white underbelly. When cleaning and trimming the fish take particular care to cut off the first dorsal fin, which is spiny. It should also be carefully scaled.

This is a fish for a special occasion and a favourite of chefs, but it is also easy to cook at home. I cannot ever remember cutlets or fillets of sea bass being sold, just the beautiful whole fish, and this is how I recommend cooking it although, of course, you can fillet it yourself. Poach it gently in a *court bouillon*, steam it, or wrap it in buttered foil or greaseproof paper and bake it in the oven. It needs careful cooking because the flesh is soft and delicate.

One of my favourite methods is to steam it in the Cantonese style: place a chopstick on an oval plate, scatter a bunch of coriander, sliced fresh ginger and chopped garlic on top, place the fish on top of this and sprinkle a little soy sauce over it all (the chopstick allows the steam to circulate underneath the fish). Steam it and just before serving, pour some hot sesame oil over it to crisp the skin. The Cantonese cook bass with the head on as the most delicate morsels can be extracted from the fish cheeks and neck with chopsticks. Sea bass is excellent cooked with these Oriental flavours but also with butter or olive oil, fresh finely chopped herbs and a hint of lemon, lime or orange zest.

In the south of France it is often baked over dried fennel twigs and splashed with a little *pastis*. I have also enjoyed it steamed over mint, an unusual and highly successful combination. (*150*)

BLUEFISH

The bluefish is not native to British waters but is found in the Mediterranean and the North Atlantic. It is particularly prized in Turkey and the United States. Although it can grow to a considerable size, specimens weighing 2–3lb (1–1·4kg) are the most likely to be available. The bluefish is most attractive, being firm and round with a silver belly and a blueish colour on its back. The body is rounded at the shoulders and tapers at the tail; the head is neatly proportioned. The flesh is white, firm and has a delicate flavour. American and Turkish cookery books are the best source of recipes, but I would have no hesitation in treating it like a salmon,

grilling, poaching or baking it, either whole or in cutlets. Subtly flavoured accompaniments are best, in order to retain its delicacy. Leave strong flavours such as garlic and soy sauce for other fish.

BONITO

A member of the same family as the mackerel. A smooth-skinned fish with a neat, slender, round body, pointed head and deeply indented, curving tail fin. The belly and sides are silvery white and the back is striped with even, horizontal, dark blueish-bronze markings on a steely blue surface. The fish has a wide-opening jaw which extends beyond the eye – helpful in identifying the whole fish. When full grown the bonito can be almost 3ft (90cm) long and weigh many pounds. Steaks and fillets taken from a large fish can be found occasionally as can smaller whole fish. When cleaning and trimming before cooking, make sure you remove all the innards, even tiny particles clinging to the backbone should be brushed or scraped away. Rubbing with coarse sea salt may help.

The flesh is pale and meaty and cooks well in casseroles, chowders and braised dishes. I like to use strong Mediterranean flavours such as garlic, thyme and olive oil to complement the robust texture of bonito, or to spread the steaks with mustard or horseradish butter and grill them. I once cooked it, freshly caught in the Mediterranean, with wild fennel and white wine. It is more often found in its canned form in Britain, as skipjack, or skipjack tuna – a useful standby in the kitchen. See also DRIED AND SALTED FISH, page 181.

BREAM *freshwater bream*

Rarely found, this is a frankly unexciting freshwater fish. It averages about 2lb (1kg) in weight. Despite its deep narrow body, it is a round fish, not a flat fish. Its colour varies according to age and habitat through various dull shades of blueish, greenish browns, with a dull bronze belly and grey fins and tail. Sadly this dullness is carried through into the flavour. The bream grubs around in muddy river, lake and canal bottoms to feed on worms, grubs and weeds. Before cooking it needs thoroughly cleaning with salt and lemon or vinegar, and then soaking for at least half an hour in lightly salted and acidulated water to get rid of its muddy flavour. Braise, grill, bake it, stuffed or seasoned with strong flavours such as garlic and pungent herbs,

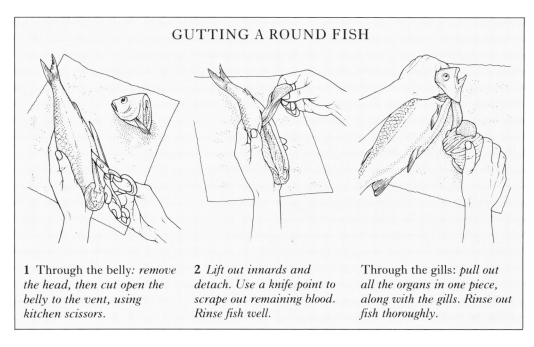

GUTTING A ROUND FISH

1 Through the belly: *remove the head, then cut open the belly to the vent, using kitchen scissors.*

2 *Lift out innards and detach. Use a knife point to scrape out remaining blood. Rinse fish well.*

Through the gills: *pull out all the organs in one piece, along with the gills. Rinse out fish thoroughly.*

and olive oil or butter to baste its rather dry flesh. Pieces of bream could be cooked with other rather better river fish in a freshwater fish stew, or *matelote*, with red or white wine (*146*)

BREAM *sea bream, porgy, scup*

This is a large family of fish which includes black sea bream, bogue, Couch's sea bream (known as red porgy in the United States), dentex, gilt-headed bream (sometimes sold as the *daurade*, its French name, not to be confused with *dorade* which is the French name for the red sea bream). Some are native and seasonal; some are imported and available most of the year. Emperor breams, such as capitaine rouge, capitaine blanc and lascar, confusingly use the name bream. Although their flesh is similar to sea bream they are not in fact from the same family.

They are usually sold weighing up to 2lb

Sea Fish

1	POMPANO	12	SNAPPER	22	SCAD (BLUE RUNNER)	32	REDFISH
2	CONGER EEL	13	SARDINES	23	BREAM (BLACK BREAM)	33	SHARK
3	SNAPPER	14	POMFRET			34	HADDOCK
4	SCAD	15	HERRING	24	GURNARD	35	MACKEREL
5	WHITING	16	HAKE	25	POMPANO	36	WHITEBAIT
6	GREY MULLET	17	MONKFISH	26	WRASSE	37	RED MULLET
7	SNAPPER	18	TUNA	27	SPRATS	38	SCABBARD
8	ANCHOVIES	19	PILCHARD	28	GURNARD	39	RED MULLET (GOLDEN MULLET)
9	JOHN DORY	20	SCAD (TREVALLY JACK)	29	COD		
10	SMELT			30	POLLACK		
11	COLEY	21	BASS	31	CROAKER		

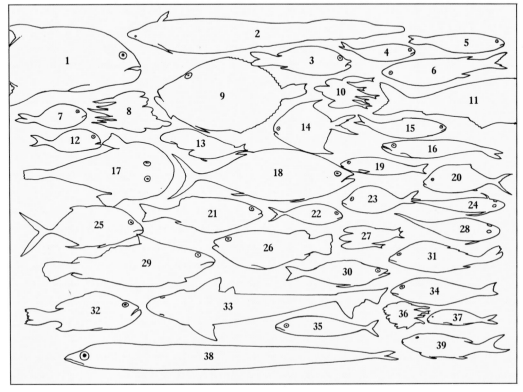

(1kg), although they also come rather larger. In colour they vary from dark grey (black sea bream) to crimson with blue spots (Couch's sea bream), through pale rosy grey (red sea bream). All have a deep narrow body, small mouth, big eyes, quite large tough scales and a single spiny dorsal fin. Because they are rather unfamiliar, and lie there on the slab in their full glory, not in neat white fillets or cutlets, there is no great demand for them and so they are relatively inexpensive.

Buy them when you see them. They are delicious. Have the fish scaled, cleaned, gutted and trimmed, and cook it whole unless you have a really large specimen which will give you good-sized fillets. Bream is excellent stuffed and baked or braised with wine and butter. The flesh is sweet, firm and delicate. One of the nicest ways of cooking red sea bream is Spanish style, baking it in the oven on a bed of thinly sliced potatoes, onion and garlic and splashing it with white wine or *fino* sherry and plenty of olive oil. (*150, 166*)

BRILL *britt, kite, pearl*

Among the large family of flat fish, this, for me, comes very close to turbot for flavour and texture. It used to be thought of as poor man's turbot and was inexpensive until it became a favourite of food writers and restaurateurs. The fish is at its best between June and February, although there are supplies through the year.

Always sold whole, brill is a flat fish with a pale underside and a brownish-grey freckled topside. The scales are small and smooth. It is quite easy to skin. The bones make excellent fish stock. About 2lb (1kg) is a good size; much smaller than this and the fillets are rather thin.

All the classic turbot and sole recipes are suitable for brill. Cook it either whole on the bone (by baking, steaming or poaching) or in fillets (by grilling, frying or poaching) and serve with any number of sauces such as those based on butter, fresh herbs and a little lemon juice. A delicate fish, it is ideal for cooking *en papillote*.

Brill also goes well with vegetables. I have cooked it with leeks, with spinach, with courgettes and with cucumbers, and have also served it with a stunning beetroot and red wine sauce. An all-round good eater, brill is hard to beat. It is not as extravagant as sole or turbot but is far more exciting than plaice. (*161*)

CARP

This freshwater fish is a favourite in many of the world's kitchens – Chinese, French, Jewish, Central and Eastern European. It lives wild in rivers – sometimes to a great age – where it feeds on water weeds, but it is also to be found in the beautiful ornamental fish ponds of great country houses and monasteries, both in Europe and in the Far East. Although they can grow to a considerable size, some to 40–50lb (18–22·5kg), they are usually sold weighing between 2 and 3lb (1 and 1·4kg).

They are handsome fish with bright skin, tight shiny scales and firm flesh. Some varieties have scales all over; one, the mirror carp, has a few large scales irregularly dotted over its back and sides. Carp is almost always sold whole and you should ask the fishmonger to clean and scale it for you.

Chinese, German, Polish, French and Jewish cookery books all have excellent recipes for preparing this fine fish. It has a sweet firm flesh and not too many bones. For this reason cook it whole, stuffed and gently braised to keep the flesh moist.

In Catholic countries carp is often the main dish on Christmas Eve and Good Friday. How fortunate then that the fish is at its best from late autumn until the spring. In the summer, as water levels drop, carp go deeper towards the bottom of the pond which can cause them to take on a muddy flavour. But you can get rid of this by skinning and then soaking them in chilled, acidulated, lightly salted water. (*146*)

CATFISH *Scarborough wolf, wolf-fish*

This fish is found off the coast of Yorkshire, and other northern waters. Catfish (or wolf-fish as it is more commonly known to distinguish it from freshwater catfish) is not a pretty fish and so is usually sold in fillets or cutlets. It is sometimes sold under the label of rock turbot or rock salmon. This is misleading and unnecessary. The whole fish is quite a sight with its fearsome mouth full of two rows of teeth, one set for biting and one for grinding, perfectly adapted to its diet of shellfish. Because of its superior diet it is an excellent eating fish, with pearly pink flesh which cooks to a firm-textured white. Like monkfish, catfish has a thick central bone and a good meaty fillet on either side with no small bones.

It is generally inexpensive, so this is an

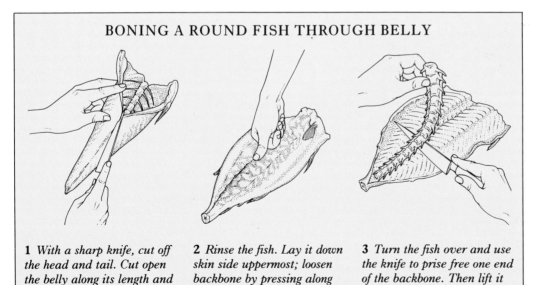

BONING A ROUND FISH THROUGH BELLY

1 *With a sharp knife, cut off the head and tail. Cut open the belly along its length and remove the gut.*

2 *Rinse the fish. Lay it down skin side uppermost; loosen backbone by pressing along its length with a thumb.*

3 *Turn the fish over and use the knife to prise free one end of the backbone. Then lift it out completely.*

excellent fish for experimenting with, particularly in casseroles and braised dishes. Try it marinated and grilled on kebab skewers, in a fish curry, a fish couscous or a mixed fish stew flavoured with saffron, tomatoes and *pastis*, or with bacon, parsley, juniper berries, gin and potatoes.

Cᴀᴛꜰɪsʜ *freshwater catfish*

In Louisiana and other parts of the southern United States catfish are now being farmed in increasing quantity to produce an important food source. They are no longer the province of small boys who would go out on a Saturday afternoon with a bamboo pole for a fishing rod and a bent pin for a hook. There are different varieties of catfish, some growing to 8lb (3·6kg) in weight, but smaller fish up to 2lb (1kg) are more common. It has a broad flat head and belly, smooth, scaleless, somewhat slimy skin and long, flexible barbels resembling a cat's whiskers, hence its name.

After cleaning and gutting the whole fish can be stuffed and baked, or its fillets breaded and deep-fried. It needs plenty of flavouring with salty powerful tastes such as anchovies, bacon or olives, herbs and olive oil or butter. (*146*)

Cʜᴀʀ *Arctic char, charr*

This rare treat of a fish is a member of the salmon and trout family, living in clean fresh mountain lakes in Britain and Europe. The grayling is a close relation as is the vendace or powan from British waters and the much larger whitefish found in the Great Lakes, Alaska and other North American lakes and streams. There are two sorts of char: one is wholly freshwater and the other is migratory, spending some time at sea and, like salmon, coming inland to spawn.

It is a distinctive fish with a red underbelly, a steely blue green back, and pinkish orange speckles on the sides. Neat and streamlined in shape like a salmon, the char reaches 2lb (1kg), but I have found smaller fish available. If you manage to obtain one, clean it, scale it, remove the gills, pat it dry and cook it gently in butter. Its sweet firm flesh will delight you. Sometimes, if the char has had a diet of small crustaceans, the flesh is pale pink, rather like that of a rainbow trout, but it is often white.

I have found it in markets in France where it is now being farmed on a small scale. If you ever see *omble chevalier* on a restaurant menu in France or Switzerland, order it. Char is what you will get. Potted char is a traditional delicacy from the English Lake District, clearly a recipe from the days when these lovely fish were more plentiful. It is simply made by mixing the cooked fish with equal quantities of softened butter and some seasoning.

Cᴏᴅ

This is the patriarch of a very large family from the North Atlantic which includes coley, haddock, hake, ling, pollack and whiting.

A round fish, it is a light sandy brown or khaki green on its back and sides, with small yellowish-brown spots. Its underbelly is a creamy silver. The fins are soft and back-sweeping; it can be recognized by the barbel under its chin. It is the largest of the family, weighing on occasion as much as 100lb (45kg) and growing to 3–4ft (90–120cm) long.

We usually see cutlets and fillets from somewhat smaller specimens, although codling (young cod) are sometimes available and these are sold whole. They are well worth seeking out, with firm, white, sweet flesh, more delicate than that of the adult, which is nevertheless an excellent and versatile fish, suitable for frying, grilling, poaching, baking, stuffing, and serving with every imaginable accompaniment. Recipes for its use abound in Scandinavian cookbooks, but also in English, French, Spanish, Portuguese and American ones.

Cod used to be plentiful and therefore relatively inexpensive. This is no longer the case, and so care needs to be taken in selecting it. Deep-sea cod from Icelandic and other far northern waters will be cleaned, gutted and frozen at sea to preserve it during the long fishing trips and voyage back to market. Inshore cod will not have been so treated and if you can get it really fresh, it is wonderful. Ask for Scarborough cod or codling. I can think of few greater fish treats for someone who does not often fry fish than a portion of cod dipped in a light batter, deep-fried in groundnut or sunflower oil and served with homemade chips. But it will take other robust treatments: cook it with a cheese and caper sauce, with bacon, olives and tomatoes, or with garlic, thyme, olive oil and onions. Curry it, bake it in a tandoori, serve it in a fish stew, a pie or a chowder. See also SMOKED FISH, page 177, and DRIED AND SALTED FISH, page 181. (*150, 154*)

Cᴏʟᴇʏ *coalfish, pollock, saithe*

A round, saltwater fish of the cod family, coley is not nearly as highly regarded as cod in Britain. It is often bought simply to feed cats, but deserves a much better fate. We usually see the fish filleted, but whole it is not unlike cod in shape, with a long body tapering from broad shoulders. The skin is often a dark charcoal grey on the back and a silvery grey underneath. It is best skinned before cooking. The flesh is a light, translucent greyish pink, which people tend to find less attractive than white fillets and cutlets, but when cooked, coley does turn milky white. It does not have a particularly distinguished flavour or texture, but is a good everyday fish, one of those which is challenging to a cook.

How to turn something basically rather ordinary into something delicious? I have successfully cooked coley in a pie with prawns, potatoes, cream and fresh basil with a crisp pastry

HOW TO SKIN A FILLET

Lay the fillet flat on a board, with the flesh uppermost; then use a sharp kitchen knife to ease this off the skin, holding the knife slightly angled away from you, and pressed down lightly on the board.

topping. It also makes very good fishcakes and can be used as the white fish in fish soup or chowder, to act as a foil for more exotic, and expensive, shellfish.

In Germany, where coley is known as *Seelachs* (sea salmon), it is salted, dyed a rather vivid orange, smoked, and served like smoked salmon. (*150*)

CONGER EEL

A voracious salt-water fish caught in the coastal waters of southern England, northern Europe and the Mediterranean, the conger eel feeds not only on smaller fish but on molluscs and crustaceans, which make it a fish of very good flavour. The long – sometimes up to 9ft (2·5 metres) – snake-like round body is covered with a smooth grey skin which lightens towards the belly. The dorsal fin runs from the shoulder to the tail.

It is usually sold in cutlets and is well worth buying because it has few bones, except in the tail, and a firm, white flesh with a good flavour.

Fish Cuts

1 HADDOCK FILLET	9 PLAICE FILLET
2 LEMON SOLE FILLET	10 MACKEREL FILLET
3 COD FILLET	11 TUNA STEAK
4 TROUT FILLET	12 DOGFISH FILLET
5 HALIBUT STEAK	13 CONGER EEL STEAK
6 TURBOT STEAK	14 SWORDFISH STEAK
7 MONKFISH TAIL	15 SHARK STEAK
8 SALMON STEAK	16 SKATE WING

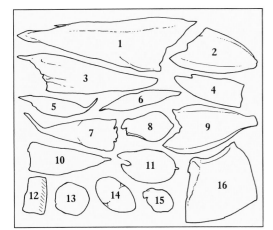

The neck end is the best piece to choose because it has a larger proportion of flesh to bone. Small sections from the tail end are best used in soup and to make fish stock. Conger eel is ideal in a mixed fish soup, because the gelatine which exudes from the bones give the soup plenty of body. A clarified reduced stock made from conger eel tail pieces would make a good base for a fish terrine.

It is close-textured, rather like monkfish, which encourages me to treat it like meat: to roast it like a joint or cook it in a variation of the traditional cassoulet with salt cod and beans, or in a rich stew with garlic, tomatoes, onions and olive oil. (*150, 154*)

CORAL TROUT *croissant*

This is one of the most beautiful groupers I have ever seen, a deep orange-pink, just like coral in fact. It has a dense, strong-looking compact body, with a large head and spiny gill covers. The dorsal fins are firm and spiny; take care when handling this fish. Smaller specimens, 1–2lb (500g–1kg) are excellent steamed in Oriental fashion; the larger ones are best either cut into steaks, using the head and tail for stock, or poached whole in a fish kettle. The flesh is deliciously sweet, firm and milky white, like a cross between a turbot and sea bass. It is a great treat. See also *Grouper* (*166*)

CROAKER *black drum, sea drum, weakfish*

This family of fish includes the drum, queen-fish, hardhead, meagre, ombrine and yellow croaker. Some, like the ombrine and the meagre, are found in Mediterranean, others in North American coastal waters, and yet others in South-East Asia. Members of the same family are found in the South Atlantic (the kabeljou) and the Indian and Pacific oceans of the Australian coast.

The single common characteristic is the ability in the male fish to make a loud croaking noise by twanging a muscle attached to the air bladder, rather like a string plucked on a bass guitar. However this is of little concern to us who are only likely to see them on a fishmonger's slab when they are long past croaking. The fish can be anything up to 2ft (60cm) long and weigh

between 8oz (250g) and 3lb (1·4kg). Some are much smaller and two or three are needed for one portion.

Fish within this group come in a variety of colours, some of which fade after the fish is caught, but are generally a rather dull, gun-metal grey or greyish yellow, sometimes with darker stripes or patches, although I have seen very fine-looking golden croakers in the fish markets of Hong Kong. Almost all are scaly fish and the scales should be removed when cleaning or gutting them. Some croakers and drums have barbels on their chin and others do not.

They are relatively inexpensive fish and are worth trying, particularly if you can find freshly caught specimens. They need careful cooking with plenty of highly flavoured ingredients; perhaps fennel and *pastis* or soy sauce and ginger. (*150*)

DAB *dab sole, garve, sand dab*

From hand-size to a more substantial 1½ pounder (700g), the dab is a member of that large flat-fish family which includes the flounder (fluke), lemon sole, witch, plaice and halibut. It is an oval fish with light sandy-brown skin on its back, and white on its belly. The skin is rough with tiny scales. Indeed, its French name *limande* comes from the Latin name for file and the skin does feel like sandpaper.

The dab is considered by many to be among the best-tasting of the cheaper flat fish. Small fish are best dipped in flour and fried whole in butter after cleaning and trimming and, if you wish, skinning. Larger specimens can be filleted and cooked in any number of ways, simple or elaborate; grilled, steamed or poached, or alternatively wrapped around a filling and baked. I tend to cook them with strong flavours: mustard, garlic, anchovy, horseradish, tomato, soy sauce and so on. (*161*)

DOGFISH *flake, huss, rigg, tope*

There are several varieties of dogfish but the one you are most likely to come across is the spur dog, which is coloured like a shark in tones of grey. You never see it sold whole. Instead you are usually offered attractive pinky boneless fillets, taken from the body and tail. There are no small bones, only a central, easily removable cartilage.

This is a good inexpensive fish, best suited to fairly robust accompanying flavours rather than the delicate classic butter sauces. It can be curried, simmered in sweet-and-sour sauces, braised in wine with herbs and garlic, baked with lemon and olive oil, or incorporated in a rich fish soup or stew. The fish can be cubed, seasoned and marinated, then threaded onto skewers with small tomatoes, mushrooms and a bayleaf and grilled. (*154*)

DOLPHINFISH *dorade, dorado, lampuka, mahi-mahi*

The four alternative names are, respectively, French, Spanish, Maltese and Hawaiian, an indication that the fish is to be found in many parts of the world, although it is not widely known. Freshly caught they are one of the most attractive fish imaginable, rather flashy looking in every way – bright silver skin with mother-of-pearl reflections, a rakishly forked tail, and a high forehead, which looks like a broken nose, behind which the dorsal fin stretches to the tail. The body is rather flat.

It is a versatile fish. Split it like a herring, dip in oatmeal and grill for breakfast. Bone and salt it as for *gravad lax* (salmon). Bake it in a pie with vegetables – a traditional Maltese dish. It is very popular in the United States where it is known by its Hawaiian name, *mahi-mahi*.

DOVER SOLE *common sole, sole*

This is the true sole, the subject of hundreds of recipes in the classical repertoire, from *sole Adrienne* (with soft roes and crayfish tails) to *sole Yvette* (with shrimps and truffles). And while it is true that recipes for Dover sole can be adapted to lemon sole or any of the flat-fish family, they will taste entirely different.

Sole is a luxury fish. It is expensive and so best cooked very simply, either grilled or, according to the classic *à la meunière* or 'miller's wife' recipe, dipped in flour gently fried in butter. It does not need all the elaborate dressing up it often gets although sometimes I skin and fillet it, and make a stock with the head and bones, roll the fillets around a small amount of delicious stuffing, sit them in a little bath of wine and stock and bake them in the oven. Fresh Dover sole is also excellent raw in Japanese *sushi*.

Sole weigh up to 2lb (1kg) and measure up to 18in (45cm) long. The blind side is white, the top side varies a little in colour according to its habitat, but is generally a light brownish-grey.

Baby sole up to 8in (20cm) long are known as Dover slips, and also make good eating, although I think it is a pity to take them too small. (*161*)

EEL, ELVER

These are freshwater fish, although at the beginning and end of their life cycle, the sea is

their habitat. Elvers or baby eels are slim, pale silvery-grey, thread-like creatures, caught after they have made the long journey across the Atlantic to swim up the rivers of Europe. In Spain, France and Portugal they are considered a great delicacy at this stage. In the Basque country they are cooked in olive oil with parsley and garlic and eaten with wooden forks. The little creatures would slip from metal prongs.

Full-grown eels can reach as much as 2–3ft (60–90cm) in length and about 2in (5cm) in diameter. They are dark, almost black on top; with pale silver sides and underbelly. They are sometimes sold live and the fishmonger will prepare them for you. The flesh is firm, white, sweet and very rich. The bones contain plenty of gelatine which, when the fish is cooked in wine and water and then allowed to cool, produces the characteristic jelly of the famous London jellied eels. There are English recipes for eel pie which have their origins in medieval cookery, such as seasoning the eel with ginger, sugar and currants, topping with a layer of hardboiled egg and then baking it under a pastry crust. In France, too, eels are combined with sweetness in the form of prunes in a Touraine recipe which also uses red wine. The Italians marinate and grill pieces of eel and serve them with the fruity, spicy *mostarda di Cremona*. See also SMOKED FISH, page 177. (*146*)

FLOUNDER *fluke*

In my view, this is one of the least exciting of the flat fish, which loses its flavour very soon after being landed. It resembles plaice quite closely, but is not as good. It is absolutely white on the blind side and a dull, dark, greenish-brown on the eye side. The skin is blotchy and sometimes has pale orange spots.

The fish can be cooked whole or filleted with or without the skin. Skinned fillets would be useful as a filler in a fish terrine, in fish balls or in fish cakes. If you do cook it as a fish dish in its own right use plenty of flavouring to counterbalance its inherent blandness. (*161*)

FLYING FISH

Found in tropical waters, this is very popular in the Caribbean and the Philippines. The wings

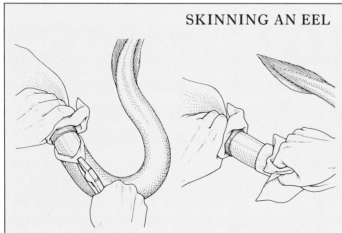

SKINNING AN EEL

Make a circular slit behind the gills. With pliers lever back a flap of skin in the direction of the tail. Gripping flap, pull off the skin; cloths will facilitate a good grip. Cut off the head, slit the belly, remove the organs.

are, in fact, enlarged pectoral fins and the fish look very pretty skimming along the water surface. They have a delicate flavour and can be cooked whole or as fillets. (*166*)

GARFISH *gar, garpike, greenbone, needlefish, sea needle*

This is an unusual fish, unlike any other in that it has an extraordinary vivid green skeleton, even when cooked. This puts people off, which is a pity since the fish is good and the colour is due only to a harmless pigmentation. Its lack of popularity, however, means that it is relatively economical.

A very slender fish, with a long needle-like jaw full of small sharp teeth, the garfish looks quite beautiful, with a bright steely blue-green back and silvery underbelly. The fish is sold whole and may be up to 2lb (1kg) in weight. If you plan to cook it whole, it needs to be cleaned and the gills removed. Any traces of blood or black skin should be scrubbed or scraped away.

One of the best ways I know of cooking it whole is to season it well, spread a little butter over it, add a little white wine or dry sherry, a slice of lemon and wrap it in buttered foil or greaseproof before baking it in the oven.

GRAYLING

This freshwater fish, a member of the salmon family, is a rare treat. It is an attractive silvery fish, with tones of heathery greens and violets which fade to silver grey when it is caught. Small fish weigh about 8oz (250g), and the larger ones 2lb (1kg).

In order to enjoy its sweet, firm, white flesh cook it simply by brushing with melted butter, seasoning and grilling. It can also be cooked using recipes for trout and salmon and is very good cold.

GREY MULLET

A handsome round fish, grey mullet is much underrated and therefore good value. It is no relation to red mullet, but instead looks like a rather rough cousin of the elegant sea bass. It is a dull blue-grey, with faint horizontal stripes, and has large coarse scales. It is available generally all

the year round but is at its best from midsummer to autumn.

Grey mullet weigh up to 9–10lb (4·1–4·5kg) but are most often available at 1½–2lb (750–1kg). The flesh is white, with a good flavour and a texture not unlike that of sea bass.

I would always cook a grey mullet whole; it makes a fine centrepiece when brought to the table, especially when filled with a good stuffing such as chopped fennel and mushrooms. One of its characteristics is that, being a weed-eater rather than a fish-eater, it has an extremely long digestive system, which when removed during cleaning, leaves an excellent cavity for stuffing. This should be rubbed with salt and lemon juice or vinegar to remove any last traces of entrails before stuffing the fish. A particularly good and unusual recipe comes from northern France where it is stuffed with a forcemeat containing minced veal. Meaty flavours go well with the mullet and I would also enhance the sauce with a little veal stock. Strongly flavoured herbs such as rosemary or mint go well with it.

Grey mullet roe is a delicacy and can be cooked on its own or mixed into a stuffing. It is the original ingredient of *taramasalata*, that delicious Greek fishy cream that is now made usually with cod's roe. Dried mullet roe is called *poutargue* in France and *botargo* in Italy. It has the pungency of truffles when grated over a steaming bowl of tagliatelle. See also DRIED AND SALTED FISH, page 181. (*150*)

GROUPER

This is a large family of fish found in the warm waters of the Caribbean and the Gulf of Mexico, South-East Asia, the Indian Ocean and the Mediterranean. The flesh is firm, white, delicate and has an excellent flavour. Groupers are prized by the Chinese and some varieties fetch extremely high prices in the fish markets of Hong Kong. Such a fish will often be the highlight of an important banquet. It will be cooked whole, simply steamed, and lightly seasoned so as not to detract from its exquisite flavour.

Some groupers can grow to a great size, 40–50lb (18–23kg), although you can also find them weighing less than 1lb (500g). They are firm, sturdy fish with compressed oval bodies,

strong tails and, generally speaking, thick lips. Colour is not much help in identifying them, since the grouper is a clever fish which can change colour to suit its habitat, and there is a rainbow of colours to choose from, ranging through muted greys and browns, to yellow, orange and red, mottled, spotted, striped or patched.

Sometimes the fish are simply called groupers, sometimes, according to their colour, red grouper, yellow grouper, and so on. If they are imported from the Seychelles they will more often than not be identified by their creole names: *croissant, vieille maconde, vieille platte* or *vieille rouge*.

A small fish, up to 3–4lb (1·4–1·8kg), will probably be sold whole. When clean remove the gills and gill spines and cut off the spiny dorsal fin, particularly if you plan to cook the fish *en papillote*. Larger ones are sold in steaks. Groupers lend themselves to many methods of cooking: steaming, baking, grilling, poaching or frying. They are also very good cold. Delicate white fillets of grouper are certainly the equal of sole or turbot fillets, and can be served with classic sauces such as *beurre blanc* (white wine and butter sauce). They can also be wrapped individually in foil or greaseproof paper with a little olive oil or butter, a splash of dry white vermouth and a twist of lemon juice and then baked. Larger pieces can be marinated and baked. The fish is firm and robust enough to take strong flavours and accompaniments. See also *Coral Trout*. (*166*)

GURNARD *piper, sea robin*

The three varieties most commonly available are the grey, yellow and red gurnard. The fish has a large head behind which the body narrows into a cone shape.

Partly because of its lovely deep red colour the red gurnard is perhaps the best for cooking. It makes a colourful addition to a fish soup or stew. The flesh is white, firm and tasty. With its large head there is a good deal of wastage, but the fish is inexpensive and the head makes good stock. Cook gurnard either whole for the smaller fish, say up to 2–3lb (1–1·4kg), or in steaks for larger fish. If baking a whole fish, try stuffing it with a herb and mushroom mixture. (*150*)

157

HADDOCK

One of the most important and popular members of the cod family, haddock comes from cold North Atlantic waters. Because of its popularity it is now in grave danger of being overfished and for the next few years we are likely to find it in shorter supply and at higher prices.

It is not as large a fish as the cod, growing to about 2ft (60cm) long and weighing up to 5–6lb (2·3–2·7kg). Small fish are sometimes sold whole – these are sweet and firm-fleshed and should be snapped up immediately. Otherwise you will find fillets or sometimes cutlets. Some people like the smaller fillets, some the tail end of the fillet and some the thicker shoulder pieces. Simply fry or grill after brushing with a little olive oil or butter, or batter and deep-fry or stuff and bake. It goes well with richly flavoured sauces such as tomato, cheese, mustard and caper. See also SMOKED FISH, page 177 (*Arbroath Smokie* and *Haddock*). (*150, 154*)

HAKE

A round, slaty-grey, saltwater fish with silvery-grey underbelly, the hake grows to a length of some 2ft (60cm) and comes from the waters of the North and South Atlantic. The fish is sold whole or in fillets or cutlets. Its flesh is milky white and delicate in flavour; smaller fillets and cutlets are rather fragile in texture. They need careful handling or they will break up during cooking, so they are ideally suited to cooking *en papillote*, or being wrapped in lettuce or spinach leaves, before being steamed. Steaks cut from larger fish are more robust.

Hake is a great favourite in Spain and Portugal. It is fried or baked, served hot with rich green herb sauces, or cold with garlicky dressings and marinades.

Hake throats were a delicacy once enjoyed by Basque fishermen as their occupational perk. It then found its way into Basque restaurants and thence to the rest of Spain where it is now extremely popular. The gelatinous content of this small triangle of flesh combines with the olive oil, garlic and parsley in which it is cooked to produce a most unctuous, richly textured dish. If you see *kokotxes* on a Spanish menu, do try it. (*150*)

HALIBUT

This is one of the largest of the fish we eat. A flat bottom-living fish, the halibut has been weighed in at over 60lb (27kg), growing to a length of 10–12ft (3–4 metres). Such specimens are rare, but steaks and fillets from very large fish are sold. Chicken halibut are small halibut and weigh considerably less: up to 5lb (2·3kg). One weighing about 2lb (1kg) makes a very good meal, or buy the equivalent in steaks. When buying steaks avoid those from the tail end, where the proportion of bone to flesh is high. Bone is a good conductor of heat and so steaks from this part of the fish will dry out in cooking more quickly than steaks from a less bony part.

The flesh of the halibut is white, firm and has a good flavour. It has a tendency to dry out easily and needs careful cooking with plenty of liquid or fat to baste it. I like to cook it very gently in a covered frying pan with butter and mushrooms which together provide a good, tasty basting liquid for the fish.

When cooking a small whole fish I find it best to leave the skin on. It is easy to remove it when cooked, and provides a further protection against over-cooking.

Living so deep in the cold waters of the North Atlantic, the halibut is scarcely affected by seasonal changes and is available most of the year. Greenland halibut is a different species of fish. Although it closely resembles the true halibut in outward appearance its flavour and texture are not as fine. See also SMOKED FISH, page 177. (*154, 161*)

HERRING

Huge shoals of this thin round fish roam around the North Atlantic and North Sea. It has been an important part of the northern European diet and economy for hundreds of years. It is a beautiful fish, steely blue backed with a silver underbelly, neat small fins and forked tail, and pointed head. An oily fish and highly nutritious, the herring is still one of the most economical fish available. For a number of years, in the late 1970s and early 1980s, herring fishing was banned because stocks had become depleted through intensive fishing.

There is not a great deal of variation in the size of herrings. Most weigh around 8–10oz (250–300g), and are about 10in (25cm) long, although slightly larger or smaller ones will be found.

The head can be left on when the fish is cleaned, but it is more usual to remove it. The bones are soft and it is easy to remove the backbone taking the smaller bones with it.

Herring is good grilled with mustard or served with a cold horseradish sauce. Dipped in oatmeal and fried it is a traditional breakfast dish. It is also good cold this way. Best of all though is herring cooked in a light vinegar or white wine. The acidity perfectly complements the rich flesh. Marinating, sousing and pickling are all traditional northern European methods of preparing the herring. See also SMOKED FISH, page 177 (*Bloater, Buckling* and *Kipper*) and DRIED AND SALTED FISH, page 181. (*150*)

JOHN DORY *St Peter's fish*

This armour-plated creature is not very easy to handle. But do not be put off by its large, flat ugly head and curving, sharp dorsal fin; this hides one of the most delicious fish around. The John Dory can grow up to 4lb (1·8kg) in weight and at least 18in (45cm) in length. We are lucky to find 1lb (500g) specimens. Because of its large head you need to allow 1½lb (750g) per person of the whole fish to give a reasonable portion for a main course. I usually serve fillets from smaller fish as a starter. If you have it filleted by the fishmonger use the bones and head to make an excellent stock in which you can poach the fish, and then reduce the poaching liquid to make a well-flavoured sauce.

John Dory is a versatile fish, as highly regarded by chefs as sole and turbot, and can be cooked with a range of ingredients and flavourings. One of the best dishes I have ever had was fillets of John Dory on a bed of butter and spinach, brushed with a light cheese sauce and glazed under the grill but I also like to cook it simply, frying it in butter with tarragon. (*150*)

LEMON SOLE *lemon dab, lemon fish*

It would be so much better all round if sole were not part of this fish's name. It suffers in comparison with the true sole, Dover sole, when really the two fish are quite different. The lemon sole is good in its own right: it is plentiful, economical, with a delicate, sweet white flesh. It is a fairly large flat fish, a roundish oval in shape, with a white blind side and a mottled, drab, brownish-grey topside.

Smaller fish, of 12–16oz (375–500g), can be cooked whole; large ones, up to 4lb (1·8kg), are usually filleted by the fishmonger and cost slightly more. The fish can be skinned before cooking, but it is easy to remove the skin when it is cooked. Simple cooking is best: grill or shallow-fry in butter, or deep fry in a light batter. Lemon sole also tends itself to some of the more elaborate fish terrines, or mousselines, or fillets can be rolled around a stuffing and steamed or baked.

Fillets of lemon sole also make a good addition to a mixed fry of fish, as in Italian *fritto misto*. Whole fish are excellent steamed in Cantonese style with spring onions and ginger, and seasoned with soy sauce and sesame oil. The very freshest lemon sole is exquisite raw, as in the Japanese preparation of *sashimi*, where neat, oblique thin slices are taken from the fillet and served alone or with other raw fish, to be dipped into a mixture of soy sauce and Japanese horseradish, and eaten with pickled ginger. But the fish *must* be absolutely fresh. (*154, 161*)

LING

More eel-like in appearance than cod-like, the ling is nevertheless one of the larger members of the cod family, growing up to 30lb (14kg) in weight. Whole fish can be identified by their long slender body, bronzed olive in colour, mottled green and brown with a white underbelly. Less expensive than cod, but not always easy to find as much of it goes for drying and smoking, it is well worth buying if you come across it.

Cook it in pies or with plenty of strong flavours such as prawns, garlic and spinach. Ask for middle or shoulder steaks rather than small cutlets from the tail end which will have proportionally less flesh on them.

MACKEREL

A handsome round fish from inshore waters available all the year round, the mackerel is highly nutritious, with a good flavour, plentiful and inexpensive. Its distinctive torpedo-shaped body is covered in a smooth iridescent skin, light silvery-blue on the underbelly, darker steely-blue-green on the back, with thick, wavy, dark stripes the length of the body.

The fish, weighing up to 1½lb (700g), are usually sold whole. The head can be taken off or not, as you wish but as it is an oily fish the head is not much use for making stock or fish soup.

A rich, oily, meaty fish, mackerel is best plainly cooked, grilled or dry-fried, or served with sharp sauces, such as mustard, horseradish or curry. It takes tart flavours too. A traditional English way of serving mackerel is with gooseberry sauce, but rhubarb makes an equally good sauce, as do freshly-cooked cranberries in the winter months. A large very fresh mackerel can be boned and filleted and prepared just like *gravad lax*, the Scandinavian marinated salmon dish and eaten with brown bread. It can also be pickled, soused and marinated like herring, as well as salted and home-smoked. See also SMOKED FISH, page 177. (*150, 154*)

MEGRIM *carter, meg, whiff*

One of the lesser flat-fish as far as flavour and texture goes, the megrim is a deepwater fish, oval, with a pointed snout, large head and eyes, and muscular-looking tail. The blind side is white and the back a dull light brown or brownish grey with scarcely visible dark spots. The megrim can weigh up to 5lb (2·3kg) but 1–2lb (500g–1kg) specimens are the ones usually available. The skin is fairly tough and can be

SKINNING AND FILLETING A FLAT FISH

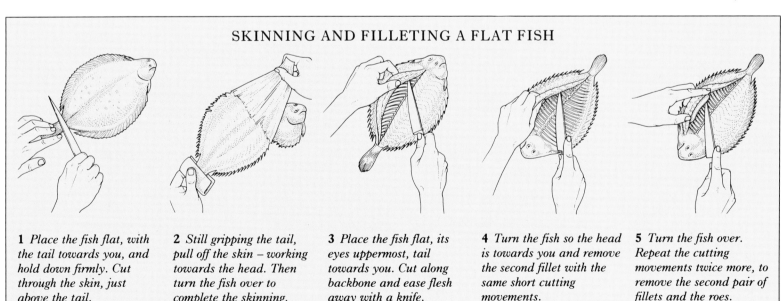

1 *Place the fish flat, with the tail towards you, and hold down firmly. Cut through the skin, just above the tail.*

2 *Still gripping the tail, pull off the skin – working towards the head. Then turn the fish over to complete the skinning.*

3 *Place the fish flat, its eyes uppermost, tail towards you. Cut along backbone and ease flesh away with a knife.*

4 *Turn the fish so the head is towards you and remove the second fillet with the same short cutting movements.*

5 *Turn the fish over. Repeat the cutting movements twice more, to remove the second pair of fillets and the roes.*

removed before or after filleting or cooking. Lemon sole and plaice recipes can be used when cooking megrim but it has considerably less merit than either one. Fish cakes or fish stock are probably the best use for it. (*161*)

MONKFISH *anglerfish*

The broad, fiercely ugly head of the monkfish is rarely seen, only its neat, firm, conical body encasing a single, narrow, vertical bone running down the centre back of the fish. The skin is smooth and mottled dark grey or brownish green. Quite often the tail is skinned before being put on display. Even then it is covered with a tough transparent membrane which should be carefully stripped off before cooking otherwise it will shrink in the heat and toughen. Tails can reach up to 8lb (3·6kg), but on average they weigh from 1½–3lb (750g–1·4kg). I do not like the fish being caught so small as to give us the 6oz (175g) tails which are sometimes seen.

It is worth trying to get a whole fish, since the liver is removed with the head and this is a most exquisite delicacy. Only once have I been lucky enough to find one. It weighed just over 1lb (500g) and looked for all the world like a *foie gras*. After some deliberation I decided to treat it like a goose liver, fried it lightly in butter, weighted it and sliced it when cold to serve with warm toast.

Monkfish (called *lotte* or *baudroie* on French menus, *rape* in Spanish and usually *coda di rospo* in Italian) is a fashionable, popular and therefore rather expensive fish, costing about the same as sole or turbot. However you are not paying for bones, skin and head since the fish is usually already prepared when you buy it, and the flesh is meaty, white and with a good flavour. Grill, fry or bake it. Cut it into chunks and use in kebabs. Slice it thinly, marinate it and serve it raw. Take advantage of its chunky, firm tail and dense texture and treat it as you would a leg of lamb: brush it with olive oil, stud it with pieces of garlic and anchovies and roast it. Monkfish lends itself to the robust flavours of Mediterranean accompaniments, but is also very good with a delicate creamy parsley sauce. I have cooked it like the veal dish, *osso buco*, with a tomato sauce. See also SMOKED FISH, page 177. (*150, 154*)

PARROT FISH *cacatois*

The brilliant hues and beak-like snout of this tropical fish really do resemble those of a parrot. Turquoise blue, viridian green, violet, all these colours and more, enhanced by the large iridescent scales, make the parrot fish one of the most spectacular. The colours fade a little on cooking, but it still looks most impressive on the table. The parrot fish, of which there are many varieties, can grow to 2ft (60cm) or more but what we usually see are 1½–2lb (750g–1kg) specimens.

To remove any chalkiness ensuing from their coral reef habitat rub them inside and out with salt, leave for 15 minutes in a cool place, then rinse and dry thoroughly.

Such a fish is best cooked whole, preferably steamed or poached, and served with a buttery sauce, or one with more Oriental flavours such as ginger. My most successful experiment with parrot fish involved a roasting bag and a bundle of seaweed. Somehow the seaweed, sealed with the fish in the roasting bag, gave it back some of the flavour of the sea which it had lost on its long journey from the tropics. (*166*)

PERCH *darter*

This is an excellent 'food fish' from the fresh waters of lakes, rivers and ponds, growing up to 1½lb (700g), but often much bigger when its habitat is the brackish waters of bays and inlets. Found in Britain, northern and central Europe and in many parts of the United States, the perch is an angler's fish and rarely finds its way to the fishmonger's slab. If it does you will recognize it by its distinctive colouring, an olive-green back with a golden-yellow underbelly, and six to eight darker bands across the back. Its fins are red and orange.

Perch has a delicately flavoured white flesh albeit somewhat coarse in texture. Cook it whole or filleted, and grill, shallow-fry or deep-fry. To keep the flesh moist and tender use the shortest possible cooking time. (*147*)

PIKE

This is a large family of freshwater fish found in the rivers of Europe and North America. It can grow to a remarkable size, over 40lb (18kg) in weight. The pike is a long-bodied fish with a pointed head and jaw and a mouthful of vicious-looking teeth. The skin is a blueish grey or olive green in colour, lightening towards the belly, and marked overall with pale creamy spots.

The best recipes come from France and the United States, where the pike is greatly respected as a fish of good flavour and texture. It is a lean fish and best steamed, poached, baked or shallow-fried, or alternatively stuffed with a good moist filling such as breadcrumbs mixed with herbs, fish stock, chopped onions and tomatoes, and larded with plenty of butter or bacon to keep the fish basted from the inside. The flesh contains many Y-shaped bones, the effect of which is lessened when the fish is stuffed. Light and airy pike dumplings, *quenelles de brochet*, are a feature of classic French cooking. (*146*)

PILCHARD

The pilchard is the adult sardine. It is a round oily fish found in the inshore waters of the Atlantic from Portugal to the southern part of

Flat Fish

1 TURBOT	6 HALIBUT
2 FLOUNDER	7 DOVER SOLE
3 WITCH	8 PLAICE
4 MEGRIM	9 LEMON SOLE
5 BRILL	10 DAB

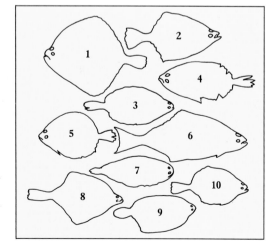

England and Ireland. It is not unlike the herring in appearance, but with larger scales and a more rounded body. It is bluey green in colour, shading through pale gold to silvery white on the underbelly.

The pilchard grows to about 10in (25cm) long and is at its best in the summer. However, most of the catch goes for processing for canned pilchards so fresh pilchards are rarely available. Freshly caught they are delicious grilled, best of all on a charcoal grill, and served with a wedge of lemon and a salad of sweet, ripe tomatoes splashed with olive oil. (*150*)

PLAICE

A flat fish, plaice is browny green with distinctive reddish-orange spots on its back and milky white fins on its blind side. It can grow up to 3ft (90cm) in length, but is usually no more than half that size. Sold whole or in fillets, the plaice is a popular and versatile fish, although I find it rather lacking in flavour. Grilled or fried on the bone, moistened with a little butter and served with lemon and parsley, a very fresh plaice is most acceptable, but even more than most fish it quickly loses its flavour, becoming dull and watery.

If you have thick plaice fillets, marinate them first in olive oil, onion slices and orange juice for example, or in soy sauce and toasted sesame oil. Then grill or steam them and serve with a really flavoursome sauce, fennel, ginger, garlic, tomatoes, anchovies or mustard. (*154, 161*)

POLLACK *greenfish, lythe*

Pollack is a member of the cod family, but not of the same quality as hake, haddock and cod. It is, however, very economical, and worth cooking in fish stews and pies with other livelier flavoured fish. If you are cooking it on its own it will need plenty of dressing up. Try marinating the fillets in a yogurt and tandoori mixture, then bake them and serve with fresh coriander leaves and rice.

Pollack is usually sold in fillets or cutlets. The whole fish can be recognized by its slender khaki or greeny brown body, spotted and blotched with pale yellowy orange. The whole fish can weigh up to 20lb (9kg). (*150*)

POMFRET *ray's bream*

A tropical fish, the pomfret is highly prized in Indian, Chinese and South-East Asian cooking. It is a beautiful fish, with a squat oval body and a mild unaggressive appearance. Its skin is silvery grey on top shading to a silvery-white belly. It is usually sold whole.

Fresh pomfret is an exquisite fish, and there are also many good Thai and Indian recipes for it. The flesh is white, and tender but firm, rather like sole and turbot in texture, although not in flavour. You can use fillets of pomfret in sole and turbot recipes but it is more enjoyable cooked with Oriental flavours – lime, lemon grass, coconut, ginger, *garam masala*. Not all at once of course. (*150*)

POMPANO

Pompano is found in the warm, temperate waters of the Mediterranean, the Caribbean and the Florida and Louisiana coast. It is a round, oily, rich fish, growing up to about 18in (45cm) long, but usually considerably smaller. The fish can be cooked whole or filleted. For recipes consult Caribbean and American cookery books. The pompano reaches the heights of gastronomy in recipes from New Orleans where it has long been a great delicacy. Pompano fillets cooked in a paper bag (*en papillote*) – a dish first created in the famous Antoine's restaurant in New Orleans – is now a permanent feature in most of the city's restaurants.

The flesh tends towards coarseness and dryness, and for this reason I prefer to cook the fillets wrapped in foil or greaseproof paper, having well seasoned them first. Several good combinations come to mind: coconut milk with shreds of lime zest and coconut flesh; chopped, peeled, seeded tomatoes, basil and olive oil; thin apple slices, butter and cider. (*150*)

POUT

A small 10in (25cm) member of the cod family found in coastal waters, pout is bony and the fillets extremely small. If you find it in sufficient quantity and at a good price it will be worth buying to make fish soup, using the flesh to mince for fish cakes or fish balls.

RABBIT FISH *cordonnier brisant, ratfish, spine foot*

The name and the appearance of this fish are somewhat at odds. It has a set of very angry looking spines. These should be removed before you clean and scale the fish, and with great care since they are venomous. If you prick yourself bathe the afflicted spot in hot water. Its skin is a dull khaki grey, striped with faint gold lines. It is a fish from the warm waters of the Eastern Mediterranean, the Indian Ocean and the Pacific feeding on seaweeds as its name suggests.

The flesh is only moderately good, rather dense but crumbly and tending to dryness. It is good in soup and can be baked with plenty of flavourings, Mediterranean or Oriental style, as you wish. (*166*)

REDFISH *berghilt, Norway haddock, ocean perch, red perch, rose fish*

This is a marvellous looking fish, bright reddish orange, with a large bony head, scaly compressed body, a strong tail and large eyes. Although it can grow up to 3ft (90cm) long, most specimens are considerably smaller.

The redfish is a deepwater fish of the North Atlantic, popular in Germany and Scandinavia.

It really is a worthwhile fish. Its flesh is quite firm, white and with a good flavour. It is related to the scorpion fish, or *rascasse*, of the Mediterranean. Although it does not have the same fine flavour, a steak or two cut from a redfish would be excellent in fish stew. But it is worth trying in other ways too: as charcoal-grilled fillets or kebabs, marinated first in olive oil and lemon; or steamed; or stuffed and baked. It can also be filleted and fried. (*150*)

RED MULLET *goatfish*

There are at least two varieties of true red mullet available. The best one is often called golden mullet, although it is actually redder than the other type. This is an excellent fish and has become very fashionable, often served most decoratively as a neat little fillet sitting on a pool of delicious sauce with a frill of chervil or some such greenery for decoration.

Red mullet is sometimes referred to as the woodcock of the sea because it is often cooked –

usually baked or grilled – with the liver still inside like the game bird. I recommend this simple method of cooking above all others since the fish has such a good, sweet, rich flavour and wonderful texture. (*150*)

ROACH

A silvery-greeny-blue fish found in British and European waters, the roach can be identified by its red-tinged fins and, even when fresh, a red iris to the eye. The tough scales are its other characteristic feature and these are best removed immediately after catching. On the other hand, if you were to bake the fish in salt – a fine old-fashioned method of cooking – when you break open the salt crust the scales will come away with it. As it is a river fish, and may have been feeding on muddy river bottoms, a good rinse, or even a 30-minute soak in lightly acidulated water will do it no harm. It can then be cooked as you would cook trout – fried, grilled or poached.

ST PETER'S FISH *tilapia*

This is an important freshwater fish, which is farmed in the lakes of East Africa. St Peter's fish also comes from the Middle East, notably Israel, and is being developed in parts of Europe, especially Belgium.

Most specimens are about 8–12in (20–30cm) long and weigh around 1lb (500g) or a little less. It is a deep charcoal grey over all its body, with only slightly paler sides and underbelly, and sometimes darker patches. It has large prominent scales.

Cook it whole, or filleted. The flesh is white, firm and with a good flavour, lending itself to poaching, steaming, frying or grilling with a good amount of well-flavoured sauce.

Do not confuse this with the John Dory which is also sometimes referred to as St-Pierre or St Peter's fish. (*146*)

SALMON

We should really refer to this wonderful fish as the Atlantic salmon to distinguish it from the Pacific, or Alaska, salmon which is more familiar as canned salmon. The five types of Pacific salmon are the king or royal, the sockeye or red salmon, the pink salmon, the coho or silver salmon and the chum or keta salmon. The last are the most similar to Atlantic salmon and are now being sold fresh in Europe.

The Atlantic salmon is a fine, majestic fish. A steely, silvery blue, streamlined fish, with pale silver flanks and belly, a relatively small head and narrow tail, black dots on the head and upper half of the body, the salmon is relatively easy to identify.

The salmon is a freshwater fish that migrates to the sea to feed for one to four years before returning to the river to spawn. It is also farmed in large cages in locks and estuaries. Farmed salmon is available all the year round. Wild salmon is available only in its season, generally from February to August. There are those who prefer wild salmon. It is a firm, more muscular fish with, in my view, a superior texture and flavour. Farmed salmon has led a more sheltered life, is intensively raised and has a softer texture. Wild salmon feeds on crustacea, which explains the pink colour of the flesh. Farmed salmon may be fed a concentrated feed that has been coloured. Unless the fish is labelled wild salmon it is likely to be farmed. Salmon is sometimes described by the river where it was caught, thus, Tay salmon from Scotland and Dee salmon from Wales.

The specimens usually sold whole are grilse, young salmon, up to 6lb (3kg) in weight, although much larger fish are caught and then sold in steaks or fillets.

The deep orangy-pink flesh is rich and firm and a little goes a long way. Despite it being an oily fish, salmon spoils more quickly through overcooking than any other fish. Perhaps this is why preparations such as *gravad lax* are so popular. This is a Swedish method of preserving boned salmon in salt, sugar, pepper and dill weed, pressing it down and keeping it refriger-

BONING A ROUND FISH THROUGH THE BACKBONE

1 *With a sharp knife, cut off the head. The hold the fish steady, tail towards you and cut along the back, above the backbone.*

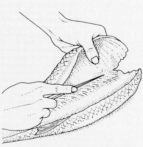

2 *Slide the knife along and down over the ribs, but leave the fillet attached by the belly skin if you wish to stuff the fish.*

3 *Flatten out fillet and lift 'head' end of backbone. Slide knife under and along towards tail. Remove bone with tail.*

4 *To fillet the fish: if you do not need to keep fish in one piece for stuffing, separate fillets simply by cutting along belly skin.*

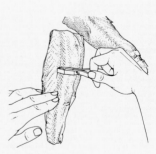

5 *Use your fingertips to feel for any remaining bones and remove these carefully, using small kitchen pliers.*

163

ated for a few days, turning it from time to time in the liquid that is given off. The salmon is thus still raw, but beautifully cured. It is served thinly sliced. I much prefer it to smoked salmon. In fact raw salmon, when it is perfectly fresh is delicious. I make it into a salmon tartare, or serve it in the Japanese style as *sashimi* (small slices of raw fish) to dip into soy sauce and *wasabi* (Japanese horseradish).

A smaller salmon is very good cooked whole, poached, or wrapped in foil and baked in the oven. It can be eaten hot, warm or cold, with appropriate accompaniments. Salmon is also a great favourite for terrines and *mousselines*.

When it is more plentiful later in the season and comes down in price a little, it is worth experimenting with other sorts of dishes – pies, flans, kedgerees and my favourite, the Russian *kulebyaka*, a pie made of brioche dough filled with fish, eggs, herbs, butter and sometimes cooked rice and mushrooms. See also SMOKED FISH, page 177, and CAVIAR, page 183. (*146, 154*)

SALMON TROUT *sea trout*

The salmon trout is closely related to the brown trout, but while the latter is entirely freshwater-dwelling, the salmon trout is, like the salmon, migratory, feeding in the sea and returning to spawn in rivers. The brown trout has a creamy-white flesh, but salmon trout lives on crustaceans which give it a pink, delicate flesh, also like the salmon. The same pigment is present in paprika, for example, and so the flesh of farmed fish can be turned pink by feeding them foodstuffs containing appropriate pigments.

You can distinguish the salmon trout from the salmon by its slightly less streamlined shape, its thicker tail stalk with slightly concave fin and a longer jawline, extending beyond the eye.

Cook salmon trout very simply so as not to detract from its delicate flavour. See also CAVIAR, page 183. (*146*)

SARDINE

Someone has only to mention Portugal to me and the first thing that comes into my mind is the memory of the smell of fresh sardines grilling over small cast-iron charcoal burners – one of the simplest and most appetizing meals in the world when served with fresh crusty bread and a salad of sweet ripe tomatoes.

Fresh sardines – baby pilchards – usually weigh about 4oz (125g), and are long, thin and silvery with a multitude of fine scales. These are soft and best removed by holding the fish by its tail under running water and running finger and thumb over the body – tail to head – gently easing the scales off. The fish can also be gutted and rinsed, although the head is usually left on.

As well as grilling them, roll sardines in flour and shallow- or deep-fry. They are very good baked with a drop of olive oil and a few slices of lemon and eaten hot or cold. Really fresh sardines with head and backbone removed lend themselves to all kinds of marinades. Sardines are used in Sicily to make the traditional dish, *pasta con le sarde*, a rich mixture of sardines, fennel, pine nuts and raisins with spaghetti or bucatini.

Canned sardines are a very good store cupboard standby. Sardines on toast is a quick delicious snack. Mashed with butter and herbs they make an excellent savoury spread. The very best quality are canned in olive oil. See also DRIED AND SALTED FISH, page 181. (*150*)

SCABBARD *espada, sabre fish*

This is a handsome fish well worth buying if you see it. A long-jawed round fish, it has a flat, narrow, elongated body, which with its silvery or dull grey, shiny skin really does resemble a scabbard. They can grow up to 5ft (1·5 metres) long, but the ones on sale are usually 2–3ft (60–90cm).

Mainly a North Atlantic fish, it is particularly appreciated in Portugal, where it is given the simplest of cooking treatments, grilled or fried in olive oil, and served with fresh coriander leaves and lemon. The fish has a firm enough texture to take a flavoursome marinade before cooking. The tail piece has little flesh on it, but if you are feeding several people it is worth buying the whole fish, keeping the head and tail for soup or stock another day, and having the body to cut into suitable serving pieces. Try it in a *ceviche*, cooked and marinated in olive oil, lime juice, onions and chillies. (*150*)

SCAD *horse mackerel*

The family of carangids to which the scad and horse mackerel belong is one of the largest families of 'food fish'. Jack, trevally jack, crevalle, kingfish, king carangid, queenfish, amberjack, rainbow runner, blue runner, yellowtail, pompano, golden thread and many others are included. They are found in the Atlantic, the Mediterranean, the Pacific and the Indian Ocean.

The flesh is a pale biscuity colour, oily like mackerel and sardines, firm and slightly coarse in flavour. The fish vary considerably in size. Some are sold whole, some in steaks or fillets.

Whole they are best baked with a good, moist, flavoursome stuffing. Otherwise marinade and grill them. Recipes for mackerel are suitable for this group of fish and excellent recipes will be found in Caribbean cookery books. (*150*)

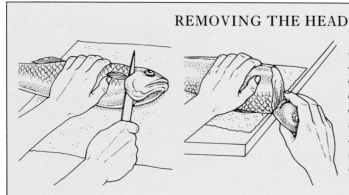

REMOVING THE HEAD

If the fish is quite small, simply cut right through, just behind the gills. If the fish has a very strong backbone, cut through as far as possible, then bend back the part severed head against edge of table to snap the bone. Cut through remaining flesh.

SHAD *allis*

This plump, handsome member of the herring family is a fine eating fish if you are lucky enough to come acoss it. It has the characteristic rounded torpedo shape, silver belly and steely blue-green back of its family but is a rounder fish than the herring. Different varieties grow to different sizes, from about 8oz (250g) to the huge American shad which can reach a weight of 14lb (6·5kg).

Like salmon, shad, which generally lives in coastal waters, swims upriver to spawn, and is best caught and eaten just before it does so, that is when it is entering the estuaries. Then it is plump and firm with, in the females, a delicious roe which is a great delicacy and should be cooked separately. May is the best time for shad in Britain and Europe. However in the United States the shad season extends from December in the warm estuaries of Florida to June for the more northerly waters.

The scales are relatively soft, flexible and lightly attached which makes shad an easy fish to scale. It has the same bone structure as herring, and the bones are similarly small, thin and quite soft. It is possible to bone the fillets by running a sharp boning knife down either side of each line of bones, lifting the whole line out with the knife point and then cutting each fillet into firm long strips. Do not remove the skin when filleting shad as the flesh is delicate and will easily break.

Rather than fillet the fish, I prefer to use cooking methods which minimize the effect of the bones. There are three traditional ways of doing this. In France, where you will sometimes see *alose* in the Loire, Ardèche and Garonne regions, it is often cooked whole or in slices, with large quantities of sorrel, the acid in which is supposed to soften the bones. The bones can also be softened by cooking the fish on a very low heat (Gas mark ½, 250°F, 120°C) for a long time (5–6 hours), making sure that the fish is first well seasoned, buttered and sealed in baking parchment or a baking dish with a tight-fitting lid. The third method is to stuff the fish and bake it. The stuffing encloses the small bones in each mouthful.

French and American cookery books have wonderful recipes for shad. My favourite is planked shad, in which a clean plank of wood is oiled and heated from cold in the oven. When it is really hot, the split fish is placed on it, brushed with butter and put into the oven for 20 minutes. A bakestone makes an excellent substitute for the plank.

SHARK *Beaumaris shark, porbeagle, tope*

A giant up to 12ft (3·65 metres) long and weighing up to 200lb (90kg), this smooth-skinned creature is now found quite often on the fishmonger's slab. Do not be put off by its characteristically sinister dorsal fin and long, pointed, dangerous-looking snout. It is remarkably good to eat. Like many members of the shark and dogfish family it has no small spiny bones, just a central bony cartilage. Usually sold in chunks or steaks of pale creamy pink flesh, it can be cooked like veal – breaded and gently fried in butter. It is a densely textured and distinctively flavoured fish, and a little goes a long way. Casserole it with onions, tomatoes, olives and herbs, or flavour it with ginger, garlic, lemon grass, soy sauce and sesame oil, not to mention a couple of fiery chillies. See also DRIED AND SALTED FISH, page 181. (*150, 154*)

SKATE

Skate and ray are large, flat, non-bony fish related to shark. They have a similar, simple cartilaginous bone structure. A whole skate or ray is dark skinned, smooth, soft and shiny, kite-shaped with a long tail. Only once have I ever seen a whole one, a long thornback ray on the floor of a fishmonger's in Le Touquet, in France. It was a least 3ft (90cm) across its 'wings'. Usually only the wings are sold, skinned on one side and with a pearly white skin on the other. The raw flesh is a most attractive pinkish white, covering the long curving wing of cartilaginous rays joined together like a fine web. When cooked the flesh is delicious, sweet, white and has an excellent texture.

An absolutely freshly caught skate or ray will be tough and tasteless, but fish about three or four days old is perfect. There should be no more than a slight hint of ammonia about it. Do not buy it if this smell is strong for it will not disappear in cooking, however much you bathe the fish in salt water or vinegar.

Skate and ray are sold interchangeably as 'skate', already skinned, jointed and prepared. Skate wings weighing about 1–2lb (500g–1kg) each are the ones to look for. Wings from smaller skate are sometimes available, but the flesh is rather skinny. Very large wings are difficult to cook in domestic-sized pots and pans, even when cut into pieces but, more importantly, their flavour and texture are not quite so fine.

This is one of my favourite fish. I like it hot, cold, or best of all, just warm in a salad with new potatoes, nut oil and some fresh mint leaves, finely chopped. It is also excellent with olive oil and capers, or with samphire. The classic French way with skate – *raie au beurre noir* – is to poach it first then finish it off with browned butter, vinegar and capers.

Occasionally skate knobs are sold. These are small pieces cut from the skinned tail which make an economical tasty dish. They are a good addition to fish soups, but I also cook them in olive oil with garlic, parsley and a drop of *manzanilla* sherry. (*154*)

SMELT *sparling*

Although at first glance you might take this for a sardine, the smelt is actually related to salmon. It spawns in rivers and lives in coastal waters and river mouths throughout Europe. The slim, slightly flattened body, 4–8in (10–20cm) long, has a metallic olive-green back and a creamy silvery belly separated by a wide bank of bright silver.

The fish are sold whole and should be gutted. The traditional way to cook them is to thread a few on to a skewer through the eyes and deep fry them in oil, draining them on paper and serving them crisp and crunchy. Alternatively, if they are absolutely fresh, shallow-fry them in a little unsalted butter to preserve their delicate and unusual flavour. (*150*)

SNAPPER *bourgeois, bordemar, job gris, job jaune, thérèse, vara-vara*

The different kinds of snapper make up a large group of important food fish from tropical and subtropical waters. They are striking fish with long domed foreheads, compressed bodies,

rounded backs and a high lateral line following the shape of the back. The front of the dorsal fin is spiny, the scales large and tough and the skin very thick. In colour they cover the spectrum of the reds, oranges and pinks, although some are greyish, others bluey green. Vertical bars, horizontal stripes, patches and spots further adorn these glorious fish. There is a huge size range, from 6in (15cm) to well over 3ft (90cm) long.

I once helped cook a 6lb (3kg) bourgeois for Christmas lunch. We poached it whole in a fish kettle, removed the skin and served portions of the delicate, yet firm white meat with a rich *beurre blanc* sauce flavoured with chives. Fillets of turbot never tasted better. The best of the snappers are excellent fish and lend themselves to many cooking methods. Cookery books from

Tropical Fish

1	BARRACUDA	10	SNAPPER
2	GROUPER (VIEILLE		(BOURGEOIS)
	PLATTE)	11	SCAD (GOLDEN
3	CORAL TROUT		THREAD)
4	SNAPPER (VARA-VARA)	12	PARROT FISH
5	SURGEON FISH	13	FLYING FISH
6	EMPEROR BREAM	14	PARROT FISH
	(LASCAR)	15	SNAPPER (BABY
7	PARROT FISH		BOURGEOIS)
8	GROUPER (VIEILLE	16	EMPEROR BREAM
	MACONDE)		(CAPITAINE BLANC)
9	EMPEROR BREAM	17	RABBIT FISH
	(CAPITAINE ROUGE)		

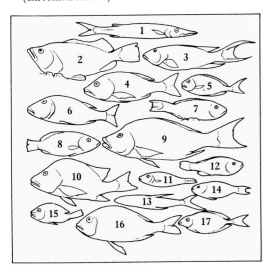

South-East Asia, South America, the Caribbean and the Seychelles will provide good guidance.

If you are choosing a whole fish, have it scaled, cleaned and trimmed and gutted, and then make sure the cavity is well scrubbed out before you cook it. The bones are rich in gelatine and make excellent stock. (*166*)

SPRAT

This small relation of the herring is found in European coastal waters and is at its best in the winter months. The long oval body has small fins, a forked tail and thin, soft scales. It is bluey-green on its back, shading through pale gold to silver on its underbelly.

Only 4–6in (10–15cm) long, sprats can be cooked ungutted, and I usually run my fingers over them, tail to head, to remove the scales. This is best done under running water.

Sprats are best cooked simply, either grilled or fried and eaten hot or cold. They can also be fried and then marinated (a typically Portugese method). This way they will keep in the refrigerator for several days. See also SMOKED FISH, page 177. (*150*)

SURGEON FISH *doctor fish*

This tropical inshore fish has a sharp blade on either side of the tail, rather like a scalpel. Still quite a rare sight in Britain it is very popular in the Caribbean and West Africa. (*166*)

SWORDFISH

Steaks of pale peachy-pink swordfish meat are occasionally available. The flesh, which cooks white, has a firm meaty texture, but is inclined to dryness and should be marinated before grilling or baking on a barbecue or a domestic grill. It can also be breaded and fried like veal. See also SMOKED FISH, page 177. (*154*)

TORSK *tusk*

A slight confusion is possible here. 'Torsk' is the name for cod throughout Scandinavia, but there is also another member of the cod family called 'torsk' in England but 'brosme' in Scandinavia.

It lives in the northernly part of the North

Atlantic and makes quite a good eating fish, treated in the manner of cod or haddock. It averages 1½–2ft (45–60cm) in length but can grow larger. It is a dull reddish or greenish brown with a lighter underbelly. The fins are edged in white.

TROUT

Two fish are dealt with under this heading; brown trout and rainbow trout.

The brown trout, sometimes also called the lake trout, lives wild in the waters of rivers, streams and lakes in North America and northern Europe. It has mottled greenish-brown skin with a creamy underbelly and is 8–16in (20–40cm) long. If very fresh it will feel slimy to the touch. The flesh when cooked is creamy white.

It is a rare treat. I have twice been lucky enough to eat brown trout, once in a small mountain town in northern Tuscany and once in the Black Forest in Germany. On both occasions the fish were cooked *au bleu*. Very freshly caught, they were poached in simmering water with a little vinegar. The natural shine on the skin turns to a soft blue during cooking, which is a sign of sparkling freshness.

The rainbow trout is now largely a farmed species. It has a pretty iridescent skin, with greenish-brown spots. Its flesh is pink. Rainbow trout is plentiful and relatively inexpensive.

For brown trout the simplest cooking methods are best. They will enhance rather than mask the delicate flavour, colour and texture of the fish. Rainbow trout can take more robust treatment and need some flavouring, such as garlic, anchovies or bacon, fragrant herbs, wine, tomatoes, lemon. Cold, both fish are excellent with mayonnaise, cream salad dressings and sauces. See also SMOKED FISH, page 177. (*146, 154*)

TUNA *albacore, bluefin tuna, skipjack, tunny, yellowfin*

Belonging to the same family as mackerel and bonito, the tuna is an excellent food fish. Fresh tuna is becoming more readily available, and no longer do we only see it canned in oil or brine (though these are a useful store cupboard standby). Different species of tuna are found all over the world in temperate and subtropical seas. They come in a range of sizes from 2–3lb (1–1·5kg) to 1500lb (675kg)! It is an oily fish with dense firm meat, from pale pink to dark red, depending on the species.

Most tuna is sold in steaks or larger pieces, often already skinned. This is always a good buy because there is absolutely no waste, and a little of this rich fish goes a long way.

My favourite way of cooking it is to marinate it overnight with ginger, garlic, soy sauce, sesame oil and a little rice wine or failing that, *amontillado* sherry, and then grill it on a charcoal or cast-iron grill, just like a fillet steak. It is delicious left rare in the middle, but it can also be cooked through for those who do not like raw fish. It has a tendency to dryness and needs careful cooking with plenty of lubrication. There are very good Spanish and Portuguese recipes for fresh tuna. It can be baked, fried, braised, marinated and stewed, alone or with other well-flavoured ingredients.

Canned tuna is worth a place in the store cupboard as it has many uses other than as sandwich fillings. It is very good flaked and stirred into a bowl of hot pasta and is equally good in cold pasta salads. It may not be authentic but a *salade niçoise* with tuna makes a very good summer lunch or supper dish. Canned tuna is also an essential ingredient in that summery Italian dish, *vitello tonnato* where cold, sliced veal is covered with a creamy tuna fish and caper sauce. (*150, 154*)

TURBOT

Without a doubt this is the king of the flat fish, although the sole also has its partisans. Turbot is expensive and a fish for just an occasional treat. It lives on the bottom of the deep waters of the north-eastern Atlantic and grows up to 25lb (11·3kg) in weight. The blind side is white and the top side a greyish-brown, covered with bony nodules and greenish-brown spots. It has a neat oval-diamond-shaped body, matched by the diamond-shaped *turbotières*, or turbot-kettles, which were important kitchen utensils in bygone days and still to be found in specialist kitchen shops. A large sauté or frying pan or roasting tin might just take a whole turbot trimmed of its tail fin, otherwise you should have it filleted, or buy

steaks cut from a much larger fish. Whatever you do, take care not to overcook this exquisitely delicate fish. The simplest methods and the lightest hand in seasoning are by far the best. Poaching, grilling or shallow-frying, with a light butter, lemon, chive and parsley cream sauce would be perfect. Serve left-over turbot cold with mayonnaise. (*154, 161*)

WEEVER

I once bought some fine-looking weevers in the market in Bordeaux in South-West France and was impressed by how carefully the fishmonger gutted and cleaned them after cutting off the first two spines of the first dorsal fin, and the gill covers which are not only painful, but venomous, if you prick yourself. It is a handsome fish, with a greyish-brownish body with darker brown spots and creamy-yellow flanks and underbelly, usually about 12–16in (30–40cm) long. They are good flavoursome fish, with firm but not dry, white flesh. To cook them I make several diagonal slashes across the flesh, on both sides, rub them with a mixture of mustard, olive oil and finely chopped herbs and grill them, serving them with an extra trickle of olive oil.

WHITEBAIT

This is the name given to the fry, or young, of a number of fish, usually herring or sprats. It is rarely on sale fresh because of measures taken to conserve herring fishing.

These tiny – no more than 2in (5cm) long – fish are delicious. Simply roll them in flour, deep-fry in oil and serve with a wedge of lemon and a scattering of sea salt for eating whole. They are a favourite treat in the bars of Lisbon and Barcelona. (*150*)

WHITING

One of the smallest members of the cod family from the eastern side of the Atlantic, whiting are about 12–16in (30–40cm) long and can weigh up to 4lb (2kg), although the ones we usually see weigh between 12oz and 1lb (375–500g). Flesh and flavour alike are delicate. The longer the fish has been out of the sea, the more the flesh breaks down and it is impossible to fillet and skin it

without tearing the flesh.

It is useful for fish soups and also to mince for fish balls, and to grind for a paste for use in fish *mousselines*. It needs gentle indirect heat, poaching or cooking in foil, rather than grilling.

Whiting has long been associated with invalid cookery because it is delicately flavoured and highly digestible. (*150*)

WITCH

This can be mistaken for a Dover sole if you do not look too closely. It is an oval flat fish, sandy or darker brownish grey in colour, with a small mouth and relatively large eyes, and fine scales that make the skin feel rough rather than scaly.

It has more flavour if cooked on the bone and I would recommend steaming or shallow frying, then adding plenty of good flavours in the sauce, for example, herbs like tarragon or chervil with a few chopped tomatoes and garlic. (*161*)

WRASSE *ballan wrasse, cuckoo wrasse, green wrasse*

A handsome picture book fish, this is a large-scaled round fish with a spiny single dorsal fin running from just behind the gills to the tail, broad-bodied with a convex tail fin 12–20in (30–50cm) long. It does not make for particularly good eating. Its rather coarse flesh is best used in mixed fish stews or soups.

Some of the mottled blue-green wrasse have a slight resemblance to the parrot fish to which they are distantly related, but they are not as good. (*150*)

ZANDER *pike perch*

This is the *sandre* of French menus in the Loire valley, a fiercely rapacious game fish from the rivers, lakes and canals of Europe, rarely found commercially in Britain. It grows to about 3ft (90cm) long. It resembles the perch in appearance and the pike in its habits, hence its alternative name. If you should come across it freshly caught, it should be scaled, cleaned and gutted immediately.

The fish can be stuffed and baked or poached and served hot or cold. It makes for good eating but needs some flavouring and moistening.

SHELLFISH

This is a large and important group of seafood that adds a delicious diversity to our diet, but which does need careful handling. It divides into three subgroups: crustaceans, molluscs and cephalopods.

Crustaceans include lobsters, crabs, prawns and shrimps and are distinguished by their five pairs of legs, one pair of which is sometimes formed as heavy front claws or pincers. The head and body is often enclosed in a shell or a tough carapace like armour plating. Quite often they are sold ready cooked, but it is much better to buy them live and cook them yourself if you want really fresh, sweet flavours.

Molluscs are a very large group of shellfish: the gastropods which use a single shell like the whelk and winkle, and the bivalves which are enclosed inside two hermetically sealed shells like the mussel, oyster and scallop.

Cephalopods are the family to which squid, octopus and cuttlefish belong and are well worth looking out for. They are not difficult to prepare and yield delicious sweet white flesh when carefully cooked.

All shellfish deteriorate rapidly, raw or cooked, and should be bought for immediate consumption.

ABALONE *ear shell, ormer*

The abalone's dwelling is a single squarish-oval shell with a beautiful pearly interior, which it carries around, moving on its single muscular 'foot'. The shell is about 5in (12cm) across. The foot is the edible part, considered a delicacy in both the Channel Islands and California. Ormers – smaller, European abalone – used to be so prolific in Guernsey that you will see there the exterior walls of whole houses decorated with the empty shells. Bearing in mind that the edible part of the abalone is the muscle with which it propels itself and clings to rocks, it is no surprise to learn that it is somewhat tough. After cutting it away from the shell, tenderize it by beating it with a wooden mallet or a rolling pin.

Slice small tender abalone thinly, marinate it, then eat it raw. Larger ones can be sliced and cooked quickly in butter or olive oil. They have a sweet flavour, not unlike scallops. Abalone is also used in Oriental cooking. (*175*)

CLAM

Found in coastal waters almost worldwide, there are very many varieties of these excellent and edible bivalve molluscs. Some are tiny, only an inch or two (2·5–5cm) across – these are the ones called *vongole* in Italy and used in some classic pasta sauces. Some resemble large round smooth stones, as much as 5in (12cm) across; some, like the Venus clam, are pale, delicately coloured and quite pretty; others, like the hard-shelled clam, look grey and muddy. Clams are very popular on the east coast of the United States, particularly in New England, which is famous for its marvellous clam soups, or chowders, and clam-bakes, a kind of beach picnic, where clams, lobsters, chicken, potatoes and corn are cooked in a steam pit dug in the sand.

Clam flesh is firmer than that of an oyster or mussel and you need to cook it carefully. Clams are bought by weight if they are small, individually if large. Make sure that none is damaged or open. Small, smooth clams only need rinsing; scrub larger, rough-shelled clams under running water to remove sand or grit. Discard any that remain open. Raw clams are popular in the United States and Japan, and are often served on the half shell on a bed of ice in France where they are known as *praires* or *palourdes*, depending on the variety.

To open clams place small ones in a lidded saucepan and steam just until they open. Put larger clams on a baking tray and heat in a fairly hot oven for a minute or two until the shells open. Large clams can also be slit open in the same manner as oysters (see page 173).

All parts of the clam are edible but cut off the black-tipped nozzle, or siphon, of large clams. Smaller clams such as *amandes* the little necks, cherry-stones, carpet-shells, Venus, steamers or soft-shell clams are usually eaten whole from the shell with a little melted butter. The larger hard-shell clams and ocean quahogs have a stronger flavour, and are the ones usually chopped or minced for chowders and sauces. Buy clams to cook and eat the same day. (*175*)

COCKLE *arkshell*

Various types of cockles are found in sandy coastal areas throughout the world. They are rarely sold fresh and in their shell, but more usually in jars, preserved in brine or vinegar. These are suitable for eating as a piquant appetizer straight from the jar, but are of little use in cooking.

Sometimes shelled cockles that have already been cooked are sold loose. If they are not too salty, these small beige and orange creatures can be thoroughly rinsed and mixed with pastas, served in a salad, or in a seafood pie.

Live cockles, which can be dug up near the water-line on sandy beaches, are bivalves – that is, they occupy two hinged shells. Cockleshells are pale yellowy beige, dirty pink, cream, or slaty blue, with ribs radiating from the hinged centre of the two shells to the curving edge. Place live cockles in a bowl of salted water or clean sea water overnight to disgorge any impurities, grit or sand. Cook them like mussels. Do not gather cockles or, indeed, any bivalves, unless you are absolutely certain that they come from an area of unpolluted sea water. (*175*)

CRAB

There are said to be more than 4500 species of crab found worldwide. They vary in size from mere fingernail size for the tiny oyster crab which actually spends part of its life in the shell of a live oyster, to the familiar common brown crab, 8–10in (20–25cm) across.

Crab meat is of two sorts, the brown meat which is soft and rich, from inside the hard upper shell, and the more chewy, dense, sweet white flesh found in the claws and the body. The male has larger claws and will therefore yield a larger proportion of white meat than the female. But the female may have a bonus of pink coral. You can distinguish the male and female by looking at the tail flap. The male's is narrower and more pointed, the female's broader.

All crabs have hard, shield-like shells, or carapaces, and ten brittle claws or legs, sometimes covered with hairs. They come in a wide variety of colours when live: green, blue, brown, red, grey, all turning reddish-brown when cooked, some brighter than others. Crabs are often sold cooked. Choose one that feels heavy for its size; this indicates that there is plenty of meat and that the crab is fully grown in its shell. You will get better results if you buy a live crab

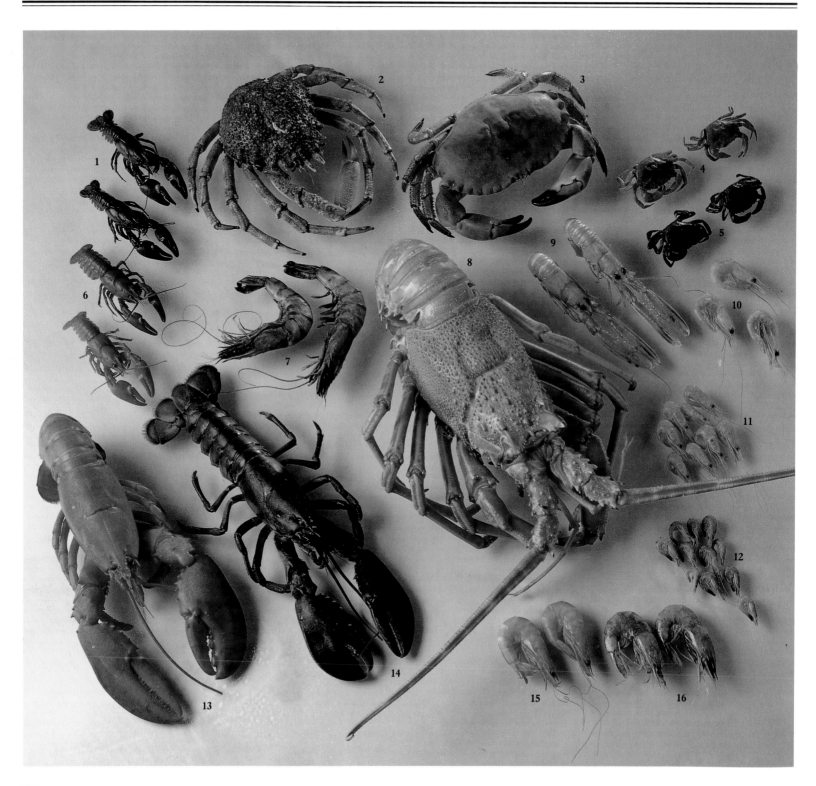

and cook it yourself – the flavour is far superior.

Brown crab, edible crab This is abundant in European waters and fished throughout the year. The largest are 8–10in (20–25cm) across the shell with very large heavy front claws. The shell is a rusty red-brown, the legs red, mottled with white, and hairy, and the large front claws have almost black pincers. A 1lb (500g) crab will serve one person.

Blue crab, Atlantic blue crab Although not exclusive to American waters, the blue crab is an important source of seafood throughout the long eastern seaboard. It grows to about 8in (20cm) across the shell, but is sold much smaller. The shell is a blueish brown, a flattened pointed oval with a serrated edge where the head is. The other edge is smooth.

Like all crabs, the blue crab moults, and it is at the stage when it has just discarded its shell that it is landed as a soft-shell crab. This is a highly prized delicacy, and the entire crab is eaten – often deep-fried – because there is no shell to crack. It sounds ghastly, but it *is* delicious.

The small green, shore crabs of Venice are treated in the same way.

Dungeness crab This is one of the most delicious crabs I have ever eaten. Native to the Pacific coast of the United States and a great delicacy in California, the crab has a large proportion of firm, sweet, white meat. The soft meat in the shell is a pale greyish-green and of a particularly fine flavour. It is large, about 8in (20cm) across the shell.

Spider crab Native to European waters, much of the catch is taken by French and Spanish fishing boats. But this spring creature is well worth buying for its sweet succulent flesh. It

really does have something of the appearance of a spider in the arrangement of its long hairy legs. Unlike the brown crab it does not have a set of large claws, and its shell is spiny and oval in shape. When live, the shell and legs are a dull reddish purply brown, which lightens to a bright red on cooking. There is plenty of meat in the legs. You will need one crab per person.

Other crabs You may come across a number of other types – Thai crabs, coral crabs, flowery crabs or smokies – varying in size, colour and markings. The larger ones can be cooked like other crabs, and the flesh picked out of them.

The smaller ones are best cooked in the manner of the French *soupe aux étrilles* (*étrilles* are small swimming crabs, dark brown in colour with navy blue markings), where the shellfish are pounded and sieved after cooking to produce a smooth soup. (*170*)

CRAWFISH *langouste, rock lobster*

This is a far-ranging salt-water crustacean which should not be confused with the freshwater crayfish. The rock lobster is found around European and American coastal waters, the

Crustaceans

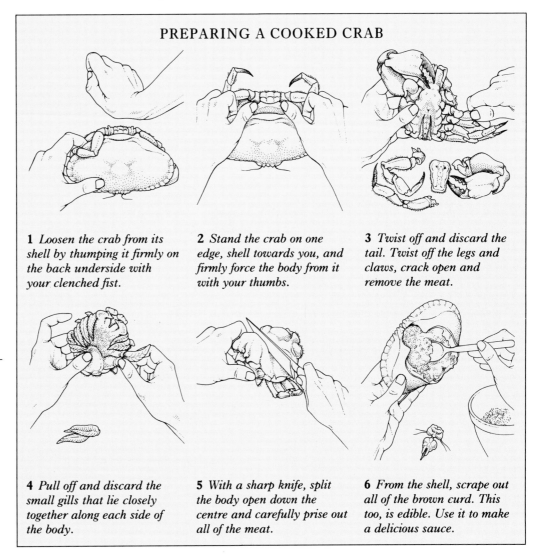

PREPARING A COOKED CRAB

1 *Loosen the crab from its shell by thumping it firmly on the back underside with your clenched fist.*

2 *Stand the crab on one edge, shell towards you, and firmly force the body from it with your thumbs.*

3 *Twist off and discard the tail. Twist off the legs and claws, crack open and remove the meat.*

4 *Pull off and discard the small gills that lie closely together along each side of the body.*

5 *With a sharp knife, split the body open down the centre and carefully prise out all of the meat.*

6 *From the shell, scrape out all of the brown curd. This too, is edible. Use it to make a delicious sauce.*

Mediterranean, the South Atlantic and the waters of South-East Asia. In size and colour it varies according to its habitat but the most familiar ones are anything from 12–18in (30–45cm) long with a rough, prickly, reddish-brown, mottled shell. The main differences between it and the true lobster are its very well-developed, long, whippy antennae, its thicker, chunkier body, five sets of legs of even size, and no heavy claws. The tail meat is excellent. Prepare and cook as for lobster. (*170*)

CRAYFISH *écrevisse*

Crayfish are still found in unpolluted freshwater lakes, ponds and streams in Britain, Scandinavia and many parts of Europe, America and Africa. Years ago in Nigeria I gave a party where the food and drink was a huge pile of freshly cooked crayfish, and large jugs of distilled palm wine,

Cephalopods

1 SQUID   3 CUTTLEFISH
2 OCTOPUS   4 BABY OCTOPUS

both liberally adorned with thick slices of fresh, fragrant, juicy lime.

About 3–4in (7–10cm) long, a dark greeny brown and quite frisky when live, the crayfish cooks to a bright pink or deep clear red, and is best eaten simply with melted unsalted butter – and fresh lime. The flavour is sweet and delicate, rather similar to that of lobster. (*170*)

CUTTLEFISH

The Latin name for cuttlefish is *Sepia officinalis*, and the inky liquid found in the small sac just behind the cuttlefish's head was, indeed, formerly used to make sepia ink. This is a very good widely distributed 'food fish', but it is not as popular as it deserves to be.

Like squid and octopus, the cuttlefish is a member of the group known as cephalopods. It grows to a length of about 10in (25cm), and its bell-shaped hollow body sac contains the hard white smooth oval shell or cuttle. The body has a frilled 'fin' all the way round the edge and eight medium and two long tentacles. The colour varies, but is often a deep brownish violet or grey.

Preparing cuttlefish (and squid) is easier than it appears to be and it really is worth doing. The flesh cooks from a pale translucent pinkish grey, to a milky white sweetness and is tender yet firm to the bite. There are many excellent Mediterranean recipes for cuttlefish, and it can be substituted in any recipe calling for squid.

There is also a very small variety of cuttlefish about 2in (5cm) long, which when cleaned is cooked whole, usually deep-fried in batter. You may come across it under its French name *supion*. Both kinds should be used immediately after buying, and not stored. See also DRIED AND SALTED FISH, page 181. (*172*)

DUBLIN BAY PRAWN *langoustine, Norway lobster, scampi*

These crustaceans come from the north-east Atlantic and the Mediterranean. They look like small slender lobsters, with rather more delicate colouring and lighter claws in relation to the body. They are a rare and expensive luxury with little meat on them, but delicious if very freshly caught and cooked. At their best from late spring to late autumn, they are cooked in the same way as lobster (although a shorter cooking time is obviously required). (*170*)

LOBSTER

These belong to the same family as crabs and prawns, the crustaceans. A lobster has three main parts: the oval head covered in a tough shield-like curved shell; a set of heavy claws ending in pincers, which project from the top of the head and are in fact the modified first set of five pairs of legs; and a flexible body, or tail, covered in overlapping hinged layers of shell joined by membrane. In its natural state it is a patched and mottled greeny blue with brown undertones and touches of orange. It turns red on cooking. Choose lobsters that feel heavy for their size. They are often sold cooked but it is preferable to buy them live and cook them.

There is very little in the lobster that is inedible, only the stomach sac, a small transparent bag that will probably have grit or sand in it, and the thin dark intestinal system which runs the length of the body and can be removed with a sharp knife point. Above all do not discard the tomalley, the creamy grey-green liver which has such an exquisite flavour. To get at the meat in the claws, you'll need to crack them open with a hammer or a special implement similar to nut crackers. The deep orange coral in a female lobster can be used to colour the sauce. Although European and American lobsters can grow up to 10lb (4·5kg), the best size is from just over 1lb (500g) to about 2½–3lb (1·1–1·4kg), which would amply feed two people. (*170*)

MUSSEL

My first, unforgettable, experience of mussels was in France, one November evening, quite chilly and miserable. On each table was placed a large bowl of steaming fragrant mussels, the bright orange meat nestling in the pearly interior of blue-black shells. They were sweet, salty, melting and chewy all at the same time.

Mussels are bivalve molluscs. The colouring of the shell is usually a dark blue-black but some, particularly the large ones from Spain, can be more brownish with a tortoiseshell effect. There is also a variety called the green-lipped mussel which has a bright viridian-green lip to the shell. Mussels are good value because their shells are much thinner than those of many other shellfish, so that pound for pound there is more meat in them.

Available from September to April, they can be kept for a day in a bucket of lightly salted water sprinkled with flour or oatmeal. This will feed the mussels and allow them to disgorge any sand or impurities. Otherwise buy them for immediate consumption. Clean them under cold running water, scrubbing off any sand or mud. Knock off any barnacles with a knife and tug off the 'beard' – the tuft which protrudes from the hinge. If any mussels remain open after this vigorous treatment, discard them because they are certainly dead and may be toxic.

To cook them, steam them in a lidded pan until they open – discard any which do not open. They can then be eaten as they are, or baked with a stuffing in the shell, or removed from the shell and added to soups, sauces or salads. See also SMOKED FISH, page 177. (*175*)

OCTOPUS

An eight-tentacled creature, growing to up to 2–3ft (60–90cm) long, octopus is the largest of the cephalopods. It is well worth buying for its firm sweet flesh. If you buy prepared octopus, check that it has been tenderized after cleaning and skinning or you may finish up with a tough octopus stew. If not, put the body and tentacles in a plastic bag and beat with a meat hammer, a wooden mallet or a rolling pin.

If you have a whole octopus to deal with, use a heavy, sharp knife to cut off the tentacles in one piece, then wash them. Turn the body (which is also the head) inside out and discard all it contains except for the small silvery ink sac which you can use to colour a marvellous risotto or pasta dish as well as octopus stew. Rinse it thoroughly and then cut off the portion at the edge with the mouth beak and eyes. To skin the octopus, blanch head and tentacles in boiling water for a good five minutes, then rinse under cold water and peel off the skin and membrane. Then, to tenderize it, give the octopus a good beating.

Very good octopus recipes will be found in Greek and Spanish cookery books. (*172*)

OYSTER

Among the many varieties of oysters found throughout the world there are four that are particularly important as a food source; the native or European oyster, the Portuguese oyster, the Pacific oyster, and the American, or Virginian, oyster.

It can be very hard to identify oysters since they change their appearance to suit their habitat, growing long or round to fit a particular rocky crevice. In general, however, the native oyster has a round shell and Pacific oysters, such as the Geiger oyster, a long one.

The outside shell of the oyster is rough and flinty. The concentric whorls show how the shell has grown and changed in shape and size. There is a flat top shell and a cupped lower shell with, at the narrower end, a hinge. Inside, the shell is a pearly grey and the oyster meat is a milky bisque colour with dark fringes. All the meat is edible. Some oysters have a greenish tinge arising from their diet of a particular plankton. These green oysters, are quite delicious. You will find them in France as *verte de Marennes* or *Marennes*, from the area in western France where they are cultivated.

Pacific oysters are now being farmed widely with considerable success. Portuguese oysters are also being cultivated in France and Britain. American oysters are found in great profusion and variety down the eastern seaboard.

The native or European oyster used to be so prolific that it could be eaten regularly by rich and poor alike. That is sadly no longer the case, but there are still healthy beds of native oysters, often sold under the name of the area of origin: Helford oysters from Cornwall, Whitstable oysters from Kent, and Colchester oysters from Essex.

Oysters are usually eaten raw, with just a squeeze of lemon juice. Or they can be cooked: try grilling them in the half-shell with butter and chopped shallots, or with white wine and finely chopped spinach, with a little hollandaise sauce on top.

Unopened oysters that are tightly shut will keep for a few days in a cold place. Open oysters just before serving or cooking them. It is better to open them yourself, so that the precious juices are not lost. First scrub them to remove any sand or mud.

To split them – known as shucking – use a special oyster knife with a broad wooden handle that fits into the palm of the hand and a short heavy-duty blade. Some oyster knives have a circular shield between blade and handle to protect your knuckles. A kitchen knife does not work and could be dangerous if the flexible blade were to snap. You can wrap your hand holding the oyster in a tea-towel for extra protection or wear a special glove. When you have split the

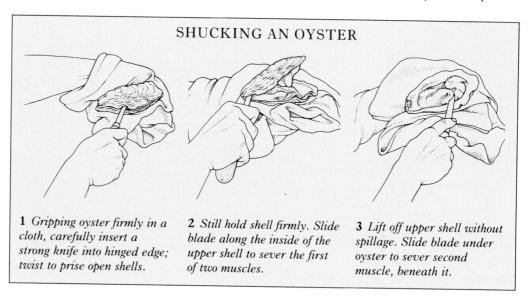

SHUCKING AN OYSTER

1 *Gripping oyster firmly in a cloth, carefully insert a strong knife into hinged edge; twist to prise open shells.*

2 *Still hold shell firmly. Slide blade along the inside of the upper shell to sever the first of two muscles.*

3 *Lift off upper shell without spillage. Slide blade under oyster to sever second muscle, beneath it.*

oyster, immediately smell it. If there are any 'off' or unusual smells, discard it at once.

Native oysters are not eaten in the summer months because this is when the oysters are spawning and not at their best. Pacific and American oysters are sold and eaten throughout the year. See also SMOKED FISH, page 177 and DRIED AND SALTED FISH, page 181. (*175*)

PRAWN

From the ubiquitous pink Greenland prawn to the large, fine tiger prawns from South-East Asia, there is a wide variety of choice under this name.

Prawns vary in size from 2–7in (5–18cm) in length. In colour they range from the translucent almost transparent pink of the small, common pink prawn, to the deep bluey brown of the Pacific prawn. King prawns, or Mediterranean prawns, grow to a size of some 8–9in (20–23cm) and have a brownish-red colour before cooking. Deep-water paler prawns are also found in the far North Atlantic and the Mediterranean and these are reddish when live, pink when cooked.

Very few prawns reach us fresh and we have to make do with frozen ones, cooked or un-

cooked. In either case, they should be thoroughly defrosted before cooking further. Ready-cooked prawns do not need further cooking, but they can be quickly fried, steamed, or peeled and added to a sauce or fish dish as it is finishing cooking. Uncooked prawns lend themselves to various cooking methods, some of the best of which are to be found in Chinese cookery books. In order to maximize their flavour and texture, prawns should be cooked through. There is no virtue in undercooking them and it may be dangerous to do so. (*170*)

RAZOR-SHELL CLAM

This type of clam is only rarely available commercially, but you might find it near the shore-line on a damp, sandy beach. It is unmistakable, looking exactly like an old-fashioned cut-throat razor with its long, slim curving shell with sharp edges and open at both ends. They are very good indeed just steamed. (*175*)

SCALLOP

These pretty, rounded, open-fan-shaped shells contain delicious seafood. Found throughout Atlantic, Mediterranean and Pacific waters in a

number of varieties, scallops are prized in many cuisines, particularly French and Cantonese. They can grow to 7in (18cm) across the shell. The small queen scallops, or queenies, are about 3in (7cm) across. In Hong Kong I came across beautiful scallops in long, grey shells, rather like half-closed, silk fans. The edible part of the scallop is the round white adductor muscle and the coral, or roe, orange at the pointed end and creamy white at the part joining the muscle. The frilly part of the scallop, the gills and mantle, should not be discarded but used for soup or stock. To open scallops, split them with a sharp knife, or put them in a hot oven until the shells separate.

If you are buying scallops loose – that is, not freshly removed from their shells in front of you – check whether they are fresh or frozen. Scallops that have been frozen are pure white and look milky, plump and moist. Fresh scallops are more translucent and creamy-grey rather than white.

It is best to buy them for immediate consumption, but if you are planning to open the scallops yourself you can keep them for a day or so in the refrigerator. Scallops can be steamed, grilled or shallow-fried in butter, but in each case, cook them gently and then serve them simply to best appreciate their rich yet delicate flavour. (*175*)

SEA URCHIN *oursin*

These fierce-looking creatures are in little danger from predators. They look for all the world like small round hedgehogs with shiny black spines, and they are very painful indeed if you step on one with bare feet or if you prick your fingers while preparing them. They are

---

PREPARING A SCALLOP

1 *With flat side up, and holding the scallop firm, carefully insert a strong blade between the shells and sever the roof muscle.*

2 *Carefully separate the two shells. Then slide the blade under the skirt of the scallop in lower shell to sever the second muscle.*

3 *Remove the scallop and separate out the best edible parts: white muscle and pink coral. Use the skirt for stock. Discard the rest.*

Molluscs

1 OYSTERS (NATIVE)	9 RAZOR-SHELL CLAMS
2 MUSSELS (GREEN-LIPPED)	10 GEIGER OYSTERS
	11 MUSSELS (SPANISH)
3 CLAMS	12 SEA URCHINS
4 SCALLOPS	13 VENUS CLAMS
5 BRITTANY OYSTERS	14 WINKLES
6 MUSSELS (BRITISH FARMED)	15 WHELKS
7 ABALONES	16 COCKLES
	17 VENUS CLAMS
8 QUEEN SCALLOPS	18 AMANDES CLAMS

about 2in (5cm) in diameter and actually contain very little – five 'tongues' of coral which are the ovaries. You need about two dozen to make enough sauce for four people, so this is an expensive and somewhat time-consuming delicacy; rather enjoy them as a free seaside treat if you happen to find them. Hold them with a folded towel and use a pair of long, sharp scissors to cut a hole in the top, large enough to insert a teaspoon and scoop out the sweet salty flesh, full of the iodine taste of the sea. (*175*)

SHRIMP

The smallest members of the crustacean family are among the most widespread, the most common being the tiny brown shrimp and slightly larger pink ones. The best I have ever tasted came from Morecambe Bay, Lancashire, where you can still buy them straight from the shrimp boat, boil them and eat them within an hour or two. These tiny brown morsels can be eaten whole or you can bite off and chew the tail, enjoying the sweet, briny flavours with a thick slice of homemade brown bread spread with unsalted butter.

Usually shrimps are bought ready-cooked. These are the shrimps for potting in butter with flavouring of mace and nutmeg in traditional English fashion. See also DRIED AND SALTED FISH, page 181. (*170*)

SQUID *calamar*

From the small 2–3in (5–7cm) translucent arrow squid to much bigger, heavier creatures, about 10in (25cm) long, squid deserve to be much more popular eating than they are. They have sweet, tender, white flesh when cooked, and relatively little waste, and once you have learned how, they are not difficult to prepare. When removing the innards, make sure you retain the small slender silvery ink sac if you want to use it for colouring the finished dish. Discard the rest of the innards. Squid is available most of the year round, frozen if not fresh, and it is one of the few shellfish that does not seem to suffer from freezing.

Squid are attractive to look at with their mottled violet-grey bodies and delicate tentacles. They can be prepared in many ways: sliced, battered and deep-fried in succulent golden rings, stewed, stuffed and served in a rich wine and garlic sauce or included in a seafood *paella*. Look to Portuguese, Spanish and Italian cookery books for the best recipes. See also DRIED AND SALTED FISH, page 181. (*172*)

WHELK

Resembling a large pointed snail, this saltwater shellfish is usually sold already cooked and without its shell. The meat is chewy, juicy and salty, but if it has been overcooked it will be rubbery. They are useful as part of a mixed seafood salad or in those lovely seafood platters or *fruits de mer*, piled high with small crabs, oysters and shellfish of every description. I would not recommend cooking them further. Nor would I advocate gathering whelks from the sea shore. You don't know where they've been – or where what they have eaten has been. (*175*)

WINKLE

These tiny dark brown or black sea snails about ½in (1cm) across make a delicious appetizer. You will sometimes be served them in a restaurant in France as you wait for your first course. Often they are sold ready cooked and you simply extract them from their shells with a pin.

To prepare raw winkles, rinse them in several changes of water, rattling them around in a colander. Then let them disgorge impurities in a bowl of lightly salted water for a few hours. Rinse and steam them in a lidded saucepan for eight to ten minutes with no more than the liquid that clings to them. Extract them from their shells to use, for example, in sauces accompanying sole or turbot. If you plan to eat them simply as they are, add some seasoning, a splash of dry white wine and some parsley or tarragon to the saucepan. (*175*)

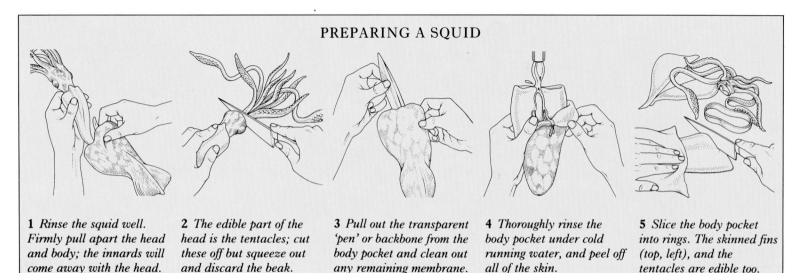

PREPARING A SQUID

1 *Rinse the squid well. Firmly pull apart the head and body; the innards will come away with the head.*

2 *The edible part of the head is the tentacles; cut these off but squeeze out and discard the beak.*

3 *Pull out the transparent 'pen' or backbone from the body pocket and clean out any remaining membrane.*

4 *Thoroughly rinse the body pocket under cold running water, and peel off all of the skin.*

5 *Slice the body pocket into rings. The skinned fins (top, left), and the tentacles are edible too.*

SMOKED FISH

Smoked fish is a traditional British delicacy and one of our most successful food exports. One has only to think of the popularity of kippers and smoked salmon all over the world to realize this. Indeed, the French have now taken smoked haddock into their repertoire. Where you see *le haddock* on a French menu, expect it to be served smoked. There are two basic methods of smoking fish, having first dry-salted it or immersed it in brine:

Hot smoked The fish is wholly or partially cooked by being suspended close to a fire or smouldering ashes and smoked at a temperature of 165–210°F (75–100°C). Hot smoked fish such as the Arbroath smokie should be eaten soon after curing. Although fish smoked in this way have been largely cooked and are ready to eat, they can be heated through briefly under a grill or lightly fried. Some people say this brings out the flavour.

Cold smoked The fish are suspended at some distance above a much lower source of heat and smoked at 115°F (45°C) or lower. Fish smoked by this method keep better and, with the exception of smoked salmon, almost always need cooking again afterwards.

Smoked salmon is something of an anomaly. Technically it is still raw, but cooking it is the last thing one would want to do. At a pinch it can be stirred into scrambled eggs or pasta, but cooking it, for example, in a quiche spoils it.

ARBROATH SMOKIE *Aberdeen smokie*

About 10in (25cm) long and a lovely (uncoloured) pale bronze, Arbroath smokies are small haddock. Headless and gutted, they are hot smoked, traditionally over peat smoke in Dundee and Aberdeen, particularly Arbroath. They are usually sold in pairs, tied together through the gills or tail. Although hot smoked, and therefore cooked, the smoking is light so the fish will keep only for a day or two.

They are best enjoyed cold, with just a squeeze of lemon and brown bread and butter. The tasty white flesh can also be flaked and made into a mousse or a fish paté. I have also enjoyed smokies boned and baked in a puff pastry case, served hot with a chilled horseradish sauce. See also FISH, page 146 (*Haddock*).

BLOATER

When the herring fleets used to fish off Yarmouth in Norfolk, they were close enough to shore not to need to salt their herrings before curing. Instead, once ashore, the herrings were lightly salted, whole and ungutted, and smoked just sufficiently to partially cook them. They are much harder to come by than they used to be but Great Yarmouth still remains the bloater capital of the world.

Bloaters are the same size as herrings, slightly swollen, and a gleaming silvery gold. Serve them grilled or fried, split open or filleted, or, once cooked, mashed with plenty of butter to make an excellent bloater paste. See also FISH, page 146 (*Herring*).

BUCKLING

This is another type of smoked herring. The head is removed and the fish is gutted before being hot smoked. This small, oily fish should be eaten within two days. It needs no further cooking. Look for firm, copper-coloured fish. See also FISH, page 146 (*Herring*).

COD

Genuine uncoloured smoked cod is a lucky find.
Cod fillets All too often cod fillets have been coloured after salting and are not smoked. Tartrazine has been used, but more often now you will see the fish described as having 'no artificial colouring'. The colouring is obtained from an organic source, but it may still be from a plant or flower that has nothing to do with fish. Use like haddock.
Cod's roe The whole roe of the female cod is removed, salted, then rinsed and soaked. The outer membrane, which is peeled off, is a rich red and the firmly packed roe inside is pink and sticky to the touch. Keep it refrigerated, well wrapped in greaseproof paper, and it should last for four or five days. Eat it on its own in very thin slices if you like its powerful saltiness and flavour. If it dries out, grate it over a pasta dish. Smoked cod's roe is used to make the Greek appetizer, *taramasalata*. See also FISH, page 146, and DRIED AND SALTED FISH, page 181.

EEL

Both conger eel and freshwater eel are smoked. The latter is much more expensive, but as it is so richly flavoured, you need very little. If it has been hot smoked, it needs no further cooking and is best simply served with lemon and brown bread. It is sold in long, thin, pale fawn fillets with a darker brownish-red stripe down the middle.

Smoked conger eel is sold in chunks cut across the fish and with the dark skin left on. The flesh is white, firm and very tasty. See also FISH, page 146.

HADDOCK

Uncoloured smoked haddock fillet is a marvellous treat and much more available than previously. It is well worth paying extra for. The flesh should be moist and translucent because it is raw (having been cold smoked), with a pale yellow outer surface, and silvery-grey skin. Small or large fillets are available. Poaching and steaming are particularly suitable cooking methods and haddock is excellent in fish pies and in soups such as the Scottish 'cullen skink' (with potatoes). It's also used in kedgeree, a traditional breakfast dish, originating in India, in which the cooked fish is mixed with rice, chopped boiled eggs and spices.

A more unusual preparation is to slice the fish thinly, like smoked salmon, and serve it with buttered brown toast. But haddock must be very fresh to be eaten raw. Alternatively, marinate the thinly sliced fish for an hour or two in, for example, hazelnut oil and lime juice. I like to add a splash of aged rum, about 20 minutes before serving it.

Finnan haddock is a small whole haddock that is soaked in brine and then cold smoked. It is sold without the head and with the silvery-grey skin split open to reveal delicate, pale yellow flesh. Finnan haddock weighs about 12oz (375g).

Finnan haddock should not be kept much longer than two to three days. Cured, but still raw, it requires further cooking. The classical way is to poach it very gently in milk and it is often served with a lightly poached egg. See also FISH, page 146.

HALIBUT

Smoked halibut needs no further cooking. It is sold both as whole sides and thinly sliced. The latter lend themselves particularly to elegant composed salads (*salades composées*) with delicate leaves, herbs, and nut oil dressings.

The fish is salted, rinsed and given a light coating of honey before being smoked over beechwood and juniper. The smoking process gives the outside of the fillets a pale golden yellow colour. The flesh is white, slightly pearly, firm, yet tender and moist with a good flavour.

The fish will keep in a sealed vacuum pack for a couple of weeks but once the packet has been opened it should be eaten within three or four days at most. Most smoked halibut comes from Greenland and Britain. See also FISH, page 146.

KIPPER

One of the best-loved fish in the whole of the British Isles, the kipper's warm-brown flesh and greeny bronze skin grace many breakfast tables. It is yet another version of the versatile herring,

Smoked Fish

1	SALMON	11	SWORDFISH
2	ARBROATH SMOKIE	12	KIPPER
3	BLOATER	13	OYSTERS
4	FINNAN HADDOCK	14	COD'S ROE
5	EEL	15	STURGEON
6	MUSSELS	16	COD FILLET
7	SPRATS	17	MACKEREL
8	TROUT	18	HADDOCK
9	BUCKLING	19	HALIBUT
10	MONKFISH		

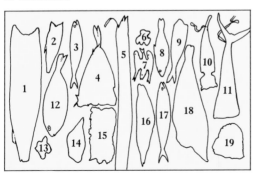

in which the whole fish – including the head – is split down the middle, gutted, salted and smoked, usually over oak. Make sure you look for uncoloured whole kippers, in preference to mahogany-brown kipper fillets.

Although it is very good thinly sliced and eaten raw or marinated, the traditional method of cooking it is grilling. Or stand it upright in a tall jug and pour boiling water over it; letting it stand for a few minutes will be sufficient to cook it. It can also be made into a delicious pâté. See also FISH, page 146 (*Herring*).

MACKEREL

Both hot and cold smoked mackerel is produced, but hot smoking is more common. The fish is gutted and beheaded, soaked in brine, then smoked, whole or in fillets.

The skin is a lovely, oily, bronzy green and the flesh a moist pale fawn. Very deeply coloured ones will probably have been coloured. Well wrapped, the fish will keep for two to three days in the refrigerator, but I prefer to buy it for immediate consumption as it has a powerful smell which is easily picked up by other food stored with it. Hot-smoked mackerel is very rich and delicious served uncooked with a little lemon juice or, for more bite, with horseradish sauce. See also FISH, page 146.

MONKFISH

Smoked monkfish is one of my favourite foods. The long fillets are removed from the central bone, cured and then smoked. (Avoid buying the thin tail piece as it will be drier than the shoulder end.) The flesh remains white and firm, the outer surface a pale tan colour. The flavour is delicate and fine and the fish needs no further cooking.

Well wrapped, it will keep for two to three days in the refrigerator. See also FISH, page 146.

MUSSEL

This tasty little brown morsel is removed from its shell, salted lightly and then smoked. Mussels prepared in this way are particularly popular in the Far East, where they are sometimes preser-ved in oil and packed into cans for export. Smoked mussels are also now processed in Britain. See also SHELLFISH, page 169.

OYSTER

Smoked oysters closely resemble smoked mussels. They are very much an Oriental speciality, prepared and preserved in the same way as mussels. See also SHELLFISH, page 169 and DRIED AND SALTED FISH, page 181.

SALMON

When buying smoked salmon you need to be aware exactly what is being purchased. Is it Pacific or Atlantic (Scottish) salmon? Has it been smoked in Scotland, which has one kind of cure, or in London or Ireland? The London cure is more delicate, some would say blander.

Pacific salmon, which is far inferior to the Atlantic salmon caught in Scotland, is frozen and exported to Scotland for smoking, so ask the fishmonger what type of salmon it is, and where it was smoked. Buy it sliced to order for preference. Any that has already been sliced may be drying out and losing its flavour.

The traditional method of smoking salmon is still the best. Large salmon are filleted and then given a liquid brine or dry salt cure. Sometimes sugar and spices are added. The fillet is then rinsed and the saltiness checked before the salmon is cold smoked for about 15 hours, at a relatively low temperature, below 90°F (33°C). Sawdust, woodchips and peat are used in the smoking and the type of wood (usually oak) used will influence the final flavour.

Good smoked salmon has moist, glistening flesh, firm yet tender, and is rosy pink with a faint hint of peachy orange. Vacuum-packed salmon will keep for a couple of weeks, but once open it should be treated like freshly sliced smoked salmon and eaten within two or three days. Smoked salmon pieces or trimmings are sometimes sold at a lower price and are particularly good for making into pâté. Best eaten on its own with a wedge of lemon and perhaps some freshly ground black pepper, smoked salmon also makes wonderful sandwiches using brown bread. Cooking ruins the texture. See also FISH, page 146, and CAVIAR, page 183.

SALMON TROUT *sea trout*

The large salmon trout is cured and smoked in the same way as salmon. It is just as fine, some would say finer, and just as expensive. The flesh is pink, moist and glistening, and has a full, rounded flavour. It is sold freshly sliced or vacuum-packed. Once open, treat the latter as freshly sliced and use within two to three days. Like smoked salmon, salmon trout is best eaten as a very special starter on its own with little other adornment apart from a piece of lemon and some toast. See also FISH, page 146, and CAVIAR, page 183.

SPRAT

This small, pale gleaming, silver fish is lightly salted in brine and hot smoked for a few hours. Smoked sprats need no further cooking and make an excellent snack or starter. See also FISH, page 146.

STURGEON

Like the caviar which comes from it, smoked sturgeon is a great delicacy, rare and expensive. Have the pale bisque fillet sliced horizontally as for smoked salmon to enjoy its full, moist texture and wonderful flavour. See also CAVIAR, page 183.

SWORDFISH

Lightly cured and smoked swordfish is a pale fawn colour, and usually thinly sliced, delicate and well-flavoured. It requires no further cooking before being served as an appetizer. See also FISH, page 146.

TROUT

Hot smoked rainbow trout is widely available as a whole fish or in fillets. The whole fish is a rich, deep golden brown; if darker, it has probably been coloured. The skinned fillets are a pleasant creamy-fawn colour and should be moist and firm. Wrapped in greaseproof paper and re-frigerated, the fish will keep for two or three days, longer if vacuum packed. It needs no further preparation. See also FISH, page 146.

DRIED AND SALTED FISH

Dried and salted fish add an extra dimension to the already rich array of fish and seafood available. Fish used to be dried in the sun and wind but now large airy sheds are used. Dried and salted fish are used in many ways, reconstituted and cooked, even as flavourings.

Dried and Salted Fish

1. COD (STOCKFISH)
2. COD (BACALAO)
3. BOMBAY DUCK
4. ANCHOVIES (SILVERFISH)
5. SQUID
6. GOURAMY
7. SHRIMPS
8. ANCHOVIES
9. HERRING
10. BONITO FLAKES
11. GREY MULLET
12. SARDINES
13. SHARK'S FIN
14. CUTTLEFISH
15. OYSTERS

There are two methods of salting fish. One is to cover the fish in dry salt, the other is to soak it in a salt solution. In fact, if you store fish in dry salt for any length of time, it produces its own liquid which combines with the salt to form a brine. Some cures are saltier than others.

Whichever method has been used, if the fish is to be cooked as if it were fresh, it must first be soaked in plenty of water. This reduces the salt (if it has been salted) and allows it to regain the moisture it lost in drying. Two days is not too long for this, and you should change the water from time to time. Once soaked, the fish should be cooked as if fresh, that is, very gently, and for a relatively short time.

Some cured and dried fish is intended to be eaten in its changed state. Dried cuttlefish and Bombay duck are eaten as appetizers and condiments respectively.

ANCHOVY

The canned anchovies imported from the Mediterranean have been filleted and salted before being packed in oil. Whole salted anchovies are also occasionally available, the silvery fish packed tight like the spokes of a wheel. Soak them in water or milk to remove some of the salt before filleting them. Their strong, piquant flavour can be used to season and garnish many dishes, including stews and pizzas, and they are a key ingredient of *salade niçoise*. In Thai

cookery baby anchovies (called silverfish) are soaked and stir-fried, or fried as they are with mung beans, and added to soups. See also FISH, page 146.

BOMBAY DUCK *bombil, bummaloe*

Small, pale, translucent bummaloe fish from South-East Asia, dried and sold as Bombay Duck in irregular, rather woody looking chunks or pieces with a strong fishy smell and flavour. These are baked or fried until crisp and served as a savoury accompaniment to Indian food.

BONITO FLAKES

Thin small flakes are shaved from a piece of dried bonito that has been smoked, dried and fermented. They have a concentrated salty, fishy flavour and are used in Japanese cooking as seasoning, particularly for clear soups and broths. When buying, check that they are really pale – the lighter the better – and that they smell fresh and clean. Store them in the refrigerator, and once the packet has been opened use them within a couple of weeks. See also FISH, page 146.

COD

Salt cod is principally prepared in Norway, Iceland and Newfoundland. First it is gutted and cleaned, then soaked in brine or laid under dry salt, after which it is dried and exported to Portugal, Spain, France, Italy and the rest of the Mediterranean. Now, salt cod is also available in Britain (mainly *bacalao* from Spain). It is usually sold in neat packets of fillets, but sometimes the whole fish is hung up in the shop and pieces are carved off. A tough-looking, woody, stiff kite shape (having been split open), it is best to have it cut up for you unless you have a very strong, heavy knife or poultry scissors. Salt cod is rather expensive so, if possible, buy prime pieces from the middle, rather than the tail and fin ends. The fish is creamy grey, with a fine dusting of sparkling salt. Before cooking salt cod, soak it for up to 48 hours – changing the water frequently.
Dried cod, sometimes called stockfish and almost identical in appearance, requires equally

long soaking. In Scandinavia and Portugal it is virtually a staple food and the cuisines of both countries include many recipes for the re-hydrated fish. See also FISH, page 146, and SMOKED FISH, page 177.

CUTTLEFISH AND SQUID

Some of the most fascinating shops in the streets of the older part of Taipei (Taiwan) are those selling dried fish. Sometimes a small shop will sell nothing but dried cuttlefish and squid, strung in neat rows, flattened and slightly hardened, tanned and light brown. The Japanese serve these as a chewy, salty snack with drinks, rather as we serve crisps. See also SHELLFISH, page 169.

GOURAMY *gourami*

This is an important freshwater fish of South-East Asia which has now been introduced to the Western hemisphere, to the Caribbean and South America. It grows up to 7½lb (3·4kg) and is usually eaten fresh. It can be dried and is used in this way in South-East Asian recipes.

GREY MULLET

Dried baby grey mullet fillets are used in Thai cookery, usually fried or steamed and often with tomatoes, spring onions and coriander leaves. See also FISH, page 146.

HERRING, MAATJES HERRING

The herring is scaled, gutted and packed in salt in tubs or barrels. Brine forms from the salt and the juices of the weighted-down fish, and preserves them. Behead, bone and soak them before adding them to salads.
Maatjes herring Amsterdam's Albert Kuyp-straat market has stalls of 'green' herrings in spring. These new season's herrings are brought in from the boats, ready salted by the fishermen. The stallholders rapidly remove the head and backbone and hand you the fillets. Locals swallow these whole, just holding their heads well back and letting the fillets slide down their throats. The more timid munch on them in a fresh bread roll. See also FISH, page 146.

JELLYFISH

Lightly salted edible jellyfish are dry, flat and translucent. Sold loose or in packets, they keep indefinitely if still sealed in their packaging. Used in Chinese cooking, they are rolled up, shredded and then soaked before use. With little flavour of their own, they add an all-important crunchy yet gelatinous texture.

OYSTER

Dried smoked oysters are used to season other dishes, particularly Chinese meat dishes. See also SHELLFISH, page 169 and SMOKED FISH, page 177.

SARDINES

These small fish are usually preserved in oil, and then canned, but they can also be smoked or salted. See also FISH, page 146.

SCALLOP *conpoy*

Dried scallops are an important feature in Chinese cooking. Only the white flesh is dried (not the coral), and it dries to a small, slightly leathery, pale creamy-fawn disc. They keep well if stored in an airtight jar or box in a cool place. Use whole or shredded as a seasoning or garnish. See also SHELLFISH, page 169.

SHARK'S FIN

This highly prized delicacy and important ingredient in several Chinese dishes is the pointed dorsal fin of a few cartilaginous species of shark. Salted and then dried, shark's fin has minimal flavour of its own but adds texture, particularly to soups. See also FISH, page 146.

SHRIMP

Small pink shrimps, lightly salted and dried to preserve them, are much used in Chinese and South-East Asian cooking. When dried they still retain both their shrimp shape and distinctive smell. They can be soaked in water before use, or used dried as a seasoning. See also SHELL-FISH, page 169.

CAVIAR

The eggs or roe of certain female fish are highly prized as a luxury food, the most famous being caviar from the huge sturgeons of the Caspian Sea. This is processed on a commercial basis by the Russians and the Iranians: the mass of eggs is removed, stripped of the membranes, then salted, drained and packed. Some fresh caviar is reserved for hotels and restaurants. The cans and jars that one buys commercially will all have a sell-by date and, once the container has been opened, the caviar should be consumed within a few hours.

All caviar should be firm, yet soft and moist – never dried out. To serve it, place it in a small glass bowl and rest this on crushed ice in a second, larger bowl. Good caviar is best savoured on its own, except for a little fresh lemon juice and thin slices of toast. Chilled neat vodka is the traditional partner. Some of the other 'caviars' can be particularly salty; a good tip is to put them into a fine plastic sieve and pour the contents of a small bottle of beer or lager through the eggs. They should not be rinsed in water.

TRUE CAVIARS

Pasteurized caviar Because of the difficulties of storing caviar at the correct temperature – it must be chilled to just below 32°F (0°C) but never frozen as the oil and salt in the caviar stop it from freezing at this temperature – most caviar that we buy in Britain, the United States and Europe has been pasteurized. This process is said to reduce the flavour slightly, but few of us will have the chance to make comparisons between fresh and pasteurized caviar. Unopened, pasteurized caviar keeps for 12 months, and fresh caviar for two to three months in a vacuum-packed container.

Beluga In Britain, this is the most popular caviar. It comes from the beluga, the largest of the sturgeon family. The eggs are quite large granules, and a soft, pearly, light to dark grey.

Oscietra (osetra or asetra) The most popular caviar in France and the United States, this comes from a smaller sturgeon; in fact, the true sturgeon. The eggs are slightly smaller than those of the beluga, grey brown to golden with a nutty flavour.

Sevruga The even smaller sevruga sturgeon produces eggs at six to eight years old, whereas the beluga only matures at 18 or so. Sevruga is, therefore, much more abundant and its caviar is less expensive than the other two. It is a fine-grained caviar of small, dark grey eggs, and no less exquisite than beluga and oscietra.

Mandarin Caviar This comes from the Chinese large white sturgeon, is greyish green in colour, and relatively inexpensive.

Pressed Caviar This concentrated, intensely flavoured caviar is made by pressing together in a much denser fashion the damaged, salted eggs of different sturgeon. The resultant dark shiny mass has a slightly, 'jammy' texture.

OTHER 'CAVIARS'

Although true caviar comes only from varieties of sturgeon, as described above, a number of other fish roes are marketed as caviar 'look-alikes'. Their colour ranges from pale gold to black, and some contain colourings. Unlike true caviar they benefit from a dash of lemon and chopped chives or sliced, hard-boiled egg.

Capelin roe The capelin belongs to the same family as the smelt. Its roe is cured in salt. The grains are about the same size as lumpfish eggs. I serve it on toast or with small pancakes and sour cream.

Keta, ketovia is the roe of a Pacific salmon, the keta or chum. The eggs are large, translucent and an orangy pink. When it is not too salty, it can be delicious and is often used by chefs to garnish elegant fish dishes. It is much cheaper than caviar and very good served in the traditional style with blinis (buckwheat pancakes) or hot toast, soured cream and a wedge of lemon.

Lumpfish roe Perhaps the most widely available of all the processed fish eggs, this is taken from the lumpfish. It is usually coloured black, red or orange, so if you are using it for decoration, do so at the last minute because the colour tends to run. Once you have opened the jar, use within a day or so.

Salmon roe This looks like the keta – translucent orangy-pink eggs although sometimes slightly smaller. If you find eggs in the salmon you buy, it is worth experimenting with your own salmon caviar.

Whitefish caviar A very delicate and fine golden 'caviar' made from the eggs of the whitefish, a North American lake fish related to the salmon family. Serve it traditionally or used as a garnish for fish or to flavour sauces.

Salmon trout roe This very pale, pearly roe has a slight golden glow. When it is not too salty, it can be extremely good.

Caviar

1 RED LUMPFISH ROE
2 SALMON TROUT ROE
3 SALMON ROE
4 CAPELIN ROE
5 ORANGE LUMPFISH ROE
6 MANDARIN CAVIAR
7 SEVRUGA CAVIAR
8 BELUGA CAVIAR
9 OSCIETRA CAVIAR
10 BLACK LUMPFISH ROE

MEAT

Since prehistoric times animals have been an important source of food for mankind throughout the world. Almost every cuisine, past and present, has a place in it for meat, although in some societies certain meats are taboo for religious reasons. In Britain and the Western world beef, pork and lamb are the main meats eaten (as well as, of course, poultry and game but these are dealt with in separate chapters). Veal is also consumed to a lesser degree, as is goat meat and mutton.

Why do we call it beef, pork and mutton and not ox, pig or swine and sheep, since those are the animals which give us our meat? When William of Normandy conquered England in 1066 he brought Norman speech and customs with him, together with Norman cooks and chefs. While the Saxon shepherds and swineherds continued to call their animals by the names they'd always used, by the time the animal was slaughtered, cooked and brought to table it was called by its Norman French name. Thus the words *porc*, *boeuf*, *mouton*, *veau* and *l'agneau* are the origins of our meat names: pork, beef, mutton, veal and lamb.

I choose my meat carefully and cook it in the most appropriate way. I will cook a casserole using inexpensive meats, say a carbonnade of beef, a navarin of lamb or a *blanquette de veau* and it goes down very well indeed. Or I might roast a rack of lamb, stuff a breast of veal with its kidneys and roast it, or roast a loin of pork stuffed with apricots and walnuts encased in its crisp, crackling overcoat. If I'm in a hurry, veal escalopes or medallions cut from the loin of lamb will fry or grill in a few minutes to make a main course, ready for enticing accompaniments in the way of sauces, vegetables and salads.

There are certain meats such as beef and lamb which are very palatable when served raw in such dishes as *carpaccio*, steak tartare and *kibbeh*. Some people, including me, like roast lamb and beef served rare. In the case of both raw and lightly cooked meat, harmful bacteria are still likely to be present and such meat should not be eaten by children, pregnant women and the elderly. It is a risk that one needs to be aware of. See also *Handling Meat*.

Good flavour and texture in meat comes partly as a result of the animal's feed during its lifetime and, indeed, from its way of life and its environment. If the animal has fed on pastureland rather than having had a corn-based diet, this will be reflected in the flavour of the meat.

NUTRITION

Because cuts of meat vary so much and animals themselves vary in the ratio of lean to fat, it is impossible to give exact nutritional information. However, as a rough guide, the protein content of 3½ oz (100g) roast or grilled meat from one of the leanest parts of the animal ranges from 29 per cent (beef and lamb) to 31 per cent (veal), the fat content from 4·5 per cent (beef) to 11·5 per cent (lamb). The carbohydrate content of all types of meat is nil.

In addition to its high protein content, which is also of high quality since it contains all the eight essential amino acids adults need, meat is a rich source of iron, zinc and other minerals and some of the important B vitamins such as niacin, riboflavin and thiamin which are so important for metabolizing other foodstuffs, and also B12, a vitamin which is lacking in a vegan diet.

CHOOSING MEAT

This will be dealt with in more detail in each section, but some factors need to be borne in mind whichever meat you are buying.

It is important to select a cut of meat appropriate to the recipe or cooking method you are planning to use. A quick lesson in anatomy will explain the reason for this. Joints or cuts of meat are taken from every part of the animal: fore- and hindquarters, back and belly. The front part of the animal – the shin, shoulders, fore ribs and neck – does most of the work. Think about it. An animal moves forward from its front legs; the neck, shoulders and fore ribs support a large head, but also work to forage for food, lifting the head up and down. It follows that the parts of the animal which do the most work have the most developed and hardest muscles and thus will produce the tougher cuts of meat such as shin and neck. They are also the least expensive cuts. However they require the most preparation and long careful cooking by indirect heat. This is something to be kept in mind when working out how economical a dish is. A piece of fillet steak is much more expensive than a piece of shin of beef but it takes only a few minutes to prepare and a few minutes to cook. A shin of beef casserole may take 20 minutes or more to prepare and then a couple of hours of expensive oven time to cook.

The back of the animal, which yields the loin, fillet and saddle cuts, does the least work and produces the tenderest meat. Such meat can be cooked quickly with high, direct heat, by roasting, grilling or frying.

Cuts from the rest of the animal such as the breast, flank and top of the rump are neither very tender, nor very tough. Pot-roasting or braising with moderate heat is the best way to deal with these meats.

Taste, appetite and recipe are the main influencing factors on how much to buy. With lean meat off the bone it is usual to allow between 3½–6 oz (100–175g) per person. With meat on the bone it is usual to allow 8–12 oz (250–375g).

When buying food it makes sense to buy from an outlet which has a steady turnover. You can be sure then that the meat has not been stored for too long and is fresh.

The meat should look good and smell good. In colour the flesh should be in the pink/red spectrum (depending of course on whether it is veal, pork, lamb or beef, and bearing in mind that mature beef is a dull, dark red) and the fat should look and feel firm, white or creamy white, not yellow, and should have a soft waxy texture. There should be no unpleasant or unusual smells. The surface of the cut joint will have a slightly moist appearance, but certainly should not look or feel wet and clammy. Usually meat is prepared so that it is ready to use when sold – excess fat, gristle, bone and skin (where necessary) will have been trimmed off.

STORING MEAT

If the meat is in a film-covered tray store it in that in the refrigerator. To safeguard against leaking, put the tray on a plate. This is especially important for meat sold in rigid containers where it has been packed in a controlled atmosphere. Keep this meat in its packaging until required. If the meat is not pre-packed, wrap it in foil or greaseproof paper on returning home and put it in the refrigerator on a plate until you are ready to use it. Always store meat in the coldest part of the refrigerator. Never let the meat, or any juices from it, come into contact with any other foodstuff especially raw foods. Wash your hands before and after handling meat. See also *Handling Meat*.

The following are guidelines for storing uncooked meat in the refrigerator (or follow the 'best before' or 'sell by' dates). Meat will deteriorate faster in warm or humid weather than in cold. Smaller cuts have a relatively large proportion exposed to the air, so chops will deteriorate faster than a large joint of meat. Beef, lamb and mutton will keep for three to five days in a refrigerator, pork and veal for two to four days and goat and kid for three to four days. Offal of any kind will keep for two days at most, and mince should be cooked within two days if it is pre-packed, and one day if bought loose.

PREPARING MEAT

If you are cooking only for yourself or for two or three people, but also make stocks and pâtés, it makes sense to do all your meat preparation at once. When I have bought my meat, for example, I cut up one batch of meat for a casserole. This cooks at the same time in the oven as a meat pâté and a stock (which will cook just as well in the oven) made from the trimmings, carcases and bones. In the same oven I also cook a sauce made from minced beef for pasta. I might put some pork fillet to marinate for later in the week and then quickly grill a piece of calf's liver for the evening meal. Stock, pâté, casserole and sauce when cooked will be cooled as rapidly as possible and then refrigerated until required. Then apart from cooking the marinated meat and thoroughly re-heating the sauce and casserole, there is no further meat preparation during the week.

No one knows if King Henry VIII really did knight a rib of beef by touching it with his sword and saying, 'Arise Sir Loin', but that is one of the stories about the origin of the name for the largest and most popular roasting joint. Or it might come from the French *sur loin* meaning on top of the loin. Beefeaters in the Tower of London and roast beef are part of the image of a traditional England. We eat something over 21lb (9·5kg) of beef per head every year, putting it ahead of chicken, and well ahead of lamb and pork.

Unlike lamb which is slaughtered at four to six months and pork at five to seven months, beef is a mature animal at slaughter, about two years old. Over recent years beef production has changed considerably. Twenty-five years ago the best beef cattle were slaughtered at five to six years old, after lengthy feeding on open pasture-land.

An average animal will yield a carcase of well over 600lb (270kg). This represents a lot of joints and cuts of beef. When freshly slaughtered, beef joints, steaks and stewing meat are a bright, coral red. If cooked at this stage it will not be particularly flavourful. Beef needs to be hung, like game, to mature and develop its flavour and improve the texture. Mature beef is a dark, rich red. Fresh or mature, the cut surface of the meat will be slightly moist. The fat will be white or creamy-white. Cattle are now being bred with a lower fat content and, indeed, during preparation more of the fat is being removed before purchase. Whether you choose cuts with plenty of fat or extra-lean ones with only a little is a matter of personal taste. Cooking and serving meat with fat does increase its calorific content, as well as the overall amount of fat consumed.

METHODS OF COOKING

A beef carcase yields joints and cuts of meat for every occasion and in every price range, from the expensive tender fillet, to the bony but succulent and delicious oxtail. There are no cooking methods unsuitable for beef but certain methods are best suited to certain cuts and this will be dealt with when each cut of beef is described.

Roasting For a special occasion a large joint of beef cannot be beaten, simply roasted and served with crisp light Yorkshire pudding, gravy made from the juices in the roasting pan, and some

HANDLING MEAT

Bacteria which are naturally present in all living organisms (including humans) are still alive when meat is brought home. Some are harmless, some cause food to spoil and some, like campylobacter, listeria and various strains of salmonella, are harmful and can be life-threatening. At room temperature bacteria increase in numbers rapidly and cause food to spoil. In the refrigerator they grow more slowly so that food keeps better there. They cannot grow in the freezer, although they can start to multiply again when the food is thawed. High temperatures used in cooking kill them off and they may still be present in raw and lightly cooked meat.

There are certain precautions that must be taken to avoid cross-contamination or the transfer of bacteria from raw meat to other food in your kitchen or refrigerator.
1. Wash hands before and after handling fresh meat. Wash knives and other utensils between handling raw and cooked food.
2. Do not prepare raw meat on wooden chopping boards as these are difficult to clean and disinfect after use. Use white non-porous chopping boards which are easy to clean with plenty of hot water and a little bleach.
3. Refrigerate all meat, loosely but carefully covered, in a shallow container as soon as possible after purchase unless the label says otherwise. Check the temperature of your refrigerator – it should not exceed 42°F (5°C).
4. Avoid contact between cooked and raw foods during storage and preparation.
5. If meat is cooked for eating later it must be cooled as quickly as possible, then covered and refrigerated. Warm food of any kind is the ideal breeding ground for bacteria when stored at room temperature.
6. To destroy the bacteria all meat should ideally be thoroughly cooked. It is cooked when the temperature in the slowest-to-heat part of the meat reaches at least 160°F (70°C). A meat thermometer gauges this accurately and takes the guesswork out of timing. Insert it into the thickest part of the meat making sure the tip is not touching any bone.
7. Any bacteria in whole meat joints will be on or very close to the surface and the outside of roast meat gets hot enough to sterilize it. However, rolled joints are different. Bacteria may be deep within the joint so extra care is needed to make sure enough heat penetrates right through the flesh to kill the bacteria.

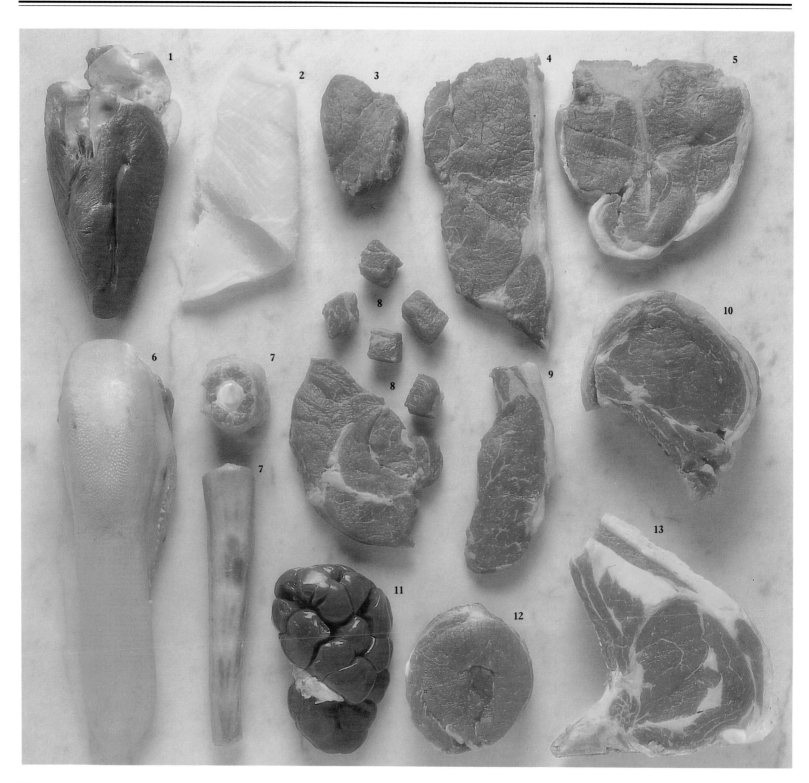

English mustard. The outside of the beef should be well-cooked and a mahogany brown and the inside pinkly tender and rare – plenty to satisfy all tastes.

For quick roasting on the bone, estimate 20 minutes per 1lb (500g) and 20 minutes extra at Gas mark 6, 400°F, 200°C. Off the bone, allow 25 minutes per 1lb (500g) and 25 minutes extra. This will give a medium-cooked roast rather than a rare one. For a rare joint, reduce the cooking time accordingly.

No fancy sauces, no herbs, or garlic are needed with roast beef. Whereas pork, lamb and veal can take all manner of accompaniments, marinades, jellies and sauces, roast beef needs none of these things.

However the quality of the meat is of prime importance. It must be tender and you must choose a joint that is suitable for roasting. Many of those sold for roasting look very tempting: small, neat, without a bone and thus easy to carve, tied around with a thin layer of fat so that the meat will baste itself as it cooks. But if those joints come from the hardworking muscles of the back legs (which is why they are lean), they are best pot-roasted or braised, covered and cooked in a low oven with liquid and vegetables to flavour them.

For a good roast you must choose a joint from the back, the ribs, fillet or sirloin. In roasting, small joints shrink more than larger ones. For this reason, try to choose a joint of beef rather larger than you need, then use the left-overs carefully, in curries, moussaka, cottage pie, soups and salads, and use the well-browned bones for the stockpot.

Boiling Boiled beef and carrots is a traditional English dish enshrined in the old music hall song. In fact slow boiling, which is closer to poaching, is the method used, and it is particularly suitable for silverside and brisket which are

Beef

1 OX HEART
2 TRIPE
3 FILLET STEAK
4 RUMP STEAK
5 T-BONE STEAK
6 OX TONGUE
7 OXTAIL
8 CHUCK STEAK
9 PORTERHOUSE STEAK
10 FORE RIB
11 OX KIDNEY
12 ROLLED BRISKET
13 WING RIB

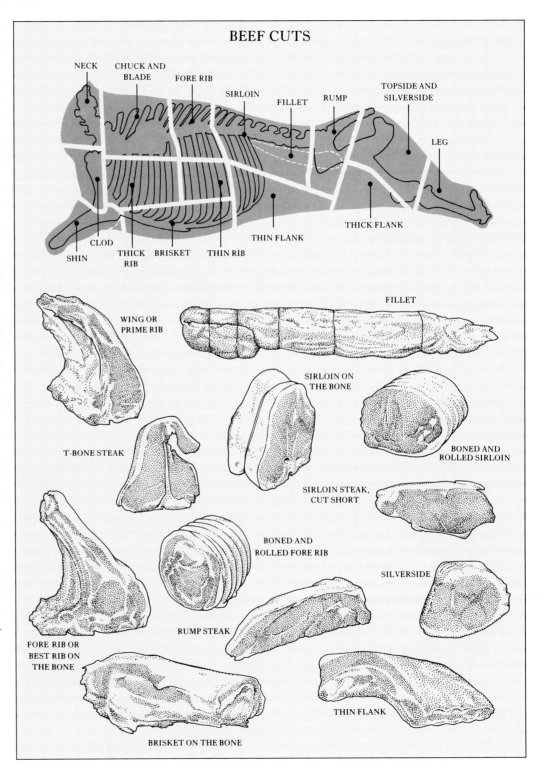

BEEF CUTS

187

cooked slowly with vegetables and then often served cold and sliced. Sometimes the beef is salted or pickled first. Surprisingly, beef can even be steamed or poached, if it is a tender piece of fillet. Although these methods may sound very modern, poached beef, or *boeuf à la ficelle* (beef on a string) is a traditional French dish. The piece of beef is tied into a neat shape with a length of string and with this it is lowered into a pot of just simmering water or stock and left in for about 15 to 20 minutes per lb (500g).

Braising and **pot-roasting** This is a very useful method for dealing with the less tender cuts of meat, such as the small lean joints of topside or silverside and blade or chuck steak. The meat is usually floured and fried all over first to seal it then it is set on a bed of vegetables and herbs with enough liquid just to cover these and the pan is covered. The meat cooks in the gentle moist heat of the scented steam, absorbing flavours from the herbs and vegetables and giving its own flavours to the cooking juices which make a rich sauce when the beef is served. *Sauerbraten* and *boeuf à la mode* are two of the most famous beef dishes cooked by this method.

Frying is a quick cooking method suitable for tender steaks, such as fillet and rump. It can be done in a dry non-stick pan, since the meat has enough fat, or with just a little butter or oil to lubricate the pan. Depending on whether rare, medium or well-done meat is required, 1in (2·5cm) thick steaks will take 7 to 15 minutes.

Grilling Appropriate for the same cuts of beef as for frying, grilling is a method which gets rid of excess fat since the meat sits on a rack which allows much of the fat to drain away. This is only suitable for the tenderest cuts of meat as the grill gives out a fierce, dry heat. Depending on whether rare, medium or well-done meat is required, 1in (2·5cm) thick steaks will take 7 to 15 minutes.

Stewing or **casseroling** Some of the most famous beef recipes use the least expensive cuts to produce extremely good dishes, warming and nourishing and full of appetizing aromas which develop during the long slow cooking. *Boeuf à la bourguignonne* (cooked in red wine), *boeuf gardien* (cooked in white wine), Hungarian goulash, rich with the colour and spicy flavour of sweet paprika, and carbonnade of beef, a Flemish dish cooked with beer, are all good examples.

Shin and leg of beef, chuck and blade, neck and clod, skirt and flank are all suitable. Stewing is also the first step to such glorious dishes as steak and kidney pie.

Stir-frying Beef is ideally suited to this method of cooking, commonly used in the preparation of Chinese recipes. Use tender cuts such as rump steak or, for even better value, see if you can buy the tail-end of fillet steak. Often this will be much less expensive than the thicker end of the fillet. The same method of cutting the beef into small strips and stirring it continuously throughout the cooking time is also used when making beef stroganoff.

Overall it would be impossible to say which country has the best beef recipes. Some are plain and simple, yet spectacular in their size and quality like the roast sirloins and standing ribs beloved of the British Sunday lunch. Others are elegant dishes for special occasions such as beef Wellington, a succulent piece of fillet wrapped and baked in a crisp pastry case. Pastry plays a part in other traditional English beef dishes, steak and kidney pie and, even nicer in my view, the classic steak and kidney pudding which used to be made with fresh oysters tucked under the suet crust.

In French *daubes* and casseroles beef is cooked slowly; and in South America where they make a large beef stew called *puchero* with sweetcorn, pumpkin and potatoes. In Belgium it is cooked in beer; in Spain they use sherry. I like to cook it in dry cider too. Beef can also make a meal in a hurry, whether it is a grilled steak or a hamburger. Steak is also used to make that favourite American dish, Swiss steak, where flour is pounded into the meat which is slowly braised with onions and served with a thick floury gravy.

Beef is also an important ingredient in mixed meat stews, such as the Italian *bollito misto*, the Portuguese *cocido* where it is cooked with chicken, salt pork, black pudding and other sausages, potatoes, vegetables and rice. One of my favourite such dishes is *baeckenoffe*, from Alsace in France, a layered casserole of potatoes, pork, lamb and beef with a bottle of Riesling poured over it and the whole baked for two to three hours in a low oven.

Unusual beef recipes will be found in Caribbean and South American cookery books. One is

the Spanish recipe for *ropa vieja* or 'old clothes' in which flank steak is cooked in a piece with peppers, vegetables and spices until it is tender enough to shred into 'rags'.

ACCOMPANIMENTS

What else to buy if you're shopping for a piece of beef? It is of course possible to serve beef with any vegetable you like, or with any kind of sauce or seasoning but just as lemon goes with fish, so several ingredients go supremely well with beef. On the vegetable front, celery hearts, celeriac, parsnips and fennel are all excellent, particularly when braised or roasted with the joint. And how appropriate these autumn vegetables are when you realize that beef is at its very best between September and November (although it is, of course, available all the year round).

Potatoes go supremely well with roast beef, whether they are roasted with the meat, or baked in their jackets, or boiled, or sliced and cooked *au gratin*. Leafy green Oriental vegetables should also be tried with beef, and not only for Oriental dishes. *Pak choi* and *choy sum* are both very tasty when steamed or quickly boiled. Gherkins and olives go well with cold roast or spiced beef. Mustard and horseradish are the perfect flavour enhancers or relishes, whereas to serve fruit with beef, in the form of a jelly or a purée, would be a culinary solecism of the highest order. On the other hand, I·do enjoy fruity chutneys and pickles on a rare roast beef sandwich and, of course, with spicy beef curries.

ENGLISH CUTS

Cuts of beef not only vary from country to country, because of the way the carcase is butchered, but within Britain there are wide regional variations. For example, the thick flank of beef has 27 different names.

Bladebone see **Chuck**

Brisket Sold either on the bone or boned and rolled, the brisket comes from the lower part of the shoulder. It can be a fatty piece of meat but has a good flavour. It is boiled, braised or pot-roasted, and sometimes salted or spiced first. Brisket is often served cold and thinly sliced.

Chuck or **blade bone** Cut from the top forequarter of the carcase, the blade bone is a large, relatively lean joint which is usually boned and sold as chuck, blade or braising steak. The meat has a little fat surrounding it and is well 'marbled' or streaked with thin seams of inter-muscular fat, which when cooked serve to baste and tenderize the meat. Chuck and blade are the best of the stewing meats and they can also be braised.

Clod and **neck** (or **sticking**) Both cuts of meat are from the neck part of the carcase, relatively lean, and usually cut up as stewing steak or stewing beef, or sometimes minced. They are leaner than chuck and blade beef, but without the flavour of shin of beef. Clod and neck are among the most economical cuts of beef and make excellent stews provided you add plenty of flavouring and cook them slowly.

Fillet This is a smallish boneless joint of beef – about 2–3lb (1–1·4kg) the 'eye' taken from within the rib bone or sirloin. It is extremely lean and tender and in prime specimens will be lightly marbled (this is particularly true of American prime beef). Although expensive there is no waste on it and it cooks quickly, which makes it worth considering for a special occasion. It can be roasted whole in a matter of 20 minutes, or for a more elaborate dish, such as beef Wellington, it is wrapped in puff pastry and baked.

Fillet is also sliced to make steaks, called variously, fillet steak, *filet mignon*, Château-briand steak (although the piece of fillet that is roasted whole is properly called Châteaubriand as well) and *tournedos*.

The tail-end of the fillet is narrow, tapers to a point and is unsuitable for cutting into steaks. My favourite way of preparing it is to trim it of all fat, chop it very finely, season it with parsley, salt, pepper, Worcestershire sauce, capers, onions and whatever else takes my fancy and serve it as steak tartare – raw, chopped seasoned steak. It is very tasty. Fillet is the right cut to use for that other delicious and fashionable beef recipe from Italy, *carpaccio*, which is paper-thin slices of raw steak, laid in overlapping slices on a plate and dressed with virgin olive oil, sea salt, freshly ground black pepper, shavings of Par-mesan cheese and a little greenery which might be celery tops, peppery rocket or thin slices of raw globe artichoke heart.

Leg and **shin** The first comes from the back legs of the animal and the shin from the forelegs, which are slightly smaller than the back legs. Sinews and connective tissue run through the lean tough leg muscle which gives the meat, when cooked, its characteristically rich, flavour-some, gelatinous quality. The shin and leg meat is perfect for stews and casseroles and is also used to make beef tea and stock.

Minced beef, mince meat This is beef which has been passed through the mincer once or twice. It is not always clear which part of the carcase has been minced, but as a general rule, if it is pale, it has a good deal of fat in it, if darker and more uniform in colour it is probably leaner. Unless the fat content is declared, there is much to be said for making your own mince by buying a piece of casseroling or stewing beef such as thin flank or neck, or the leaner chuck, trimming it of all fat (you can always add extra fat in frying) and then mincing it in a table-clamped mincer or in a food processor. Mince is ideal for cottage pie, meat sauce for spaghetti or lasagne, to mix with rice for stuffing peppers or aubergines, for making meat balls, meat loaf or hamburgers.

Rib The fore rib or best rib next to the sirloin is sold on the bone or boned and rolled as a traditional roasting joint. It is a lean tender joint. The middle rib, which is the cut made up of the top and back ribs, comes between the fore rib and the blade bone. It is a large joint usually divided into two, the top and back, and is often boned and rolled. They are lean joints, with less bone than the fore rib. The bone helps conduct heat to the centre of the joint; and without it the meat is best braised or pot-roasted.

The wing or prime rib is one of the largest, most expensive and certainly one of the best roasting joints, with the perfect proportion of bone, lean meat and fat. It should have a large central eye of meat and a good outer layer of creamy, white fat.

Rump If cut across the saddle with both back ends of sirloin, this becomes a large, traditional joint called a baron of beef. Rump is usually sliced for steaks.

Shin see **Leg**.

Silverside This is the lean outside thigh muscle. I do not think it roasts successfully unless you give it constant attention, basting it and check-ing the temperature. It is far more successful (and delicious) when braised or pot-roasted.

Silverside can also be salted, spiced or 'corned' and then boiled, pressed when cold, and sliced for serving.

Sirloin This is a fine majestic piece of beef for roasting, coming from the back or loin, the tenderest part of the animal. It is sold boned and rolled or on the bone. Either way the lean tender fillet, which is the small 'eye' of meat enclosed within the rib bones, can be removed for cooking separately either whole, or cut across the grain into fillet steaks.

Skirt This comes from the belly of the animal: thick or goose skirt is part of the inner muscle of the belly wall which is attached to the rump; thin skirt is the muscular part of the diaphragm, and body skirt is also part of the diaphragm.

Steak Châteaubriand is a thick cut of steak from the fillet which can be grilled or fried. Entrecôte literally means 'between the ribs'. This is a lean tender steak cut from the thin end of the boneless sirloin. Sirloin steaks also come from the sirloin. They are boneless and can be cut short or long. Porterhouse steaks are cut from the wing end of the sirloin and T-bone steaks are cut right across the sirloin, to include the bone and the tender fillet. Mignon is a small steak cut from the fillet, sometimes called *filet mignon*. Rump steak is a large, long cut of steak taken from the top of the rump. It is tender and full of flavour when grilled or fried.

Thick flank or **top rump** This comes from the hindquarter at the front of the thigh. It is lean, like topside and silverside, and more suitable for braising and pot-roasting than roasting. When sliced it can be fried slowly until tender.

Thin flank This is the under muscle towards the belly. It can be rather fatty and gristly, and is usually cut up or minced for stewing or use in pies. When left whole it can be salted or pickled and boiled.

Topside Sometimes called round or buttock steak, this is a lean boneless joint from the top of the inside hind leg. It is inclined to be dry as it is fine-grained with no marbling of fat. For this reason, braising or pot-roasting can often be more successful than roasting.

AMERICAN CUTS

Brisket One of the less tender but none the less tasty cuts of meat, brisket is inexpensive and

189

makes an excellent meal when braised with herbs and vegetables and served with a good horse-radish sauce. Brisket is also used for corned beef and salt beef.

Chuck roast The chuck or shoulder quarter of the carcase is large and can yield a number of different cuts: inside chuck roll, chuck tender, blade pot-roast or blade steak, boneless shoulder pot-roast or boneless shoulder steak, chuck short ribs, arm pot-roast or arm steak and Boston cut. These are less tender cuts than the prime loin and rib cuts but are nevertheless extremely tasty and nutritious when properly cooked. A moist heat is required, which makes all these cuts suitable for braising and pot-roasting, as well as for casseroling.

Flank steak Cut from the belly area below the loin, this is a narrow, flat cut of meat. It can be grilled or fried if from a tender animal and is often seen on menus as London broil. Inexpensive, boneless and easy to cook, fine quality flank steak is a very good buy.

Ground beef is minced beef.

Loin steaks Cut from the short loin between the sirloin and the rib are three types of steak. The porterhouse, cut from the large end, has more tenderloin or fillet. The club steak is from the small end of the loin and has no fillet, and the T-bone lies between the two. The porterhouse and T-bone are usually cut about 2in (5cm) thick and one will feed two people.

Rib steaks These are large steaks, usually one rib bone thick, with quite a lot of internal marbling fat as well as an outer layer. The Delmonico or Spencer steak is the eye of the rib, with the bone, fat and coarser meat removed. Cut between 1–2in (2·5–5cm) thick they are treated like fillet or tenderloin.

Rolled rib roast The same cut of meat from the fore rib, it has been taken off the bone, rolled and tied. Whether you choose this or the standing rib is very much a matter of preference. The quality of the meat is the same. Many people feel that the rolled boned joint is easier to carve, but perhaps it does not look quite as impressive as the standing rib.

Round steak Sliced from the top of the hindquarters, round steak is not the tenderest of steaks but it is very tasty. It is not suitable for hot dry cooking such as grilling or barbecuing, but it is suitable for pan-frying as in the traditional

Swiss steak recipe where flour and seasoning is pounded into the steak before it is fried with onions and then cooked very slowly, until tender enough to eat with a fork. Top round steak is a more tender, prime cut towards the rump.

Rump roast or **standing rump** This is the same cut of meat, the top of the hindquarter, which is used for the English cut of rump steak. Without the bone it becomes rolled rump. If the meat is from very tender, high-quality beef, these joints can be roasted, otherwise it is safer to pot-roast or braise them.

Short ribs From the short plate, rib or shoulder section of the carcase, short ribs are the equivalent of the English rolled rib joint. It is a good piece of meat for braising whole or in pieces.

Sirloin steaks These are tender, juicy, prime steaks cut from the loin. They contain the bone and a marbling of fat, as well as an outer layer of fat. Depending on where in the sirloin they are cut from, the steaks can be pinbone, flatbone, wedgebone or boneless. The New York strip or strip steak is the boneless strip of loin left when the fillet or the tenderloin is removed.

Standing rib roast This is the prime joint, and can weigh up to 8lb (3·6kg), depending on how many ribs you ask for. It corresponds with the English cut of best rib, and is taken from the fore rib of the animal. It is a very easy joint to roast, fat side up. No rack is needed underneath as the bones keep the meat away from the fat on the bottom of the pan.

Stew meat Cut from the shank or forelegs of the animal, this is the same as shin of beef. Use it for stocks, beef tea and well-flavoured stews, but cook it slowly for a long time.

FRENCH CUTS

Aiguillette Cut from the top of the rump or flank, this is the cut the French consider best for braising, being neither too fat nor too lean. It is also used for *boeuf à la mode* as well as *boeuf braisé* and in each case it is usual to lard the beef by threading strips of thin pork back fat through the lean parts.

Aloyau This is the large boned joint from the loin, equivalent to the sirloin, and marvellous for roasting for a special occasion.

Châteaubriand This is the thick end of the fillet, usually roasted and served to two people.

Contre-filet, faux filet Taken from the eye of the sirloin, this is a very tender and expensive roasting joint. It can also be cut into steaks called *faux filet* or *contre-filet*.

Côtes couvertes The rolled ribs are left on the bone as a roasting joint. Not as tender as the cuts from the sirloin, the *côtes couvertes* are best roasted slowly.

Entrecôte A thick, juicy, well-marbled steak, the *entrecôte* is cut, literally, from 'between the ribs'. Excellent for grilling, it is one of the classic French steaks. Often served with a sauce such as *marchand de vin* or *à la bordelaise* with red wine and beef marrow, or simply with a flavoured butter as in *entrecôte grillée maître d'hôtel*.

Filet This is the whole fillet taken along the backbone and can be roasted whole when it is usually larded, or it can be sliced into *filet mignon*, *tournedos* or Châteaubriand.

Onglet and **hampe** Cut from the breast or lower ribs of the carcase, the *onglet* and *hampe* are thick, juicy pieces of meat, somewhat like skirt steak. Occasionally, if from a particularly tender animal, the *onglet* is served grilled or fried as a steak, but both are probably best braised as in *carbonnade* or *daube*.

Paleron Somewhere between the chuck and the neck, this is an excellent cut of meat for stewing or braising, whole, or in pieces.

Plat de côtes Taken from between the ribs and the brisket, the *plat de côtes* is the equivalent of the short ribs or rolled ribs. Whether boned and rolled or on the bone, braise or pot-roast it. It is one of the French cuts used for boiled beef.

Poitrine A good, lean shoulder cut, the *poitrine* is suitable for braising and pot-roasting. It is one of the French cuts used for boiled beef.

BEEF OFFAL

Cheek Not often found for sale any more, the ox cheek is inexpensive and nutritious, but requires long, slow cooking. It needs to be carefully trimmed and washed.

Heart A very large organ, the ox heart can be stuffed and braised, but it is best cut up or sliced and casseroled. The meat is dark, dense and more fibrous than that of other offal.

Kidney These are large and dark, divided into many small lobes, a whole kidney weighing

VEAL

about 1lb (500g). It has a strong flavour which can be diminished by soaking in milk or water (or water and lemon juice) for half an hour or so before cooking it. Prepare it for cooking by removing any fat. This is suet and thus valuable for pastry making. (You can grate it yourself after chilling it, and then store it.) Peel off the membrane and cut out the core and gristle. Ox kidney should only be used for slowly cooked dishes such as steak and kidney pie or pudding.

Liver Coarse, dark and strongly flavoured, this is an acquired taste. Like all liver, it is highly nutritious, being rich in iron and protein. To minimize the strong flavours and dense texture, soak the slices or pieces of liver in milk overnight. It is best suited to slow cooking methods such as braising or casseroling and it is as well to add other powerful flavourings such as pungent herbs or curry spices, and wine or cider as the cooking fluid.

Marrowbone Marrow is a soft, rich, fatty substance contained in the large shin and leg bones of the animal. It is a delicacy, used for enriching sauces, for serving on toast or, traditionally, eaten with a long silver spoon from the roasted bones wrapped in a napkin.

Oxtail This remains one of the best bargains on the butcher's counter and makes some of my very favourite dishes in winter – oxtail soup, oxtail stew and oxtail terrine. The tail is usually chopped across into chunks. The thick bones can be used in a casserole, the small pieces added to the stockpot. The meat is richly flavoured, and the gelatine released from the connective tissues enriches the dish even further.

Tongue This usually weighs 3–4lb (1·4–1·8kg) but can be heavier. Sold fresh or salted, the tongue is tough and needs soaking before cooking, for two to three hours if fresh, eight to ten hours if salted. Cooking time will be shorter, by about an hour or so if salted; otherwise long, slow cooking is needed.

Tripe Tripe comes only from the ox and is the lining of the first three stomachs. It is wet, white, slithery and an acquired taste, and I love it. Traditional tripe recipes are found all over the world – Mexico, Portugal, Taiwan, Normandy and Lyon in France and Lancashire in Britain. In Britain almost all the tripe we buy has been scraped, bleached and pre-cooked, requiring only a further hour of cooking.

Escalopes, *schnitzel, piccata*, Milanese, Florentine, *osso buco*, *blanquette*, just a few of the culinary terms used to describe veal are a powerful illustration of the fact that it has never really been a British meat. Although the Normans brought with them from France the practice of killing very young calves for food, it never found favour with Anglo-Saxon farmers, who could not see the point of 'wasting' a perfectly good animal. In later times veal was regarded as a suitable food for invalids and then, after the French Revolution when the emigrés brought with them their cooks and recipes, more veal began to find its way into the British kitchen. In the last 30 years, since we have begun to travel much more and become familiar with French and Italian cooking, veal is more widely available, although with the exception of certain cuts, it is an expensive meat.

Some veal is reared in Britain, fed on powdered milk and slaughtered at 13 to 20 weeks. The young calf produces a pale pink, finely grained meat with a very firm, creamy white fat. In fact, there is little fat on it and it has no interior marbling of fat at all. In Italy, France and the United States very young animals are slaughtered, producing very pale, greyish-pink meat. The palest veal comes from animals which have been fed on milk, not on grass. This means too that the meat will be very tender. In fact, most veal cuts and joints are extremely tender and almost all can be roasted or, if cut into steaks or chops, fried or, with care, grilled.

METHODS OF COOKING

Roasting The most memorable veal I have ever tasted was a whole leg, bathed in lemon juice and olive oil, stuck with slivers of garlic and encircled with sprigs of rosemary. It was roasted before an open charcoal fire in the homely kitchen of the Antica Trattoria Suban, a big stone barn of a restaurant high above the city of Trieste in North-East Italy. The veal was crisp and brown on the outside, tender and moist on the inside. Veal should be roasted in a moderate oven, Gas mark 3, 325°F, 160°C for about 35 minutes per 1lb (500g), if on the bone, and 40–45 minutes per 1lb (500g) if boned and rolled. The leg, the loin and the rib joints are all suitable for roasting, as is the boned and rolled shoulder. As it is a dry meat, remember to baste frequently.

Veal should be thoroughly cooked and not served rare.

Frying and **grilling** Because veal is so lean, great care needs to be taken when grilling it. In my view the only cuts suitable for grilling are the massive Florentine chops, rather like a T-bone steak and cut from the loin, which are sometimes served in good Tuscan restaurants. Even then great care must be taken to baste the meat with olive oil during grilling to stop it drying out. Chops, fillets and escalopes cut from the leg are best pan-fried in butter or olive oil. They are sometimes breaded first 'Milanese' style, which gives an extra protection against drying out.

Braising and **pot-roasting** Such a lean, tender meat lends itself to these methods where the moist heat gently cooks the meat, and the herbs and vegetables added to the pot provide flavourings for this sometimes bland meat.

Stewing and **casseroling** Some of the cheapest cuts of veal make the tastiest stews. Think of the French *blanquette de veau* with its creamy, lemony sauce tasting of cloves and onions, or the Italian stew, *osso buco* with its sticky, glossy white wine and tomato sauce and piquant garnish of lemon, parsley and garlic.

French and Italian cookery books are usually the best source of recipes for veal. Veal Marengo uses the same ingredients as the chicken dish of the same name, which was said to have been cooked for Napoleon just before the battle of Marengo. Fortunately his chef had to hand some tomatoes, garlic, wine and parsley to turn the chicken into a tasty stew. *Fricandeau à l'oseille* is an old-fashioned French dish made from the small, plump cushion-like muscle from the leg. It was barded and braised on a bed of carrots and onions and served with a purée of sorrel. *Paupiettes de veau* and veal birds are small stuffed parcels of flattened veal escalope. *Cima alla genovese* is a marvellous recipe for stuffed breast of veal from Liguria in Italy. *Vitello tonnato* is another favourite of mine, a joint of roast veal sliced cold and served with an unusual sauce, almost like a mayonnaise, of tuna fish and capers. I make a version of the sauce with cooked salmon and often roast the veal especially to have it cold.

Another northern Italian recipe for veal is *vitello al uccelletto* in whch diced rump of veal, or other tender pieces, are quickly fried in olive

191

VEAL CUTS

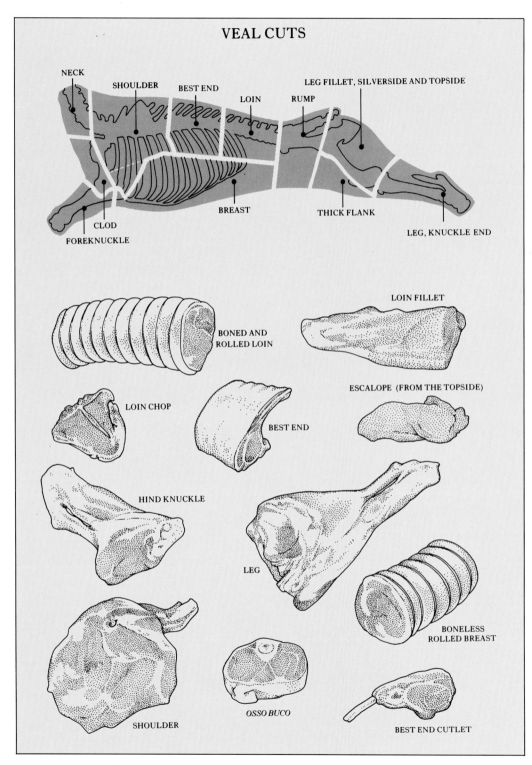

NECK

SHOULDER

BEST END

LOIN

RUMP

LEG FILLET, SILVERSIDE AND TOPSIDE

CLOD

FOREKNUCKLE

BREAST

THICK FLANK

LEG, KNUCKLE END

LOIN FILLET

BONED AND
ROLLED LOIN

LOIN CHOP

BEST END

ESCALOPE (FROM THE TOPSIDE)

HIND KNUCKLE

LEG

BONELESS
ROLLED BREAST

SHOULDER

OSSO BUCO

BEST END CUTLET

oil with a little chopped sage and moistened with white wine. Boneless roasting joints can also be substituted for pork in the Tuscan recipe *maiale al latte* in which loin of pork is pot-roasted in milk.

For a whole piece of veal that needs plenty of moisture in cooking, braise it on a bed of small onions and fresh garlic cloves, together with a dozen or so small sweet tomatoes, a sprig of rosemary and a little olive oil and white wine. Veal escalopes can be quickly cooked with a slice of ham and cheese on each escalope, the whole thing then being dipped in egg and breadcrumbs before frying.

ACCOMPANIMENTS
Although veal is lean, it has a gelatinous, sticky, suave quality when cooked, which is best complemented by sharp, piquant, fragrant scents and flavours. Lemons should go into your shopping bag if you're buying veal, and other lemony-flavoured things such as lemon thyme and lemon grass. Although the latter is an Oriental ingredient and veal is not, a sauce flavoured with lemon grass and nutmeg is a perfect match for braised veal. Oranges and limes are also compatible flavours for veal. Try marinating diced pie veal in orange juice and cardamom before making a casserole, or grating lime zest into a sauce for veal medallions. Summer savory, rosemary and lavender are also excellent herbs to flavour a veal roast. Sharp-flavoured greens such as sorrel, rocket, spinach and watercress provide the right sort of colour contrast with veal. Look too for the crisp textures of broccoli, green beans or stir-fried cabbage, rather than Jerusalem artichokes, salsify and other root vegetables.

Purées of vegetables are not generally associated with veal dishes, yet creamy mashed potatoes and garlic are the perfect accompaniment to a plain roasted veal kidney. Homemade

Veal

1 LOIN CHOP
2 FILLET (SLICE)
3 FILLET
4 CALF'S LIVER
5 LOIN
6 ESCALOPES
7 OSSO BUCO
8 SWEETBREADS
9 CALF'S KIDNEY
10 SHIN
11 BRAINS

pasta or noodles also go very well with roast or braised veal or medallions – any dish that has plenty of veal gravy.

ENGLISH CUTS

Best end, best end of neck This joint corresponds to the ribs of the animal. It is sold on the bone for roasting, like a smaller version of rib of beef, or in cutlets for grilling or frying. In either case it is best to remove the chine bone – this is the thick part where the rib joins the backbone. I like to roast this joint with a herb, mustard and breadcrumb crust, pressed all over the thin outer layer of fat.

Breast The thin underside of the body, corresponding to the belly, this is a marvellously economical piece of veal, with an excellent flavour and texture when carefully cooked. It can be roasted on the bone, braised on a bed of vegetables, diced for stew, minced for a meat loaf but, best of all, it should be boned, stuffed, rolled and braised or roasted. It has enough fat on it and in it to stop it drying out too much.

A seventeenth-century English recipe for stuffed breast of veal used breadcrumbs, currants, rosewater, cloves, mace, saffron, chopped dates and a little sugar served with a sauce made from meat juices, claret, nutmeg and a little orange juice.

My favourite recipe combines the inexpensive breast with the more expensive kidney, but a 2½lb (1·1kg) prepared breast and 1lb (500g) kidney will feed six to eight people and thus it is still very good value. I like to leave some of the fat on the kidney which then bastes from the

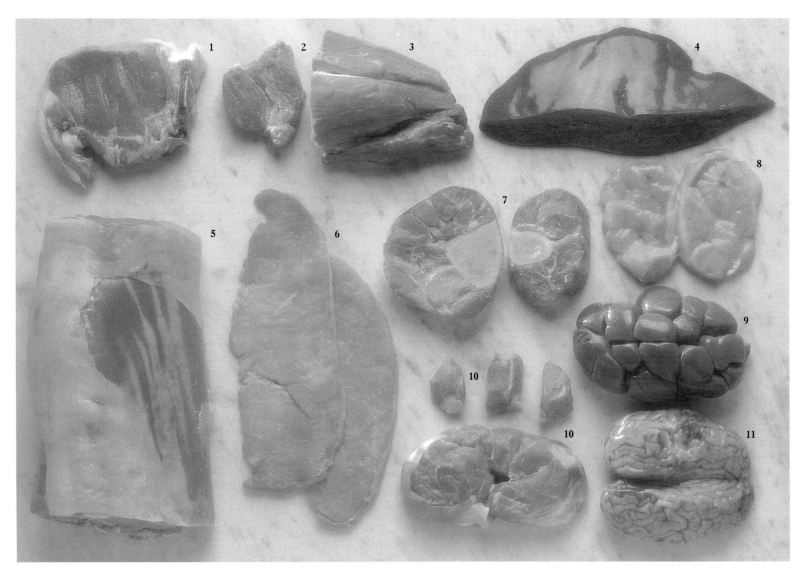

inside. Season the kidney, wrap it in spinach leaves and then roll the breast round it. It looks very good when sliced, and is absolutely delicious when cold and thinly sliced.

The foreknuckle or shin next to the breast has little meat on it but makes very fine, rich, pale stock.

Leg This is one of the largest, leanest, tenderest joints on the carcase, and consequently one of the most expensive. It is possible to buy and roast the whole leg from a small animal, but it is more usually divided into several cuts from both the fillet end and the knuckle end. Topside or cushion of veal is the small, lean cushion-shaped muscle from which escalopes, or very thin slices, are cut along the grain, about ¼in (0·5cm) thick and then beaten even thinner. The cushion can also be larded and braised or pot-roasted.

Thicker slices called fillets are also cut from the top end of the leg for grilling and frying, or a large thick fillet can be removed for roasting. Knuckle, the bonier end of the hind leg contains plenty of rich marrow and gelatinous connective tissue. The hind knuckle is sawn into 2in (5cm) rounds to make *osso buco*. It can also be braised. Occasionally I have braised the knuckle in one piece and then served it with a white risotto enriched with the marrow scooped out of the bone. This makes a very tasty dish.

Loin Either left whole for roasting or cut into loin chops for grilling or frying, loin is another prime veal joint. It is taken from between the hindquarter and the ribs or best end. Sometimes it is sold boned and rolled around a stuffing and sometimes includes the fillet. The fillet can be sliced into thick rounds, called medallions, for grilling or pan frying. If roasting a whole fillet, add plenty of flavourings and baste well during cooking.

It is well worth boning a loin yourself, trimming it of as much fat as you wish and then mixing your own stuffing. If you buy the whole loin, you may or may not get the kidney with it. Since veal kidney is a particular delicacy, it is expensive so it is usually sold separately.

Middle neck and **scrag** Both cuts come from the forequarter, between the head and the best end of neck. Bony but well flavoured, these can be chopped up for casseroles, the bonier pieces being used for stock, or the bones can be removed and the meat used for pies or mince.

Minced veal A pale pink mince which you will sometimes find ready-made, although it is more usual to select your own piece for mincing. Minced veal combines very well with other minced meats, particularly pork and beef, as its gelatinous quality prevents the mixture from crumbling, which beef tends to do if it is used alone. Use minced veal in meat loaves, in sauce for pasta, as a filling for cannelloni or lasagne, and as a stuffing for cabbage leaves and other vegetables.

Pie veal This is the diced meat taken from the cheaper secondary cuts and is suitable for pies and casseroles. It usually comes from the middle end, scrag or shin and also includes the breast trimmings after the carcase has been cut up.

Shoulder or **chuck** An awkward shape, the shoulder is nevertheless a good, inexpensive roasting joint. It can be roasted on the bone or boned and stuffed. Because of its round, flat shape, after the knuckle has been removed it is sometimes called the oyster.

Stewing veal is taken from the same cuts as pie veal but not diced. Both need slow, careful cooking with plenty of liquid and flavourings. These are the cuts I sometimes use for cold meat pies, often combined with rabbit or ham. While the pies are still hot I make a hole in the crust and pour in stock made from veal bones. This turns to a marvellous clear jelly when cold which makes the pie very good for slicing.

AMERICAN CUTS

Because of the extensive Italian influence through immigration in the past and the present large cattle industry, veal is popular in the United States and a wide selection of cuts is available for roasting and for braising as well as smaller ones for grilling and frying.

Casseroling, braising and **stewing cuts** Neck slices, riblets, foreshanks, brisket pieces and brisket roll, and the forequarter generally. 'City chicken' is diced veal on skewers, the meat is usually cut from the lean part of the shoulder. For meat loaves, patties and meat sauce the meat is usually cut from the lean part of the shoulder.

Grilling and **frying cuts** are boneless cutlets, round steak, escalopes (scallopini), rolled cutlets (veal birds) and heel of the round, all from the leg; loin chops, kidney chops, sirloin steak and cube steak from the loin; rib chops and Frenched rib chops; arm steak and blade steak from the shoulder; and stuffed chops which come from the breast.

Roasting cuts are standing rump, shank half of leg, rolled leg and centre leg, all from the leg; loin roast, rolled stuffed loin, sirloin roast and rolled double sirloin all from the loin; rib roast and crown roast from the rib; arm roast, blade roast and rolled shoulder from the shoulder; breast of veal and stuffed breast.

FRENCH CUTS

These resemble English cuts quite closely.

Côte The ribs are divided into the *côtelettes premières*, the four cutlets from the best end of neck nearest the loin, and the *côtelettes secondes* or *découvertes* which are the four cutlets nearest the shoulder. Both are excellent roasting joints, but are also divided up into cutlets for grilling or frying.

Crosse This is the heel end of the hind leg, suitable for the stockpot.

Épaule, collet and **bas de carré** The shoulder, neck and scrag end joints are not as tender as the prime cuts and are usually braised whole on the bone, or boned, rolled and braised. Neck meat is often cut up for casseroles.

Grenadin is a small thick steak cut from the leg.

Jarret is the knuckle or shin which contains the large leg bone and marrow and is surrounded by juicy, succulent meat. It can be braised whole with vegetables or cut into chunks.

Poitrine The breast of veal, also known as *flanchet*, is braised, boned or on the bone and used for such dishes as *blanquette de veau*.

Quasi Escalopes are cut from this lean rump piece, or the *quasi* can be roasted whole.

Rognon is so called because it contains the kidneys. The *longe* (loin) and *filet* (fillet) are the prime roasting joints cut from this part of the carcase. *Médaillon* is a small, thick steak cut from the fillet in the loin.

Rouelles This is the thick, lean part of the leg between the *quasi* (rump) and the *jarret* (knuckle) and contains the *cuisseau* or *noix* which corresponds to the topside or cushion of veal, and the *noix pâtissière* which corresponds to the thick part of the flank. To roast successfully, it would be best to lard these cuts.

VEAL OFFAL

Most offal is a good bargain because there is not a great demand for it, but veal offal is the exception. It is highly prized by chefs and discerning cooks, which has helped to raise the price, particularly of kidneys and liver. Prices were always higher than those of other offal simply because there is less veal about than beef and lamb. Veal or calf's offal is well worth buying, preparing carefully and turning into a dish for a special occasion.

Brains Although no longer available in Britain you may come across these abroad where they are still considered fit to eat and prized as a delicacy. One brain, weighing about 8oz (250g), makes one serving. To prepare, soak in very lightly acidulated water for about half an hour to remove all traces of blood, and then blanch by bringing it to the boil in lightly salted water, drain, rinse in cold water and then allow to rest. Remove all traces of filament. Modern Viennese chefs serve them with artichoke hearts, with mushrooms, cold in salads with leeks and broccoli, and in savoury strudels with spinach.

Calf's foot Rarely available, but if you do find a calf's foot it is a marvellous thing to cook in stews and casseroles because of the amount of gelatine it contains which adds a rich, sticky quality to the dish. It is the origin of the nourishing calf's foot jelly beloved of Victorian cooks, especially those cooking for the sick room. If you are making jellied meat terrines this is what you need.

Calf's head is the basis of mock turtle soup, brawns and *tête de veau vinaigrette*. You are not very likely to come across one often. It takes quite a lot of preparation to bone, blanch and trim, but the end results give a feeling of great satisfaction.

Heart This makes a good, inexpensive roast when stuffed and basted well. The meat has a good flavour, and it is pleasantly chewy, unlike most offal. It can also be sliced and fried, and cooked with spices and plenty of strong flavours.

Kidney Veal or calf's kidney is a great delicacy. As they are quite richly flavoured, I think one is sufficient for two servings. A traditional French way of cooking is to roast it in its suet overcoat, if you are ever lucky enough to find calf's kidneys in this state. The kidneys can be sliced and grilled or fried, quickly so that the inner part is still just pink and juicy. Kidneys are also marvellous with a creamy sauce, flavoured with mustard or Roquefort cheese and served with rice. Because they are so delicate, do guard against overcooking them.

Liver Calf's liver is as fine and delicate as veal kidney. It, too, should be lightly cooked, preferably grilled or fried in thin slices. *Fegato alla veneziana* is a favourite Italian dish, requiring the simplest, quickest of cooking, just searing the thin slices of liver on both sides in some hot butter and then serving it with the pan juices and some crumbled sage leaves. Deglazing the pan with a drop of raspberry vinegar adds a nicely sharpened counterpoint to the meltingly soft liver. A whole calf's liver can weigh 3–4lb (1·4–1·8kg) and it is possible to turn it into a spectacular dinner dish by seasoning and roasting it, taking care to baste periodically, and then carving it into neat, tender slices at the table.

Marrowbone The hind legs of the animal have a thick, sturdy shin bone which contains the rich marrow. It is excellent for lubricating sauces and casseroles and the marrow can be used also as a garnish for other dishes. The roasted bones can be served as a starter, the marrow being scooped out with a long silver spoon and eaten on toast.

Sweetbreads Although no longer on sale in Britain, *ris de veau*, calves' sweetbread, is one of the classics of French cookery. Mild, delicate and with an unusual texture, the sweetbread lends itself to a vast range of preparations and garnishes. It consists of two parts of the thymus gland, the 'throat' bread which is long and the 'heart' bread which has a rounder shape. The pancreas, or 'stomach' bread, is not a sweetbread but is sometimes referred to as such. If you come across them abroad where they are considered fit to eat, this is how to prepare them. Soak them in lightly acidulated water to remove all traces of blood, blanch in lightly salted boiling water, rinse them and remove all skin and fat except the very fine membrane which holds them all together. Then weight them down until cold when they can be sliced or diced and used in a number of recipes. I like to cook them in butter with mushrooms, tarragon and cream and then use the mixture to fill a pastry case. Large slices can be breaded, fried and served with lemon wedges.

A plump, healthy porker rooting around the farmyard is no longer a familiar sight in the countryside. Pigs today are, for the most part, raised indoors, fed on a concentrated diet and slaughtered as young as six months old for pork joints, a little older for bacon and manufactured pork products.

Until the Industrial Revolution, when people left the land to seek work in the towns and cities of Britain, many families relied on the pig as their main source of meat during the winter months. A piglet born in early spring would forage in the farmyard and on common land until November, when it would be killed. The first meals when the carcase was cut up would be the fresh offal. The large joints would be packed away in a brine tub and the trimmings made into sausages packed into the cleaned out intestines which even today are used for sausage skins. The pig's head might well have made its appearance as the main dish of the Christmas celebrations. Some of the joints, instead of being salted would have been lightly cured and then hung up to dry as ham or bacon.

In China the pig was domesticated some 5000 years ago and it has been an important food source in many other parts of the world. Pork meat is forbidden to Jews and Muslims and it is not therefore to be found in the cuisines of the Middle East and North Africa, and other areas where Islam is the main religion.

BUYING PORK

As pork is a young meat, expect to find it with firm white fat; pink, smooth velvety flesh; pale bones with a tinge of blue to them, and pale pinky-fawn, smooth, hairless skin. Avoid any meat that looks in any way damp or clammy, or with oily, waxy-looking fat.

Pork is available and quite safe to eat all year round and not just in the winter months. Modern storing and refrigeration techniques mean that that restriction is no longer necessary. In the summer months pork seems to be less in demand because it is regarded as a winter food. It follows, therefore, that it is often to be had at bargain prices during the summer.

METHODS OF COOKING

The modern pig is a slim young thing, developed over the years to have much less fat and more lean meat. Every part of the pig from its head to its tail is said to be edible, with the exception of the squeak.

Roasting, grilling and **frying** Because it is young, tender meat, most cuts of pork can be roasted, grilled or fried. Whereas pork was once considered too fat for many people's taste, it is now so lean that some cuts need basting as they roast. Alternatively lean pork can be roasted in foil or a roasting bag to eliminate the need for basting. For many people the attraction of roast pork is that marvellous, crisp, crunchy, golden,

mahogany crackling. To achieve the perfect crackling, the skin must be scored in deep parallel lines, not too far apart, and right down through the fat. The rind can be removed and roasted separately or it can be left on the joint. Whichever method you choose, do not baste the skin and do not let it come into contact with any fat, liquid or cooking juices in the roasting tin. It will become like leather if it does. If roasting pork on the bone, allow 25 minutes per 1lb (500g) and 25 minutes at Gas mark 6, 400°F, 200°C. Pork is best roasted slowly off the bone,

for 35 minutes per 1lb (500g) and an extra 35 minutes at Gas mark 4, 350°F, 180°C. Allow an extra five to ten minutes if the joint is stuffed.

Braising is a suitable method for large, lean joints which will benefit from the addition of lightly browned vegetables, herbs and some well-flavoured stock or wine.

Stewing and **casseroling** Slow cooking of pork either on top of the stove or in a heavy sealed pot in the oven is an excellent method for this tender, succulent meat. A pork casserole is an extremely good-tempered dish, one which is

difficult to spoil and which will just go on cooking gently until you are ready for it.

Boiling This is something of a misnomer since meat is never boiled, just allowed to simmer gently. This is a good method to use for a joint of salt pork. The meat should be soaked in water overnight, then put in a large saucepan of clean water together with vegetables, suitable herbs and spices, brought to the boil and simmered for 25 minutes to the 1lb (500g).

Apart from the traditional pork roasts there are many marvellous pork dishes from around the world which we can reproduce in our own kitchens. Among the countless Chinese recipes some of my favourites are from the south, particularly the Cantonese *char siu*, a rich red roast pork which is marinated in soy sauce among other things before cooking, and then used almost as a seasoning for other dishes, such as fried rice and noodle dishes. Barbecued spare ribs and stir-fried pork tenderloin are also dishes borrowed from China. Cassoulet, that fragrant stew of beans, meat and garlic from South-West France, has pork in it, as well as lamb and preserved duck or goose. Boston baked beans, which is surely a first cousin of the cassoulet, has a succulent piece of salt pork buried in among the beans. In Germany and Austria cuts of fresh and salt pork are served with sauerkraut and boiled potatoes. Spain, too, is a rich source of pork recipes. Indeed, the Iberian pig is one of the great gastronomic treasures of the country, making as it does, cured ham (*jamón de Jabugo*) to rival that of Parma and San Daniele in Italy. Suckling pig is the speciality of Segovia, just north of Madrid. Clever Portuguese cooks invented what has become one of my favourite pork dishes – *porco alentejana* (pork in the Alentejo style), which consists of small cubes of pork tenderloin, lightly seasoned and fried in olive oil until almost cooked, when handfuls of

Pork

1 KIDNEY (SKINNED)	8 HAND AND SPRING
2 LIVER	JOINT
3 SPARE RIBS	9 SPARERIB OR
4 TENDERLOIN	SHOULDER CHOP
5 KIDNEY (UNSKINNED)	10 LOIN CHOP
6 TROTTER	11 LOIN
7 LOIN CHOP AND KIDNEY	12 TOP LEG

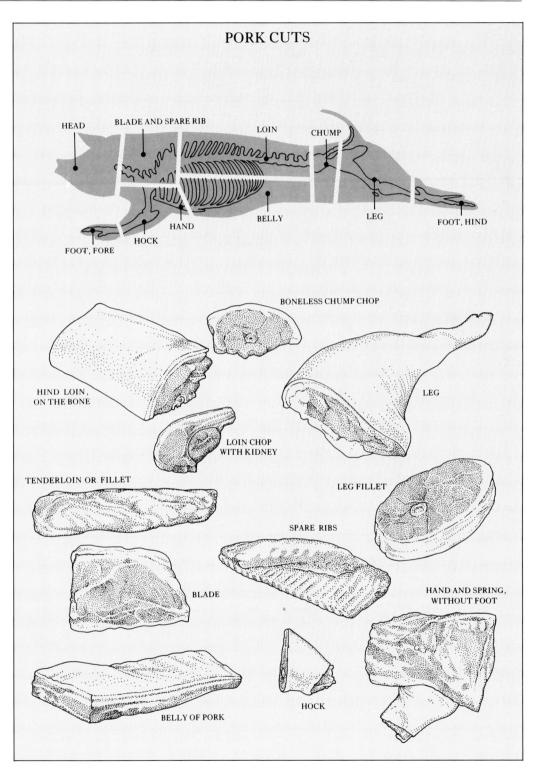

PORK CUTS

HEAD · BLADE AND SPARE RIB · LOIN · CHUMP · FOOT, HIND · LEG · BELLY · HAND · HOCK · FOOT, FORE

HIND LOIN, ON THE BONE · BONELESS CHUMP CHOP · LEG · LOIN CHOP WITH KIDNEY · LEG FILLET · TENDERLOIN OR FILLET · SPARE RIBS · BLADE · HAND AND SPRING, WITHOUT FOOT · BELLY OF PORK · HOCK

freshly cleaned, small clams, still in their shells, are thrown in and the lid tightly clamped on. The resulting heavenly stew, with both meat and shellfish cooking juices, is flavoured with coriander before serving.

ACCOMPANIMENTS

From the foregoing it will be seen that pork is a very companionable meat that goes with a whole range of ingredients. The single most striking accompaniment to pork, however, is fruit. Many pork dishes are unthinkable without it. In the Touraine region of France it is traditionally served with prunes. Due north in Normandy it is served with apples, as it is in Britain and Germany. In New England it is served with cranberries, in Georgia with peaches, in Hawaii with pineapple. Pork is a meat to experiment with. Try it with plumped-out dried apricots or pears. This pale rich meat needs sharp fruity or acidic flavours, which is why sauerkraut is also a perfect companion, and spiced red cabbage another. Pickles go beautifully with cold pork in Sichuan and South Korea as well as in any Suffolk pub. Pulses and pork are good companions; dried beans in the winter and autumn, fresh broad beans in spring and summer.

The pungent oily herbs such as sage, rosemary, myrtle, savory and thyme are appropriate for pork, as are juniper berries, cardamom, ginger, allspice and nutmeg. For me, pork and Mediterranean flavours have little in common, and I rarely cook it with tomatoes, olives, garlic or basil, for example.

ENGLISH CUTS

Belly Also known as streaky and flank, this is the same cut as the breast of lamb. It is a thin cut of meat with approximately the same proportion of fat to lean in thin layers. The long rib bones can be removed from the belly and divided up for roasting or barbecuing. These are the spare ribs. The belly can then be stuffed, rolled and roasted. This meat is also invaluable for terrines, and is the cut I buy for mincing when, as with terrines, a good proportion of fat is required. It can also be chopped up and added to casseroles where it adds flavour and richness. A tripe casserole, for example, benefits hugely from a few chunks of belly pork.

Leg This is the largest joint of the carcase, weighing in excess of 10lb (4·5kg). It can be roasted whole, on the bone or boned and stuffed. It is more usual, however, for the leg to be chopped into two large joints, the knuckle half (or hough as it is known in Scotland) and the fillet half leg. Sometimes this includes the chump. Both are excellent roasting joints, the knuckle having rather more bone than the fillet end, which is the top half of the leg. This is sometimes sliced into leg chops which can be braised or grilled.

Loin Hind loin is the choice half of the loin, the prime roasting joint. It contains the kidney and the fillet or tenderloin. The hind loin will weigh about 4–5lb (1·8–2·3kg). If buying it to roast on the bone, check that the chine bone (the half backbone) has been sawn for easier carving.

Foreloin is the rib end of the loin, and it looks like a larger version of a best end of neck of lamb. Boned, stuffed and rolled this makes a marvellous dinner party dish which slices beautifully. It is also extremely good served cold, in thin slices, with fresh bread, unsalted butter and homemade pickles. I sometimes stuff this joint with apricots, walnuts, herbs and breadcrumbs.

The tenderloin is often sold separately from the hind loin. It is a lean, tender and very succulent piece of meat, weighing 10–14oz (300–425g) which makes it a perfect choice for two. It can be sliced into medallions and pan-fried, split lengthways, stuffed, tied and roasted, or marinated and cooked Oriental style. If roasting it, a roasting bag is a good idea; it allows the meat to baste itself.

Chops are also cut from the loin. Loin chops from the fore loin and chump chops from between the loin and the leg are best grilled or fried on a moderate heat rather than on a very high heat as you would do for lamb. The skin and fat need cutting into at intervals with a sharp knife or kitchen scissors to prevent them curling in the heat.

Neck and **shoulder** An assortment of cuts come from this part of the pig. One of the best is the tasty and inexpensive spare rib or shoulder joint. It is sometimes cut into sparerib or shoulder chops (not to be confused with spare ribs from the belly). Sparerib chops are not quite as lean as loin chops because they have a good deal of marbling, but this is what helps to keep them sweet and

succulent as they cook. The chops can be grilled or fried, cut into slivers for stir-frying, or the whole piece of spare rib can be braised. The blade from the neck end of the shoulder is a slightly soft and fatty joint and can be roasted or braised.

Hand and **spring** The lower part of the forequarter is divided into the hand and spring (also known confusingly as the shoulder) and the knuckle or hock. Either singly or together, these make excellent braising joints. They are inexpensive and have a very good flavour. The gelatinous content of the skin, bones and connective tissue give a wonderfully smooth texture to casseroles. I find these pork cuts particularly good when cooked slowly, with beans, for example, in a clay pot.

AMERICAN CUTS

The leg of pork is called the ham, whether it is fresh or cured. More of the cuts are sold cured or smoked than in Britain.

Ground pork (minced pork) is usually taken from one of the forequarter cuts, and is used as a stuffing for vegetables, or for mixing with minced beef or veal to make excellent meat loaf. Less tender cuts for braising, pot-roasting or casseroling are the shoulder slice, shoulder butt, spare ribs and pork knuckle.

Ham roast This is the leg of pork, sometimes sold off the bone as boneless ham roast; it is a very large joint weighing up to 10lb (4·5kg).

Pork loin roast This is taken from the front or rear of the loin, or indeed can be the whole loin, weighing about 12lb (5·4kg). Grilling or frying cuts are taken from the loin as chops such as the butterfly pork chop, rib chop, loin chop, sirloin chop or top loin chop. The tenderloin (fillet) is cooked whole, or cut into noisettes or medallions and pan-fried.

FRENCH CUTS

Carré The equivalent of the best end of neck, this joint is taken from the fore ribs (*côtes*) and can be roasted on or off the bone, rolled and stuffed if the latter. The joint can also be divided into *côtelettes*, or chops which are usually grilled or pan-fried, and often served with creamy mashed potatoes, a marvellous combination.

Échine The top part of the shoulder has the

equivalent of the spare rib joint, which is braised whole, pot-roasted or cut into chops. The *palette* is the blade bone joint which can be roasted on or off the bone.

Filet This is the prime roasting joint, the centre or middle loin to which the kidney is attached. The *pointe de filet* is the tenderloin.

Jambon The *jambonneau* is the narrow, bony part of the hind leg between the trotter and the top end of the leg or *jambon*. It has plenty of flavour and gelatine and thus is good in soups and casseroles. It is also a nice piece to salt, then cook and serve with sauerkraut or beans. The *jambon* is usually roasted.

Plat de côtes The forequarter flank is suitable for braising or pot-roasting, or cutting up for casseroles.

Poitrine The belly is sold whole or in slices, and is a very versatile meat. It enriches other dishes such as stews and pâtés, and comes into its own in the preparation of *rillettes*, that very superior potted meat made by slowly cooking belly pork until it falls apart and then shredding it and packing the meat loosely into pots which are filled with the clear, liquid pork fat. When cool the fat solidifies around the meat.

PORK OFFAL

Everything but the squeak, remember. While some pork offal such as heart and liver is fairly coarse, and a poor substitute for lamb's heart and liver, there are parts of the pig that are invaluable for cooking with other dishes. One of the most important of these is pork fat.

Fat The back fat is sliced into thin sheets which are used for barding (or wrapping around) lean joints of meat, pork or beef, and larding, or inserting thin slivers of fat into lean pieces of meat such as fillet of beef. Back fat also makes lard, a fat used in cooking and baking. Leaf lard is the crisp white fat from around the kidney. This is considered excellent for pastry making. Caul fat is the thin, veil-like membrane around the stomach lining, through which run thin veins of fat. It is invaluable for making home-made sausages, faggots and *crépinettes* (from *crépine*, the French word for caul fat). In its natural state it is stiff and needs soaking in warm water for five minutes or so to make it pliable.

Head It is a very long time since I have seen a pig's head for sale. It used to be a popular dish, made into brawn (*fromage de tête* or *hure* in French). Like so many bits of offal and odds and ends, a pig's head needs a great deal of careful preparation, cleaning, singeing, scalding and soaking. Pig's cheek is sometimes sold separately and this is cooked until tender, then shaped and coated in egg and breadcrumbs to make a 'Bath chap'. Brains can be prepared like lamb's or calf's brains and soaked in cold water, then blanched in lightly salted water before cooking them.

The ears are still very popular in France but not often seen for sale in Britain. When washed and singed, they are simmered for an hour or two to soften them, then pressed until cold, cut in half, dipped in melted butter and breadcrumbs and fried to be served with a mustardy vinaigrette. They have a crunchy, gelatinous quality.

Heart makes a good, inexpensive dish when well-trimmed and braised with herbs or spices, on a bed of vegetables.

Kidney Pig's kidneys have a good flavour and texture. Sometimes they are chopped up with the loin chops, but they are also sold separately. They can be grilled or fried.

Liver Although not as delicate as lamb's liver, if it is soaked in milk first, pork liver can be gently cooked or fried to make nutritious and inexpensive dishes. I have to say I have been put off pig's liver ever since eating a traditional Christmas dish from Albi in South-West France of cooked, sliced radishes and pork liver. It was truly one of the least enjoyable things I have ever eaten but it is excellent in terrines and pâtés.

Tail Even this small, pink, curly object is worth having. Chop it up and add it to the stock pot as it is rich in gelatine.

Tripe Pork tripe and intestines are the main ingredients of chitterlings (or tripe sausage, also known as *andouille* and *andouillette* in France).

Trotters or **feet** are one of my favourite parts of the animal. I often buy a couple to cook in the stockpot. There are two benefits here. They become tender and the stock takes in enough gelatine to allow it to set when cold. This makes a good homemade aspic. The tender pig's trotters are then brushed with melted butter, rolled in soft breadcrumbs and grilled or baked brown and crisp. Served with chips, watercress and a mustardy sauce you have a dish straight out of the best French bistros.

Lamb is the meat from a young sheep, up to about a year old, after which the animal is called a hogget, and the meat becomes known as mutton. Mutton is a darker meat than lamb and has a slightly stronger flavour.

Grasslands, both hillside and lowland, of temperate and cold climates, provide the right conditions for rearing sheep. These are widely distributed and so is lamb. It comes from the barren Asian steppes of Mongolia to the islands in the North Sea off the Netherlands where the famous Texel lamb is found; from the lush grassy pastures of Kent and Sussex to those of the North Island of New Zealand where there is a far greater population of sheep than of humans. Human migration around the world helped to spread and develop sheep farming, both for wool and for food. The Welsh hill farmers took sheep with them to hilly Patagonia in South America. Basque shepherds from South-West France and northern Spain, said to be among the most skilled in the world, took sheep to the Pacific North-West states of the United States, along with their spices and methods of cooking.

The lamb has always been associated with springtime, both in a culinary and a symbolic sense. It has featured in ancient Chinese spring rituals, as well as the Jewish Passover and Christian, Greek and Russian Orthodox Easter festivals.

In many Western countries roast lamb is the traditional dish to serve on Easter Sunday. It is my favourite meat for roasting, one of the least intimidating and the one best suited to this method of cooking. It is a young meat and will be tender. Because it is reared outside in the early part of the year in a cold temperate climate lamb has an adequate covering of fat which, when cooked by fierce direct heat as in roasting, stops the meat from drying out. And if it has been reared outside and fed on good things such as pasture with wild herbs, heather or salt marshes, the meat will have a fine, fragrant flavour. (Milk-fed lamb, that is lamb not yet weaned, is not readily available in Britain, but it is a great delicacy in Italy and Spain.)

The other reason I like lamb is that it is a relatively small beast and produces joints of a size that two people can manage quite easily rather than something that will feed a whole Victorian Sunday-lunch tableful of people.

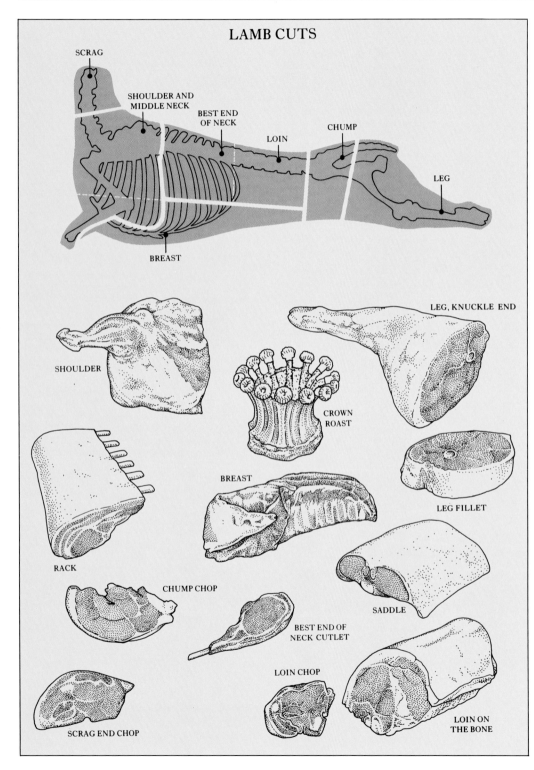

LAMB CUTS

SCRAG

SHOULDER AND MIDDLE NECK

BEST END OF NECK

LOIN

CHUMP

LEG

BREAST

SHOULDER

CROWN ROAST

LEG, KNUCKLE END

RACK

BREAST

LEG FILLET

CHUMP CHOP

BEST END OF NECK CUTLET

SADDLE

SCRAG END CHOP

LOIN CHOP

LOIN ON THE BONE

As a young meat, lamb is tender and should have a fine grain when you see a cut across the muscle. The younger the animal the paler pink the meat will be, although its feeding also has a bearing on the colour: some hill breeds have quite dark meat even when young. The fat is white, firm and brittle, yet waxy.

METHODS OF COOKING

Roasting The British taste for lamb is to prefer it well done, although that is changing. To well roast a leg or loin of lamb in the oven, it needs about 25 minutes per 1lb (500g) at Gas mark 4, 350°F, 180°C plus 25 minutes extra. To roast it so that the meat is still pink inside, you need to cook it at the same temperature for only 15 minutes per 1lb (500g) and then rest it in a warm place for 25 minutes more, which relaxes the meat fibres and distributes the pink juices throughout the meat. If I am roasting a small best end of neck of lamb for two people I roast it at Gas mark 6, 400°F, 200°C for 20–25 minutes, then let it rest for 10–15 minutes more.

On the subject of roasting, let us consider the question of roasting on or off the bone. A boneless joint is undoubtedly easier to carve, but there are those who maintain that a joint roasted on the bone has a better flavour and texture. Let me pass on a trick which chefs use. If you decide to serve a saddle of lamb, before you cook it cut away the meat from the bone for easy carving, but then tie it back on to the bone in its original position so that the joint will retain maximum flavour during basting. For carving, simply untie the string.

Because lamb can be a fatty meat, I prefer it to be well-trimmed before roasting. If you are buying a special joint such as a crown roast or a

Lamb and Mutton

1	LAMB'S HEART	9	LEG OF LAMB
2	LAMB'S KIDNEY ENCASED IN FAT	10	BEST END OF NECK OF LAMB CUTLET
3	LAMB'S KIDNEYS	11	LOIN CHOPS
4	LAMB'S LIVER	12	MIDDLE NECK OF LAMB CUTLETS
5	LEG OF MUTTON		
6	MUTTON CHOP	13	CHUMP CHOP
7	SCRAG END OF NECK OF LAMB	14	BEST END OF NECK OF LAMB
8	BREAST OF LAMB	15	SHOULDER OF LAMB

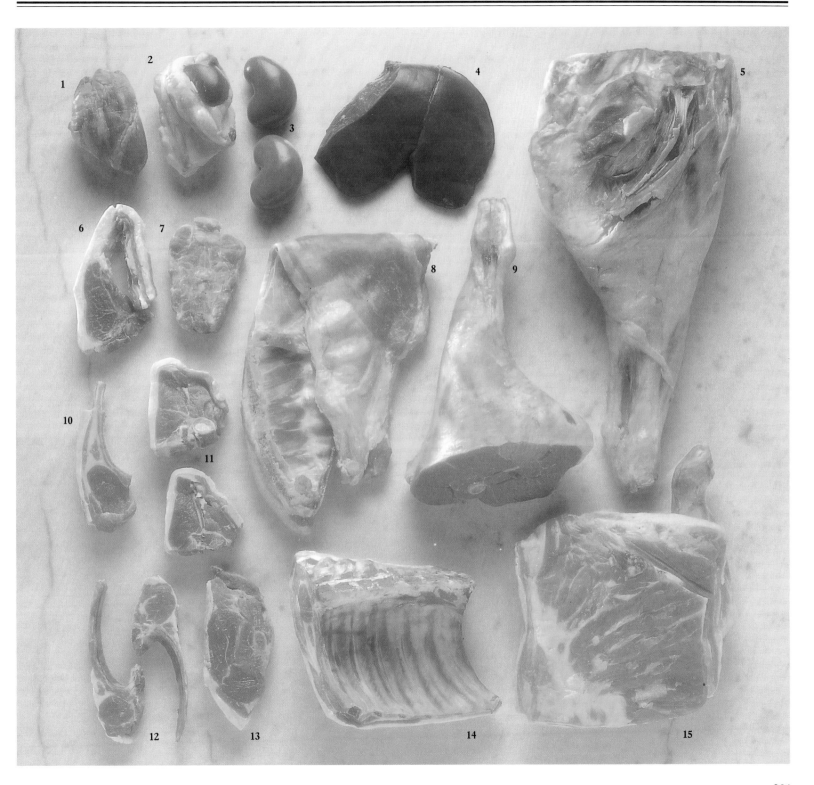

guard of honour ready prepared, you may need to dismantle it at home and trim off more of the fat, then reshape it before roasting.

If you spit-roast or barbecue lamb the fat just runs off and is not a problem. This is the very best method of all for cooking a juicy, tender shoulder or leg of lamb. I have eaten it like this on several occasions and it cannot be bettered.

Braising and **pot-roasting** Lamb joints are on the whole so tender that they do not require this slow moist method of cooking to tenderize them, and indeed, with the amount of fat they contain, it is not a particularly good idea to braise them. However, some of the extremities such as the shanks are tougher and leaner, as you would expect, and can be made into extremely tasty and inexpensive dishes using these methods.

Stewing and **casseroling** The scrag and middle neck are often cut across the bone, or the shoulder is boned and sold as casseroling lamb. Well-trimmed of fat it makes a good stew with the addition of herbs and vegetables. The leaner best end chops are the foundation of some famous traditional British stews such as the Lancashire hotpot and Irish stew.

Lamb is a curious meat. On the one hand many lamb dishes are simple and rustic, tending to come directly from areas where sheep are raised and the recipes are not in any way dressed up or sophisticated. One of my very favourite lamb dishes in this style is a Basque leg of lamb, well-cooked rather than pink, for which the leg is boned and the bone is replaced with a length of pork fillet. The whole is seasoned, tied and roasted. When sliced you get a large tender piece of lamb encircling a small slice of pork fillet. I highly recommend this dish for those who like their lamb well done. On the other hand lamb has also found its way into the kitchens of top chefs. A loin or fillet of lamb, for example, will divide into the neat round pieces so well suited to *nouvelle cuisine*, with its small portions of meat sitting in pools of reduced, glazed sauce, garnished with a sprig of this and a curl of that and accompanied by a few green beans or tiny carrots tied in a bundle with long green chives.

You will find recipes for lamb in every kind of cookery book, from the masterworks of the European chefs through books on regional French and Spanish cooking, Greek cooking, the rich and spicy cooking of the Indian sub-

continent and, perhaps most abundantly of all, in the cookery books of the Middle East where lamb is the main meat consumed. There tender cubes of lamb are charcoal-grilled as kebabs, similar to the Russian Caucasian dish of *shash-lik*. Whole lambs are roasted with spices, nuts and fruit and served with light, dry rice. Lean raw lamb is minced and mixed with cracked wheat in a flavoursome and savoury dish called *kibbeh*.

Apart from Lancashire hotpot and Irish stew, not too far from home we can also enjoy some of the delicious French recipes for lamb such as the *navarin d'agneau* which is a light lamb stew with spring vegetables. Brittany, home of the famous salt-marsh or *pré-salé* lamb, is a source of excellent recipes. There, lamb is cooked in a casserole with small turnips (*navets*) and another Breton speciality, little raisin dumplings called *kun pods* which are added 20 minutes before the end of cooking.

ACCOMPANIMENTS

Garlic, French mustard, tarragon, rosemary, tomatoes, olive oil, olives, aubergines; as I think of appropriate accompaniments for lamb, the ones that come immediately to mind are the strong, clear flavours of the Mediterranean. I think of a leg of lamb stuck with garlic cloves and sprigs of rosemary and served with baked aubergines or ratatouille. But lamb also goes well with sweet, tender young vegetables: new potatoes, baby carrots and kohl rabi, peas and beans. Then I'm reminded also of fragrant lamb *tagine* from North Africa, flavoured with cinnamon, coriander and cumin, combined with almonds and dried apricots and served with couscous; or the spicy Middle Eastern, Indian and Persian lamb dishes served with saffron-flavoured rice. In Britain we share a fondness for the lamb and mint combination with the Middle East. I wonder if Crusader knights brought back this idea in the Middle Ages. I enjoy the flavour of mint, but I am not keen on mixing it with sugar and vinegar, which I find overpowers everything else in the meal, particularly the kind of wine that goes with a fine roast leg of lamb. I tuck a few sprigs around the joint while it is roasting for a more subtle effect.

Although lamb is not much featured in Oriental cookery, Oriental spices are marvellous

used with it. I have marinated a leg of lamb in soy sauce, rice wine and rice wine vinegar, fresh ginger, a little honey and some star anise, and then brushed it with the same marinade as it was roasting.

ENGLISH CUTS

Best end of neck (sometimes called rack of lamb). This is the rib joint between the middle neck and loin and is one of the most economical and most versatile pieces of lamb. Its chops or cutlets, when trimmed of much of their fat, are the cuts to use for Irish stew and Lancashire hotpot, as well as for a tasty quick grill. These are thinner chops than those from the loin or from the chump.

A best end of neck has six or seven small chops on it, which makes it a perfect joint to roast for two people. A trimmed best end of neck is often called rack of lamb. With two best ends and plenty of time you can produce one of two rather spectacular roasts. A crown roast is formed by joining two trimmed best ends together, ribs to the top and fatty side in. The cavity in the centre is usually filled with a stuffing and when roasted and ready to serve, paper frills are slipped on the trimmed cutlet bones. A guard of honour is made by joining together two trimmed best ends so that they face each other, fat side out, ribs to the top and interlocking like hands at prayer.

Noisettes can also be made by boning best end chops and tying them into neat rounds.

Breast This is an inexpensive cut of meat from the belly of the animal. It is quite fatty and is best boned and well trimmed before stuffing it, rolling it and tying it. Roasting is one way of cooking it – there is certainly enough fat on and in the meat to baste it. If well-trimmed of fat it can be braised.

Leg (called by its French name *gigot* in Scotland). This is one of the prime roasting joints, and one of the largest, weighing 4–6lb (1·8–2·7kg). Often it is divided into two, the knuckle or shank end and the leg fillet, which is the top end of the leg next to the chump. Occasionally the top end is sliced across into leg chops which grill beautifully to produce a tender, juicy piece of meat quickly cooked and needing little adornment except perhaps a garlicky green salad. The leg lends itself to more traditional treatments and can be roasted on the bone or boned and stuffed.

Loin The large saddle area of the carcase between the leg and rib yields the tenderest and most expensive joints and cuts, the largest of which is the truly magnificent saddle of lamb. Weighing up to 8lb (3·6kg) this really is a special-occasion joint. Whereas each carcase is usually divided into two sides and then cut into joints, the saddle is taken from right across the carcase and includes both loins, the kidneys and the tail, which are tied and skewered to the joint in a decorative fashion ready for roasting. With a good covering of fat the saddle will need little attention in the oven, and is best cooked quite plainly.

Each loin divides into the chump end near the tail, and the loin at the rib end. These joints can be roasted, on or off the bone, or stuffed, rolled and roasted. Quite often it is these cuts which are divided up to provide chump chops and loin chops for grilling or frying.

To make noisettes, the eye of the loin is completely boned out and the resulting fillet is tied around, usually with a layer of fat, to be fried or grilled. This is an expensive cut of meat since there is much wasted bone. If you prepare noisettes at home, either from loin chops or the loin, you do at least have the bones from which to make a stock for sauce.

Middle neck and **scrag end** This is the bony end of the forequarter nearest to the head, sometimes sold as one piece, sometimes chopped up and sold separately. With quite a lot of fat, and a considerable amount of bone, these are cheap cuts which make exceedingly tasty casseroles when cooked on a gentle heat. They will take plenty of spices – I sometimes use them for lamb paprika or lamb *tagine* (a Moroccan stew), and they can be used for excellent curries. Occasionally the neck fillet is boned out and sold separately, at a higher price. This is a nice lean piece of meat suitable for grilling or frying and is the perfect size to cut up for kebabs. Middle neck cutlets are sometimes cut and these too are best used in stews and casseroles. They can replace best end cutlets in hotpot and Irish stew, for example.

The rib is the whole forequarter section, including the scrag end, middle neck and best end, but it is rarely sold whole as the three cuts within the rib are so different and not suited to the same cooking methods.

Shoulder This is a good, large roasting joint from the forequarter, weighing about 4lb (1·8kg). It has an excellent sweet flavour and because it is fattier than the leg it is ideally suited to being barbecued or spit-roasted. It is an awkward shape as it contains the blade bone and the shank. Boned shoulder can be turned into rosettes. The opened-out shoulder is stuffed – about 4oz (125g) stuffing per 1lb (500g) meat – then folded over and tied across three times, star-fashion, to give it a round, rosette-like appearance. I use an olive, walnut and lemon zest mixture with some soft breadcrumbs and a little chopped ham. It makes a very good, inexpensive roast. Shoulder is also sold boned for kebabs or casseroles, and well-trimmed boned shoulder can be minced.

AMERICAN CUTS

Apart from slices from the neck, brisket pieces, shanks, ribs and breast, most American cuts can be roasted, although some of the larger ones, such as the boneless rolled breast and boneless rolled shoulder, can be braised.

Ground lamb is meat taken from the neck, breast, shanks and flank and minced for patties and 'lamburgers'.

Roasting, grilling and **frying** joints are as follows: sirloin half of leg roast, leg roast, sirloin on or sirloin off, American leg roast, centre leg roast, combination leg, rolled leg roast, French leg roast, leg chop, shank half of leg and hind shank, all from the leg; saddle or loin roast, rolled double loin roast, sirloin roast, rolled double sirloin roast, English chops, loin chops and sirloin chops from the loin; rib roast, crown roast and rib chops; square cut shoulder roast, rolled shoulder roast, cushion shoulder roast, mock duck, Saratoga chops, blade chops and arm chops from the shoulder; and breast, rolled breast, breast with pocket and stuffed breast.

Stewing lamb is generally taken from the forequarter cuts, neck and shoulder.

FRENCH CUTS

Baron d'agneau is the whole leg of lamb, suitable for roasting.

Carré The rack or best end of neck is one of the most popular smaller roasting joints. The *côtes premières* or *côtelettes premières* are the four cutlets from the best end of neck nearest the loin. The *côtes secondes* or *côtelettes secondes* are the four cutlets from the best end of neck furthest from the loin. The *haut de côtelettes* is taken from the part between the best end and the breast. The *côtes découvertes* are cutlets taken from between the *carré* and the *collet* or neck. The cutlets can all be grilled, or they can be braised in a *râgout*.

Collet or **collier** This is the scrag end of neck and is used for casseroles and stews.

Épaule The shoulder of lamb is a popular French roasting joint, sometimes sold on the bone, sometimes boned, rolled and tied in a half shoulder, *épaule d'agneau roulée*, or a whole shoulder, *épaule roulée*, or boned, stuffed and tied in a ball or melon shape as in *épaule roulée en ballon*.

Filet This is the loin of lamb, sold whole for roasting or as loin chops, *côte de filet* or *côtelettes dans le filet*.

Gigot is the top end of the leg, suitable for roasting.

Gigot d'agneau is the shank end of the leg, suitable for roasting. A French recipe I like very much is *gigot d'agneau à l'anglaise* where the leg is wrapped in muslin and lowered into a large pan of boiling water. It is simmered for 15 minutes per 1lb (500g) and served rare, as if it was roasted, with spring vegetables. The caper sauce served with it indicates this recipe does indeed come from the traditional English boiled leg of mutton.

Poitrine The breast of lamb is used boned and rolled as in the English cut and is also used to make *épigrammes*. The breast is cooked in stock, allowed to go cold, boned and cut into small pieces, breaded and baked in a hot oven or grilled. This is a delicious and inexpensive dish.

Selle d'agneau With the *gigot*, this is the other prime roasting joint. It is the saddle taken from the two sides of the carcase.

LAMB'S OFFAL

Brains Smaller than calf's brains, weighing about 4oz (125g) each, lamb's brains are delicate but some people maintain that they are not as good as calf's brains. They need to be soaked in cold water first to disgorge any blood, then blanched in lightly salted boiling water before being cooked. One set (that is, two brains) is sufficient for one serving.

Heart Lamb's heart is a small, inexpensive item and makes a very good homely casserole. You will need one heart per serving. This should be trimmed of excess fat and tubes and then stuffed and braised, or sliced and casseroled. The meat is full-flavoured, dense and fibrous, producing a rich meaty gravy. Cook hearts with plenty of spices or herbs and other ingredients such as nuts and dried fruits.

Kidney Two or three kidneys quickly fried or grilled make an excellent meal. Take care not to cook this tender meat too much as it becomes tough. Devilled kidneys, spiced with mustard and pepper, remains a favourite dish today, more often served at lunch or dinner rather than at breakfast which is when the Victorians used to eat them.

If the kidneys are still enclosed in their crisp, firm white fat (or suet) they can be roasted in this. Otherwise remove the fat, the thin transparent membrane and, when you slice the kidneys in half, strip out as much of the gristly core as possible before cooking.

Lamb's fry Looking rather like white kidneys these are lamb's testicles. Fry or grill them and serve as you would kidneys. They are delicious.

Liver Although not as tender and delicate as calf's liver, lamb's liver is not as expensive either. When gently cooked by grilling, frying or braising, it is tender and full of flavour.

Paunch and **pluck** Of interest mainly to those who make their own haggis, the paunch is the lamb's or sheep's stomach which is used as a casing, and the pluck is the heart, liver and lungs (or 'lights') which are chopped up and mixed with oatmeal and spices for the filling.

Sweetbreads Fresh lamb's sweetbreads are small, pale pink and delicate in flavour and texture. After soaking and blanching they can be turned into all manner of dishes, particularly creamy *râgouts* and *fricassées* with mushrooms, lemon and herbs, also terrines.

Tongue Available fresh or salted, tongues need soaking before cooking, then skinning and pressing, or serving when freshly cooked. A lamb's tongue weighs 3–4oz (75–125g).

MUTTON

If you have cookery books of at least 20 years ago, you will find them packed with delicious-sounding mutton recipes – mutton chops baked with layers of potato and garlic; Hungarian sweet pepper stew, using mutton cooked with bacon, potatoes, paprika and caraway seeds; mutton stewed with ginger, soy sauce, sherry and orange peel; braised haunch of mutton; *haricot de mouton* cooked with beans and plenty of herbs and spices. All marvellous homely dishes for serving to a hungry crowd, but mutton is scarcely part of modern cookery at all.

Mutton is now rare because sheep are slaughtered much younger. Mutton comes from the larger carcase of a mature animal. The meat is darker and the fat yellower than that of a lamb. The joints, though larger, will look the same shape. You will find legs and loins of mutton as well as mutton chops.

It is a meat well worth trying, with lots of flavour and a good texture. Trim it of as much fat as possible. Marinate it in wine or cider with herbs and spices and then cook it gently, by braising or pot-roasting. Then serve it with other robustly flavoured food, perhaps roast potatoes. If it is Welsh mutton, what better than a dish of laver, the dark rich seaweed? If it is mutton from the salt marshes, then samphire would go very well with it. Try a thick, white onion purée and a bitter orange (Seville orange) marinade which you then make into the gravy.

Better still, revive some of the delicious old mutton recipes. I once wrapped a boned leg of mutton in pastry, having partially roasted the meat first. I then baked it to a crisp golden brown and served it with a spicy fruit jelly and sliced potatoes baked with cream and garlic. Try a mutton pudding using the suet from the kidneys to make a light suet crust and then fill it with mutton, herbs and onions. In hilly sheep-rearing districts it was traditional to flavour the pudding with wild thyme flowers in the summer and late redcurrants in the autumn. Quite a different recipe was very popular with Victorian ladies. Minced mutton was gently cooked in a white stew with lettuces, spring onions, green peas, cucumber and button mushrooms and served with a generous platter of plain steamed or boiled rice.

Kid is a favourite dish to order when we go to Lisbon. There is a restaurant across the Tagus, near the huge shipyards of Lisnave, called *O Cabrito*, which specializes in succulent casseroles of kid and pieces of roast kid. It is a popular venue if one takes a trip out of the city on a Sunday. Kid is also very popular in Spain, Italy, Malta and other parts of southern Europe, particularly the mountain regions where goats are reared.

Kid is usually a young male of from six weeks to four months old. The female kids are generally kept for their milk. Kid is at its best between mid-March and May and can be a real delicacy. The meat is pale and tender and sweet, though thought by some to be insipid, so it lends itself well to strong seasoning. To prevent the meat drying out if you are roasting it, it is often best to marinate it in oil, vinegar, herbs and pepper before cooking. Slipping slices of onion or herbs, such as rosemary, into slits in the meat, is another good way of flavouring the joint, though remember that it will need a lot of basting while it is roasting, in order to keep it succulent. Most recipes for lamb and veal can be used for kid. It is a meat which also freezes well.

In addition to roasting this tender delicious meat, use it to make excellent white stews, enriched with cream and flavoured with an onion stuck with cloves and mace like the French veal dish, *blanquette de veau*.

Goat is a tougher, firmer, darker meat as it is more mature, although most of the goat I have bought here has come from quite young animals, judging from the size of the bones, and it is a pleasant pinkish red, and what fat there is on this lean meat is white. Meat from older animals needs careful preparation before cooking, using similar methods to those that would be used for mutton or venison. It lends itself well to strong seasonings such as cumin, cloves, cardamom, chillies, ginger and garlic. The flavour and smell of the meat when cooked is considerably less strong than that of lamb. However it is very hard to come by, which I think is a great pity as it is a versatile meat and well worth trying.

METHODS OF COOKING

Roasting Shoulder, leg or loin of kid or young goat can be roasted or treated as you would spring lamb. Barbecuing or spit-roasting would be excellent as well, but for all methods baste the meat frequently.

Braising In order to keep kid and goat moist you might prefer to braise it. I have cooked pieces of kid in an unglazed chicken brick with stock, almonds and dried apricots and then served it on a bed of saffron rice.

Casseroling *Chan fana* is a marvellous Portuguese dish from the Coimbra area for which lamb, kid or young goat can be used. The meat is marinated for 24 hours in red wine with bay leaves, cloves, garlic, onions and paprika; then put into a hot oven which is then turned down for slow cooking.

One of my most successful goat casseroles was cooked with sumac, black cumin, fenugreek leaves and white wine in a fine disregard for culinary boundaries.

I have also cooked goat with fruit, nuts and spices in the style of a Moroccan *tagine* which I then served with couscous. In fact, it is a mistake to think of goat as an inferior meat needing lots of spices to disguise its supposed strong flavour. I find it very tasty and wholesome, and it has a permanent place in my repertoire.

Since most recipes for lamb are also suitable for kid and goat, it follows that the accompaniments will be similar. Try redcurrant jelly with one of the roasting joints or serve one of the sharper fruit chutneys. Rowanberry jelly would be excellent with a simple roast or pot roast, with which I would also serve a creamy, garlicky gratin of potatoes and some parsnips or celeriac roasted around the meat.

CUTS

Kid is generally cut in the same way as lamb – so the joints available are comparable.

Best end of neck of goat This cut comes from the rib joint between the middle neck and loin and, if basted, can be successfully roasted. The boneless cutlet which can be cut from the bone is usually rolled and tied into a medallion and then grilled or pan-fried.

Chump chop of goat This comes from the end of the loin near the tail and is best suited for gentle pan-frying or braising.

Forequarter or **shoulder of kid** Although this joint can be roasted it might be safer to braise it, since it could be tough, and the stock will help to prevent the meat becoming dry and unpalatable. The joint can be boned, if wished, and the meat then minced or sliced.

Leg A leg of goat is best casseroled or braised to produce the tenderest result since the meat is lean and will dry out if roasted over a fierce heat. Hindquarter or leg of kid, can be roasted whole or it can be boned and the meat then cubed and braised since it will be quite tender. The cubes of meat can be used for kebabs. If the meat is minced it can be used for an authentic moussaka.

Loin The saddle area of the carcase between the leg and rib produces some of the tenderest meat. Both goat and kid loin can be roasted if the joints are pre-larded or well-basted to keep the meat succulent. Loin chops can be grilled or pan-fried with careful attention so that they do not dry out. It is best to marinate them first, or cook them with a small amount of liquid.

Offal The flavour is similar to lamb's offal and can be used in the same way.

Kid and Goat

1 BEST END OF NECK OF GOAT
2 GOAT CUTLET
3 LEG OF GOAT
4 SADDLE OF KID
5 LOIN CUTLET OF GOAT
6 GOAT CHUMP CHOP
7 FOREQUARTER OF KID
8 LEG OF KID

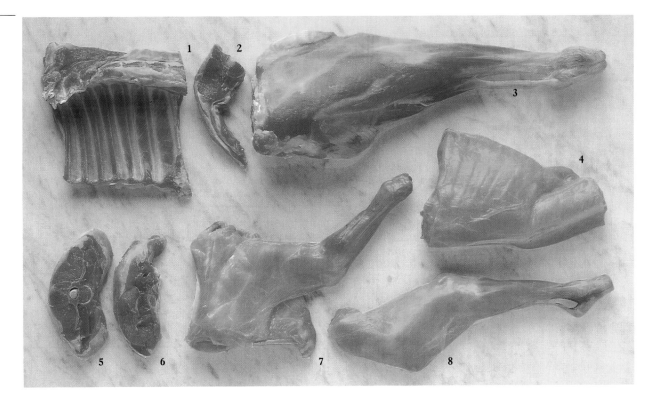

POULTRY

The word poultry describes all domesticated birds raised for the table: chicken, duck, geese, guinea fowl, squab, quail and turkey. Originally some of these birds, like turkey and quail, were wild birds. As man came to realize their value as a source of food, he first hunted them almost to extinction, but then had the good sense to tame a few and raise them in the barnyard which was, I suppose, the very beginning of the huge present-day poultry industry.

Much poultry is now reared according to very intensive methods. A cookery book published 18 years ago described broilers reaching a weight of 3–4lb (1·4–1·8kg) at the age of six to twelve months. They now reach that weight at six to seven *weeks*. Some farmers prefer to rear their birds, whether chickens or turkeys, free range according to more traditional methods and they are fed less intensively and slaughtered older. More expensive of course, but many feel that it is worth paying a premium for mature, well-flavoured birds.

Intensive rearing methods have enabled producers to keep prices low, putting chicken and turkey in a price bracket that more people can afford. What used to be a once-a-year luxury is now a regular part of our diet. Geese and duck continue to be more expensive as they do not adapt nearly as readily to intensive methods of rearing.

Poultry is a most versatile food, lending itself to a huge range of recipes and cooking methods. The poultry section is often the largest chapter in a general cookery book.

NUTRITION

Poultry is an excellent source of protein, a complete protein containing all the essential amino acids. It also contains important minerals such as phosphorous and potassium and some B vitamins. Its fat content, especially without the skin, is lower and its fatty acid content less saturated than that of red meats. Thus poultry is recommended for low-cholesterol diets and for calorie-controlled diets generally. An average portion – 3½oz (100g) – of roast chicken contains 220 kilocalories and without the skin 145 kilocalories. The same amount of roast turkey without skin contains 130 kilocalories. Skinless roast duck has about 190 kilocalories and 340 kilocalories with the skin left on. Goose is slightly less rich with about 320 kilocalories per portion with the skin on.

BUYING AND STORING

Chicken, duck, guinea fowl and quail are available all year round. So, to a lesser extent, is turkey although, like goose, it is still seen rather as a seasonal bird to be enjoyed at Christmas and Easter. The more expensive free-range birds and squabs, which are only raised in limited numbers, will often need to be specially ordered.

Fresh poultry Most poultry today is sold as oven-ready – that is, plucked and drawn – either fresh or frozen. But a fresh bird may also be sold 'clean-plucked', that is plucked but with its head and legs still left on. This is also called 'New York dressed'. The bird will be drawn after weighing and pricing so remember to allow for this extra weight when estimating the size of bird you need. About one third of the bird's weight will be lost in drawing.

Poultry is a product which deteriorates relatively rapidly. When choosing a fresh bird it is a good idea to smell it. There should be no 'off' taint whatever; a fresh bird will smell perfectly agreeable. Limbs, flesh and skin should look sound and undamaged. The breast should be firm and plump and there should not be too many traces of feathers.

Unwrap the bird when you get it home, wipe it with kitchen paper all over and remove any giblets that may be stored in a plastic bag in the cavity. It is all too easy to forget them and roast the bird with them inside, plastic bag and all. The giblets should be unwrapped and stored separately in a covered container. They should be used within a day or two. These can be cooked with the bird, for example, using the chopped heart and liver in stuffing, or use them in a risotto or to make gravy. The giblets from larger birds such as geese and turkeys are even more interesting. You can, for example, stuff the neck. See *Poultry Offal*.

After wiping, place the bird in shallow container, loosely but carefully covered, in the coldest part of the refrigerator and cook within three days.

Frozen poultry Frozen oven-ready poultry is often as freely available as fresh. Most commercial poultry such as chicken and turkey is frozen by being immersed in a water chiller so remember that the weight of the bird you buy includes a certain amount of water which will drain off when it is thawed later on. Do not refreeze once it is thawed.

Check that the packaging is intact and that there are no lumps of ice between the underneath of the bird and the wrapping as this is a sign that the bird may have been partially thawed and refrozen.

It is important to thaw all poultry completely before cooking. The chart on page 214 gives guidelines on how long to allow for different sizes of bird, thawing in a cool place. Thaw the bird in its polythene bag with one end open. Remove any giblets as soon as possible during thawing. The bird is thawed properly when there are no ice crystals in the cavity and the legs and thighs are soft and flexible. Once thawed the bird should be cooked as quickly as possible.

PREPARATION AND COOKING

Chicken, turkey and duck, as well as being sold whole, are sold in pieces ready for grilling or casseroling. As you can see on page 209, jointing birds is straightforward and once you have done it a couple of times it is quite easy. As well as giving you individual pieces for cooking, you also have the bonus of a carcase to make rich, tasty stock. Boning a bird is a little more time-consuming (see page 211) but if you want to make, for example, a ballottine of duck for a special occasion, it is well worth the effort.

Oven-Ready Poultry

1 BOILING FOWL	8 CAMBRIDGE BRONZE
2 BROILER OR	TURKEY
ROASTING CHICKEN	9 WHITE-FEATHERED
3 CORN-FED CHICKEN	TURKEY
4 GUINEA FOWL	10 DUCKLING
5 GOOSE	11 BARBARY DUCK
6 QUAIL	12 GRESSINGHAM DUCK
7 POUSSIN	

Poultry lends itself to simple everyday cookery too. Fried chicken, grilled duck breasts, pot-roasted guinea fowl, spatchcocked quail all cook relatively quickly and are not difficult to prepare.

The varieties of chicken or turkey casserole must be endless; there are so many ingredients which combine with this pale, firm, well-flavoured meat, from just a few fresh herbs to the full panoply of rich ripe Mediterranean flavours such as sweet, juicy tomatoes, courgettes, garlic, peppers and pungent rosemary or thyme.

Poaching, steaming, frying, grilling, barbecuing, roasting and braising are all methods that can be used for whole chicken or turkey or individual pieces. Quail, squab and guinea fowl can also be cooked by this range of methods.

One of my favourite ways of preparing a bird that I am going to roast quite simply is to take some fresh herbs, such as chervil, tarragon, coriander and flat leaf parsley, and, easing the skin away from the flesh, lay the herbs all over the breast, and then pull the skin back over it. I then season the bird and rub it with lemon juice and marinate it overnight before roasting it. This also works as well with turkey as it does with chicken, duck and quail.

The fattier birds, goose and duck, are best cooked by dry heat – roasting or grilling – but there are exceptions. A cassoulet, for example, benefits hugely from the addition of some duck or goose pieces and that is by no means a dry cooking method.

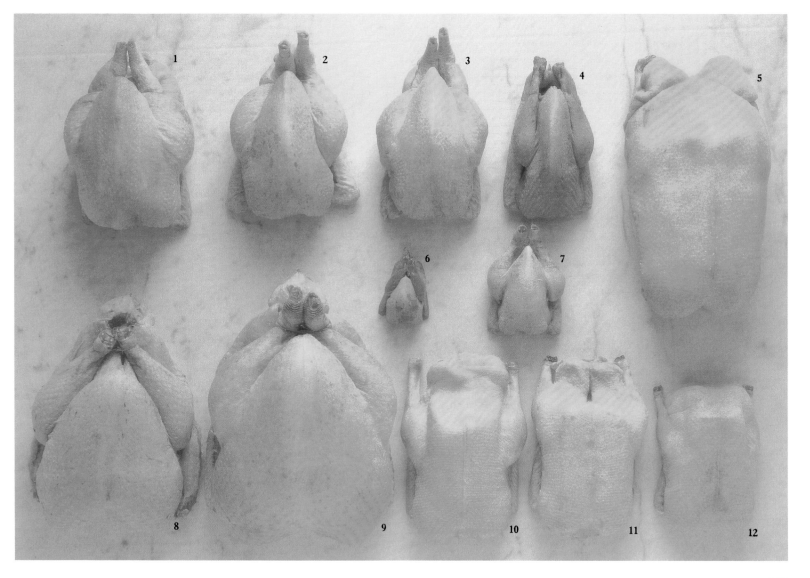

CHICKEN

My favourite monarch is Henri IV of France, who is commemorated in one of Paris's most striking statues, the Vert Galant on the Île de la Cité. What has this to do with chickens? It was the coronation wish of this benevolent ruler to secure the economy to such an extent that each of his subjects could enjoy *la poule au pot* (pot-roasted chicken) on Sunday. Today chicken is still the most popular meat for Sunday lunch, whether a roast, as it often is in Britain, part of a boiled dinner as it might be in New England, a *bollito misto* (mixed boiled meats) in Italy, or a French *poulet de Bresse à l'estragon* (chicken with tarragon). But chicken is common to all cuisines, not just European and American. Its versatility in cooking, whether used whole or jointed, and its importance as part of a low-cost, healthy diet has made it one of the most popular meats worldwide.

BUYING CHICKEN

With no shortage of ideas on what to do with a chicken, what are the different types available?
Broiler or roasting chicken From being almost literally a backyard concern, poultry-raising is now big business. Most chickens eaten in Britain today are broilers reared intensively in large buildings housing thousands of birds. They are sold when they have reached 3–4½lb (1·4–2kg) in weight, which takes six to seven weeks. These broilers are sold oven-ready, either fresh or frozen; allow at least 12oz (375g) per person. Look for a plump white breast and smooth pliable legs. Fresh oven-ready chickens are normally sold chilled, with or without the giblets or edible innards wrapped inside. Always choose one with giblets if possible as these make a good-flavoured stock to use when cooking the bird. See *Poultry Offal*.

Broilers are tender with plenty of meat on them in proportion to the carcase. The meat on the legs and thighs is darker than the pale, almost white breast meat. There will be some fat, just inside the cavity and under the skin around the sides and back. Excess cavity fat can be pulled out before cooking, but the fat on the body helps to baste the bird, particularly if you are roasting it. A good tip is to roast the bird breast side down so that the juices flow into the breast rather than away from it. You can turn the bird the right way up for the last 15 minutes or so to brown and crisp the breast.

Cooking the chicken in a chicken brick, a roasting bag, wrapped in foil or in a slow cooker will all keep it juicy as it will be protected from direct heat. As well as being roasted, whole broilers can be steamed, poached or braised on a bed of vegetables.

Chicken joints Broilers are also sold jointed into portions but, although convenient, this is a more expensive way of buying chicken. It is not difficult to joint your own chicken at home and need only take a few minutes (see page 209). Chicken portions are available in a wide variety of packs, from single breasts, drumsticks or thighs to mixed packs. Pieces of chicken are suitable for grilling, frying and barbecuing – methods that are not suitable for the whole bird because the outside would be overdone, not to say burned, before the meat in the centre has cooked. These methods are also very suitable for cooking marinated joints, thus adding a range of interesting flavours.

Double poussin This weighs about 2lb (1kg) and is a young broiler of about six weeks old. It is enough for two people. This small tender bird may lack flavour; after all, it has hardly had time to develop any. Consider marinating or stuffing it before roasting it, or roasting it with plenty of other flavours. I insert slivers of garlic and fresh ginger into the flesh, rub it all over with soy sauce and a little rice wine or vinegar and brush it with sesame oil. Leave it for a few hours to absorb the flavour and then roast, steam or pot roast it. Garlic, lemon, onion and sherry are also good flavours for a double poussin. Sometimes you may find two single poussins packaged together on one tray and sold as 'a double poussin'.

Poussin This is the smallest broiler chicken, a mere four to six weeks old, weighing between 12 and 20oz (375 and 625g). The smaller size is perfect as a single serving. Also called a spring chicken, a poussin makes a very neat attractive dish and is fun to serve and eat, but frankly it does not taste of much as the meat has had even less time than a double poussin to develop any flavour. These birds really benefit from a moist,

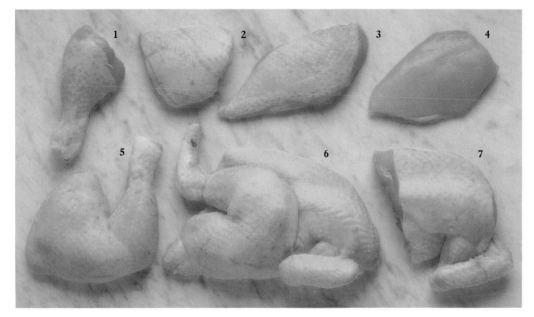

Chicken Joints

1 DRUMSTICK
2 THIGH
3 BONED BREAST WITH SKIN
4 SKINLESS BONED BREAST
5 QUARTER CHICKEN, LEG JOINT
6 HALF CHICKEN
7 QUARTER CHICKEN, WING JOINT

richly flavoured stuffing, such as a mixture of chopped giblets, onions and mushrooms cooked in a little butter and mixed with herbs and cooked rice or soft breadcrumbs.

Boiler or boiling fowl This is an elderly laying bird that has outlived its usefulness but makes a tasty dish. From the age of about five months female birds not destined for the table become layers. For 12 months they are intensive egg layers and then they are slaughtered. Tough stringy birds with a good deal of fat, boiling fowls weigh 5–7lb (2·3–3·2kg). Roasting is quite out of the question for a boiling fowl, but gentle cooking, such as slow braising or poaching, will tenderize the meat and give plenty of excellent stock for sauce or broth. The best chicken soup is made by chopping up a boiling fowl and cooking it slowly in plenty of water with herbs and vegetables. The larger, more developed bones of these birds give body to the stock.

To make a classic *poule au pot* make plenty of stock with a boiling fowl and then poach a tender younger bird in the stock with a second batch of vegetables. Broth, chicken and vegetables are served separately, with perhaps some mustard, and a dish of coarse salt to sprinkle on the chicken and vegetables.

Capon These are castrated cock birds and although you may come across them in your travels abroad, it is illegal to produce them in Britain. Large roasting chickens are sometimes called capon-style, but this is a misnomer.

Corn- or maize-fed chicken Most corn-fed chicken in Britain are very healthy looking, with yellow-tinged skin and fat. However in France, where they are very popular, a *poulet de grain* or *poulet de maïs* is not necessarily a different colour as the breed can determine the colour of the skin. A real plump corn-fed chicken is indeed a gastronomic treat, and they are usually sold fresh, though some are frozen. The birds weigh on average 3–5lb (1·4–2·3kg). A corn-fed chicken responds best to simple cooking. Roasting it with a few sprigs of tarragon inside and some of the leaves inserted under the skin produces an exquisite taste.

Free-range chicken There are two sorts of free-range chicken: those that have access to the open air with space to move around and feed at will for a minimum of 28 days and which are slaughtered at eight to ten weeks, and those that

JOINTING A CHICKEN

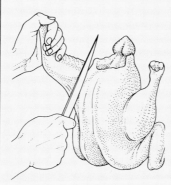 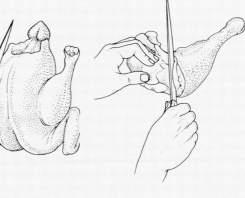 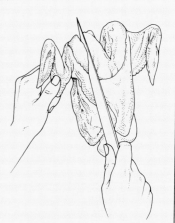

1 *Place the chicken breast side up. Remove the legs by pulling them away from the body. Use a sharp cook's knife to cut down through the skin between the thigh joint and the carcase.*

2 *Large leg joints can be divided into two pieces, thigh and drumstick, by cutting down through the joint.*

3 *Remove the wings by cutting down from the breast towards the wing joint. This ensures that each wing joint has some breast meat attached. Cut off and discard the wing tips.*

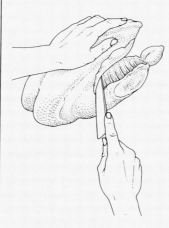 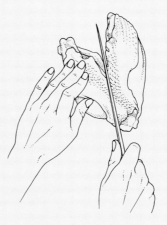 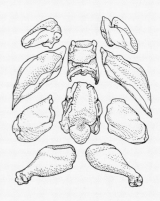

4 *Hold the top of the breast and split the carcase by cutting along the natural break in the rib cage to separate the breast from the lower carcase.*

5 *Place the breast skin side up and cut down just to one side of the ridge of the breast bone to make two pieces. The breast of a larger bird such as turkey or goose can be cut again widthways. Cut the carcase across into two pieces.*

6 *Using this method a chicken or other bird can be jointed in only a few minutes.*

are traditionally reared in the farmyard. These farmyard chickens are slaughtered at 10–12 weeks and because the birds are more mature, they are much bigger and quite a different, broader shape than the familiar oven-ready broiler. Because of the extra cost of maintaining the chickens they are, of course, more expensive. Around Easter and Christmastime large free-range chickens, weighing as much as 8lb (3·6kg) or more, are sometimes available.

Poulet de Bresse The Bressan chicken from Bresse in Burgundy is a special breed which can very occasionally be bought outside France. They are large plump-breasted birds with white plumage and blue feet, weighing between 3 and 6lb (1·4 and 2·7kg). They are used in the best traditional recipes from Burgundy, such as the unusual *poulet à l'écrevisses*, chicken with a crayfish sauce.

DUCK

Domestic ducks are descended from two species. The common duck comes from the wild mallard, native to the northern hemisphere, and the Barbary duck comes from the Muscovy duck of Central and South America. The common duck is a waterfowl, with webbed feet, oily feathers covering a layer of down, and a layer of fat under the skin to protect it from the cold. It swims and flies. It is to be found in every continent except Antarctica and in most climatic zones. The Chinese domesticated and bred the duck for food over 2000 years ago and the white Peking duck with its delicate flavour was bred especially for the emperor's table.

In Britain duck production was traditionally centred on Aylesbury, and the Aylesbury breed, a white duck bred for the table, was the best known, although there were other breeds, such as the Orpington, the White Pennine and Danish strains. Lincolnshire is now the centre of duck production and many of the strains developed there are exported all over the world, including China.

Duck or duckling? A bird becomes a duck when it reaches the second-feather stage at two months old. Commercial ducklings are killed at seven weeks old. Depending on the breed a duckling can reach 9½lb (4·3kg) live weight – the equivalent of 7lb (3·2kg) oven-ready weight –

by this stage. Despite their size these large birds are not ducks, and still have the tender meat of a duckling. Ducklings as small as 3–3½lb (1·4–1·6kg) are also available. Oven-ready birds are almost always ducklings but you can sometimes find ducks on sale. These will probably be sold in the feather or 'clean-plucked' with head and feet on and not eviscerated.

BUYING DUCK

Most duck are sold as frozen oven-ready and are available all the year round. When choosing frozen duck make sure that the package and the bird are undamaged. Ducks freeze well as their relatively high fat content ensures they retain maximum flavour and succulence when they are defrosted. Fresh oven-ready ducks are also available all the year round. The larger sizes, 6–7lb (2·7–3·2kg), tend to be on sale in any number around Easter and Christmastime but are available at other times of the year too. When buying fresh duck in the feather the bird's underbill should be soft enough to bend and the feet pliable (in old birds they are tough). Look for a plump breast with plenty of meat on. Allow at least 1lb (500g) duck per person and slightly more when buying the smaller ducklings.

Fresh and frozen duck portions are also available. These are either a quarter duckling, divided into breast or leg portions, or boneless breast fillets and supremes. Both are increasingly popular and can be used in many different ways.

Aylesbury duckling Although the name Aylesbury continues to be widely used no pure Aylesburys have been bred commercially since the 1950s. The birds called Aylesbury by today's catering trade are incorrectly labelled and are descended from a variety of strains of the common duck. Most of the common ducks on our table today are either Lincolnshire or Norfolk ducklings.

Gressingham This is the brand name of a new cross-breed of English duck which has recently come on to the market. It is not yet widely available as very few are produced but it is already very popular with chefs and restaurateurs. The birds are small, 1½–3lb (700g–1·4kg), and so are an ideal size for two people. The Gressingham is a lean bird full of flavour and texture, as it is killed slightly older than

most other ducklings. For a special occasion for four people I think it is worth getting two ducks and cooking the breasts only. Use the carcases and leftover trimmings for an excellent duck soup, and use the legs in a casserole, a *confit* or a cassoulet.

Nantais duck This is one of a few traditional breeds still found in France but only in small numbers. It is the origin of the traditional *canard* (or *caneton* more properly) *aux petits pois* (duck with green peas). Brittany is famous for its peas (most of the French crop is grown there) and Nantes is famous for its special breed of duck, a strong-flavoured bird. A Nantais duck usually weighs 4–5lb (1·8–2·3kg) and will feed four people. In France it is traditionally roasted in a hot oven (Gas mark 7, 425°F, 220°C), turning it during cooking and removing it when the breast meat is still slightly pink.

Barbary duck This is a different species of duck descended from the Muscovy and is bred in large quantities in France. It is occasionally sold oven-ready in Britain. It is slaughtered when a duck, up to three months old and well into its second-feather stage. The male ducks are nearly twice the size of the females and so there is a huge weight range from 3lb (1·4kg) to 7lb (3·2kg). A 6–7lb (2·7–3·2kg) duck makes a handsome meal for four to six people. As the bird is killed at a later stage than most other ducks the meat has a more mature flavour altogether. The Barbary duck is a far less fatty bird than the common duck and has a thin skin with no layer of fat underneath. It should be cooked more slowly and when roasting needs the addition of plenty of moist flavouring such as a good stuffing. The breast should also be basted from time to time. It is often cooked with a sauce to moisten the meat.

COOKING DUCK

The meat of a duckling is darker than chicken meat, with plenty of flavour and a good texture when carefully cooked. It is rich in protein but is often said to be a fatty meat. Such are the wonders of modern animal husbandry and breeding techniques that ducks are being bred with less fat, more lean meat and a smaller carcase. There are easy ways of dealing with the fat on the bird, and indeed, of making the most of it. I like a good layer of fat on a duckling as it provides the bird with its own basting which I then do not need to do. It also provides me with a lovely pot of soft white duck fat at the end of the day to cook potatoes in or to use in baking. Covered, this will keep well for weeks in the refrigerator. It can also be frozen.

To make sure that the fat drains away during roasting prick the skin of the bird all over with a larding needle or fork before cooking and stand the bird on a rack or trivet while it is being roasted. Every 20 minutes or so remove the duck from the oven and drain off the fat. In this way the fat will not burn, and it is less dangerous than leaving it to the end of cooking time and draining away up to a pint of boiling fat. Cool the fat before storing it for later use.

For roasting a duck allow 30 minutes per 1lb (500g) at Gas mark 4, 350°F, 180°C and raise the heat to Gas mark 6, 400°F, 200°C for the last 30 minutes to crisp the skin. While roasting is one of the most popular methods of cooking duck it is by no means the only one. The bird can be jointed and then braised or casseroled. The duck breasts can be grilled or pan-fried and served as a meal for two, or for four if from one of the larger birds. The legs can then be added to that delicious traditional Languedoc dish, cassoulet, fragrant with herbs, sausage, lamb and plenty of tender beans. Or use the legs in a casserole with green olives and a little orange peel for flavouring. A single piece of duckling can be boned and finely sliced or chopped to use in an Oriental-style stir-fried dish with ginger, garlic and mangetout peas.

There are hundreds of wonderful Chinese recipes for dealing with duck but perhaps the best is the well-known Peking duck. Here the bird is allowed to dry out thoroughly before cooking which produces extremely crisp skin when roasted at a very high temperature in a special oven. The tender meat is then served with pancakes, plum sauce and sliced spring onions.

In Scandinavia and northern Europe duckling is served with apples, with spicy braised red cabbage or with sauerkraut. In France it is often served with wild sour cherries or bitter oranges. Note how most of the classic accompaniments to duck are sharp or sour fruits or vegetables. Their bitter flavours combine perfectly with the rich, moist meat.

BONING A DUCK

1 *With the duck breast side up, cut off lower parts of wings at the second joint. Turn the duck over. Make a cut down the backbone, from the neck end. Cut away the flesh from the rib cage down one side to the leg joint.*

2 *Cut through the ligaments and carefully scrape the flesh away, working along the thigh bone and then the drumstick. Pull the bones free and remove.*

3 *Continue cutting down the rib cage until you reach the wing. Hold the wing joint and carefully scrape away the flesh. Cut through the ligaments and twist the bone free. Then scrape the flesh off down to the breast bone.*

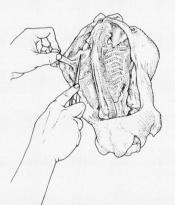

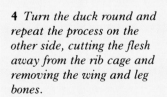

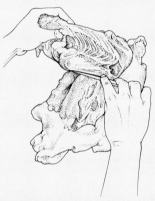

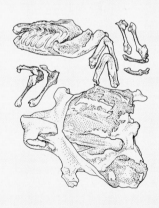

4 *Turn the duck round and repeat the process on the other side, cutting the flesh away from the rib cage and removing the wing and leg bones.*

5 *Lift up the rib cage and cut along the ridge of the breastbone to free it. Be careful not to break the skin at this stage. As duck skin is tougher than chicken this should not be too difficult.*

6 *Scrape off any remaining sinews. Turn the flesh of the legs and wings to the centre to form a neat shape. The duck is now ready to be stuffed, trussed and cooked. Other poultry can be boned in the same way.*

GOOSE

In Britain and northern Europe the goose has long been a favourite bird to grace the table on high days and holidays. Most domestic geese are descended from the greyleg goose but they have never been as domesticated as chicken and turkey and still conjure up an image of fierceness. The goose's legendary ability as a vigilant guardian once saved the Romans from a barbarian invasion and they certainly do have a way of making their presence felt with their hissing attack and noisy honking at any sign of an intruder to the farmyard.

BUYING GOOSE

Goose is still very much a seasonal bird and animal husbandry techniques have not been able to change the natural cycle. A young goose, called a gosling or green goose because its diet is mainly fresh summer grass, is hatched in the spring. It is ready for the table by late September when it is six months old and weighs between 10 and 14lb (4·5 and 6·3kg), oven-ready weight. A roast goose with sage and onion stuffing has long been an English tradition on Michaelmas Day (29 September) and is said to ensure a prosperous year ahead. By December the goose is that much more mature and larger, weighing up to 18lb (8·1kg). This sounds huge, but because the goose has such a broad rib cage, there is less meat on it, pound for pound, than on a chicken or turkey. Before turkey became popular roast goose was the traditional bird to serve on Christmas Day and still is in many parts of Europe.

Fresh goose is mainly available from September to December and an adult bird is not sold for the table after eight months, although geese can live as long as 40 years. If choosing a fresh young goose still in feather or 'clean-plucked', look for a plump breast and downy feathers around the legs. The bird should have soft, flexible legs and webs, a supple windpipe and a soft, pliable underbill. As the goose matures its various extremities will harden.

Frozen oven-ready goose is increasingly available all the year round. Check that the packaging and the bird is undamaged and buy in plenty of time for the bird to thaw out before cooking. See *Handling Poultry*.

Allow about 1lb (500g) per person and slightly more when buying a smaller goose. There is little or no waste as the carcase can be used to make a delicious stock, and rendered goose fat keeps well, covered in the refrigerator. This fat has many wonderful uses, including baking and roasting potatoes (see COOKING FATS, page 238).

COOKING GOOSE

Roast goose served with a sage and onion stuffing is the traditional way of eating goose in Britain. A more exotic stuffing I learned from a friend is a mixture of breadcrumbs, chopped rum-soaked apple, chopped prunes, parsley, lemon, salt and pepper. As with duck it is best to roast goose lying on a rack and drain off the fat periodically. Roast in a hot oven, Gas mark 7, 425°F, 220°C for 30 minutes and then turn the heat down to Gas mark 4, 350°F, 180°C and cook for a further 3½ hours.

Cold roast goose is excellent in salads with potatoes, fennel and walnuts dressed in walnut oil, for example, or shredded and mixed with rendered goose fat as *rillettes*, a traditional potted meat from the Touraine and Sarthe regions of France.

Goose is not normally casseroled, braised or in any other way cooked covered or in a container, since it is difficult to drain off the fat. The legs are, however, often added to a slow-cooking cassoulet, where the fat is absorbed by, and enriches, the dried haricot beans. In Germany goose is often served with sauerkraut, in Denmark with red cabbage, in Italy with chestnuts and in France (Normandy) with apples and Calvados.

GUINEA FOWL

Originally a game bird, native to the Guinea coast of West Africa, the guinea fowl has been domesticated in Britain and Europe for the last 500 years. A smallish bird no bigger than about 4lb (1·8kg) and usually weighing about 2½lb (1·1kg), the guinea fowl's flesh and flavour has some similarities to that of chicken and pheasant; tender like chicken, but slightly darker in colour and with a hint of game. The smaller guinea fowl serve two people and the larger birds three or four. Guinea fowl are now usually sold ready for the table and can be recognized by their dark scaly legs, yellowish fat and skin and darkish breast meat.

COOKING GUINEA FOWL

With a tendency to dryness, the guinea fowl needs careful cooking. If you wish to roast it, either bard it by tying a strip of pork fat over the breast, or lay buttered muslin on the breast. You can also lard the breast with tiny slivers of pork fat. If you like bacon-flavoured roast guinea fowl, lay strips of bacon over the breast. Baste it frequently during cooking. It is best roasted at a moderate temperature (Gas mark 4, 350°F, 180°C) for about 35–45 minutes per 1lb (500g).

Guinea fowl can be stuffed, either with a traditional breadcrumb and herb stuffing or with a more exotic fruit stuffing. In the autumn I have cooked guinea fowl stuffed with grated quinces and moistened with cider. Casseroled guinea fowl using the same ingredients is also very successful, and apples and Calvados can stand in for quinces and cider.

QUAIL

Originally a game bird with native species found in many parts of the world, the wild common quail is now a protected species in Britain. The Japanese quail is the species bred for the table in Britain and Europe and it is available throughout the year. Quails weigh between 4 and 5oz (125 and 150g) each. They are usually sold oven-ready, fresh or frozen and need nothing doing to them before cooking. Although very small, a quail has a surprising amount of meat on it, and one bird can be sufficient for a single serving with other accompaniments, and especially if you stuff it beforehand.

COOKING QUAIL

It is a delicately flavoured bird, juicy and tender when not allowed to dry out during cooking. Although it can be roasted or grilled, it lends itself best to pot-roasting, braising or casseroling. Because it cooks in 25 minutes or so, it is a marvellous standby for an impromptu dinner party. The quail is also amazingly good-tempered when it comes to accompaniments. Sometimes I treat it in a very rustic fashion and after frying it all over, I casserole it in a heavy iron pot with new potatoes, baby globe artichokes, a little tarragon and some white wine. This is a great springtime treat. For those who have their own vine leaves, quails can be wrapped in Cognac-soaked vine leaves and pork or bacon fat, stuffed with a mixture of breadcrumbs, bacon and their own livers, roasted and then served with a few peeled grapes.

If you are cooking quails for a dinner party, it is worth cooking a few extra as they are delicious cold. For grand picnics there is nothing finer.

SQUAB

Weighing about 12oz (375g), the squab is a young pigeon which has not yet fed on whole grain or been allowed to fly. Long a favourite in France and the United States and indeed in former times in England when country properties had their own dovecotes and pigeon lofts, squabs are now being bred for the table in Britain. They are usually available only in late spring when the birds are about four weeks old. They are considerably more expensive than the wild or wood pigeon but because they are young birds their flesh is very tender. It is a light cherry red colour with a surprising amount of flavour. The birds should look plump, rounded and firm.

COOKING SQUAB

Different cooking methods can be used, such as roasting, braising or grilling (after splitting down the back and flattening them out). There are recipes for squab casseroles, but since one bird is such a perfect individual portion I think it is best cooked and served whole. One of the most memorable lunches I have eaten, in one of the famous châteaux in Bordeaux, included a boned stuffed squab, roasted slowly until crisp on the outside and meltingly tender inside, served with *petits pois*, morel mushrooms and a delicate clear gravy made from the cooking juices. An excellent stuffing can be made from breadcrumbs, herbs, ham, a few walnuts or pine nuts and some chopped prunes or apricots.

Squabs should be roasted at a low temperature, Gas mark 3, 325°F, 160°C, for about an hour or so for a stuffed bird. If grilling squab, make sure that it is about 8in (20cm) from the heat source. Squabs should be well cooked and

not served rare or pink. Roasted squab are delicious cold and make very fine, if rather expensive, picnic fare. See also GAME, page 216.

TURKEY

As far as I can tell the world divides at Christmas into two distinct camps: those who always have turkey and would not dream of having anything else and those who will go to great lengths to avoid it, with their 'alternative Christmas dinners' of wild boar, a baron of beef, roast goose, small game birds and all manner of exotica. For a number of years I was firmly in the second camp, but now after two or three very good turkeys, I hover between the two. And there are clearly plenty of other turkey-eaters around too. At Christmastime in Britain something like 10 million whole turkeys are eaten.

Apart from its versatility and ready availability all the year round the turkey is a good source of protein, with a relatively low fat content.

White-feathered turkey or Broad-breasted white This bird with its familiar white plumage is the result of modern husbandry and accounts for most of the turkeys sold today. When plucked the skin is left smooth and unblemished unlike the more traditional breeds which have a speckled skin when the dark feathers are plucked. In good condition the white-feathered turkey will have a firm, broad, round breast and a white unblemished skin with a faint blueish hue to the flesh underneath. The thighs and drumsticks will be meaty. The fresh bird should have a short neck, bright eyes, and parts such as the comb will be red and fresh-looking. The hen bird is said to be the better buy since it is somewhat plumper and has lighter bones than the male.

Bronze turkeys Before the white-feathered turkey became popular these were the most common turkeys and were so called because of their distinctive plumage. Both Norfolk Black and Cambridge Bronze turkeys are once again available and are well worth looking out for as their flesh is juicy and full of natural flavour. The birds are reared on a small scale, according to traditional non-intensive farming methods. This means they take longer to mature and put down a layer of fat under the skin which contributes to the flavour.

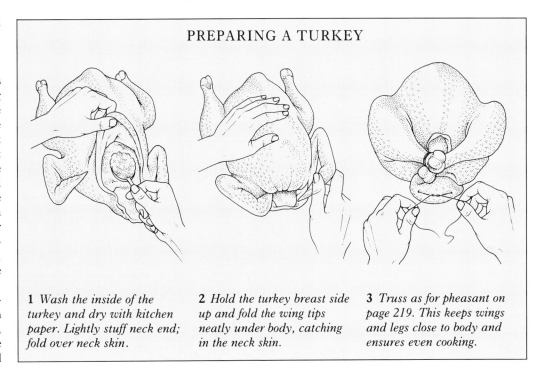

PREPARING A TURKEY

1 *Wash the inside of the turkey and dry with kitchen paper. Lightly stuff neck end; fold over neck skin.*

2 *Hold the turkey breast side up and fold the wing tips neatly under body, catching in the neck skin.*

3 *Truss as for pheasant on page 219. This keeps wings and legs close to body and ensures even cooking.*

HANDLING POULTRY

Poultry birds are not reared, slaughtered or stored in sterile conditions and thus the bacteria which are naturally present in all living organisms (including humans) are still alive when we bring the poultry home. Some bacteria are harmless, some cause food to spoil and some, like campylobacter, listeria and various strains of salmonella, are harmful and can be life threatening. At room temperature bacteria increase in numbers readily and cause food to spoil. In the refrigerator they grow more slowly so that food keeps better. They cannot grow in the freezer, although they can start to multiply again when the food is thawed. High temperatures used in cooking kill them off.

There are certain precautions that must be taken to avoid cross-contamination or the transfer of bacteria from raw poultry to other food that you might have in your kitchen or refrigerator.
1. Hands must be washed before and after handling poultry. Knives and other utensils must be washed between handling raw and cooked food.
2. Raw poultry should not be prepared on wooden chopping boards which are difficult to clean and disinfect. Use white non-porous boards which are easy to clean with hot water and a little bleach.
3. Refrigerate all poultry, loosely but carefully covered, in a shallow container as soon as possible after purchase. Check the temperature of your refrigerator – it should not exceed 42°F, 5°C.
4. Take care to avoid contact between cooked and raw foods during storage and preparation.
5. If poultry is cooked for eating later, it must be cooled as quickly as possible, then covered and refrigerated. Warm food of any kind is the ideal breeding-ground for bacteria when stored at room temperature.
6. All poultry should be thoroughly cooked through to destroy the bacteria. It is cooked when the temperature in the slowest-to-heat part of the meat (for example, the thigh of a chicken) reaches at least 160°F, 70°C. A meat thermometer gauges this accurately. Otherwise test by piercing the thigh with a skewer – the juices should run clear, not pink or red.

POULTRY SIZES AND THAWING TIMES

Type of bird	Size	Number of servings	Thawing time in hours in a cool place
CHICKEN:			
POUSSIN	12–20oz (375–625g)	1–2	6
DOUBLE POUSSIN	2lb (1kg)	2	8
BROILER	3–4lb (1·4–1·8kg)	3–4	9–12
FREE-RANGE	up to 8lb (3·6kg)	6	14–18
DUCK	3lb (1·4kg)	2	9
	5lb (2·3kg)	4	14
	6–7lb (2·7–3·2kg)	6	18
GOOSE	10lb (4·4kg)	4–6	30
	15lb (6·8kg)	6–8	36
	18lb (8·1kg)	10	48
GUINEA FOWL	2½–4lb (1·1–1·8kg)	2–4	9
QUAIL	4–5oz (125–150g)	1	6
SQUAB	12oz (375g)	1	6
TURKEY	5–8lb (2·3–3·6kg)	6–10	15–18
	8–11lb (3·6–5kg)	10–15	18–20
	11–15lb (5–6·8kg)	15–20	20–24
	15–20lb (6·8–9kg)	20–30	24–30
	20–25lb (9–11·3kg)	30–40	30–36
	25–30lb (11·3–13·5kg)	40–50	36–48

Wild turkey In the United States turkey enjoys the status of national dish, if not national treasure. The wild turkey was once found in large flocks over the American continent, and the Pilgrim Fathers learned from the North American Indians how to rear them. The wild turkey was domesticated by the Aztecs and Indians of Central and South America, and was then introduced to Europe by the Spaniards following their New World conquests. Although wild turkeys are still to be found, the domesticated turkey in the United States today is like the one known in Europe. Wild turkeys are smaller and gamier than the domesticated bird with a delicious flavour.

BUYING TURKEY
You can buy turkey in a variety of different ways but the breast should always be plump and white and the drumsticks firm and rounded.
Traditional farm-fresh These birds are reared less intensively and traditionally are hand-plucked on the farm and hung for up to 14 days depending on the flavour required. These are the only sort to be hung as under EEC regulations for large producers turkeys must be slaughtered and prepared in one process. They are sold either 'clean-plucked' or oven-ready, in which case the farm name should appear on the label.
Frozen turkey This is the cheapest way to buy turkey but remember that the weight includes extra water, which accounts for approximately 5 per cent. Lengthy, slow thawing is necessary to make the bird tender and safe to eat.
Chilled turkey Some oven-ready turkeys are also sold air-chilled, a process which involves no intake of water, unlike freezing, so that there is no weight loss later on. The giblets are usually wrapped separately inside.
Self-basting turkey The basting agent inserted underneath the skin may be a butter-based, vegetable-oil or stock solution. This keeps the bird moist during cooking and flavours the meat as well but the juices given off are often extremely salty. It is always preferable to buy a straightforward turkey and do your own basting. The most effective method of basting turkey is the buttered cloth. Take a large square of cheesecloth or muslin, dip it in melted butter and drape it over the whole turkey, breast and

drumsticks, and then roast it in the usual way.

Turkey joints and breasts Roasting is not the only method of cooking turkey. While a whole turkey is ideal for a large gathering, it can also be regarded as a collection of various cuts of meat. Portions of turkey are now widely available, or you can joint one yourself. The darker meat on the wings and drumsticks is perfect for casseroles and pies, the thighs can be boned, stuffed with an exotic filling, rolled, roasted or braised and then sliced. The light breast meat can be cooked in the same way, or it can be sliced into escalopes, marinated and grilled. The giblets and carcase make plenty of excellent stock and the liver can be cooked to make a separate dish.

Turkeys vary enormously in size, from 5–8lb (2·3–3·6kg), which will serve eight to ten people, to 25–30lb (11·3–13·5kg) which will serve 40–50 people. When judging the size of the turkey you require allow up to 12oz (375g) per person if the turkey is oven-ready. If buying a 'clean-plucked' bird, allow 1lb (500g) per person to take account of the discarded weight when the turkey is eviscerated.

COOKING TURKEY

The traditional way to cook turkey as a celebration bird at Thanksgiving and Christmas is to roast it, but cookery books are full of the most ingenious recipes for using up turkey leftovers. In Mexico, where the turkey is very popular, one of the best known dishes is turkey with a chocolate sauce, *mole poblano*. The other ingredients of *mole poblano* are various types of chilli, herbs and spices, all items native to Mexico.

Traditionally, two stuffings were used in roast turkey, one in the body cavity and one at the neck end, but it is best to stuff the neck end only as a dense stuffing inside the body may prevent the inside of the turkey from cooking properly. For the neck cavity of an average 10–12lb (4·5–5·4kg) turkey allow about 8–10oz (250–300g) stuffing. Do not put the stuffing in the neck until just before cooking. The basic bread stuffing with herbs, onion and celery can be flavoured in various ways – chopped raw oysters; chestnuts; sausagemeat; fruit and nuts such as chopped apples, prunes and walnuts or almonds; or a rice stuffing can be made by substituting raw or cooked rice, brown, white or wild, for the breadcrumbs.

While we are familiar with chicken livers and, increasingly, turkey and duck liver, other bits of the bird are well worth having, such as the neck, gizzard and heart.

Giblets The collective name for the edible innards of poultry is giblets. When buying a fresh bird always buy one with giblets and refrigerate them separately when you get home. Giblets, as with all offal, should be bought for immediate consumption and not stored for more than one to two days, well covered, in the refrigerator.

It is possible to buy chicken, turkey and, increasingly, duck livers separately, either fresh or frozen. A chicken liver weighs about 2oz (50g) and is usually dark red, and separated into two lobes joined by sinews. A duck's liver weighs about 2–3oz (50–75g) and is similar in appearance. Turkey and goose livers are somewhat larger and can weigh between 4 and 6oz (125 and 175g) depending on the size of the bird. Duck and goose livers can be specially fattened to make *foie gras*.

Chicken or other poultry livers make an excellent quick and inexpensive meal and 3½oz (100g) is an ample serving. Like all liver it is a rich source of iron as well as protein. It can be grilled, fried or stir-fried in a matter of minutes and served with rice, or used to fill a jacket potato. Fry it in olive oil, add a splash of white wine and a couple of crumbled sage leaves and you have a marvellous sauce for pasta. Serve chicken livers on a piece of toast with a fried apple ring for a quick midday snack. An unusual starter can be made by quickly frying chicken livers and then encasing them individually in puff pastry with some herbs and garlic before baking them.

Poultry livers also make excellent terrines and pâtés. A quick way is to fry them, cool them and put them in the food processor with some unsalted butter, herbs and spices. Pack the pâté into small ramekins. The classic, and more time-consuming way, is to rub the livers through a sieve, mix them with cream, port and spices and cook them slowly in a *bain-marie* until set.

The larger poultry livers can be sliced and fried and served on a bed of salad leaves, as indeed can the gizzards. A *salade de gésiers* is one of those tasty French dishes which you feel very virtuous in preparing because it costs so little. In France it is often served with sliced cooked potatoes in olive oil.

The gizzard, heart and liver can be chopped up and added to whatever stuffing you are making for the bird. To prepare them for cooking remove any sinews, fat, skin, and from the liver any traces of green from the gall bladder which will give it a bitter taste. The rough skin can be sliced away from the gizzard with a sharp knife and it should be well rinsed to remove any traces of grit or small stones that poultry pick up with their food to help their digestion.

Foie gras This method of producing, literally, fat liver is not practised in Britain. Geese and ducks are force fed on grain for the last few weeks of their lives which gives them a much enlarged liver. A goose liver prepared in this way will weigh around 1½lb (700g) before cooking. It is a pale pinky beige, in two long lobes, quite firm to the touch, but as it gets warm, even as you handle it, it begins to melt. Most people leave the cooking of *foie gras* to the experts and buy it ready cooked *en bloc* or *en terrine*.

If you cook it yourself, you need to open it out and remove all the tiny red thread-like veins and filaments. Season it, moist with a little port or cognac, pack into a terrine and gently cook in the coolest possible oven in a *bain-marie*. Otherwise you will be left with a terrine full of fat. When cold, the liver is still just pink and covered with a layer of dense yellow fat which looks like butter.

Neck In the geese-rearing parts of France, particularly the south-west, very little of the bird is wasted. A marvellous coarse rustic sausage is made from the neck. This is a very easy dish to prepare and one that can be adapted to the turkey too.

Make sure that the head is cut off leaving the neck as long as possible, and then carefully cut the neck away from the body. The skin is peeled back, the meat taken off the neck, minced and mixed with, for example, chopped giblets, minced pork, herbs, spices and some breadcrumbs and stuffed back into the skin. The sausage is tied at both ends, poached or steamed and then finished off by grilling or baking. It can be eaten hot or cold.

Feet Chicken feet and duck webs are not used in Western cooking but do feature in Chinese cooking. When cooked they are crunchy and gelatinous at the same time.

215

GAME

Traditionally this term covers every edible form of furred and feathered meat not raised on the farm. Thus our ancestors ate heron, swan, peacock, bittern and wild boar as well as the more familiar hare, rabbit, pheasant and venison. But over the centuries, many of these species, such as heron and swan, have diminished in numbers and are no longer eaten. In their place some of the birds and animals which formerly lived only in the wild, such as quail, are now reared for the table. Nowadays most game is protected by vigorous laws and can only be shot at certain times of the year. Feathered game is in season during the autumn and early winter months up until the end of January. In Britain this begins as early as 12 August with the open season on grouse. There is no close season for pigeon and rabbit. Hare has no close season but cannot be sold between March and July. The availability of venison depends on the breed of deer but it can usually be found throughout the year.

The old saying that we are what we eat is equally true of animals and birds. A partridge that has fed on corn left behind after the harvest and a young grouse that has eaten nothing but heather shoots are both going to taste very different from the creature who has been fed a carefully balanced, formulated and processed foodstuff. In addition the game bird or animal exercises, both in searching for its food and escaping from its predators, and does not get contentedly fat sitting in a farmyard being fed regular meals. All this has an effect on the flavour and the texture of the meat. The meat from true game birds and animals is lean and firm with subtle flavours. Its relative rarity means that it is often considered to be an expensive food but this is by no means true, and it is even cheaper if you can do most of the preparation yourself at home.

TELLING THE AGE OF A BIRD
In general young birds have pointed flight feathers at the tip and edge of their wings, soft, pliable feet, short rounded spurs on the legs and downy feathers on the breast and under the wings. However some young birds have rounded flight feathers, and even on older birds these look pointed if they are wet.

The most conclusive way of judging an old from a young bird is to apply the bursa test, which you can only do on birds that are in feather. The bursa is a small opening, found on all young game birds, just above the bird's vent. In mature birds the opening becomes much smaller and may close entirely. A bursa open to a depth of 1in (2·5cm) in a pheasant, and ½in (1cm) in a partridge or grouse, is a reliable indication of a young bird. Gauge this by inserting a matchstick or cocktail stick.

HANGING GAME
If game is cooked without hanging its flavour will be mild. Hanging tenderizes the meat and allows the gamy flavour to develop. How gamy you like your meat is a matter of personal preference. What the hanging process does is to allow the various enzymes and microbes naturally present in the flesh to react with it, breaking down the tissues. Clearly the final result is putrefaction, and that must not be allowed to happen. It is nevertheless difficult to set hard and fast rules for hanging.

Hanging a freshly shot pheasant for three days in mild autumn weather will be sufficient, whereas it might take ten days hanging in a cold snap in mid-winter to reach the same stage. A badly shot bird will decompose more quickly than one cleanly shot.

PREPARATION AND COOKING
After hanging fresh game must be cleaned and trussed. Feathered game is plucked and drawn and hares and rabbits are skinned and paunched (this is done to venison *before* hanging). Game meat is then often marinated to tenderize it still further. Oven-ready game can be frozen (up to nine months for game birds and six months for furred game) but it does have a slightly adverse effect on the texture as well as the taste. Once thawed it is best cooked by a slow moist method such as braising. In general young tender game is best roasted or grilled, and older tougher game is suited to slow methods such as braising. Game meat is lean and care must be taken not to let it become too dry during cooking. The weights given are for undressed game – oven-ready birds will weigh about 25 per cent less. Whether you serve game rare or well

cooked is a matter of personal preference. Generally pale game such as partridge or pheasant tends to be served well done, but many people, and I include myself, like grouse, venison, hare and wild duck served very pink. Pink or rare meat means that it has not been thoroughly cooked and harmful bacteria may still be present.

SELECTING OVEN-READY GAME
Examine the bird or joint. Is it fresh or frozen? If frozen it may show traces of watery blood in the wrapping. If there are any particularly bloody patches, this may indicate where it was shot and you will need then to look out for small lead shot which can literally break a tooth if bitten on inadvertently. Avoid any game with very misshapen limbs as this is an indication that it was badly shot.

Look at the 'best before' date. Is it beyond the date on which you want to cook it? Smell the package. It should not have any 'off' taints, nor should it in any way smell rotten or putrid. If you buy oven-ready game it will probably already have been hung but I have yet to come across a label which tells me for how long. Properly hung game will smell rich and 'ripe' but not in any way unpleasant.

Unwrap the meat once you get home. Feel over it with your fingers and if you detect any shot, ease it out gently. Remove any bits of fur or feathers and loose fat. Paying particular attention to any bloody patches, wipe it over with kitchen paper moistened with vinegar. Dry it and put the meat on a plate. Cover it loosely but completely, making sure that nothing can drip from it on to any other food. You can put the meat, whole or jointed, in a large bowl and marinate it. I have found this is also quite a good way of flushing out lead shot.

Feathered Game

1 WILD DUCK (TEAL)	7 PARTRIDGE
2 PHEASANT (COCK)	(RED-LEGGED)
3 WILD DUCK (MALE MALLARD)	8 PARTRIDGE (GREY)
	9 PHEASANT (HEN)
4 WILD DUCK (FEMALE MALLARD)	10 WILD DUCK (WIDGEON)
5 PIGEON	11 GROUSE
6 SNIPE	12 WOODCOCK

FEATHERED GAME

GROUSE

The red or Scottish grouse, the smallest of the many grouse species, feeds on the young heather shoots of the Scottish, Irish, Yorkshire and Derbyshire moors and it is this food which is said to give the red grouse its intense unique flavour. There are many who claim that grouse is the finest of all game birds and its gamy flavour is much admired, not to say coveted, by the French who, while they have many breeds of game bird, have no native grouse. I know of more than one French chef who has taken a dozen brace back with him to serve in his fine restaurant in guises far removed from the traditional roast grouse served with bread sauce, fried breadcrumbs, watercress and game chips.

It really is best to roast young grouse, which are those shot in the same year they are born. Although the season runs from 12 August, known as 'the Glorious Twelfth' by those who shoot, until 10 December, they are at their best in the first half of the season. The glossy dark-feathered young birds have soft downy breast feathers and pointed flight feathers at their wing tips. The spur at the back of the leg above the claws is soft and rounded. Grouse can be eaten within 24 hours of killing, although if necessary can be hung for a short period, on average between two and four days depending on the age of the bird and the weather. They are usually only available fresh.

A plump grouse with an undressed weight of about 1½lb (700g) will feed one person. The meat is dark red, rich and gamy in flavour yet delicate and unusual at the same time. It is much better not to hide its qualities with sauces and too many accompaniments and it should be roasted quickly and allowed to rest briefly before serving. It is traditional to serve this tender meat on the rare side but it can be roasted for longer if preferred. Grouse are dry birds and need a little assistance by way of liberal basting during roasting to keep the flesh moist.

An older grouse, one that has escaped the guns for a season or two, is no good for roasting. The meat is tougher and drier though it still has a fine flavour. There are several very good ways of dealing with an older grouse: either marinate it in red wine, then braise or casserole it, or add the diced breast meat to a mixed game pie. A salmis or game stew is another excellent method.

Other members of the large grouse family include the black grouse found in southern England and the capercaillie, a large bird weighing about 9lb (4·1kg) and found in mountainous areas of northern Europe.

PARTRIDGE

Partridge is a fine game bird and is related to the pheasant. There are many different species, including the more common English or grey partridge which has the better, more delicate flavour and the French or red-legged partridge which is slightly larger. Young birds have soft, pale yellow-brown feet and legs and pointed flight feathers. The flesh of the partridge is pale, almost like that of a chicken, and has a very delicate fine flavour that should not be spoiled by allowing the bird to become too gamy. Three or four days' hanging is sufficient.

Partridges are at their best in October, near the beginning of the season, having eaten their fill of grain left behind among the stubble in the harvested wheat fields. They are also available oven-ready, both fresh and frozen.

With an undressed weight of 14–16oz (425–500g), a bird is sufficient only for one person. Like much other game, roasting and serving with plain accompaniments such as watercress, fried potatoes and a gravy made from cooking juices is the best way of preparing young birds.

With older birds there are many excellent recipes. Use them in pâtés, pies, casseroles and soups. Among the many partridge recipes in the classic repertoire perhaps the most famous is chartreuse of partridge. The meat from two partially roasted old partridge is layered with cooked cabbage in a *chartreuse* mould (similar to a charlotte mould) decorated first with slices of turnip and carrot. It is baked, turned out and served with a sauce of reduced cooking juices.

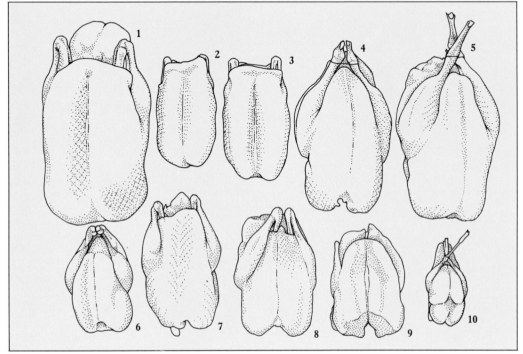

Oven-ready Game

1 WILD DUCK (MALLARD)	6 PIGEON
2 WILD DUCK (TEAL)	7 PARTRIDGE (RED-LEGGED)
3 WILD DUCK (WIDGEON)	8 WOODCOCK
4 PHEASANT (HEN)	9 GROUSE
5 PHEASANT (COCK)	10 SNIPE

PHEASANT

The cock pheasant with its beautiful brightly coloured plumage and distinctive long tail feathers is a common sight in the British countryside in winter. Although native to the Far East the pheasant was introduced to Britain hundreds of years ago. It is a very tame bird and you will often see some feeding by the roadside, at the edge of fields or in country parks.

Because pheasant are easier to rear than most other game they are more available and consequently one of the cheaper game birds. The flesh is pale and, like that of all lean birds, has a tendency to dryness. The brown hen pheasant is slightly smaller than the cock, which weighs 3-3½lb (1·4-1·6kg), with a plumper rounded breast and supposedly a finer flavour. Young birds, both cocks and hens, have soft beaks and feet and smooth legs. A young cock has rounded short spurs which become longer and more pointed later in the season. Pheasant are often sold by the brace, meaning a cock and a hen. Freshly shot birds, at their best in November and December, should hang for at least three days for a good flavour to develop and as long as three weeks if the weather is very cold. Hanging is important if the bird is to be plain roasted, otherwise it can prove dull. Pheasant are also available oven-ready, both fresh and frozen.

Hen or cock, one pheasant will make four servings, dividing neatly and obviously into two legs and two breasts. Note that I do not say that it serves four people. The meat on the legs is so different from that on the breasts that ideally it needs quite a different method of cooking. The breast is delicate and tender and the legs darker, tougher and sinewy, even on a young bird. So I buy two pheasants to feed four people. The meat left over from roast pheasant can be removed from the carcase and made into potted pheasant or chopped finely to make a rich sauce for pasta. The carcase itself will make fine game stock. Another good method is to remove the breasts, marinate them and then shallow-fry them in a little butter. Serve them with a good reduced pheasant glaze, some fruit jelly and a purée of celeriac and potatoes.

Almost any chicken recipe can be adapted to pheasant. Unless you are absolutely certain that it is a young, tender, roast-worthy bird, then it is far better to joint and casserole it following one of the many excellent chicken recipes to which, sadly, many of today's tasteless broilers do not do justice.

Pheasant legs can be casseroled, cooked in a Moroccan *tagine*, served *à la Normande* with cream, apples and Calvados, added to a mixed game pie or used to make a veal and pheasant pie. Cold roast pheasant is very good, too. Mixed with chunks of apples, some crunchy slices of celery, a few shelled wet walnuts and a creamy dressing it becomes a delicious autumn salad.

PLUCKING, DRAWING AND TRUSSING PHEASANT

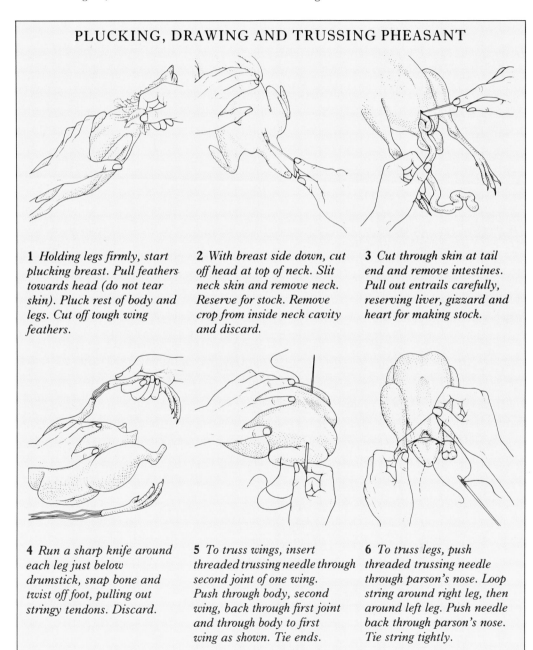

1 *Holding legs firmly, start plucking breast. Pull feathers towards head (do not tear skin). Pluck rest of body and legs. Cut off tough wing feathers.*

2 *With breast side down, cut off head at top of neck. Slit neck skin and remove neck. Reserve for stock. Remove crop from inside neck cavity and discard.*

3 *Cut through skin at tail end and remove intestines. Pull out entrails carefully, reserving liver, gizzard and heart for making stock.*

4 *Run a sharp knife around each leg just below drumstick, snap bone and twist off foot, pulling out stringy tendons. Discard.*

5 *To truss wings, insert threaded trussing needle through second joint of one wing. Push through body, second wing, back through first joint and through body to first wing as shown. Tie ends.*

6 *To truss legs, push threaded trussing needle through parson's nose. Loop string around right leg, then around left leg. Push needle back through parson's nose. Tie string tightly.*

PIGEON

Pigeons are found wild in most parts of the world and are also reared domestically in some countries. The squab is a young pigeon and is now reared commercially for the table. The wood pigeon, plentiful in cereal-growing areas, has no close season, being considered vermin by farmers and landowners, such is the damage it is said to do to crops. Because of its feeding habits, eating first unripe and then ripe corn, a wood pigeon in late summer makes for excellent eating. It is also a meaty little bird, about 1lb (500g) in weight, and relatively inexpensive. Unless it has soft supple feet without scales you can assume it is a wily old bird that has escaped the guns for a season or two.

If you have freshly shot pigeons, hang them for one day before plucking and cooking. Pigeons are easy to cook and full of gamy flavour. A pigeon has a surprising amount of meat on the breast and as it is so rich and highly flavoured, I find one bird ample for one serving. If it is a young plump bird, it can be quickly roasted and served quite rare. The flesh is dry but the bird can be well larded or wrapped in buttered foil. For those who do not like rare game, you can make a salmis of pigeon: first roast it on a high heat for 15 minutes, then remove the breasts, slice them in two horizontally and finish them off in a frying pan, gently cooking them in a sauce. Just one small, scrawny, old pigeon can make all the difference to the stockpot to make very good soups and sauces. Pigeon pie is an old country favourite and braising pigeon on a bed of moist vegetables is another excellent way of cooking it.

Pigeon goes well with other strong flavours such as gin and crushed juniper berries, port and Muscatel raisins or prunes, and, my favourite combination, chocolate, raisins and pine nuts, producing a dense, dark, savoury sauce, highlighted with a little balsamic or wine vinegar. This is the basis of the classic Italian *agrodolce* or sour-sweet sauce. I once took these ingredients and turned them into something quite different: pan-fried pigeon breasts served with chocolate ravioli stuffed with ground pine nuts, raisins and Ricotta cheese

One of the very best staple foods to serve with pigeon, and all dark richly flavoured game such as wild duck and hare, is polenta or cornmeal. The combination looks very good on the plate – the rich yellow cornmeal next to the dark velvety sauce and meat. See also POULTRY, page 206 (*Squab*).

SNIPE AND WOODCOCK

These two birds with their distinctive long beaks are very closely related, the snipe being the smaller of the two and weighing about 4oz (125g) as opposed to 11oz (325g) for the woodcock. They are pretty birds, dappled brown and cream, and the woodcock has slightly redder plumage and a deeper, plumper breast. Snipe and woodcock are rarely found on sale and you are more likely to come across them by way of friends who shoot. Both birds are highly prized for their flavour.

Three days is considered sufficient for hanging snipe and woodcock and it is customary to roast them undrawn, that is with the innards or 'trail' still inside, which adds to the flavour. The head is usually left on but skinned and the neck twisted to allow the beak to be pushed sideways through the legs and body to truss it neatly. The eyes are removed from the head. Allow one to two snipe and one woodcock per person.

To roast put the bird on a rack and place a piece of bread brushed with melted butter under the rack to collect the dripping from the bird. This makes the 'toast' or roasted bread even tastier than the bird itself. When cooked, the 'trail' is spooned out of the bird and spread on the toast and the little bird itself then served on top.

WILD DUCK

Mallard, widgeon and teal are the species of wild duck most often found on sale. Living on the coast and in marshy places, wild duck feed mainly on plants growing below the water and so their flesh is relatively oily and strong-tasting, with sometimes a supposedly fishy flavour.

The male mallard is a familiar sight on our ponds and lakes with his handsome head covered with iridescent green feathers, a white necklet, downy breast and flashes of dark blue on his wings. The female is brown in colour. The largest and most readily available of all wild duck, it averages about 2½lb (1·1kg) and will feed two or three people. When ready for the oven it resembles a duckling with its broad, flat breast and light-coloured legs. Although the flesh is lean, dark and inclined to dryness if not properly cooked, because the mallard is a water fowl there is a layer of fat under the skin.

Widgeon weigh about 1½lb (700g) and are prized for their delicate but distinctive flavour. One bird will serve one to two people. The teal weighs about 14oz (425g), and will serve only one person.

Wild duck are at their best in the late autumn, between October and December. Young birds of the new season have soft, pliable thin feet and brighter bills than older birds. They should be hung for only 24 hours or so as the flesh deteriorates rapidly. So buy from a reputable game dealer who will give you accurate information on the age and hanging of the duck, or check 'best before' dates on ready-packaged ones.

Before cooking wipe the body inside and out with a damp cloth. Wild duck should never be washed. To safeguard against any possible fishiness, insert a peeled halved onion and a halved lemon into the cavity, cover the bird and refrigerate overnight. Remove the 'deodorizers' before roasting. Leaner and drier than domestic duck, wild duck is best larded and should be basted frequently. Serve it juicy and slightly pink; the longer it cooks the tougher it becomes.

Smaller wild duck such as teal and widgeon can also be spatchcocked, that is split down the back with the backbone removed, and then grilled. Older duck can be braised or stewed gently in butter and a little red wine or port. Wild duck and oranges are a good combination, especially in the form of a sharp sauce made with Seville oranges. You can also put kumquats inside the duck's cavity with a little butter, herbs, port and seasoning before roasting it.

After slicing the breasts off for one meal, I usually take the meat off the legs and carcase and use the bones to make a rich stock. Then I chop the meat finely and use it to make a delicious sauce to serve with chunky pasta.

Alternatively make a delicious pâté by processing the meat with an equal quantity of butter, some mace, a tablespoon of port and after packing it into a terrine dish seal the top with clarified butter. Keep in the refrigerator.

FURRED GAME

HARE

Hares belong to the same family as rabbits but are larger and longer legged; their dark meat has a rich gamy flavour. Hare remains one of the best bargains of all game and is very popular throughout Europe. Traditional cooking methods in Britain include jugged hare and roast saddle of hare and the latter is becoming increasingly popular in fashionable restaurants. The saddle is cooked quickly, carved into narrow strips and served quite rare. Hare is very popular in Europe. In Germany a spicy stew called *Hasenpfeffer* is made from hare and in France *civet de lièvre à la royale* is the famous dish of Limousin and much prized. The hare is boned and then stuffed with a mixture of its own kidneys and offal, other meats, *foie gras* and brandy. It is then formed into a sausage shape, wrapped in pork fat and casseroled in brandy and red wine. In Italy *pappardelle alla lepre* is a Tuscan speciality – a wonderfully rich dark hare sauce is served with broad flat homemade egg noodles. In Belgium hare is often cooked with beer or with prunes and chestnuts, and in Spain with wine, wine vinegar, chocolate and pine nuts.

In Britain the hare will either be the more common English brown hare or the smaller Scottish or blue hare found in the Highlands. On the Continent there are many species: blond hares from Champagne and russet-coloured ones from Germany, to describe but two. The so-called Belgian hare is, in fact, a domestic breed of rabbit. In the United States there is no clear distinction between hares and rabbits and the names are used interchangeably. For example the American jack rabbit is most definitely a hare to European eyes.

Hare is best eaten when young and you can easily tell a leveret, as hares under one year are called, by its soft, thin ears which tear easily, small, sharp, white teeth and a soft, smooth coat. An adult hare will have large, yellow teeth, a pronounced lip and sharp claws. The best months for fresh hare are October to January.

A freshly shot hare should hang for about a week, unpaunched and head downwards over a bowl to catch any blood which is much prized in cooking later on. They lose about one-third of their weight when cleaned. A young hare,

unskinned and unpaunched, will weigh about 6–7lb (2·7–3·2kg) and feed four people. An older larger hare will feed between six and eight people. You can either buy hare whole or already cut into joints such as the saddle or hind legs.

An adult hare is a very economical buy and will provide a range of dishes. The saddle can be roasted and, with plenty of vegetables, will serve four. The massive hind legs can be jointed and then 'jugged' or casseroled to serve four. The meat from the forequarters or shoulders will make a good sauce for pasta, a terrine, coarse pâté or potted hare, and the carcase and head make a rich stock for a soup. Hare soup with celeriac and dumplings is a fine winter dish. On an older, larger hare the legs will be considerably tougher than the saddle or back, and while the saddle can be casseroled, braised or roasted, the legs should only be subjected to slow gentle heat with plenty of lubrication, and not roasted.

The young hare or leveret has a delicate pale meat and can be roasted provided it is basted frequently to stop the outer flesh from hardening. A stuffing helps to keep it moist and basted from the inside. All hare meat should be well cooked.

The blood saved when paunching a hare is essential for an authentic jugged hare or *civet de lièvre*, the classic French dish, as it enriches and thickens the sauce perfectly. The blood is added to the dish only about five minutes before the end. It is stirred in, then heated through without boiling which would curdle it. If you order a hare, remember to ask for the blood to be put to one side. When you get home stir a teaspoon of wine vinegar into the blood to stop it coagulating, cover and refrigerate it until required.

Both young and older hares benefit from a marinade, the first for flavour, the second for tenderness. Oil, wine and wine vinegar should be the basis of the marinade, then add herbs, spices and vegetables according to taste and what you have available.

RABBIT

The European rabbit, originally a native of the Iberian peninsula, has had a chequered existence. Before the onset of myxamatosis in the 1940s and 1950s when much of the world's rabbit population was wiped out, wild rabbit was

so plentiful that it could hardly be given away. But rabbits are a hardy breed and they survived and continue to multiply. From the same family as the hare, a wild rabbit has darker flesh than a tame rabbit, often with a gamy flavour; much depends on what it has been eating. A young rabbit feeding on a field of corn will be fat and deliciously tender.

The rabbit has been domesticated for many centuries and rabbit farming is big business. Tame rabbit makes good eating if properly prepared and its delicate, well-flavoured white meat is inexpensive.

Rabbit and Hare

1 FOREQUARTER OF RABBIT
2 SADDLE OF RABBIT
3 HINDQUARTER OF RABBIT
4 WHOLE RABBIT
5 FOREQUARTER OF HARE
6 SADDLE OF HARE
7 HINDQUARTER OF HARE
8 WHOLE HARE

PREPARING RABBIT

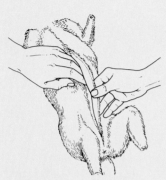

1 *Remove ears and paws. Slit open skin along belly with sharp scissors. Ease away skin from flesh, along cut and around body.*

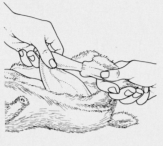

2 *Pull skin over each hind leg so that flesh of lower half of animal is completely freed.*

3 *Holding body firmly, pull skin up and over front quarters and head. Remove head.*

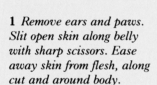

4 *Cut open belly up to breast bone. Remove entrails, reserving heart, liver and kidneys. Discard rest.*

5 *Cut away skin flaps below rib cage. The rabbit is now ready for roasting whole or it can be jointed.*

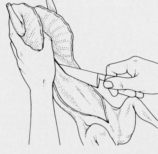

6 *Holding carcase firmly, divide it in half lengthways down the centre.*

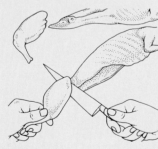

7 *Remove both hind legs from carcase at thigh.*

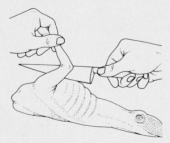

8 *Remove both forelegs from carcase.*

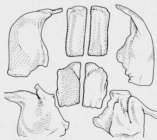

9 *If you want equal-sized portions for casseroling cut saddle crossways in half.*

Wild rabbits are smaller than tame ones and average 3lb (1·4kg) or so. They are best in autumn in their first season. Tame rabbits can grow to a huge size, and reach as much as 9lb (4·1kg) by six months. Young rabbits should have soft ears that tear easily and small white teeth. If the claws are rough and blunt it is an old rabbit fit only for the stewpot. Rabbit is best eaten fresh and needs no hanging. If you want to hang your rabbit it must be paunched beforehand, unlike a hare, and then hung by the hind legs. Fresh rabbits for sale are usually tame rabbits and are available all the year round. They can be sold whole in fur or ready-jointed. Frozen rabbit is also widely available, mainly imported from China, but has a tendency to dryness if not cooked carefully and it does lack the flavour of fresh rabbit.

Very often rabbit has much more flavour than the average broiler chicken and I often use tame rabbit in recipes designed for chicken. It can be grilled, fried, barbecued or roasted but care must be taken to keep it well basted and thus moist as rabbits have little natural fat, especially wild rabbit. As you would expect wild rabbit is tougher than tame rabbit and needs slower, gentler cooking.

Rabbit casserole is my favourite way of cooking rabbit, whether wild or tame. Cook the meat in red wine with prunes, in white wine with baby onions and mustard or in beer with celery or chunks of celeriac. Tarragon is the perfect herb to accompany rabbit and will turn it into a really fine dish. In summer serve a cold jellied rabbit terrine using white wine and tarragon.

A clay chicken brick is an excellent way of cooking rabbit. Soak the pot first, put a layer of small onions on the bottom and place the rabbit pieces on top. Scatter uncooked rice into the spaces (enough for the right number of servings), add twice the amount of stock or white wine, and saffron threads soaked first in a tablespoon of hot water. Extras such as chopped apricots, almonds and cumin seed give a faintly Middle Eastern or North African touch to the dish. A similar Portuguese dish includes rice and rabbit cooked in strong red Dão wine and the result is a dark rich dish. One of my favourite paellas is a simple combination of rabbit, green beans and some chopped asparagus cooked with rice, saffron and stock.

VENISON

Venison is the name of all meat from the deer family. There are four types of deer used in Britain for food: the roe deer, the fallow deer, the red deer and the Sika deer. The season depends on the breed, whether the deer is male or female, and varies from one part of the country to the other. Some of the venison comes from truly wild deer and some from park or farm deer. Scotland, Wales and the New Forest in Hampshire are the major sources of deer in Britain. Venison is also imported from New Zealand. It is an extremely popular meat in Europe, and much British venison is exported to the Continent, especially Germany.

Fresh venison is found mostly in the autumn and early winter, though is available at other times whenever herds are culled. Frozen venison is available all the year round and is increasingly popular.

Venison is better from an older deer when the meat will have had time to acquire its true flavour. The animal is skinned and cleaned after shooting and before hanging. Although young deer may be eaten fresh older ones need hanging in a cool airy place, head downwards, often for two or three weeks.

Venison meat is quite unmistakable, being a very fine-textured, dense, dark red meat which has little fat on it and little marbling of fat in the flesh. What fat there is will be white if the animal is young and yellower if mature. Because it is high in protein and low in fat, it is a meat with good nutritional properties. Covering it with a rich cream sauce or basting with lots of butter will, of course, change the balance entirely.

As with all other game, meat from the older animal needs slow careful cooking, while venison from a young animal can be roasted. Venison is sold already jointed and there is a wide choice of cuts available. To many people's surprise the cost of venison is often less than that of beef. The different parts of the animal require different treatment. Meat from the loin and the saddle does not come from such hard-working muscles as the shoulder and leg. It follows, therefore, that a saddle can be roasted, and loin chops or medallions cut from the fillet can be grilled or best of all, pan-fried in butter.

The leg or haunch and the saddle are the choicest joints. A haunch can vary in size depending on whether it is cut short or long; a saddle will be sufficient for six to eight people. The shoulder can be braised or cut into cubes for stewing. Venison is often marinated first, up to four or five days depending on the weather, to develop the gamy flavour. You can make a good marinade from port, olive oil, red wine, herbs and spices, including juniper berries, bay leaves and peppercorns. Any roasting joint should then be larded well with thick strips of pork back fat and basted frequently during cooking. Be careful not to overcook the meat as roast venison should be fairly pink.

Stewing venison, diced from a boned shoulder or leg, makes a marvellous game pudding, cooked with stout inside a suet crust, or else chop it very small and use it to make a venison chilli in the style of *chilli con carne*.

The neat lean medallions cut from the fillet cook very quickly and are fine for one of those smart dinner parties where your guests can be left for a few minutes while you quickly fry the meat, deglaze the pan and swirl up a few tablespoons of delectable sauce enriched with the meat juices in the pan, redcurrant jelly, butter and a little cream.

When trimming venison be careful to remove all traces of fat as these will spoil the flavour of the meat.

WILD BOAR

These handsome aggressive-looking beasts, hunted since ancient times, have been extinct in Britain in the wild for about 300 years, although they are still found in the more remote hilly areas of Italy, southern Germany and eastern France among our close neighbours. Once in Italy in the winter, after driving through snow and sleet to Castelnuovo di Garfagnana in the unfashionable and remote part of north-western Tuscany near Lucca, we had a hot, steaming, rich, gamy stew of wild boar heaped over freshly cooked polenta and it was one of the most welcoming dishes I have ever eaten.

Some enterprising British farmers now farm wild boar, some are pure bred and others are cross-breeds. About five years ago I visited a farm in North Wales with a small herd of pure-bred wild boar. They were fine but very fierce animals and made excellent food. Our host had made us a huge, raised hot-water crust pie, full of wild boar, grouse, pork, chicken livers, pistachio nuts and plenty of seasoning, and served cold with some spiced plums. It was quite marvellous.

Wild boar looks like a slightly denser, darker version of pork and should be cooked in the same way: roast the lean or tender cuts, casserole the tougher cuts, and make soups and pâtés from the trimmings or a rich meat sauce for pasta. Particularly good casseroles can be made when the meat is cooked with a few wild mushrooms such as ceps or in the sour-sweet style with a little dark chocolate, some wine or sherry vinegar and a handful of pine nuts, raisins and capers. There is little fat on the meat and the flavour is excellent. Unlike venison, boar should always be well cooked.

Venison and Wild Boar

1 BOAR LOIN CHOPS	4 VENISON LOIN CHOPS
2 SADDLE OF BOAR	5 SHOULDER OF
3 VENISON STEAKS	VENISON

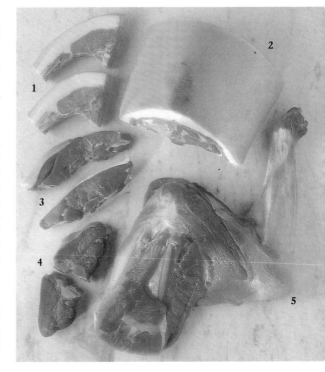

BACON AND HAM

How fortunate it was for our ancestors that the curing of pork, which they had to do from necessity to preserve it, produced such a tasty meat. It was so full of character that a little went a long way, eking out quantities of potatoes, beans or cabbage. Even though we no longer need to cure pork, we still do because we like the flavour of bacon and ham.

BACON

Bacon is made by curing the meat from the back or side of a pig and sometimes by smoking it. There are two main methods: tank curing in brine (the most common) and dry curing, which produces a fuller flavour, but is less often practised. Pork that has been cured and matured is called 'green' or unsmoked bacon and has a mild flavour. The smoking of cured bacon helps to preserve the meat further by retarding the growth of bacteria. It gives a special flavour, and improves the colour. There is also a special milder cure available known as tendersweet.

Good quality bacon should have a pleasant smell. The lean should be firm and deep pink in colour. A dark, dry appearance suggests that the bacon has been cut for some time and exposed to the air. There should be no yellow or greenish stains on the meat and the fat should be white and firm. The rind should be thin, elastic and smooth, though the colour will depend on the process by which the bacon has been cured and smoked. Bacon is not intended to be eaten raw.

HAM

Ham is the hind leg of a pig, taken from a side of pork and cured very much more slowly than bacon. The term is also applied to shoulder of pork that is cured in the same way, but ham-cured shoulder generally has a less delicate flavour than ham. (Note that in French cookery, *jambon* not only means ham, but also can mean a leg of fresh pork.) Some hams are intended for further cooking, others are eaten in their cured 'raw' state.

A variety of factors influence the flavour and texture of ham, as you would expect. These include the breed of pig and its diet; whether it has been dry-salted or brined, how long it has been cured (it could be as long as two years) and whether it has been air-dried or smoked and if so whether over applewood, beechwood, hickory, juniper, oak, or even peat. All manner of other ingredients may be added to the curing solution, such as beer, treacle and vinegar. Some of the finest hams come from the Iberian peninsula, the southern United States, France, Italy and Britain.

COOKING BACON AND HAM

Some hams are sold ready for baking. These are the milder cures, the ones with less salt. Otherwise, to prepare a ham for baking or indeed any other method of cooking, you should soak it first, for up to 24 hours if it is one of the traditionally cured hams. The rind is left on during most of the cooking as this keeps the meat in shape and helps to flavour and baste it.

A whole ham can be prepared by first soaking it, then simmering it in water very gently for approximately 25 minutes for each 1lb (500g). The water should never boil and the ham must be kept covered with water. When the ham is cooked the pan should be removed from the heat until the ham is cool enough to handle. The rind is then removed, to make carving easier, and the fat underneath can be trimmed off, or scored and basted with syrup, honey or some other form of glaze before being baked in a hot oven for 20 minutes.

Although this is the most usual method of cooking ham, smaller joints and joints of bacon can also be braised, casseroled or steamed. Both need careful cooking if they are not to be dry and hard, but this effort will amply repay you with a moist and succulent piece of meat, full of good flavour and with a fine texture. I see no reason why ham and bacon should not be marinated before cooking. Of course the curing process it has already undergone is a type of marinade. Try marinading a bacon joint (after soaking) in cider or beer, wine, apple juice or pineapple juice with some ginger, cinnamon and cloves.

BACON AND HAM IN THE KITCHEN

Because they share a similar flavour and texture, bacons and hams will take the same kind of accompanying flavours. Mashed potatoes, lentils, peas, beans, cabbage and sauerkraut make the perfect partners. Fruit complements the sweet, salty flavours, as in pineapple glazed ham or ham stuffed with peaches or apricots. Apple sauce is very good with a bacon joint and the Italian mustard fruit preserves are excellent.

Whole hams have their place at the festive table, burnished and glistening with a sweet glaze, studded with cloves and bejewelled with fruit. Rather than canned pineapple or glacé cherries, use dried apricot halves which you have soaked, and 'nail' them in with cloves.

At the other end of the scale, rashers of smoked streaky bacon are endlessly versatile in the kitchen. Use them to line tins in which you make pâté. This will enrich the pâté and keep it moist, as well as giving it a good pink colour. Make a simple and inexpensive bacon and egg pie by lining a pie dish with pastry, spreading blanched, rindless rashers of bacon on the bottom, cracking in some raw eggs and adding a few slices of sausage. Top with a pastry lid and bake until the eggs are firm. It is marvellous picnic food when cold. Streaky bacon rashers make excellent wrappings for food that you want to grill or bake: scallops, oysters, chicken livers, herring roe, small pieces of monkfish or eel. The bacon bastes and flavours the food and prevents it drying out. And of course, it is essential to the BLT, a substantial American sandwich of grilled bacon, lettuce and sliced tomatoes.

In France a popular salad is made from batavia or endive, dressed with 'lardons' of hot cooked bacon and bacon fat, which wilt the leaves. Spinach and bacon salad can be made in the same way, and hot potato salad served with crisp bacon bits is delicious.

Cook ham or bacon with beans in a soup or a stew. Black bean soup is excellent made with a ham bone stock, as are all the bean soups and stews of Spain, Italy and Portugal. All pulses are the perfect accompaniment to hams and bacons, as are root vegetable purées and cabbage dishes. The finest raw hams, however – the Italian *prosciutto di Parma* or *di San Daniele*, the French *jambon de Bayonne* and the Spanish *jamón serrano* – need nothing more than fresh bread and a piece of ripe fruit: a fig, a wedge of melon or some pawpaw.

A sweet- or mild-cured ham sometimes described as ready to bake will not need to be soaked before it is cooked. For stronger cures, soaking for between 8 and 24 hours may be necessary. Although these preserved meats have a robust character, their flesh is in fact, quite delicate and they spoil with over-cooking, becoming dry and stringy. Although one might read of boiled ham or bacon, it should never boil, just simmer gently.

Wrapped closely in food wrap, bacon and ham joints can be stored in the refrigerator for up to ten days. Sliced cooked hams should be eaten within three days.

CUTS OF BACON

In Britain, bacon is usually divided into the following cuts, with slight regional variations in name and cut.

Back bacon is divided into four cuts: long back weighs about 2½lb (1·1kg), and is usually thinly sliced for frying or grilling; short back, about 5lb (2·3kg), is the best cut of bacon for rashers; back and ribs weighing about 6¾lb (3·1kg) make good joints for boiling or braising and lean rashers for grilling or frying; top back, about 2¼lb (1kg), is good for boiling or braising and also makes good lean rashers.

Collar bacon is divided into two cuts: prime collar weighs about 6lb (2·7kg) and is the best joint for boiling, either whole or cut into pieces;

end of collar, about 2lb (1kg) in weight, is an economical cut, good for boiling or baking (soak it first).

Flank bacon is about 2¾lb (1·2kg) in weight. It may be boiled, or sliced and fried.

Forehock may be whole or divided into two: the hock knuckle weighs about 3lb (1·4kg) and should be boned, and minced, or used in casseroles; prime hock is a small fatty joint, which weighs 1¼lb (600g) and is good for boiling.

Gammon There are four gammon cuts from the hind leg of the pig: gammon slipper is a small lean joint, weighing about 1½lb (750g), and is good for boiling or roasting; gammon hock is a joint of about 4½lb (2kg) which can be boiled, or

baked after being partly boiled, and is very good cold; middle gammon weighs about 5lb (2·3kg) and is the best gammon joint for boiling or roasting, and for steaks and lean rashers which are good for grilling, in fact perhaps the best cut for a mixed grill; corner gammon is a lean boiling or roasting joint weighing about 4lb (1·8kg) and provides good grilling rashers.

Middle bacon or **through cut** is back and streaky undivided, and produces excellent grilling rashers.

Oyster is from the end of the long back and weighs about 1½lb (750g). It produces good rashers for frying or grilling.

Streaky bacon is divided into three cuts: top streaky weighs about 1¼lb (600g) as a small

Bacon and Ham for Cooking

1 GAMMON STEAK
2 STREAKY BACON RASHERS (RINDLESS)
3 TENDERSWEET BACON RASHERS
4 STREAKY BACON RASHERS (UNSMOKED)
5 HAM (HALF-GAMMON)
6 STREAKY BACON RASHERS (SMOKED)
7 BACK BACON RASHERS (RINDLESS, UNSMOKED)
8 BACON (SLIPPER)
9 BACK BACON RASHERS (SMOKED)
10 BACON (FOREHOCK, UNSMOKED)
11 BACON (PRIME COLLAR, SMOKED)
12 BACK BACON RASHERS (UNSMOKED)
13 LONG BACK BACON RASHERS (UNSMOKED)
14 BACON (PRIME HOCK, UNSMOKED)
15 OYSTER-CUT BACON RASHERS

boiling joint, or can be cut into thin rashers for grilling or frying; prime streaky is a joint of about 5½lb (2·5kg) for boiling, or can be cut into rashers for grilling or frying; thin streaky, sliced into small rashers, is good for frying crisply, for lining pâté tins and for wrapping small food items before grilling them, for example chicken livers or scallops.

OTHER BACONS

Lard de poitrine is a French version of streaky bacon, made from belly of pork and very fatty. It is used for flavouring stews or in warm salads.

Lard fumé is smoked *lard de poitrine* which may be sliced and fried or used in omelettes, salads or sprinkled on baked potatoes.

Pancetta is an Italian streaky bacon, smoked or green and used to flavour dishes such as spaghetti *alla carbonara* (with an egg and bacon sauce). It is also used in the Italian *soffrito*, the basic flavouring of a casserole which is chopped vegetables, herbs and pancetta, fried until just lightly brown, which adds a remarkable depth of flavour to the dish. *Pancetta coppata* is cured, unsmoked *pancetta* which has been rolled up with a bit of *coppa* (shoulder ham). It is generally served sliced as a cold meat.

Schinkenspeck is *Speck* or *Spek* with more lean in it, like streaky bacon. It is often served in the piece with lentils or in a thick pea soup.

Speck or **Spek** is German or Scandinavian fat bacon which is almost entirely fat. It may be smoked or green. Rendered speck can be used for frying. *Tocino* is the Spanish equivalent.

TYPES OF HAM

Asturias is one of the best-known of Spanish hams. It is delicate in flavour and eaten hot or cold after being boiled.

Bradenham This well-known English ham comes from Chippenham in Wiltshire. It is first dry-cured and then placed in a 'basting cure' of molasses, brown sugar and spices in which it is turned and basted daily. It is hung to dry and mature for several months and smoked until the outside is completely black. The ham may need to be soaked for as long as a week before it is boiled, as it may be very salty. It has a sweet flavour and is usually served cold.

Coppa The Italian equivalent of ham from the shoulder, this is more fatty than *prosciutto*, but also less expensive.

Coppa crudo Cured collar of pork is, pressed raw into sausage skins and left to dry and mature for two to four months. Served thinly sliced, Coppa crudo is an important part of the traditional Italian antipasto.

Coppa di Corse is a similar type of ham from Corsica: dark, dry and sweet flavoured.

Culatella di zibello or **di Parma** is ham from the Italian province of Parma. Made from the rump of pork it is cured in a similar way to *prosciutto*. The ham is often soaked in white wine for two or three days before it is cut. It has less fat than *prosciutto* and a more spicy flavour.

Danish hams These are a side product of the Danish bacon industry and are usually green (unsmoked). They are also boned and canned.

Gochaer is a German ham which may be braised, baked or boiled, and eaten hot or cold.

Irish ham Irish hams are produced in Northern Ireland. Belfast hams or Ulster Rolls are dry-salt cured, and well trimmed. Boneless Irish hams are usually cured and boned before they are smoked – often with peat smoke.

Jambon blanc is French cooking ham, and can be lightly smoked, or unsmoked. It is also known as *jambon demi-semi, jambon de Paris* or *jambon glacé* after it has been boiled.

Jambon d'Ardennes is a Belgian ham which is sliced very thinly and eaten raw. It can also be sliced and gently heated in butter.

Jambon de Bayonne This French ham from the Basses-Pyrénées is dry-cured and smoked. It should be eaten raw, in very thin slices.

Jambon de Grisons is a Swiss ham which is lightly salted and dried in the open air. It has a delicate flavour.

Jambon de Toulouse is a French ham which is salted and dried. It is eaten raw.

Jambonneau is a small ham, usually covered with breadcrumbs, and sold ready to eat.

Jambons de campagne These local French hams are usually sweet-cured and well smoked. They can be eaten raw as an hors d'oeuvre, or used in cooking. Among these hams are those, for example, of Alsace, Auvergne, Brittany, Burgundy, Lorraine, Limousin, Montagne-Noir (Cevennes), Morvan, Touraine, Savoy and the Vosges.

Jamón de Jabugo is a sweet Spanish ham from the region of Huelva. It is a very well flavoured ham, rosy pink in colour, and is eaten raw. The pigs are the long-legged Iberian pigs which roam freely, feeding on acorns and foraged food. The hams are usually displayed with the black hoof to demonstrate their authenticity. Similar hams come from Granada, Caceres and Salamanca where they are known as *jamón serrano* or mountain ham. Some hams are left in the snow to mature.

Kentucky is an American ham, from Hampshire hogs. The pigs are fattened on acorns, beans and clover and finally on grain. The hams are dry-salted for about one month and then smoked for another month over corn cobs, hickory bark and apple or sassafras wood. They are then matured for up to a year.

Lachsschinken is a German delicacy, made from smoked foreloin, wrapped with white pork fat and tied with string. Pink and moist, it is always eaten raw, often with horseradish.

Lomo Ahumado This is loin of pork from Spain, cured and smoked. It is well-flavoured and eaten raw as a popular *tapas*.

Picnic or **shoulder ham** Not true ham because it comes from the fore-hock or front leg of a bacon pig. The meat is cut round like a ham and cured separately. It is much cheaper than true ham and can be used in the same way.

Prague (Pragerschinken) The best Czechoslavakian hams are Prague hams which are salted and then left in a mild brine for several months. After being smoked with beech wood, they are matured in cool cellars. The hams are cooked whole, have a sweet flavour and are often served before the main course.

Presunto is the lightly cured and smoked ham of Portugal. It is served sliced as an appetizer.

Prosciutto di Parma, prosciutto crudo (Parma ham) The classic Italian ham, said to come from pigs fattened on a diet of parsnips. In fact, the pigs are fed on a diet of whey left over from making the local cheese, Parmeggiano-Reggiano, or Parmesan. The ham is dry-cured for part of the time under weights, which gives it a flattened shape. After it has matured for about a year, it is soaked in tepid water to soften the rind. After being dried and stored for a short time, it can then be very thinly sliced and served raw, or lightly fried.

Prosciutto di San Daniele Many consider San Daniele the equal of Parma ham. It has a more pronounced flavour and a richer colour.

Prosciutto Veneto This is a light and delicately flavoured ham. Similar raw, cured hams are made elsewhere, in Tuscany, in Friuli and in Emilia-Romagna.

'Quick-cure' hams Some American hams are specially treated to produce a quick and economic cure. They can be cooked more rapidly than slow-cured hams, but I do not find the flavour as good.

Schwarzwalder (Black Forest) A German ham which is cured in a strong brine and smoked. It has strongly flavoured flesh and the fat is very white. It is eaten raw.

Seager (Suffolk) is one of several county hams produced in England and cured by the 'basting cure' method. A mixture of salt and saltpetre is rubbed into the surface of the meat. It is then covered by a 'pickle' of old ale, black treacle, brown sugar and spices. After being turned and basted for a month, it is hung to dry and mature for four months. After being boiled, baked or braised, it can be eaten hot or cold and has a full, mild flavour.

Smithfield is an excellent ham from Virginia in the United States. The pigs are at first allowed to roam wild, feeding on acorns, beech nuts and hickory nuts, then they are fed mainly on peanuts and finally on corn. The ham is dry-cured, rubbed with black pepper and heavily smoked over hickory, apple and oak. It is then matured for up to a year. It can be served raw, or braised, baked or boiled and eaten hot or cold.

Sugar-glazed Cooked ham prepared with a glaze made from sugar, treacle or honey.

Virginia The true Virginia hams of the United States come from a breed of pig known as 'razor-back'. The pigs are fed on peaches and peanuts, and the meat is dry-cured for about seven weeks. After the salt is brushed off, the ham is basted in a cure of brown molasses, brown sugar, black pepper and saltpetre for two weeks. It may then be drained and hung to mature for a year, or it may be smoked over apple and hickory before being matured. It is boiled, baked or braised and served hot or cold.

Westphalian A German ham with a distinctive flavour that is produced by smoking the ham over juniper twigs on a beechwood fire. It has an attractive chestnut colour and is served raw.

Wiltshire The so-called Wiltshire ham is in fact a gammon which has been cured on the side of pork instead of separately as for a true ham. It is milder than true ham and will not keep as long.

York The traditional English ham, this is dry-cured with salt and a little saltpetre for about three weeks then baked in the oven and matured. Green York ham is dry-cured and then washed and placed in a calico bag where it is allowed to mature for about six months. Green ham needs cooking. Usually boiled or baked and eaten hot or cold, it has a delicate flavour. It is sold either raw (when it must be cooked), or already cooked and thinly sliced.

Hams and Bacon

1 WESTPHALIAN HAM	9 PANCETTA
2 SUGAR-GLAZED HAM	10 COPPA
3 LOMO AHUMADO	11 PROSCIUTTO
4 LACHSSCHINKEN	12 JAMBON D'ARDENNES
5 JAMBON DE	13 JAMBON DE BAYONNE
GRISONS	14 JAMÓN DE JABUGO
6 YORK HAM	15 SCHWARZWALDER
7 BRADENHAM HAM	HAM
8 VIRGINIA HAM	16 PANCETTA COPPATA

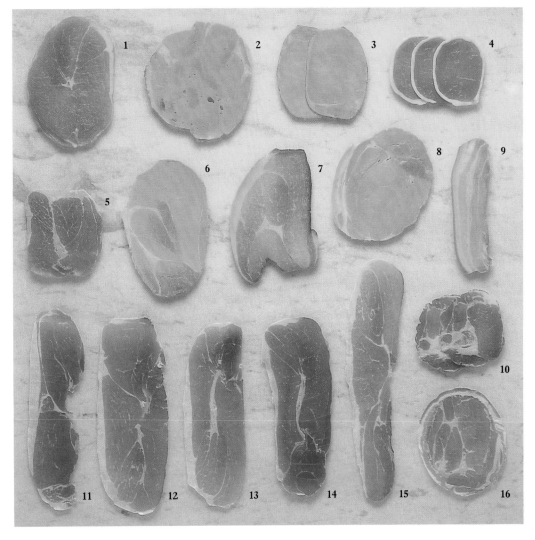

OTHER PRESERVED MEATS

These meats have all been 'cured'; that is, some of the moisture has been removed by drying, salting and/or smoking to preserve them. In the past this was done to ensure a winter supply of meat. The practice continues today mainly because it extends the variety of flavours of a major food.

BILTONG *jerky*

The original biltong was a South African invention: narrow strips of meat cut from game and pounded vigorously to release the juices, then air- or sun-dried, salted and spiced, or smoked. Now it is also used for biltong beef. Whatever the meat, after curing it looks like an offcut from a well-worn leather belt. It can sometimes be a good meaty chew – just bite off pieces.

BRESAOLA

This is an Italian speciality from Lombardy, where lean, tender cuts of beef are air-dried and matured for several months. Finely sliced and marinated in olive oil, lemon juice and black pepper, it makes a tasty hors d'oeuvre.

BÜNDNERFLEISCH

This is the air-dried beef of the Grisons, Switzerland, and, like bresaola, it is an expensive delicacy. Serve it Swiss style, as an appetizer, in wafer-thin slivers with an oil and vinegar dressing and some pickled gherkins.

CORNED BEEF, SALT BEEF

In Britain corned beef consists of compressed pieces of cured, cooked, gelatinous beef. It is mainly served thinly sliced in salads and sandwiches, or cooked with potato to make corned beef hash. Corned beef was the early American settlers' method of preserving beef. They 'corned' the meat by covering it with large granules or 'corns' of dry salt, or brine-cured it with salt, sugar and saltpetre. The American version still consists of a whole piece of meat, usually brisket (in Britain known as 'salt beef'). This is cured in a spiced brine, then cooked and served hot or cold and eaten with dill pickles and rye bread. Beef silverside is prepared similarly.

OX TONGUE

The salted poached tongue of an ox is strongly flavoured, dark reddish-brown and slightly gelatinous, yet with a grainy texture. Serve it cold, sliced, in salads or in sandwiches.

PASTRAMI *pastrama*

In the United States pastrami is underside or brisket of beef, cured in a non-liquid mixture of sugar, spices and garlic for about seven days, then smoked. The Romanian version – *pastrama* – may also be cured meat from a goat, pig or goose. This, too, is dry-cured with salt and spices, then smoked. Serve with rye bread.

SMOKED POULTRY AND GAME

Smoked duck, turkey and poussin all have a delicate smoky flavour which comes from an initial cold-smoke, followed by a brief hot-smoke. The cured meat is then rested for a short while in cool storage to let the flavour mature.

Venison is hung for at least seven to ten days, then given a cold-smoke followed by a hot-smoke cure. Its flavour will depend on the species of deer and its grazing, though the roe deer is generally considered to be supreme. Venison, particularly haunch, is the most popular of game meats but reindeer can also be bought smoked.

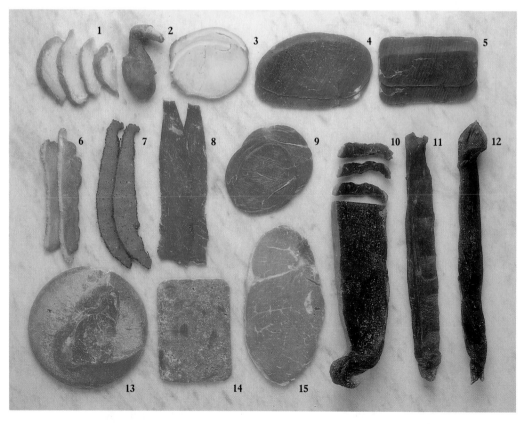

Preserved Meats

1 SMOKED POUSSIN BREAST	8 SMOKED VENISON
2 SMOKED POUSSIN LEG	9 SMOKED REINDEER
	10 BILTONG (BEEF)
3 SMOKED TURKEY	11 BILTONG (JERKY)
4 BÜNDNERFLEISCH	12 BILTONG (VENISON)
5 BRESAOLA	13 OX TONGUE
6 SMOKED DUCK	14 CORNED BEEF
7 PASTRAMI	15 CORNED BEEF (SILVERSIDE)

The history of the sausage dates back to when most meat, particularly pork, was home-reared and killed to provide the family's staple diet. Every morsel of the animal was used. Sausages were made up from the scraps that were left over. These scraps were stuffed into casings made from the animal's guts, seasoned, eaten fresh, or salted or dried to preserve them. Nowadays most major producers use only meats from the animal's forequarters. The casings used for sausages can be natural – made from the cleaned guts of pigs, sheep or cattle – or commercially made from reconstituted collagen, cellulose and sometimes plastic.

Sausages are no longer the poor man's convenience food but play an important part in the world's cuisines. Almost every country has its own type of sausage – some with as many varieties as regions.

Sausages can be divided into three main categories: those for cooking, those for slicing or spreading and salami. Within each category there are further variations. Fresh cooking sausages can be made from any meat, though pork and beef are the most popular.

Some sausages are salted and smoked but still need cooking, and others like the frankfurter, are already cooked but still need reheating in hot water (never boiling or their skins will burst). Slicing sausages are cooked and often smoked and have a firm consistency. They are usually sold sliced for sandwiches or for part of a cold meat plate. They must be eaten within a day or two of purchase if sliced, otherwise they become stale. It is therefore better to buy them in the piece and slice them as required. Spreading sausages are also cooked but have a soft texture, similar to paté, ready for spreading on bread.

COOKING SAUSAGES

Like meat, fresh sausages are highly perishable and should be cooked within a few days of purchase. They require slow cooking over gentle heat to ensure that they are cooked through, pricking them beforehand to prevent their skins bursting. Sausages come in many varieties, flavours and textures which lend themselves to a range of dishes, from the simple sausage served in a bowl of steaming hot soup, to richly garnished sauerkrauts or the Italian *zampone* sausage served as part of an elaborate New Year's Eve dinner.

Italian, Polish, Spanish, German, French and Portuguese cookery books are full of traditional recipes for using sausages: try a Polish hunter's stew or *bigos*. One New Year's day in Paris we had a marvellously simple meal of *boudin blanc, boudin noir* and apple purée. Good-quality coarse sausages make an excellent sauce for dried pasta when skinned, chopped and fried with garlic, tomatoes and aubergines. Use Mortadella as part of the traditional stuffing for homemade pasta. Cook sausages in beer before serving them with a purée of garlic and potatoes. Fry them gently so that they give off fat, drain them and add a good splash of beer to the pan.

ACCOMPANIMENTS FOR SAUSAGES

Lentils, split peas, broad beans, borlotti beans and other pulses are excellent foils, with their floury earthiness, to the rich meat of sausages. Polenta, potatoes and rice go well for the same reason. And cabbage in all its varied methods of preparation – spiced red cabbage, sauerkraut or *choucroute* (fermented cabbage) – and raw cabbage can be used with cooked sausages cut up in mixed salads. Sausages can be cut into dice or strips and mixed with cooked diced potato, apple, onion and chopped gherkin, all folded into a mayonnaise or soured cream dressing.

Salamis and other sliced sausages need nothing more than fresh bread – crusty Italian or French bread, or chewy moist rye bread from Germany and Scandinavia – unsalted butter and a bowl of olives or gherkins.

The page numbers in brackets at the end of an entry refer to the relevant photograph.

ANDOUILLE

This is a large thick French slicing sausage made from pork meat, chitterling, tripe, calf mesentery, pepper, wine, onions and spice, first marinaded, then salted and finally smoked. Although not a very attractive sausage – wrinkled and knobbly and brown or black from the smoking – it has an excellent taste.

ANDOUILLETTE

This French sausage contains almost the same ingredients as the *andouille* but is much smaller as it is packed into the small intestine. Usually bumpy in appearance with coarsely chopped meat, it varies in colour from white through to black, depending on whether it has been smoked. It is often sold covered in fat or wrapped in paper.

Andouillettes are usually grilled or fried, and served with mashed or fried potatoes and fried onions for preference, although like most sausages they go very well with lentils. *Andouillettes*, like *andouilles*, are an acquired taste, with strong, earthy flavours.

They will keep for up to two days only. *(231)*

AP YEUNG CHEUNG

A hot air-dried Chinese sausage containing preserved duck liver, pork, pork fat, sugar, soy sauce and Chinese wine, this is similar in appearance to a small, thin, knobbly salame. Chinese sausages are traditionally steamed over boiling rice but they can also be grilled on a barbecue. *(231)*

BASTOURMA

This is a Turkish cooking sausage made of minced lamb and flavoured with paprika. It is usually grilled or steamed. *(231)*

BIERSCHINKEN

A large German slicing sausage, Bierschinken contains pork, ham, ham fat, peppercorns and pistachio nuts. When sliced the chunks of ham and pistachio are clearly visible. It is eaten cold with bread or as part of a meat plate. *(235)*

BIERWURST

A large coarse-textured German slicing sausage made from pork, or pork and beef, this is flavoured with spices such as juniper berries and cardamom. Garlic is also sometimes added. It is one of the most popular of German slicing sausages and is a common ingredient in a plate of German cold cuts. *(235)*

BLACK PUDDING

Also known as blood sausage pudding, this sausage originally came from the Midlands and North of England and usually contains pig's blood (and occasionally a mixture of other bloods), fat, cereal, onions, groats and spices and is traditionally flavoured with the herb pennyroyal. In Scotland black pudding is made with sheep's blood. As the name suggests it is black and shiny in appearance and varying in size from a small U-shaped link sausage almost to salame size. Although already cooked, it is generally sliced and fried.

Black pudding is traditionally regarded as a breakfast food, but try it sliced and fried and served with a warm salad of leeks or potatoes. It may be kept for just a few days in the refrigerator and can be frozen. (*231*)

BLUTWURST

The German name for blood sausage, of which there are many different varieties. One of the most popular varieties contains pig's blood, pork, bacon fat, marjoram and allspice. It can be eaten sliced and cold as well as fried like black pudding.

BOCKWURST

A German smoked scalded sausage made from veal and pork or spiced beef and pork, finely minced with back fat and spices, this looks like a large frankfurter and is cooked in the same way – gently heated in hot water. (*231*)

BOLOGNA

Known as polony in Britain, this is a finely ground, smoked pork slicing sausage originally based on the Mortadella sausage from Bologna in Italy, but now found in the United States where it is called bolony.

BOUDIN BLANC

There are many varieties of this French sausage which, translated into English, is 'white pudding', but with the name the resemblance to the British variety ends. This is a delicate creamy white sausage about 6in (15cm) long which may contain finely minced veal, chicken, pork, rabbit or hare plus milk or cream, onions, eggs, spice and a little breadcrumbs or rice. Although they are already poached they should be served hot – gently grilled or fried in butter or poached in milk and water. They are highly perishable and should be eaten on the day of purchase. In France it is traditional to eat them with apples as part of the Christmas festival food. (*231*)

BOUDIN NOIR

This French blood sausage contains pig's blood, pork fat, cream, onion and spices. There are many regional varieties containing additional flavourings. It is generally served hot, either very gently grilled, or sliced and lightly fried, accompanied by mashed potatoes and sometimes apples. In Alsace it quite likely to be served with *choucroute*. (*231*)

BRATWURST

A pale-coloured German smoked sausage made from finely minced pork or veal and spices, this is similar in appearance to a rather meaty, large, British pork sausage. It can be gently grilled or fried, and is for same-day consumption. (*231*)

BRITISH BEEF SAUSAGE

These cooking sausages are very popular in Scotland, where they prefer mutton and beef to pork. The sausages are generally made from lean beef, fat, bread, and seasoning (although legally British pork and beef sausages can contain some other meats). They are similar in size and appearance to British pork sausages, but are generally redder in colour. They are usually fried or grilled. (*231*)

BRITISH PORK SAUSAGE

There are many different regional varieties of British pork sausages – also known as bangers. They are all fresh cooking sausages made from pork, pork fat, spices and cereal with spices or herbs added, depending on the variety (Lincolnshire sausages, for example, are flavoured with sage). They are served as part of the traditional English breakfast with bacon, egg, tomatoes, mushrooms and fried bread. They can be fried, grilled or barbecued. Two traditional English dishes are 'bangers and mash' (fried sausage with mashed potatoes) and 'toad-in-the-hole' (sausages baked in a batter pudding). (*231*)

Cooking Sausages

1 SMALL ITALIAN COOKING SAUSAGES
2 SALSICCIA
3 BLACK PUDDING (SCOTTISH)
4 BRITISH PORK SAUSAGE (SMOKED)
5 BLACK PUDDING (ENGLISH)
6 LUGANEGHE
7 WILD BOAR COOKING SAUSAGE
8 BRATWURST
9 BOUDIN BLANC
10 CUMBERLAND SAUSAGE
11 ANDOUILLETTE
12 SAUCISSE DE TOULOUSE
13 VENISON SAUSAGE
14 BRITISH PORK SAUSAUGE (LINCOLNSHIRE)
15 BRITISH BEEF SAUSAGE

16 BRITISH PORK SAUSAGE
17 CHIPOLATA
18 BRITISH PORK SAUSAGE (COCKTAIL SAUSAGE)
19 AP YEUNG CHEUNG
20 LAP CHEUNG
21 BOCKWURST
22 FRANKFURTER
23 VIENNA
24 KNACKWURST
25 CERVELAS
26 PEPERONE
27 ZAMPONE
28 COTECHINO
29 LOUKANIKA
30 MORCILLA
31 HAGGIS
32 BLACK PUDDING (ENGLISH)
33 BOUDIN NOIR
34 CHORIZO (MILD)
35 CHORIZO (HOT)
36 BASTOURMA

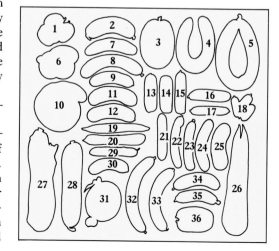

BUTIFARA

A Spanish pork sausage from Catalonia, seasoned with garlic and spices, it is first boiled, then air-dried and generally eaten cold, though it may also be gently cooked. It is less spicy than many of the other Spanish sausages.

CAMBRIDGE SAUSAGE

A very meaty English pork sausage with twice as much lean as fat, it contains pork, herbs and spices and should be grilled or fried.

CERVELAS

This French sausage was originally made with brains, which accounts for the name, although brains are not part of the ingredients today. Short in length, it contains lean and fat pork and is usually flavoured with garlic. It is generally poached in water and eaten hot. See also *Saveloy*. (*231*)

CERVELAT

A large, smoked German sausage containing finely minced pork and beef, this is generally sliced and eaten cold and is similar in appearance to a fine salame. (*235*)

CERVELLATA

A pork sausage made in northern Italy, flavoured with spices, Parmesan cheese and saffron, this originally contained pig's brains which explains its name.

CHIPOLATA

The name for a small British pork sausage which refers to the size – approximately half the size of a normal pork sausage – rather than the contents. Cook in the same way as ordinary British sausages, either fry or grill. (*231*)

CHORIZO

This well-known Spanish sausage comes in many varieties, but all have ingredients in common: pork and the paprika which gives them their distinctive colour. Some are hotter than others. Some varieties are for slicing and eating raw while others are for cooking and are similar in size to the British pork sausage. The cooking variety is an important ingredient in the Spanish dish, *fabada asturiana*, a rich, warming bean and sausage stew. They are generally quite spicy and are used a great deal in Mexican cooking as well as Spanish. They are available both smoked and unsmoked, and are excellent grilled, gently fried or added to a stew. *Linguica* is the Portuguese version of *chorizo*. (*231, 235*)

COTECHINO

A speciality of Emilia-Romagna, this large Italian sausage – (each one weighs between 1–2lb (500g–1kg) – is made from both lean and fat pork, white wine, cloves and cinnamon. It is made both fresh and part-cured for export. The fresh variety should be cooked for several hours, whereas the part-cured variety needs only about half an hour. It is generally served with beans, lentils or mashed potatoes or as part of a *bollito misto* (mixed boiled meats). *Mostarda di frutta*, preserved fruits in a mustard syrup, is the ideal accompaniment. (*231*)

CUMBERLAND SAUSAGE

A popular English pork sausage containing coarsely chopped pork and black pepper, it is sometimes unlinked and sold by the length rather than the weight. It is usually baked. (*231*)

DRISHEEN

An Irish black pudding made with sheep's or pig's blood mixed with cream, breadcrumbs and herbs. It is also known as 'packet' in parts of Ireland. Both are traditionally eaten with tripe.

FRANKFURTER

The original frankfurter sausage comes from Germany and bears little resemblance to the American frankfurter or hot dog which must surely be one of the world's most famous sausages as well as one of the most frequently debased. A genuine German frankfurter should contain finely chopped lean pork and a small amount of salted bacon fat, which are blended into a smooth paste and smoked. The American version contains beef and pork. Frankfurters should be gently heated in hot water, and never boiled or they will split. (*231*)

GARLIC SAUSAGE

This is a smoked slicing sausage made of pork and beef and flavoured with garlic. It is generally served as part of a plate of cold cuts. (*235*)

HAGGIS

A large Scottish sausage made from diced sheep's liver, lungs, heart, oatmeal, onion and suet, seasoned with spice and packed into a sheep's stomach. It requires long slow cooking – simmering in boiling water – and is traditionally served on festive occasions, particularly Burns' Night, with boiled, mashed potatoes, mashed 'neeps' (turnips) and whisky. (*231*)

JAGDWURST

A scalded smoked pork sausage from Germany. It is eaten cold and sliced and is an important ingredient in 'Brunswick salad' (strips of Jagdwurst, mixed with pickled cucumber, tomato, grated apples and cooked French beans with an olive oil dressing). (*235*)

KABANOS

A hard, thin, smoked spicy pork sausage from Poland. Each link is about 12in (30cm) long. Eaten as a snack or cooked with lentils. (*235*)

KATENRAUCHWURST

A large, firm salame-type German sausage made from coarsely cut smoked pork. Eaten in thick slices with bread. (*235*)

KIELBASA *kolbasi, kolbassy*

A highly seasoned sausage of Polish origin, but now very popular in the United States. Made of coarsely ground lean pork and beef, it can be fresh or smoked, cooked or uncooked and is the sausage in *bigos* or Polish hunter's stew.

KNACKWURST

A rather stumpy type of smoked sausage from Germany containing lean pork, beef and fresh fat pork, finely minced and flavoured with spice and garlic, this is served poached or grilled with potato salad. (*231*)

KRAKOWSKA

As the name suggest, this sausage comes from Kraków in Poland. A slicing sausage, similar in size to a salame, it contains smoked pork and beef, garlic, nutmeg and pimento.

LANDJÄGER

A hard, square, German cured sausage containing mostly beef mixed with pork, caraway seeds and garlic. It is both smoked and air-dried and is eaten raw.

LAP CHEUNG

This fairly common Chinese sausage is made from pork, soy sauce, paprika, cereal and alcohol. See also *Ap Yeung Cheung*. (*231*)

LOUKANIKA

A Greek sausage made from coarsely ground pork seasoned with coriander and marinated in red wine. Usually served sliced as part of a Greek mixed hors d'oeuvres, or *meze*. (*231*)

LUGANEGHE

A pure pork sausage from the north of Italy which is unlinked, and is sold by length rather than weight. It can be boiled or grilled. (*231*)

MERGUEZ

A short spicy Algerian sausage, usually grilled, this is made from mutton and sometimes goat meat, it is often served with couscous.

MORCILLA

A Spanish blood sausage which has many different varieties. The most famous is from Asturia and along with *chorizo* is an important ingredient of that province's national dish *fabada* – a stew made from bacon, belly of pork, onions and white beans, *chorizo* and morcilla. (*231*)

MORTADELLA

A very large, slicing sausage from Bologna in Italy made from pork, garlic, coriander seeds and sometimes pistachios, it is often eaten cold, thinly sliced, and is used as a stuffing for some of the homemade pastas in Emilia-Romagna. (*235*)

PEPERONE

This is a hot, dry Italian sausage containing a mixture of coarsely chopped pork and beef, seasoned with red pepper, fennel and spices, often served with pizzas. (*231*)

SALAME

There is a huge range of salami available from all over the world, including Germany, Austria, France, Denmark, Hungary, Romania, Israel (kosher – made with beef), Bulgaria and Spain, but these sausages are essentially Italian. New varieties are constantly being introduced; some are smoked, others have interesting casings, such as black peppercorns or grated apples. They are basically made from uncooked meat, usually a mixture of pork, pork fat, often beef, veal and sometimes wild boar. Various flavourings are added, different spices such as peppercorns, coriander or garlic, paprika, sugar and wine. Some are pickled, others air-dried or smoked. There are as many different types as there are regions.

Danish salame This rather fatty salame has a distinctive bright red or pink colour, due to the colouring added. It may be made from a mixture of pork, beef, veal and pork fat, and has a fine texture and a very salty, smoky flavour.

Hungarian salame Hungarian salami are also made in Italy. They are lightly smoked and contain paprika and other spices.

Italian salame A general guide to Italian salami is that those from the south of Italy tend to be more highly spiced than those from the north.

Salame d'Abbruzzo A flat Italian salame about 12in (30cm) long that is hard and peppery.

Salame dei cacciatori A small salame, about 7in (18cm) long, that is quite soft. The name means hunters' salame; as it is easy to carry in the pocket to eat while out hunting.

Salame calabrese A very peppery salame containing large pieces of fat. It is only about 7in (18cm) long and the links are tied with string, running along each sausage.

Salame di cinghiale A small strong-flavoured salame made from finely minced wild boar meat, sugar, salt and spices.

Salame di Cremona Cremona is supposed to be the place where salami originally came from. It is a large, coarsely chopped salame.

Salame di Felino A good-quality salame made from pure pork, white wine, garlic and whole peppercorns. Many claim this to be the best salame. It comes from near Parma, and is certainly my favourite.

Salame finocchiona A large pure pork salame, mottled with pieces of meat and fat and subtly flavoured with fennel.

Salame fiorentino A larger-than-average salame, about 4in (10cm) in diameter, from Florence. Similar in texture to the *salami finocchiona*, but without the fennel.

Salame genovese This salame is made from a mixture of pork and veal, and additional fat to make up for the dryness of the veal.

Salame milanese A finely mottled salame containing 50 per cent lean and 20 per cent fat pork and the remaining 30 per cent may be either beef or veal. It is seasoned with spice, garlic and peppercorns.

Salame napoletano A long, thin, quite peppery salame from pork and beef, seasoned with red and black pepper.

Salame romano This large, square-shaped salame with chunks of fat and peppercorns is a regional variation from Rome.

Salame toscano A large, rich, dense salame with large chunks of fat and flavoured with white wine, peppercorns and garlic. (*235*)

SALAMELLA

A speciality of Mantova and Cremona in the Lombardy region of Italy, *salamelle* are fresh pork sausages about 5in (12cm) in length. They can be boiled or fried. (*235*)

SALCHICHÓN

The finest *salchichón* comes from Vich in Catalonia. These are Spanish slicing sausages made from pork and spices and smoked. *(235)*

SALSICCIA

These are Italian pork cooking sausages which contain pure pork flavoured with garlic and peppercorns, and can be poached, grilled or fried. (*Salsiccia* is simply the Italian word for sausage.) *(231)*

SAUCISSE

This is the French name for sausage, and generally refers to small fresh sausages which are for cooking and eating hot. There are as many varieties as there are regions of France.

Saucisse de campagne A country-type sausage which is a mixture of lean pork and fat bacon; used in soups and stews.

Saucisse d'Espagne A spicy pork sausage, similar to the *chorizo*.

Saucisse de Frankfort, saucisse de Strasbourg These are both frankfurter-type sausages which should be gently heated in hot water.

Saucisse de Toulouse Made from coarsely chopped pork, this is perhaps the best known of all the French cooking *saucisses*. Similar to the British cooking sausage in appearance but slightly larger, it also can be sold in continuous lengths and is an important ingredient of cassoulet. *(231)*

SAUCISSON SEC

This is the French name for large sausages which are mostly dried and often smoked but are ready to eat and not generally cooked; the only exception is *cervelas*, which is boiled. They are often sold sliced to be eaten as a snack with bread or as part of a plate of cold cuts. The best-known varieties are the following:

Saucisson d'Arles A mixture of finely minced beef and coarsely chopped pork seasoned with garlic, black pepper and peppercorns.

Saucisson de campagne, saucisson de ménage This sausage is made from finely minced lean pork and coarsely chopped hard

back fat, and flavoured with spice and garlic.

Saucisson de Lyon This consists of finely minced leg of pork, diced hard back fat, salt, saltpetre, white peppercorns, ground white pepper, French spice and garlic. The longer it is left to mature the better it tastes.

Jésus A very large, coarsely chopped, pure pork sausage, this is very wide in diameter and can weigh up to 7lb (3·2kg). It is regarded as one of the better-quality *saucissons secs* and is generally eaten raw and sliced.

Rosette A pure pork sausage made from the shoulder of pork wrapped in a natural skin casing, which dries and matures very slowly. *(235)*

SAVELOY

The British version of *cervelas*, this is made from minced smoked and cured pork and cereal. It is most often found in fish and chip shops, where it is deep-fried before serving.

SCHINKENWURST

A mildly flavoured slicing sausage made from flaked ham, ham fat and pork, sometimes flavoured with peppercorns and caraway seeds. Smoked over beech and ash wood to which juniper berries are added, it tends to be quite soft, so chill it in the refrigerator before slicing.

VENISON SAUSAGE

A British sausage containing four parts minced venison to one part either pork or veal, plus spices and herbs, this can be grilled or fried. Wild boar sausages are also available. *(231)*

VIENNA SAUSAGE

This is a common name given to kosher beef sausages with finely minced flesh. They are bright red in colour, vary in size from tiny cocktail ones to finger size, and should be warmed in hot water before serving. *(231)*

WHITE PUDDING

This is a British white sausage containing either pearl barley or groats, suet, leeks, rusk, milk, herbs and sometimes cloves, salt and pepper.

WIENERWURST *Wiene*

It is believed that the *Wienerwurst*, or *Wiene* as it is called in the United States, rather than the frankfurter was the origin of the hot dog. These smoked sausages are sold in amazing quantities on the streets in America, sandwiched between a split bun. Made from beef, pork, coriander and garlic, they should be cooked in the same way as frankfurters.

ZAMPONE DI MODENA

An Italian pork sausage similar to a *cotechino*, except that the meat is stuffed into a boned pig's trotter, it has to be soaked for many hours before it is poached. It is traditionally served with lentils, beans and *mostarda di frutta*. *(231)*

ZUNGENWURST

This is a large smoked sausage from Germany containing pork fat, and sometimes liver and blood, with distinctive chunks of tongue. *(235)*

ZWYIEKA

A Polish slicing sausage made from pork and beef, this is made in long spindly links. *(235)*

Ready-to-Eat Sausages

1	BIERWURST	18	SAUCISSON SEC
2	CERVELAT		(JÉSUS)
3	GARLIC SAUSAGE	19	MORTADELLA
4	SALAME FINOCCHIONA	20	SALAME MILANESE
5	SALAME TOSCANO	21	SALCHICHÓN DE VICH
6	SALAME NAPOLETANO	22	KATENRAUCHWURST
7	HUNGARIAN SALAME	23	LANDJÄGER
8	GERMAN PEPPER SALAME	24	SALAME ROMANO
9	BIERSCHINKEN	25	ZUNGENWURST
10	SALAME GENOVESE	26	KABANOS
11	JAGDWURST	27	ZYWIEKA
12	CHORIZO (HOT)	28	SAUCISSON SEC (SMOKED)
13	SAUCISSON D'ARLES	29	SALAMELLA
14	SALCHICHÓN	30	SALAME DEI CACCIATORI
15	DANISH SALAME	31	CHORIZO HERRADURA
16	PAPRIKA SALAME		
17	GERMAN SALAME		

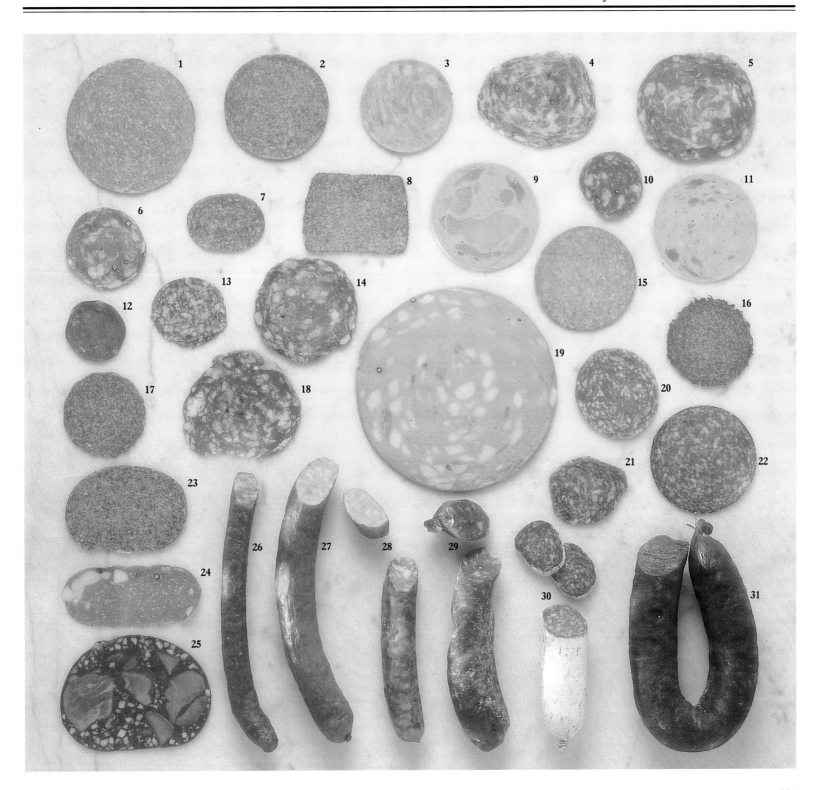

Eggs are a basic and important food in many cultures. They are the subject of myth and legend and have played a major role in religious rites and customs. The Christian tradition of giving eggs on Easter Sunday dates back to the pre-Christian Anglo-Saxon festival of Eostre and symbolizes the arrival of spring, rebirth and fertility. Eggs are acceptable to many non-meat eaters and vegetarians (though not to vegans).

As a form of 'top-class' protein, eggs have no equal. Not only are they a most valuable natural food, they are readily available, easy to prepare, easy to digest and inexpensive. A plainly cooked size three egg contains just over 80 kilocalories and 11 per cent of the recommended daily protein requirement. It contains vitamins A, B and D and several important minerals: iron, calcium and iodine.

COOKING WITH EGGS

Many types of cooking would be impossible without eggs. Egg combines well with other ingredients to produce quite different creations. Among the egg's properties are the following:

Aeration By whisking egg white you trap air into it. When this is folded into other ingredients and baked, the air remains trapped inside and thus soufflés, whisked sponge cakes and meringues stay light and airy.

Thickening By mixing egg yolk into hot but not boiling liquid, the liquid thickens, whether it is a custard, a soup or a sauce.

Emulsification Egg yolk is an emulsifying agent and combines with oil or butter to produce sumptuous mayonnaise or hollandaise sauces. The yolk of the egg will hold many times its volume of melted butter or oil in suspension.

Stabilization The protein (albumen) in egg white is used in making sorbets because it stabilizes the mixture during freezing, minimizing the chance of ice crystals forming.

Coagulation The proteins in egg start to combine or coagulate when heat is applied – cakes, pancakes and batter puddings are all possible because of eggs.

EGG DISHES

As with all really good fresh food, the cook can scarcely improve upon what nature has produced. A fresh egg, lightly boiled so that the white is just set and the yolk rich, golden and runny, then served with some buttered toast or wholemeal bread-and-butter fingers, is one of the tastiest ways to enjoy this versatile food.

But for variety there are many other delicious egg dishes from around the world that can form the basis of inexpensive and quickly prepared everyday dishes, as well as more elaborate dishes for special occasions. Here are a few of my favourites:

Brik à l'oeuf An exciting dish from Tunisia in which a fresh raw egg is enveloped in paper-thin *filo* dough and deep-fried in oil. When you bite into it, the egg yolk spurts all over your fingers if you are not careful.

Eggs benedict, eggs florentine, eggs hussarde are marvellous breakfast dishes which were served originally in New Orleans' restaurants. Poached eggs are served on muffins, or on a bed of spinach (florentine) often with a slice of ham, and then coated with a rich sauce, either hollandaise (benedict) or red wine (hussarde).

Frittata is an Italian version of an omelette where vegetables are cooked in the egg mixture in the frying pan until set, then the top browned lightly under the grill. It can be served hot or cold

Oeufs meurette From Burgundy in France, this is poached eggs served with a rich red wine sauce flavoured with bacon and small onions.

Tortilla is a thick Spanish omelette served in wedges like a cake, often made with potatoes and spinach or green pepper.

Zuppa pavese is a soothing soup from Italy in which boiling hot broth is poured over a raw egg in a heated bowl. Similar soups are found in Spain, Portugal, Malta and Greece and make excellent supper dishes. The Chinese egg drop soup is different in that the beaten raw egg is stirred into the hot broth which sets it in strands.

T*YPES OF EGGS*

Hens' eggs These are usually sold in boxes of multiples of half dozen and dozen. Eggs are graded according to weight by grams. These are: Grade 1 – 70g and over (about 2½oz); Grade 2 – 70–65g (about 2½–2¼oz); Grade 3 – 65–60g (about 2¼–2oz); Grade 4 – 60–55g (about 2oz); Grade 5 – 55–50g (about 2–1¾oz); Grade 6 – 50–45g (about 1¾–1½oz); and Grade 7 – under 45g (under 1½oz). Most cookery book recipes are based on size 3 eggs. Eggs are also graded A, B and C according to quality. A is the freshest grade, B is less fresh (the eggs may have been refrigerated for several weeks) and C is sold only to food manufacturers. Boxes of pre-packed eggs

HANDLING EGGS

Chickens, like many other animals including humans, are subject to a variety of bacteria, many benign and some harmful. Although eggs look as if they are hermetically sealed, the shell is porous. The contents can occasionally become contaminated by bacteria such as salmonella through the birds' feed, through the laying process or through handling, whether from battery reared or free range birds. The risk of contamination is reduced if high standards of cleanliness are practised by the producer.

Storing eggs Refrigerated eggs keep well for up to two weeks. Eggs absorb smells easily so always store them away from strong-smelling foods. Bring them to room temperature about 30 minutes before using and don't use cracked or dirty eggs. Eggs should be stored, unwashed, with the pointed end downwards. A fresh egg should feel heavy and well-filled, and will sink to the bottom if put in water.

Cooking eggs The application of a certain degree of heat kills bacteria, but many of the egg's unique properties require that it should be only lightly cooked or indeed used in its raw state. We must be aware of the risks we are taking if we use fresh or raw eggs to make homemade mayonnaise and lemon curd, runny omelettes, moist scrambled eggs, light soufflés, gently poached eggs, three-minute boiled eggs, airy pavlovas and meringues or silky custard sauces. For those susceptible to or anxious about infection, pasteurized eggs, heat-treated to kill any potentially harmful bacteria, are available, either in a frozen or dried form, as whole egg or whites or yolks only, and this circumvents any possible risks, although the products are not suitable for mayonnaise and lemon curd.

are stamped with the packing date and size of egg and sometimes with a 'sell by' date too.

Over 90 per cent of egg farming in Britain uses the battery system but these eggs do not have to be labelled as such. Other intensive systems include deep litter and perchery.

Commercially raised free-range eggs come from hens which have continuous daytime access to open-air runs and are limited to a maximum of 404 birds per acre. It is still possible, however, to buy eggs from farms and smallholdings where the hens live, roam and feed freely on wheat, maize and whatever they pick up in the barnyard, rather than on specially formulated animal protein feed.

There is no difference in flavour or nutritional quality between white and brown eggs. The colour is solely dependent on the breed of hen and not on how the hen is fed. Brown eggs, particularly speckled ones, have an image of rural wholesomeness but this is pure illusion. The colour of shell does not determine quality.

Specialist hen breeders may sometimes have surplus eggs for sale. Use these in exactly the same way as you would use any hens' eggs. Some of the types available are: Aracana (a medium-sized, blue egg, not unlike a small duck egg); Black Peking (a small pale creamy-grey egg); Buff Plymouth Rock (a small pale egg, very similar to the Black Peking); and Wellsummer (a relatively large dark-brown egg).

Duck eggs These are available all the year round but mainly in the spring and summer laying seasons. Duck eggs should always be well cooked and never eaten with runny yolks. Because of their size (they tend to be a little larger than hens' eggs) and rich flavour, they are particularly suitable for baking. Some of the types available are: Barbary or Muscovy (a largish egg, rounded and a pale creamy colour); Blue (a medium-sized, greyish-blue egg); Khaki Campbell (a medium-sized white or pale grey egg); and White (a tapering oval egg, quite large and creamy white in colour).

Goose eggs Because geese are not reared intensively they follow the natural breeding cycle, laying eggs from spring onwards. The eggs are available from about Eastertime and are very popular with those who like to blow and colour eggs for the Easter table as they are about twice the size of hens' eggs. Geese are farmyard animals and likely to lay their eggs in all kinds of places without any regard for hygiene. The eggs should therefore be thoroughly cooked and are particularly good in baking.

Guinea fowl eggs These small, pretty, brown eggs are not widely available commercially. Those that escape predators are more likely to be used for hatching than for the table. They are rich, with an excellent flavour, and are usually served hard-boiled in salads.

Gull eggs Seagulls nest in such precarious positions that this in itself protects their eggs from human predators. Slightly smaller than hens' eggs, gull eggs are said to be a delicacy with their fishy flavour and are sometimes available, particularly from Scottish game dealers. They are usually hard-boiled and eaten with a sprinkling of celery salt.

Pigeon eggs These are small white eggs, although not as small as you might think given the size of the bird. Often found in Chinese and French restaurants, they are usually served lightly poached in a rich consommé made from pigeon meat.

Red-legged partridge and pheasant eggs Some game dealers dispose of their surplus stocks of these small eggs, and they have an excellent flavour.

Quail eggs Once a hard-to-find delicacy and quite expensive, these attractive, small, dark-speckled eggs are now quite common because of the increase in quail farming. Often eaten soft- or hard-boiled, they are extremely difficult to shell when still warm so you need to allow plenty of time for this if serving them at a dinner party. The traditional accompaniment to hard-boiled quail eggs is a sprinkling of celery salt.

Quail eggs make perfect cocktail snacks or starters – one idea might be to serve a selection of quail egg dishes as a starter; choose from among tiny individual eggs benedict, miniature omelettes filled with cream cheese and tied with a chive stalk, poached quail eggs in small pastry cases and soft-boiled quail eggs arranged on salad greens.

Turkey eggs Large, brown and delicately flavoured, turkey eggs are much too expensive to be a commercial proposition. But they are of excellent quality so chat up your local turkey farmer!

Eggs

1 BARBARY OR MUSCOVY DUCK	7 KHAKI CAMPBELL DUCK
2 LINCOLNSHIRE DUCK (WHITE)	8 BUFF PLYMOUTH ROCK HEN
3 WELLSUMMER HEN	9 ARACANA HEN
4 LINCOLNSHIRE DUCK (BLUE)	10 GUINEA FOWL
5 WHITE HEN	11 BLACK PEKING HEN
6 BROWN HEN	12 PIGEON
	13 QUAIL

COOKING FATS

Butter, margarine, lard and suet, ghee, drippings and synthetic fats all have their different uses in cooking. They can be chosen for flavour, texture or cooking properties, depending on what you are making.

There are two main types of fats: unsaturated and saturated: the unsaturated fats can be mono-unsaturated or polyunsaturated, are usually of vegetable origin and are soft at room temperature or in oil form. These are used in some low-calorie spreads, soft margarine and the white vegetable fats. From a health point of view, polyunsaturated fats are preferable as they do not build up deposits of cholesterol in the blood.

Saturated fats are usually of animal origin and will remain solid at room temperature. They include butter, dripping, lard, suet and hard margarine.

Fat has many uses in the kitchen apart from just cooking. It can be used to give flavour and richness to food, for instance dressing vegetables just before serving with a knob of butter. Fat moistens food and makes it easier to swallow, for instance, butter on bread.

Deep- and shallow-frying require fat of some kind as a cooking medium. If the fat has a flavour of its own it will impart this to whatever is cooked in it, so it is important to choose a bland, neutral fat, or one with a flavour you like. All fats have a 'smoke point' and should not be heated to this point as they begin to deteriorate and produce toxic fumes. Dispose of any fat heated to smoking point and start again. Pure oils, such as corn oil, rather than a blended vegetable oil, are better for frying as their smoke point is at a higher temperature. Margarine should not be used for deep-frying as it contains about 16 per cent water and is prone to spattering. All of the low-fat spreads also contain water. In shallow-frying, fats and oils can be mixed in order to raise the smoke point. The best example is oil added to butter for cooking. Butter adds flavour, oil helps to prevent burning.

It is also important to choose a fat rather than an oil for greasing tins, since butter or lard, for instance, do not break down at high temperatures and become sticky, as do some oils when they are spread in a thin film.

Another use for edible fats is in baking where they soften and 'shorten' what would otherwise be a tough flour and water dough. Some cooks prefer to use butter for a good flavour; some say lard is best because they like a very short, crumbly texture; others use a mixture of butter and lard. Some people prefer not to use animal fat and so will choose one of the hydrogenated vegetable fats.

The solid fats keep well in the refrigerator but should be tightly covered as they readily absorb other flavours. Some of the rendered (melted) fats, drippings and suets, as well as butter, will be at their best for only two to four weeks; others will last much longer. The hydrogenated fats will keep for a couple of months. See also OILS, page 121, and BUTTER, page 243.

COCONUT OIL

This is used as a cooking medium in South-East Asia, India and other parts of the tropics where the coconut palm grows. Dense, white, rich and buttery, more fat-like than oily, it imparts a coconut flavour to food cooked in it.

CONCENTRATED PALM OIL *dendê*

When I first came across this in Nigeria it looked for all the world like orange shoe polish, so thick and waxy was it. It comes from the oil palm and is one of the main cooking fats of West Africa, the Caribbean and Central and South America.

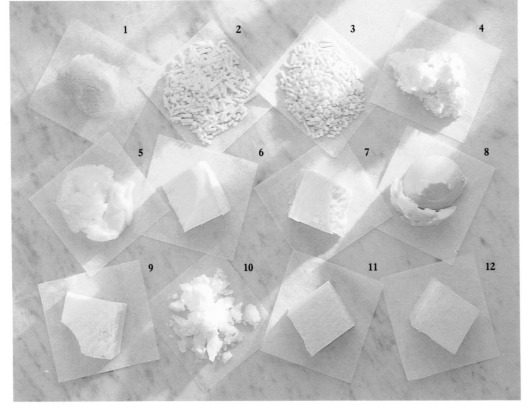

Animal Fats

1 VEGETABLE GHEE	7 DRIPPING (BEEF)
2 SUET (BEEF)	8 MARGARINE (SOFT)
3 SUET (VEGETABLE)	9 HYDROGENATED
4 CONCENTRATED PALM	FAT
OIL	10 COCONUT OIL
5 GOOSE FAT	11 MARGARINE (HARD)
6 HYDROGENATED FAT	12 LARD
(SOLID VEGETABLE OIL)	

It is rather tasty and nutty. Much palm oil finds its way, decoloured and deodorized, into vegetable fats and margarines identified simply as 'vegetable oils' or 'vegetable fats'. I would use it in highly spiced and coloured dishes, but remember that it is very high in saturated fats.

DRIPPING

This homely product is derived from the fats and juices released from a joint of meat when it is being roasted. When the fat cools there is a thick layer of clear jellied meat juices underneath. The fat portion is high in both saturated and mono-unsaturated fats. It can be used for frying and for making pastry.

Beef dripping is the most common but dripping can be derived from lamb and bacon too. If you are collecting dripping, fats from different meats should be kept separately. Melted bacon dripping can be used to 'wilt' a green salad and adds a good flavour. Beef dripping is often used for frying chips. See also *Goose Fat*.

GHEE

Traditionally ghee is a form of clarified butter – butter which has been heated gently until all the water in it has evaporated and the milk solids fall to the bottom; the fat left on top will cook at high temperatures without burning. It is used particularly in Indian cooking.

A special vegetable ghee is made for those vegetarians who do not eat any animal products. This is processed from hydrogenated vegetable oils and is not unlike vegetable margarine. See also BUTTER, page 243.

GOOSE FAT

This is used mainly in Alsace and south-western France where it is produced commercially, for export as well as for domestic purposes. You can obtain it yourself when roasting a goose simply by setting the goose on a rack in the roasting pan and draining off the fat periodically. Store it, when cool, in the refrigerator. Like all animal fats it is high in saturated fats, but is nevertheless an extremely good cooking medium. It is a soft, well-flavoured fat which produces marvellous roast potatoes; it can also be used for pastry.

HYDROGENATED FAT

Usually sold in blocks in Britain and in cans in the United States, hydrogenated (hardened) fats were first developed around the turn of the century in France and in Britain. It was an important development in which liquid oils were converted into semi-solid fats. In this way inexpensive oils from seeds and grains, such as cotton seeds, corn and soya bean, could be substituted for the much more expensive butter and lard in cooking and baking, both on a domestic and a commercial scale. The oils are processed into a bland white fat which can be used in place of lard or butter, although it is without the texture or taste of either one.

Vegetable ghee, solid vegetable fats and hard margarine are all hydrogenated fats. However, it should be noted that the hydrogenation process which hardens the fat, also changes poly-unsaturated fats into saturated fats. Hydrogenated fats contain as many calories as other saturated fats such as butter.

LARD

This is rendered, purified and clarified pork fat, the fat being taken from the back and around the kidneys. Traditionally lard was the main fat used for cooking in Scandinavia, Western Europe above the olive oil belt, both North and South America, Eastern Europe and Russia, and it is still widely used today. Even in Spain, a large producer and user of olive oil, lard is also used, often coloured and flavoured with paprika or annatto seeds. Many home pastrycooks maintain that lard is the best fat for making crisp, flaky, tender pastry. For much general cooking lard has now been superseded by hydrogenated fats and cooking oils.

MARGARINE

The name is derived from the Greek word for pearl, *margaron*. Margarine was 'invented' in the late nineteenth century by a French chemist, as an inexpensive substitute for butter. Basically it is a smooth, pale yellow fat, suitable for some cooking and baking and for table use. But the subject is much more complicated than that. Margarines are made from a wide variety of ingredients and combinations of ingredients. Hard margarine will be made up of hydrogenated fats. Soft margarine may be made up of unhydrogenated fats. Some margarines contain animal ingredients in the form of whey, skim milk or butter fat, other margarines are made solely from vegetable sources. Some are high in polyunsaturated fats; others simply labelled 'vegetable oils or fats' may contain palm oil or coconut oil, high in saturated fats.

Margarine is not lower in calories than butter. Some margarine may be lower in cholesterol than butter; but since it has the same fat content of around 80 per cent it is as high in calories as butter. Margarine usually contains additives – to emulsify, to stabilize, to colour and to flavour. Margarine by law also has to contain certain levels of Vitamin A and Vitamin D.

Use margarine in the same way as you would use butter; but do not expect it to taste the same.

MUTTON FAT

This is the rendered fat of mutton and lamb. It is hard and creamy white. The flavour is strong, distinctive and noticeable in any dish which has been cooked in mutton fat. It is used mostly in Middle Eastern cookery where lamb and mutton are the main meats.

SHORTENING

This now is more commonly used as a cooking term in the United States. It refers to any edible fat, in solid or liquid form, used for pastry-making to give a rich, crisp or 'short' texture to the basic flour and water mix which would otherwise be tough when cooked. When no particular type is specified you can use butter, lard or one of the hydrogenated fats.

SUET

The very hard, crisp white fat surrounding beef kidneys is grated and floured for domestic use, or processed further for commercial use. This is known as suet and it is a traditional fat used in baking, particularly for pastry and puddings. Hard or hydrogenated vegetable oils are now prepared in the same way so that vegetarians can enjoy 'suet' puddings and pastry.

Milk has been an important source of food for thousands of years and today is highly valued for its versatility, too. As well as a good variety of milks (from cows, ewes and goats), there are the byproducts – cheese, butter, cream, buttermilk, whey, yogurt and soured cream.

MILK IN THE KITCHEN

Milk contains fat, protein, carbohydrates in the form of milk sugar (lactose), calcium, phosphorus, sodium and potassium; also vitamins A, C, D, and the B vitamins riboflavin, thiamine and B12, and small amounts of minerals and salts.

Apart from its use in drinks, favourite puddings such as rice or tapioca pudding cannot be made properly without milk. Use milk also to enrich vegetable soups. Combine it with flour and butter for the traditional béchamel and roux sauces. Enrich meat sauces, such as an Italian *ragù* that you serve with pasta, by adding milk in the early stages of preparation before you add any other liquid. Let it evaporate then add wine, tomatoes or other ingredients.

Milk curdles or separates easily, so if you are using it, say, in a sauce, or heating it to serve with coffee, heat it gently and remove it from the heat before it boils.

COWS' MILK

Pasteurized milk Much of the fresh cows' milk sold in Britain is pasteurized and there are *no* exceptions in the United States. This heat treatment kills harmful bacteria in the milk but does not prevent later contamination.

This general-purpose milk, sold in silver topped bottles or in labelled cartons, contains about four per cent fat. It keeps for four to five days in a refrigerator.

Homogenized milk Sold in red-topped bottles or appropriately labelled cartons, it has the same fat content as pasteurized milk, but has been further subjected to homogenization, which permanently breaks up and disperses the fat through the milk. It can be used in all recipes requiring milk.

Semi-skimmed milk With a fat content of 1·5–1·8 per cent, this tastes less rich than full-cream milk, but it is perfectly good for use in

tea and coffee, and for making sauces and pancake batter. It is sold in bottles with silver and red-striped tops, or in labelled cartons.

Skimmed milk A fat content of no more than 0·3 (but more typically 0·1) per cent makes this ideal for anyone wishing to cut down their fat intake. But it is not suitable for babies and children. Since most of the fat has been removed, along with it has gone the fat-soluble vitamins A and D, although the other nutrient levels remain the same. The milk looks thinner and some prefer it in tea and coffee because it is less fatty tasting. Sold in bottles with blue and silver checked-tops, or in labelled cartons, it can also be used in soups, sauces and cakes.

There is also available a type of skimmed milk which has had some of the skimmed solids added back to give it body, together with vitamins A and D.

Channel Islands and **Jersey milk** This is the very best for milk puddings, bread-and-butter pudding, caramel cream and anything that requires rich milk as it has four to eight per cent fat. It is sold in gold-topped bottles.

Raw, untreated, unpasteurized milk is clearly labelled 'raw unpasteurized milk'. The milk undergoes stringent testing and comes from cows certified as brucellosis free. It is also filtered before bottling. Many consider it to have a very good flavour, arguing that pasteurization produces comparatively bland milk, but it is a contentious issue and this type of milk should be avoided by the very young or old, and by pregnant women.

Acidophilus milk Pasteurization of milk not only kills dangerous bacteria but also the harmless, even beneficial bacteria which act upon milk to ripen and mature its flavour. Acidophilus milk has been pasteurized and then the benign acidophilus bacteria, in a dormant state, is put back into the milk. It is said to help balance the bacteria in the digestive tract which, in turn, helps the digestion and absorption of food generally.

Buttermilk is a byproduct of butter-making and is the thin, rather unstable liquid which remains after the fat globules have coagulated to form butter. What is usually sold as 'buttermilk' is a 'cultured buttermilk' – a skimmed milk, pasteurized, cooled and inoculated with a special culture which ferments under controlled condi-

tions. This produces the characteristic acid quality which makes it so good for use in making scones and soda bread.

COWS' MILK – CREAM

This liquid butterfat content of whole cows' milk is separated from the milk, pasteurized (except where it is deliberately made into unpasteurized cream, which I find has an exquisite flavour) and then cooled and packed. Or it may first be given further treatment such as homogenization, UHT (ultra-heat treatment) or sterilization. A variety of creams are available, each one suitable for particular dishes or usages. The calorie content of each type depends on its fat level and ranges from 140 for 3½fl. oz (100ml) for half cream to 590 for clotted cream.

All cream should be kept refrigerated and used within two to three days. Keep it tightly covered so that it does not pick up the flavours of other stored foods. Treat UHT creams as fresh creams once opened.

Half cream The thinnest, lightest cream, this is suitable for pouring, and particularly good in coffee and on breakfast cereals. It also enriches milk puddings or homemade yogurt. However it cannot be whipped nor can it replace heavier creams in sauces as it dilutes rather than enriches. UHT half cream is also available.

Single cream Although its fat content is too low to allow for whipping, single cream has many uses. As well as being perfect with fresh fruit salad, breakfast cereals and in coffee, I stir it into soups just before serving them. It is also available in UHT form.

Whipping cream The high butterfat content of this cream, and the fact that it has not been homogenized, allows for whipping. The cream, bowl and whisk should be cold to achieve at least double the volume. A wire whisk lets you feel the texture of the cream changing and you will know to stop before you have whisked it irrevocably into butter and whey. An electric beater or rotary whisk is heavier and there is slightly less control over the texture. Once whipped, it can be piped into decorative whirls on cakes, trifles and other cold desserts, but it will not hold its shape on a hot dish. Fold it into sweets and mousses for a light texture. The cream is also suitable for pouring and can be added to soups and sauces. It is also available in UHT form.

Double cream adds richness of flavour and texture to a wide range of dishes, and is the basis of desserts such as *crème brûlée* and ice-creams. For an even quicker sweet, fold a flavouring such as coffee essence or orange liqueur into whipped double cream and sprinkle toasted almonds, hazelnuts or coconut on top.

Double cream can be whipped but take care not to overwhip it into butter. Adding 1–2 tablespoons of milk to a ¼pt (150ml) double cream helps avoid this and gives extra volume.

Extra-thick double cream A spooning cream rather than a whipping cream, this has been homogenized to disperse the butterfat globules. Serve it with pies, puddings and fruit salads.

Clotted cream The richest of all, this thick yellow cream is a speciality of Devon, Cornwall and Somerset. Spread it thick on warm scones. It is marvellous, too, with apple pie and steamed puddings.

Crème fraîche This important ingredient in French cooking is treated with a culture that gives it a light acidity without sourness. I make a version which is quite close. On the yogurt principle, as a starter I mix buttermilk into whipping or double cream, in a one to two or one to three ratio, heating it to about 75°F (25°C). Then I partially cover it and let it stand for six hours before placing it in the refrigerator, where it will keep for two to three weeks. Soured cream or yogurt can also be the starter.

Smetana, smitane, smatana A soured cream, much used in Russia and Eastern Europe as a sauce or liaison ingredient, both in sweet and savoury dishes, this is also made commercially in Britain, from skimmed milk, single cream and a souring culture. It is a good, low-fat substitute for cream. In cooking, add it towards the end

and do not let it boil, or curdling will occur.

Soured cream This is not a cream which has gone sour through age, but a commercial preparation, with approximately the same fat content as single cream. (Pasteurized cream does not turn sour through age; it becomes bitter and unusable even in cooking.) It is made from homogenized cream with a 'souring' culture added. Use it to enhance casseroles such as goulash, to enrich soups, as the basis of flavoured dips, and spooned on to baked potatoes.

Spooning cream To give it a thick, spoonable consistency, this has been vigorously homogenized. It is high in butterfat but will not whip because of the homogenization. Serve it as a table cream with puddings, pies and other sweets. It can also be used for sauces but will not behave like double cream; it becomes thinner on contact with heat.

Whipped cream Sold ready whipped, this has the same fat content as whipping cream, contains stabilizers to maintain the texture and may also contain sugar.

COWS' MILK – LONG LIFE

This does not taste quite as good as fresh milk but is a useful 'reserve' and is perfectly accept-

able in cooking. Once opened, it should be treated as fresh milk.

Condensed milk can be sweetened or unsweetened, and made from whole, partly skimmed or skimmed homogenized milk, which is heated to 176°F (80°C) for 15 minutes, during which time the sugar may be added. The mixture is then subjected to further very high heat until it is 2½ times more concentrated than the original milk. Condensed milk is rich and creamy, with a sticky texture. It makes wonderful toffee and fudge.

Dehydrated milk, dried milk, milk powder, powdered milk For the most part this is made from spray-dried skimmed milk. Some has vegetable fats added which give it the same nutritional value as whole milk once reconstituted. It can be used in cooking, but is inferior to the other long-life milks in tea and coffee.

Evaporated milk As its name suggests, some of the water content has been removed from this to achieve twice the concentration of ordinary milk. This rich, thick and creamy liquid can be used in cooking, reconstituted with water or as it is. Because it has been subjected to high heat it has a slightly cooked flavour. A milk pudding made with evaporated milk will have a rather pronounced 'creamy' flavour.

Milks, Creams and Yogurts

1	NATURAL YOGURT (FULL CREAM)
2	CRÈME FRAÎCHE
3	FRENCH-STYLE YOGURT
4	SKIMMED MILK
5	GOATS' MILK
6	CLOTTED CREAM
7	DOUBLE CREAM
8	GREEK YOGURT
9	JERSEY MILK
10	SINGLE CREAM
11	NATURAL YOGURT (GOATS' MILK)
12	SOYA MILK
13	PASTEURIZED WHOLE MILK

241

Sterilized milk Homogenized, bottled and sealed, the milk is then further heat-treated (sterilized). This caramelizes the milk sugars slightly, giving the milk a lightly cooked flavour. Unopened, it keeps for two to three months.

UHT In the ultra-heat treatment, homogenized milk is briefly heated to 270°F (132·2°C). Packed into sterile, foil-lined cartons, it has a shelf life of several months, but once it has been opened it should be used as fresh milk. Whole, skimmed and semi-skimmed milk are all available in UHT form.

EWES' MILK

Ewes' milk is very rich, with a higher fat content than cows' milk. Very white, slightly thick and a little sweet, it is ideal for milk puddings and can be used in the same ways as cows' milk.

GOATS' MILK

Goats' milk is drunk by more than half of the world's population, but in Britain only now is it becoming more widely known. It looks like cows' milk, has a similar composition and can be used in the same ways although it is a little stronger and tangier in taste.

SOYA MILK

Milky substances can be derived from various nuts, roots and beans. Soya milk retains most of the high nutritional value of the soya bean. It can be used in cooking though it has a tendency to curdle in very hot tea. It does not taste like dairy milk: some brands have a slightly bitter flavour, while others contain sugar to counteract this. Soya milk is acceptable in the diet of people who are lactose intolerant.

YOGURT

With the exception of pasteurized and 'long-life' yogurts, yogurt is a live product: two active beneficial bacteria, *Lactobacillus bulgaricus* and *Streptococcus thermophilus*, are introduced into pasteurized and usually homogenized milk. This culture breaks down lactose (milk sugar) into lactic acid, and gives yogurt its sharp, refreshing flavour.

The nutritional qualities of yogurt vary enormously according to whether it has been made with whole or skimmed milk, and whether it has had cream, sugar or fruit added. It may also contain gelatine, starch, preservatives and colouring which may or may not be natural; check the label.

Store all yogurt except the long-life type in the refrigerator, covered to prevent it from absorbing off-taints or drying out. Do not use after the 'best before' date, because it will begin to go off as the bacteria continue to develop.

YOGURT IN THE KITCHEN

While yogurt is a delicious food in its own right it is also very useful to add to casseroles and soups, and as the basis for sauces and dips. Its natural acidity makes it a good marinade for meats and it also makes an excellent salad dressing. The traditional Greek *tzatziki* is a refreshing mixture of yogurt, cucumber and garlic.

A variety of cold drinks, too, can be made in a blender with ice or iced-water. Try yogurt with ripe mangoes or peaches, or with blackcurrant and fresh mint leaves.

Using yogurt as a replacement for cream in hot dishes such as soups and casseroles is not so easy because boiled yogurt curdles, but it can be stirred into a hot dish just before serving. In order to cook with it, yogurt needs to be stablized first: stir a teaspoon of cornflour into a tablespoon of cold water, then stir this into up to 1pt (600ml) of yogurt. Pour into a pan, bring to simmering point and simmer gently for ten minutes.

There are several different types of yogurt which themselves may vary somewhat in their characteristics with different producers.

Natural, plain yogurt This is simply milk to which 'yogurt' cultures have been added. It may be set or not depending on whether incubated in the carton, or in churns or tanks then sliced. It has a clean, slightly acidic, refreshing flavour and is a most useful ingredient for sweet and savoury dishes, in soups, salad dressings, drinks and with breakfast cereals. Use it as a starter for making more yogurt.

Low-fat yogurt Made from concentrated skimmed milk, low-fat yogurt has between 0·5 and 2 per cent fat. Very-low-fat yogurt is made from skimmed milk and contains less than 0·5

per cent fat. Low-fat yogurt comes in plain, and sweetened fruit varieties. The plain can be used as you would other natural yogurts.

Greek or **Greek-style yogurt** This can be made from either cows' or ewes' milk. The ewes' milk yogurt is rich and creamy, with a fat content of about six per cent. Much of the cows' milk Greek yogurt is strained to concentrate the flavour, the texture and the fat content (around 9–10 per cent). This yogurt is marvellous with a compote of dried or fresh fruits. Its higher fat content neutralizes the acidity to some extent and makes it seem sweeter than other natural yogurts. For a very quick sweet, spoon it into glasses or bowls, run a layer of clear honey over the top and scatter with toasted flaked almonds. It is excellent in soups and sauces when stabilized first as described earlier.

French or **French-style set yogurt** This is made from low-fat homogenized milk which has been allowed to set in the pot. In France it is possible to buy a type of set yogurt made from unhomogenized milk which has a layer of rich, golden cream on the top. Although it can be used in cooking, its full, smooth flavour is best appreciated when it is eaten on its own.

Goats' milk yogurt Ideal for those who are allergic to cows' milk products, this tastes rich, yet has the characteristic slightly acidic flavour. Because its composition is slightly different from that of cows' milk it does not curdle when cooked so it can be used without first being stabilized.

Long-life yogurt To increase the shelf life by weeks, if not months (it is not refrigerated), some yogurt is pasteurized – which kills off the yogurt culture. In flavour and texture it resembles live yogurt but as it contains no live culture it cannot be used as a starter for making more yogurt.

Drinking yogurt, fruit yogurt It is easy to make your own drinking yogurt by thinning down a plain yogurt with milk (whole, skimmed or semi-skimmed). If you want sweetened yogurt, simply stir in honey or sugar. Fruit yogurts are delicious. In summer, stir chopped peaches and raspberries into a bowl of stirred plain yogurt. In autumn, try blackberries or blueberries. In winter, add grated pears and chopped walnuts. In spring, use ginger and fresh cooked rhubarb.

BUTTER

Butter is made by vigorously shaking milk until the fat globules become a solidified mass. This usually contains about 80 per cent fat, not more than 16 per cent water, and may also contain salt and/or lactic acid cultures. Unfortunately, it has to be said that its very high fat content makes butter high in calories also: 740 calories in 3½oz (100g).

Incidentally, butter can be made from the milk of many mammals. In India, for example, a clarified butter or ghee is made from water buffalo milk. In Tibet yaks' milk is used in butter-making, and in the Middle East ewes' milk.

BUTTER IN THE KITCHEN

Butter is ideal for making rich flavoursome cakes and biscuits and exquisite pastry. However it is not the easiest of fats to use for frying because it also contains water, milk deposits and salt, and therefore burns at a lower temperature than many other oils. A teaspoon of oil added to the butter prevents it from burning so easily. Clarified butter, concentrated butter and ghee, which all have a higher fat content and fewer deposits, are generally more suitable for frying.

Most often butter is added at the end of cooking to season or enrich dishes such as broccoli or mashed potatoes. But use a light hand; it is easy to overpower their individual flavours.

Many classic sauces use butter; *beurre meunier* (butter and lemon juice); *beurre blanc* (white wine and/or stock, seasoning and chilled butter whisked in at the end of cooking time); *beurre noisette* (butter which has been allowed to cook to a nut brown and to which vinegar is added); hollandaise sauce (made with eggs on the same principle as mayonnaise).

Flavoured butters are easily made at home: just mix the chosen ingredient into softened butter. Herb butters are delicious with fish, poultry or vegetables. Garlic, onions or chives turn butter rancid after a while so only make such mixtures as and when required. Sieved anchovies or sardines, mustard, tomato purée, crushed walnuts or hazelnuts, capers, olives, watercress and celery are just a few other ingredients which can be added to butter with good effect.

TYPES OF BUTTER

There are two main types: sweet cream and lactic butter; both may be salted or unsalted.

Sweet cream butter is made from pasteurized cream and is usually lightly salted.

Lactic butter is the type traditionally made in Denmark, Holland and France. The cream is mostly pasteurized, inoculated with a culture which ripens the butter, then pasteurized once more to arrest the ripening process.

Salted butter This popular butter was originally salted to preserve it for the winter months when fresh butter was not made. Later, imported butter from New Zealand was salted to preserve it during its long sea voyage. With 3 per cent or more of salt, it is labelled 'salted'. With only 1–2·5 per cent salt it need not be so labelled, although some is marked 'slightly salted'.

Unsalted (sweet) butter Pale, creamy and 'sweet', unsalted butter is now produced in Britain as well as imported from France, Denmark and Holland. That from the Normandy countryside around Vire, towards Brittany, and Poitou-Charente in the west of France is the finest I have eaten. The best unsalted butter stays firm, so it is excellent for puff pastry.

Clarified butter You can make this at home by gently heating cubed butter up to boiling point, then allowing it to separate and straining off the pure melted butter. Because the water and solids have thus been removed the butter is more stable and can be cooked to a higher temperature, but it is not used for deep-frying.

Ghee is a clarified butter originating in India but now made elsewhere. It has a more distinctive flavour than other clarified butter because it is cooked a little more in the clarifying process. It is also made from a stronger-flavoured cream.

Whey butter A byproduct of cheese-making, this is made by separating the residue of cream from the whey drained from the cheese curds. The cream is then made into butter.

Concentrated butter As the moisture and other deposits have been removed to give a butterfat content of 96 per cent, this can be cooked at a higher temperature – like clarified butter – and is excellent for shallow-frying. It is also very economical for baking – you need less. But add a little extra liquid since there is so little in the butter, and recipes normally take account of the

water content of ordinary butter. It will keep for at least three months in a refrigerator.

Butter substitutes There are something like 200 'yellow fats' on the market, many designed to taste and look like butter. They are made from combinations of animal and vegetable fats, colouring, stabilizers and preservatives. Some have the same fat content as butter or margarine. Others have a large proportion of water whipped in; these contain less fat and fewer calories. See also COOKING FATS, page 238.

Butters

1 SWEET CREAM BUTTER (SLIGHTLY SALTED)
2 SALTED BUTTER
3 UNSALTED BUTTER (NORMANDY)
4 WHEY BUTTER
5 CONCENTRATED BUTTER
6 SWEET CREAM BUTTER (SALTED)
7 GHEE

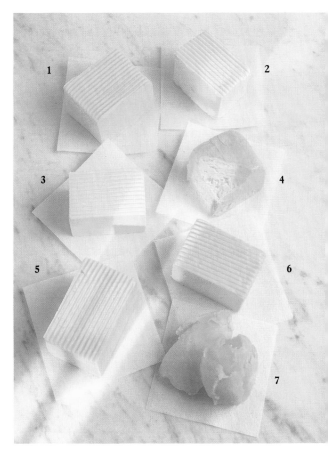

CHEESE

Cheese, once described as 'milk's leap to immortality', goes back thousands of years to the first livestock farmers who discovered, probably by accident, that surplus milk – left to curdle then drained and salted – was good to eat. From these simple beginnings, cheesemaking has evolved into a sophisticated process with endless variations – but the basic principles remain the same and begin with milk.

MILK
Although goats' and ewes' milk cheeses are common in some regions – and in Italy the milk of water buffaloes is used for cheesemaking – most of the world's cheeses are made from cows' milk. It may be whole, skimmed, semi-skimmed or cream-enriched and this determines the fat content of the cheese and helps shape its character. Whether the milk comes from a morning or evening milking (many cheeses are a mixture) is also significant. So is the grazing: hay, young spring grass or – best of all – rich summer grass.

Ewes' and goats' milk cheeses are traditional in harsh inhospitable landscapes where these animals can thrive better than cattle. But the availability of their milk is highly seasonal, so production is relatively limited – unlike cows' milk cheese which is made all year. Sheep and goat cheeses have distinctive flavours: the former has a sharper flavour than a cows' milk cheese, the latter tastes tangier.

Another factor that affects milk – and thence cheese – is pasteurization: partial sterilization which destroys potentially harmful bacteria and ensures consistency. Most cows' and goats' milk used for cheese-making is pasteurized, especially for factory-made cheese. Ewes' milk generally remains unpasteurized. Although pasteurization is necessary to mass production, experts – both those who make cheese and those who eat it – often claim it dilutes a cheese's character; hence some cheesemakers prefer unpasteurized milk. Given the high standards of hygiene applied to modern cheesemaking, the use of unpasteurized milk does not present a threat to normally healthy adults, though unpasteurized cheeses that have been ripened for a few weeks only, such as Brie and Camembert, should be avoided by small children, the elderly or sick, and pregnant women.

HOW CHEESE IS MADE
Essentially, cheesemaking comprises five stages. First the milk is acidified, or soured, by warming it and introducing a starter culture, and when the correct acidity has been reached rennet (or a vegetarian equivalent) is added; this coagulates the milk, separating it into solid curds and liquid whey. Then the curd is cut, or broken up, and drained. The fineness of the cut affects the amount of whey left in the cheese which in turn determines its character. Fresh soft cheeses are cut sparingly, but hard cheeses are cut into very tiny pieces. With extra-hard cheeses the curd is 'cooked'; this shrinks it, making it easier to extract the maximum moisture.

Next the curds are put into moulds which vary in shape and size from the small pyramid shapes typical of many goats' cheeses to the huge drum shapes for Emmental and Parmesan. In some cases they are hand-moulded. They may be left to finish off draining naturally, or pressed – the extent affects the firmness of the cheese.

Finally, except for very fresh cheeses such as cream cheese and Mozzarella, the cheese is ripened: as little as a month for soft cheeses like Brie and Camembert, up to three years for extra-hard types such as Sbrinz and Parmesan. During the maturation period some cheeses develop blue veining; others acquire holes. The rind also develops during ripening. It may be a tough crust, formed naturally as the cheese dries out; it may be artificial – perhaps wax, leaves or ashes; or, on a soft cheese, a bloomy white mould or an orange-yellow mould may be encouraged to develop.

CHOOSING AND STORING
Most cheese today is sold pre-packed but, if possible, it is preferable to buy pieces cut from a whole cheese. With the soft cheeses such as Brie and Camembert it is a good idea to smell them. A hint of ammonia means that the cheese is overripe and not worth eating. The interior of these cheeses should be plump, but not runny. Harder cheeses such as Cheddar should be firm and fresh looking, not dried out or cracked. Resist the temptation to buy too much: once cheese is cut it deteriorates, so limit yourself to just enough for two or three days. Careful buying also minimizes the problem of storage, for although refrigeration is the only practicable option, it does not enhance flavour or texture. Wrap cheeses individually in foodwrap or foil, and take them out of the fridge 30 minutes (for soft cheeses such as Brie) to an hour (for hard cheeses such as Cheddar) before use. If re-wrapping them after use for further storage, use fresh wrapping.

COOKING WITH CHEESE
Cheese was the cause of one of my very early culinary disasters. We were giving a small late-night supper party whose main dish involved large quantities of melted cheese. (I have also learned a great deal about menu planning since then – cheese is not the most digestible of foods.) I decided to do some advance preparation, grating and melting the cheese. I would then need only to reheat it later. Total disaster. I learned three lessons there about cooking with cheese. Never reheat cheese unless it has been blended with other ingredients as in a sauce, and even then, reheat very gently. Reheated cheese simply solidifies in a block of rubbery protein sitting in a pool of yellow oil. Apart from dishes that are being quickly browned, such as Welsh rarebit or cauliflower cheese, never cook cheese with a high heat. Two things may happen if you do. It may 'oil' – that is separate into solid protein and liquid fat, or it may burn, giving off bitter, acrid, toxic fumes.

Fortunately that experience did not put me off cooking with cheese. It is an important food item in its own right, and a marvellous one when served with crusty bread for lunch or to round off an excellent dinner with port, which is the English style, or before the sweet course with the last of the red wine, which is the French style. But cheese is also an enormously versatile ingredient that figures in dishes to be served at any course in the meal. While some cheeses are particularly suited to certain dishes because of the same national origins, such as Parmesan with risotto, Gruyère for fondue, Lancashire for cheese on toast, it is well worth experimenting with different cheeses. I have used Hawkestone goat cheese in place of Parmesan, Jarlsberg in fondues, and toasted Mimolette, all of which have been delicious.

Cheese has a great affinity with vegetables, particularly the leafy green vegetables such as spinach, or the strongly flavoured ones such as onions, leeks and artichokes. Cheese also adds interest to root vegetables – think of a gratin of potatoes or celeriac, or indeed a mixture of root vegetables. Eggs and cheese together make countless classic and traditional dishes – soufflés, omelettes, eggs florentine (with spinach) and eggs benedict (with ham and

hollandaise sauce). In some cooked dishes cheese plays the main part rather than a supporting role – *gougère* (a crisp cheese-flavoured puffed up ring of baked choux pastry), *aligot* (a mixture of cheese, potatoes and garlic beaten to a cream), fondue and the Italian and Swiss versions of melted cheese – *fonduta* and *raclette*. Many soups require cheese – German beer soups, French fish soups and onion soup, Italian *zuppa pavese* (with bread, eggs and Parmesan). The first and last course of a meal, hors d'oeuvre and savouries, also rely heavily on cheese. One of my favourites is a cold mousse of Roquefort cheese served on a bed of sliced cucumber.

Although cheese is versatile and lends itself to experiments in cooking, it is important to choose carefully – it does not do to assume that because it is to be cooked, quality does not matter. Badly stored, overripe or immature cheese will not produce an appetizing dish.

The page numbers in brackets at the end of an entry refer to the relevant photograph.

Hard Cheeses

1 GRANA PADANO
2 PARMESAN
3 SBRINZ
4 SAPSAGO
5 PECORINO SARDO
6 PECORINO ROMANO

APPENZELLER

A semihard cows' milk cheese made in north-east Switzerland for over 700 years, this has a hard orange-brown rind – washed in white wine or cider – a firm yellow interior with a few small holes, a delicate smell and a rounded fruity flavour. (*247*)

BAVARIAN BLUE

A modern semisoft blue cheese made in southern Germany from pasteurized cows' milk, this has a soft white Camembert-type rind, supple creamy texture, and is spattered with blue mould. It has a spicy flavour. (*258*)

BEAUFORT

A French Gruyère-type cows' milk cheese from the high mountain pastures of Savoie, this is buttery yellow with a smooth hard texture, fresh aroma and rich, fruity, brine-edged flavour. It can be used as a dessert cheese and for cooking. (*247*)

BEAUMONT

A French semihard cheese, factory-produced from pasteurized cows' milk in Haute-Savoie, Beaumont is buttery yellow with a yellow rind, supple texture, and a mild creamy flavour. (*253*)

BEENLEIGH BLUE

This is an English veined cheese made in Devon from unpasteurized ewes' milk. It is semihard and has a smooth creamy texture with dark-blue veining and a clean, sharp, slightly nutty flavour. Made only in spring and early summer – and matured for at least three months – it is available from late July to the end of March. (*258*)

BEL PAESE

A popular semisoft Italian cheese invented in the early 1900s, this is factory-made from cows' milk. Bel Paese (meaning 'beautiful country') is pale yellow with a dark yellow waxy rind, smooth pliant texture, light smell and mild fruity flavour. (*253*)

BLEU D'AUVERGNE

'Bleu' is the French generic term for veined cows' milk cheese, normally semisoft and mostly from upland areas in the Jura and Massif Central. Bleu d'Auvergne is one of the best-known. It is pale and creamy with dark blue marbling throughout. It has a clean sharp flavour. Bleu des Causses is similar, yet stronger and saltier. The popular Bleu de Bresse is creamy and milder with a hint of spice. But it over-ripens quickly: pungent rind or pinkish paste indicates a cheese past its prime. (*258*)

BLUE SHROPSHIRE

Despite its name, this hard, veined English cheese – instantly eye-catching by its lightly veined, deep golden colour – is not made in Shropshire, but in Leicestershire. Produced from pasteurized cows' milk, it has a speckled brown rind, firm texture and mild savoury flavour. Primarily a dessert cheese, it crumbles easily, making it good for cooking as well. (*258*)

BLUE VINNEY *Blue vinny, Dorset blue*

Also known as Dorset Blue from its place of origin in southern England, this is a hard, dry cheese with a crusty brownish rind, off-white firm-textured interior and mottled, all-over blue veining. Made of skimmed cows' milk, it has a sharp sour flavour and strong aftertaste. Authentic Blue Vinney is now rare. (*258*)

BOULETTE D'AVESNES

This is a small, cone-shaped cheese from Flanders in northern France. Made using buttermilk, the drained curds are kneaded with parsley, tarragon and paprika, then left to ripen for three months. The result is a soft cheese with a red rind, emphatic smell and strong spicy taste. Traditionally made on farms, but there is also some factory production which uses Maroilles curds rather than buttermilk solids. (*253*)

BOURSAULT

A French triple-cream cheese made using pasteurized cows' milk, and factory-produced in the Île de France and Normandy, Boursault is soft, creamy and very rich, with a white rind tinged with pink and a mellow, nutty taste. Overripe cheeses are excessively pink. (*249*)

BOURSIN

A small French triple-cream cheese made from pasteurized cows' milk in Normandy, comes foil-wrapped and boxed and is soft, creamy white with a light tangy taste. It is available both plain and flavoured (with garlic and herbs or with crushed peppercorns). (*257*)

BRIE

The royal family of French cheese, Brie has been known since the 1200s. It traditionally belongs to the Île de France and although the best Brie still comes from this region, around Paris, the cheese is now produced all over France and abroad. Made from cows' milk – pasteurized in creameries, unpasteurized on farms – Brie has a distinctive shape: a large, round, flat moon-like disc. Its rind is downy white; the interior is smooth, plump and glistening pale yellow – with a full, fruity, tangy taste.

Brie is a soft, unpressed cheese, left to ripen for three or four weeks and then distributed for sale; it quickly matures and just as quickly deteriorates. Avoid cheese that has a chalky centre – it has been cut too soon and cannot continue to ripen properly – or one that is

Semihard Cheeses

1 EMMENTAL	15 LEICESTER
2 CACIOCAVALLO	16 MAHON
3 APPENZELLER	17 FARMHOUSE
4 CACIETTO	CHEDDAR
5 ORKNEY	18 DOUBLE
6 HERRGARDSOST	GLOUCESTER
7 CHESHIRE (WHITE)	19 ROYALP
8 PROVOLONE	20 LEIDEN
9 SINGLE GLOUCESTER	21 BEAUFORT
10 DERBY (SAGE	22 RACLETTE
DERBY)	23 GOUDA (MATURE)
11 MANCHEGO	24 GRUYÈRE
12 KEFALOTIRI	25 TÊTE-DE-MOINE
13 EDAM (MATURE)	26 MIMOLETTE
14 DERBY	27 CANTAL

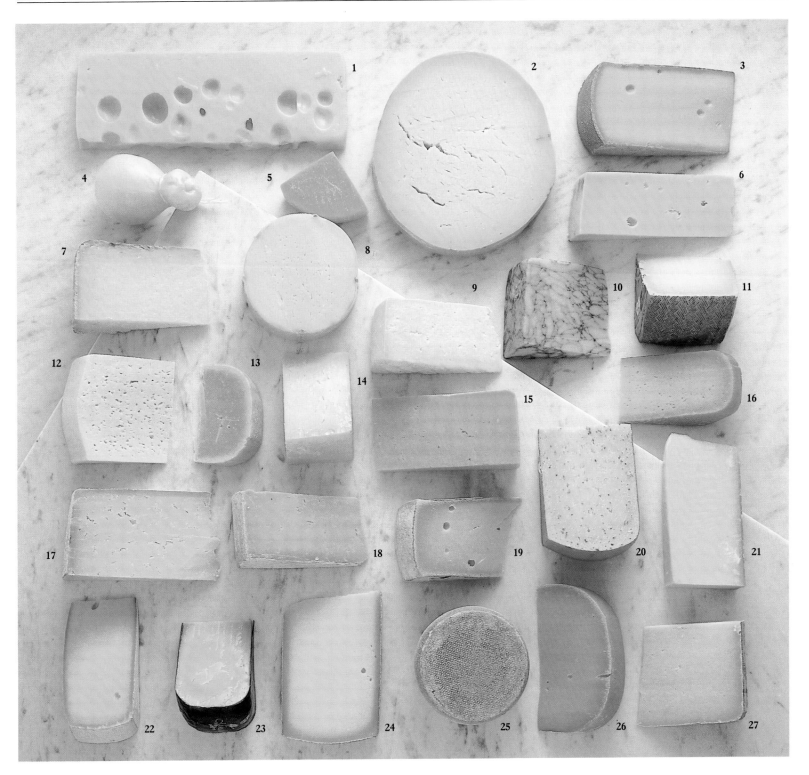

half-melted as it is past its prime. If it is runny and smells of ammonia, it is dangerously over-ripe.

There are several special types of Brie. Brie de Meaux is the classic Brie from the area around Meaux, south-east of Paris. It is farm-made using unpasteurized milk, and is ripened for four to six weeks. It has the characteristic white bloomy rind, but with more reddish-brown speckles than ordinary Brie, a deeper golden interior and a stronger, fuller flavour that evokes cream and mushrooms and fruit.

Brie de Melun is an unpasteurized Brie sold at various stages of maturity: unripened (*frais*) or ripened for ten weeks or so (*affiné*) which makes it deep yellow with a strong smell and fruity, salty flavour. Brie de Melun *bleu* is Brie de Melun *frais* dusted with powdered charcoal. (*249*)

BRILLAT-SAVARIN

A soft triple-cream cheese made from pasteurized cows' milk in Normandy, France, this is factory-produced in smallish flat discs. It is rich, firm-to-soft and buttery, with a white downy rind and a creamy lactic taste.

BRUDER BASIL

This German smoked cheese, made in Bavaria, is produced from pasteurized cows' milk. It is buttery yellow with a mahogany-brown rind, firm texture with small holes, and a light piquant smoky taste. It is also available flavoured with ham. (*253*)

CABOC

A rennet-free double cream cheese from the Scottish Highlands, this is made using cows' milk cream, then rolled in toasted pinhead oatmeal which gives a crunchy coating to the soft, very rich, buttery paste. It has a delicate, creamy flavour. (*257*)

CABRALES

This semihard veined cheese from the mountains of Asturias, north-west Spain, is traditionally made of goats' milk, but may also contain cows' or ewes' milk. It is off-white, with brownish patches and blue-brown veins; and is sometimes wrapped in leaves. It has a powerful smell and pungent taste.

CACIETTO

This is an Italian cows' milk semihard cheese hand moulded into small pear shapes and of the same spun-curd family of cheeses as Cacio-cavallo and Provolone. It is pale in colour with a slightly tangy flavour.

CACIOCAVALLO

An Italian semihard cows' milk cheese, originally from the south but now manufactured throughout the country, this is moulded into large pear-shapes. The cheeses are strung together with a cord and hung over poles to ripen – three or four months for table use, at least a year for grating. Caciocavallo is pale yellow with a shiny yellow-grey rind, and a delicate flavour. (*247*)

CACIOTTA

A type of farmhouse cheese made throughout Italy, using whatever milk is available – cows', ewes', goats' or a mixture – Caciotta's characteristics vary from region to region but generally the cheese is semisoft and has a firm rind, pale yellow paste and a gentle flavour that can range from sweet to mildly piquant. Commercial Caciotta, made with pasteurized cows' milk, is blander. (*253*)

CAERPHILLY

Originally Welsh, this is a moist, white, semi-hard cheese, with a crumbly, springy texture, and a delicious fresh, salty flavour (it is soaked in brine). Caerphilly matures quickly, being ready for consumption within a week to ten days, but because it is a young cheese it is relatively short-lived. In addition to the commercial creamery production, some cheese is also made on farms using unpasteurized milk (and at least one of the farms is in Wales). Although farm-house Caerphilly can be eaten a few days after manufacture, it can also be kept for several weeks, becoming yellower, smooth-textured, full-flavoured and tangy. Caerphilly is easily digested and is generally eaten uncooked – although it melts well which makes it a good cheese for rarebit and fondue-type dishes. (*253*)

CAMEMBERT

France's best-known cheese came originally from Normandy, especially the Pays d'Auge, but is now made throughout the country – as well as elsewhere – and accounts for almost a quarter of all French cheese manufacture. Production is predominantly factory-based using pasteurized cows' milk to create the familiar small, round, soft, white-rind creamy cheese with a light fruity flavour. This commercial type, however, never quite matches the authentic Camembert *fermier*, hand-made on Normandy farms and using unpasteurized milk from local herds. Such cheeses have a stronger fragrance and flavour. At its best, Camembert has a smooth, supple rind and a voluptuous pale golden paste which when pressed should bulge, but not run. When buying, choose a cheese that is plump and yielding – and that fills its box; avoid ones that are hard, or that are either swollen or sunken, or that have a bitter smell. Once ripe, Camembert deteriorates quickly and is at its prime for only two or three days – sometimes less. (*249*)

CANTAL

This is probably France's oldest cheese, made in the Auvergne for more than 2000 years. The farmhouse Cantal (labelled *fermier*) using unpasteurized cows' milk, is produced only in summer when the herds are grazing upland pastures. It is a semihard yellow cheese with a dry grey rind, smooth close texture, earthy smell and a mellow nutty flavour. Cantal *laitier*, from pasteurized milk, is made in creameries throughout the year. The two are very similar except that the farmhouse cheeses tend to be heavier, weighing up to 100lb (45kg) each; but there is a small farmhouse version weighing 8–20lb (3·6–9kg). It is eaten as a dessert cheese and is particularly good with a ripe, juicy Williams pear which is how I first tasted it. Since then it has remained one of my favourite cheeses. It is also used in regional dishes, the best known of which is *aligot*, a mixture of mashed potatoes and milk into which the cheese is beaten to produce a soothing fondue-like dish. *(247)*

CARRÉ DE L'EST

A small square-shaped cheese, factory-produced from pasteurized cows' milk in north-eastern France, this is a Camembert type – soft, with white bloomy rind, but a bland, slightly salty taste. There is also a stronger orange-rind version with the same name. *(254)*

CASHEL BLUE

A semisoft farmhouse blue cheese made from unpasteurized cows' milk in County Tipperary, Ireland, this was first produced in 1983. It has a mottled brownish rind, creamy paste, all-over blue-green veining and a buttery, piquant flav-

our. It's normally sold between six and ten weeks maturity, but can be eaten older – up to four months – when it is stronger and richer. Like most of the blue cheeses it is excellent with celery at the end of a meal. *(258)*

CHABI *Chabichou*

This is a soft goat cheese from Poitou, South-West France. There are two basic types, each easily distinguished by their rind: pale grey with red streaks on the farmhouse variety, but white and bloomy on Chabichou *laitier* which is made in small dairies. Both have a strong goaty taste and smell. Chabichou *cendré*, ripened in wood-ash, is even more pungent. *(250)*

CHAOURCE

A soft silky cheese made from unpasteurized cows' milk in the Champagne district of France,

Chaource is smooth and milky with a downy rind, light texture and a nutty flavour with a refreshing acidic edge. Most of the cheese comes from small dairies but there is still some farmhouse production. *(249)*

CHEDDAR

Britain's favourite cheese, developed on West Country farms during the Middle Ages, Cheddar is now mass-produced throughout Britain and is imitated worldwide. Made from pasteurized cows' milk, it owes its hard dense texture and slow-ripening properties to the special 'cheddaring' process: before milling, the drained curds are cut into blocks which are stacked on top of each other and then turned frequently to squeeze out even more whey. Cheddar has a cream to deep yellow colour, depending on age, and a flavour that evolves from fresh and sweet in a young cheese to rich

White-Rind Cheeses

1 GAPERON
2 BOURSAULT
3 BRIE
4 BRIE DE MEAUX
5 CAMEMBERT
6 NEUFCHÂTEL
7 COULOMMIERS
8 ST-MARCELLIN
9 CHAOURCE

and nutty when mature. Factory-produced Cheddar is available at various stages of its maturity, ranging from 'mild' – sold between three and five months old, to 'mature' – ripened for at least five months, often more. Farmhouse Cheddar – still made in the West Country, sometimes from unpasteurized milk – may be aged for as long as eighteen months and has a

full, strong flavour quite unlike the younger cheese. It is well worth hunting out farmhouse Cheddar – it is the equal of any of the world's fine classic cheeses.

Cheddar is a versatile cheese, excellent both cooked and uncooked. There are numerous Cheddar variants, some newly invented, others derived from traditional recipes. The better-known include: Charnwood and Applewood, both smoked – the latter over apple logs and coated with paprika; and Windsor Red, with elderberry wine mixed in at the curd stage. (247)

CHESHIRE

Britain's oldest cheese, mentioned in 1086 in Domesday Book, Cheshire may even have been known to the Romans. It is a crumbly loose-textured cheese with a mild tangy flavour and a subtle saltiness derived from the unique soil of the Cheshire plain, which covers huge salt reserves. Made using pasteurized cows' milk, it is naturally creamy white, but is often coloured with annatto to an apricot shade (called 'red'). Production is concentrated in creameries but the traditional unpasteurized cheese is still made on two farms, one in Cheshire and one in Shropshire. It is generally aged between four and eight weeks, but is occasionally matured for over a year – giving a mellower flavour. There is also some farmhouse production of the rare blue Cheshire which has a rich full flavour. All Cheshires are lovely eating cheeses; red and white also cook well. (247, 253, 258)

CHÈVRE

This is the French generic term for goat cheese. By law, cheeses labelled *chèvre* or *pur chèvre*

Goats' Milk Cheeses

1	MENDIP	6	STE-MAURE CENDRÉ
2	HAWKESTONE	7	STE-MAURE
3	GJETOST	8	VALENÇAY
4	CROTTIN	9	CHABI
5	CROTTIN DE CHAVIGNOL	10	CHABI CENDRÉ

The remaining cheeses are a collection of *chèvres* in various shapes and sizes.

must be 100 per cent goats' milk; cheeses using a minimum of 25 per cent goats' mixed with cows' milk are called *mi-chèvre* and have an identifying yellow band on their label. Made throughout France, goat cheeses are small, generally shaped in rolls, rounds, pyramids or ovals and range in flavour from fresh and creamy to strong and tangy. The names of many local types often incorporate words derived from *chèvre* such as *chevret, chevreton, chevrette, chevrotin*. Goat cheeses, traditionally in season from late spring to late autumn, are best eaten within a few days of purchase – except for matured varieties. They also cook well. A popular and delicious way to serve them is to slice them, place on a round of French bread, toast them and serve with a salad of mixed pungent, bitter leaves. Goat cheese soufflés are also delicious. (250)

COMTÉ

A French Gruyère-type cows' milk cheese made since Roman times in the Jura mountains bordering Switzerland, Comté is deep golden yellow with a tough rind – which may be dark or straw-coloured – a firm smooth texture, scattered with marble-sized holes, and a rich, fruity flavour. When buying, avoid a cheese that is bulging or has too many holes. On the other hand, if it 'weeps' salt 'tears' and exudes moisture around the holes, buy it; it is a sign that it is perfectly mature. This also applies to Beaufort, Gruyère and Emmental. It is used extensively in cooking and also as a dessert cheese.

COTHERSTONE

An English farmhouse cheese made from unpasteurized Jersey cows' milk in the Yorkshire Dales, this is semihard and has a soft crust, loose texture, creamy paste and a delicate sharp-edged flavour. It can be blue or white. (253)

COTTAGE CHEESE

This is a type of curd cheese made from skimmed cows' milk which is warmed before the starter is added. This heating causes the curds to form in large soft lumps – a distinctive characteristic. They are then drained, washed and coated with thin cream. Cottage cheese – stark white, granular, low-fat and with a clean, mild taste – is generally sold prepacked in tubs, and is available plain or flavoured with herbs, fruit, nuts, or vegetables. Eat it fresh or use in cooking. (*257*)

COULOMMIERS

This soft, white-rind cheese is made from cows' milk in the same area of France as Brie. Although similar – and even sometimes called Petit Brie – Coulommiers is smaller in size, eaten younger (after about one month) and has a less mellow taste. If allowed to ripen longer, it becomes more like a Camembert in flavour than a Brie. It is eaten as a dessert cheese. (*249*)

CREAM CHEESE

This is unripened cows' milk cheese made from single or double cream. It is very soft and white, with a smooth texture and rich buttery taste, and is available plain and flavoured. Full-fat soft cheese is similar but with a lower fat content. It can be used to make cheesecake and, more unusually, can replace butter or margarine to make a very successful short pastry. (*257*)

CROTTIN DE CHAVIGNOL

A small round goat cheese made on farms in Berry, central France, it is dry and firm inside the slightly wrinkled rind which darkens as it matures to full ageing — at around three months — when it has a full, pungent flavour and a hard texture. The commercial version is softer and milder with a light-coloured rind. (*250*)

CROWDIE

A traditional unripened cheese made on Scottish farms from unpasteurized skimmed cows' milk and enriched with cream, this is similar to cottage cheese but with a finer texture and a sharper taste. In the past, crowdie was also made from goats' milk.

CURD CHEESE

This unripened soft cows' milk cheese was traditionally made by allowing the milk to sour naturally; but nowadays it is generally produced through the addition of a lactic starter. The resulting curds and whey are separated, and the curds then drained and salted. It has a slightly tart, refreshing flavour. Use it fresh or in cooking. (*257*)

DANABLU *Danish blue, Jutland blue*

A well-known, Danish, veined cheese made from cows' milk, this is semisoft with a buttery, crumbly texture. White, densely veined, with a rich, strong, quite salty taste, it is popular for dips, spreads and dressings. There is also a stronger version, sometimes marketed as Jutland Blue, which has a softer texture and a creamier, less salty, flavour. (*258*)

DERBY *Sage Derby*

One of England's lesser-known commercial cheeses, and made from cows' milk, Derby is pale with a close firm texture, and mild buttery flavour. It is usually available young when I find it lacks personality, but sometimes it is sold mature, after six months' ageing when I find it makes an excellent dessert cheese. The more popular Sage Derby – marbled green with the juice of sage leaves – has a sharper taste. (*247*)

DEVON GARLAND

An English farmhouse cheese made in North Devon from unpasteurized Jersey cows' milk and using vegetarian rennet, this is semihard and creamy yellow with a flaky texture, and is flavoured with chopped fresh herbs. (*253*)

DOLCELATTE

This Italian blue-veined semisoft cheese is made from cows' milk. It has a smooth, creamy texture and a delicate piquant flavour. (*258*)

DOUBLE BERKELEY

This is now being made again to a traditional recipe in Gloucester from the unpasteurized milk of Gloucester cattle. It is a semihard, full fat cheese with a sweet nutty flavour marbled with vegetable colouring.

DOUBLE GLOUCESTER

This rich English cows' milk cheese is traditionally made by adding to evening milk the following morning's milk. Its deep gold-to-orange colour comes from the natural colour annatto but there is also a little farmhouse production of uncoloured cheese. Double Gloucester is semihard with a firm, satiny texture, and full, mellow flavour, and is at its best after four months. Variants include Cotswold which is Double Gloucester flavoured with chopped chives; Huntsman, layered with Blue Stilton; and Sherwood, flavoured with sweet pickle. (*247*)

DUNSYRE BLUE

A recently introduced semihard blue cheese made from unpasteurized cows' milk in Lanarkshire, Scotland, using traditional methods, this is creamy white with strong vertical veins and a mild, slightly tangy taste. (*258*)

EDAM

This popular Dutch semihard cheese is distinguished by its bright red wax coat and ball shape. Named after the town where it originated some 700 years ago, Edam is now commercially produced all over Holland. Made from pasteurized skimmed cows' milk, it is low in calories and keeps well. It is golden yellow with a firm supple texture, a sparse scattering of holes and a gentle nutty flavour. Most Edam is sold at two to four months but with age, a year or more, it becomes darker, stronger and harder. The red wax jacket (black for mature Edam) is for export only; at home, Edam's natural yellow rind stays unprotected.

Very mature Edam is a fine cheese for cooking and grating over dishes such as pasta, vegetable gratins and risottos. (*247, 253*)

EDELPILZ *Pilzkäse*

A semisoft German blue cheese made from cows' milk, this is white, with a crumbly texture and fine dark-blue veins running vertically through the centre. Its strong fruity flavour makes it a popular dessert cheese. (*258*)

EMMENTAL

One of the world's great cheeses comes from the mountain cantons of central Switzerland, and is named after the Emme valley, near Bern, where it originated. Famous for its large, round holes, Emmental is deep golden yellow with a firm smooth texture, and a flavour that is mellow and sweet with a lingering hint of hazelnuts. Made with unpasteurized cows' milk and ripened for at least four months, often longer, it comes in an enormous wheel weighing up to 220lb (100kg) and, to guarantee authenticity, has 'Switzerland' stamped all over the rind. There are many imitations worldwide but none has quite the same fragrance or subtle sweetness as the original Swiss. When buying, avoid cheese that has too many holes or that shows signs of cracking. Emmental keeps well and is excellent for both dessert use and cooking, particularly in fondue when it is combined with white wine, kirsch and sometimes a proportion of Gruyère. (247)

ÉPOISSES

A full-flavoured, soft cows' milk cheese from Burgundy, France, this is characterized by its pungent aroma and rich, orange-red rind, sometimes wrapped in leaves. Produced in small rounds, it has a smooth supple paste with a penetrating, tangy taste. It is traditionally eaten fresh in summer but matured – for at least three months – from November to May. (254)

ESROM

Esrom is a pale yellow semisoft cheese from Denmark with a butterlike texture and numerous irregular holes. It has a rich lightly aromatic flavour which becomes spicier with age. It is made from pasteurized cows' milk and comes in a long, foil-wrapped loaf. (253)

FETA

A Greek cheese traditionally made from ewes' milk, but now more usually from cows' milk, and preserved in brine, Feta is brilliantly white with a firm, crumbly texture and a bland salt-edged taste; but with a longer time in brine, it becomes harder and develops a sourer, saltier flavour. In Greece, Feta is sold from its brine bath and eaten fresh – either by itself, with olives or in salads; it also features prominently in Greek cooking. Outside Greece, the cheese is generally sold in vacuum packs. Feta imitations, produced in several other countries, are usually made from pasteurized cows' milk, but Bulgarian Feta, a particularly good version, is made from ewes' milk. (257)

FONTINA

Fontina is one of Italy's most delectable cheeses. It comes from the high alpine meadows of the Valle d'Aosta and is made with unpasteurized cows' milk in mountain chalets during the summer months. In winter the cheese is factory-made in the valleys. Fontina is deep golden yellow with a tough almond-brown rind, a firm slightly springy texture and random tiny holes. The flavour is delicate with subtle hints of honey, fruit and nuts. It makes a memorable dessert cheese and is also an essential ingredient of *fonduta* – Piedmontese fondue – along with white wine and shaved white truffles. (253)

FOURME D'AMBERT

A semisoft French veined cheese made from cows' milk in the Auvergne, this looks like a small Stilton. It has a grey mottled rind, and is white with blue veining. It has a sharp tangy taste, and is best in autumn at four to five months old. Cut it horizontally, like a Stilton. (258)

FROMAGE FRAIS

This is fresh curd cheese made from pasteurized skimmed cows' milk sometimes enriched with cream. Its consistency varies from soft, light and pourable to relatively firm and thick. The taste also ranges from mildly acid to rich, according to the amount of cream added, and this also affects the fat content which ranges from almost nil to eight per cent. Traditionally French, fromage frais is now also made in many other countries. It is widely used in cooking and is also eaten fresh as a dessert – often flavoured with fruit or just sugar. (257)

GAPERON

This is a semisoft low-fat French cheese made from skimmed cows' milk or buttermilk (*gape* is an old country word for 'buttermilk'), and flavoured with garlic. Traditional to the Auvergne, it is shaped like an upturned cup and has a light garlic smell and taste. (249)

GJETOST

This semihard Norwegian whey cheese is made either from a blend of goats' and cows' milk or entirely from goats' milk (and then labelled *ekte*, 'genuine'). Caramelization of the milk sugar (lactose) gives the cheese a distinctive toffee-brown colour and sweet sticky taste. In Norway it is sliced very thinly and eaten for breakfast, and with Christmas cake. (250)

GORGONZOLA

Italy's Gorgonzola is one of the world's oldest and greatest veined cheeses. It originated over 1100 years ago in the village of the same name near Milan; today production is still concentrated in Lombardy. Made from pasteurized cows' milk and ripened for three to four months, this semisoft cheese characteristically has a reddish-grey rind, creamy yellow interior, pale green marbling and a piquant flavour that is both seductively rich and delicate. When buying Gorgonzola, avoid any cheese that is hard or discoloured or that has a bitter smell. It is eaten as a dessert cheese – classically with pears –

Semihard Cheeses

1 MORBIER	13 CAERPHILLY
2 EDAM	14 CACIOTTA
3 SWALEDALE	15 TOMME DE SAVOIE
4 HAVARTI	16 BRUDER BASIL
5 CHEDDAR	17 HALLOUMI
6 BEL PAESE	18 COTHERSTONE
7 WENSLEYDALE	19 LANCASHIRE
8 ST-PAULIN	20 GOUDA
9 DEVON GARLAND	21 BEAUMONT
10 ST-NECTAIRE	22 FONTINA
11 TILSIT	23 CHESHIRE (RED)
12 BOULETTE	24 ESROM
D'AVESNES	25 JARLSBERG

but also makes an excellent sauce for pasta. Torta Gorgonzola is a cheese consisting of layers of Gorgonzola and Mascarpone. (*258*)

GOUDA

The most important Dutch cheese, Gouda is made from pasteurized cows' milk, and aged two to four months. It has a smooth shiny yellow rind, firm straw-yellow paste with random holes and a mild buttery flavour. Mature Gouda, with a black-waxed jacket, ripened for up to a year, develops a deeper colour, a much fuller, spicier flavour, and harder texture. When buying, avoid cheese that appears crumbly or that has too many holes. It is suitable for cooking, but is best eaten raw – the Dutch enjoy it thinly sliced for breakfast. Very mature Gouda is a fine grating cheese. (*247, 253*)

GRANA PADANO

This very hard cows' milk cheese from the Po valley in Italy is similar to Parmesan. Young Grana Padano is pale yellow, moist and mild, and is an ideal dessert cheese. Mature – at about two years old – it has a deeper colour, drier texture and a fuller flavour and is generally grated for cooking. The word *grana*, meaning 'grainy', is applied to various Italian fine-grained hard cheeses. (*245*)

GRUYÈRE

A celebrated Swiss cheese from unpasteurized cow's milk, Gruyère is pale yellow and very firm and close-textured with a sprinkling of small holes. The flavour is sweet and nutty with a briny aftertaste. Like Emmental, a genuine cheese has 'Switzerland' stamped all over its rind. A good Gruyère, at its best, has a slight glistening of moisture round the holes. It is a wonderful dessert cheese and widely used in cooking and especially in the traditional Swiss cheese dip, *fondue*. (*247*)

HALLOUMI

This Greek semihard cheese is generally made with ewes' milk, but a little is produced from cows' milk. It has an elastic texture and a creamy, slightly salty taste. It is used fresh or ripened for about a month, and is very popular in cooking. Rinse with water or milk before use. It is often sliced and grilled as part of the Greek *meze* (hors d'oeuvre); eat it while it is hot. Once cold it is like chewing India rubber. (*253*)

HAVARTI

Factory-made in Denmark from pasteurized cows' milk, Havarti has a springy texture and buttery yellow paste – spattered with holes of all shapes and sizes. Its full spicy flavour and piquant aftertaste become stronger and more pungent with age. (*253*)

Orange-Rind Cheeses

1	LIVAROT	7	PETIT MUNSTER
2	CARRÉ DE L'EST	8	ÉPOISSES
3	LIMBURGER	9	TALEGGIO
4	PONT-L'EVÊQUE	10	MILLEENS
5	MUNSTER	11	REBLOCHON
6	MAROILLES		

HAWKESTONE

A hard, orange-rind English goats' milk cheese farm-made in Cheshire, this has a rich, full, nutty flavour. It reminds me more than anything else of a fine Parmesan, and I have seen Italians fall into raptures over Hawkestone. (*250*)

HERRGARDSOST

A popular Swedish semihard cheese, factory-made all over the country from pasteurized cows' milk – either full-fat or semi-skimmed, it has a firm texture, and is pale straw-coloured with a scattering of small holes, yellow-waxed rind and delicate flavour. It is similar to Swiss Gruyère, although not so fine. (*247*)

JARLSBERG

A very popular Norwegian cheese, Jarlsberg is factory-made from pasteurized cows' milk. It is semihard, yellow-waxed and has a springy texture – rather like Dutch Gouda – and is light gold in colour punctured with irregular-sized round holes like Emmental. The distinctive flavour is nutty and slightly sweet. (*253*)

KEFALOTIRI

A strong-flavoured Greek cheese made from ewes' milk – sometimes goats' milk – it has a tough rind, drab yellow paste and is mainly grated for cooking. The little amount of Kefalotiri found abroad comes mostly from Cyprus. (*247*)

LANARK BLUE

This modern semihard blue cheese made from unpasteurized ewes' milk in Lanarkshire, Scotland has a rich, creamy white paste with blue-green veins and strong, salty flavour. (*258*)

LANCASHIRE

At its best, this creamy-white, crumbly, semihard English cheese has a rich tangy brine-edged taste. It is traditionally produced by mixing together separate cool curds, drained, salted and lightly pressed from two days' milk. This authentic cheese still exists, made from unpasteurized cows' milk on a couple of local farms. But most Lancashire is produced in creameries, using just a single day's curds (pasteurized) and has a milder flavour. Lancashire is a good dessert cheese and, as it melts easily, is ideal for cooking, making marvellous cheese on toast. (*253*)

LEICESTER

Instantly identified by its rich russet-red hue – from the vegetable colour annatto – Leicester is one of England's hard cheeses. Virtually all Leicester is now factory-made using pasteurized cows' milk. It ripens quickly and is therefore quite moist with a short life-span (compared with Cheddar): at its peak between three and six months, past its best at a year. Leicester has a granular buttery texture – impossible to cut cleanly – and a mellow flavour which combines a lemony tang with a touch of sweetness. When buying, avoid any cheese that has a 'bleach' blotch on the cut surface – it will be unpleasantly strong. (*247*)

LEIDEN *Leyden*

A Dutch cheese spiced with cumin seed, made from pasteurized cows' milk – part skimmed, part buttermilk – Leiden has a firm texture and a natural yellow rind (orange if farm-made), but for export the cheese is red or yellow-waxed. It has a mild taste dominated by the cumin. There is a variant flavoured with cloves. (*247*)

LIMBURGER

This very strong cows' milk cheese originally came from Belgium but is now made in several other countries, especially Germany. It is a soft cheese with a smooth yellow-brown skin, formidable smell and assertive spicy flavour. (*254*)

LIVAROT

One of Normandy's oldest and strongest cheeses and made from skimmed and whole cows' milk, Livarot is soft with a shiny dark-brown rind; rich, gently yielding yellow interior, vigorous aroma and spicy flavour. Best in autumn and winter, it is eaten with cider or Calvados. (*254*)

MAHON

This Spanish cheese – traditionally a mixture of cows' and ewes' milk – is made in the Balearics, especially Menorca. Inside the tough, blotched brown rind, the paste is supple and creamy – becoming firmer and darker with age. The cheese is soaked in brine then coated in olive oil. It has a slightly sour, sharp taste. (*247*)

MANCHEGO

Spain's premier cheese originated in La Mancha but is now produced all over the country. Made from ewes' milk, it has a firm ivory-to-gold paste and a taut nuts-and-butter flavour. With age it becomes harder and drier. Manchego is sold at various stages of maturity from *fresco* (fresh) through to a very rich version aged in olive oil, *en aceite*. A traditional accompaniment for Manchego is quince jelly, *membrillo*. (*247*)

MAROILLES

This ancient cows' milk cheese has been made near Lille, in northern France, for over 1000 years. Produced in small square slabs, it has a reddish rind, soft pale-gold paste, penetrating smell and piquant flavour. (*254*)

MASCARPONE *Mascherpone*

An Italian soft cream cheese made from cows' milk in Lombardy, it has a rich butter-coloured paste, silky smooth texture and a luscious, light whipped-cream taste. It is eaten fresh as a dessert – often with fruit and sugar, flavoured with coffee, chocolate, or liqueur. (*257*)

MENDIP

A hard goats' milk cheese made to a Pecorino-based recipe in Avon, this is matured for two to six months, and has a full rich flavour. (*250*)

MILLEENS

This is an Irish farmhouse cheese made from unpasteurized cows' milk. It is aged for six to eight weeks ripening to a creamy soft texture, full strong flavour and a pungent aroma. (*254*)

MIMOLETTE

An Edam-type Dutch cheese made from pasteurized cows' milk, Mimolette is a hard bright orange cheese with a drab darkish rind, and strong appetizing flavour. A French Mimolette – very similar in looks and taste – is produced in various parts of France but especially in Flanders. It is a good cheese for grating and cooking. (*247*)

MONTRACHET

A soft goat cheese with a mild, creamy taste from Burgundy, France, this is ripened for a few days in vine or chestnut leaves and sold still wrapped in the leaves.

MORBIER

This semihard cows' milk cheese from the Jura mountains in eastern France is distinguished by a black band running horizontally through its middle: traditionally a layer of charcoal or soot was put on top of the morning curds to protect them until the evening curds were ready. Morbier has a dry grey rind, firm pale yellow paste and fairly strong flavour. (*253*)

MOZZARELLA

Mozzarella is an unripened cheese now produced all over Italy and beyond, but originating in Latium and Campania and properly made from water buffaloes' milk. Nowadays cows' milk is more commonly used although, in southern Italy, some cheese is made using a mixture of both milks. Mozzarella – traditionally shaped into balls – is white and spongy with a mild, creamy-sour flavour. Cows' milk varieties are sometimes blander and more rubbery than the authentic Mozzarella di Bufala. In Italy, the cheese is kept in whey and sold from the bowl. Mozzarella, which becomes stringy and elastic when cooked, is a standard ingredient of many Italian dishes as well as the classic cheese for topping pizza. In Italy it is also eaten fresh – traditionally dressed with olive oil, salt and ground black pepper – with tomatoes and olives. A smoked version called Mozzarella Affumicata is also available. (*257*)

MUNSTER

A French aromatic cheese from the Vosges mountains in Alsace, this was developed by monks in the seventh century. Made from unpasteurized cows' milk, it has a brick-red rind, soft buttery-yellow paste, assertive smell and strong sharp taste. Munster comes in a disc shape and is aged from two to three months – but locally is often eaten younger. The farmhouse type is traditionally made in summer and autumn; the commercial version, Munster *laitier* uses pasteurized milk and is produced throughout the year. Sometimes flavoured with caraway (known in French as *cumin des près* so it is often wrongly translated as cumin) and in Alsace often served with a spoonful of caraway seeds on the plate, and a glass of Gewürztraminer Vendange Tardive, which is one of the best cheese and wine marriages.

There is a German cheese called Münster – a gentler version of the Alsace original (the umlaut distinguishes German from French) – made from pasteurized cows' milk. It has a thin reddish-brown skin, yellow paste, medium-strong smell and a mild, spicy taste. (*254*)

MYCELLA

A semisoft Danish blue cheese made from cows' milk, this is creamy-yellow with greenish veins and, for a blue cheese, a surprisingly mild flavour. It is sometimes known as Danish Gorgonzola. (*258*)

NEUFCHÂTEL

A very rich and creamy soft cheese from the Pays de Bray in Normandy, France, this is made from cows' milk, the curds being milled to give an extra smooth velvety texture. Neufchâtel can be eaten either fresh or ripened, *affiné*. Fresh, it has a bloomy white rind and a moist, lightly sour taste. Neufchâtel *affiné* develops reddish tinges on the rind and a stronger flavour. It comes in a variety of shapes – square, loaf, roll and heart. (*249*)

ORKNEY

This Scottish semihard cheese from the remote Orkney Islands is made using skimmed cows' milk. The cheese is naturally white but is also available coloured orange (with annatto) or smoked. It was traditionally matured in a barrel of oatmeal, but this is now rare. (*247*)

PARMESAN *Parmigiano Reggiano*

This world-famous cheese comes from a small specified area around the rivers Po and Reno in north-central Italy. Made with semi-skimmed unpasteurized cows' milk, the cheese is straw-coloured with a brittle, grainy texture and a fruity fragrant flavour. The thick, hard, brown rind is stamped all round with Parmigiano Reggiano as a guarantee of origin. At one or two years old, Parmesan is pale, supple and crumbly – good for dessert use, especially served with pears, apples, nuts and grapes. It is also served in Italy with a dressing of olive oil. Thin shavings of Parmesan are served on top of the classic dish *carpaccio*, paper-thin slices of raw beef. At three or four years, it is darker, drier and very hard, and is the classic grating cheese for pasta, risottos and other dishes. It is also used to make *pesto* sauce and stuffings for homemade ravioli. It is best to buy Parmesan in a piece and grate it as required. (*245*)

PECORINO

Pecorino is the Italian generic term for ewes' milk cheese, which is made all over the country but especially in the centre and south. The most celebrated varieties are the aged, hard Pecorino Romano and Pecorino Sardo; but there are numerous other everyday sheep cheeses which are generally younger and milder. Fresh Pecorino – soft with a light sour taste – should be eaten within a day or two unless heavily salted. The firmer Pecorino *da tavola*, matured for a few months, has a strong, sharp flavour.

Pecorino Romano is probably Italy's oldest cheese. Originally from Latium, it is matured for at least eight months, and has a tough rind – which may be dark grey or yellow according to treatment – and a dense, whitish-yellow paste with a sharp, dry flavour. Young Pecorino Romano makes a delicious dessert cheese; with age, it becomes very hard – a quality grating cheese much used in Italian cuisine. Pecorino Sardo, from Sardinia, is similar. (*245*)

PONT L'EVÊQUE

One of France's best-loved cheeses from around the same part of Normandy as Camembert, this is made from cows' milk – unpasteurized on farms, pasteurized in commercial dairies – it comes in a plump, square shape with a gold-to-tan rind. Inside, it is soft, supple, pale yellow and has a savoury scent, full rich tangy flavour and a sweet aftertaste. When buying, avoid a skin that is hard, rough or cracked as the cheese will be overripe and bitter. (*254*)

PROVOLONE

This Italian cheese was originally from the south but is now also produced in the Po valley. Made using unpasteurized cows' milk, it is either coagulated with calf's rennet (Provolone *dolce*) or kid's rennet (Provolone *piccante*). The *dolce* version, aged for two or three months, has a thin waxed rind, yielding texture, creamy-white paste and a mild, slightly acid taste; it is used as a table cheese. Provolone *piccante*, cured for up to two years, has a tough natural rind, hard texture, darker colour and sharper flavour, and is a good grating cheese. Both types are hand-moulded into a variety of shapes and are often tied together in pairs. Some of the other shapes have names like Provole and Provolini, but are essentially the same cheese. (*247*)

QUARK

This is a fresh curd cheese made throughout Germany from cows' milk – which can be skimmed, whole, buttermilk – and sometimes enriched with cream. It is milky white, with a spoonable texture and a delicate sour flavour which becomes creamy in types with a higher fat content. It is widely used in cooking, for curd cheese tarts and cakes. I like to mix it with herbs and garlic, then drain it through a sieve or cloth to make my own soft cheese. (*257*)

RACLETTE

Raclette is a family of Swiss cheeses, mostly from the south-west canton of Valais, and made with unpasteurized cows' milk. It is typically semihard with a thick grey rind, firm texture,

dull yellow paste – lightly holed – and a full flowery flavour. The name, 'scraper', refers to the local Valais speciality also called *raclette*: a half cheese is held before an open fire, scraped off as it melts and eaten with potatoes, pickled onions and gherkins. (*247*)

REBLOCHON

One of France's great mountain cheeses is made in Haute-Savoie and is semisoft, with a yellowish brown rind, and a gentle fruity flavour which becomes bitter if aged too long. It is sold in flat rounds set on thin wooden discs. (*254*)

RICOTTA

Ricotta is an Italian whey cheese and is most familiar in its fresh, unripened form when it is white and creamy with a soft, smooth texture, and a bland, slightly sweet flavour. It also exists dried and salted; and, aged, as a harder grating cheese. Traditionally Ricotta is produced from ewes' milk whey, but cows' milk whey is used in Piedmont. Nowadays the whey is sometimes enriched with whole or skimmed milk. Ricotta is an exceptionally versatile cheese: eaten fresh as a dessert with fruit or with liqueur, powdered chocolate or coffee added, and also featuring extensively in Italian cooking – especially as a filling for pasta dishes and pastries. It should be used within 24–36 hours. (*257*)

RIGOTTE

A French soft cheese made in upland areas from either cows' or goats' milk or a mixture of both, it is small and round, and cured for just two weeks – sometimes in wine or oil. Naturally-ripened Rigotte has a flavour ranging from mildly sour to strong and nutty, according to the milk used. (*257*)

ROQUEFORT

This remarkable veined French cheese is produced from ewes' milk and ripened for three months in the limestone caves of Les Causses. Made in this barren wasteland of south-central France for thousands of years, Roquefort is a creamy-white, semisoft crumbly cheese with

all-over marbling – more green than blue – quite unlike any other blue cheese. When buying, avoid a cheese with a very white paste or too few veins. It is a superb dessert cheese, especially with a sweet wine like Sauternes. (*258*)

ROYALP

This Swiss semihard cheese, originally from the Thurgau canton in the east, is known as Tilsit in Switzerland and Royalp abroad. It is buttery yellow with a firm but supple texture and sparse holes, a full flavour and a spicy aftertaste. (*247*)

SAINGORLON

A creamy semisoft cows' milk cheese speckled with green mould, it is made in various parts of

Fresh Cheeses

1	CABOC	9	QUARK
2	RIGOTTE	10	MASCARPONE
3	CREAM CHEESE	11	FROMAGE FRAIS (8
4	MOZZARELLA		PER CENT FAT)
	AFFUMICATA	12	FETA
5	MOZZARELLA	13	RICOTTA
6	FROMAGE FRAIS	14	CURD CHEESE
	(ALMOST FAT-FREE)	15	CREAM CHEESE
7	COTTAGE CHEESE	16	BRILLAT-SAVARIN
8	BOURSIN		

France, but especially the Auvergne. It has a sharpish taste, and was originally developed as a Gorgonzola substitute during World War Two. (*258*)

SAINT-MARCELLIN

Originally a farmhouse goats' cheese, this is now factory-made using pasteurized cows' milk in the Isère valley, in Dauphiné, France. It is soft and pale yellow in colour, with a thin bluish rind and a very mild, but refreshing, slightly sour taste. (*249*)

SAINTE-MAURE

This soft and creamy French goat cheese comes from the Touraine region. Cylindrical, and with a long straw through the centre, it has a pink-tinged, downy white rind, a goaty smell and full flavour. It is available in both *fermier* (farmhouse) and *laitier* (creamery) varieties. (*250*)

SAINT-NECTAIRE

An ancient French cheese made in the Auvergne for over 1000 years from cows' milk, it is semihard with a greyish rind, supple texture, and a gentle nutty flavour. It is good for cooking and is best between June and December. (*253*)

SAINT-PAULIN

This is commercially produced all over France and in other countries from pasteurized cows' milk. It is a semisoft golden cheese and has an orange rind, springy texture, light smell and a bland, buttery flavour.

SAMSO

A popular Danish cheese produced from pasteurized cows' milk, this has a biscuit-coloured rind, firm buttery texture, with a scattering of holes and a gently sweet, nutty taste.

Blue Cheeses

1 WENSLEYDALE (BLUE)
2 BABY STILTON
3 DANABLU
4 CHESHIRE (BLUE)
5 BLUE VINNEY
   (DORSET BLUE)
6 EDELPILZ
7 BLEU DE BRESSE
8 BLEU DES CAUSSES
9 STILTON
10 BLUE SHROPSHIRE
11 FOURME D'AMBERT
12 BEENLEIGH BLUE
13 DANABLU (JUTLAND)
14 BLEU D'AUVERGNE
15 GORGONZOLA
16 LANARK BLUE
17 MYCELLA
18 CASHEL BLUE
19 DUNSYRE BLUE
20 SAINGORLON
21 DOLCELATTE
22 BAVARIAN BLUE
23 ROQUEFORT

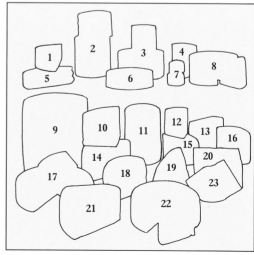

SAPSAGO

This very hard Swiss cheese made from skimmed cows' milk or whey is flavoured with the leaves of melilot, an aromatic plant of the clover family, which gives the cheese its pale green colour and distinctive strong pungent taste. Sapsago is used only for grating. (*245*)

SBRINZ

An ancient cheese made from unpasteurized cows' milk in central Switzerland for some 2000 years, Sbrinz is very hard with a dark yellow rind and paste and has a very strong, piquant flavour. Cured for at least two or three years, it will keep much longer. It is is excellent for cooking. (*245*)

SERRA

This is a traditional Portuguese cheese made on farmsteads in various parts of the country from ewes' milk; the varieties from the Serra da Estrela mountains in the north are particularly good. It is semisoft with a smooth golden rind, buttery interior and a slightly sour taste. When found in perfect, buttery condition you can see it ripening before your eyes. I once watched one in a restaurant in Lisbon. It looked perfectly neat at the beginning of the meal, but by the time we left it had sprawled all over its platter and was about to descend on to the table.

SINGLE GLOUCESTER

This rare English farmhouse cheese from Gloucestershire is like its better-known relation, Double Gloucester, made from the milk of Gloucester cows. But Single Gloucester is quicker-ripening – ready after six to eight weeks – thinner and lighter than the Double. It is a semihard cheese with an open texture, creamy-coloured paste and a mild fresh flavour.

STILTON

The king of English cheese, Stilton is produced only in Leicestershire, Nottinghamshire and Derbyshire. It is most commonly blue-veined or, less regally, white. Blue Stilton, made from pasteurized cows' milk is ripened for three to four months; it has a grey crinkled crust, moist crumbly texture, creamy-yellow paste, all-over blue-green veining and a rich tangy flavour. Available throughout the year, but at its best in late autumn (made from rich summer milk), it is traditional fare at Christmas – accompanied by port. When buying, avoid cheese with a dry brownish paste (except at the edges) or patchy veining. Cut Stilton flat, across its face; never scoop it out from the centre. And never pour port into it – such a practice spoils two superb natural foods. White Stilton, without the mould, is a younger, milder cheese. (*253, 258*)

SWALEDALE

This is semihard cheese similar to Wensleydale made from unpasteurized cows' milk. It is pale creamy-white in colour with a dark yellow firmer rind and the flavour is mild and refreshing. (*253*)

TALEGGIO

A rich, soft cows' milk cheese from northern Italy, this is traditionally farm-produced from unpasteurized milk. It has a rosy-grey rind and – after ripening for six to seven weeks – a tender, springy texture, delicate yellow paste and mild fruity taste. As it ages the cheese becomes darker with a deeper, more aromatic flavour. (*254*)

TÊTE-DE-MOINE

This creamy Swiss cows' milk cheese was originally from Bellelay Abbey but now is produced by small dairies elsewhere in the Bernese Jura. It is made during the summer and sold in winter. A small, drum-shaped cheese, semihard with a rough brownish rind, firm texture and a full fruity flavour, it is traditionally eaten in thin slivers, sprinkled with pepper and cumin powder. (*253*)

TILSIT

A very popular semihard German cheese, Tilsit is made from pasteurized cows' milk – whole or skimmed. It has a firm springy texture, straw-yellow paste peppered with small holes and a light creamy taste, and is sometimes flavoured with caraway seeds. (*253*)

TOMME DE SAVOIE

This is a family of French semihard pressed cheeses made in Savoie by farms and dairies using cows' milk – either whole or semi-skimmed. It generally has a rough grey rind, firm smooth texture, yellowish interior, strong smell and mild nutty flavour. When ripened in grape spirit, it becomes much stronger and is called Tomme *au marc*. (*253*)

VACHERIN MONT D'OR

A celebrated Swiss cheese made from unpasteurized cows' milk in the Jura mountains, this has a thick pinkish crust, matt yellow paste, voluptuous near-liquid texture, resiny aroma and a mild creamy taste, and is bound with a band of spruce bark. Ripe after two to three months, Vacherin Mont d'Or becomes so meltingly soft that it is traditionally eaten with a spoon, straight from its box. It is a winter cheese, not available in spring and summer. The Swiss version is very like its French counterpart of the same name.

VALENÇAY

A soft goat cheese from west-central France made in a squat pyramid shape, the farmhouse type has a blue-grey rind dusted with wood ash, a light goaty smell and mild taste. The commercial version is coarser and stronger with a white bloomy rind. (*250*)

WENSLEYDALE

Originally a blue cheese with a close texture and delicate flavour, this is now more usually a white unveined cheese, though the blue version is still occasionally found. Made from pasteurized cows' milk, it has a flaky texture, moist creamy-white paste and a mild milky flavour with a honeyed aftertaste. Usually eaten young – around a month old – traditionally with apple pie or fruit cake. Some unpasteurized farmhouse Wensleydale is made in Cheshire. It is perfect with celery after a meal, or with pickles and crusty bread for lunch. In the north of England it is traditionally eaten with apple pie. (*253, 258*)

Sugar

Most of the sugar we consume today, both off the shelf and in processed food products, comes from two sources: the sugar cane grown in the tropics, and the sugar beet grown mainly in temperate climates.

Sugar is either refined or unrefined and either white or brown. A refined sugar has had all impurities removed and been separated from its molasses – residue of sticky syrup produced during the initial sugar-extraction process. All white sugar is refined, and there is no difference in taste between beet and cane. An unrefined sugar is only part-purified and contains some molasses; how much affects colour, texture and taste. As beet molasses is inedible, all unrefined sugars come from cane. Traditionally brown sugars are unrefined but today many are made from refined white sugar lightly coated with cane molasses. Identify them by the ingredients list on the packet. An unrefined sugar does not have any 'ingredients', but for emphasis may have a label saying 'raw' or 'unrefined'. Unrefined sugars have the best flavour and aroma.

Sugar is pure carbohydrate, a simple carbohydrate which is quickly absorbed and metabolized by the body to produce an instant – but relatively brief – energy boost.

Refined sugar is 99·9 per cent sucrose and contains 375 kilocalories per 3½oz (100g); 64 kilocalories per tablespoon. Unrefined sugar, because of its molasses, contains a minute proportion of minerals, vitamins and proteins. But the amounts are so small that their nutritional value is negligible.

USES OF SUGAR

As well as sweetening, sugar acts as a preserving agent, inhibiting the growth of bacteria, yeasts and moulds. Fruits can be preserved in sugar syrup, and sugar is used in the making of jams, jellies and chutneys – it acts with the pectin and acid in fruit to form a 'set'. This can be used to advantage in other types of cooking. If you want fruit to keep its shape, cook it with sugar. If you want a soft pulpy mass, add the sugar when the fruit has been thoroughly cooked.

Other flavours, even savoury ones, are enhanced by sugar. Ingredients on the packages of many supposedly savoury items often list sugar near the top. In home cookery a pinch of sugar can be added to bring out the flavour of a fresh tomato sauce if underripe tomatoes are being used.

Sugar has a stabilizing effect on some frozen desserts: homemade sorbets with the smoothest, most appealing texture are those with the most sugar in them. Reduced-sugar sorbets have a nice fruity flavour but are hard, granular and uneven. Sugar is also important in baking, both in yeast cookery and cake-making, in that it encourages rising and aerating. When using eggs in the making of sauces, soufflés and custards, the addition of sugar retards the thickening process, so helping to produce the correct texture.

CASTER SUGAR *superfine sugar*

White free-flowing sugar with very small crystals, this is particularly suitable for baking (it creams easily) and for sifting decoratively on to cakes and pastries. It is also quick-dissolving which makes it popular as a table sugar to sprinkle over desserts, especially fruit. Golden caster is made from crushed and sieved golden granulated.

CRYSTAL SUGAR *rock candy, sugar candy*

This is white sugar produced in large crystals and often coloured amber for use as coffee sugar. It is also available multi-coloured (rainbow), generally with slightly smaller crystals, and used both in coffee and to decorate cakes and biscuits. Make your own by putting a few crystals in a saturated sugar solution; as the water evaporates, the sugar joins with the 'seed' crystals to form larger ones.

CUBE SUGAR *loaf sugar*

This is made from white granulated sugar, moistened with water and moulded into blocks, then dried and cut into cubes. Cube sugar is more expensive than loose sugar, so there is little point in buying it for kitchen use with one exception – I know no better way of extracting the essential oils from an orange or lemon than by rubbing a sugar cube hard over its entire surface. Brown varieties are also available.

DEMERARA SUGAR

Golden-brown sugar with quite large sparkling crystals, this is named after its place of origin in Guyana. Demerara is traditionally an unrefined (raw) cane sugar; it has a relatively low molasses content – hence its pale colour and mild flavour. Today some demeraras are made from refined white sugar with molasses added. Use this sugar on breakfast cereals and yogurt, in coffee and for glazing hams. Its large crystals make it less suitable for baking, but good for decorating cakes and biscuits.

FRUCTOSE

Sweetest of all natural sugars, fructose is found in honey, fruit and vegetables but for commercial purposes is extracted from sucrose. In the body fructose metabolizes without insulin which makes it suitable for diabetics – provided the calorific content is monitored. For cooking, use as sugar but reduce amounts by one-third.

GOLDEN GRANULATED SUGAR

Pale honey-coloured granulated sugar, this is either refined cane sugar with a slight residue of molasses or refined beet sugar coloured with molasses. A good general-purpose sugar, its largish crystals are ideal for making jams, preserves and marmalade as they do not compact in the pan, but are unsuitable for use in pastry and biscuits since they blend badly and show up as dark specks. Golden caster and icing sugars are also available.

GRANULATED SUGAR

The most common and inexpensive sugar, this is refined from cane or beet. It is white, free-flowing with medium-sized crystals. This general-purpose sugar cooks best when it has time to dissolve well as in syrups, jams and jellies. It is less successful for pastry and biscuits where it shows up as brown flakes.

ICING SUGAR *confectioners' sugar*

This is very fine white sugar, made by grinding granulated into a powder – with an anti-caking agent such as calcium phosphate added. It dissolves instantly, and is commonly used to make icings and other cake toppings, confectionery, and syrups for fruit; also to dust on pastries and cakes. Golden icing sugar is made from golden granulated.

MOLASSES SUGAR

Soft, fine-grain, dark brown, unrefined cane sugar with a very high molasses content making it almost-black and sticky with a strong treacle-toffee taste, molasses sugar is used in dark-coloured foods like Christmas pudding, chutney, gingerbread and, of course, treacle toffee.

MUSCOVADO SUGAR

Soft, fine-grain, brown sugar, this is traditionally made from unrefined (raw) cane sugar. There are two main types: light and dark. Light muscovado is pale gold with a delicate, fudge-like flavour, and is suitable for making cakes, biscuits, excellent meringues and marvellous fudge. It can also be used as a table sugar. Dark muscovado, with a higher molasses content, has a moister texture and a strong lingering flavour that goes well with other rich flavours – as in gingerbread, coffee and chocolate cakes.

PRESERVING SUGAR

White sugar with large coarse crystals, this is designed for making jams, jellies and marmalade. It does not form a dense mass at the base of the pan, which helps prevent burning, and also produces very little surface froth so eliminating frequent skimming. Some jam sugars now contain pectin to assist setting.

RAW SUGAR *crude sugar*

Traditionally this is the dark sticky mass of sugar and molasses produced by boiling down cane sugar juice – local names for it include *jaggery* (India), *piloncillo* (Mexico), and *panda* (Colombia). In many cane-growing countries this is poured into moulds, left to harden and then used as a sweetener in cooking.

But as part of the sugar-making process, the term 'raw sugar' is more specific. After boiling, the resultant gooey mixture is separated into molasses and raw sugar – which is then either refined into white sugar or purified and sold as a brown sugar.

SOFT BROWN SUGAR

This term refers to a range of fine-grain, moist sugars, light or dark brown in colour – and in flavour – varying according to molasses content. It is made either from unrefined (raw) cane sugar or, more generally, from refined white sugar with molasses added. Both types are mainly used in baking; the dark varieties are especially good for rich fruit cakes or spiced tea breads.

VANILLA SUGAR

This is caster sugar to which at least 10 per cent pure vanilla extract or essence has been added, and is used to flavour pastries and sweet dishes. But you can easily make your own by burying a vanilla pod in a closed jar of caster sugar and leaving it for a couple of weeks. Similarly, make other spiced sugars with cloves, cardamom seeds or cinnamon sticks; if the spice is ground first, even more flavour penetrates the sugar.

Also available is vanilla-flavoured sugar – caster sugar flavoured with synthetic vanilla.

Sugars

Honeys and Syrups

Honey, the world's oldest sweetener, is made by bees from the nectar of flowers. What type of flower the nectar comes from affects colour – ranging from creamy white to dark brown – and flavour. Rosemary honey, for example, is pale and delicate, while pine honey is dark amber with a strong resinous taste. Flavour is also influenced by weather and season: springtime honeys are soft and sweet; summer ones have a richer aroma. The tendency of honey to crystallize depends on the natural balance of sugars it contains – although most clear honeys will crystallize with time, especially if kept at a low temperature. Similarly a set honey will become runny if heated. But essentially there is no difference between clear and set and many honeys are produced in both forms. Two common exceptions are acacia honey which is always thin and runny, and clover which is generally thick and creamy. Sometimes honey is sold on the comb or bottled together with part of its comb; in both cases the comb is edible.

For most cooking purposes choose a clear runny honey as it blends easily and dissolves quickly. Use it to replace sugar in cakes, pastries and biscuits. It is excellent in mousses, jellies, creams, bavarois and ice-creams. It makes a lovely sweetener for fruit salads, stewed fruit and baked apples. There are also various cakes and sweetmeats based on honey, such as *halva* and *baklava* from Greece and nougat from France.

Honey has its place in savoury dishes, too – especially as a glaze or in marinades. And, of course, use honey straight from the jar – spread on to bread, and trickled over ice-cream, waffles, pancakes, yogurt or cereals.

Syrups, normally less sweet than honey, are widely used both in home cooking – especially baking – and in the food industry. Some, such as golden syrup and treacle, are byproducts of sugar-refining. Others come from the sweet juices which occur naturally in certain trees and plants like the maple, palm and sorghum; these juices are reduced by boiling into concentrated syrups.

When using honey or syrup as a sugar substitute in recipes remember they are liquid sweeteners and that other liquid ingredients should be reduced accordingly.

TYPES OF HONEY

Honey can be divided into two categories: blended honey and single-flower honey. Much honey is blended, which ensures consistency of taste, texture and colour – but I find the flavour is generally rather bland. Jars labelled simply 'honey' or more evocatively 'wild-flower honey', 'meadow honey', or 'mountain honey' are blends, often from more than one country. Major honey producers include Australia, Canada, China, Greece, Hungary and other parts of Eastern Europe, Mexico, New Zealand and South America, particularly Argentina.

Single-flower honey, as its name implies, is predominantly made from the nectar of just one flower variety – and is honey at its best. The variety is enormous, ranging from well-known types like clover and acacia to the rare pohuta-kawa honey from New Zealand and the rich chestnut honey from the forests of France. Some of the most important single-flower honeys are:

Acacia From Canada, China, France, Hungary, Italy and Romania, this is a very pale, clear liquid honey with a delicate scented flavour. It is one of the few honeys that does not crystallize with age.

Alfalfa honey is very common in the United States. Thick creamy-yellow with an agreeably sweet taste, it is often used in blends and is good for cooking.

Buckwheat A reddish-brown, strongly flavoured honey from North America and Europe, this is traditionally coarse and granulated, but is also available clear.

Clover Very popular both in Europe and North America, clover honey is light coloured, thick and full flavoured. It is a good all-purpose honey. English clover honey is delicious but, like all English honey, expensive.

Colza (**rape**) honey is pale, smooth and very sweet; useful in cooking. Sunflower and lucerne honeys are similar.

Eucalyptus honey is a burnished-brown, pungent, powerful honey from Australia and the Mediterranean.

Heather One of my favourites, from Britain and mainland Europe, this is reddish-brown with a crystallized, soft-butter texture. With its distinctive, intense flavour, it is too special for cooking. Heather honey made from ling is curiously gelatinous, with a full bitter-edged taste.

Hymettus Not honey from a single flower but from a specific area – Mount Hymettus in Greece – this is one of the world's most expensive honeys. Dark brown and aromatic, it has thyme as a dominant flavour.

Lavender Mainly from Provence, this is a deep-golden thick honey with a strong perfumed flavour and lingering aftertaste.

Leatherwood Australian honey made from the blossom of the Tasmanian leatherwood tree, this is amber-coloured with a delicate flavour.

Lemon blossom is a fine, pale-gold, clear honey from Mexico with a light delicate flavour.

Lime flower (**linden**) From France and Eastern Europe, this is a greeny-gold honey with a rich soft flavour.

Manuka This is a New Zealand honey made from the blossom of the manuka or 'tea tree', and is a clear, thick, deep golden honey with a rich flavour.

Orange blossom From Spain, Florida and other orange-growing areas, this is a clear liquid honey with a pale reddish-gold colour, delicate flavour and light perfume.

Rosemary A pale clear honey with a fragrant flavour which becomes stronger if mixed with thyme honey, this comes principally from France and Spain.

Honeys and Syrups

1	ACACIA HONEY	14	BUCKWHEAT CLEAR HONEY
2	BLACKSTRAP MOLASSES	15	BUCKWHEAT SET HONEY
3	ENGLISH HONEY	16	MEXICAN SET HONEY
4	FRENCH CHESTNUT HONEY	17	MEXICAN CLEAR HONEY
5	DARK SYRUP	18	CARIBBEAN SET HONEY
6	WEST INDIAN TREACLE	19	LIME BLOSSOM HONEY
7	TROPICAL WILD HONEY	20	CANADIAN CLOVER HONEY
8	CORN SYRUP	21	NEW ZEALAND MANUKA HONEY
9	MAPLE SYRUP	22	GREEK MOUNTAIN HONEY
10	GOLDEN SYRUP	23	CARIBBEAN CLEAR HONEY
11	LEATHERWOOD HONEY		
12	COMB HONEY		
13	NEW ZEALAND POHUTAKAWA HONEY		

Types of Syrup | HONEYS AND SYRUPS

TYPES OF SYRUP

Syrup can be thin or thick, pale or dark. In general the dark heavy varieties – such as molasses and black treacle – have a stronger flavour which makes them ideal for use in gingerbread, rich fruit cake and spicy sauces. Lighter types like maple can be poured over pancakes, waffles and ice-cream.

Cane syrup This is boiled-down intermediate syrup from the sugar-cane refining process. A popular table syrup, especially in the United States, it is often blended with maple syrup to create a less expensive product than pure maple.

Corn syrup An all-purpose syrup made from corn (maize) starch, corn syrup is available light or dark; the darker variety is less refined and has a stronger flavour. It is used as a table syrup and in baking; and is also good for sweetening frozen desserts and preserves – it gives ice-cream a smooth texture and makes jams and jellies clear.

Dark syrup is a blend of golden syrup and black treacle. Use it as golden syrup, but for a darker colour and a less sweet flavour.

Fruit syrup is a blend of concentrated sugar syrup and fruit juice. If buying, check the label for 'pure fruit juice' not 'fruit-flavoured'. But these syrups are easy to make at home – especially from soft fruits like blackcurrant, raspberry, strawberry and blackberry. Used to flavour ice-creams and sorbets, cakes and cake fillings, fish and meat sauces, they are also delicious poured over desserts.

Golden syrup Light and sweet, with an amber colour and butterscotch flavour, golden syrup is a byproduct of sugar refining which is then further refined in its own right. It is popular as a table syrup and in home-baking, especially for gingerbread, flapjacks and treacle tart.

Maple syrup The boiled-down sap of the North American maple tree, this distinctive syrup – reddish-brown with a smooth rich flavour – is expensive, especially if it is 'pure' 100 per cent maple sap. Less expensive varieties are often blended with corn or cane syrup; check the label when buying. Pour it on to pancakes, French toast, waffles and ice-cream; also used to glaze vegetables and hams.

Molasses A dark, thick concentrated syrup left over when sugar cane is refined, this is not as sweet as other syrups. Its strong rich flavour enhances fruit cakes, Christmas puddings, gingerbread and treacle toffee – as well as chutneys and pickles. It is also a traditional ingredient in various North American dishes, including Boston baked beans. The colour ranges from mid-brown to black; the darkest variety, blackstrap, has a bitter edge.

Palm syrup is concentrated sap from various species of palm tree. Very dark and sticky, it is produced in the Middle East, Far East, India and Latin America and used in local dishes.

Sugar syrup (**simple syrup, stock syrup**) is syrup made from sugar and water. To four parts water use either two parts sugar (thin syrup) or three parts sugar (medium syrup) or 4¾ parts sugar (heavy syrup). Stir the sugar into the water, heat gently until dissolved, bring to the boil and simmer for three minutes. Use it for bottling fruits, making sorbets and ice-creams and for sweetening drinks and fruit salads.

Treacle is a blend of refinery syrup and cane molasses, ranging in colour from gold to black (often called West Indian). It is used in baking and confectionery for a strong sweet flavour.

COFFEE

Two species of the coffee plant produce the major part of the world's coffee supply. The best, and most widely cultivated, is *Coffea arabica*, which flourishes at high altitudes – from about 2000ft (600 metres). This small evergreen tree, which grows right across the world's tropical belt, has glossy green leaves and fragrant white flowers, followed by berry fruits. The sweet pulp of the berries houses two pale green seeds or 'beans'. This coffee is the lowest in caffeine and may be kept unblended.

Coffea canephora, used to produce *robusta* coffee, grows best at lower altitudes. It has larger leaves but smaller, heavier-cropping berries than *Coffea arabica*. It also has a higher caffeine content, and is often used in blending.

Coffee also has particular characteristics according to its country of origin. It is interesting to experiment not only with different types and roasts but the various methods of making the coffee. It is quite possible to create your own particular blend of beans, roasted to the degree you want and prepared by your favourite method.

COFFEE-MAKING EQUIPMENT

Jug This is the simplest method, requiring the minimum equipment. Pour boiling water into a china or earthenware jug to heat it while you grind the coffee, coarse or medium ground, and boil fresh water. Empty the jug, then spoon in the coffee. Slowly pour on water which has just boiled (but is not boiling). Stir once, then allow it to brew for four minutes. Strain into cups, or into another heated – and preferably lidded – coffee pot.

Cafetière or **plunger** I like this method, both for the excellent coffee it makes and the pleasing design of the pot. A heat-proof glass pot with a pouring spout, sometimes in a steel girdle, sometimes sitting in a metal rack, has a plunger attached to the lid. Fine wire mesh keeps the coffee grounds separate from the liquid when you pour it. Use medium-ground coffee and let it brew for four minutes, then push the plunger down.

Filter method Another method which gives rich, clear coffee. Heat a china or heat-proof glass jug with hot water, then pour this away.

Place a filter paper in the special holder that fits over the jug and spoon in fine-ground or filter-ground coffee. Pour on just enough freshly boiled water to moisten the coffee and when it has dripped through, carefully pour on the rest of the (measured) water. The only drawback to this method is that the coffee can cool too quickly. This is avoided with an electric automatic filter machine.

French drip pot The pot has three parts. An upper container is filled with just-boiled water. This drips through medium-ground coffee placed in the central filter compartment and into the bottom container which has a handle and pouring spout. Individual over-cup filters can be purchased to fit over coffee cups.

Neopolitan flip This also comes in three parts: a container for the water, a second container for the ground coffee and a third container for the product of the two – freshly brewed coffee. The water is heated in the pot, which is then turned upside down so the hot water drips through the coffee into the third section.

Espresso pots and **machines** This method requires the most expensive equipment, either mechanical or electrical. It produces a most powerful, fully flavoured extraction because water is forced by steam through the very finely ground coffee, which is usually a high roast. This is the coffee served in bars and restaurants all over Italy. It is a tiny strong mouthful of a very potent and high-roasted brew.

Percolator This system allows water to drip through the coffee until the extraction is complete. To my taste, this results in a cooked flavour.

Ibrik This small, specially designed, long-handled copper pan, rather like a small milk churn in shape, broad at the bottom and narrow at the top, is used to make 'Turkish' (or 'Greek' – both countries lay claim to it) coffee. Alternatively you can use a narrow, high-sided saucepan. Grind medium- or high-roast coffee to a very fine powder. Put coffee, sugar (this type of coffee is usually sweetened) and water into the pan and bring to the boil, allow it to froth, remove from the heat and stir. Do this twice more before pouring the

coffee, without straining, into tiny, warm coffee cups – after which it is not stirred further. Milk is never used in this type of coffee.

COFFEE-MAKING METHODS

There are many ways of making a good cup of coffee, but even the best equipment will give a poor cup of coffee unless certain basic principles are followed:

1. Whereas weak tea is drinkable and to many tastes enjoyable, weak coffee is not, so do not try to economize. One to two tablespoons of ground coffee per cup is needed. I use ten tablespoons to fill an eight-cup cafetière for breakfast time coffee; 12 tablespoons for the same size cafetière for a stronger after-dinner brew.

2. Use freshly drawn water, just off the boil.

3. Make sure that the container or utensil is clean and free of coffee oils build-up; soaking in a mild detergent will strip away any oily residue.

4. Use the freshest-possible beans; ideally, grind them as you need them. Ground beans lose their freshness more quickly than whole ones because there is more surface contact with the air. It is advisable to buy your coffee beans regularly and in small quantities so they do not go stale on the shelf. Storing coffee beans in the freezer compartment of the refrigerator is also said to help keep them fresh.

5. Choose a blend *you* like. Experiment rather than follow slavishly those who tell you that such and such is best. If you do not like the flavour why drink it?

6. Make sure that the coffee is ground appropriately for the method you use. For example, coarsely ground coffee is not suitable for the filter method since not enough flavour will be extracted; and fine filter-ground coffee will fall through the perforated basket of a percolator and the coffee will be rather muddy.

SERVING COFFEE

There are many ways of serving this fragrant, stimulating drink. The *café au lait* that you drink from a large green cup in a Paris café and perhaps dip your croissant into is a very different drink to the tiny *espresso* served in a bar in Rome, often with a sliver of lemon zest which you twist over the coffee. In New Orleans you might order a *café brûlot* (or *café au diable*): cinnamon, cloves, sugar, orange peel and brandy, burning in a bowl with a hazy blue flame with hot, strong coffee poured over them. A similar flaming coffee, *quemada de la casa* served in Galicia and the cool northwest of Spain, is perfect for a winter evening. On a hot, sticky day in New York, few things are as refreshing as a tall, frosty glass of iced coffee. Irish coffee is a heady concoction of black coffee and Irish whiskey topped with thick cream. It has many derivatives: Norman coffee with Calvados, Caribbean coffee with rum, Mexican coffee with tequila or the coffee liqueur Tia Maria.

COOKING WITH COFFEE

Coffee is an important flavouring in cake-making, especially for light sponges and cake fillings. Ice-creams, *granitas* and cold soufflés, chilled custards and mousses all benefit from its subtly distinctive, rich, slightly bitter flavour, and it marries particularly well with chocolate. Not long ago in a Paris restaurant I ate an exquisite ice-cream with an indefinable flavour. Green unroasted coffee beans were the magic ingredient. It was one of the best ice-creams I have ever tasted. There are chefs who have also experimented using coffee as a condiment, marinade or sauce ingredient to accompany savoury dishes!

TYPES OF COFFEE

Brazilian What happens to the coffee harvest in Brazil affects the world coffee market, since that country is now the largest producer and exporter of coffee. Santos, named for the port through which it is exported is probably the best-known of the Brazilian coffees. It produces a smooth sweet brew.

Colombian Very fine coffee produced from the *arabica*, this flourishes in the Andean foothills and the plains around Medellin which yield the best-quality beans.

Costa Rican This is a distinctively sharp yet rich-flavoured *arabica* coffee.

Ecuadorean Grown at rather high altitudes, this is neither very full-flavoured nor a particularly interesting coffee.

Indian One of the best-known Indian coffees is Mysore, which has lots of flavour and character and is often included in blends.

Indonesian and **Javanese** coffees are very full-flavoured, rich and distinctive.

Jamaican Not all Jamaican coffee is as smooth and mild as the renowned and very expensive Blue Mountain coffee, which is named after the area where it is grown; nevertheless all Jamaican coffees are very good.

Kenyan One of the most widely available coffees, it has a good straightforward yet appealing flavour and fine aroma.

Mocha is a very loose term, applied also to coffee and chocolate mixtures. Smooth, strong flavoured, *arabica*-type Mocha or Moka coffee is produced by several countries. The traditional pulverized coffee used for Turkish coffee is Mocha.

Others Coffee also comes from many other countries, including Angola, Cameroon, Dominican Republic, El Salvador, Ethiopia (the original home of the wild *arabica* coffee plant), Guatemala, Haiti, Ivory Coast, Madagascar, Mexico, New Guinea, Nicaragua, Puerto Rica, Tanzania, Venezuela and Zimbabwe.

TYPES OF ROAST

Roasting gives the beans their flavour and aroma by reducing their moisture content and thus releasing their aromatic oils. It also changes the colour of the coffee, which darkens the more it is roasted.

Light roast is best for mild beans, bringing out their full but delicate flavour, and is suitable for breakfast coffee.

Medium roast subjects the beans to longer heat treatment for a stronger flavour and aroma. The beans will be a rich mid-brown and look dry, and are perfect for morning coffee.

Full or **high roast** produces a strongly flavoured, slightly bitter coffee. The beans will be dark brown with a slightly satiny surface. These are good for after-dinner coffee.

Continental roast This is the highest roast, producing a rich black coffee with a burnt, slightly bitter flavour. The beans are black and oily-looking. It is the roast for espresso coffee, served in tiny cups.

Coffees

1 COSTA RICA BEANS (UNROASTED)
2 JAVA BEANS (UNROASTED)
3 KENYA BEANS
4 BLUE MOUNTAIN
5 SANTOS BEANS
6 SOHO-BLEND BEANS
7 TURKISH GRIND
8 ESPRESSO GRIND
9 FILTER GRIND (FINE)
10 MEDIUM FINE GRIND
11 MEDIUM GRIND
12 COARSE GRIND

TEAS AND TISANES

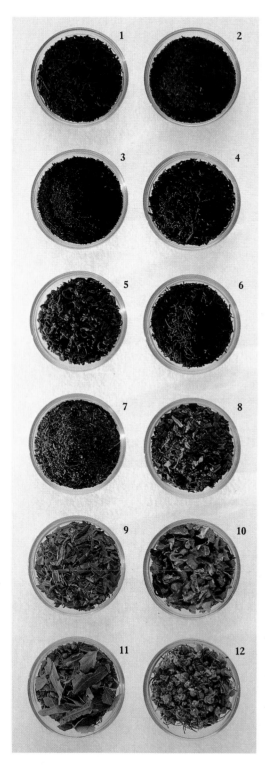

This almost universal drink is made from the processed leaves of the evergreen bush, *Camellia sinensis*. Native to China and India, now it is also grown in Asia, East Africa, South America and parts of Eastern Europe.

We know it as a rich golden-brown breakfast time cuppa, and as a more genteel high tea beverage served in delicate porcelain cups. In the United States it is served iced, and this is where I first tasted 'sun tea'. A few teabags were placed in a large jar of water and this was left in a sunny porch. After eight hours in the hot sun, the liquid had turned golden red and we drank it from tall, frosted glasses part-filled with ice cubes and garnished with fresh mint leaves.

In Tibet black tea is served with yak butter. In Russia it is sweetened with jam. In China and Japan tea has a long and important history, from the first writings about it by Lu Yu in 800 AD to the tea ceremony which is still an important part of life. In both these latter countries, tea houses tend to serve a similar function to that of the pub, bar and café in Western society.

TYPES OF TEA

Once you are familiar with the various terms used to describe teas, reading a tea packet becomes something like reading a wine label. The country of origin will give you some hint of what you will drink, as will the description 'black' or 'green'. But what about 'pekoe' or 'souchong'? No, these are not types of tea but descriptions of the tea leaf. Tea is classified by the type of processing it undergoes, and also graded by leaf size.

Green tea has been heat-treated by steam to prevent the tea leaves fermenting. After picking, they are withered (the initial drying process in which the leaves lose about 60 per

cent of their water content), then heat-treated, dried and packed. It is most commonly drunk in China, as a delicate pale brew, without milk or lemon. Green tea is also common in Japan.

Black tea The characteristic colour and much of the powerful flavour of black tea come from the fermentation process. After the leaves have been picked and withered, they are broken to release their juices or enzymes and acids. On exposure to air the leaves oxidize and turn bright brown and then, when dried under temperature-controlled conditions, they become black. Black tea is produced in China, South-East Asia, East Africa and Eastern Europe.

Oolong tea For this type of tea, the fermenting process of the green tea leaves is stopped halfway through, then the leaves are dried. It was perfected in Taiwan, and the tea is still called by the island's earlier name, Formosa Oolong, although some Oolongs are also produced in China. Drink this fine-flavoured pale tea without milk, sugar or lemon to best appreciate its distinctive peach-like flavour.

Smoked or **tarry teas** are fermented black teas which have been smoke-dried to produce the characteristic tarry taste. These teas are drunk without milk, sugar or lemon.

LEAF SIZE

Black teas are graded by the leaf size, which determines the necessary brewing time. The smaller the leaf, or fragment of leaf, the quicker the tea will brew.

Small-leaf teas are fine leaf particles or small leaves, and are used mostly in teabags. They brew very quickly.

Broken-leaf teas include broken pekoe and broken orange pekoe, and are used for dark strong teas because the brewing time is relatively short.

Leaf teas Flowery orange pekoe is a large-leaf tea containing a high proportion of tips which have a slightly golden colour. If it has an even higher proportion of tips, this is sometimes called golden flowery orange pekoe. Orange pekoe has long, thin, tightly rolled leaves. Souchong is another large-leaf tea, but whereas pekoe (although derived from a Chinese word) is used to describe Indian and Sri

---

Tea and Tisane Leaves

1 EARL GREY	8 COMFREY
2 NILGIRI	9 THYME AND
3 DIMBULA	CINNAMON
4 DARJEELING	10 ROSEHIP AND
5 GUNPOWDER	HIBISCUS
6 KOKEI CHA	11 LIME BLOSSOM
7 MINT	12 CAMOMILE

Lankan teas, souchong is used only to describe large-leaf black teas from China.

These large-leaf teas need longer brewing than the broken- or small-leaf teas in order to release their flavours.

MAKING TEA

Whether using loose tea or teabags the method is the same – unlike coffee-making. No one has been able to improve upon the teapot, but for preference, use a glazed china or earthenware pot as both retain heat and will not taint the tea. Scald the pot by rinsing it out with hot water. Put in one teaspoonful of tea or one teabag per person and, if you like it strong, one extra for the pot. Always use freshly drawn water which must be boiling as it is poured on to the tea; this is why you take the pot to the kettle. Put the lid on the pot immediately so that the fragrant steam does not escape. Let the pot stand for three to five minutes according to the leaf type (just two for small-leaf tea). Then stir the tea to ensure an even strength before pouring it through a strainer. Add milk or lemon and sugar according to preference.

After the tea has brewed it will begin to go bitter and there will be an excess of tannin if the leaves are left in the pot. With teabags simply fish them out. With loose tea, contain the leaves in a tea ball.

COOKING WITH TEA

One summer, while lunching on the terrace of a restaurant in the Loire valley, we were served a pudding described on the menu as a lemon mousse in a tea sauce. It sounded fascinating, but tasted just as if a cold cup of tea had been poured over the rather delicate mousse. The French chef had infused the tea leaves in a thin cream and sweetened it, exactly as I would make a mint or a lavender sauce. Yet to English taste buds the dish did not work.

On the other hand I have made syrups with jasmine tea and served them with ice-cream. An excellent green tea ice-cream is often served in Japanese restaurants, and jasmine or even Darjeeling tea sorbet would work well.

Tea is traditionally used to steep prunes and other dried fruit. And you can use tea in rich

dark cakes such as barm brack, as a substitute for some or all of the liquid that is required in the recipe.

CEYLON TEAS

Although the country is now called Sri Lanka, the tea is still referred to as Ceylon tea. The best types are 'high grown', particularly those at 6000ft (1800 metres) above sea level, but 'middle grown' are also good. Tea from the tropical rain forest area is known as 'low grown' tea. There are various types available.

Dimbula has a golden colour and a mellow rich flavour. It is excellent for breakfast and throughout the day, and can be drunk with or without milk.

Kandy is a strong, full-bodied tea grown in the area around Kandy, the ancient royal capital.

Luaka is high-grown, high-quality tea, with less tannin and caffeine than other teas.

Nuwara Eliya is delicate light tea that makes a perfect after-dinner drink.

Uva The Uva Highlands are said to produce the very best Ceylon tea, strong, full-flavoured, aromatic and with a fine rich colour. An excellent breakfast tea, drunk with milk.

CHINA TEAS

Much of the tea now exported from China is blended and known by the name of the blend rather than by the name of the tea plantation which produced it, although some blends, such as Keemun, are named for the original region of production. The tea, whether black or green, is, on the whole, of the large-leaf or souchong grade.

Brick tea is an exception to the above statement. In earlier times, when transportation was difficult and expensive, black teas were steamed and pressed into bricks for ease of transport. The tea

Teas and Tisanes

1 CEYLON UVA
2 LAPSANG SOUCHONG
3 English BREAKFAST
4 SENCHA FUKU JYU
5 DARJEELING
6 ROSE CONGOU
7 HIBISCUS
8 PEPPERMINT
9 HONEYSUCKLE
10 APPLE AND LEMON
 BLEND
11 ORANGE FLOWER
12 ROSEHIP

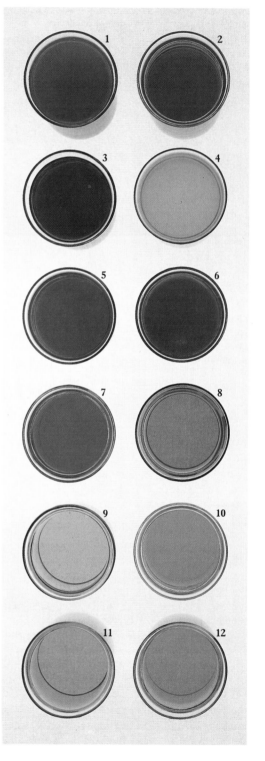

was not of the highest quality, a mixture of dust, stems and coarse leaves being used. Brick tea is still produced today and makes an interesting souvenir to bring back from China as the bricks are embossed with an attractive design and lettering. Just grate or break off the amount that you need.

Chrysanthemum tea Small, dried, yellow and white chrysanthemum heads are mixed with black or green tea to make a refreshing drink, often served in Chinese restaurants as an alternative to jasmine tea. As it does not have the sweet fragrance of the jasmine flower, it perhaps also interferes less with the tastes of whatever foods you are eating.

Congou (Pouchong) A large-leafed black tea, using not the very tip of the plant but the third or fourth leaf. Sometimes dried rose petals are added to make rose congou.

Earl Grey Originally blended for the second Earl Grey in the 1830s, Earl Grey is now a generic name for black tea flavoured and scented with oil of bergamot. It makes a pale to medium golden-brown tea best drunk alone – although some people like it with a thin slice of lemon or a little milk.

Formosa Oolong This is a lovely aromatic tea, pale golden when properly brewed, with a distinctive flavour. To appreciate its quality fully drink it without milk, sugar or lemon.

Fukien Oolong Although the Formosa Oolongs are said to be superior to those from China, one of my very favourite teas is a blend called Ti Kuan Yin, or Iron Goddess of Mercy, which comes from Fujian Province. The leaves are large and show a good deal of paler tips. It is served at the end of a Chinese meal.

Green tea Probably the best known is gunpowder tea, so called because the leaves are tightly rolled into small balls (the leaves expand dramatically when infused). It produces a fragrant, pale greeny-yellow tea with a delicate aroma. Other green teas are hyson, young hyson and lung ching.

Jasmine tea Black or green tea is mixed with the dried flowers of the scented white jasmine, which makes a fragrant and refreshing drink before and after a Chinese meal. Although it has the appearance of a summery drink, it is traditionally served in winter in China.

Keemun A rich yet at the same time delicately flavoured, slightly sweet black tea.

Lapsang souchong The best known of the smoked or 'tarry' black teas, large-leafed lapsang souchong has an unusual flavour that is best enjoyed on its own.

EAST AFRICA TEAS

Kenya Throughout East Africa tea production is a growing industry. Much of it is blended, but some estates – particularly in the Kenyan Highlands – produce excellent strongly flavoured tea, rather like Assam.

Malawi produces black teas known for their superb colour and brightness, which are used in many British blends.

INDIA TEAS

Assam and Darjeeling teas are justly famous in their own right, but much of India's huge tea harvest goes into blending. 'English Breakfast Tea' is a blend that varies from merchant to merchant, but will contain a good proportion of Assam tea which is valued for its rich golden colour and powerful flavour which can stand up to the addition of milk.

Assam The largest tea-producing area of the world, and one of the three main tea-growing areas of India, the Assam valley produces strong, mature teas.

Darjeeling Grown high in the foothills of the Himalayas, the finest Darjeeling from India's second most important tea area are exquisite: light, fragrant and fruity. 'The Champagne of teas' is a frequent description. Pure Darjeeling from the best tea gardens is very expensive. That grown lower down the valley still retains some of the character and is less expensive. It can be drunk with milk or lemon, and is very good iced, when its Muscat grape aroma can be detected.

Nilgiri The third tea-growing region, Nilgiri, is in the hills of southern India. Tea is plentiful here, with a good colour and flavour, often used in blends, but also enjoyed alone.

INDONESIA TEAS

Both black and green teas are produced in Sumatra and Java. These have a good colour and flavour, and are used mainly in blends.

JAPAN TEAS

Only two per cent of Japan's tea is exported. **Sencha Fuku Jyu** is the most often seen. It is a richly coloured green tea served, not by the potful as in Chinese restaurants, but by the cupful. It is a high-grade leaf.

Banch is the everyday Japanese tea.

Gyokuro is the finest tea leaf, called 'jewel-dew'.

Kokei Cha This is a fine and fragrant green tea that is made from a particularly thin and needle-like leaf.

Matcha The powdered version of the above, this tea is whisked into very hot water to form a bright green frothy tea that is used in the tea ceremony.

TISANES AND FLAVOURED TEAS

Tisanes, or herb teas or infusions, are not teas at all because they are not made from the leaves of the tea bush. However, they are made in the same way, by infusing leaves, flowers, seeds or roots in nearly boiling water until the flavour has been extracted.

Many herb teas are held to have specific therapeutic properties: camomile tea, for instance, is used as a sedative. But perhaps one of the main reasons for their increasing popularity, particularly for after-dinner drinking, is that they do not contain caffeine or tannin. Another reason must surely be that they taste so good and there are so many different flavours.

As well as being used to make single herb teas, some blend very well together, such as linden and peppermint, or thyme and cinnamon.

Flavoured teas In China, black and green tea has long been flavoured with other ingredients: jasmine tea, chrysanthemum tea and rose congou tea, for example.

This idea spread to the West, and now black tea is flavoured with all manner of ingredients. Dried fruit and fruit peel make apple and lemon tea, grapefruit tea, mango tea. Oils and essences produce blackcurrant tea, kiwi tea, lime tea, passion fruit tea and strawberry, vanilla and wild cherry teas.

These are made in exactly the same way as the more traditional teas, sometimes served iced and not normally drunk with milk.

À la bourguignonne Food cooked in a red wine sauce with small onions, mushrooms and diced bacon. A speciality of Burgundy, France.

À la grècque Literally from Greece. Usually refers to vegetables cooked in water with olive oil, lemon juice and other flavourings and then cooled. Usually served as an hors d'oeuvre.

Acidulated water Water to which lemon juice or white wine vinegar has been added. It is then used for immersing vegetables or fruit to prevent their discolouration, for example celeriac and apples.

Al dente Literally the Italian for 'to the tooth'. It is used to describe the texture of food, especially pasta, when it is properly cooked but just firm to the bite. The term also refers to vegetables.

Aromatic Any fragrant plant used for flavouring foods. Different parts of the plant can be used depending on the variety. Aromatics are widely used, both directly in cooking and, indirectly, in marinades, court-bouillons mustards and flavoured vinegars, for example. See also *Court-bouillon*.

Aspic Transparent savoury jelly made from clarified meat or fish stock. Used to glaze cold foods.

Bain-marie A water bath. A roasting pan of hot water or a double saucepan with water in the lower half for cooking food slowly at low temperatures or for keeping food hot.

Ballottine A dish of boned and stuffed meat, poultry or game.

Bard To cover meat, poultry or game with a piece of pork fat or bacon fat to keep the flesh moist during roasting.

Baste To spoon fat or pan juices over food during cooking to prevent it from drying out.

Bavarois A moulded pudding made from egg custard and gelatine, mixed with whipped cream and sometimes fruit purée.

Béchamel A white sauce made by adding infused milk to a roux base. It is often used as a basis for other sauces. See also *Roux*.

Bind To add egg or other liquid to dry food to hold it together.

Blanch To pour boiling water over foods such as tomatoes to remove the skin. Also means to cook briefly in boiling water for a few seconds or minutes before, for example, freezing the food, usually vegetables.

Bollito misto A meat stew from Piedmont, Italy, containing a wide selection of several meats and vegetables.

Braise To brown food in fat and then cook it slowly in a minimum of liquid in a tightly covered pan.

Brine A salt-water solution used to preserve fish, meat and vegetables.

Brown To sear the outside of meat before stewing or braising to seal in the juices.

Caffeine A substance present in coffee, tea and cola nuts which acts as a stimulant.

Caramelize To turn sugar into caramel by gently heating it so that it becomes brown. Small vegetables are often caramelized by cooking them in a small amount of water, sugar and butter to produce a glazed effect.

Cassoulet A French stew originating from Languedoc and consisting of dried haricot beans, pork or lamb, sausages and preserved goose (*confit d'oie*).

Charlotte A cold, moulded pudding prepared in a special large round mould.

Chine To separate the backbone from the ribs in a joint of meat for easier carving.

Clarify To remove impurities from fats, especially butter and stocks by slow melting and then straining.

Compôte Fresh or dried fruit cooked in a sugar syrup and served as a dessert.

Condiment A seasoning used to flavour foods or to act as a preservative. Most condiments come from vegetables and are used either raw or untreated, such as fresh herbs, or after preparation, such as sauces and chutneys.

Court-bouillon Flavoured liquid used for poaching fish. Made from water and wine or wine vinegar with herbs and vegetables for flavouring.

Couscous A North African dish made with hard wheat semolina. Using a special double boiler, the meat and vegetables are cooked in the lower half and the semolina steamed in the top half.

Crystallize To preserve fruit in sugar syrup.

Curd The coagulated or thick substance produced in milk when it is soured. Milk can be coagulated either by adding rennet or by natural souring. The flowering head of cauliflower and broccoli is also called curd.

Curdle To cause sauces made either from egg and butter or oil, or from egg and milk or cream and yogurt mixtures to separate into solids and liquids.

Cure To preserve fish or meat by drying, salting or smoking.

Daube A French term for braised meat and vegetables, often cooked with red wine.

Deglaze Scraping the cooking juices from the bottom of the pan and diluting with the use of wine or stock to make gravy or sauce.

Dress To prepare poultry and game for cooking by plucking, cleaning and trussing. With salads it means to add the vinaigrette. It also means to prepare crab and lobster meat. See also *Vinaigrette*.

Eaux-de-vie Dry fruit brandies which are higher in alcohol than liqueurs. The finest come from Alsace, France, southern Germany and Switzerland.

Emulsify To bind fatty foods such as butter and oil with water, vinegar or lemon juice using an emulsifier such as egg yolk to prevent the combined ingredients from separating.

En croûte Cooking food, especially meat, poultry and pâté, entirely in pastry.

En papillote Food cooked and served piping hot in paper bags, made from oiled or buttered greaseproof paper.

Entrails The internal organs of an animal, bird, or fish. Also called innards. The giblets are the edible entrails.

Essence A concentrated aromatic liquid used to flavour foods.

Eviscerate To gut an animal, bird, or fish. See also *Gut*.

Ferment To cause certain yeasts and bacteria to react with other food substances to form acids or alcohols. A wide range of foods are fermented, for example yogurt is produced from fermented milk and sauerkraut from fermented cabbage.

Filo A type of pastry made in thin sheets. A speciality of Greece and other eastern Mediterranean countries.

Fillet To cut the breast of poultry or flesh of fish from the bones.

Flake To separate pieces of, for example, cooked fish into small slivers.

Fritto misto From Italy, literally 'fried mixture'. Usually includes small pieces of vegetables and meat.

Fumet A concentrated stock, usually fish, used to give flavour to other stocks and sauces.

Galantine A mixture of meat, poultry or game, spices and other ingredients pressed into shape, cooked in aspic stock and glazed with aspic.

Glaze To make food glossy by coating it with beaten egg or milk before cooking, or after cooking with sugar syrup or aspic, for example.

Gluten The protein contained in some grains such as wheat or rye, which, when mixed with water, makes dough elastic.

Granita A frozen water ice flavoured with fruit. A speciality of Italy.

Gratin The golden crust on top of a dish after it has been browned in the oven or under the grill. Usually achieved by adding breadcrumbs or grated cheese towards the end of cooking.

Gut To remove the entrails from fish, animals or birds. See also *Eviscerate*.

Hang To suspend meat and game from hooks in a cool place for a number of days to make the flesh more tender and to allow the flavour to develop.

Hors d'oeuvre The first course of a meal, to whet the appetite.

Hull To remove the stalk and centre core or calyx from soft fruits such as strawberries.

Infuse To extract flavour from food such as herbs and tea leaves by steeping it in hot liquid.

Innards The entrails of an animal, bird or fish. See also *Entrails*.

Jugged A stew made from pieces of game, especially hare.

Julienne Strips of vegetables cut matchstick thin. Used as a garnish.

Junket An English pudding made with milk, sweetened and flavoured, and then set with rennet. See also *Rennet*.

Kilocalorie A measurement of the energy value of foods.

Kosher Food prepared according to strict Orthodox Jewish laws.

Lard To insert strips of fat or lardons into meat before roasting, using a larding needle, to make the meat more succulent.

Liaison A thickening for a sauce or soup, using an emulsion such as oil and egg in mayonnaise or a starch such as flour in a liquid.

Liqueur An alcoholic drink usually made with some sort of spirit and flavoured with different fruits, herbs or even coffee beans. They can vary in strength enormously.

Macerate To steep fruit in sugar, liqueurs or spirits to soften it. See also *Liqueur*.

Marinate To soak raw foods, especially meat, in liquid to make them more tender and full of flavour. A marinade also helps to preserve food and is usually a blend of wine, oil, vinegar, herbs and spices.

Medallion Food cut into a round shape. Often applied to veal and chicken.

Parboil To boil for a short time to partially cook food.

Pasteurize To sterilize by heating to a temperature of 140–180°F (60–82°C) to destroy the bacteria.

Pastis A generic name for liqueurs made with aniseed and liquorice. A speciality of southern France.

Pâté A mixture of finely chopped meat, poultry and game which is baked and then served cold.

Pectin A natural gelling substance found in fruit and vegetables and important in the setting of jams and jellies. Some fruits have an especially high pectin content, such as apples, oranges, lemons and blackberries.

Pickle To preserve meat and vegetables in a brine solution.

Pith In citrus fruits the bitter white part of the skin next to the zest.

Pluck To remove the feathers from poultry and game. Also refers to offal.

Poach To cook food gently by immersing it in simmering liquids.

Pot-roast To cook meat in a tightly closed pan with some fat and a little liquid.

Purée Cooked food, often vegetables or fruit, that has been mashed and then sieved.

Ratatouille Originally from Nice in southern France, a vegetable stew containing aubergines, peppers, courgettes, onions, tomatoes and herbs cooked in olive oil.

Reduce To concentrate or thicken a liquid by boiling it rapidly so that it evaporates partially.

Render To melt fat slowly to a liquid. It is then strained to eliminate any impurities.

Rennet A substance extracted from calves' stomachs. Used to coagulate milk for cheese-making or junket. See also *Junket*.

Risotto An Italian dish of rice cooked in butter or oil with the addition of stock, meat, seafood and vegetables and often grated Parmesan cheese.

Roe Fish sperm and eggs. Soft roe is from the male and hard roe the female eggs.

Roux The basis of savoury sauces made from fat, usually butter, and flour mixed together and cooked before the liquid is added. See also *Béchamel*.

Salmis A game stew cooked in red wine.

Saltpetre The common name for potassium nitrate. The small white crystals have been used to preserve food since ancient times.

Sashimi Thinly sliced raw fish served with soy sauce. A speciality of Japan where a great variety is found.

Sauerkraut Finely sliced, salted and fermented white cabbage. It can be served hot or cold. It is a speciality of Germany and also Alsace in France where is is called *choucroute*.

Skim To remove the froth and scum from the top of boiling liquid.

Spatchcock To split a small bird lengthways, flatten it out and then cook it, usually by grilling.

Steep To soak in liquid.

Stir-fry A cooking method much favoured in the Far East, especially China. Usually using a wok, equal-sized ingredients are quickly cooked over a high temperature.

Stock A well-flavoured broth made from meat, poultry or game with vegetables and used instead of water to cook many dishes.

Sushi Rice cooked with seaweed, moulded into small thin circles, then flavoured with vinegar and garnished with ingredients such as fish or cooked egg. A speciality of Japan where they are a popular snack and 'take-away' food.

Syrup A thick liquid made by heating sugar in water so that it dissolves.

Tagine From North Africa a deep earthenware dish with a tight-fitting conical lid. The name is also used for the flavoursome meat and vegetable stews cooked slowly in a *tagine*.

Truss To tie poultry and game into a neat shape before cooking, using a trussing needle and string or skewers.

Vinaigrette A mixture of oil, vinegar, salt, pepper and sometimes herbs used to dress salads and other cold dishes.

Whey The watery liquid that separates out when milk or cream curdles.

Yeast Fungus cells used to produce alcoholic fermentation or to cause dough to rise.

Zest The oily outer part of the skin of citrus fruit, used for flavouring.

INDEX

Acknowledgements

The publishers are grateful to the following individuals and
institutions for the help, advice and information which they
contributed towards the preparation of this book:
Agricultural Scientific Services, Bridget Ardley, Judy Bastyra,
Sid Brassington, British Goose Producers' Association, British
Poultry Federation, British Trout Association, British Turkey
Federation, Brogdale Research Station National Fruit Trials, CAB
International Mycological Institute, Antonio Carluccio, Julian
Clokie, Coffee Information Centre, Catherine Dell, Delicatessen and
Fine Foods Association, Roz Denny, Lesley Downer, Duck Information
Service, Food from Britain, Fresh Fruit and Vegetable Information
Bureau, Paul Fry, Rachel Grenfell, Rupert Hastings, Steve Hatt,
Elizabeth Henderson, George Hill, Mary Hitch, Caroline Macy, Meat and Livestock
Commission, Tom Main, David Mellor, Milk Marketing Board, Sonya
Mills, Ministry of Agriculture, Fisheries and Food, Mushroom
Growers' Association, National Institute of Agricultural Botany,
Chris Newnes, Mary Pickles, Sandra Pickles, Potato Marketing Board, Royal Botanic
Gardens at Kew, Royal Horticulture Association, Seafish Industry
Authority, Barbara Segal, Martin Tabbenor, Tea Council, Thompson
and Morgan, Dr Roy Watling, Susannah Webster, Frank Wilson.

Editorial Director Sandy Carr
Art Director Douglas Wilson
Editors Margaret Daykin, Fiona Holman
Home Economist Bridget Sargeson
Designers Chris Legee, Alison Leggate, Annie Tomlin
Illustrator Coral Mula
Indexer Naomi Good